ABUNDANCE
FOR WHAT?

ABUNDANCE FOR WHAT?

DAVID RIESMAN

WITH A NEW INTRODUCTION BY THE AUTHOR

Transaction Publishers
New Brunswick (U.S.A.) and London (U.K.)

New material this edition copyright © 1993 by Transaction Publishers, New Brunswick, New Jersey 08903. Originally published in 1964 by Doubleday & Company, Inc.

All rights reserved under International and Pan-American Copyright Conventions. No part of this book may be reproduced or transmitted in any form or by any means, electronic or mechanical, including photocopy, recording, or any information storage and retrieval system, without prior permission in writing from the publisher. All inquiries should be addressed to Transaction Publishers, Rutgers—The State University, New Brunswick, New Jersey 08903.

Library of Congress Catalog Number: 93-18093
ISBN: 1-56000-599-8
Printed in the United States of America

Library of Congress Cataloging-in-Publication Data

Riesman, David 1909–
  Abundance for what? / David Riesman.
    p. c.m.
  Originally published: Garden City, N.Y. : Doubleday, 1964. With new introd.
  Includes bibliographical references.
  ISBN: 1-56000-599-8 (paper)
  1. Quality of life—United States. 2. United States—Social conditions—1945– 3. Wealth—United States. 4. Leisure—United States. 5. Social history—20th century. I. Title.
HN58.R5 1993
306'.0973—dc20
                                                                    93-18093
                                                                         CIP

Acknowledgments

"National Purpose" Copyright © 1963 by the *Council for Correspondence Newsletter*. Reprinted by permission of the *Council for Correspondence Newsletter*.

"The American Crisis" by David Riesman and Michael Maccoby. Reprinted by permission of Doubleday & Company, Inc.

"The Nylon War" Copyright 1954 by The Free Press of Glencoe. New material copyright © 1962 by Quincy Wright, William M. Evan, and Morton Deutsch. Reprinted by permission of The Free Press of Glencoe, and Simon and Schuster, Inc.

"Some Observations on the Limits of Totalitarian Power" Copyright 1954 by The Free Press of Glencoe. Reprinted by permission of The Free Press of Glencoe.

"The Cold War and the West" Copyright © 1962 by David Riesman. Questions copyright © 1962 by *The Partisan Review* and reprinted by permission of *The Partisan Review*.

"Careers and Consumer Behavior" by David Riesman and Howard Roseborough. Copyright © 1955 by the New York University Press. Reprinted by permission of the New York University Press.

"A Career Drama in a Middle-aged Farmer" Copyright 1954 by David Riesman.

"Work and Leisure: Fusion or Polarity?" by David Riesman and Warner Bloomberg, Jr. Copyright © 1957 by Harper & Row, Publishers, Incorporated. Reprinted by permission of the publishers.

"Leisure and Work in Postindustrial Society" Reprinted with permission of the publisher from *Mass Leisure*, edited by Eric Larrabee and Rolf Meyersohn. Copyright © 1958 by The Free Press, a Corporation.

"Some Issues in the Future of Leisure" by David Riesman and Robert S. Weiss. Copyright © 1961 by the Society for the Study of Social Problems. Reprinted by permission of *Social Problems*.

"Sociability, Permissiveness, and Equality: A Preliminary Formulation" by David Riesman, Robert J. Potter, and Jeanne Watson. Copyright 1960 by the William Alanson White Psychiatric Foundation. Reprinted by permission of *Psychiatry, Journal for the Study of Interpersonal Processes*.

"The Suburban Dislocation" Copyright © 1957 by David Riesman.

"Flight and Search in the New Suburbs" Copyright 1959 by David Riesman.

"Autos in America" by David Riesman and Eric Larrabee. Copyright © 1958 by Lincoln H. Clark. Reprinted by permission of Harper & Row, Publishers, Incorporated.

"The Found Generation" Copyright © 1956 by David Riesman.

"The Social and Psychological Setting of Veblen's Economic Theory" Copyright 1954 by The Free Press of Glencoe. Reprinted by permission of The Free Press of Glencoe.

"The Relevance of Thorstein Veblen" by David Riesman and Staughton

Lynd. Copyright © 1960 by David Riesman and Staughton Lynd. Printed by permission of Charles Scribner's Sons.

"Self and Society: Reflections on Some Turks in Transition" by David Riesman and Daniel Lerner. Reprinted by permission of *Explorations*.

"The Oral Tradition, The Written Word, and The Screen Image" Copyright © 1956 by David Riesman. Additional material reprinted by permission of the Beacon Press, copyright © 1960 by the Beacon Press.

"Law and Sociology" Early version copyright 1957 by the Board of Trustees of the Leland Stanford Junior University. Reprinted by permission of the editors of the *Stanford Law Review*. Revised version reprinted here with permission of the publisher from *Law and Sociology*, edited by William M. Evan. Copyright 1962 by The Free Press of Glencoe.

"Tocqueville as Ethnographer" Copyright © 1961 by David Riesman.

"Introduction to Crestwood Heights" Copyright © 1956 by Basic Books, Inc. Reprinted by permission of Basic Books, Inc. and the University of Toronto Press.

"Orbits of Tolerance, Interviewers, and Elites" Copyright © 1956 by Princeton University. Reprinted by permission of *The Public Opinion Quarterly*.

"Interviewers, Elites and Academic Freedom" Copyright © 1958 by the Society for the Study of Social Problems. Reprinted by permission of *Social Problems*.

"The Study of National Character: Some Observations on the American Case" Copyright © 1959 by the President and Fellows of Harvard College. Reprinted by permission of *The Harvard Library Bulletin*.

To Erich Fromm

Author's Note (1964)

Several of the essays included in this volume are joint products, and I am indebted to my colleagues for their generosity in allowing me to reprint here work on which they contributed as much as I. Michael Maccoby is the coauthor of "The American Crisis"; Eric Larrabee, of the paper on the auto; Mark Benney, of the article on "The Sociology of the Interview"; Howard Roseborough, of "Careers and Consumer Behavior"; Robert S. Weiss, of "Some Issues in the Future of Leisure"; Robert J. Potter and Jeanne Watson of "Sociability, Permissiveness, and Equality."

Over the past seven years a number of foundations supported some of the work represented here. The Behavioral Sciences Division of the Ford Foundation financed the Center for the Study of Leisure of which I was Director at the University of Chicago (1955–58); the Foundations' Fund for Research in Psychiatry supported the work on the interview (of which two out of half a dozen papers and monographs are reprinted here); the National Institute of Mental Health supported the Sociability Project, one of whose publications is included; the Carnegie Corporation has assisted work on higher education reflected in the essays, "Some Continuities and Discontinuities in the Education of Women" and "Law and Sociology." I am indebted to these foundations for their flexibility as well as their generosity.

The editorial help of Anne Freedgood and Phyllis Klein is gratefully acknowledged.

Contents

Introduction to the Transaction Edition	xiii
Section I: The Impact of the Cold War	1
Preface	3
National Purpose	19
The American Crisis	28
Reflections on Containment and Initiatives	52
The Nylon War	67
Some Observations on the Limits of Totalitarian Power	80
The Cold War and the West: Answers Given in a *Partisan Review* Symposium	93
Section II: Abundance for What?	103
Preface	105
Careers and Consumer Behavior	113
A Career Drama in a Middle-aged Farmer	138
Work and Leisure: Fusion or Polarity?	147
Leisure and Work in Postindustrial Society	162
Some Issues in the Future of Leisure	184
Sociability, Permissiveness, and Equality: A Preliminary Formulation	196
The Suburban Dislocation	226
Flight and Search in the New Suburbs	258
Autos in America	270
Abundance for What?	300
The Found Generation	309
Some Continuities and Discontinuities in the Education of Women	324
The Search for Challenge	349
Section III: Abundance for Whom?	369
Preface	371
The Social and Psychological Setting of Veblen's Economic Theory	374

CONTENTS

The Relevance of Thorstein Veblen	388
Self and Society: Reflections on Some Turks in Transition	402
The Oral Tradition, the Written Word, and the Screen Image	418
Section IV: Social Science Research: Problems, Methods, Opportunities	443
Preface	445
Law and Sociology	454
Tocqueville as Ethnographer	493
Introduction to *Crestwood Heights*	506
The Sociology of the Interview	517
Orbits of Tolerance, Interviewers, and Elites	540
Interviewers, Elites, and Academic Freedom	568
The Study of National Character: Some Observations on the American Case	584
Acknowledgments and Notes on Previous Publication	604
Index	611

Introduction to the Transaction Edition

In this new preface[1] I shall focus first on the question of totalitarianism. Then I shall turn to the title essay and to the assumption which permeates this volume—and also *The Lonely Crowd,* published in 1950—that affluence was here to stay, and that a problem for the future would be how to make good use of that affluence, not how to recapture it. The third theme to which I shall turn in the last segment of this new preface is the one that has been my major research arena, namely, education, and herein primarily higher education.

As I indicated in the preface to the first section of this volume, "The Impact of the Cold War," the playful idea of "The Nylon War" occurred to me during a 1947 conference among social scientists to discuss "the world community." I thought we were being unduly solemn in our attempts to be realistic. When I then wrote the essay in the late 1940's, there were few channels by which my fantasy might come to the attention of Russian readers and be regarded as a criticism of their greed and materialism! American readers need to be reminded that nylon stockings were once a precious commodity; were the essay to be written today, it might be called "The McDonald Franchise War." My fantasy assumed that parachute drops of consumer goods would disrupt the Soviet Union which, although effective in making tanks and other heavy equipment, was not then or later adept in producing consumer goods; lacking were the skills needed for motivating workers and managers prepared to service customers rather than often grudgingly to obey orders from above. As I have reflected recently both on "The Nylon War" and on "Some Observations on the Limits of Totalitarian Power," I have recalled my own extremely mixed reaction to George Orwell's *1984* at the time of its publication and thereafter. I thought it a far less realistic anti-utopian fantasy than Aldous Huxley's *Brave New World,* for in Huxley's version it is material bounty that keeps the society together, in contrast to Orwell's fearsome imagery of near-total terror amid scarcity.[2] While Orwell's work might have been useful vis-à-vis fellow travelers of Communism in the West, whose small number but considerable influence down to the time of the Korean War it is easy to forget, I thought his book presented a far too defeatist view, and indeed resembled Aldous Huxley's in its assumption of the malleability of human beings (then referred to by the generic term "Man" in this and other essays of that period).

"Some Observations on the Limits of Totalitarian Power" was an address to a November 1951 meeting of the American Committee for Cultural Freedom, an organization later discredited by the discovery that it got some CIA money.[3] My questioning of the degree of total control possessed by the Nazi and the Soviet societies evoked passionate criticism. Although Bruno Bettelheim had himself survived a Nazi concentration camp, he joined my other critics, Hannah Arendt and Nathan Leites, also emigrés, in insisting that totalitarianism succeeds in controlling all aspects of life; I was the "innocent American," naive in not realizing the full extent of submission resulting not only from the coercive powers of "the system" but also from the internalization of its aims and ideals by virtually everyone. I was also morally at fault, since an effort to suggest that the goals of totalitarian leaders were unattainable might minimize American resistance and, to the degree that my outlook would be shared, undercut American fears that helped to sustain this country's Cold War efforts.[4] Especially after Stalin's death in 1953, when I thought that it might have been possible to work out a less bellicose balance of power with the Soviet Union and those who were presumed to be its allies, it seemed to me that Khrushchev and other Soviet leaders were frightened of those vocal Americans for whom containment was insufficient, who were demanding a rollback of Soviet advances in Eastern Europe and elsewhere. Moreover, what President Eisenhower had referred to as the military-industrial complex, which should more accurately have been called the military-industrial-scientific-intellectual complex, moved the country beyond minimum deterrence toward developing "counterforce," that is, first-strike armaments accompanied by the aggressiveness disguised as fear that went into building bomb shelters.[5]

I never regarded myself as more than an amateur when it came to Soviet affairs and issues concerning nuclear arsenals. But I do believe I had a certain advantage in having visited the Soviet Union in the summer of 1931, after my graduation from Harvard College. Unable to obtain an individual visa in Berlin (the United States had

INTRODUCTION TO THE TRANSACTION EDITION   XV

not yet recognized the USSR), I traveled with an Intourist group led by the photographer Julien Bryan. I had learned some Berlitz Russian, and I carried a pocket dictionary on the long "hard" or third-class train rides and while going down the Volga on a steamer. Ordinary Russians met en route or elsewhere were patient with my limited vocabulary. I did not avoid, but rather sought out Americans, meeting with a Hearst reporter who had gone over as a fellow traveler and had become disillusioned; with the bombastic pro-Soviet Walter Duranty of the *New York Times*; and with William Henry Chamberlain of the *Christian Science Monitor*, still writing sympathetic stories while already embittered vis-à-vis the cruelties of the Stalinist regime. American engineers joked about how Russian peasants never put oil in their tractors, so that the machines soon broke down. I met other engineers at the Stalingrad tractor plant, where a few Stakhanovites, that is, fanatically dedicated workers, proceeded furiously while the rest of the plant loafed, and where I also learned that a mistake could be interpreted as sabotage and one could be shot. After the group left, Bryan, another young man, and I stayed on to visit a collective farm founded by former emigrés to Australia who had returned to help the socialist fatherland, only to find themselves in an impoverished and tyrannical setting, where our very presence created some anxiety, all the more so when I injured my knee and needed hospitalization. My two American companions left, and I was greatly helped by a husband and wife, trained in the old regime as artists, who had come to the farm to do paintings of rural scenes that could pass as "Socialist Realism"; with the door of my room closed, one could keep watch outside while the other could tell me in candid French that I needed to get myself to a hospital in Moscow. A stolid young woman was my escort on the again "hard" train ride to Moscow, where in the hospital I had the luck to be on a ward served by an idealistic young woman, fluent in English, who said she had wanted before the Revolution to become a painter but now she painted with iodine! In the bed next to me was a German Communist who had also come in the hope of helping the regime and out of fear of the rising power of Hitler and the Nazis. He was treated with callousness. At that time, and now as I read in the papers again today, even in the more prosperous cities there was a lack of sutures, of anaesthetics, and of other medical equipment we take for granted. Paradoxically, as it seemed to me, the male director of the hospital— all the other physicians I saw were women—who had heard of my father, then Professor of Clinical Medicine at the University of Pennsylvania, demonstrated to me an apparatus of which he was proud and which, had it worked, would have given him the temperature of each bed in the hospital, thanks to a thermometer in each mattress. I did not understand how this would help report on patients; moreover, like ever so much else, the apparatus simply failed to function. Yet despite much awkwardness—the Russians seemed to lack the gifts of thingmanship of the Japanese, the Swiss, the Germans, and many other peoples—a few operations did work, and the first tractors came out of the Stalingrad plant while I was still in the hospital, triumphs reported daily in the pages of *Pravda*.

This personal background facilitated my discounting all the claims shared by Communists, fellow travelers, and the fiercest Cold Warriors about the success of what often used to be referred to as the "Soviet experiment." I found it hard to understand how Lincoln Steffens had come to the Soviet Union in the 1920's and said, "I have seen the future and it works." Perhaps had Hitler's armies, as they drove into the Soviet Union, been less hostile to the occupied Polish and Slav peoples, they might have won more individuals to their own side; instead, they made it possible for Stalin, himself a Georgian nationalist, to rally the nationalist fervors whose legitimacy Communism had not erased or replaced, and so eventually, along with bad weather and some American aid, to defeat the German armies, who had captured a third of the country by December, 1941.

I had no comparable personal experience against which to measure the extent to which the Chinese Communists under Mao had managed to create a totalitarian regime in so enormous a country. When I came to Harvard in 1958 I met the psychiatrist Robert Jay Lifton and discussed with him the interviews that went into his books, *Thought Reform and the Psychology of Totalism: A Study of 'Brainwashing' in China* (Norton, 1961) and *Revolutionary Immortality: Mao Tse-tung and the Chinese Cultural Revolution* (New York: Random House, 1968). The Chinese seemed to me to be seeking much more than outward obedience. They insisted on inner transformation, illustrated by a woman who had been a pianist and allowed her fingers to be broken as punishment for so bourgeois a pursuit. Yet it seemed inconceivable to me that in that enormous population, with varying dialects and some ethnic diversity, there would not be islands of unvoiced resistance, coupled with whatever professions of assent were requisite. In my view, President Richard Nixon deserves great credit for recognizing China; the more ties, economic and otherwise, the United States can have with China, the less opportunity the regime possesses to insulate the Chinese from the acids of modernity.[6] There are still many people alive who have not lost the entrepreneurial spirit that is so impressive in overseas Chinese. Still, "Some Observations on the Limits of Totalitarian Power" was focused primarily on the Soviet Union and to a lesser degree on Nazism. I was not thinking of China, nor of North Korea, not to speak of Albania.

One notion in the essay may be read with a critical eye today, namely, where (p. 85) I suggest that women under the Nazis "were more immune than men to impersonal and abstract ideals; they are more conservative in the good and in the bad sense—more 'realistic.'" Such a remark would appear to be consonant with Carol Gilligan's perspective on the moral development of girls overall, as distinct from that of boys overall. Gilligan, in *In a Different Voice* (Harvard University Press, 1982), presents evidence that girls develop a more contextual, less abstract morality in contrast to boys.[7] However, in a later essay in this volume (p. 550) I report my own experience when I spoke to a politically active women's organization in the middle 1950's and defended the urban party bosses and their brokerage among fanatical ethnic groups and ideologies; the women in my audience, at that time mostly homemakers, were righteously indignant, whereas men of similar social class might well have had more exposure to class and ethnic differences and have become more cynical about politics.[8] However, to an international observer today, the United States would appear to be the country with the strongest women's movements—and backlashes against these—resulting in perhaps the largest quotient of angry and extremely idealistic women, some of whom believe that gender differences are no more than cultural creations by men of power, old and new.[9] Women were more opposed than men to the Vietnam war and also more opposed than men to going to war against Iraq, and in that sense less captured by nationalistic fervor. (Some girls become cheerleaders in school and continue in college, but it is boys and men whose passionate interest in competitive sports at their school, college, or locale can be extrapolated to their vision of an embattled USA.)

The term "containment" during the Cold War era drew on the judgment of George Kennan that the task of the United States was to contain the Soviet Union, to prevent its further extension, not to try to overthrow the regime. My essay on pages 52–66, "Reflections on Containment and Initiatives," was originally presented at a symposium, "Studies on War and Peace," at the 1962 meeting of the American Sociological Association; I took for granted my judgment that the Soviet Union was more a status quo power than an expansionist one. The Russians found Berlin a great irritant, spreading "contamination" even to the severely controlled East Germans; but other than Berlin, I could not imagine a Soviet desire to incorporate more unruly and unreliable "allies" such as Poland, Czechoslovakia, or Hungary, in the latter two of which brutal intervention occurred, whereas in Poland a Communist general, Jaruzelski, was able to contain Soviet fears while also not completely extirpating Polish national aspirations. A Soviet invasion of Western Europe (beyond the issue of Berlin) never seemed credible to me. Rather, my concern was with the question of "containing" the expansionist, interventionist impulses within American democracy. These populist pressures, I argued, limited the prospects for initiatives for peace which might be interpreted as "soft on Communism." I noted how frequently Americans in letters to the editor refer to themselves as "sick and tired." "Jingoes say that they are 'sick and tired' of Castro or Khrushchev or the United Nations." (page 66).[10] Moreover, I observed that American atmospheric tests of our nuclear arsenals signaled to us that we needed to expose ourselves to the dangers of radiation because our Soviet adversaries were sufficiently powerful, as well as evil, to require us to undergo this hazard.[11] Believing as we Americans were then inclined to do in our own morality and honor, it was in these years hard for us to imagine how much we threatened the Soviet Union, and the possible effects on Soviet military and civilian leaders of John F. Kennedy's running for the Presidency in 1960 emphasizing the "missile gap" (which ran enormously in America's favor) and Cuba, "90 miles from home." I realize now from recent disclosures that I underestimated the dangers in the Cuban missile crisis in the fall of 1962. Among other things, I did not realize that Fidel Castro might have had some independent power to use these missiles against the United States, feeling threatened as he did by the fear of another attempt at invasion. Of all Kennedy's foreign policy actions, I most admired the partial test ban treaty of 1963, regretting that, because of what even at the time seemed small differences about the number of inspections the Soviet Union would allow, a complete ban was not achieved.

Always for me the fear of use of nuclear arsenals was central. Thus when in this 1962 essay I referred to South Vietnam as a possible point of collision (I had become attentive to the question of Vietnam when the United States refused to back the Geneva Accords of 1954), my concern was not with South Vietnam per se, but with the nuclear issue. Like a number of military men and quite a few scientists, I saw nuclear arsenals as carrying the irrationality of some earlier total wars to a Samson-like or suicidal degree—this was the principal hazard to which I was alert in the repeated conflicts between Israel and its neighbors, fearing that Israel might draw the United States in, or Syria or Egypt propel the Soviet Union.[12] With the dissolution of the Soviet Union, American concern with nuclear nightmares has evaporated, but I have not lost my own anxieties concerning what Robert Jay Lifton has termed "nuclearism." (I imagine that biological armaments also have similar planet-destroying potential.) I watch uneasily as different nationality groups in the former Soviet Union contend, if not for hegemony, then for some deterrent of their own; nuclear scientists, engineers, and even equipment might end up in Pakistan or some other country seeking not only a deterrent but the status—so clearly enjoyed in an earlier day by General deGaulle—of being among the nuclear powers.

Today in 1992 one can only dream about an American-inspired program which would simultaneously help the recovery from Communism and from fragmentation of the former Soviet and East European states while also taking steps toward a world free of nuclearism. People of my generation remember the Marshall Plan. The buoyancy of victory in World War II and the development of a foreign policy elite, patrician in origin or adoption, made creation of the Marshall Plan feasible to assist our former enemy, Germany, as well as other European countries, to recover from the devastation of the war. (The incipient Cold War already meant that, had the Soviet Union insisted on participation, the Marshall Plan could probably not have won Congressional approval.) But there has been no comparable buoyancy resulting from the collapse of the Soviet Union and its loss of control of its former East European satellites. This is so even though Poland has substantial lobbies of former citizens now in the United States. There is instant rejection of the slightest suggestion of raising taxes in order to contribute any substantial help (other than to Israel, and Egypt in the Israeli context) outside America's borders. During the 1992 presidential campaign,

President George Bush was assailed from the Right by Patrick Buchanan, an isolationist of an old-fashioned anti-statist, even-handedly xenophobic sort, and by Democratic leaders such as Congressman Richard Gephardt of Missouri who are avowedly protectionist whether toward Mexico or toward Japan, and felt impelled in the spring of 1992 to take "welfare king" Lee Iacocca and other American auto executives to Japan in an embarrassing effort to reduce the Japanese exports our consumers can actually use.[13] Currently it would seem that the xenophobia once focused on the Soviet Union, and for part of the population and its leadership on Communist China, with a bit of room left for Castro's Cuba, is likely to be targeted against the Japanese, who sell us goods we want (originally with help in making them from Americans like W. Edwards Deming), made by methods some of which we could learn, and sold for money we borrow back.

A reflective essay by John Lukacs discusses the centrality of nationalism in American politics in the Civil War and increasingly thereafter, to the point today where nationalist populists exercise power in both the Democratic and the Republican Parties, even while Lukacs suggests that American nationalism ". . . may devolve into tribal struggles of a peculiarly American kind."[14]

Although the essays in this section on the Cold War reflect my own and others' earlier concerns about a potential nuclear catastrophe, they nevertheless reflect an underlying sanguinity which contrasts sharply with our current discontents. An essay written with Michael Maccoby, "The American Crisis," first presented to a group of liberal Democratic Congressmen in 1960, expresses the hope that if the critical years of the Cold War could be overcome, the country could "move away from the anarchy of nationalism, reducing arms to the level of police forces" (p. 42). We refer to an America where "people feel there is plenty for all, but little joy in using the things we have made" (p. 45). The entire essay is a reminder of the degree to which it was still possible to assume that the engine of the American economy was the world's most powerful and that it was conceivable that it could be turned from war production to national munificence. This observation leads me to the perplexity I would imagine any contemporary reader would bring to the sections in this volume with the headings "Abundance for What?" and "Abundance for Whom?": how could I so readily have assumed increasing affluence as an American inheritance? The title essay, "Abundance for

What?," was originally a contribution to a 1957 conference of the Committee for Economic Development under the title "Abundance for What?—How to Use the Rising Income that Economic Growth Makes Possible." It was published the next year in *Bulletin of the Atomic Scientists*. The essay assumed, as did *The Lonely Crowd* and other writings of the late Forties and many years thereafter, that the problems of industrial production and of mass distribution had on the whole been resolved; abundance was here to stay, kept in place by what I assumed to be the "permanent war economy" (p. 152). What might our country (and also some smaller countries where the dream of plenty seemed within reach, referring to Switzerland, West Germany, and several Scandinavian countries) spend our money on, once we had satisfied desires for consumer goods and brought more people into the educated strata who would have diminished needs for invidious consumption?[15] I saw a fairly unlimited desire for education, although I recognized that spending for schools, public and private health, and non-slum redevelopment faced political obstacles and that no "needs" could compare in imperative and in political leverage with those that could in some fashion be tied to defense.[16]

I did not arrive at my view out of illusions concerning the efficiency of American business and industry. I had worked from 1943 until the end of 1945 at Sperry Gyroscope Company, first as Assistant to the Treasurer and then as Contract Termination Director. I could observe plant managers who hid scarce materials from each other, sometimes in cooperation with the Navy, which appeared more antagonistic to the Army Air Force than to the Nazis and the Japanese. I experienced controversies with the holding company and designedly kept away from conflicts with the United Auto Workers, who had unionized the plants.[17] I recognized that Sperry, which had exploded from a small engineering-dominated company of 1,000 to 33,000, was discombobulated in ways quite different from large, established companies such as General Electric or the Studebaker plant I visited in Indiana. Still, Sperry served as a prime contractor for much war matériel. The idea never occurred to me that Germany and Japan, Korea, Singapore, and many other countries could learn to produce more effectively than the Americans.

Repeatedly in the essays in this volume there is the assumption of continued and growing affluence. In "The American Crisis," we noted that "none of the problems of scarcity has been dealt with in a wholly satisfactory way: not all Americans are affluent, many are destitute, and many of the traditional issues of welfare and social justice—markedly, of course, the race issue—remain exigent" (pp. 50–51). Several paragraphs earlier, we referred to "the highly unlikely prospect of another depression" (p. 49) because we assumed that an increase in what we ironically termed "defense" expenditures could be used as a Keynesian stabilizer "to maintain the flow of income." So confident was I about incrementally increasing affluence that in the essay "Abundance for What?" I wondered what we Americans would do to find uses for our productivity, even suggesting ironically that New Orleans "be made a national park, with its homes inhabited by subsidized families (much as bear or deer are 'subsidized' to live in Yellowstone)."[18]

The GI Bill of Rights in effect subsidized bringing into higher education young men who prior to the Second World War would never have dreamed of going to college, and certainly not of attending one beyond commuting range. I recall the great confidence an enormous proportion of them had concerning their post-baccalaureate futures. Today, despite the often nearly requisite "cool" manner one finds among college students, most, even among the affluent, are aware of the hazards the economic future portends for them. Over three-quarters of them are not so deprived as to lack access to an automobile. In an essay written in 1955, "Orbits of Tolerance: Interviewers and Elites," I remarked that "to be young today means to have a larger orbit than the previous generation" and went on to suggest that women had a greater orbit than previously and a greater equality in the home (p. 566). In an essay the following year, "Some Continuities and Discontinuities in the Education of Women," I suggested the limits of that orbit: "Young college women today, it is my impression, feel that they can fulfill themselves *only* in marriage and child-rearing, and an exciting career is not really an escape route even from the prospects of a dull and trying marriage" (page 332). However, I also observed: "Whereas in an earlier day, a small handful of feminists wanted careers and the vast majority of 'femininists' wanted homes, today the entire college generation wants, not a career, but a job as a supplement to marriage," including jobs "before marriage, before the children come, and after the children have grown" (page 327). In the same paragraph I noted that married women were "even helping put an end to the famous schoolteacher shortage." The paragraph continues: "Through these jobs, few of them lucrative and hardly any of them eminent, college-educated women contribute to meeting the costs of a standard of living which pushes ever higher, thus making it possible for them to raise three or four children in middle-class circumstance with not much assistance from accumulated or inherited capital" (page 327).

The essay was an address at Bennington College, then a women's college noted for its cultural and also political radicalism.[19] I remarked that Bennington College women were not always satisfied to marry "merely" a young man from nearby Williams College (page 333); such outlooks anticipated those of the women's movements at a time when I could take for granted that the single-sex colleges in the Eastern half of the country, public as well as private, would remain that way. It was a time when women, notably Catholic women, went to college less often than men did. It was expected that they would channel their surplus energies into the work of the voluntary associations which, as I noted in the essay "Tocqueville as Ethnographer," impressed Tocqueville as the main civic bond of the individualistic Americans, their principal protection against tyranny. A related notion appears in the essay "Autos in America," written jointly with the late Eric Larrabee in 1958; we remarked that "... our postwar prosperity, above its cushion of defense spending, rests on the twin supports of new cars and new suburbs; in fact, the latter depend primarily on the former," with the two-car garage "freeing the wives for sociability, shopping, and chauffeuring of children" (pp. 286–287). There are still such families among the well-to-do. Robert S. Weiss describes a cohort of successful executives living in some of the affluent Boston suburbs in his book *Staying the Course*; some of these men encourage their homebound wives to pursue a vocation for the sake of their mental health, since it is not necessary for the support of the menage—the more so since the husband sees his role as the good provider as his principal *raison d'être*.[20]

Even before it dawned on people that to maintain, let alone improve, their standard of living required two wage-earners in the family, the efflorescence of the women's movements, coming in the wake of and in some respects in response to the civil rights, student, and anti-Vietnam war movements of the late Sixties, had transformed the aspirations of many girls and women. The movements, accompanying as they did a general loosening of constraints, contributed to a situation in which few women could count on their marriages as insurance for life—or wanted to do so. No-fault divorce, as Lenore Weitzman found in her research, has had the consequence more often of liberating husbands than of emancipating their spouses, especially if the latter are left to take care of the children, as is generally the case.[21] Not only do girls and women now have to look to themselves to secure their own futures, but the ideology of the women's movements compels them in the more selective institutions to put their own careers first and subordinate or forget about what used to be thought of as romance.[22] In *A Lesser Life: The Myth of Women's Liberation in America*, Sylvia Ann Hewlett poignantly describes her experience when she taught economics at Barnard College while also taking care of a small child. When she had arranged for child care during her classes and her office hours, her scheduling would be upset when her colleagues would sometimes call a previously unscheduled meeting at lunch and, if she brought her child, she would receive coldness rather than empathy; she would be told she was not taking her career seriously enough.[23] As someone who believes in the importance of the women's colleges, Barnard among them, I was troubled by her account and was reminded of those wings of the women's liberation movements that have maintained that there are no differences between men and women other than those created by power and concomitant cultural history. Tragically, there have been some situations in which women's liberation amounted de facto to men's liberation, facilitated in some measure also by much more widely available contraceptives and, in the case of mischance, abortion.[24] How far we have moved in the last decades is illustrated by my now archaic comment in the Bennington College address already mentioned, that while Catholic women had the option of becoming nuns, other women feel pressure to marry lest they be thought perverse (pp. 331-332).

In "The Self-Centered Society," written in 1979, I assumed not only continuing affluence for the majority of Americans, but also the availability of jobs for the growing number of the college-educated young. After referring to examples of young people devoting themselves to a variety of crusades, including both segregationist youth who supported George Wallace and civil rights activists (today one would want to add anti-abortion and also animal rights activists engaging in civil disobedience), I wrote: "There is also strong movement for environmental protection, notably in the anti-nuclear power demonstrations and sit-ins—an unconscious kind of social-class combat with the less well-to-do, who would also like amenities and protection against hazards, but for whom jobs and standard consumer goods, taken for granted by the affluent, are a first priority."[25]

I have come to see my assumption of continuing affluence under which the college-educated would do better than their less well-educated parents as an indication of my provincialism, my lack of appropriate comparative historical perspective on the United States. My personal experience reached only to the Great Depression of the 1930's, which continued into the New Deal years despite the many initiatives such as the Civilian Conservation Corps and the Works Progress Administration which put some of the unemployed to work. With the demands of the Second World War, not only did male unemployment end, but for just a few years women were pulled into the factories and service agencies of wartime, only to be sent back again to their homes when the men returned. Since the Great Depression had followed only a few years after the end of the First World War, many believed that there would be a similar economic slump after the Second World War. Since I did not believe that, and since the war was followed by a boom, including the "baby boom," I became too complacent about the Keynesian formulae, including my belief that defense expenditures would continue to be used as stabilizers.

For at least two decades now the American industrial and service economies have not been creating high-paid jobs of the old-fashioned labor-intensive kind. I have learned from the comparative studies by Michael Maccoby of companies in Sweden, France, Japan, and the United States that high-paying jobs are available for skilled mechanics who understand computer-driven machines and how to repair them or are able quickly to learn the newest technologies, are handy with things and, in sufficient measure, with people.[26] There are also well-paying though not necessarily durable positions for those in the fields that my Kennedy School colleague Robert Reich refers to as the symbolizing professions, including finance, law firms, and at a less exalted level in terms of income, medicine and the whole new arena of consultants to companies and to institutions more generally.[27] Even in the high-paying fields, there is little assurance today that the jobs will always be there. Even the college-educated children of the affluent in the well-paying professions cannot take for granted that their positions will last as long as they do, especially as old age now stretches out well beyond what would even several generations ago have appeared a normal life span.[28] The college-educated children of the affluent working in the minor service fields cannot take their jobs for granted either; some for lack of steady work must live with their families of origin and lack the opportunity their parents had to buy a home and start a family of their own.[29] If the parents, like so many American parents even in the well-off top quartile of the population, did not save for their children's college education, the latter may also be paying off student loans.[30]

The assumption in these essays that affluence could be taken for granted and that anyone who wanted either a job or a career and worked steadily toward this end could find opportunity is not the only assessment which experience has taught me to reject. In the essays in this volume dealing with work, I assumed that everyone would like to have meaningful, non-redundant work. I later discovered that this was an exaggerated view. I had several opportunities to visit the Harman Industries auto parts plant in Bolivar, Tennessee, where under the combined impetus of Sidney Harman and the United Auto Workers, an experiment was under way to increase workers' role in management and the redesign of plant operations. The experiment was studied by Michael Maccoby and his associates, who uncovered the reality that there were some factory workers, many women and quite a few men, who actually preferred factory routines to having to be more involved in the production process. Their emotional lives were outside the plant—some were part-time farmers—and following well-known routines was more important than having to take the responsibility of being in partial charge.[31]

In two essays, "The Suburban Dislocation" and "Flight and Search in the New Suburbs," I made some of the same kinds of misjudgments that Herbert J. Gans has criticized as those of intellectuals who are snobbish, inexperienced city folk.[32] I envisaged, for example on page 239, the suburbs as lacking the "critical masses" of individuals with specialized interests, for instance, Mozart lovers as distinct from Bach, Wagner, and jazz lovers. This was a mistaken assumption, failing to appreciate the ability of people to connect with each other through "thin" non-contiguous networks, in some measure annihilating geographic distance. There is another mistaken assumption in the essay with Eric Larrabee on autos in America, published in 1956, in which (although we referred to Volkswagen and Renault in a 1962 coda) we took for granted the hegemony of the American Big Three with their annual model changes and with their assumption (as Bruce

Kimball has reminded me) that Americans would permanently want "big" and also fuel-inefficient cars. Today, the Big Three (with many parts actually made in Japan) still have hegemony in those segments of the country where nativism is strong and where resentment of Japanese success can be ferocious. But our earlier outlook did ignore the extent to which market research and new modes of production allow the targeting of specific audiences and the tailoring of consumer goods, automobiles among them, geared, so to speak, to particular ZIP codes and age, class, gender, and ethnic variations among these. The old-style large movie house has nearly disappeared, replaced in the cities and as a feature of many suburban malls by market-segmented multiplex theaters, allowing a variety of types of film to be shown simultaneously—a highly visible illustration of this shift. Furthermore, the spread of varying amounts of higher education, although uneven in quality, carries with it the potential that in any residential or large metropolitan college or university there will be some audience for tastes once considered esoteric. Fundamentalisms remain strong; because they are "isms," they are not inherited traditions but rather ideological and evangelical in composition. To put it differently, although the country is bitterly polarized along cultural lines involving in varying degrees class, race, ethnicity, region, and generation, there are not many boondocks around: the philistinism we have now, politically and culturally powerful, is much more sophisticated than its predecessors.

To climb just a little bit out of my own North American boondocks, I began when I came to Harvard to audit courses on the Far East, particularly Japan, including the introductory course students nicknamed "Rice Paddies," taught by John Fairbank and Edwin Reischauer for many years; Robert Bellah's course in traditional Japanese religion; Albert Craig on modern Japanese history; in addition, there was the continuing influence of my colleague Ezra Vogel's scholarship. I also benefitted from the work of Robert Jay Lifton. In the fall of 1961 my wife and I were for the months of October and November the guests of International House in Tokyo; International House offered to bring us together with any Japanese we might want to meet, whether in university, business or other professional life, or in the arts; our then-young sociologist friend, Hidetoshi Kato, teaching at the University of Kyoto, took time out to become our guide and interpreter.[33] It is interesting that my effort to meet with politicians from the Diet was unsuccessful in this otherwise hospitable atmosphere, where we met with leaders of the teachers union and with radical student leaders. My hosts could not believe that I truly respected politicians. Even the fact that I had written a sympathetic foreword to Stimson Bullitt's *To Be a Politician* could not convince them that I detested the prevailing snobbery and contempt for politicians![34] My wife Evelyn and I greatly appreciated Japanese courtesy and the sense of mutuality we instantly felt, especially with some younger Japanese scholars, Hidetoshi Kato among them, who referred to themselves as the "third generation" in terms of their distance from the more nationalistic and self-limiting Japanese of earlier eras. Some of the few Americans we met, including then reporter Abe Rosenthal, later managing editor of the *New York Times*, and some officials at the American Embassy, appeared to be disgusted by just the courtesies and delicacies we respected among their Japanese counterparts: as one of them put it, arguing with Japanese men was like wrestling with spaghetti! In a book of selections from the diaries my wife and I kept while we were in Japan, I described my visiting Konusuke Matsushita at his plants near Osaka in 1961, and my astonishment to discover that a Left Wing union was devotedly cooperative: the dedicated workforce included many young women who never glanced up from their work as, accompanied by photographers, our party toured their work rooms.[35] The radical students, the *zengakuren*, had in 1960 helped lead the protests that caused the cancellation of President Dwight D. Eisenhower's planned visit to Japan. But these same students, after what was often termed the "pink shower," the Marxist indoctrination of their rather leisurely undergraduate years, went into the big companies or into government service, bearing hardly a scintilla of rebellious or counter-cultural baggage with them.

In the last three decades Japan has greatly changed, illustrated by the beginnings of a women's movement and the decision of many young women to think of the future not only in terms of marriage, which they now tend to postpone, but also in terms of careers, in contrast to jobs; fecundity has not been high, and there is a demographic downturn. Indeed, Japan has been forced to depend on immigrants from the Asian continent to take not only the low-level jobs but also some of the highly skilled ones for which the great national universities no longer provide enough trained workers but rather graduates who, as in the United States, prefer working in the financial marketplace to becoming highly skilled engineers and other technical professionals.

It helps me to understand the United States less badly than I had earlier done to consider the cultural and moral sources of Japan's competitive ability in contrast to our own. Thomas Lifson is a sociological practitioner who works as a consultant to Japanese and American firms. In "Innovation and Institutions: Notes on the Japanese Paradigm," he refers to the inherited tradition of cooperation and mutual reciprocity which began in the Meiji period and which has been adapted to the needs of mutually responsive corporations.[36] He describes an instance where a subcontractor to a large company was suddenly faced with an enormous increase in the price of the material that it used to make its products, so that it would quickly go bankrupt if held to its contract without adjustment on the prime contractor's part; the latter arranged for others to purchase the subcontractor's products in order to ease the latter's situation and to maintain the prized relationship, even at some additional cost. But this very mutuality central to Japanese relationships, as Lifson notes, is viewed in this country in an extremely negative way: it is an "old boy network"; it is "back-scratching"; it is patronage; it is blatant favoritism. The anti-trust laws which were of doubtful relevance even when the United States was more insulated from the rest of the world illustrate and enforce American notions as to what is fair, norms which are individualistic rather than cooperative.[37]

The reciprocity and mutual trust that foster the international competitiveness of Japanese products and services are not wholly absent in the United States, but they tend to be looked upon, as I have just suggested, with suspicion. Lawyers operate hardly at all in Japan. The degree to which in the United States lawyers, and the fear of litigation, play central roles in inter-institutional relations is illustrated by the fact that the Vice President and General Counsel's Office at Harvard University has a staff of nine lawyers. In my own experience in working with Harvard College undergraduates on their senior honors theses, I have observed a considerable majority of them head to the top law schools. In increasing measure, science is left to those of non-American background, at Harvard mainly but not only of Asian American background, being regarded in school and even in the university as the work of "nerds" and other dehydrated folk. Biology in all its variety is not deprecated in the way that physics and chemistry tend to be; many women are drawn into biology who may then find themselves in one of the many niches in biology which involve physics and chemistry. Many women are also attracted to premedical programs, although medicine is not seen as the especially idealistic calling that once drew outstanding students, perhaps reflecting in part recognition of the maze of regulation and the pressures for defensive medicine out of fear of malpractice suits about which so many practicing physicians complain. The law does attract some idealists, on occasion inspired by legal activists fighting "the system," such as Ralph Nader. Increasingly, law attracts women, who now number 40 per cent of law students, so that my judgment on pages 483-84 that young recruits in the big offices are no longer driven by the "all-male atmosphere of night work" is mistaken in terms of gender, but also in terms of the hours the major law firms require. Domesticity for either sex takes second place.[38]

Law school offers, in comparison with graduate school in arts and sciences, the assurance of its lasting only three years. (It is partly due to students' snobbery that I make few converts among Harvard undergraduates when I occasionally suggest to them that business school takes only two rather than three years, and that the cases used at the Harvard Business School can in some cases be richer—although the graded class discussion may be thinner—than the appellate opinions which comprise so much of standard legal education but where class discussion, being ungraded, can be freer.) Perhaps no less important, to go to graduate school suggests the claim that one is capable of some originality, of making a contribution to the field and to one's potential students and colleagues. Going to law school makes only the minimal claim that one has high enough scores on the LSAT, the law school aptitude test, and good enough grades and recommendations to get in.[39] Lawyers have shown an enormous ability to make work for one another. When I was a law professor I studied libel and slander in cross-national perspective, a topic which interested virtually none of my colleagues; I was puzzled why we Americans were then supposed to be able to "take it" under the fallacious maxim that "sticks and stones can break my bones but words can never hurt me," in contrast to Austria, Argentina, the United Kingdom, and elsewhere in the European tradition, where defamation was taken with great seriousness.[40] I have lived long enough to see develop what might be termed a libel malpractice bar, often intimidating to the press and to publishers. A great variety of arenas exists in which, often through triple damages under the anti-trust laws, or punitive damages in other situations, we observe the cost to society of using the clumsy avenues of the law as a way of rather unevenly regulating conduct and adventitiously distributing wealth, a goodly share of which remains with the legal profession.

In an essay, "The Dream of Abundance Reconsidered,"[41] written as the Reagan Administration was coming into office in 1981, I expressed my misgivings concerning those public interest lawyers who with the aid of social scientists ". . . can decide that almost any group in the population—prison inmates, mental hospital psychotics, those who suffer from any definable handicap, including many school children—have had their Constitutional rights violated, and the state must somehow find the money for a remedy. . . . The adversary process spreads outward from the legal process to the larger American society and is inadequate to deal with the kinds of tradeoffs and compromises necessary when abundance can no longer lift all boats or grease all squeaking wheels" (p. 36).[42] I envisaged the disenchantment among Americans deprived of their anticipated standard level of consumer goods. I could not imagine Americans satisfied to live "at a lower level of abundance not based on credit," and then added, "Instead, I fear that many who voted for President Reagan, with the expectation that all these bounties would prove compatible, may become even more cynical about politicians and 'bureaucrats,' to the further weakening of the already strained bonds of what has been since the beginning, as the Civil War reminds us, a bitterly divided country."

My essay in part 4, "Interviewers, Elites, and Academic Freedom," was a preliminary report on my inquiry into the interviewing that took place in 1955 in a study of the impact of what we loosely term "McCarthyism" on social scientists in higher education. The study was commissioned by Robert M. Hutchins in his capacity as President of the Fund for the Republic, which was an offshoot of the Ford Foundation; Hutchins had asked Paul M. Lazarsfeld, founder of the Bureau of Applied Social Research and Professor of Sociology at Columbia University, to undertake a study. Professors at some elite institutions complained about what they regarded as the superficiality of the questions; at Smith College, for example, professors who had been interviewed complained to Robert Hutchins that the interviewer was too obtuse to understand their complicated responses, and that the questions in any case could not possibly capture their own idiosyncratic reactions.[43] Nevertheless, at this level also, hardly any refused altogether to be interviewed. The same receptiveness held true for the general population.

However, in recent years there has been a notable increase in resistance to surveys. A small element fueling popular anxiety and resistance has been the experience of salesmen posing as interviewers. But there is an additional factor which I did not find when I studied interviews done in the late Forties and in the Fifties, namely, a refusal to contribute one's own opinion out of a lack of any civic sense, perhaps rationalized on the basis that "nobody cares about what I think anyway." Careful understanding of the limits of interviewing helps to indicate some of the cleavages which in recent years have become more pronounced, so that it takes an unusual white person and an unusual effort, perhaps especially for a white male, to gain entrée to a black neighborhood and black respondents[44]—and black interviewers might in some white neighborhoods also meet resistance, particularly if male. One element here is the zealous insistence on personal privacy as technologies develop which make it more difficult to protect.[45] What has occurred in the realm of survey research can be seen as an indicator of the anarchic individualism and the fragmentation that have grown in the United States over the last three decades.

As Richard Hofstadter recognized, notions of paranoia are not new in America. Not only was there fear of the Masons, but of the fictional Illuminati, and in much of the country in much of the last century, of the Roman Catholics. One of the things that has changed is the speed with which television and other modern modes can carry outrage from one end of the country to the other. What also has changed is the diminution of the parties as filters for the political process, with a large increase in the last two decades of the de-aligned voters.[46] Careful survey research shows, however, that many of those voters who declare themselves to be "independent" lean toward the Democratic or toward the Republican Party, and that in the voting booth they commonly vote for the party representatives, even in many cases at the presidential level, toward whom they had expressed a leaning. Even so, to label oneself "independent" when one's voting behavior shows that this is not really the case, is another suggestion of the strong pull toward an anarchic individualism. In the Democratic Party, the George McGovern reforms virtually eliminated the centrality of the party bosses in choosing presidential candidates who they hoped could win an election, in contrast to the small activist groups who can now dominate the state primaries with little or no scrutiny by party regulars. It was the professionals, the party bosses, who chose Dwight Eisenhower for the Republicans and Adlai Stevenson for the Democrats in 1952, and Richard Nixon and John F. Kennedy in 1960.[47]

Writing these observations in the course of the 1992 presidential season, I have the sense that the traditional American antagonism to politicians has become even more extreme, leading some of those now in Congress and in office elsewhere to decide not to run for re-election, even while they and many in the public at large are frustrated by the inability of our divided governments to resolve conflicts between the things we demand and expect from government and the price in taxes or self-restraint we also need to reduce the deficit and accomplish a bit more of our goals. The rancor often focuses on trivial issues of minor privileges and "perks," but it is also the case that the legislature can be overwhelmed by the mobilization of unanticipated pressures.[48] The animus is illustrated by the effort at term limitations. A considerable number among the angry, commonly de-aligned Americans believe that their own Congressman or local legislator possesses serviceable seniority and is helpful to the district or area, even perhaps quite decent, but they become willing to sacrifice their own representatives because all the other citizens out there, all those dumb and gullible people, are not aware how all the other Congressmen or legislators are the captives of all-powerful "special interests" whose money and clout is essential for what is regarded as near-automatic permanent incumbency. There is an arrogance in that attitude about the validity of one's own vehemence, one's own version of being "sick and tired" or "mad as hell."

And what we have seen in recent years is a return to plebiscitary process propounded originally by Hiram Johnson and the Progressives in the earlier part of this century and now used in California, inter alia to pass Proposition 13, which dramatically and dangerously cut property taxes on those already owning homes.[49] Positioning himself as an outsider, as if he had never been to Washington, Ross Perot made two brief stabs for the Presidency on a plebiscitary platform in the 1992 presidential season, eliciting many enthusiastic and not always previously de-aligned volunteers. He proposed to call an electronic "town meeting" of Americans to decide, disregarding Congress and the executive agencies of the federal government, what ought to be done—a combination of technocracy and autocracy by someone Thorstein Veblen would have termed a Captain of Industry. Such an instantaneous procedure collapses the necessary space that should exist between the unevenly informed general population and the more or less professional politicians and civil servants whose education, experience, and relative—although of course not universal—tolerance vis-à-vis one another provides some protection against impulsiveness. The essay in this volume "Orbits of Tolerance, Interviewers, and Elites" discusses the relative broad-mindedness of people in public affairs who deal regularly with their opponents in contrast to the attitudes of their constituents who tend to be surrounded by the like-minded, some of the most vocal of whom are the closed-minded. There are times when I am inclined to regard the United States as a huge ferryboat with a very shallow draft and minimal keel, whose passengers are tempted to run first to one side of the boat and then to the other, nearly tipping it over, with Congress and the despised bureaucracy and the federal courts, with their lifetime tenure, serving as partial stabilizers.[50] The plebiscites, and here I include amendments to the federal Constitution, make the ferryboat more likely to tip over, because they circumvent the stabilizers.[51]

Many of the passengers on the ferryboat, even in the company they keep, feel that things are out of control, particularly since the end of the Cold War has deprived the country of the stability a national adversary can evoke. Some of Ross Perot's appeal was that he declared war on the deficit, and boldly said that he would raise taxes on gasoline over five years by fifty cents a gallon, and argued that with egalitarian populist support he could mobilize consensus, take charge, and replace drift with mastery. Ross Perot too campaigned "agin the guvmint." Some public figures and commentators have made an effort in recent years to refocus resentments, not against politicians, their hardly ever egregious pay and only occasional corruption, but rather against those who looted savings and loan institutions in the Reagan years; there has also been an attempt to focus on the enormous disparity of pay and benefits granted many American CEO's in contrast not only to the relatively declining pay of many members of their own workforce, but also with the executives of European or Japanese corporations; salaries often run into seven digits, along with less visible benefits in stock options and set-asides for retirement.[52] Taxpayers' resentments appear especially anguished among the two-income families of the middle class, many of whom look back to a nostalgic picture of a more equable time of rising affluence at the end of the Second World War until the oil shock crisis of 1973. I admire those who in this climate are willing to run for office as politicians, not as outsiders, and to become civil servants as a career, not as a brief step in an anticipated business or legal career. Class resentment against the very rich, with an exemption for those in sports and other entertainments, does exist, but not in vehemence comparable to that mobilized against the poor, perceived primarily as black and in major metropolitan areas visibly black.[53]

In January 1946 I began to teach in the undergraduate Social Science program of the University of Chicago, an intense experience for the GI's returning from the Second World War as well as for its in many cases, like myself, neophyte staff.[54] My policy concerns, as Section I of this book indicates, were with the dangers of nuclear weapons and their testing; I have already mentioned my support of Leo Szilard and the Council for a Livable World that he initiated. I have also served on the Board of Sponsors of the Federation of American Scientists, primarily concerned also with the dangers of war and preparation for war.[55] However, my major involvements with public policy have been on educational issues, primarily but not exclusively in higher education. I served on Nelson Rockefeller's Special Study Project; Lyndon Johnson's Task Force on Education; the Carnegie Commission on Higher Education and its successor Carnegie Council; also on several boards of trustees (Sarah Lawrence College as parent-trustee, Lewis & Clark College, and the Academic Advisory Board of Marlboro College).

An article I published in 1954 in the *Harvard Educational Review*, "Teachers Amid Changing Expectations," aroused fierce criticisms. I had argued that social studies should not be taught in precollegiate education, but rather schools should concentrate on the subjects best learned when young, such as foreign languages, mathematics and science, speech and writing (now I would also add musical instruments).[56] Social studies programs then were subject to McCarthyite scrutiny by Right Wing vigilantes, but in any case I regarded such studies as a topic requiring maturity, best studied by students who already knew a good deal of history and geography and had had some experience of life. I contended that social studies would be taught for those who went on to post secondary education by less intimidated teachers; if they did not go on to college, I declared that I had more confidence in the media (not that I regarded them as invulnerable!) than in many local schools. Understandably, I received angry letters from social studies teachers in secondary schools who declared that they were not intimidated and that their students needed an early introduction to social studies. I do not doubt that indeed many were not intimidated, nor would I deny that many secondary schools would do better in social studies than a great many colleges; I would not today generalize as I did in that essay. But in 1954 I could assume that teachers in general had somewhat more education than most of the parents of their students and that they carried a certain authority in their schools, including the authority of screening those intending to pursue college education. One can glimpse a vignette of that period in the quotations on page 597 of this volume, drawing upon the cues used in a 1952 study of the attitudes of 2500 ninth and tenth grade students in the high schools of eight middle-class New Jersey communities.[57] Parents shared with peers the value of being popular and friendly, but in this cohort, rebels who hated school work and believed ". . . that the teachers don't understand too well the things that really count" were rejected, while serious students who were sufficiently friendly won wide respect. A vivid ethnographic study of a public high school, Gerald Grant's *The World We Created at Hamilton High*, illustrates how different matters are today, where teachers appear to be ganged up on by their students, backed by their parents.[58] Grant describes the trajectory which led the school he disguises as Hamilton High to lose its magnet school quality and after being disrupted by racial integration, to achieve a certain measure of equanimity at a far lower level of academic expectation. Students have learned how to talk about their rights, to rebel at restraints (although some public schools have succeeded with dress codes), and to count on parents and other adults to side with them against the teachers rather than, as I have suggested would have happened in an earlier day, generally to support the teachers.

Student cynicism and resistance to authority are not of course only a legacy of the protest movements of the 1960's. Studies in the 1950's of campus life at the University of Kansas and of student attitudes at the University's medical school revealed a high degree of student skepticism and a resistance resembling that of workers who "soldier" on the job, and yet by an inchoate majority the students saw that the major part of the job got done.[59] Many more students, including for the first time more women than men, are coming to college today;

there is also an enormously increasing older population engaged in adult education. With huge variations by institution and hence in terms of region, class, gender, ethnicity, race, and field of study, the undergraduates arrive with a somewhat more hardened veneer of sophistication than did their predecessors. The sophistication disguises the fact that their level of verbal skills is considerably lower even at the top than it was a generation ago. We are all familiar with the difficulties schools face in areas of urban poverty, where even physical safety is not assured. We are less aware of what Daniel J. Singal, professor of history at Hobart and William Smith Colleges, terms "The Other Crisis in American Education," namely, what he refers to as the "dumbing down" of the curriculum, the rejection of excellence as "elitist."[60] Ability grouping in precollegiate education continues to be attacked as "tracking," even though it would seem that a mingling of able students with those who are inept and even disruptive harms both groups, the former by boring and perhaps alienating them from school, and the latter by making them feel inferior even while they reject school. The greatest decline has been in girls' verbal scores, which now, to the astonishment of many, are slightly lower than those of boys, even while the great gender disparities in mathematical scores, which have fallen much less dramatically, remain relatively unchanged.[61]

Whether one has in mind the competitive position of the United States in world markets or the capacity to enjoy continuous learning that some Americans do possess, but not enough in the typical urban or suburban setting to provide a peer group for each other, school reform and increasingly college and university reform are on the nation's agenda. But what seems lacking in virtually all discussions is a recognition of how badly we need experiments to see what might work at every level of schooling. Along with my former colleague James S. Coleman of the University of Chicago, I began over thirty years ago proposing an experiment in single-sex boarding schools for black boys; we had in mind schools that would focus on mathematics and science, employ a kind of Outward Bound quality for outdoor learning and discipline, and aim to send graduates on to college in science and engineering. Invariably, I emphasized that I was not confident that such a proposal would work, but could only be confident that a large proportion of what we had was not working. Any proposal for inner-city boarding schools for black boys was rejected as racist as well as sexist until quite recently when, for example, an effort to establish three such elementary schools—day schools, not boarding schools—in Detroit was struck down by litigation brought by the National Organization of Women in combination with the ACLU.[62] With the loss of parental authority any day school has to compete with the peer group and the peer group's choice of media influences. The North Carolina School of Mathematics and Science illustrates the kind of boarding school I would like to see attempted elsewhere. Like the much earlier and hence braver North Carolina School of the Arts, it has been racially integrated. Moreover, parents of prospective students are given money in order to visit the school to reassure themselves that their youngsters will be in the hands of careful educators.

When Franklyn Jenifer, now the President of Howard University, of which he is himself a graduate, was Chancellor of the Massachusetts state system of higher education, he came in 1989 to speak at the Harvard Graduate School of Education, his topic having been announced as "on higher education" (I was to be the discussant). He discarded that topic on arrival, declaring that the problems in the United States do not lie in postsecondary education but in the earlier years. He then declared that what was needed was to develop boarding schools in the inner city—and if this meant a politically and otherwise doubtful voucher system, so be it. Against his proposal was thrown the experience of the inadequacy of the American Indian boarding schools on the reservations. But these, it was noted, are run by the Bureau of Indian Affairs, whereas Jenifer of course had in mind schools which would have black leadership. Even if such schools took on the character of de facto orphanages for some abandoned youngsters in the inner city, they would seem worth trying. Even in the absence of the isolation of boarding schools, Catholic parochial schools, as Coleman's and other studies have shown, have been extremely effective at much lower per-pupil cost than the public schools, not only because they can exclude disruptive students, but because they have an ethos which tends to minimize disruption. Moreover, like a few other schools, including some public ones, they may require students to wear uniforms, which reduces peer jealousies and competition, including the resort to crime to get the money to buy sneakers and other requisite equipment.

I have already, in my reference to *Mississippi University for Women* vs. *Hogan*, indicated my belief in the importance of single-sex schools for girls and women. I marshall and cite some of the evidence in my

1991 contribution to a *Festschrift* for the feminist sociologist Rose Laub Coser (who does not agree with me), "A Margin of Difference: The Case for Single-Sex Education," cited earlier. Women and on occasion men as well have attacked me as sexist for contending that girls would profit from single-sex schools. One line of such attack has been that the "real world" is coeducational and hence preparation for it should also be coeducational. Moreover, some feminists contend that girls of whatever age should always be with the boys and the men because that is where power lies.[63] To be sure, the "real world" of coeducation is always present because schools do not operate year-round, any more than the boarding schools do, and peer competition in dress or in sexual games, as well as in the realm of sports, has social space in which to operate.

In "The Search for Challenge," an address in 1958 at the University of Chicago and at Kenyon College, reprinted in this volume, I raise the possibility of a revival of the Civilian Conservation Corps on a voluntary basis, suggesting that this was a "... moral equivalent for basic training which could be applicable to all young people and to women as well as to men" (p. 361). The Civilian Conservation Corps was one of many improvised relief measures of the New Deal, which took only young men, often from urban areas, out to clear forest trails in Vermont or Colorado, install soil conservation ponds, build firebreaks, and other such tasks. I refer in a footnote (p. 362) to Senator Hubert H. Humphrey's proposing such a plan in 1959. In recent years a number of efforts to re-establish a national volunteer service have been made, with Robert McNamara, former Secretary of Defense in the Kennedy and Johnson Administrations and former head of the World Bank, being one of the leaders of this movement. On page 362 in "The Search for Challenge," I take account of the fact that some of the noncom types who were in charge of Civilian Conservation Corps camps were more brutal than they needed to be. Today I have been reluctant to join in promoting such a plan, because it has been my observation that we do not have sufficiently capable young men and women who could put still younger people productively to work in a way that would not create continuous controversies, including perhaps ACLU litigation, over who is in charge. In this respect I am reminded of my experience on the National Advisory Council of the Peace Corps, where in the early years of the program, beginning in 1961, Volunteers were willing to endure the hardships of their two-year overseas assignments under not always magnetic Peace Corps leadership, but as the decade went on and the student revolts became endemic, the needed minimum of discipline often was insufficient to hold people to their commitments, so that there were many sites where some 40 per cent of Volunteers quit before their two years were up.[64]

Service in the Peace Corps did not earn Volunteers support for any further education they might wish to pursue. But if something like the CCC is to be revived, with small-scale experiments to help train leaders, one would want, as in some of the programs currently being suggested, some compensation either to provide a mid-career moratorium or to provide support for further education.[65] There is a small number of colleges where students are required, indeed where everyone, including the faculty and the administration, is required to do jobs necessary for the campus. Berea College in Kentucky is the best-known example, but others are Warren Wilson College in North Carolina and Blackburn College in Illinois. The School of the Ozarks in Point Lookout, Missouri, also depends on its Scholarship Work Program, in which students meet their tuition and room and board costs in return for work in campus jobs or industries. Obviously there is no huge demand to attend these colleges. Indeed, if one is well-to-do one cannot be admitted to Berea or the School of the Ozarks.[66] Still, such idiosyncratic locales can serve as experiment stations in order to learn what kinds of demands students are prepared to put on themselves in the face of the endemic pose of cynicism which, as I have suggested, appears obligatory, at least in much of bicoastal America.[67] The annual studies of entering students done by Alexander Astin of the School of Education at UCLA indicate an inclination to reject the self-absorption seen as characteristic of the Reagan era; there are other evidences of latent and in an increasing number of cases overt idealism especially among the well-to-do but not only among them. But if service were made a requirement, it might then provide more of an outlet for defiance than for idealism. Between service, so to speak, for its own sake and rewarding it by college credit or tuition credit one has to strike a delicate balance.

Such issues of balance are not escaped by the national military academies, which are often readily exploited by young men and women to obtain a fine undergraduate education while successfully avoiding actual service in the military.[68] Two state-supported military academies have not admitted women, namely, The Citadel in

Charleston, South Carolina, and Virginia Military Institute in Lexington, Virginia. In 1990, Claire Guthrie, Assistant Attorney General of the state of Virginia, asked me if I would testify as an expert witness in defense of the single-sex status of Virginia Military Institute against a suit brought by the Department of Justice which would require the admission of women. Claire Guthrie was aware of my dedication to the cause of women's colleges, thanks in part to my several visits to Chatham College in Pittsburgh, where she had served as chair of the board and acting president, and which was under severe pressure to follow the prevailing model and become coeducational. When Governor Douglas Wilder pulled out of the case, Claire Guthrie was forced to withdraw; the defense was taken up by the Alumni Association, whose counsel came to Cambridge to take my deposition; I was cross-examined by a lawyer from the Department of Justice. To prepare for my deposition I watched videotapes of the intensity and severity of basic training at VMI (whose physical ferocity was more than matched by the closeups of a football game in which VMI was playing some more powerful competitor). One could see the Spartan quarters and severe drill under which VMI cadets live, four or five to a room, where the beds have to be rolled up to find a place to study. Women in Virginia who want military training in addition to an academic program can receive both at Virginia Polytechnic Institute and State University, a much larger and incomparably less demanding locale. (In my testimony I called attention to the four women's colleges in Virginia—Mary Baldwin, Hollins, Sweet Briar, and Randolph-Macon Woman's College—which though private get some modest state support and which provide, along with VMI, diversity of opportunity for single-sex education.[69]) Virginia Military Institute is a wholly undergraduate college with 1300 students, rarely from privileged backgrounds, located (as is selective and only recently coeducational, private Washington & Lee University) in Lexington, a town of 7600, in the foothills of the Blue Ridge Mountains. Some students apply to VMI because they recognize that they would benefit from the discipline. Among those who do benefit have been a number of black students, in a setting where all of the "rats," as the first-year students are called and as they are treated, recognize that they are not singled out for the circumambient severity. Each senior is mentor to a rat, and in going through the mud or other obstacles, the cadets encourage one another, developing a kind of competitive cooperation that serves well not only the 20 per cent who enter the military directly but the great majority who, though potential soldiers, pursue careers as often civic-minded civilians.

I also contended that VMI serves Virginia and the country well as an exemplar of single-sex education. As I have already suggested in these pages, girls and boys develop at different rates through adolescence, with enormous variations by ethnicity and race, social class, and a constellation of individual circumstances. Boys tend to be more prideful than girls, less emotionally connected, "hanging out" with other boys, but not always in school or college intimate with them—even the "old boy network" in later life is often more of a grouping for sport and other play than for career enhancement or intimacy. Girls seem to be somewhat less prideful and more cooperative. But by middle school they like to be with those girls, the potential cheerleaders, whom boys like. Despite the schisms this setting engenders, females often maintain through life their friends from school and college. (When men are asked who their best friends are, they commonly reply that their wives are their best friends, whereas married women commonly say their best friends are other women.) By middle school, and in varying measure through high school and on into college, coeducational institutions are commonly boys' schools. There are exceptions, notably the Honors Program at Swarthmore College where women and men prepare cooperatively for external examiners, using their own professors as coaches rather than as bestowers of competitive commendation. Even at Harvard College, where some women thrive in combat for classroom and professors' time, other women are surprised that, in a locale where they had anticipated they would find men not as threatened by bright women as they had experienced in secondary school, there is a scarcity of such men; many women resign themselves—despite much mobilization of feminist opinions—preferring to demur and defer to men in class and out.[70]

The Citadel in Charleston, South Carolina, is all male at the undergraduate Corps of Cadets level, but has women in its graduate and evening programs.[71] Wabash College in Indiana is sufficiently well endowed so that its recent decision to remain a private men's college and not become coeducational can be sustained. The same is true of Hampden-Sydney College, a Presbyterian college with 800 students, also in Virginia. Warily, Texas Woman's University retains its single-sex program at the undergraduate level, hoping that men can be persuaded to attend North Texas State University in the same town of Denton. Men are admitted to its graduate programs.

Many critics of VMI regard it as an anachronism, a relic of patriarchy; they regard single-gender education as no less reprehensible than the earlier policy at most Southern institutions, including VMI and The Citadel, of racial segregation. This linkage is ironical in view of the success I have already mentioned that both institutions have—even in so "Confederate" a city as Charleston—in the relatively high percentage of blacks who make it through to graduation. The political and cultural illegitimacy of VMI has been insisted upon by Alexander W. Astin, one of the country's leading authorities on higher education, who joined in an amicus brief appealing the decision to support the single-sex status of VMI by the Federal District Court in the Western District of Virginia.[72]

Just as environmentalists cherish vanishing species we do not yet know how to recreate in a laboratory, so we must do the same with institutions, which in our own virtuous era we would not be able to invent *de novo*. I fear that both ideological and juridical constraints limit the diversity permitted *among* educational institutions, in contrast to the often isomorphic diversity encouraged, if not legally and administratively enforced, *within* institutions throughout much of the academic procession. One of the sources of that enforcement is that diversity of color and of course of gender has become an advertising staple, evident in catalogues and other consumer-oriented materials. (Rarely is it held against the "diversity" image of a highly selective private college or university that most of its students belong to a single age cohort and do not have the advantage that, for example, Chatham College offers of recruiting older women as students to live in the dormitories with their children and to act, as some of the younger students see it, as "rate-busters" by spending too much time preparing for class.) In this situation of forced, superficial homogenization, there is all the more reason, then, to hang onto VMI and pursue what might be learned from it. I discovered, for example, in the student magazine, *Sounding Brass*, some remarkably sensitive poems and short stories whose authors in that setting had no fear of appearing insufficiently manly to themselves or to their peers.

I have for similar reasons defended the historically black colleges and universities, and have opposed the efforts by litigation to require the merger of what have sometimes been called the black land-grant institutions with their formerly all- or virtually all-white counterparts.[73]

By the title *The Academic Revolution,* Jencks and I meant to refer to the hegemony of the faculty vis-à-vis administrators, trustees, and the public at large. Several years later, the student revolts with faculty assistance at a number of highly visible primarily residential colleges and universities helped diminish the authority of previously regnant faculty and brought students into governance processes, where now in some measure they remain. Nowhere did students even with faculty allies gain hegemony. Rather what occurred was the triumph of the student in his or her role as a consumer, free of adult parietal authority and in most institutions less constrained by curricular authority.[74]

There do remain a few institutions where adult authority, including parietal authority, still holds sway. One of the largest and most impressive is Brigham Young University. Edward B. Fiske, in the *Fiske Guide to Colleges 1993,* writes: "BYU might seem like a 1950s timewarp to most Americans; and at times it may seem, in one student's words, like a 'clean-scrubbed complacency farm that churns out nice, quiet students.' But its students seem to thrive in the university's caring, albeit squeaky-clean atmosphere. 'Can you imagine a university where an honor system actually works for 27,000 students?' queries one student." Actually, in terms of the prevailing passion today for multicultural diversity, there is a very high proportion of male and now also female students who have spent two years of proselytizing for the Mormon faith overseas before coming to BYU; there is a growing though still small cohort, seven per cent, of foreign students. Goshen College, with about 900 students in Goshen, Indiana, is Mennonite with correspondingly strict rules; yet an effort is made to deprovincialize faculty members as well as the students by study-service trimesters overseas. (See Victor Stoltzfus, *Church-Affiliated Higher Education: Exploratory Case Studies of Presbyterian, Roman Catholic and Wesleyan Colleges,* Goshen, Indiana: Pinchpenny Press, 1992.) Wheaton College in Illinois, with several thousand students, and its less well-known sister college Gordon College on Cape Ann, northeast of Boston, with 1100 students, are non-denominational Christian colleges with rules unimaginable in most adolescent locales. (Gordon's President came under criticism a few years ago when he decided to permit dancing on the campus.) The colleges founded by Roman Catholics vary considerably, even among the 28 varieties founded by the Jesuits; but even the culturally and politically conservative University of Dallas, which like most but by no means all colleges founded by Catholics has no fraternities or sororities, has no religious requirements, but students are required to take twelve credits in philosophy and also in English.

The University of Chicago remains the most eminent institution where curricular authority appears to reside largely in faculty hands. During the celebration in 1991-92 of the hundredth anniversary of the University's founding, a newspaperman asked me my opinion about Chicago and I expressed my great admiration for its having maintained, all through the 1960's and thereafter, an unyielding striving for excellence in scholarship and teaching, its leadership bowing neither to McCarthyite pressures in the 1950's nor to student protests thereafter; when students took over the Administration Building, Chancellor Edward Levi refused any compromise, dismissed many of the students over passionate protests from parents and some faculty members, and continued to maintain the authority of the faculty and the administration. In *General Education in the Social Sciences*, I describe my own experiences in the College of the University of Chicago and compare them with the quite different constellation faced as a teacher at Harvard College in 1958 and thereafter, when I could not count on roommates being in the same courses, or a class in a lecture sharing much of a common culture in any respect. In my essay, "My Education in Soc 2 and My Efforts to Adapt It in the Harvard Setting," in that volume (pp. 178-216), I refer to a further effort I made in the initial year of Harvard's Freshman Seminar program to develop a course for 40 men and 20 women, admission to which would require their taking a common program in the humanities and a similar, not so successful, effort in the natural sciences.[75] When I taught in the College of the University of Chicago, from 1946 to 1958, I took full advantage of the fact that the students were reading the same books—in the social sciences by no means always classics or a canon—and could share conversations beyond banalities, unlike the situation in most institutions, where students share very little common learning. When the inquiring reporter from Chicago then asked me why, if the University of Chicago was so magnificent, there were not more exemplars of that approach, I responded that it was not what most customers wanted. Many people do not realize how small is the College of the University of Chicago, with 3400 students, or that despite its eminence it must accept 46 per cent of its applicants (in contrast, for example, to Princeton's 17 per cent) to recruit a first-year class. Students do not come to Chicago for social life or to build a resumé as they might in the Ivy League or Stanford or Duke. Not only the consumer mentality of students and their families but also the solipsism of so many scholarly faculty members make it difficult to imagine re-creating such an institution as the University of Chicago.

The two St. John's Colleges in Annapolis and in Santa Fe, with their entirely required "Great Books" programs, have tiny enrollments of under 500 students, and must accept over three-quarters of their applicants. Faculty members all have the status of tutors, and must eventually accept responsibility for teaching in every subject, a requirement that denies most of them visibility beyond the locale. (Along with my admiration, I have serious misgivings about the preoccupation of the St. John's College Program with oral discourse and lack of attention to writing—a more serious problem today than a generation ago, when more high school graduates knew something about how to write and were not so allergic to it and awkward at it as they often are today.)[76] A few public institutions have sought to position themselves as liberal arts colleges in the public sector and to make serious demands on students, for example, proficiency in a foreign language. The University of Minnesota campus at Morris, with less than 2,000 students, is such a place. New College in Sarasota, initially private, is now a branch of the University of South Florida; it became experimental in what is now the more conventional mode of granting almost complete autonomy to its 530 students in their choice of what to study; still, the New College atmosphere is intellectually strenuous. Edward B. Fiske in his *Guide* writes critically about New College, which in other respects he admires, that fewer than three per cent of students are black. At the more elite institutions, including the major "flagship" state universities and often well beyond these, "diversity" now means a standardized, so to speak photogenic diversity, including an ample number who can be defined as people "of color." I am reminded of two Hispanic young women whom Wendy Griswold, then at Harvard, and I taught in a conference course on the sociology of higher education in 1978, who had been recruited from migrant worker families and did not realize until they got to Cambridge that Harvard College exists in a metropolis, a setting for which they were totally unprepared, just as Harvard, despite its black Dean of Students, black Chaplain, and other African

American forms of support, was in my view being exploitative, in part I should add as the result of idealism as well as of fashion.

My hope remains what it has been in my years as a cautious reformer in higher education, namely, that we need to think of policy alternatives to cope with our present discontents. Much as a new drug needs to be carefully tested before it can be widely marketed, so with a new idea or a revived old idea such as national volunteer service or a required curriculum of "Great Books." Again, my aim is to encourage experiments and thorough research to see what may have worked and what may have done less well, meanwhile creating as well as maintaining a variety of models from which to choose.

David Riesman

Notes

1 Acknowledgements: Lewis Dexter, Martha Fuller, Bruce Kimball, Robert Jay Lifton, Wilfred McClay, Michael Maccoby, Richard Robbins. Financial support: Stimson Bullitt, Lewis Dexter, Michael Maccoby, Richard Hunt.

2 Somewhere in the files of *The Listener*, a now defunct weekly publication of the BBC, is an article published by a public school classmate of Orwell's who said that the latter when he saw his fellow students saluting the masters thought that these students, unlike himself, were obedient conformists, when in fact, being more cynical than Orwell, they were going through the motions without the proper emotions. This classmate thought that *1984* was Orwell's image of his own experience at Eton. Michael Shelden in *Orwell: The Authorized Biography* (London: Heinemann, 1991) suggests that prior to Eton Orwell had begun preparatory boarding school at age eight at St. Cyprian's under even more severe conditions of oppression than at Eton, helping frame the portrait of Winston Smith in *1984*. See the essay review by Michael Scammell "Sense and Censorship" in *The New Republic* issue 4 039, June 15, 1992, pp. 31–38.

3 I had resigned publicly from the Committee because it had refused to come to the defense of J. Robert Oppenheimer when the latter was attacked as a national security menace by Edward Teller. I regarded Teller with enmity during all the Cold War years, and even now when he remains the chief proponent of fanciful and often disingenuous "Star Wars" notions; I had allied myself with Leo Szilard, founder of the Council for a Livable World, an organization opposed to nuclear weapons development and testing (I recall my astonishment at going to see Szilard not long before his death at his Washington, D.C., hotel, and finding Edward Teller, his fellow countryman and still his friend, in the room with him). One of the ironies of the present situation is that many Russian intellectuals during the Gorbachev thaw expressed their admiration for the steadfastness of the American right

wing, including Edward Teller and my civilized and erudite colleague, Richard Pipes, seeing them as among those responsible for forcing the Soviet Union into an arms race that could only embarrass it and cause the country to fall ever further behind in almost every other respect. As for the CIA, I have invariably defended its recruiting on campuses for its intelligence branches (in contrast to its dirty tricks branches), for I have seen the CIA, as was evident during the Vietnam war, as more likely to give a candid picture of America's opponents than the other intelligence agencies linked to the military services. However, the Senate hearings which confirmed President Bush's appointment of Robert Gates to be Director of the CIA indicated that Gates himself had, perhaps opportunistically, greatly exaggerated Soviet military and even economic power and until near the end dismissed Gorbachev's accomplishments as part of a sophisticated effort to deceive the United States.

4 When the immensely gifted and exquisitely sensitive Erving Goffman, seeking to do participant observation in a mental hospital, went as a presumptive patient to St. Elizabeth's in Washington, D.C., he emerged with the concept of the "total institution." He may not fully have appreciated the extent to which the constraints and restraints of the hospital were experienced as protective by some of the patients. Along with the attacks on professional psychiatry by Thomas Szasz, M.D., and also on medicine more generally (on schooling as well) by the radical priest Ivan Illich, Goffman helped support the later de-institutionalization of enormous numbers of mental patients. Even today, when formerly hospitalized patients provide a large cohort of the homeless, bright lawyers feel justified in getting hospital patients (including many of those committed because they pleaded insanity as a defense to murder, child abuse, and other crimes) set free, especially when patients—frequently on medication that they will drop upon release— can plausibly "pass" as sane for a brief time in the courtroom and when in the society at large an increase in the already extravagant American antagonism to "bureaucracy" and to institutions helps power the crusade.

5 Many of the concepts in the earlier debates about nuclear arsenals have nearly vanished from the American vocabulary. What was meant by "minimum deterrent" was deterrence through fear of reprisal, the threat of unacceptable devastating damage to the presumptive enemy's first strike. In contrast, building bomb shelters implied that the United States might take the initiative, that is, use "counterforce" weapons to attack the enemy's own deterrent while insuring or rather appearing to insure that bomb shelters protected Americans from what would then be "acceptable" reprisals. In other words, to build bomb shelters made it look to our opponent as if we were contemplating an attack, granted the opponent's continuing inferiority in weapons of destruction and in modes of detection.

6 However, in my comments for a *Partisan Review* symposium, "The Cold War and the West" (vol. 29, no. 1, 1962, pp. 63–74), reprinted in this volume (pp. 93–102), while declaring "I have never been convinced that totalitarian governments are here to stay, whatever their own boasts or the fears of their enemies . . ." (p. 101), I had earlier remarked in passing that vis-à-vis Communist China ". . . the ideology and fanaticism of the Chinese have not

been dimmed by history or thawed by Western contact" (p. 99). This was true of the leadership and the cadres whose minds it could reach, but for the country as a whole it was a superficial and mistaken over-generalization.

7 Robert Jay Lifton, in a clarifying comment on an earlier draft (letter of September 11, 1992), reminds me that their very personal context did lead some women to become among the most fanatical of Nazis, which he illustrates by Leni Riefenstahl and her film, *The Triumph of the Will*, "probably one of the most powerful of all Nazi propaganda documents." She had, Lifton indicates, a particular talent for rendering the abstract mythology in an earthy way.

8 As I write these sentences in the midst of the 1992 presidential campaign, I find it hard to overstate my dismay at the extravagant cynicism of both men and women, leaving them prey to the paranoia of the gullible, who believe those candidates who pretend not to be politicians, to be "above" politics. Men and women alike have disdained party affiliation, prideful that they can judge candidates on their individual merits, arrogant enough to despise mere politicians and bureaucrats without any personal experience and without appreciation for the complexities of our nearly ungovernable federal non-system.

9 In a forthcoming essay, "The Family of the Future" (1992), Michael Maccoby observes that gender differences tend to be smaller in the increasing number of families where both parents have careers, in contrast to the earlier, more patriarchal family where the mother, depending on children and their ages, might have a succession of jobs but not aspire to a career. Carol Gilligan's influential work does not assume that all girls and young women develop "in a different voice," but appreciates the need for disaggregation among both genders.

It is paradoxical and sad that prior to the renewed and new women's movements which began so energetically in the 1960's girls did better in school in comparison to boys than they do now, when there is so much attention to actual and supposed gender bias. For several of my many efforts to understand this development, see "A Margin of Difference: The Case for Single-Sex Education," in Judith R. Blau and Norman Goodman, Eds., *Social Roles and Social Institutions: Essays in Honor of Rose Laub Coser* (Boulder: Westview Press, 1991), pp. 241–257; and "Foreword" in George H. Hanford, *Life with the SAT* (New York: College Entrance Examination Board, 1991), pp. ix–xxi.

10 In footnote 5 on page 57 I refer to a 1961 conversation with "an influential opinion-maker who was sure that there would be a nuclear war, since it was impossible to do business with Khrushchev. I asked him whether he thought it impossible to do business with Jimmy Hoffa. He grew red in the face, pounded the table, and screamed imprecations against Hoffa." For readers of a later generation, I should note that Jimmy Hoffa was head of the Teamsters Union, then regarded as the most corrupt union in the whole country, with Hoffa regarded as someone who generally got his way.

11 In later years, I have found myself defending nuclear power against a number of colleagues, students, and others who found it more compelling and rewarding to try to close down a local nuclear power plant such as

Seabrook in New Hampshire or (successfully) Shoreham in New York than to mount quixotic attacks against America's nuclear tests, especially after these went underground (where it turned out that really quite enormous bombs could be tested). For nuclear power in this country to be less hazardous, it would need to be run as the French do, perhaps by the nuclear Navy or the Corps of Engineers, rather than by local public utilities, which by their very nature as low-profit enterprises rarely attract great managerial skill, entrepreneurial ingenuity, and pertinacious watchfulness for things that might go wrong.

12 In the light of hindsight, I was probably too critical of Israel's attack on the Iraqi nuclear reactor, although I would still stand behind my criticisms of Israel's bombing and later invasion of Lebanon. A letter I wrote in the *New York Times* (July 9, 1982) criticizing the bombing brought me for a time telephone harassment that I assume came from the Jewish Defense League, because the caller, always male, would say either "Never again," the JDL slogan, or "Yasser Arafat thanks you."

13 Bernard Sarachek, in "Japan-Bashing and the American Malaise," contends that American business schools, in order for their graduates to help the United States become more competitive in world trade, should include science, engineering, and technology in their actual programs. *Business & the Contemporary World*, vol. IV, Summer 1992, pp. 40–48, at pp. 47–48.

In footnote 5 on page 57 I refer to the belief Americans held in 1961 that in business matters we must make compromises and that we are pragmatists, in contrast to national affairs, where we should be moralistic and idealistic.

14 John Lukacs, "American History: The Terminological Problem" (*American Scholar*, Winter 1992, vol. 61, pp. 7–32, at p. 32). Lukacs assesses the irrelevance of the traditional terms "conservative" and "liberal" in the current era.

On the particularistic forms taken by American ethnic cultures, see the observations of Werner Sollors, Professor of Afro-American Studies and of English Literature at Harvard University, *Beyond Ethnicity: Consent and Descent in American Culture* (New York: Oxford University Press, 1986). See also Mary Waters, *Ethnic Options: Choosing Identities in America* (Berkeley: University of California Press, 1990).

15 "Invidious consumption" is a Veblenian term. It can serve as a reminder that there are other strains in American life from which affluence is seen as menacing. There is a Malthusian strain which fears over-population and, in its current "green" garb, destruction of the environment. There is a strain, hauntingly represented by the Amish, whose intelligent this-worldly asceticism resembles Thorstein Veblen's own preference for an unadorned life, hostile to all forms of display. In the preface to the third section of this volume, I refer to Veblen's anticipating the Beats in his cavalier attitude toward convention, including the conventions of the consumer-dominated affluent society. But Veblen differed profoundly from the pietist sects such as the Amish and other opponents of modernity in his passionate belief that society should be run by engineers, by people who know machines, rather than by Captains of Industry who know only finance and clandestine

monopoly. The Technocrats of an earlier era saw themselves as followers of Veblen, wanting production to be efficient, not to produce the affluence which led to what Veblen labeled as conspicuous consumption but to diminish poverty, inequality, and waste. Veblen would have no sympathy with the anti-scientific outlook so common today; coming from a poor Scandinavian-American farming family, he had no nostalgia for the pastoral.

More generally, I now believe that the emphasis on affluence in these essays accepted too readily the assumptions of progress which Veblen himself would have shared, and which much of the world, looking enviously at its image of America, also shares. The religious and secular traditions of restraint have much to say to us in the light of American history and also much to say in the light of world hunger and nearly world-wide conflicts over scarce resources among ethnic, religious, and nationalist groups.

16 Even the national highway system was given some justification as the National Defense Highway program. We must remember that the development of the nuclear bomb was begun in academic settings, notably the University of Chicago. Defense agencies initiated the federal enterprise of funding research in the social as well as in the natural sciences. The Office of Naval Research was one of the initiators here. But with the end of the Cold War and the increasing pressures on the federal budget, the defense connection is no longer so exigent.

For many years the Office of Naval Research was the prime contractor for federal research support for Stanford University, which negotiated with the Office to decide upon the overhead rate charged on government research contracts, under which Stanford could recoup costs for maintenance, administration, and other forms of support for research. This arrangement came unraveled and the cause of a major scandal because it appeared that charges for presidential entertainment were being borne by "taxpayers' money." However, depreciation charges on a Stanford yacht were included by mistake and should not have been included under the Stanford and ONR agreement to take 20 per cent off the accumulated costs to allow for individual items that might not be appropriate for research overhead or, despite the argument that presidential entertainment is one of the costs of doing academic business, might look inappropriate in the press and in the purview of Michigan Congressman John Dingell and his watchful subcommittee. Stanford's former President, Donald Kennedy, was forced to resign. Stanford and many other universities were then and now continue to be targeted for similar expensive excavation of previously agreed-upon arrangements. For an earlier discussion of the costs sometimes unthinkingly imposed on universities, see the contribution by Stanford's former President, Richard W. Lyman, "Federal Regulation and Institutional Autonomy: A University President's View," in *Bureaucrats and Brainpower: Government Regulation of Universities*, Paul Seabury, ed. (San Francisco: Institute for Contemporary Studies, 1979), pp. 27–45.

17 I learned about the issues concerning appropriate overhead charges, which now are salient at many research universities, from Stanford to Harvard Medical School and to MIT and far beyond, through my experiences in negotiating an overall overhead rate with the Army Air Force. No

Sperry product went to a civilian purchaser. How could we then include in overhead any of the expenses for the radio broadcasts from London of Edward R. Murrow under Sperry's aegis? I argued that we were entitled to recover a portion of the amount because it was important for the morale of our employees to believe that there was a future for them after the end of the war when defense production, we naively assumed, would come to an end. The Army Air Force contracting officer agreed that we could allocate a portion of the costs to overhead.

18 A similar thought recurs in a later essay, "The Search for Challenge," where I satirically consider that underinvolved adolescents in Kansas City, Missouri, might build mountains up which they could climb and down which they could ski (pp. 360–61).

19 See Theodore Newcomb, *Personality and Social Change: Attitude Formation in a Student Community* (New York: Dryden, 1957).

20 Robert S. Weiss, *Staying the Course: The Emotional and Social Lives of Men Who Do Well at Work*. New York: Free Press, 1990.

21 Lenore Weitzman and Mavis MacLean, *Economic Consequences of Divorce: The International Perspective*. Oxford University Press, 1992.

22 What is said in the text needs to be qualified in terms of region, religion, and social class. For example, in a Southern state university which I think is almost certainly Chapel Hill, and to my surprise in a neighboring black state university, almost certainly North Carolina Central University, older patterns still appear to prevail: women entering as first-year students have higher occupational goals than those with which they emerge, as they cool down their aspirations in order not to threaten the available males. See Dorothy C. Holland and Margaret A. Eisenhart, *Educated in Romance: Women, Achievement, and College Culture* (Chicago: University of Chicago Press, 1990). A very different picture of coed life is provided in Michael Moffatt, *Coming of Age in New Jersey: College and American Culture* (New Brunswick: Rutgers University Press, 1989). Moffatt, an anthropologist, lived for several seasons in the Rutgers College coed dormitories, whose prevailing atmosphere is "cool" and cynical. The women have learned to use the same vulgar language as the men. They bait and taunt each other; some of the men choose to leave for fraternities or to live off-campus, not finding it easy to deal with women who cannot be defined in the old vocabulary as either "good girls" or "sluts."

23 William Morrow, 1986. See also the critical, yet not wholly unsympathetic essay-review of *A Lesser Life* by Beth Cagan and Neil McLaughlin, "Women's Liberation and the Politics of Family Policy Reform." *Socialist Review*, Vol. 1, Winter 1988, pp. 154–161.

24 For a reflective analysis of the backlash of traditional women who in order to mobilize had to leave tradition behind, see Rebecca Klatch, *Women of the New Right* (Philadelphia: Temple University Press, 1987).

25 The essay first appeared in the Yearbook supplement to *Collier's Encyclopedia* (New York: Macmillan Educational Corp., 1980), pp. 80–86; then in 1980 in the now defunct British magazine *Encounter* under the title "Egocentrism: Is the American Character Changing?" (vol. LV, nos. 2–3, August–September 1980), pp. 19–28.

26 See the cross-cultural comparisons in Maccoby, "To Work Globally, Seek Common Values" in *Research-Technology Management*, vol. 35, no. 5, September-October 1992, pp. 50–52. See in addition Larry Hirschorn and Thomas Gilmore, "The New Boundaries of the 'Boundaryless' Company," *Harvard Business Review*, May-June 1992, pp. 104–115.

27 For an account at once historical and contemporary of how law, medicine, and the academic professions developed far beyond the original profession of theology and the ministry, see Bruce A. Kimball, *The "True Professional Ideal" in America: A History* (Oxford: Basil Blackwell, 1992). In the chapters on the legal and the medical professions, Kimball discusses their rise and the contemporary distrust both now elicit.

28 The widespread practice of relatively frequent changes of jobs, something which has only recently come to Japan, carries risks in terms of health and retirement benefits. One of the most difficult issues facing two-career couples is how to achieve equity between the job choices available to each of the spouses, for in the past it has generally been the man's moves which had priority, and it is only in recent years in the United States that for example women college presidents' husbands have had to find sometimes lesser roles within reasonable commuting distance. Outside the heavily unionized parts of the public sector, unions have lost much of their earlier power, including the power to protect seniority. In 1994 academic institutions will lose their power to terminate tenured faculty at a specified age, often at age 65, potentially allowing many faculty members who achieved their positions during the baby-boom years to remain in their costly places. This is one of many examples of legislation which endangers American competitiveness, and here I would include the Americans with Disabilities Act and the to me unjustified legislation in many states forbidding employers from taking account of employee health-risky behavior off the job, notably smoking. (This last is an issue where the ACLU cooperated with the lobbyists for the tobacco companies in defense of employees' privacy rights.)

29 Richard B. Freeman in *The Over-Educated American* (New York: Academic Press, 1976), foresaw the societal strains likely to result from the disappointments of the college educated unable to achieve their expectations of highly remunerative steady work.

30 When educated people think of "college" or "university," they commonly have in mind a private and residential setting. However, over three-quarters of contemporary students are non-residential, some of them living in apartments adjacent to a campus, but the majority are commuters, and the great majority depend on scholarship aid, work-study, and loans, with the need to pay off the latter partially limiting their options for future careers.

A quotient of the resentments arising from stalled opportunities in the faltering economy has been turned against the increasing tuitions charged even in the "Public Ivies," which already educate many of the children of the wealthy at the expense of the general less-educated population in the state. Richard M. Huber focuses these resentments on the faculty who in his view have been reducing their teaching loads and become negligent toward students in their pursuit of often meaningless research. See *How Professors*

Play the Cat Guarding the Cream: Why We're Paying More and Getting Less in Higher Education (Fairfax, Virginia: George Mason University Press, 1992). Yet there are ever so many "invisible colleges," both public and private, where students would be much better off if faculty members retained some tie to adult worlds rather than competing through entertainment and grade inflation for student customers, even while there are also unduly research-aspirant primarily state colleges which seek to duplicate graduate programs already in existence nearby. See my observations in "Can We Maintain Quality Graduate Education in a Period of Retrenchment?" David Henry Lecture (University of Illinois: 1975). Moreover, it is not sufficiently appreciated that tuition increases have in part been driven by the demands of student consumers and their parents that adequate health care and other student services be provided and, in the more visible and especially the residential institutions, that the student body and the faculty be "diverse" in terms of blacks, Hispanics, and, to a much lesser degree, scholarship-assisted low-income whites. For black students especially, the market for recruiting has become national, and for aspirant institutions this is true for able students generally, driving up recruiting costs even for non-aspirant colleges which could once depend on a local primarily commuter market. For now somewhat outdated discussion, see Chapter 4 in Riesman, *On Higher Education: The Academic Enterprise in an Era of Rising Student Consumerism* (San Francisco: Jossey-Bass, 1980), pp. 105–61.

31 For discussions of work today see Michael Maccoby, *Why Work: Leading and Motivating the New Generation*. New York: Simon & Schuster, 1988.

32 In addition to Gans's own explorations in *The Levittowners: Ways of Life and Politics in a New Suburban Community* (New York: Pantheon, 1967), see his *Middle American Individualism: The Future of Liberal Democracy* (New York: Free Press, 1988). See also the brilliant and acerbic defense of lower-middle-class values by Christopher Lasch in *The True and Only Heaven: Progress and Its Critics* (New York: Norton, 1991), a book which in my judgment goes overboard in its self-critique of intellectuals' snobberies.

33 Professor Kato had met us while studying in this country. See Kato, "Development 19th-century Style: Some Historical Parallels between the United States and Japan," in Herbert Gans et al., eds., *On the Making of Americans: Essays in Honor of David Riesman* (Philadelphia: University of Pennsylvania Press, 1979), pp. 173–90; he is now at the National Institute of Multimedia Education in Chiba, Japan. His continuing interest in Japanese popular culture is illustrated in his book *Media, Culture, and Education in Japan: A Collection of Papers*, published by the National Institute of Multimedia Education, 1992.

Robert Jay Lifton had also encouraged us to come to Japan and with his wife B.J. Lifton also helped our introduction there.

34 Stimson Bullitt, *To Be a Politician* (Garden City, NY: Doubleday, 1959).

35 See David and Evelyn Thompson Riesman, *Conversations in Japan: Modernization, Politics, and Culture* (New York: Basic Books, 1967), pp. 74–79.

36 "Innovation and Institutions: Notes on the Japanese Paradigm," in Paul Adler, ed., *Technology and the Future of Work*, Oxford 1992, p. 17. See Seymour Martin Lipset, "American Exceptionalism, Japanese Uniqueness,"

for an excellent account of the continuing role of hierarchy in contributing to the communal efficacy of Japanese society [forthcoming].

37 In August 1992 District Judge Louis Bechtle in Federal District Court for Eastern Pennsylvania ruled that the Massachusetts Institute of Technology violated the anti-trust laws in sharing data on the financial aid requests of candidates who applied to more than one of the Ivy League and other cooperating universities. Judge Bechtle harshly swept aside MIT's argument (which I had strongly and publicly supported) that the purpose of the cooperation was not to raise consumers' costs of higher education (already highly subsidized even if full tuition is paid) but to prevent a bidding war for scholars comparable to that engaged in throughout much of the country for athletes, and to spread financial aid to those in need, thus diversifying their student bodies. Ironically, there was no university with which MIT could at the time of suit conspire, since the other institutions had all withdrawn their challenged programs. A small group of liberal arts colleges, mainly in the Northeast and not all of them highly endowed, also belong to the Overlap Group which shared and often adjusted their respective judgments on the financial aid requests of those who applied to more than one of the Group; when also targeted by the Justice Department as a price-fixing conspiracy, they ended this cooperation. MIT, having already spent something like a million dollars in its defense, plans to appeal to the Circuit Court of Appeals.

38 A prize honors thesis in 1992 by Madhavi Sunder, "For the Record: Discrimination and 'A Different Voice' at *The New York Times*," describes the quite similar demands of work for the *New York Times* if one wants to rise in the paper's hierarchy, where there is a quasi-military sense of urgency.

Many years ago an undergraduate with whom I had worked was tempted to go on in sociology, but he followed his many peers into law school. After he had worked several years in one of the big firms in Chicago, he turned up to report that his cohort were all working on weekends and that he had no time to enjoy his immense salary, let alone to establish a family. When the cohort was about to be offered a raise, he proposed that instead of a raise, they all ask to take Sundays off. Everyone else refused. He resigned, took a low-paying position with the American Civil Liberties Union, and several years later was able to enter another firm with the stipulated basis of time he would have for his own pursuits—an arrangement sufficiently unusual to have been reported on the Friday law page of the *New York Times*.

39 I have found illuminating Bruce Kimball's account of the rise of the legal profession in the United States and its relation to such older professions as theology and to its contemporary competitors, in *The "True Professional Ideal in America": A History* (Oxford: Basil Blackwell, 1992).

40 Cf. my series of essays, "Democracy and Defamation," *Columbia Law Review* 1942.

41 *Nieman Reports*, vol. xxxv, no. 3, Autumn 1981, pp. 29–37.

42 I recognize that what is said in the text is a vast over-generalization concerning public interest lawyers. I have worked on projects and theses with a number of outstanding undergraduates who have used their training imaginatively. A recent example who comes to mind is Jeff Rosen, who has just now (fall 1992) become Legal Affairs Editor of *The New Republic*. I

worked with him on a senior project in the academic year 1984–85. After two years as a Marshall Scholar at Oxford he attended Yale Law School, worked for Judge Abner Mikva, during which time he began writing both for the *Yale Law Journal* and for *The New Republic*, for which he now serves as a commentator on major constitutional themes. Right after graduating from Harvard College he served as a speechwriter for former Secretary of Education William Bennett. Just from my own limited purview, I have seen ever so many who put law school to work in the public interest in reflective rather than fanatical fashion, not seeking the enormous post-graduation stipends to which they would have entrée, but not seeking either to attack what many young people still regard as the nearly immutable "system" in the fashion that I sometimes associate with the present litigiousness of the ACLU.

43 So great was the outcry from such locales that Lazarsfeld asked me, as someone with an interest in academic freedom and in survey research, to undertake a review of the survey. I first read all the interviews, kept confidentially at the Bureau of Applied Social Research. I selectively interviewed a number of interviewees, and recruited the late Mark Benney, who had done survey research in England during and after the Second World War, to join me in interviewing the interviewers of these same respondents. After this preliminary "triangulation" as I term it in the essay (p. 572) I sent out a mail questionnaire to some 750 of the 2500 respondents (I obtained a 55 per cent response). Lazarsfeld had followed the example set by Samuel A. Stouffer, reported in his book *Communism, Conformity, and Civil Liberties* (New York: Doubleday, 1955; New Brunswick, NJ: Transaction Press, 1992), of using two quite different survey research agencies to help get a better grasp of the potential biasing effects of the interviewers. (The Stouffer work is discussed in "Orbits of Tolerance, Interviewers, and Elites," reprinted herein, pp. 540–67.) Benney and I found that although the NORC interviewers were better educated and more cosmopolitan and liberal than those from the Roper organization and had obtained more free-answer responses, there was no substantive difference between the interviewing groups in the overall survey results; women of both cohorts impressed me, as I have repeatedly been impressed throughout my work, by their willingness to go anywhere— most of the Roper interviewers were older and married and went far beyond their husbands' orbits—and to be scrupulous about their tasks. See Riesman, "Some Observations on the Interviewing in the Teacher Apprehension Study," in Paul F. Lazarsfeld and Wagner Thielens, eds., *The Academic Mind: Social Scientists in a Time of Crisis* (Glencoe, Illinois: The Free Press, 1958), pp. 266–370. To read this essay over in 1992 is to be reminded of how enormous has been the shift in higher education, taken as a whole, since 1955, in terms of what Jencks and I were later to term "The Academic Revolution," which freed professors pretty much the country over, at least in the major state and private colleges and universities, from extramural censorship and intimidation. At many of the colleges I visited McCarthyism was, as the essay printed herein reports, in the stratosphere. Apprehensions came from the president, the regents, the governing religious order, the local business community. I have often thought of the visit I made in the summer

of 1955 to what was then North Carolina A & T College in Greensboro, now North Carolina Agricultural and Technical University, still predominantly black. Answers faculty members had given to the survey were of such unruffled complacency that we wondered whether or not the interviewees might have felt intimidated. Hence I talked with a local journalist and with a local minister who assured me that yes, this is exactly how things are at the Negro college; there is no dissent. It was at just this college that four freshmen in 1960 went downtown to stage a sit-in at the local Woolworth's. They had been dared by one another to take such a radical step—the first such sit-in to draw national attention.

44 See, however, Alex Kotlowitz, *There Are No Children Here: The Story of Two Boys Growing up in the Other America* (New York: Nan A. Talese/Doubleday, 1991), the exceptional work of a journalist who gained the confidence of some residents of a black housing project on the West Side of Chicago, focusing on small children who, as the book explains, can hardly have a childhood in the traditional sense.

45 The privacy of figures in the public eye and of institutional procedures is something else again, for here there is, powered again by distrust, an insistence on "the public's right to know" and a belief that no negotiations or decisions should go on "behind closed doors." This echoes an older Wilsonian insistence on "open covenants openly arrived at," in the face of widespread recognition among the experienced that compromises can generally only be reached in a setting of confidentiality. For illustrations from searches for college and university presidents, see Judith Block McLaughlin and David Riesman, "The Shady Side of Sunshine," *Change*, vol. 21, no. 1, January/February 1989, pp. 45-57, and more generally McLaughlin and Riesman, *Choosing a College President: Opportunities and Constraints* (Princeton: Carnegie Foundation for the Advancement of Teaching, 1990), Chapters Six and Seven.

For a haunting, wide-ranging discussion of what we do and what we should owe to one another in the overlapping, contradictory, and not always concentric circles of our engagement with society, see Alan Wolfe, *Whose Keeper? Social Science and Moral Obligation* (University of California Press, 1989). Commenting on mass communications, I observed in 1964, 'In this country, it would seem, we are too sophisticated to be enlightened." See "Comments by David Riesman" in Lewis Anthony Dexter and David Manning White, eds., *People, Society, and Mass Communications* (Glencoe: The Free Press, 1964), pp. 512-516, at p. 515.

46 I have not changed the position taken in *The Lonely Crowd* and (with Nathan Glazer) in other writings that political apathy per se is not problematic. It is the mobilization of the apathetic by what *The Lonely Crowd* termed the curdled indignants that is frightening. See Riesman and Glazer, "Criteria for Political Apathy," in Alvin Gouldner, Ed., *Studies in leadership* (New York: Harper & Brothers, 1950), pp. 505-56.

47 For my own judgment that President Nixon has been subjected to the specifically American moralism that astonishes Europeans, who admire Nixon's achievements in foreign policy even while they might concede, as I do, that he has a bad character, see "Attitudes toward President Nixon: A

Case of American Exceptionalism in Relation to Watergate," Address at the Tocqueville Society Annual Meeting, 8 October 1982, *Tocqueville Review* vol. IV, no. 2, pp. 280–302. On the shortening attention span that Americans devote to presidential politics, see the description by Kiku Adatto of the extent to which the length of "sound bites" diminished between the 1968 and 1988 elections. Adatto, *Picture Perfect: Imagery and Artifice in American Culture* (New York: Basic Books, 1993).

48 A dramatic example is what happened when the American Association of Retired People, the most prominent established lobby for the elderly, got Congress to pass legislation for health care for the elderly, some of whose costs would be absorbed by increasing taxes on the well-to-do among the elderly—who as a social cohort are much better off than the suburban, let alone the inner-city children. Another group claiming to speak for the elderly used the devices of modern communications for nearly instantaneous mobilization, so that there were frenzied scenes of members of Congress being hooted at and booed in old-age homes. Before the new law had a chance to go into effect, it was with near unanimity repealed. Of course in such situations, if it is clear that a majority is turning against a measure, and there is anger out there about it, it takes a quixotic or especially prideful person to vote against a bill which is certain to pass. Congress is now understandably wary of any efforts to help the elderly, beyond the large entitlements already in existence.

49 One ironic element in Proposition 13 was the fact that Governor Ronald Reagan had accumulated a huge surplus in the state's budget, leading many who voted for Proposition 13 to believe that they were being unduly and unfairly taxed by a state already amply endowed with resources.

50 Albert Hirschman, in *Shifting Involvements: Private Interest and Public Action* (Princeton: Princeton University Press, 1982), suggests that modern societies tend to shift from belief that the state can resolve problems and then disillusionment with outcomes, to the belief that only private non-state efforts can be of any use. But this proves an illusion also; thus again people begin to have confidence that government might help. I have myself had peripheral involvement with the group headed by the sociologist Amitai Etzioni of The George Washington University which publishes the journal *The Responsive Community: Rights and Responsibilities*, a group whose ethos is sometimes referred to as "communitarian." See for its bearing on the text Aaron Wildavsky, "Representative vs. Direct Democracy: Excessive Initiatives, Too Short Terms, Too Little Respect for Politics and Politicians," *The Responsive Community: Rights and Responsibilities*, vol. 2, Summer 1992, pp. 30–40.

51 In an occasional nightmare, I envisage a Constitutional Convention which would abolish many if not all of the provisions of the Bill of Rights, partly in response to the understandable fear of crime from which black inner-city populations are among the worst sufferers, although whites and especially Asians are far from immune. My uneasiness over the amendment process was one reason for my opposition to the Equal Rights Amendment, although I was in sympathy with many of the Amendment's aims of improving the economic, political, and indeed cultural situation of women in the

United States. I believed the amendment would bring women nothing not already provided under the equal protection clause of the Fourteenth Amendment, except litigation whose outcomes might not always be to the advantage of women. The amendment lost primarily because of opposition by aroused traditional women, in part because some of the amendment's sponsors, including a number of feminist lawyers, contended that an appropriate consequence would be to remove the military's restrictions on using women in combat: there should be no situation in which women received special protection and correspondingly none in which men would set themselves apart from women. See for discussion Jane Mansbridge, *Why We Lost the ERA* (Chicago: University of Chicago Press, 1986).

Those wings of the women's movements that believe that there are no significant genetic or biological differences between men and women—there are other wings which believe that women are indeed different and also superior—insisted that there remain in this country no sanctum, no sports locker room, no old boys' club, no fraternity on a campus, that should not be open to women. (At the extreme I think of a lawsuit brought by parents to win their daughter a place on the boys' football team in a public high school.) In my own view, women would be the main losers if all single-sex educational settings were forced by law or ideological pressure to become coeducational. Indeed, I could envisage the ERA being used by a man to gain entrance to a women's college in just the kind of unanticipated litigation to which I saw the ERA potentially giving rise. The Equal Protection clause was the basis for the suit brought by William Hogan, a resident of Columbus, Mississippi, seeking to enter the nursing program of Mississippi University for Women, which is located in Columbus and which had successfully fended off an effort by the state to merge it with Mississippi State University, much as Texas Woman's University in Denton, with the support of dedicated alumnae, maintained its single-sex status at the undergraduate level in the face of efforts to merge it with North Texas State University, also located in Denton. William Hogan had been told that he would be eligible for the nursing programs of four Mississippi state universities, including the Ole Miss nursing program in Jackson. However, in Mississippi University for Women v. Hogan, 458 U.S. 718 (1982), Justice Sandra Day O'Connor wrote for a five-to-four majority that the University was required to admit Hogan, declaring that to do anything else would stereotype women as associated with nursing; Justice Harry Blackmun, writing for the dissenters, responded that something that the state was justified in considering to be educationally viable and valuable was being jeopardized for the convenience of a commuter.

52 Boards of directors call in consultants to advise on executive pay, using as a measure what is paid elsewhere in the same line of work; the consultants' own interests lie in raising, certainly not drastically curtailing, executive pay.

53 In "Two Americas, Two Value Systems: Blacks and Whites," Seymour Martin Lipset summarizes studies showing the tremendous advances made by the black middle class in the last several decades, contrasting the numerically small but incendiary black "underclass" in the inner city with the suburban well-off two-parent black families (which, like comparable white

families, are not philoprogenitive). *The Tocqueville Review*, vol. XIII, no. 1, pp. 137-78, at pp. 159-65. For a poignant account of the pressures put on successful blacks to follow the party line of the alienated "blacker than thou" leadership, see Glenn C. Loury, "Free at Last? A Personal Perspective on Race and Identity in America" in *Lure and Loathing: Essays on Race, Identity, and the Ambivalence of Assimilation* (forthcoming, 1993).

54 For a reflective history of this program, see Michael Schudson, "A Ruminating Retrospect on the Liberal Arts, the Social Sciences, and Social Science 2," in John J. MacAloon, ed., *General Education in the Social Sciences: Centennial Reflections on the College of the University of Chicago* (Chicago: University of Chicago Press, 1992).

55 After the United States entered the Second World War, I served on a committee set up by the American Law Institute to draft an international bill of rights with the hope that our work would become useful for some postwar counterpart to the earlier League of Nations. We were mostly Americans, joined by a handful of jurists from other countries, mainly Latin America, then living in the United States. I proposed that there be included the "right to a reasonable leisure," which one of my colleagues dubbed "Riesman's Freedom from Work Amendment"! Ever so many years later, I found myself critical of the use of human rights issues to make the Cold War more inflammatory or in other ways contrary to what I regarded as America's interests. I saw human rights as creating conflicts among American ideals; see, e.g, my essay "The Danger of the Human Rights Campaign" in Carl Marcy, ed., *Common Sense in U.S.-Soviet Relations* (New York: W. W. Norton, 1978), pp. 49-55.

56 Reprinted first in *Anchor Review* as "Thoughts on Teachers and Schools" (1954, pp. 27-60) and then revised as "Secondary Education and 'Counter-Cyclical' Policy" in *Constraint and Variety in American Education*, 1956, Chapter 3, pp. 107-60.

57 Matilda White Riley, John W. Riley, Jr., and Mary E. Moore, "Adolescent Values and the Riesman Typology: An Empirical Analysis," in Seymour Martin Lipset and Leo Lowenthal, eds., *Culture and Social Character: The Work of David Riesman Reviewed*, Free Press, 1961, pp. 370-386.

58 Cambridge: Harvard University Press, 1988. Shortly after the Second World War, Howard S. Becker studied the preferences of Chicago school teachers when seniority allowed them to exercise choice among schools. Most did not want to teach in schools where the parents had more education than they, nor in schools where the parents had minimal education, but rather in schools where the parents appreciated education but had less of it than the teachers. See Becker, *The Role and Career Problems of the Chicago Schoolteacher* (Chicago: University of Chicago Press, 1951).

59 See Howard S. Becker, Blanche Geer, and Everett C. Hughes, *Making the Grade: The Academic Side of College Life* (New York: Wiley, 1968; and Becker, Geer, Hughes, and Anselm Strauss, *Boys in White: Student Culture in Medical School* (Chicago: University of Chicago Press, 1961; New Brunswick, NJ: Transaction Press, 1980). Students also come to college bearing "legacies" from families and peer groups, in some cases a mandate to do better than one's parents and yet a recognition that to do ever so much better would

be seen as a betrayal of origins. Howard London, Chairman of the Sociology and Anthropology Department at Bridgewater State College in Massachusetts, has explored this theme in interviews with students at all levels of higher education and also in his book, *The Culture of a Community College* (New York: Praeger, 1978).

60 Daniel J. Singal, in *The Atlantic Monthly* (vol. 268, no. 5, November 1991, pp. 59–74). Reprinted in *News & Views: Educational Excellence Network*, vol. 10, no. 12, December 1991, pp. 75–82.).

61 In an understandable attack on the messenger, the SAT tests have been assailed as gender-biased—also, a somewhat different issue, race-biased. The argument is made that women in high school and in college get better grades than boys and men do, but this reflects courses taken and perhaps also more decorous behavior. I discuss this issue in my introduction to George Hanford, *Life with the SAT*, New York: College Entrance Examination Board, 1991. For an elaborate statistical account, not disaggregated by gender, see Charles Murray and Richard J. Herrnstein, "What's Really Behind the SAT Score Decline?" *The Public Interest*, Winter 1992, vol. 106, pp. 32–56.

62 The Detroit proposal and others like it also raised concerns and opposition because the curriculum was going to be "Afrocentric," with the aim of encouraging black students' self-esteem. Self-esteem is a complex matter. Some will not attain it even after overcoming great obstacles because they will believe that they were lucky or that they could have done a great deal more; in any case, self-esteem per se does not translate into learning. I am skeptical of what is regarded as Afrocentrism, for one thing because it is a mythical and not either an historical or contemporary Africa that is the focus, but I am willing to give it a try. I say this despite being in general agreement with Arthur Schlesinger, Jr.'s *The Disuniting of America* (Whittle Books, 1991).

In 1968 I had the opportunity to address Peace Corps Volunteers in Senegal when they gathered in Dakar along with their Senegalese co-workers of Action Communale. The latter were in the hundred-degree heat wearing French cuffs and dark suits, while the Volunteers were being "natural" in cutoff jeans and ragged t-shirts. The black Volunteers were so clearly American that I was confirmed in my quixotic notion that blacks coming to the more selective colleges and universities in the United States, where they will come under pressure, some for the first time, to be authentically African American and resist assimilation, would gain from a term or a year spent in a European or African country. Of course, an interim year during or after high school and before college might help the maturation of many entering first-year students, provided they were not simply tourists abroad. The black students would in particular, I anticipate, come to realize how fundamentally American they are. My Jamaican-born sociologist colleague, Orlando Patterson, has concluded that blacks are almost ultra-American, having been for decades more religiously Christian than most Americans in what remains today, as evidenced by surveys reported by Andrew Greeley, a decidedly religious nation. See also Patterson, *Ethnic Chauvinism: The Reactionary Impulse* (New York: Stein & Day, 1977). See the discussion of juridical and educational issues in Sonya R. Jarvis, "*Brown* and the Afrocentric Curriculum," *Yale Law Journal* vol. 101, pp. 1285-1304.

63 The argument about the location of power often overlaps with the judgment that the "real world" is coeducational, and therefore one must prepare for it in a coeducational setting. Applying such a mandate strictly would prevent girls from playing ice hockey or basketball and perhaps some other sports, because they would always have to be with the boys. For discussion of how boys can benefit from a single-sex setting, see Richard A. Hawley, "About Boys' Schools: A Progressive Case for an Ancient Form," *Teachers College Record*, vol. 92, no. 3, Spring 1991, pp. 433-444.

There is no concern for "underrepresented" ethnic and racial groups in sports, nor is there a fear of outstanding performance as "elitist." There has been, and I am grateful for it, emphasis through Title IX and more generally on achieving a bit of equity in coaching and other support for sports for girls and women, which can often serve in an exhilarating way to increase their self-confidence. Perhaps one reason why the standards are different in schoolwork and sports is that sports is recognized, even by the adult "boys" who dote on collegiate and professional teams all their lives, as an achievement that has a short half-life and rarely leads anywhere.

64 In 1964 at the invitation of then Associate Director Harris Wofford, I joined with a Peace Corps official to run a Termination of Service Conference for Volunteers who had served in Colombia. We met in Bogota at a time when activist Jesuits were influential in developing Liberation Theology in the area. The Volunteers' idealism had been challenged by radical students in Bogota who emphasized the *Corps* rather than the Peace part of their label; many Volunteers had shifted toward an anti-American defiance, including antagonism toward President Kennedy, although their strong idealism prevented their seeking early termination. They identified very much with the peasants they were seeking to help in the villages. Correspondingly, many had been jolted by experiences they had had at the time of John F. Kennedy's assassination: peasants, who often displayed Kennedy's photographs in their shacks, had come bearing to the Volunteers condolences for the President's death. Volunteers had been moved, and many were led to reconsider their own outlook. For an extreme example of Volunteer animosity that seemed to me especially marked in Latin America, see Paul Cowan's account of his experience as a Volunteer in Ecuador, *The Making of an Un-American: A Dialogue with Experience* (New York: Viking, 1970).

In *Making a Difference: The Peace Corps at Twenty-five*, Alan Guskin, now President of Antioch University, describes the intense excitement that he and his co-workers helped engender at the University of Michigan, which encouraged John F. Kennedy to call for a Peace Corps during his presidential campaign. See Guskin, "Passing the Torch," in *Making a Difference: The Peace Corps at Twenty-five*, Milton Viorst, ed., Peace Corps Twenty-fifth Anniversary Foundation, 1986, pp. 25-41. The book is full of illustrations of Peace Corps impact in schools and in other arenas. But in my own sense of the Volunteers, they often performed their most useful service on their return, being among the few Americans who knew something about places like Malawi or Senegal or Afghanistan, which was particularly formidable for women Volunteers confronted by men not used to seeing unescorted, and in their culture inadequately dressed, young women. For example, I learned about the Biafran revolt in Nigeria, not from Boston University's African Studies program, but from Volunteers who had had their training at Harvard in 1961. In 1965 Harris Wofford took me with him to visit a Peace Corps training program at St. John's College in Annapolis, one of the first to send Volunteers for rural, in this case chicken-farming, development in India. Most training programs incorporated an effort to bring trainees into contact with an impoverished group, sometimes in the Caribbean and sometimes in the United States itself; these trainees had been to the Eastern Shore of Maryland to see something of the life of blacks who were living there. A fervent trainee just out of Yale College argued forcefully that the cohort ought to stay at home and push the cause of these victimized blacks rather than go to India. I asked him whether the Urban League in Baltimore was in contact with the blacks of whom he was speaking, and he said they were, but that did not matter—for him and for some of the others, the Urban League was not radical enough. Of this group of trainees, as I recall, only one young woman from the University of Kansas had had experience outside the country, in her case a volunteer stint in Mexico. I made the case that there were already many liberal and radical whites concerned with the cause of American blacks, but there were hardly any Americans who could speak for the rural areas of India in their own locales when they got back or for wider American audiences. (I also had in mind what Congressional representatives from Maryland would say if it turned out that Peace Corps Volunteers being trained in their state got into what was then the incipient student rebellion business; it certainly would not help the Peace Corps.) The looseness of Peace Corps organization, to which *Making a Difference* makes ample reference, facilitated such expressiveness on the part of some of this group who were simultaneously studying Hindi, poultry farming, and evenings with the Great Books, St. John's College style. Fortunately, as I thought, they decided to go on to India.

65 C. P. Snow's *The Two Cultures and the Scientific Revolution* (New York: Cambridge University Press, 1959) created an enormous controversy in the United Kingdom and to a lesser degree in the United States. C. P. Snow urged his readers toward a campaign of sacrifice to help the pre-industrial countries, notably India, and in general to apply scholarship to the less developed world. In an appendix to a new edition of Snow's book I wrote: "The best Americans, whether trained in the literary or scientific spheres, are restless in the affluent society, and I think they would respond to leadership which offered them another alternative. But the leadership must promise not only sacrifice, but the broadening of intellectual range and the opportunity to come to terms with what matters in life. It has not been my experience that most scientists understand the scientific revolution in its world-wide aspects." I go on then to discuss the snobbery of the "pure" as against the "applied" scholarly work in terms of the ladder of prestige; I suggest that in order to become whole, we in academic life need to connect our scientific and our aesthetic sensibilities, and that one way to do so is through connections between science and its social consequences. Riesman,

"The Whole Man," in C.P. Snow et al., *The Two Cultures: A Discussion* (New Delhi, India: Congress for Cultural Freedom, undated), pp. 12-15.

66 In the New Deal era some of my friends were involved in the creation of a volunteer camp, Camp William James, in Vermont, to give privileged young men a similar opportunity; the guiding spirit was Eugen Rosenstock-Huessy, a refugee from Nazi Germany and a Dartmouth College professor of philosophy.

67 Many of the cynics harbor latent idealism which can be mobilized for causes which can be seen as working "against the system": often fervent environmentalism, less often animal rights activism, occasionally a political crusade by an anti-politician such as Jerry Brown.

For an intellectual and social history of the development of America's often anarchic individualism—"individualism" in the sense that Tocqueville meant—beginning with the Civil War and down to the present, see Wilfred McClay, *Masterless Men: Self and Society in Modern America* (University of North Carolina Press, forthcoming).

68 The service academies, along with ROTC programs at many of the more enlightened and progressive colleges and universities, have come under attack because of their discrimination against homosexuals. Before coming to Harvard College in 1927, I had for seven years attended William Penn Charter School, a Friends academy, of course then single-sex, in Philadelphia; on the *Harvard Crimson* I criticized ROTC as militaristic and asked for its abolition, leading to many letters of complaint from veterans' groups and others. However, when in the late 1960's pressure developed to eliminate ROTC because of antagonism to the Vietnam war, and beyond that to "the system," I defended ROTC at Harvard, insisting that I did not want all military officers to be trained only in the more conservative locales—I felt the same way about CIA recruitment on campus. Now the issue has arisen again at more progressive institutions over the ban on homosexuals in ROTC programs: in this case also, we want to be sure that the ROTC experience exists in the sophisticated academic centers as well as on the provincial perimeter, even at the cost of accepting a certain measure of discrimination. In this context it is important that today's military is perhaps the most racially integrated of all American enterprises.

69 Only after my testimony did I discover that there is also a private junior college for women, Southern Seminary Junior College, in Virginia; it recently selected as its President Colonel John Ripley, a graduate of the Naval Academy and former official there who had earlier been in charge of the Marine Corps ROTC unit at Virginia Military Institute.

70 The sensitivity of most women to interpersonal considerations can show up in ways quite different from what is suggested in the text. I have in mind my conversation with a 1992 honors graduate of Harvard who entered the Government Department, which has so male an ambience that references are common to "Gov jocks." She described her experience in being by chance the only woman in a large section in an introductory class, I think in economics, where she was one of the most outspoken participants. She believes that had there been other women there, she would not have wanted to compete with them, or shine by her very assertiveness; in other classes she

took, she muted her voice out of concern for the other women rather than out of obeisance to the men. However, when I told her that Linda Wilson, Radcliffe College's President, was interested in my proposal that Harvard experiment with single-sex sections in mathematics and physics, much more than in Government predominantly "boys' games" among the undergraduates, she declared that she would have profited greatly from such sections, where she would not have been anxious about being outspoken when men were absent; she recognized that such a proposal would be likely to come under attack as sexist from the student paper, the *Crimson*, and from some feminists.

71 In the summer of 1992 the American Civil Liberties Union brought suit on behalf of two female veterans of the Gulf War to compel their admission to undergraduate classes but not to the Corps of Cadets itself at The Citadel (Johnson et al. vs. The Citadel et al.). Shortly thereafter, in the United states Court of Appeals for the Fourth Circuit in an opinion by Circuit Judge Niemeyer, joined by two colleagues, a complicated decision on the VMI case was handed down. It vacated the decision on behalf of VMI's single-sex status by District Court Judge Jackson L. Kaiser in the Western District of Virginia. The Appellate Court asked for evidence that the Commonwealth of Virginia itself believed in providing support for ". . . offering the unique benefits of a VMI-type of education to men and not to women." United States of America vs. Commonwealth of Virginia et al., no. 91–16, 90, October 5, 1992. The Appellate Court emphasized the withdrawal from the litigation of Virginia's Attorney General, responding to Governor Douglas Wilder's own withdrawal of the support he had earlier offered when he ran for governor. The Court in effect asked how Virginia could claim that VMI served a state purpose when the Attorney General and her superior, the Governor, did not support this. She declared in a letter to the Governor, "You have indicated that VMI's admission policy served no legitimate public policy objective. . . . In the absence of a statute explicitly expressing the General Assembly's view on the policy issue, your statement of the Commonwealth's policy is persuasive." (United States vs. Commonwealth of Virginia at page 8) However, Judge Niemeyer accepted the findings of fact of the District Court that single-sex education offered VMI undergraduates substantial benefits which could not be maintained with the admission of women. The case was thus returned to the District Court in case Virginia could show in some fashion its equitable treatment of women. The Citadel litigation, in which I have been asked to take part, would have been a more difficult prospect than VMI, even had there not been such a decision in the Court of Appeals. With over 2,000 undergraduates, it is not only larger, but it is located in Charleston, a benefit to students with ascriptive connections whose potential salience is suggested in Pat Conroy's novel, *The Lords of Discipline* (Houghton Mifflin, 1980). Pat Conroy graduated from The Citadel in the Class of 1967; his book is a fierce, gripping attack on the brutal hazing and what amounted to thought control by the cadet corps and its traditional leadership. (Indeed, the almost incredibly heroic Vietnam prisoner of war, Vice Admiral James B. Stockdale, whom Ross Perot chose as his Vice Presidential running mate, served as President of the Citadel for just one

year, 1979–80, during which he unsuccessfully sought to reduce the extent of hazing.) "Endangered species" may not in all respects be admirable, and yet they deserve to survive and have chances to improve, as The Citadel has notably done in success with black undergraduates, 52 per cent of whom graduate in four years, much the highest percentage of any college, including the traditionally black institutions, in the public sector of South Carolina.

72 Astin's own highly regarded book, *Four Critical Years: Effects of College on Beliefs, Attitudes, and Knowledge* (San Francisco: Jossey-Bass, 1977), especially at page 246, based on years of study of entering freshman cohorts and "value added" during their collegiate years, shows that single-sex institutions offer clear advantages for women and the possibility also of benefits for men.

73 When in 1967 Christopher Jencks and I published an article, "The American Negro College," in *Harvard Educational Review* (vol. 37, no. 1, 1967, pp. 3–60), *Time* magazine picked it up and reported on it in a one-page synopsis, with a photograph of Howard University buildings above the heading: "Academic Disaster Area?" Without the *Time* story, I doubt if Jencks and I would have been subjected to the stream of abuse still not forgotten in some quarters, primarily from people who had not read the article or seen it as a chapter in our critical book, *The Academic Revolution* (Garden City, NY: Doubleday, 1968; paperback edition with a new foreword by Martin Trow, Chicago: University of Chicago Press, 1977). We had secured criticisms of drafts of our article from a number of professors at what were then the Negro colleges, whose help we acknowledged, and some of them too came under blistering attack. It has not become easier for either white or black scholars critically to address issues of race without encountering an understandable but sad defensiveness.

In the Spring Term, 1992, the United States Supreme Court by an eight-to-one majority decided under the sequence of litigation, sometimes referred to as the *Adams* case, that the formerly all-black and formerly all-white public universities of Mississippi were insufficiently desegregated, although blacks are now free to attend all the previously white universities with for example six per cent coming to Ole Miss, the University of Mississippi, and twelve per cent to land-grant Mississippi State University; I need hardly add that the more eminent colleges and universities all over the country actively recruit capable blacks from everywhere, not excluding Mississippi. The black state universities in Mississippi have not attracted any considerable number of white students—but they have lost most of their capable black faculty to predominantly white institutions the country over, which is sad for students at an institution like Jackson State University, where they are serious and eager to learn and do not face the challenge they would, for example, at Harvard University, to exhibit themselves to their fellow blacks, not only in the student body but among some of the faculty and administration, to be fully "authentic" and non-assimilationist. Even so, Justice White sent the case back to the District Court from which it had arisen, with instructions to compel a greater equivalence of student recruitment and faculty salaries and opportunities in order to overcome the heritage of segregation. Only Justice Antonin Scalia, in his characteristically acerbic fashion, dissented, declaring that his brethren were following the path now often termed "Politically Correct" rather than examining the realities. As part of the *Adams* litigation begun by the primarily Northern NAACP in 1972 and over the early objections from Southern black academic leaders, two Savannah institutions were required to give up their most salient programs for transfer to the other; thus Savannah State gave up its education program and Armstrong State gave up its business program; but the aim of producing greater racial integration failed since black students did not transfer to Armstrong State for business, nor Armstrong State prospects to Savannah State for education. One may point to a number of contrasting situations produced by the independent judgments of students in a particular locale; for example, West Virginia State College in Institute, near Charleston, is now predominantly white, and the University of Arkansas at Pine Bluff, another black land-grant college founded for Negroes, attracts day students—the great majority of students are commuters—and is only 80 per cent black. Lincoln University in Pennsylvania attracts a substantial number of white commuters to a campus which is for blacks almost entirely residential.

74 A number of institutions remain, not invariably but mostly church-related, where there are single-sex dormitories and some degree of control over visitors of the opposite sex to the dorms. Some public and private institutions offer students a choice between coeducational and single-sex dormitories. When I served in 1972 on the committee that made Harvard and Radcliffe coresidential—Radcliffe had previously had separate dormitories—I proposed that one dormitory wing be reserved for women who wanted a single-sex setting. I was not really surprised when no women expressed any interest in such an option. To have done so might have suggested that they were lesbians (then not nearly as outspoken and mobilized a group as at present), or that they feared men—the same anxieties that make it difficult for the women's colleges to recruit high school seniors from the families of the educated strata; women need to spend a year or so at a women's college before they fully appreciate how much they gain from it.

75 See John N. Gardner and Betsy Barefoot, "Reflections on the Freshman year: An Interview with David Riesman," *Journal of the Freshman Year Experience*, vol. 3, no. 2, 1991, pp. 7-28.

76 See "The Neoclassical Revival: St. John's and the Great Books," in Gerald Grant and David Riesman, *The Perpetual Dream: Reform and Experiment in the American College* (Chicago: The University of Chicago Press, 1978), pp. 40-76.

Joseph Tussman of Berkeley briefly tried an experiment of a required curriculum for student volunteers chosen by lot at the very height of the Berkeley student protests. After several years, facing resistance from the teaching assistants he had recruited, the effort collapsed. However, a follow-up of Tussman College graduates of the two-year program currently in progress by Katherine Trow of Berkeley suggests the profound effect that the experience had on those who took part in it and who came to regard themselves as somehow anointed despite being in the Program by the luck of the draw. See Katherine Trow, "The Experiment at Berkeley Revisited" [tentative title, forthcoming].

SECTION I

The Impact of the Cold War

Preface

Professor Carl J. Friedrich of Harvard introduced me to the study of contemporary foreign policy, and his book, *Foreign Policy in the Making: the Search for a New Balance of Power* (Norton, 1938), has had a profound influence on my thinking (though he would, I believe, disagree with some of my views as set forth here). In this book Friedrich describes the misphasing that he believes occurred between France and Germany after the First World War, in which the peace party in each country was always in power when the peace party in the other country was out of power, thus paving the way for Hitler. I worked under Friedrich in the Council for Democracy, a group concerned with civil liberties and the fight against fascism, and I was a reluctant interventionist before the Second World War.[1]

The American reaction to Pearl Harbor separated me still further from the interventionist outlook, for while many anti-Fascist Americans greeted the attack with relief as proof that their warnings had been right all along, it seemed to me that the result would be a largely mindless, unpolitical war, fought on the one side against "the damned yellow bastards" who had stabbed us so sneakily, and on the other, less against the Nazis than against the German people themselves.

As the war went on, I came more and more to share the outlook of Dwight MacDonald's magazine, *Politics;* as I said in my contribution to the *Partisan Review* symposium, "The Cold War and the West," I felt as he did about the mass bombing of German cities by the British and Americans—and a fortiori about the dropping of atomic bombs on Japan. Not a pacifist then or now, I felt it important to maintain the fragile distinction between ordinarily terrible war, fought by profes-

[1] How reluctant is indicated by my essay, "What's Wrong with the Interventionists?" *Common Sense,* Vol. X, pp. 327–30, published in the fall of 1941.

sionals or specially trained people against other professionals, and total war fought against whole populations.²

The very strength of grass-roots democracy in America makes this country in some respects more prone to fighting total wars. In their writings, S. M. Lipset, Edward Shils, and others have pointed out the extent to which the United States, lacking feudal traditions, has invited the participation in political life of strata who elsewhere would be voiceless or powerless.³ Perhaps "invited" is not the right word: the various immigrant groups, and now the Negro, have had to battle for the right to participate in politics, including the making of foreign policy. Although our military services, notably in the Navy, have contained elements of elitism, once we have gone to war the whole civilian population, or at any rate its politically articulate sections, has taken part. And, given the role of middle-class moralism and idealism in those sections, this has meant that our wars have been hard to stop. The Civil War saw Grant's demand for unconditional surrender; the First World War, Wilson's facilitating the total defeat of Germany and the Central Powers (instead of compelling a negotiated settlement); the Second World War again was fought—in part, to appease the suspicious Russians—under the banner of unconditional surrender. Many recent critics of the American style in war and diplomacy, such as George Kennan and Hans J. Morgenthau, have tried to understand and to discredit the moralistic and crusading excesses of that style, while historians of our wars, from that of 1812 to Korea, have criticized the fervor, demagogy, and overreaching that either brought on the war or inflated its aims. (There is the danger of an overreactive despair both

---

² I am opposed to pacifism not because I like war or cannot imagine living in a warless world, but because I regard pacifist tactics as unrealistic. And I think that the effort to use the nuclear threat, and even the danger of escalation, as leverage for the total abolition of war may divert effort from the more practical and, hopefully, possible goal of keeping some marginal restraints on the totalism of war. I believe that by reducing the habit and destructiveness of wars, we may eventually facilitate the growth of the consciousness of the oneness of mankind. In other words, I am a short-run militarist and long-run pacifist.

³ See e.g., Lipset, *Political Man: the Social Bases of Politics* (Doubleday Anchor, 1963); Shils, *The Torment of Secrecy* (The Free Press, 1959); Louis Hartz, *The Liberal Tradition in America* (Harcourt Brace, 1955); and see also Robert Lane, *Political Ideology* (The Free Press, 1963). Lipset's forthcoming book, *The First New Nation*, suggests helpful comparisons with the nationalism of the developing countries of the present era.

about democracy and idealism among the sophisticated who have learned these lessons almost too well.)

Moreover, the fact that America is a federal nation of migrants and immigrants has tended to make problematic who is an American and at times to exacerbate our nationalism; since our early days as a new nation set off from Europe, Americans have often vacillated between touchy defensiveness and the proud hope that our country would be a beacon to the world. The energies and tensions of American life, as well as the idealism and the promise, have constantly underlined for me the importance of William James's quest for a moral equivalent for war.

I owe a good deal of my further education in these matters to my colleagues at the University of Chicago in the period from 1946 to 1958. Such men as Leo Szilard, Morton Grodzins, Edward Shils, and later John Platt alerted me to the politics of atomic energy, although like many others I was a reluctant pupil and wished that I could avoid the awareness and the nightmares that the men of the Manhattan Project first faced alone.

"The Nylon War," written in the late 1940s, was an effort, couched as satire, to invent a moral equivalent for war and for mass-obliteration bombings.[4] The essay took for granted that there would be no radical

[4] When the essay was written I did not have to worry about offending Russian sensibilities, for the thaw had not yet occurred, and Soviet readers discovered what people like myself were writing only from reading attacks by party hacks in Soviet or American party-line journals. Today, there is a more welcome interchange (although it is a precarious one, depending as it does both on political developments within the Soviet Union and the changing climate of the cold war). Russians are understandably extremely sensitive to American snobbery, whether moral or material. Hence I hope that any Russian readers who chance on this essay will not feel that I was poking fun at Communist material "backwardness" simply out of amusement, let alone out of pride in American industrial efficiency and consumer opulence. On the contrary, the essay was a serious attempt to suggest ways of channeling American energies "short of war"; in one aspect it can be considered a foray in Keynesian economics in reverse.

The idea for the essay arose in my mind during a 1947 conference of a group of social scientists to discuss "the world community." Many of my fellow conferees tended to gravitate toward immediate policy questions— and to bind themselves to the alternatives the State Department might be willing or able to accept at the moment. Since we were a bunch of professors, not the State Department, since we lacked its channels of information and misinformation, but also had less of an emergency mandate, I felt we should liberate ourselves from the conventions of thought that

diminution of the combativeness endemic to American life and sought to play within the given system of pressure politics and nationalistic attitudes. In one sense, the essay can be read as a backhanded defense of "materialism" as against more honorific attitudes; it is striking that no country has ever been called materialistic for its war matériel, but only for its consumer goods. And, the essay was written at a period when many Americans believed that the Stalin regime was efficient, but few thought that it used the United States as a model, albeit a disguised one, for its own development.

There was, in fact, a time not so long ago when intelligent people sought to interpret totalitarianism either in terms of the ideological smoke screens of Communists or Nazis, or in terms of some conspiracy theory of history. As against such largely extrapolative interpretations, it was an intellectual advance to insist (as Hannah Arendt did in her brilliant and evocative *The Origins of Totalitarianism*) that modern totalitarianism brought something new into the world, not simply a new version of an older despotism or lust for power and destruction. Historians, to be sure, can find precursors for anything which exists now, and scholars have emphasized totalistic elements in the French Revolution, or for that matter, in the work of the Puritan reformers. Still, these earlier efforts at "permanent revolution" did not have quite the built-in psychological and political dynamism attained by specifically modern totalitarianism.[5]

The other older essay in this section, "Some Observations on the Limits of Totalitarian Power," was presented in 1951 at a meeting arranged by the American Committee for Cultural Freedom to discuss totalitarianism. I chose to emphasize not the savage, mysterious, terrifying aspects of totalitarianism (all of which we can find in some measure in ourselves) but the ordinary aspects that connect with our own more routine experience of human frailty, caprice, and jurisdictional dispute. I was emphasizing that the real world puts limits—not enough, to be sure—on the wishes of even the most powerful and cruel tyrants. I could safely do so without encouraging complacency toward the Com-

---

pass as realism. The notion of the Nylon War was intended to counterbalance the excess of realism in American domestic policy, as well as to underline a fact that some of the anthropologists at the conference understressed, namely that Americans as well as Russians have a culture, and one possessing characteristic energies, ambitions, and ideals.

[5] Concerning the radical aspirations of the Chinese Communists to reform man, see Robert J. Lifton, *Thought Reform and the Psychology of Totalism: A Study of "Brainwashing" in China* (Norton, 1961).

munist countries, since I was on the program with such experienced antitotalitarians as Hannah Arendt, Bruno Bettelheim, and Nathan Leites. But in the discussion it became clear, as it often has since, that many experts on the Soviet Union believe that no move is made anywhere in the Soviet sphere without Politburo planning and approval—doubtless the leaders wish it were so! Certainly, totalitarianism does make an effort to politicize all of life (just as both antifascism and anticommunism do when pushed to fanatical extremes); but it is a mistake to assume that such a movement, no matter how terrible its aims or clever its methods, can step outside of history entirely and cut all connections with social structures of an ordinarily inefficient sort.

I have no doubt that there has been created, in the phrase employed by Raymond Bauer, a "new Soviet man": dogmatic, puritanical, mechanical, and exploitative of his own and others' best human qualities. Even so, what the essay suggested was that the Soviet regime could not completely cut the bonds of human solidarity, extirpate weakness, and restructure human personality—yet. Many of my listeners and readers resented this idea; they seemed to feel that I, an unhurt outsider, was necessarily innocent, unable in my rationalistic liberalism to grasp the terrible monolithic quality of "the system." Because too many Americans had been inert in earlier decades when first faced with the challenge of totalitarian domination, the idea that there were elements of inertia and tradition even under Soviet communism seemed to many a kind of willful blindness.[6]

[6] Many anti-Nazis have contributed, I think, to wrong evaluations of Hitler's aims and accomplishments. When I was briefly in Germany in 1931, my colloquial German (learned from a nurse "just off the boat" who knew no English) was just enough to allow me to talk with students and other young men who were Nazis. Many of them were very idealistic—indeed, it was their ideals, as well as their unconscious aggressions, that were betraying them. I then thought it likely that Germany would fall to Hitler, and wondered at the complacency of the older people who felt, with the wisdom of experience, that if Hitler did reach power the responsibility would sober him—as it had sobered the Social Democrats. To be sure, when Hilter took power in 1933 he was in many ways quite inhibited and cautious; he was less confident of the outcome in the early years, both before and after 1933, than many who now retroactively see a malign logic in all that he did. Without tacit or open support from the Western democracies before 1939 and from the Soviet Union after that, he might neither have stayed in power nor brought on the war, and but for the war it is unlikely that he would have achieved his aim of totalitarian domination (or his extermination of the Jews); even at the height of the war, scholars now believe, his industry was less geared to war production than that of the United States.

It is still common in Europe and elsewhere to regard Americans as inherently innocent, unable to grasp what communism is *really* like (and, increasingly, what poverty is *really* like). The charge has often been accurate. But with respect to communism, an overreaction may have occurred, so that Americans often show a greater and less controlled fear (and perhaps concealed admiration) of communism than do people who have lived more closely under its shadow. Americans on the whole were not prepared for the Hungarian Revolution, or for the riots that broke out in East Berlin in 1953, or later in Poland.[7] The reminder that totalitarianism can kill men and silence them, but not permanently crush them, was a salutary one, even though the outcome was tragic for those who were trapped.

My paper was also criticized at the symposium by those who suggested that social science, in its effort to probe and understand our times, must necessarily miss the basic evils and deeper irrationalities of totalitarianism and remove our indignation and will to fight. I think I recognize these dangers. When I have made myself read some of the literature on concentration (and labor) camps, I have been aware of my wish for mechanisms to put this terrible material at a distance. Science can serve many concurrent aims; it can both disclose the truth and give a safe-conduct pass to the scientist—an asbestos coating in hell. But at the present time there are many thinkers to warn us that their tragic sense of life is more tragic than other people's tragic sense of life. In this atmosphere, people can plead rank on the basis of more intense suffering; and a refusal to use all available techniques for examination can appear as a noble disdain for evil and, at the same time, a recognition of its depth. We need both satire and sermon, both psychology and theology.

One kind of "crisis theology," which has become more and more common, is the talk about national purpose. This talk, greatly aggravated since Sputnik, reflects the malaise of many educated people about where America is going and, as I suggest in the essay, "National Purpose," perhaps also about where they are going. The essay raises questions that continue to perplex me. Is the concept of *national* purpose merely a form of idolatry, in which men look to the nation-state to harness their otherwise unoccupied energies and to drive them toward otherwise irrelevant ends? Can one think of better and more appropriate forms of

[7] Granted, there are some Americans whose idea of communism is so primitive that they see it *only* as a conspiracy, with whole populations simply waiting to be liberated from enslavement.

solidarity, more evocative of the best impulses of Americans? More empirically one might ask, is all the talk about national purpose something that goes on primarily among advertising men, employees of the mass media, and others in the communications industry? It is a displaced form of generational combat, by which the older generation discusses the apparent self-indulgence or aimlessness of the younger? The essay itself, which is short, only begins the discussion.

Somewhat comparable problems are raised in the second essay in this volume, "The American Crisis," which was originally presented as a talk to a small, informal group of liberal Democratic congressmen in June 1960, and later published in *The Liberal Papers*, a collection of essays written for this group—essays primarily concerned with the exploration of foreign policy. The short-lived and bitterly attacked Liberal Project itself was an outgrowth of the congressional elections of the fall of 1958, when a group of mostly newly elected Democrats sought to establish contact with academicians and intellectuals.[8]

Those who founded the Liberal Project were frustrated to discover that the Democratic victory in the elections was not to be translated into public policy; but they realized that, even if they were to have a larger voice in affairs, there were very few ideas on which they could draw for measures that went beyond what might be regarded as the mopping-up operations of the New Deal. Hence they turned, for what was in effect a series of seminars, to a group of university professors and writers whose books and articles they had read, and who, they thought, might begin to provide not only specific proposals that would point in new directions in foreign and domestic policy, but also a philosophy of liberalism that would locate specific measures in a larger social and philosophical context. In seeking such contact, they had to overcome the characteristic attitude of American scholars and intellectuals toward politicians, whom many (along with Americans in gen-

[8] Several of the congressmen had attended the University of Wisconsin or fallen under the influence of men trained there. That university has been a kind of unofficial Fabian Society for the state government, especially during the Progressive era—one of the few examples in the United States of continuing relations between government and academic life. Nothing quite comparable exists in Washington, D.C., which, although somewhat less of a cultural and intellectual desert than when Henry Adams lived there, still remains a city dominated by middle-level civil servants, the military, the lobbyists, and the service trades dependent on all of these, and not a city tied to the growing edge or height of the times, intellectually speaking, in American life.

eral) condescendingly regard as either cynical opportunists or stupid windbags.

In my own work as a teacher, first in the law and then in the social sciences, I have sought to overcome the patronizing attitude toward politics and politicians that passes for sophistication among many students. My own limited experience with congressmen and senators has been that many are intellectuals in the best sense, in their openness to ideas; and their willingness to take risks, though far from saintly, often seems greater than that of most professionals.[9] And it should be remembered that American congressmen are virtually on their own—a better example of "free enterprise" than is to be found in most businesses: they are dependent on local support, rather than on any over-all party effort on their behalf, though they can, of course, be greatly helped or hurt by the way the national presidential campaign goes in their home districts or, in off-year elections, by the positions their party has taken on "gut" issues in Washington.

"The American Crisis" was first published in the summer of 1960; in November of that year five members of the Liberal Project lost their seats. Although local issues were involved, and although President Kennedy's Catholicism was a factor in some predominantly Protestant areas, the collapse of the summit in Paris,[10] and the brash chauvinism of much of the presidential campaign may also have played a part in the defeat of these men. Indeed, immediately after publication in early 1962, *The Liberal Papers* became the object of the most violent Republican abuse: Senator Barry Goldwater, a number of right-wing congressmen, and Representative William Miller, chairman of the Republican National Committee, assailed the essays as a prelude to a new Munich, and as virtually treasonable. This attack tended to associate the Republican congressional leadership with the most jingoistic elements in our national life, those most hostile to ideas and to serious discussion. Since I do not think the Democrats have a monopoly of virtue, and since I like to see thoughtful and outspoken young people attracted to both major parties, I have been distressed by the eagerness of these Republicans to recapture from the Democrats the label of "war party."

[9] For a sympathetic picture, see Stimson Bullitt, *To Be a Politician* (Doubleday Anchor Books, 1961).

[10] For a fuller discussion of this, see my article, "The U-2 Affair and After," *The Commonweal*, Vol. 76, pp. 273–76, June 8, 1962; and for a longer version see *Council for Correspondence Newsletter*, September 1962, pp. 4–12.

More important, the attack led some liberal Democrats in the House of Representatives, already shaken by the defeat of some of their number in 1960, to feel that they would be even more endangered if they continued to participate in the consideration of any ideas that ran counter to the most narrow stereotypes for the conduct of foreign and military policy. (There are many congressmen who are liberal in domestic affairs, but whose minds are closed, or perhaps one should say bipartisan, when it comes to foreign affairs.) The unanimous or near unanimous votes by which Congress now passes defense bills or any bills that can be labeled "anti-Communist" would shame many a dictatorship.

The extreme right wing is relatively small in terms of numbers and constituents who share its one-eyed view of the world; but its ability to stir up a storm, as in the attack on *The Liberal Papers*, influences the whole temper of political discourse and shifts politics continually toward the enforcement of consensus based on slogans. Thus, any cabinet member or other administrator who goes before Congress, or before representatives of the press or television, is well aware of what the right wing will or will not permit. And responsible public men in the Democratic party fear to say something that can be pounced upon to show that the party, or the Kennedy administration, is "soft on Communism," either at home or abroad. The process of finding justification for desired policies within the rhetoric governed by the right wing's ability to misinterpret current history has become almost automatic.

In the attacks on *The Liberal Papers* Republican leaders were arguing in effect that the Democrats had better get rid of their "left-wing extremists" in the same way that the Republicans were being pressured to dissociate themselves from the John Birch Society. *Life* magazine in an editorial [May 12, 1961,] took a somewhat analogous position. Speaking of the Committee of Correspondence, a small group of intellectuals and Quakers, and referring to my colleague, Professor H. Stuart Hughes, and me as its main sponsors, *Life* attacked the group as at least as dangerous to the Republic as the extremists of the radical right wing. Possibly, the magazine was trying to show the fellow travelers of the right wing in its audience that it was fair-minded and not in the least "soft on Communism." But such a view, however comfortable for those who regard themselves as holding a centrist or moderate position, is wholly unpolitical. The Committees of Correspondence (now the Council for Correspondence) were formed by twenty individuals comprising a variety of positions; a handful of the membership is responsible for the occasional appearance of a newsletter which is open to diverse and contending viewpoints and which struggles anemically to survive. The Council for Correspondence does not exist otherwise; it has no money and has not yet got a librarian fired, let alone a congressman elected. The right wing, in contrast, is well-heeled, aggressively if diffusely organized, and has many outlets in the mass as well as the class media. The implicit notion that "both extremes" are equally strong, thereby giving the center some freedom of movement, seems inaccurate.

The very terms of discourse are confusing here: "right" and "left" have lost their nineteenth-century meanings. It is absurd to suppose that the truth, or the proper course, lies in the middle between two extremes, as if political positions could be laid out on a continuum instead of being related to each other in dialectical and oblique ways.[11]

Current definitions of where the center is located in American politics have compressed within a too narrow range the variety of opinions, outside of the radical right, that are opposed to the bipartisan consensus on the cold war. Unconventional views, which require time to be explored fully, are lumped together by their enemies[12] and those who hold them cling to one another for solidarity against the dangers of being totally crushed and silenced. This compression helps to cut America off from the rest of the non-Communist world where positions that barely exist within this country are more developed, or are at least taken more seriously.[13]

[11] The very term, "the radical right" (first coined by Seymour Martin Lipset), is an effort to combat the notion of the right as inherently conservative. I regard my own position as quite conservative in some ways, since I want to conserve America as a going concern and the rest of the world with it, and am opposed to nuclear and other experiments and adventures, from whatever side, that seek to upset the status quo with which we must live and work. For further discussion, see both my essay (with Nathan Glazer), "The Intellectuals and the Discontented Classes," and "Some Further Reflections," in Daniel Bell, ed., *The Radical Right* (New York: Doubleday, 1963).

[12] To perhaps a lesser degree, various shadings of opinion on the conservative and radical right-wing side also tend to be compressed, at least in liberal discourse: people are always more conscious of differences among strata or sects to which they are close, while those further away look alike. What is for shorthand purposes referred to as the right wing is by no means monolithic, as any reader of its journals can ascertain for himself.

[13] One should not exaggerate the solidarity among intellectuals who share apparently similar views. Each of us can always find personal and professional as well as political reasons for differentiating himself from his colleagues, and we are often tempted to do so when they come under attack. For example, when someone more conservative than ourselves is

The strategic balances and imbalances of the cold war change with tremendous speed. The nuclear arms race and its political and economic repercussions at home have their own built-in dynamic, but diplomatic crises where the two great power blocs confront each other have an even greater primacy in creating a mutual climate in which the freedom of diplomatic give-and-take is imperiled. Such freedom has never been great on the American side, since we have always regarded deals as immoral and refused to define the national interest in terms of bargain and sale.[14] The demand for unconditional surrender is, so to speak, the other side of an ambivalence about conflict and a reluctance to assume international responsibility. The State Department found it difficult even to consider the Japanese "offer A" and "offer B" just prior to Pearl Harbor. The opportunities for a settlement with the U.S.S.R. that may potentially have existed at the time of Stalin's death were never explored, let alone taken advantage of, on the American side.

This leads me to a specific misunderstanding I have encountered regarding "The American Crisis" essay. What Mr. Maccoby and I say in the first section about the American military tradition, which focuses on "destruction of the enemy at the least immediate cost in American lives, or even the least budgetary cost," has been misunderstood by some readers as a plea for pacifism. Our contention was entirely different: we were criticizing the unpolitical nature of the American military tradition, pursuing total victory regardless of everything else, as illustrated in the refusal to think about the political consequences of bringing the Soviet Union into the already nearly concluded war against Japan in 1945. In World War II there was a striking contrast between Churchill's concern as to what the relationships of the big powers would be

---

attacked by the right wing for his supposed radicalism, it is easy to be amused rather than to come to his defense. And if someone who has been attacking us for our own conservatism is then attacked, it is not hard to think twice before coming to *his* defense. Vanity and caution are not the only factors here: this is an enormous country with many dispersed centers and quite without the centralized intellectual communities of London or Paris or Tokyo. Furthermore, the general rhetoric of the mass media, quite apart from content, often makes it difficult for intellectuals to come to each other's support because in that rhetoric there is room only for the quick comeback, which is not everyone's forte.

[14] Whether there is such a thing at all as the national interest is for me an open question. See, e.g., my comments on Walt W. Rostow's essay on "The National Style" in Elting E. Morison, ed., *The National Style: Essays on Value and Performance* (New York: Harper, 1958).

at the end of the war and his willingness, if necessary, to prolong the war to protect what he regarded as British interests, and the dominant American desire, once in the war, to get it over with as simply and, in short-run terms, as efficiently as possible, whatever the long-run costs. This, and the traditional American lack of concern for military affairs during peacetime, is the sort of thing we were referring to in speaking of America's lack of "a politically sagacious military elite."

I return to these matters in "Reflections on Containment and Initiatives," a paper delivered at a symposium on studies of war and peace at the annual meetings of the American Sociological Association in September 1962. This essay, like "The American Crisis," treats in a rather cursory way the domestic consequences of American strategic doctrines. These doctrines have been changing rapidly, reflecting Soviet progress and also the struggles for supremacy within the Department of Defense and within NATO. Shifts have also been under way within the Soviet Union, influenced by the competition with Communist China for the allegiance of the developing nations; and undoubtedly the containment essay, like many of the topical essays in this section, will appear obvious in some respects and obsolete in others by the time this book is published. Given so fluid a situation, I prefer to leave the essays standing as signposts of the time in which they were written or published, rather than to annotate them to take account of later developments.[15]

However, since all of the essays in this section were written prior to the Cuban crisis in the fall of 1962, I want to say a few words here (which in turn may be rendered obsolete) about the implications of that crisis. In the spring of 1962, Secretary of Defense McNamara publicly abandoned the idea of a balanced minimum deterrent (based on possession of hardened or otherwise virtually invulnerable weapons, such as the Polaris, poised to retaliate against enemy populations), and claimed to seek instead the goals of what has come to be termed "counterforce" superiority, a policy that aims less at a last-resort deterrent than at the possibilities of greater flexibility, including, under sufficient provocation, a judiciously limited first strike and conceivably what the Air Force happily calls "prevailance."[16] McNamara's statement accompa-

[15] A discussion of some of the technical issues of strategy as these presented themselves a few months ago can be found in Arthur Waskow, *The Limits of Defense* (Doubleday, 1962).

[16] There is some evidence that McNamara's statement was aimed at the French, not at the Soviet Union, and his later statements have backed away from counterforce and suggested the advantages of stability through mutual deterrence.

nied evidence of an enormously heightened American superiority both in hardened and "soft" missiles as well as continued power of SAC bombers to deliver hydrogen bombs, while the Soviet Union has primarily relied on a relatively small number of ICBMs. The American search for supremacy in the arms race, like many other forms of overreaching and possessiveness (such as the German naval race with the British after 1900), was bound to provoke retaliation. And while speculations abound as to why the Soviet Union upset the political (but not the military) balance of power by seeking to put strategic missiles into Cuba, I am inclined to think that this was in considerable part a response to the missile build-up and counterforce doctrine on the American side for, although the Russians have broken out of the cautious European isolationism that governed their policy (except for Korea) from 1946 to 1952, I would still maintain that the Khrushchev regime is not basically and unmalleably expansionist, whatever its ideological claims and periodic millenary fantasies. As against a rejuvenated and booming Western Europe, the Russian satellites in Central Europe are a liability; and, faced with Communist Chinese expansionism and fanaticism, the Russians would like to stabilize that sector of their empire, by putting pressure on us both in Berlin and in the formerly colonial world, including Latin America, where the West is on the defensive.

To put the matter oversimply: I see the major drives of both American and Soviet policy as resting on the status quo, which both powers alternately upset, in part because of internal pressures and even more because of pressures from allies or clients. The Russians upset the status quo in crude and obvious ways: after having pressed for a moratorium, they resume testing of bombs, or they renew pressures on Berlin, or they put IRBMs into Cuba. They also take advantage of revolutions whenever they occur, at the same time cutting their losses, as in the Congo or Cuba, when we counterattack. We Americans, on the other hand, are less innocent and acquiescent than we appear to ourselves to be. I have just mentioned the counterforce doctrine that steps up the arms race. As suggested above, this doctrine stems in part from an effort, less to put pressure on the Russians, than to satisfy our European allies that our nuclear deterrent suffices for NATO, and hence to prevent the spread of separate nuclear deterrents in France and West Germany. But at the same time, the French nuclear tests have been an irritant, if a minor one, in the effort to obtain a test ban, making it more difficult for the Russians to do what has never seemed very likely: to obtain Communist Chinese assent to a test ban. And West German rearmament, along with continuing claims to recover the "stolen territories" now occupied by the Poles east of the Oder-Neisse line, makes the American position on Berlin not merely a defense of the status quo but also a tacit surrogate of West German efforts to undo the concededly unfortunate way the boundaries fell or were fixed in 1945.

I believe that President Kennedy would like to come to some sort of settlement with the Soviet Union on outstanding issues—Berlin, a test ban, and possibly moving toward disarmament. He is hampered by having to move as leader of an international coalition, some of whose members count on the cold war as a guarantee of American support. He is also confined by a domestic population that, as "The American Crisis" and other essays in this section suggest, is moving in very uneven stages toward a less simplified picture of itself, its Communist adversaries, and the problems of contemporary military strategy.

Critics of the general position I have taken contend that, although the Russians have not had a war plan for invading Germany or even seizing West Berlin, what has stopped them has been the American readiness to fight, and that, if we withdrew our threat of a nuclear first strike, we might tempt them to greater adventurousness. To answer this argument at appropriate length would require treatment of the nature of NATO, of American and Soviet domestic politics, and of the international system itself. It is perfectly true that our nuclear credibility inhibits small wars in central Europe and is an insurance against Soviet probes there. But one price of the insurance is that we Americans must be kept sufficiently worked up about the dangers of a Soviet advance to provide most of the support for NATO and all the domestic accoutrements of a potential first-strike policy, eventually, no doubt, including civil defense.[17] The interplay of American and Soviet moves on Berlin have made it extremely difficult for President Kennedy to arrive at a settlement the American people would be willing to accept.

My argument rests on the basic but obviously arguable proposition that, in a revolutionary world, the United States and the Soviet Union have many conservative interests in common, including the preservation of a status quo in which they are the major nuclear powers. A tacit *modus vivendi* between them seems to me the only way in which

[17] For an argumentative discussion of some of the potential dangers for a democratic policy of a large-scale shelter program, see Arthur Waskow's pamphlet, *The Shelter Centered Society* (Peace Research Institute, Washington, D.C., 1962), reporting a conference of social scientists, of whom I was one.

the spread of nuclear weapons can conceivably be checked and the Chinese Communists restrained. A world resting on such a *modus vivendi* would not be a comfortable or a just or peaceful one. From the standpoint of revolutionaries it would be conservative, even reactionary, and I would not, myself, envisage its enduring for very long.

In some respects, such an agreement already exists and was made manifest after the Cuban crisis. President Kennedy and Chairman Khrushchev, despite their enormous mutual distrust and misunderstandings, understand each other less badly than do some of their own allies. The difficulty with a tacit understanding is that it does not bind either allies, domestic opponents, potential rivals, or successors. For example, a treaty on Berlin would safeguard Western rights there, including access; it would restrain Americans, and perhaps also Germans, from pressing for reunification, while making it possible for Khrushchev further to restrain Ulbricht.[18] Similarly a test ban, while it would probably not, at this point, inhibit either the French or the Red Chinese, might make it conceivable for the American Government to reopen the question of the balanced deterrent and to face in a more realistic way what would be the domestic military, political, and economic consequences of serious rather than Sunday-sermon efforts toward reducing the level and pace of the arms race.

I realize, of course, that any interim program of stabilization faces enormous obstacles from technological breakthroughs, military surprises (such as the unexpected speed with which the Russians put missiles into Cuba), and shifts in the balance of political power within each bloc.

The cold war presents twin dangers, whose salience shifts constantly with events. One danger is the external threat of communism, doubtfully stable, nonmonolithic rival, whose victims' fate must be one of the concerns of a wise policy for the United States. Given the history of the postwar years and the nature of Soviet society, it is not surprising that Americans felt it necessary, first, to seek to contain and, then, also to deter the Soviet Union. What has not made sense, since it can not be accomplished without war, has been our repeated toying with the idea of liberation or rollback achieved through force; our failure to act both in East Germany in 1953 and in Hungary in 1956 (where

[18] See for fuller discussion my essay, "Dealing with the Russians over Berlin," Committee of Correspondence *Newsletter*, July 21, 1961; reprinted *The American Scholar*, Vol. 31, Winter 1961–62, pp. 1–27.

apparently Secretary of State Dulles, far more cautious in deed than in word, advised the Soviet Union that we would not intervene) indicated as much to our adversary. But the other danger of the cold war is what it does to ourselves domestically, and it is to this danger that these essays are primarily devoted.

One aspect of this danger is that tacit assurances of the sort Dulles gave the U.S.S.R. in 1956 are not binding on our own people, many of whom continue to live with delusions as to what is possible—much as the West Germans, when they are roused from the feast of affluence, are permitted to live with the possibility of recapturing the eastern territories and achieving reunification on Western terms (which neither Chancellor Adenauer nor many other Germans may actually want to see). In a dictatorship, illusions may be opiate or bait; they shape policy only marginally. In a democracy like ours, where an educated elite seeking to exercise leverage over an enormous, barely manageable country is itself sometimes marginal and torn by internal divisions, popular illusions become the very stuff of politics. They helped imprison President Eisenhower in his weak and sadly ineffective moves to reach a *détente* with the Russians over Berlin and over a test ban, although other illusions linking household budgets to national ones came to his aid when he used the budget to keep within limits what he called "the military-industrial complex." I have sympathised with President Kennedy who, far more intelligent and energetic, seeks room to maneuver vis-à-vis these cramping illusions; and, as the "containment" essay argues, in some ways it has been easier for him to contain the Russians than to contain the Americans. This can be only a temporary solution. It leads nowhere.

Readers of this section, especially those familiar with my earlier, somewhat more sanguine writings, may feel that I exaggerate the dangers of war and of the current right-wing recrudescence. I recognize that the middle-class intellectual like myself is part of society's membrane: vulnerable to storms and alarms. Needless to say, I would be glad to have my prophecies proved false. I cannot help my keen sense of the fragility as well as the splendor and misery of civilization, or my fear of the explosive mixtures of nationalism, democracy, dictatorship, and nuclear technology. I find what mankind has accomplished thus far extraordinary and awe-inspiring, and I would like to see the story continue.

National Purpose
(1961, 1963)

Even small, nonliterate societies may feel that by virtue of their very existence they are carrying out some larger plan of a cosmic sort, that they represent, for example, the Hopi Way, or even mankind as such. But in a larger, more complex society like our own, the problem of finding a "national purpose" seems to occur as a result of an accretion of opportunities, responsibilities, and unemployed energies at the top of society. It is a sort of capital accumulation, spent by leaders on behalf of all of us, and to some degree carrying out our own aspirations as well as theirs. Correspondingly, the idea of national purpose represents in some measure a deficit of purposes in the society at large. To participate as a citizen in national purpose is perhaps not inevitably a form of alienation, for both the best and the worst goals of men may be vicarious, transcending one's own immediate interest. But before looking at the nation it may clarify matters to look at groups and corporations.

It is a mistake to attribute to all members of an organization or even a nation the purposes held or set forth by the leaders. The capacity to be preoccupied by the goals of an organization is unevenly distributed. And morale may depend less than one might think on shared goals. Thus, Edward Shils and Morris Janowitz showed in their study of the *Wehrmacht* in World War II that men fought primarily because of loyalty to their small combat units and their immediate leaders and peers, rather than out of any dedication to or interest in Nazi ideology. Other studies of small groups, whether of military teams, factory work groups or street gangs, show much the same phenomenon. In many such instances, the personal qualities of the leader provide for the followers a tacit assurance that the aims of the group will be consonant with their shared though unexpressed values. Since the leaders are assumed to be good guys, the members also trust that their vested inertias will not be interfered with.

But the group leaders themselves, at the lower middle levels of the hierarchy of authority, are in a somewhat different situation. As retailers in the goals business, they need at least to believe in the goals of the wholesalers above them. Often, although they may enjoy the elbow room and prerogatives of their position in comparison with the greater constriction of those below them, they may not want the luxury or dilemma of choosing among goals, but prefer to be given a single goal by those above them which can absorb their own and their men's energies. This very preference for simplified goals in the lower ranks of an organization, by increasing obedience and diminishing flexibility, may through a process of cumulation provide multiplicity of choices for those in the upper ranks. Mussolini's relative freedom was hence the unearned increment on the unused freedom of many intermediate leaders below him.

Organizations obviously differ from each other in the extent to which top leadership possesses a monopoly (never of course wholly complete) on the setting of goals. In one of his series of articles on executive communities in America, Seymour Freedgood described in the July 1961 *Fortune* the style of life of the auto executives of Bloomfield Hills outside Detroit. As compared with the executives of large managerial businesses of similar size centered in New York City, these men are devoted to making automobiles with a single-mindedness that approaches fanaticism—a single-mindedness not uncommon in small entrepreneurial business where the founder and owner is the same hard-driving man. In the lower leadership ranks of the auto industry, supervisors may devote themselves to the task of shaving a few cents off the cost of a fender or an engine block. The pressure to do so comes down from the top, and is enhanced by small suppliers who, living on the margins of the big companies, compete to make parts cheaper than they can be made inside.

General Motors has notably institutionalized the drive for savings at all lower levels of the company whose divisions engage in fierce "socialist competition" with each other. But the result is to provide the upper ranks of General Motors and the other large companies with huge surpluses whose distribution is not automatic. To decide what to do with the money leads to concern as to what this company or any company's purpose is or ought to be: how much shall be paid out to stockholders, how much should be reinvested, how much put into institutional advertising, and how much into the increasingly variegated philanthropies inside and outside the company, ranging from the Community Chest to patronage of a congeries of local and national educational and cultural enterprises. Some auto executives, along with executives elsewhere, resent having to make such seemingly unbusinesslike judgments and choices. One man quoted in the *Fortune* stories speaks of the unenlightened "locker room conservatism" of those who, starting out in life as poor boys, never had a chance to enlarge their horizons and who are now too immersed in their accustomed detailed work to want to think about anything else.

One reason for this is that between such top executives and the lower echelons of leadership there may exist something of the relationship between a parent and a child when the child is attempting tasks which are big for it, but no longer quite so big for the parent: the parent will urge the child on, encourage him, and take very seriously what the child is doing. That is, the executive may be in the position of urging a foreman to take seriously saving a few cents here and there although the executive may not know what to do with the money thus saved. Identification here minimizes manipulation. So, too, one of the most striking features of big-business mentality in America is its identification with small-business ideology, as is clear in the mutual good fellowship of talk about free enterprise or the evils of government intervention. For, while the experience of the big businessman is very different from that of the small businessman, he likes to pretend that it is not. Hence we witnessed during the Eisenhower regime big businessmen such as "Engine Charlie" Wilson applying to the largest concerns of the nation the private and parochial small moralities of thrift and common sense, shared with semi-educated Chevrolet dealers in a small town and learned at home and school and in the plant.[1]

Increasingly, however, the men at the very top even of the auto industry, despite the conservatism of their traditional small-business purposes, cannot avoid the larger questions forced on them by their surpluses and visibility. Men like Henry Ford II, George Romney, and Robert McNamara when he was president of Ford are among those who cannot help realizing that they are doing something more than

[1] Emmett Hughes's revealing portrait of the Eisenhower cabinet in *The Ordeal of Power* suggests that Wilson's and President Eisenhower's provinciality were partial protections against the more global and dangerous moralism of John Foster Dulles, who was impressive perhaps partly because his one-eyed but at the same time global vision held a certain ambivalent appeal for men whose own horizons were more limited, not transcending the folk homilies that pass for common sense.

making autos, more even than making ancillary community decisions, such as whether to give more to the Red Cross this year than last, or to introduce new grievance machinery in cooperation with the local union.[2] These major auto executives, like their fellows in Wall Street, have come to realize that they are symbols: they are major pacesetters in dealing with labor, with problems of racial integration in their plants, with foreign countries, and with the American economy (vitally affected as it is by their investment decisions, and vitally affected as their companies are by the nation's investment decisions).

Moreover, while men lower down in the system can focus not only on narrow goals but on very short timetables for measuring performance against them, such as a day's or a week's output, these top executives must think of the survival of their companies over the long run, a span only punctuated by the annual verdict of the balance sheet, and in the auto industry by the annual model race against competing firms.[3]

Many executives are at the top (or would like to be there) because they have the capacity to invent purposes for their organizations and only at the top can they employ this capacity. Others, however, have been forced by the success of their organizations to move faster into complexity of choice than they can psychologically endure. The pressure to discover a single goal, a single purpose, whether that of an institution or that of a nation, would seem partly to arise as the cumulative pressure of those men who are looking for a way to simplify their lives and to subordinate themselves to an apparently single destiny. As many have pointed out, among the appeals of communism has been the desire of actual or potential elites to subordinate themselves to

[2] For a good many years the company president, facing outward at least as much as inward, has sometimes been pushed and sometimes pulled into the larger political arena or the quasi-political arena of national commissions or local ones, such as the Constitutional Convention in Michigan which led Romney toward the governorship.

[3] Men lower down, of course, can participate at least as spectators in this gamelike competition, though they themselves cannot make the gambles which can bet $100 million on a new model (as happened with the Edsel) against a competitor's still opaque plans and a market whose uncertainties can only be partially clarified by market research and economic forecasting. Furthermore, the men at the top are in their jobs for rarely more than ten or fifteen years. This may mean that the excitement of the race can last them the term of their active working lives. Problems of their own purposiveness can then arise only if failure, intrigue, or accident forces them out, cushioned financially but not psychologically against the loss of command.

History in order to make life more austere and more apparently meaningful. (In the Soviet Union today, many people actively or apathetically reject such simplifying impoverishment of aims.) Correspondingly, some of the late emphasis on the national purpose of America would seem to be an effort to bring the simplicity of the balance sheet into the process of deciding where the surplus of assets and choices concentrated at the top of our society should be allocated. To be sure, this is not entirely new—no large movement of this sort ever is. The middle class has often found in the emotions of nationalism compensation for and additions to its own more limited purposes and horizons. Yet during the hegemony of the concept of Manifest Destiny, there was less of the concentration of focus and unification around a single national goal than has since occurred. Even when Manifest Destiny was a factor leading to war, as in the war with Mexico, it had by no means the full support of the country. Different groups defined the mission of America in very different ways; and while expansion had a wide appeal, interlaced of course with the struggle over the limitation or expansion of slave territory, it was not a nation-wide goal. And the lack of a unified or common purpose in the United States was demonstrated by the ability of the competing sections to engage with an extraordinary parochialism (as if the rest of the world did not exist or, as the South expected, could be counted on to help) in a ferocious civil war.

At the close of the last century, in part to lift the country's eyes from the business of business, men like Theodore Roosevelt, Brooks Adams, and other patricians wanted to see the United States assert itself in the concert of nations, standing for something, or at least making its weight felt as a nation. In a society divided by the ethic of Social Darwinism, however, the search for a national consensus did not necessarily have totalitarian implications. And political scientists sought to limit as well as guide national purpose away from moralistic and over-ambitious aims by developing the concept of the "national interest"—a concept that tends to crumble when one asks in whose interest within the country are the various definitions of the supposed national interest.[4] Other efforts to define national goals have even been explicitly pluralistic, as in Arthur Schlesinger, Jr.'s *The Vital Center*.

What would seem to be new in these developments is the widespread self-consciousness of the quest for a national purpose as illustrated in

[4] For further development of this idea, see my comments on Walt W. Rostow's essay in Elting Morison, ed., *The National Style: Essays in Value and Performance* (New York, Harper, 1958).

the *Life* magazine series (now published under the title, *The National Purpose*); the effort to define America by a single idea or connected set of ideas is occurring at the same time that the country is growing greatly in population while also discovering limits to its outward reach.

The attraction of an apparently clear-cut single definition is illustrated by the discussion as to whether the country has a "win" or a "no-win" policy of victory over communism. A good many of the reservists called up by the President during the Berlin crisis in the summer of 1961 could see no relation between their bits and pieces of half-baked training with irrelevant weapons and the nation's "standing firm" on Berlin. Not being unionized, they resorted to political pressures on their congressmen and also complained to their home-town papers in order to have their own private purposes recognized in the face of the alleged national purpose. Such experiences may only intensify the pressure on the top leadership to assert an unequivocal goal to which all must conform. Until very recently and perhaps to some extent even now, the Strategic Air Command has maintained a much higher, more demanding level of morale than many other military services. One element in this morale comes from the group solidarity of a volunteer and highly selected force which can keep its personnel together; another element has been the realistic training based on such manageable micro-purposes as getting bomber crews faster into the air, making their runs more accurate and in other ways breaking performance down into man-measurable units—the military equivalents of annual budgets, model changes, and inventories. This tight leadership, however, has also been reflected in assertions by SAC leaders that talk of nuclear "stalemate" betokened lack of will and that any true American could only aim at victory. (The Marines have apparently managed to maintain high morale without generating a comparable ideology of hatred for the Communist enemy.)

However, a certain fanaticism and rigor may continue in the lower ranks of the service even while top military leadership may come to doubt whether the additional minutes "saved" by crack bomber pilot training can any longer be used for tasks which make sense. Some members of the armed services, like some auto executives, may no longer be able to believe that they have no real choices but only a simple goal measurable in unidimensional terms: more weapons, more "victory," more profits, a larger share of the globe market.

For what I have been arguing here is that as people rise in an organization or country, they come into positions where the quantity saved lower down, whether of time or of money or other resources, turns into quality and presents a problem in the making of more complex choices. The closer one nears the top, the greater the necessity appears for reconciling conflicting purposes. One of these purposes must inevitably be the purpose of each individual to sustain himself so that he can perform his main or principal purpose effectively and uninterruptedly. Obviously, when a leader or a group do not survive, they cannot perform other functions or discover other purposes—this is one of the inescapable dilemmas of existence.

As long as nations are the units for decision-making in the world, including the decision to make war or peace, the President of the United States "possesses" the savings which result from the accumulations below him. It would seem that affluence has forced millions of Americans out of our traditional purposes of getting along, making a living, keeping a job, and attending intermittently to our Creator. These Americans have projected onto the nation and onto its leader their insistent need to define where they are going.

One reason for this pressure is the fear that the men lower down, like the Berlin reservists, will conclude that their small savings, sacrifices, or minor rationalities are of no consequence. We all of us know many organizations where the men lower down have rightly or wrongly concluded that what they do doesn't make the slightest difference. One of my students in a recent term paper described a can company where he had worked for the summer, where men on the assembly line were fantastically wasteful, often tossing hundreds of perfectly good cans onto the ground simply for the fun of it or out of boredom, or turning out many that were needlessly imperfect. In fact, although the plant lost money, the strongly unionized men could not take seriously endless pleas that they be more careful, for they saw that the company as a whole was rich, they were not afraid for their jobs, they enjoyed showing their independence, and they had lost whatever they may once have possessed of what Veblen called the instinct of workmanship. Our whole society is full of such operations, and we have in this country a reputation for efficiency only because other countries have in the past been even more wasteful or have concealed their waste less well. Such lower-level sabotage can deprive an organization or the society as a whole of the surplus and the maneuverability that will permit choice. By such erosions, businesses do go bankrupt and nations do undergo revolutions or disintegrate. It is partly as a desperate measure to prevent this that some of our elite have stressed the concept of national purpose, as a way of making shapeless men shape up. And of course there is the nostalgia for the apparently simpler purposes of an earlier day, just as there is among big businessmen who find that their organizations, like junior unbounded welfare states, are pushed into increasingly complex purposes such as the training of their higher personnel to discover purpose and the preparation of future personnel through assistance to educational institutions throughout America.

Any going concern, then, sheds old purposes and acquires new ones perhaps with some of the same resistances that an individual himself presents against the discontinuities forced on him by life. In a democratic organization or country, one purpose must therefore be to keep open the possibility of other purposes being discovered, while present avowed purposes become disestablished.

I do not think that a monolithic national purpose will stave off the erosion of individual and group purposes in our society as a whole although it may cover over such erosion for a time. In a new nation, seeking to emerge by giant strides out of tribal and kinship ties, the quest for national purpose may appear necessary to make possible the simpler quest for a rising standard of living or even one which keeps up with burgeoning population growth. As an ideology of sacrifice and devotion, such a concept may organize people who would otherwise seek only the semiliteracy of mass consumption. But in fact the new nations engaged in this quest often imitate the vanished imperialists whose sometimes self-defeating gains of conquest and national prestige took the form of an unbounded expansionism.

But there seems to me something oddly regressive in the spectacle of the United States reducing itself to the size of a new nation that needs a manifest destiny to compel the newly liberated to postpone traditional gratifications. Affluence ought to mean abundance of purposes, and intense exploration and discovery of new ones, both individual and collective. It might mean a stronger concern for the purposes of others who have not yet reached the dilemmas of abundance. To some extent it has in fact done so, as well exemplified in the Peace Corps or private projects of a Peace Corps type at home and abroad. Such concern for the new nations might help them over the phase of violent nationalism, the more so if we ourselves could set a better model in this respect.

Just as this essay goes to press, President Kennedy has taken the initiative both in his commencement address at American University on the test ban and in his address to the nation on the struggle for racial justice to raise the sights of America and to ask for postponement at least of the traditional gratifications of undiscriminating hatred of the

Russians (some fanatical right wingers have objected to Secretary McNamara's "no-cities" doctrine on the ground that it will spare too many Russian lives!) and of the Negroes. To achieve a modicum of disarmament in the cold war and in the race struggle will certainly demand intense national efforts, and these provide more universalistic purposes than expansionism or chauvinistic competition. In such measure as they succeed, they will create a more tolerable plateau from which to raise more profound questions about the kind of a country and a world we would like to inhabit. For it should be clear that not even these exigent and indispensable goals provide us with a sufficient agenda for a large, multifarious nation. Not even an institution, let alone a country, can survive and prosper over any considerable period of time by serving only a single goal or purpose. If individuals try to purify their own lives to dedicate them to a single purpose only, they become fanatics. If they use their occupations and callings to define their purposes, even as artists and thinkers, they run the danger of becoming overprofessionalized and less than fully human. And if, in relative default of group and individual purposes, we use the nation to absorb the surplus, the chances are that we shall become more nationalistic—and in a world where others are doing the same, threaten the very goal we seem to cherish.

In Budd Shulberg's novel, *What Makes Sammy Run?*, when Sammy gets to the top of the heap in Hollywood, he finds himself lost: there is no one to be mad at, no one to put down, no one to deny him things. Some Americans would like the United States to act like Sammy, discovering, in the ever useful Communist adversary, those thwartings and frustrations and denials that can give life meaning again. The grandiosity of "winning" is a mean-spirited goal for a diverse people. Indeed, it is curious that the right wing, which seeks to cut down the national power to the size of the Articles of Confederation, is at the same time eager to inflate the national power to deal with alleged (and only very rarely actual) subversion at home and Godless Communists abroad: the latter aim allows the Administration to dispose of the national product by a kind of dumping operation. The President himself in the addresses just mentioned, and in other efforts such as the desire to overcome unemployment, has sought to set goals of wider range. Yet the fundamental paradox remains about the nature of goals for a huge rich country, whose solidarities cannot be those of a poor small one: if the nation itself is not transcended by the search for larger and more inclusive units of solidarity, it becomes an idol. In this sense it is too small a vehicle for our aspirations as in other perspectives it is too large.

The American Crisis
(WITH MICHAEL MACCOBY, 1960)

I

Although America has been for much of its history a belligerent and expansionist country, it has not been a militaristic one, and up until the present it has resisted military control of political policy. While this encapsulation of the military might have been a protection for the peacetime life of the country, for only rarely did generals as such get involved in politics, one consequence has been that during wartime America has lacked a politically sagacious military elite. With a few famous exceptions, our generals have considered destruction of the enemy at the least immediate cost in American lives, or even the least budgetary cost, to be their sole concern. In the Second World War, this outlook gave a mindless justification for the mass bombings of German cities (also participated in by the British) and for the terrible and unnecessary destruction of Hiroshima and Nagasaki (when in fact the Japanese had given much evidence that they were prepared to surrender).

Only as the Second World War progressed did the American military begin to enlist advisers from civilian life, and a large number of intellectuals (a number of them ex-New Dealers) became involved in its planning and execution, while the physical scientists were of course heavily engaged. At the end of the war, in order to maintain this link, the Air Force set up the Rand (Research and Development) Corporation; the Army has a similar "brains trust" in the Operations Research Office of Johns Hopkins University; and the Central Intelligence Agency, while not outside the government, has a somewhat similar immunity from immediate supervision. Science and social science departments in a number of major universities have close personal and professional ties with these agencies. It would not be accurate to say that all these men have been mobilized on behalf of the policy of deterrence through the threat of mass destruction either of a counterforce or "balanced" deterrent force. Indeed, there are probably men working for Rand who have done as much to subject defense policy to rational scrutiny as have men who are known to be dedicated workers for peace.[1] Furthermore, men working for these agencies are involved in a great number of technical studies, not only of military but also of political problems and of foreign policy, so that on the one hand the strategy of deterrence may be viewed in a wider ambit than within the AEC or SAC, while on the other hand many policy matters of a general sort are colored by a cold war filter, as if this were the only possible background for an extrapolation of the present.

Not only the exigencies of the cold war per se but the exigencies of interservice rivalry in the Pentagon have led to the recruitment of many exceptionally intelligent men whose full-time task it is to explore the justifications—and in some measure also the limitations—of the defense dogmas relevant to their arm of the service (including the Atomic Energy Commission). Thus, while some of the men at Rand and elsewhere have been intrigued by the possibilities of stabilizing the arms race by maintaining what Albert Wohlstetter has termed "The Delicate Balance of Terror," others have bent their scientific efforts to discovering holes in any possibility of a test ban which could be negotiated with the Russians.

Such holes are not so very difficult to find, for the Russians—valuing secrecy for military, political, and cultural reasons—are very reluctant to permit inspections (which some of their own scientists regard as the first opportunity for a genuine window to the West), while American scientific polemicists are prepared to denounce any treaty which does not offer the impossible, that is, a hundred per cent security against any opportunity for Soviet evasion. Take, for example, the fantastic idea, developed in Edward Teller's Livermore Laboratory, that deep holes might be dug in salt mines and bombs exploded therein without anybody's noticing—a notion that is fantastic, not because the Russians couldn't do it, but because it would take a long time, require immense commotion of men and machines, and would therefore be very hard to keep secret both from us and from the Russian people themselves. As more recent events have shown, when the Soviets decided to test both small and large bombs, they openly broke the moratorium, demonstrating their cynicism but not stealth.

[1] See, for a sympathetic account, Joseph Kraft, "Rand: Arsenal for Ideas," *Harper's*, Vol. CCXXI (July 1960), pages 69-76.

Once upon a time, the Navy in its own interest opposed reliance on massive retaliation, and its experts were therefore free to explore the dangers of this doctrine. But then, faced with a declining strategic role, the Navy traded doctrine for budget—reaping a harvest in big carriers and atomic submarines—and joined the Air Force in alliance against the remaining Army men (such as Generals Ridgway, Gavin, and Taylor) whose recurrent protests have usually led to their leaving the intraservice battlefield altogether.[2] For reasons we hope to explore in this paper, there is no organization comparable to the Rand Corporation, dedicated to disarmament; in fact, only a few journalists (among whom Walter Lippmann is outstanding), some university professors, and in the government the members of the Liberal Project and a few others are free fully to explore the risks of current military policy and the foreign and domestic policies to which it is tied.

The authors of this essay are experts neither on defense nor on foreign policy. At the same time, we have had some experience in seeing the experts make mistakes by virtue of their expertise. This does not mean that amateurs are necessarily better than professionals; but until a serious effort is mobilized for peace, amateurs will probably have to be relied upon for new ideas in the field of defense and foreign policy.

Among the most important and interesting problems of education is that of exploring the means by which people can learn to make a proper judgment of expert opinion. One way is to become expert in a particular field oneself. Another approach is to gain some sense of the kind of perspective or style of perception that the experts use, as a basis for seeing what might be the possible limitations of their view in a given instance. Thus one can find experts privy to discussions concerning deterrence who talk about the American ability to "accept," let us say, ten or thirty million casualties—experts who are familiar with the post-Second World War disaster studies but who fail to ask what sort of backwoods reactionaries would take over whatever would be left of America if our major urban centers were destroyed in a nuclear (or biological or other mass) war, nor in the same connection do they ask what the effect would be on the survivors of the sudden death of millions of their countrymen in a holocaust so extreme as not to be justifiable by the rationalizations that have in the past sustained mass killing. Some who

[2] Our understanding of these matters owes much to Eric Larrabee's work on postwar military policy. We have also profited from the discussion of absolutist military thinking in Morris Janowitz, *The Professional Soldier* (Glencoe, Illinois: The Free Press, 1960).

do concern themselves with this issue assume on the basis of the disasters of the Second World War that recuperation is possible at astonishing speed, but they are thinking at best of economic and not of cultural or moral recuperation, and at worst of the now ample possibilities of a military so-called second or third strike.

So, too, there are other men, intelligent enough to grasp some of the inherent weaknesses in the strategy of deterrence, who have speculated about an automatic deterrent, protected from the possibility of human frailty on our side. One mechanism that has been proposed for achieving this is a cobalt bomb, aimed at all countries having nuclear power themselves and primed to go off without reference to a human chain of command the moment any nuclear weapon is fired at us. The argument for such a scheme is that if a potential enemy thinks that we, as human beings, might decide for some reason or other not to hit back (despite the fact that we are equipped to do so), then our deterrent, though still terrifying, loses its absolute value; therefore we must try to set up a system over which none of us has any control. This reasoning, logical as far as it goes, typically leaves other variables out of account altogether—like the fact that becoming the prisoners of our own mechanisms would intensify the dangerous feelings of helplessness which the policy of deterrence has already succeeded in producing. It would mean surrendering the hope that the human race can get control of the arms race—even though it has been argued that once the automatic cobalt bomb was known to exist, no one would tempt fate.

One further point about experts: they have fended off outsiders, including many intelligent congressmen, by establishing as a condition of entering the debate on armaments a knowledge of highly technical matters (frequently "classified") and the possession of a polished rationality of the game-theory sort. We want to make it amply clear that we are of course not opposed to rationality, whether polished or unpolished: human reason, slender thread though it be, is the thread on which our hopes hang. Rather, the difficulty is that there are styles of rationality, based on eliminating certain variables from consideration and pursuing others as far as they will lead. These have become accepted by many strategists as the only available styles—one is said, in a boyish and overworked phrase, not to have "done one's homework" if one is not fully at home in this particular style. (The phrase about "doing one's homework" is one of the many by which the real terrors of the arms race and the human situation today are glossed over by cavalier phrases—quite "American" in their derivation from the lingo of sportsmen or juveniles.) To repeat: this sort of rationality can be very useful in dealing with problems, provided that its limits are well understood and that other sorts of rationality are also available. And there is the further difficulty that both we ourselves, that is the public at large and our allies and prospective enemies, listen in on our discussions; and if the tone of discussion seems inhuman because of its icily strategic style, then enemies may assume that they must develop analogous intellectual as well as military weapons. Thus our strategic approaches become eventually both self-confirming and self-defeating.

In criticizing the experts, furthermore, we are not supposing that the gentlemanly amateur is better at these things and that it is best to muddle through, without disciplined thought. Indeed, if we had to choose we would surely prefer to trust our fate to the experts of Rand than to some of the blustering generals (or senators) who have enjoyed talking tough (a great help, no doubt, to their opposite numbers in China and the U.S.S.R.). Our hope is that the practicality of ethical considerations may become more widely understood, and that discussion of deterrence and its alternatives can be enlarged, and more differentiated modes of thought encouraged.

II

The tone of the 1960 election campaign indicates the fringe position of the pacifist groups in American life. These groups have tried to state their case in a variety of ways: through mass meetings and leaflets, through the picketing of missile bases or the bases of nuclear-powered submarines, through lobbying and personal appeals. They must constantly combat the charge of being "un-American," while in more serious circles they often appear to be all heart and no head. They have had no extensive pocketbook to tap (and of course the politically active groups have lacked even the fringe benefit of tax exemption). In spite of these handicaps, the Committee for a Sane Nuclear Policy has had some influence in keeping ideas afloat that would otherwise not get a hearing and especially in acquainting Americans—millions of whom have yet to learn the news—with the dangers of fallout and nuclear disaster. Understandably in this situation, Americans concerned not only with disarmament but with opening up the political climate to debate on the issue have looked at Britain as a country where issues confined to the margins of discourse in the United States are openly debated. For example, George Kennan's BBC lectures of a few years ago excited much greater response than any comparable talks he has given in this country.³ While the British government in power has been somewhat less effective as a restraining force on the Americans and the Soviets than would have been salutary for both, and while the Suez adventure showed that the British blimps had enough air left for another flotation, the Americans can indeed envy the ease with which Englishmen discuss alternatives to nuclear war, ranging from unilateral disarmament to diplomatic maneuvers aimed at easing particular points of tension in the cold war, whether in China or in Germany. As against the tiny handful of American university students who feel anything can be done about the Bomb (a far larger number are concerned with the struggle for racial integration), Americans look on the Aldermaston marchers as something quite inconceivable at present in this country.

What accounts for this difference between Britain and America? The problem of dealing with experts is the same in both countries, although in Britain—which is smaller and still partially aristocratic in nature—political leaders are less cut off than ours have been from intellectuals and literary men. It may be that people feel safer in this country because it is big and powerful and seemingly remote from the traditional areas of danger. This is an irrational feeling in the modern world of deterrence, since our fearful power and our weapons themselves become a lightning rod inviting attack; nevertheless, the feeling does seem to exist. A Gallup poll in January 1960 roughly mirrored the results of a poll taken by Samuel Stouffer a few years ago: when people in a national cross section are questioned about their worries a large proportion of them mention health and family troubles, and another fraction money troubles, but only one in fourteen alludes to the international situation.⁴ Yet half the Gallup sample also thought that there would be another war before too long—a war that, as the general texture of their answers indicates, has very little reality for them. Mothers, for instance, said that they didn't want their sons to serve overseas—evidently still unaware, despite the headlines, that in effect there is no "overseas" in modern war. The mothers, in fact, often quietly favor the Republicans as the "peace party," but they do not want to seem either unpatriotic or

³ See Kennan, *Russia, the Atom and the West* (New York: Harper & Brothers, 1958).

⁴ Stouffer, *Communism, Conformity and Civil Liberties* (New York: Doubleday & Company, 1955). The Gallup poll is reported in *Look*, January 5, 1960.

timid; and for many of them, of course, foreign affairs are really "foreign"—something to be left to the menfolk.

Furthermore, whereas war in other countries has left a legacy of fear or fatalism, there is little comparable popular antiwar feeling in America. The frightful catastrophe of the Civil War has left a romantic halo both in the North and in the South. The First World War was a shock for some; it led others into a rejection of Europe rather than of war itself. Whatever suffering the Second World War involved for a few was more than matched, for millions, by the fact that the war brought the great depression to an end. Besides, the war left a legacy of wild Keynesianism that continues in a new war economy to sustain prosperity: as Gerald Piel pointed out in the April 1960 issue of the *Bulletin of the Atomic Scientists*, it is the war economy which during the last fifteen years has brought a full third of the population into relative affluence. The Korean War was popular nowhere, but it had the paradoxical result of allowing the Republican party to appear as both the party of peace and the party of anti-communism, forcing the Truman-Acheson wing of the Democratic party to continue the effort to prove, over the dead body of Senator McCarthy, that it is even more ferociously and belligerently anti-Communist than any Republican.

Americans are famously generous. There is great and admirable concern for individual life, as when somebody falls down a well or into the sea, or is captured by the enemy. In recent decades, Americans have become less cruel, enjoying less barbaric sports and appreciating gentleness in personal relations. Still, the lack of suffering leads to a certain callous lack of sympathy for the suffering of others, particularly when this can be rationalized in terms of American ideals and explained as not the result of visible injustice.

There is still another difference which Edward Shils has noted in his book, *The Torment of Secrecy*. The British, protecting their privacy better, fear spies, secrets, and invaders less than we do and have never been as hysterical about communism. Even after the Klaus Fuchs case, they in effect decided that they would rather risk losing a few secrets to a few spies than turn the country upside down in the almost certainly vain hope of flushing all enemy agents out. One result is that the ex-Communists in Britain are not nearly so eager to prove their virtue as are many ex-Communists in this country.

Though McCarthy is dead, the fear of invasion by spies and secret agents on which he played is endemic in American life and operates locally even when it is quiescent nationally. In the last decade, for example, a great many municipalities have been aroused against the chimerical and imaginary dangers of fluoridation in their water supplies (chlorination as a safeguard against the pollution of American streams and subsurface waters is already an accomplished fact); the doctors and dentists and local civil servants who have proposed fluoridation have met a barrage of suspiciousness and have been regarded as poisoners, alternately puppets of the aluminum companies (which manufacture fluorides) or the Communist party. Of course it is safe and even patriotic to attack these men, who have no great vested interests behind them, either contractual or ideological; and correspondingly it has been extraordinarily difficult to rally people in America against the real poisons of fallout or the dangers of chemical and biological warfare. For in the latter case, fear of realistic dangers, if openly expressed, might invite the accusation we ourselves have often met from student audiences when we have discussed these matters, as to whether we would rather live on our knees (as appeasers of world communism) than die on our feet. The trail-blazer attitude behind this rhetoric was well expressed a few months ago in a conversation with a nine-year-old and very bright little boy. We had been talking with his parents about the news that day in the paper that Khrushchev would come to America, and were expressing our hope that perhaps there would be a *détente* in the cold war. The boy piped up to say, "They're both chicken," meaning by this that both the United States and the U.S.S.R. were afraid. We asked him if it was chicken to fear the end of the world, and he said, "Well, we all have to die sometime"; and then after a moment he added, "Anyway, I'll go live on the moon."

It is along just this line that we see perhaps the deepest difference between ourselves and the British, namely that American men seem constantly pursued by the fear of unmanliness and therefore feel the need to present themselves as hard and realistic. This way of being realistic may have nothing to do with reality. Often "realism" becomes no more than the opposite of idealism, reasonableness, or morality. Many men of an older generation, having witnessed the excesses to which sentimentality and self-righteousness can take us, and completely sure of their own morality and dedication, are sometimes unwitting models for what is only a seemingly similar realism in others, a pseudo-realism that springs from fear about masculinity. The British seem less obsessed than we are on this score. Nor do they have a proponent of tragic realism as brilliant as Reinhold Niebuhr.⁵ What produces the difference? What is the aim that in America has been distorted into a need to feel tough?

One possibility is that for those to whom being American means being a pioneer—a trail blazer and producer—the lack of new frontiers creates a fear (felt within and reinforced from outside) that the country is going soft. Perhaps, having escaped the bombing and much of the suffering of the Second World War, many Americans have never established their courage in their own eyes. To recognize and admit the enormous dangers that grow every day the cold war continues would feel like weakness to these people; it would seem but another step leading to a retreat from the heroic stand against nature, a stand that makes sense when, in order to survive physically, man must fight, but which now becomes merely a "posture"—a term that is increasingly and symptomatically coming into use in describing American policy (along with the somewhat analogous word, "position"). This "posture" which so many people insist upon becomes self-destructive in a world of fantastically rapid change, where survival depends on flexibility and on willingness to accept some responsibility for what is happening in the world as a whole.⁶

⁵ Niebuhr's contention that man in this vale of folly cannot be wholly rational, just, or disinterested has led a number of his disciples merely to an intense distrust of the Soviet Union and hence a suspicious negativism toward any efforts at a *modus vivendi*. Paradoxically, the logic of the arms race means that such men put their trust in having both the United States and the Soviet Union behave rationally, as in a game with missiles and hardened bases as the pieces, even as the cold war and the arms race intensify the pressures toward irrationality. The realists today would seem to be those who know full well that the arms race is not likely to go on without something going amiss just because of the nature of man. For a further discussion of such game-theory logic, see Maccoby, "Social Psychology of Deterrence," *Bulletin of the Atomic Scientists* (September 1961). As to Dr. Niebuhr's own views, compare his preface to Harrison Brown and George James Real, *Community of Fear* (Fund for the Republic, Pasadena, 1960).

⁶ Here again is a difference between the British and the American situations, because many Americans who feel responsibility for defending what they perhaps too glibly term the "free world" see no alternative to adding military strength to military strength (although the total may only, in fact, in the weird nuclear arithmetic, increase weakness), whereas a number of people in Great Britain believe that their country could restore itself to the status of an important power only outside the American alliance, becoming once more the "honest broker" between nations and leading the nations of Asia and Africa by taking a position on nuclear arms that appeals to the neutrals in all countries.

Such people have been brought up to feel that worthwhile national action is to be defined mainly in terms of military or semi-military attacks on obstacles, either physical or human. They view with horror their countrymen who, captured by the ideology of consumption, have none of the Spartan virtues, and in fact seem drones heralding the collapse of the state. A number of these men are the American analogues of Tory patricians (or, in some cases, would-be patricians) who since Theodore Roosevelt's day have seen war and preparation for war as the condition of national health.[7] Having no goals for America in its own terms and (like most of us) more attuned to what they despise in their countrymen than to what they hope for, they cannot help being preoccupied with the Communists as a possible barbarian threat (often failing to realize how necessary we in turn are in the Soviet Union as a model for emulation, frequently for our worst Victorian excesses). So much, in fact, do these Americans depend on frightening their own countrymen with the not entirely fanciful bogeymen of a Soviet takeover, and so much do they rely on generating and maintaining a mood of crisis, that we ourselves are troubled lest the title and themes of this paper, too hurriedly read, add to the image of menace, when our own spirit, though no less critical, looks further and more hopefully ahead. It is one of the many ironies of the current situation that people who fear the missile gap (a presently unrealistic fear, as the U-2 flights have helped to show) and those like ourselves who fear the arms race as the gravest danger serve to some extent to cancel each other out, thus maintaining the existing complacency among the many and feeding hysteria among the few.

These contradictory images of our hardness and of our softness cannot help but cloud the vision of those military men and political leaders who are charged with the defense. Because they fear softness, they

[7] President Kennedy was quite in the patrician tradition when he concluded a Senate speech, "An Investment for Peace," of February 29, 1960, by saying, "I urge that this Congress, before the President departs for the summit, demonstrate conclusively that we are removing those doubts [about the missile gap and like weaponry] and that we are prepared to pay the full cost necessary to insure peace. Let us remember what Gibbon said of the Romans: 'They kept the peace—by a constant preparation for war; and by making clear to their neighbours that they are as little disposed to offer as to endure injury.'" In fairness it should be added that President Kennedy in this and more explicitly in other speeches has called for active steps toward disarmament and for something comparable to a Rand Corporation for peace, and we hope the responsibility of the presidency will strengthen his promise to negotiate seriously for disarmament.

seek to maintain a climate in which only hardness can thrive—so much so that perhaps a general is best able to move toward peace, since a general is less vulnerable to accusations of softness. Correspondingly, many people who have different goals in mind seek to hitch them to the defense star, with the result that something so magnanimous in conception as the Marshall Plan very soon after its inception became a weapon in the cold war. By the time of the Mutual Security Act, economic aid took second place to military assistance, so that now we find ourselves propping up or even creating military regimes in countries, like Pakistan, whose officials can persuade us that they are real made-to-order anti-Communists.

III

Obviously it is not so hard to be anti-Communist if that is the way to build up one's military faction in a still emerging nation. But as the cold war continues, it becomes increasingly difficult for decent Americans, humane enough to prefer peace to an egocentric national honor, to be outspokenly and genuinely anti-Communist. For example, we had very mixed feelings about the idealistic and dedicated Americans, some of them our colleagues, who in the summer of 1959 went to Vienna and set up shop to oppose the propaganda of the Communist Youth Festival. We had misgivings because it was impossible to escape the fact that, whatever their personal motives, these students became, in effect, emissaries of our State Department and our national cold war line. While this is the last thing many of these students wanted, the Iron Curtain creates just such ironies.

And the problem is equally grave for the radical opposition. As Margaret Mead observed in a recent address, a student in this country a generation ago who had radical ideas had the advantage of being powerless, of being on the side of a future which did not yet exist. Today, however, such a student may find that his particular idea happens at the moment also to be part of the Communist party line, in which case he is not in alliance with a nonexistent and therefore uncontaminated future, but with an extremely menacing and totally unwelcome power.[8]

[8] Some politically inexperienced students may so resent being lumped with the Communists whenever they take an unpopular position as to conclude that the cry of "communism" is simply a reactionary myth; hence, they may be susceptible to the propaganda of Communists and fellow

On the reverse side, someone like Pasternak, or many young Polish writers, because they are acclaimed in this country, may feel themselves betrayed by their very courage and virtue. Thus, as long as the cold war goes on, we lack an uncorrupted political debate.

Under such conditions, it is not surprising that so many people prefer to withdraw from the field altogether. Although they are willing to countenance arms spending, a large number of Americans cannot bring themselves to contemplate the true horror of war, and so they simply go to sleep when they are asked to "wake up" to the dangers that face them. They have learned that the thing to do with anxiety (whether based on real danger or not) is to rid oneself of it through drink, drugs, or canned fantasies.

There are other Americans, however, whose anxiety and escape take more productive forms. Like many of the Soviet intelligentsia who hate the system but feel powerless to change it, certain American elite groups have chosen the road of "inner emigration," retreating from social responsibilities into, at best, a concern with their immediate surroundings, family, and friends. Though such people are often aroused by issues like education, urban renewal, or mental health, they are estranged from the system because it seems to them run for political motives in the narrowest rather than in the best sense. Unlike the escapist security seekers, they are not alienated from themselves as human beings; yet the fact that they remain without political purpose beyond their small civic circles limits their vision and hence their growth. It is for this reason that they may today be ready to give enthusiastic support to a far-reaching idealistic political movement that will provide them with a way of reasserting their faith in democracy.

Still others who are intelligent enough to be concerned with the world have escaped into cynicism, considering the system as corrupt and finding a sense of purpose in expertise, even if this means selling themselves to the highest bidder. Such people, amorally working for personal gain within the system, have in fact supported many of its worst elements. But perhaps "support" is too strong a word, for one often finds in talking to them that they have a streak of buried idealism hidden as much from themselves as from others by this mask of cynicism. Whereas the hypocrisy of the Victorians consisted of concealing mean motives under noble rhetoric, our own hypocrisy often conceals a can-

---

travelers, small and splintered as these latter groups are today in this country. Such students may prefer to accept "guilt by association" to what they regard as the cowardly course of vigilance against the Communists.

kered decency beneath a cloak of *Realpolitik*. Sometimes the decency manifests itself only in the family and in intimate relations, sometimes in the restlessness that underlies the purposive exterior, sometimes merely in the aggressive defense that is put up by these people against any suggestion that their public and private selves need not always remain so completely at odds.

Whether in foreign policy or in personal life, Americans appear today to suffer from an inadequate formulation of their alternatives. It has become extremely common among the well educated to denounce "blind conformity" and "mass society," often symbolized by such minor irritants as tail fins, TV, or gray-flannel suits. But the only alternatives many people see to the organization man is the nostalgic image of the cowboy or the rebellious artist; hard-shelled individualism and a rejection of human solidarity are mistaken as signs of strength and independence. Even the best students in our colleges tend to assume that they must eventually make their peace with "the system"—which they see as even more monolithic than in fact it is—and they will then often become vicarious fellow travelers of the Beats, whose passive and almost entirely nonprogressive defiance serves to publicize a private helplessness.

Students in recent years have frequently said that helplessness is realistic: "What can you do about nuclear war?" Searching for a guarantee that life never provides, a guarantee not only that action will be effective but that all its consequences will be good, such young people never get started and therefore never gain the realistic political experience necessary to make them less helpless.[9] Again, there is a tendency to jump to extreme alternatives: either total control of the total weapons or total inaction.

The sit-in strikes in the South and their support in the North may be the first sign of a change in these attitudes, for they have shown how much can be done even by relatively powerless and unorganized students. We ourselves have a very vivid sense of the rapidity of this change, for a few years ago we visited briefly several of the southern Negro colleges that have been in the forefront of activity; and at that time they appeared to be quite somnolent institutions, run by despotic Negro patriarchs who were used to wheedling support from white lead-

---

[9] For further discussion, see Riesman, "The College Student in an Age of Organization," *Chicago Review*, Vol. 12, No. 3 (Autumn 1958), pages 50–68.

ers, at the same time dominating their own faculty and student bodies, while the students themselves appeared to hope for a safe passage into the world of the black bourgeoisie behind the wall of segregation. No doubt recent visitors to West Africa are equally struck by the speed with which things can change: at the very moment when the "system" appears impregnable to the realist, it often turns out to be vulnerable to the quixotic. Of course we are not saying that "where there's a will, there is always a way," but we are saying that many of the most gifted and sensitive American students have been oversold on cultural and historical determinism—in which, incidentally, there may be self-serving elements, since determinism allows us publicly to accept the existing political structure while we privately deplore conformity, perhaps even showing by minor and irrelevant rebellions like sexual promiscuity or wearing a beard that we are rebels at heart.

IV

If we see only two choices in our personal behavior, such as conformity as against individualism, or adjustment as against neurotic loneliness, then it is likely that a similar dichotomizing tendency will capture our political life. Thus, the American is asked to choose between democracy and communism, when in fact neither system is monolithic, and both have many things—literally things—in common, in contrast with the less industrialized and bureaucratized parts of the world. As already implied, our relationship with Russia is similar to that of a big brother who is obsessed with the fear that his little brother will overtake him, and this overconcern keeps us, the older brother, from realizing our unique potentialities. In this case, the sibling rivalry runs both ways, for the Russians gear their system to show that they are as good or better than we in those areas we most prize—technology, sports, and education. The tragedy is not only that because of our obsession we are rejecting Utopian possibilities and ignoring more pressing problems (at the lowest level the much greater threat of Red China) but also that we are missing a chance to provide a better goal for Soviet growth. We may hope that the Russians will get rich enough to be preoccupied by the problem of national purpose which currently plagues us; and in the American-like desires of the Soviet elite, we find signs of this development. Conceivably if we were to show that our system can be mobilized to produce a better life, drawing its meaning from activity rather than from consumption per se or from national might, we would eventually shift the emphasis of Soviet emulation.

In fairness it should be added that a surrender to apocalyptic alternatives is sometimes found on the more humane side of current American debates concerning deterrence. It would be surprising if this were not the case, for the dominant ways of perceiving in a culture generally turn up, sometimes in a disguised form, in the very models of opposing such ways. There are some pacifists, among the many different schools of pacifist thought, who see the present situation as demanding either preparation for total destruction or a complete cessation of all military measures through unilateral action. We believe that if the world survives these next critical years and becomes less uncivilized, we shall move away from the anarchy of nationalism, reducing arms to the level of police forces and handling as imaginatively as we can the problem of coping with despotic governments. Naturally, it is hard to see how the transition from the fully armed nation-state to the fully disarmed nation-state can be accomplished. It is easier to envisage a diplomatic give-and-take between ourselves and the Soviet Union that (without complete disarmament) would settle outstanding conflicts of interest in Europe and Asia—even though attempts at such a settlement would encounter the opposition of Adenauer and Ulbricht, Chiang and Mao, American cold warriors and their Stalinist opposite numbers in Russia. Efforts at disarmament not coupled with diplomatic moves to settle the cold war will make Americans as uneasy as high-flying spy planes must make the Russian people, and hence may boomerang. In our judgment, one must work simultaneously on both fronts, diplomacy and disarmament, keeping in mind the long-run pacifist goal of a world in which conflict is settled without weapons and war. Perhaps however we should not speak of this goal as "long run," analogous to some New Jerusalem that will never come; for we are faced with a situation in which the very preservation of life and social order requires political and technical measures that now seem "impossible," if they can be envisaged at all. We need as much inventiveness and confidence in what man can accomplish as were possessed by the framers of the American Constitution.

What we wish to emphasize here, however, is not the details of the various positions, but rather the way in which the American style of thinking has suffered from a tendency to oversimplify alternatives and to leap always to absolute positions. It is wrong to insist that one must choose between conformity and individualism, slavery or freedom, absolute toughness or unilateral disarmament. Our need to plan distant as well as short-run goals, to work out the full implications of alternative actions, is confused with simplistic self-definitions, and thus we militate against graduated approaches. Where the arms race is concerned, a graduated approach would start with a definition of the goal as disarmament and would continue with a step-by-step attempt to find ways of overcoming our fears on the one hand and Russia's distrust of inspectors on the other. An illustration of the kind of imaginative plan that is needed is Leo Szilard's idea of an inspection game.[10] Recognizing the reality both of our fear of secret Soviet operations (and of the unreliability of any government's promise, including our own) and theirs of foreigners poking around, Szilard would allow inspection in detail any time that either party suspected clandestine atomic activity or decided that a tremor might not merely be an earthquake. However, if we turned out to be wrong we would have to pay the Soviets a huge indemnity and vice versa. The goal of such a game is greater trust through experience rather than an idea of security through armaments which suggests either a statuesque posture or a swaddled, unrealistic existence, perhaps lived underground in concrete shelters.

To think in these terms requires something of a science-fiction mentality, coupled with this sort of understanding of political inspection that one finds in Ithiel Pool's contribution to the *Daedalus* symposium on arms control.[11]

V

How does one begin the effort to change current patterns of thinking about security through armament? Because different people in the United States are at different stages of alertness and health or flight and cynicism, answers will vary depending on which group in the population one addresses.

When a man is being overmanipulated to the point where his very existence has become unreal, he cannot be "made" human by more and better manipulation from the "right" direction, by mere bombardment with pressures and appeals. It is this very habit of ignoring the human qualities of men in order to get them to run smoothly that has caused much of our trouble.

Manipulation "downward," from the elites to the public, inevi-

[10] *Bulletin of the Atomic Scientists* (April 1960).
[11] See Ithiel de Sola Pool, "Public Opinion and the Control of Armaments," *Daedalus*, Vol. 89 (Fall 1960), pages 984–99.

tably intensifies apathy and saps the strength of an alert public just when it is most needed. Thus—to return to an earlier point—by a propaganda campaign which persuaded people to view the Marshall Plan—Mutual Security Program as a semimilitary stroke against communism rather than as an idealistic and ultimately practical acknowledgment of our new world responsibility, we increased the chances of a quick acceptance of the program at the expense of setting a pattern in which all economic development of underdeveloped countries would carry the imprimatur of our particular sort of idealism. By reinforcing the ideology of cageyness, we have been killing the very quality in ourselves which might save us from a moral disintegration that armaments can never arrest.

However, while manipulation downward or sideways leads to dysfunctional precedents which narrow future alternatives, lobbying "upward" is necessary and in the best traditions of keeping our leaders responsible. Today, as free citizens, we need energetically to influence the military, industrial, political, and educational leaders into letting go of their investments in the cold war and into working not only for a safer but for a better world. These investments are very seldom "vested interests" about which we hear so much. There are of course vested interests in the armaments industries, but there are very few businessmen who would rather make weapons than make consumer goods for the civilian population. Many of these businessmen consider themselves realistic idealists and are men of good will whose economic advantage makes it easier for them to rationalize their work by putting full blame on the Russians and by parading the horrors of communism. Many of them know deep down that this is dangerous and that the economic advantage is precarious also, especially since their customers in the armed services are constantly changing their requirements, as contractors for another service may come up with a better or more salable weapons system. Most of these industrialists would probably not object to studies such as Seymour Melman has been making on the economics of disarmament—or to plans, for example, for deploying part of Raytheon into a government-supported project for the renewal of downtown Boston. One could argue that some of the scientists are more wedded to the arms race than their commercial employers, although even the scientists could certainly be retrained and much of what they now do could be applied to nonmilitary developments. Or, to take another instance, programs might be developed for the retraining of officers of SAC and other agencies whose existence depends on the cold war. Fortunately, many men and much equipment can be deployed into inspection for disarmament; but in a less bellicose climate others may not find jobs with defense contractors. Still, such men often have unusual organizational ability and remarkable dedication and with retraining could be prepared for many governmental, corporate, and educational positions. There would seem to be less technical but graver political difficulties in the workers and their unions now involved in defense activities, for these cannot as readily afford as the businessmen and military leaders to take the "long view." Many are making more money than they ever did before and if their companies were to close down would be stranded in an economically depressed area. The situation is far more serious than in the period at the end of the Second World War when there was a great demand for civilian products; and it seems essential for the federal government to give assurances to the labor force now employed directly or indirectly in defense work that it will not suffer in a period of transition.[12]

It has been our experience that there are elements of idealism in even the most apparently cynical men who engage in defense activities for short-run gains while letting the future take care of itself. This cynicism often reflects a feeling of powerlessness to change anything important. The irony is that in an age when so many feel so powerless a single irate letter can often have a totally unanticipated impact. The men in positions of power are often both divided and confused, and a "grass roots" complaint about a TV show or a congressional measure can, as often for the worse as for the better, show the fallacy of those who believe that there are no channels left for effective political action. Even a freshman congressman who asks questions of the State Department or the Defense Department and persists at it is often able to exercise leverage that would astonish the defeatist.

VI

Yet, if we get out of the immediate crisis, we shall still be faced with the underlying disorder in a society in which—partly as the result of its great past achievements—people feel there is plenty for all, but little joy in using the things we have made.

[12] Despite the threat to the defense worker, Chester Bowles reported after his 1958 congressional campaign that many New London submarine makers supported his anti-cold-war position although they recognized it threatened their jobs. They were, however, close enough to the actual weapons of destruction to feel a healthy fear.

For the Russians, a decrease in defense spending means the beginning of television and toasters for all, and perhaps a slight loosening of despotic controls. For us, much more is involved, and more difficult problems—those of "abundance for what?"[13]

We have been trained for a world of scarcity and we have developed an image of man under the psychology of scarcity. The maturation of America and correspondingly of world civilization requires that we begin a program for abundance with a new view of man and his potentialities: neither the inherently weak and sinful Puritan nor the self-indulgent consumer, but instead a being whose nature is fulfilled through work that truly engages him, both because it draws upon his creative power and because it gives him the responsibility for helping to decide the form and use of what he makes. In this way we would be able to consider human destructiveness as the manifestation of a thwarted need to create and to initiate—a need thwarted by inadequate education and opportunity (as Paul Goodman declares in his book, *Growing Up Absurd*). In *Man for Himself* and later writings, Erich Fromm argues that man does not live merely for the release of tensions (as Freud's writings often suggest), but that when this is all society asks of him, his passive-receptive orientation to life can fill him with a nagging self-doubt—which may in turn be exploited in the fantasies of omnipotence that virulent nationalism demands.

These conflicting ideas concerning man's nature are dramatized in contemporary American arguments about the educational system. A belief in the spontaneous potentialities of human nature, and in the relevance of schooling to those potentialities, animated some of the original leaders of the progressive-education movement, notably, of course, John Dewey. In practice, however, many followers of this movement simply came to terms, as new social strata swamped the schools, with the latter's diluted demands for a laying on of educational hands. Now, in reaction against this laxity, many American leaders have found in the cold war an opportunity to "tighten up" education. Men like Admiral Rickover espouse a climate of rigor, based not on the intractable tasks set both by knowledge and by life, but by a need to keep up with the Russians. One of the most profound lessons a child learns in school is how he is to feel about his later lifework, and if he is taught to approach the idea of work only with a sense of duty, competitiveness, and fear of failure, he

[13] For a fuller development of this theme see "Abundance for What?" page 300.

will never develop the capacity to impose meaning on whatever tasks he comes to undertake.[14]

The problems, political and technical, of reorganizing work along lines we can now only dimly envisage are so enormous as to be almost inhibiting. If one ponders on these matters, one finds oneself facing into a new frontier that is neither physically nor politically simple, but that requires as much resourcefulness and tenacity as the older frontiers did. For example, one might consider the changes involved if every job in America were reanalyzed, not with an eye only to its efficiency in terms of traditional output, but in terms of its long-run effect on the worker, his family, his friends, and his political life. We now assume that production will go on as usual, and that humane progress demands only ancillary adjustments, fringe benefits, which repair some of the ravages of work, on the one hand by making the work place less physically exhausting and despotic, and on the other by trying to shore up the leisure life of the worker with a variety of welfare measures. It is difficult to change this pattern, even if management is willing to initiate the attempt. Edwin Land has found that workers in his Polaroid factory are not eager to leave the assembly line, to whose routines they have become accustomed, for an unspecified job in a laboratory. They doubt their ability to cope with a larger untried situation, just as some students

[14] Of course many people today will say that while they may not be "mad" about their work, neither do they mind it. In *The Lonely Crowd* (1950) the senior author took a sanguine view of the attenuation of meaning in work, arguing that in an affluent society arduous and demanding work would become increasingly unnecessary, and that the productive impulse would have to be expressed in leisure and play. Further reflection has convinced us that here we are not necessarily the prisoners of our technological fate, of our given forms of mass production, and of the organization of work. We now believe that a rich, heavily automatized society is precisely one that can afford to reorganize work so that attention is focused no longer exclusively on the product, but on the worker himself as a product of his work. We have been greatly excited and impressed by a few pioneering examples, like Edwin Land's Polaroid factory. There, deep involvement in work and a concept of the factory that continues the process of education for the workers have significantly enlivened many workers (without any loss in productivity when measured by the traditional standards of the balance sheet, although this must not be the sole or even the crucial measure of success). To be creative in leisure while mindless and passive in work demands a schizoid attitude which even if psychologically possible would put too great a burden on leisure, just as the family bears too great a burden when it becomes the only reservoir of decency in a disordered civic and national life.

prefer rigid routines, which give them the assurance they are learning something, to less predictable programs of self-directed study. In Dr. Land's experience, workers, like students, need support and encouragement to attempt new tasks.

Another example of inertia is provided by Professor Chris Argyris of the Yale Department of Industrial Administration. The president of a small corporation, Argyris reports, decided that all foremen should determine their own rates of reimbursement. One day he announced that there was a payroll of so many dollars to which he would add an annual increment, and that the workers should divide it among themselves as seemed equitable to them. At first they jumped at the chance, but not long after they asked to be relieved of the responsibility. The president, however, did not give up. It took him seven years to create a work milieu in which the foremen could develop respect for themselves and one another. In the course of making his innovations, the president discovered how deep were the feelings of alienation, of separateness, and how low was the sense of self-esteem among the foremen. He found also that these feelings could not be changed by propaganda, that such persuasion merely increased self-hate and alienation. The foremen preferred paternalism until they had developed a confidence in themselves based on an altered work situation in which they made decisions about style and methods of production. And the president was secure enough not to feel that he had to hang on to traditional prerogatives; as the workers took over more activities, he was freed for new ones.

VII

When in discussion we have stressed hopeful illustrations like these as models for social change, we have sometimes found them quickly dismissed by people brought up in the shadow of Marxism. Such people believe that the coming of abundance does not change the vested interests, and that political commitments will continue to reflect economic advantage. They look to what is left of the American disinherited as the potential cadre to displace the power elite, and they see hostility rather than hope as the principal lever of political change; therefore, they do not even try to move men by rational appeals. One might ask whether they are in fact good Marxists. However, one need not be entirely theoretical: recent student rallies for Negro rights at leading universities; the interest of a number of students in problems of disarmament; and perhaps above all the enthusiastic response of students in many parts of the country to the possibilities of a Peace Corps all illustrate what seems to us to have been generally the case in historical development: that it is not the most underprivileged who are most concerned about justice and about the future. Even the hangovers of scarcity psychology—for example, the prevalent notion that, even if their should be enough of the good *things* of life for all, there would always remain a short supply of status—do not alter the fact that those who worry least about having enough (including enough status) frequently show the clearest sense of responsibility. This is true not only for the Tory patricians referred to earlier but also for many of their opponents in politics and in intellectual life. What is lacking today is an audience of restless poor (save among Negroes) awaiting the leadership of the better off.

As higher education expands and as blue-collar work gives way to white-collar work, the often denigrated bourgeois idealist, the pilot fish of the Marxian theory of revolution, becomes a member of a class quite as large in number as the factory workers. This group is only residually a "class" in the traditional sense, for it lacks much sense of identity of interest and any large reservoir of hatred or of solidarity. Unlike the well-to-do of other times, it is not supported by servants—indeed, its lack of the habit of command is one of its present political weaknesses. On the whole, its members, children of the industrial revolution, have thought that any increase in productivity automatically spells progress; but today this has become a tarnished belief, and little as yet exists to take its place. The answer for which many radicals look is the highly unlikely prospect of another depression. In our judgment a depression is unlikely at present, less because the Keynesian weapons of fiscal and other governmental intervention are well understood and politically available than because, as we have already argued, an increase in "defense" expenditures can again be used, as it was in the recession of 1957–58, to maintain the flow of income. But even if such measures should fail and another great depression would threaten, the result at best would be another New Deal—if one could imagine such coasting on inherited ideals which were barely adequate in their own day, let alone in our era of potential abundance. Another formula, occasionally suggested by the engineering-minded, is to regard the race for outer space as a safety valve for the arms race, furnishing an outlet at once for imperialistic energies and cowboy imaginations. While it goes without saying that this latter "solution" is preferable to the arms race, it seems to us a fictional frontier, reflecting a nostalgia for a long-past day when the West had to be settled, the industries developed, the cities built, the immigrants "Americanized."

To summarize our argument: many Americans think that the only changes needed in our national life are minor ones, or choices between starkly stated alternatives. In this they are like patients who come to a psychiatrist and say, "There is nothing basically the matter with me except that I have this ulcer." So it is with the ulcer of the cold war which, as much as it is a reaction to a real conflict, also exposes the failure of a style of life. Though the immediate peril demands the beginning of disarmament as one first step toward ending the cold war, in doing this we only patch a symptom. Disarmament and eased international tensions are not the end of therapy, and true peace is not merely the absence of war but a state in which the quality of existence becomes humane and generous rather than destructive.

The analogy goes further. Just as no therapist can cure anyone but merely provides the support for another's steps toward health, so our leadership cannot manipulate us into Utopia. In order for us to live with our abundance, there must be greater participation in the political life of the United States and of the world. The traditional American ideology which is concerned only with equality of economic and political opportunity and freedom from control—in other words with the major problems of scarcity alone—must readjust to face the problems that have suddenly become visible because of abundance: lack of participation in life and lack of opportunity and education for self-expression. Once these problems can be faced, a people of plenty may be able to use its power for helping other people toward economic prosperity (as an essential step toward further difficult alternatives).

As has been suggested, if really promising steps could be taken, the release of fear and anxiety that people would feel—the ability to breathe freely again and to make long-term plans—will have at once a productive and an unsettling effect: old agendas and ways of regarding the world will have to be scrapped and new ones discovered. Our imagination must focus on other frontiers, work at bringing more people into participation by forming many small groups, by decentralizing industry, by creating better means for continued education not merely for children but for adults throughout life. To be sure, none of the problems of scarcity has been dealt with in a wholly satisfactory way: not all Americans are affluent, many are destitute, and many of the traditional issues of welfare and social justice—markedly, of course, the race issue—remain exigent. But a movement of renewal dedicated only to these issues is not conceivable. We shall move faster on these older fronts if they do not usurp all our attention and if we can invent an American future which is exciting, active, and responsible, but neither murderous nor imperialistic. It is for this that political programs are needed which transcend the details of the present.

Reflections on Containment and Initiatives
(1962)

Eric Larrabee likes to distinguish between the "Federal" and the "Confederate" styles in war. The Federal is reactive, waiting for the hotheads to begin something and then more slowly, relentlessly, and unconditionally finishing matters. Ordinarily, the Federal style comprises a cautious waiting for overwhelming logistical supremacy; it is in this respect a style befitting an industrial democracy. The Confederate style is more dashing and honorific, glorifying the military rather than seeing it as a last and punishing resort. Our present-day military services are differentially influenced by these two styles, which bear obvious analogies to Morris Janowitz's discussion of absolutist and pragmatist orientations in the armed services.[1] Individuals, of course, may deviate from the tradition of their arm of the service. For example, one could argue that General Billy Mitchell, for whose court-martial the country is still "paying" in the sense of having to cope with air force feelings of mistreatment, may be said to have represented the Confederate personal style during a particularly complacent and inhospitable time, although the Air Force today contains representatives of quite contrasting styles.

In the Second World War, the American commanders in the European theater, save for General Patton, were characteristic representatives of the Federal style: sober, unflamboyant men like Generals Eisenhower, Bradley, Hodge, Devers, and so on. But in the Pacific theater, General MacArthur notably harked back to the Confederate style and surrounded himself with many men who admired him and

[1] See Morris Janowitz, *The Professional Soldier: a Social and Political Portrait* (The Free Press, 1960). Alexis de Tocqueville's discussion of the democratic pattern of warfare in *Democracy in America* suggests that democracies would be slow to become committed to action, but once in motion would push through massively and brutally to the finish.

shared his values.[2] These men constantly felt that their theater was subordinated to the fight against the Nazis; and to this day, they resent the fact that they were never able to "finish" the war in the Pacific. The unsatisfactory endings—unsatisfactory even in Federal terms—of Japan's surrender and the truce in Korea have tended to create a kind of *Zeigarnik* effect among many men who are today the leaders of the military right wing (General Walker, for example). Incomplete involvement in guerrilla war in South Vietnam does not satisfy such men. Pragmatic solutions seem to them temporizing ones, unmanly and un-American.

Yet the fact is that neither the Federal nor the Confederate styles are appropriate to today's nuclear world. The Confederate style is much too rash and provocative. And the Federal style, with its insistence on unconditional surrender of the enemy, tended to become totalistic even in the mass bombings of the Second World War and would become even more so if nuclear weapons were to be employed. Indeed, the very term "weapons" applied to nuclear capabilities is a misnomer, hiding from us the radical discontinuities created by the atom. Such concealment is true even of more seemingly appropriate terms such as "general war" or "all-out war" which, along with "nuclear exchange," simply extrapolate from traditionally destructive wars.

Another semantic index of the same sort is the phrase, "finger on the trigger," which is endlessly applied to the problems of independent or co-ordinated nuclear forces in Europe. The effort still to find a line where quantity changes into quality is shown by the use of the word "unacceptable." Thus Herman Kahn, in effect, warns air force generals of Confederate orientation that there is a point beyond which millions of American dead are "unacceptable" while at the same time he seeks vis-à-vis civilians or the ground army to blur the distinction between nuclear and other weapons. Or Morton Halperin talks about "our ability to react to unacceptable Soviet provocation" (*The New Leader,* August 20, 1962). But the question of acceptability is a political one not likely to be decided on rational grounds. In July 1961, a friend of mine, talking to people in the Pentagon concerning the Berlin crisis, was told that the United States would have to resort to nuclear weapons since

[2] In the last several years, however, General MacArthur has insisted that nuclear weapons make a real difference, that a war employing them cannot be won, and that much greater efforts must be made for peace. His sobriety has not won him the acclaim that his charismatic political and military leadership did.

we could not defend Berlin by conventional means. My friend suggested jokingly that Dean Rusk call in the Soviet Ambassador, shoot him, put him in a box and send him back to show that Soviet behavior in Berlin was "unacceptable." People, of course, were shocked at this idea although they were not shocked at the idea of the prospects of a duel over Berlin escalating into nuclear catastrophe, for this could be viewed as an extrapolation of conventional warfare.

The present civilian leadership in the Pentagon finds too dangerous the Confederate style of some of the more vocal generals and admirals, and too inert and simply inactive the Federal style (marred by periodic Confederate rhetoric) of the preceding Administration. But its effort to apply pragmatic logic to the enormous political tensions within NATO and within America (quite apart from the Communist world) has led to building up weapons for various contingencies to such a point that war now seems conceivably manageable and controllable; it is seriously thought about in a way that was not done under Eisenhower, where credibility rested on bluster rather than on actual preparations of carefully graded responses—"punishments" to fit the crime. Increasing our weapons-lead over the Soviet Union helps (though insufficiently) to sop up unemployment and to satisfy various senators, but it has plainly not been a success vis-à-vis General De Gaulle, who wants his own nuclear force as a way of keeping the United States within his range of influence. He is not satisfied to be told by Secretary McNamara that the American panoply of weapons can keep everything under control if only the Europeans will increase their conventional contributions to NATO. And it also seems unlikely that a Soviet society built by parvenus will find "acceptable" their present position of drastic inferiority: they may be kept in line this way for a while, but hardly indefinitely.

What I am suggesting here is that it may be easier in the short run to contain the Soviet Union than to contain our own allies or the American energies mobilized behind the cold war. The right wing's rhetoric within America is a nostalgic reminder of our Confederate past. It asks for a policy of victory, not of temporizing, and charges the Administration with a "no-win" policy. And the strength of this rhetoric is such that the Administration, rather than trying to exhibit the complexity of affairs to the public, argues back that it does after all have a "win" policy: to change the rhetoric itself would be inordinately difficult. Samuel Lubell makes an interesting comment that such a reaction may underestimate popular awareness of the complexity of events. "Today it is the 'expert' who is likely to be proposing the one-shot remedies, while the public tends to feel that most problems are bigger than the solutions put forward for them." (See "Reporting Change," *Columbia University Forum*, Spring 1962.) The form of debate, however, makes it almost impossible for anyone, except perhaps President Kennedy, to state publicly that a proposed remedy will probably not do much good and that the very idea of "winning" is obsolete. For some time I have been haunted by the probable reaction in the United States if two or three more of the Latin American countries go Communist, or what we define as Communist, or if South Vietnam is overrun, especially if all this happens when we feel that we are stagnant domestically and that our leadership is in doubt as to its direction.

Curiously, perhaps the majority of the civilian strategists who deal with these matters think in terms of deterring the Russians and not the Americans. For example, Thomas Schelling and Henry Kissinger in recent articles engage in elaborate and brilliant calculations as to how to deter the Russians, on the assumption that they are just waiting to invade Western Europe and are kept from this, not by inertia, dislike of adventure, or any factors in their own society, but only by American power.[3] Schelling wants to be sure that we are sufficiently *unsure* of what we ourselves may do so as to intimidate the Soviets by an apparent willingness on our side to take risks of escalating warfare; this is his rational strategy of irrationally leaving something to chance. And while his paper shows a commendable awareness that even so-called tactical nuclear weapons are not "weapons" in any traditional sense, he shares the general American assumption that the existence or the importance of NATO need not be questioned. But NATO must be seen as a somewhat delayed reaction to the Berlin blockade and the Korean War—a means which, as so often happens in human affairs, has now become its own end under the umbrella of new rationalizations. Our retroactive thinking here, in which we worry about another Munich or Berlin blockade, resembles that of a new nation which fears with dis-

[3] See Schelling, "Nuclear Strategy in Europe," *World Politics*, Vol. XIV, April 1962, pp. 420–32; Kissinger, "Tactical Nuclear Weapons," *Foreign Affairs*, Vol. XL, July 1962, pp. 515–41. Cf. S. F. Griffin, "Tomorrow's Military Matrix," *World Politics*, Vol. XIV, April 1962: on page 436, "Khrushchev threatens to cross the Elba, sweep through West Germany, and attack France with conventional forces. . . ." Griffin is a former brigadier general in the U. S. Air Force; generals must think in terms of remote contingencies, but what is striking is the similarity of such thinking to that of political theorists and entire populations.

proportionate anxiety the return of the recently expelled colonialists. Such fears then lead us to build up elaborate defenses, the provocativeness of which escapes us, since we claim that our purpose is no more than the preservation of the status quo.

At the same time, the focus on NATO serves as insurance against the return of domestic isolationism (which was seldom really that, so much as a dislike of *Europe's* wars, as against forays into the Pacific or Latin America) and serves also as an incipient form of internationalism built around the ideal of Atlantic Union. But in the American forensic climate, this ideal is pursued through constant discussion of the dangers of Communist military and political expansionism.

A large proportion of the intellectuals and strategists who deal with defense and foreign policy seems to me to have an insufficient appreciation of the cumulative impact on American public opinion of such discussion. Communist military and political power is a potential danger, and reasonable insurance against the possibility of a Soviet advance in Central Europe is desirable, since Russian intentions are subject to change, just as are our own, and our influence on those intentions remains very great. But a focus primarily outside America, characteristic of the Atlantic Seaboard elite which is oriented toward NATO, leads to underestimating the problem of containing American as well as Soviet bellicosity. It is plain that any political *détente* or major steps toward disarmament will be interpreted by large sections of American opinion as appeasement, for our own people and opinion leaders are not deterred by *American* nuclear credibility.

When the question of the Canadian border was settled, Americans neither got possession of 54'40" nor fought, but it is difficult to think of other instances where all American political factions consented to a negotiated settlement. (The by no means auspicious settlement of the War of 1812 was in part rendered acceptable by General Andrew Jackson's stirring victory at New Orleans a few days after the signing of the peace treaty.) The Yalta and Potsdam agreements helped undo the Democratic party,[4] and the Korean War could only be settled by a man

[4] On the basis of the foregoing phrase, one embittered correspondent has charged me with "whitewashing" the Yalta and Potsdam agreements and trying to cut off justified criticism of them by conservatives and right-wing publicists. Of course I had no intention of going into the merits of these agreements or of defending Franklin D. Roosevelt's wartime foreign policy, of which I was critical at the time. I was referring only to the experience of Democratic party encumbents that their party can be caught between the cross fires of being the "war party" and at the same time the

who was a general and a Republican, namely President Eisenhower. Deals and negotiations are of course thought to be perfectly proper and even desirable among contenders in the market place of the domestic economy, although there are still a good many businessmen who regard bargaining with labor unions as a concession to the devil.[5] However, once an adversary is defined as the devil, whether it be a tavern keeper prior to prohibition or a slaveholder prior to emancipation, the attitude toward compromise and negotiation can radically alter, and we begin to talk as Lincoln did of a house divided rather than consulting a marriage counselor or a divorce lawyer. These traditional American attitudes have been greatly strengthened by the repudiation of appeasement that resulted from the experience before and during the Second World War. If Americans are presented with a *fait accompli*, there is a tendency to accept the apparently inevitable, but if there is discussion and controversy about possible agreements that involve concessions on both sides, there is a strong tendency to regard any concession as a sign of weakness. The child who declares "You're not the boss of me" grows up to be readily mobilized against the authority of an agreement that appears to hem the country in.

Professor Roger Fisher of the Harvard Law School has pointed out that the cold war pulls into a single vortex every incident abroad and at home remotely having to do with "communism."[6] This has happened at the same time that industrial development and social mobility within

---

party of appeasement and procommunism. Since no article or even book on complicated issues can say everything one believes at once, readers who chance upon one or another essay often appear to misunderstand the context of thought out of which it arises.

[5] At the height of the Berlin crisis in the summer of 1961, I talked with an influential opinion-maker who was sure that there would be a nuclear war since it was impossible to do business with Khrushchev. I asked him whether he thought it impossible to do business with Jimmy Hoffa. He grew red in the face, pounded the table, and screamed imprecations against Hoffa. I regarded it as fortunate that neither he nor Hoffa were equipped with an atomic arsenal. But of course the fact is that he *does* do business with Jimmy Hoffa, much as he may resent it; indeed, it sometimes seems as if the compromises we all must make within America in order to "do business" lead us to project an image of uncompromising purity on to the largest entity with which we identify, namely the nation. And this is in contrast with our simultaneous admiration of ourselves as pragmatic and nonideological.

[6] See Fisher, "Fractionating Conflict," unpublished paper to appear in report of Summer Study Group, Craigsville, Mass., 1962.

the United States and the assimilation of the immigrant groups have nationalized our society as never before, so that the loss of local identities and loyalties is more than compensated for (as happens so obviously in the new nations) by a rising tide of nationalism. Or, to put this in other terms, the United States as a nation is the entity into which American energies are increasingly thrown, since they cannot so readily be invested in local (even southern) loyalties which have declined in relevance: national unity is bought as elsewhere at the price of chauvinism. By the same token, the small minority who reject the nation-state are put in the position of identifying with the "enemy" state in a bipolar world—only a few can identify with a world community which is not yet more than a dream.

All of us concerned with these matters are a tiny minority, and among us there tends to be a characteristic sectarianism in which we criticize our accessible and vulnerable peers rather than the great mass of unreachable people somewhere "out there." On the other hand, if we do not criticize each other's work even within this small band, we cannot advance beyond it. Charles Osgood has been one of the most stimulating pioneers: what I regard as his errors are therefore among the most productive ones. (I will refer hereafter to the paper he presented at the American Sociological Association meetings on September 1, 1962, trying to write so that this discussion will be clear without the reader's having seen Osgood's paper.)

For the majority of our countrymen, it is important to stress, as Osgood does, the symmetry of the perceptions of the adversary in the United States and in the Soviet Union. But we should look also at the differences and asymmetries. While Osgood is right that each side, for reasons of its own ideology and perceptions, misunderstands the other, these misunderstandings are of different sorts, precisely because they are projective. Soviet leaders and even sophisticated academicians assume that we, too, are run by a power elite, that all our moves are calculated and part of an overall plan. Since their own population is genuinely afraid of war and in large measure pacific, it is hard for them to realize that millions of Americans are more afraid to show fear than afraid of war itself—or interpret "war" in traditionalistic terms. Furthermore, if Soviet leaders recognized the full force of American anti-communism among working-class people and intellectuals, they might be forced to ask themselves some pretty disagreeable questions about the basis for this outlook in the evils of Soviet society and the behavior of the Soviet leadership, rather than interpreting American anticommunism as the outcome of the plots and plans of the capitalists, or of their adjuncts among the power elite.

And on our side, we project onto the Soviet Union the intent actually to do what we might only be tempted to do if we had similar opportunities. The legend of the "missile gap" of the last Eisenhower years owes something to the cautionary mood of the intelligence services, something to the use of these services on behalf of the Air Force, something to journalistic zeal, and a good deal to political partisanship. But the legend could grow as it did because it was generally assumed that, since the Soviets could build ICBMs at a great rate, they would undoubtedly do so. The evidence could as well have supported an interpretation that the Soviets pursued a policy of minimum deterrence throughout the 1950s. In fact, when Malenkov and Beria came to power, a real *détente* might have been possible had we been ready to explore it, but the initiatives very tentatively suggested on the Soviet side were out of phase with the domestic politics of the American side, just as the opposite has also been true at various times during the cold war years.

Professor Osgood's thesis reminds me of the silent trade which ethnographers have described among preliterate tribes. Undoubtedly he is right that words without actions are not useful in a situation of distrust, but actions themselves in such a situation are ambiguous. We are not dealing with a people with whom one cannot talk and sound out possibilities of tacit agreement. And while Osgood is primarily concerned with signaling to the Soviet Union that we are peaceful, my own concern is that we signal to *ourselves* that we are peaceful in fact and not simply in rhetoric. And the best way I see to do this is through mutual agreements which will bind our country and thus make it possible for our leadership to hold a restless population against demagogic swings of mood by appealing to a structure of international agreements. As suggested above, such agreements are not attractive to those Americans whose theme song is "Don't Fence Me In." And the proponents of unilateral initiatives perhaps hope to appeal to the American frontier feeling of possessing elbow room and flexibility of movement, by stressing American initiatives rather than simply reactive behavior and delayed "Federal" responses. But unfortunately, those who do not like agreements would also be opposed to unilateral moves that appear to concede something to the other side or to lay the groundwork for reciprocation. Unilateralism therefore does not seem to me to offer a way out of the obvious difficulties of bilateral negotiation.

Since Professor Osgood argues in his paper that Americans fear the Russians and vice versa, I have been asking acquaintances in the government whether high officials actually do fear the Soviet Union militarily—I recognize that millions of ordinary Americans do have such fears. The range of my contacts, of course, is limited, but I have still to talk to any highly placed person who does fear the U.S.S.R. The general view seems to be that our missile superiority is now so great that the Soviets can move only at their peril; this is one meaning of our counterforce capability. They can escape that peril only by an aggressive rearmament effort which will cramp them economically even more than they are presently cramped; and there are plainly some in the government who want to keep up the pressure to force the Soviet Union into a competitive arms race or possibly into giving up the race, even if this means closing the widening gap between the Soviet and Chinese leaderships. (The Cuban crisis of October 1962 may be seen in one perspective as an effort by the U.S.S.R. to break out of this vise.) Thus I think Professor Osgood is mistaken in believing that high American policy is primarily influenced by reciprocating fear of the Soviet Union or that this is the chief reason why we do not take measures to limit armaments.[7] To be sure, high policy makers do fear the Russians in the sense that they fear being estopped by Russian power from compelling the Soviets to obey them. They want to be able to conduct what they regard as the right or self-evident policy without regard to Soviet power, and thus they fear the Russians as they fear any obstacle to their plans. Still, I believe that popular fears of Russia are even more important than elite desires for flexibility in making disarmament a goal to be desired on Sundays but not on weekdays.

In fact, I would go further: any unilateral initiative toward disarmament within America, not coupled with domestic activities to heighten our national sense of strength and well-being, may only increase the move toward greater armament by those who think that the

[7] Since the foregoing was written, Secretary of Defense McNamara's testimony on the new military budget to the House Armed Services Committee, January 30, 1963, makes clear his own effort to achieve stability rather than prevailance. He declared, "The U.S. and the Soviet Union, as the two great nuclear powers, are the nations most directly endangered by these [nuclear] weapons and therefore have a great mutual interest in seeing to it that they are never used." It is interesting to see the acceptance by this highly competent executive of the idea that nuclear weapons are basically self-defeating, adding to the danger of the nation which possesses them, while nations not possessing them are not similarly endangered.

country is about to be given away to the Communists—or if not that, given away to indolence and stagnation.

Even the top policy makers are wrong to assume that they can manage the country, that they can follow a Grand Design which can be understood by their constituencies. American leaders need the help of both allied and enemy powers to shape American policy. Tacit agreements, which is what responses to unilateral initiatives would be, are possible among a scientific or aristocratic elite who understand each other's signals and are not swayed by Populist pressures. The charge either by America's allies or by the latter's constituencies within America that such an agreement has been made will often be enough to unravel the agreement, or to prevent future agreements, much in the way that the Missouri Compromise of 1850 was one of the last agreements before the ideologues North and South forced the compromisers, so to speak, to run out of negotiable territory. Thus, while tacit agreements may now and then be made by diplomats or by the President, they can give no assurance either to our own policy makers or to the Communists that they can ever serve to contain America. They may not be possible in our democratic world.

Let me take one example. In the winter and spring of 1962 when the United States decided to resume bomb testing (responding in this needless way to the Soviet initiative of the previous autumn), many scientists argued that bomb testing is not really important one way or the other, and took the position that opposition to American resumption of testing would be a waste of scarce resources among that small minority already referred to, actively engaged in opposing or seeking to control the arms race. For one thing, they saw bomb tests as leading to slight qualitative improvements in nuclear warheads and perhaps guidance systems, but not to a new level of military expenditure which would seriously alter "the delicate balance of terror."[8] Such considerations pay too little attention to the political consequences within America of our renewed testing. As Urie Bronfenbrenner has observed, bomb tests can be signals to the people on the side which is testing that the other side must be terribly aggressive—else why would one's own honorable gov-

[8] Cf. Samuel Huntington, "Realities of the Arms Race," *The New Leader*, August 14, 1962. Concerning the step-up in American missile production and the search for superiority rather than stability, see "An Open Letter to President Kennedy: Why Are We Arming on Such a Scale?" the New York *Times*, August 21, 1962, and for fuller discussion, P. M. S. Blackett, *Studies of War* (Hill and Wang, 1962).

ernment expose people to the dangers of fallout? (Much in this same way, a major civil defense program is likely to signal to one's own side the heightened dangers posed for that side by the unreliability and aggressiveness of the other side.) It seems to me that, in the relations of the great powers to each other, the technical arms race is important, but the psychological effects of the arms race with its different cycles and cumulative tensions are even more important. An end to bomb testing might signal to our own people that the enemy is not quite so vicious as we had supposed, and on these grounds it might be worth great efforts to reach agreement. Such a signal is relevant also to the domestic struggle within America, for it would make clear that our atomic policy is a product of compromise between different points of view and is not controlled by Dr. Edward Teller and his associates or by a faction within the AEC or within the Joint Congressional Committee on Atomic Energy.

Here I return to the great asymmetry between the United States and the Soviet Union, namely, the different weight and bearing of popular pressures in the two countries. There are, of course, different factions within the Soviet elites; but various party groups, managers of heavy industry, high army officers, and other influential men have no tradition of taking their case directly to the public at large, and when the press is employed in these intramural struggles it is only obliquely channeling popular pressures and discontents. Criticism of Khrushchev may be voiced by Chinese and Albanians and indirectly at home by generals or managers, but he retains considerable freedom of maneuver, and the groups which must be conciliated are few in number. In contrast, President Kennedy's administration is subject not only to elections every two years but to an almost continuous plebscitory process which amplifies the pressures from many sizable groups of Americans who take part directly or through their organizations in the political process and who, whatever their differences, join in the patriotic consensus. Hence President Kennedy can easily move decisively against the Communist powers with virtually no domestic protest despite the risks of war, for here nearly the whole population can be readily mobilized. But the slightest move by the President to explore a *détente* exposes him to savage popular attack and leads officials who make such moves to proceed erratically and marginally, fearful lest they suffer the fate of Harold Stassen in the previous Administration.

This is especially so since those of our allies who require the tension of the cold war to remain our allies are in general much less afraid of nuclear disasters than either the Americans or the Russians; they can demand that America "stand firm" without really believing that they will suffer the consequences. They can do so in part because, except for the British, who possess the weapons and who know what this means, and the Japanese, who have suffered from atom bombs, they have not really been exposed to nuclear weapons. (The French, while they have the bomb, do not think it is very real, and moreover the importance of it has been overshadowed by the Algerian war and its domestic impact.) But it is also in part because many of our allies have a juster appraisal of the Russians than Americans do and see them as cautious, or despise them as Slavs and think that they can be kept in their place. However, it is true that many West Europeans, admiring President Kennedy, have a greater confidence that he is in charge of American policy than they might have if they lived in this country, read our nonelite press, or listened to our many jingo broadcasters, and came to realize that the House of Representatives is in many ways truly representative of American opinion. I am not speaking here of American opinion simply in terms of numbers, but rather of numbers multiplied by passion, organizational weight, and the salience of various issues. A minority of congressmen, who speak for the best elements in American life, regard issues of foreign policy as far more salient and sensitive than do their more apathetic or less aroused constituents. Thus there are many congressmen who are more enlightened, dispassionate, and internationally minded than their constituents "deserve," while others represent the more belligerent, gerontocratic, and parochial constituencies in the United States. And since it is the ability to mobilize latent hopes and passions that decides elections (or at least congressmen think so), congressmen are naturally attuned to the national rhetoric, whether Federal or Confederate, which they share in a somewhat greater degree than the more cosmopolitan Administration.

Professor Osgood would, I am sure, agree with much of what I have just said. He is right to suggest that American fear of being misled by the Soviet Union stems in part from our lack of understanding of what is in the interest of the Russians and hence what they are likely to do. Everything they do remains opaque. Morris Janowitz points out that when the Soviet Union was inaccessible to scholars after World War II, important work was done on the basis of reading of documents, analysis of ideology, and interviews with refugees. "Today," he continues, "when the Soviet Union is more directly accessible, but not available for systematic data collection, there has been a marked decline in sociological and social psychological studies of Soviet man." ["Mass Persuasion in International Relations," *Public Opinion Quarterly*, Winter 1961.]

Janowitz also makes clear the extent to which the concept of totalitarianism has now subsumed Communist and Nazi experience under a single label. One element here is a counterreaction against the American tendency in the Second World War to assume that our allies were necessarily democratic. (We made the same assumption in World War I.) It is extremely difficult for most people to keep in mind two different problems at the same time, in this case the short-run problem of Nazi Germany and the long-run problem of Communist Russia. This same tendency influences Administration leaders and intellectuals who focus on the NATO countries and the Soviet Union while underestimating the domestic pressures within the United States that affect the chances of peace. When China explodes an atomic bomb, we will focus only on this truly ideological society and wish we had not concentrated for so long on what we provincially speak of as the struggle of East and West, which is really a struggle of West and West or North and North. It is almost as if people tend to cling even to a familiar enemy in preference to an unknown one, as well as to see the enemy (as Professor Osgood emphasizes) through the most familiar but most misleading simplifications.

I say this is no tone of moral upbraiding or chiding. Americans are not different from other peoples who have been suddenly forced by history to speed up developments of thought and perspective that ordinarily take decades if not centuries. Americans *are* different in being more democratic, not only in the sense of popular pressures on decision-making but also in the sense that most of us for most of the time share the current rhetoric and the current preoccupations, even when we are critical of these at marginal points. Though we manage to preserve a somewhat greater detachment, we can hardly help but be torn between a desire for intellectual purity and moral clarity that may limit our effectiveness and our desire to influence popular American attitudes even if this means talking that language. For example, to influence men who are apathetic and feel impotent, it may seem advisable to offer hope. Will one then stretch the tenuous limits of one's own hope to make this appeal? How practical must one appear to be, by current versions of the practical? Or, to take another example, how many avowals of anticommunism should one make to legitimize one's unorthodoxies? Perhaps this is an especially difficult question for someone like myself who is strongly anti-Communist vis-à-vis both the totalitarian regimes and the local Stalinist cadres that in this country, in an earlier period, did so much damage to the liberal causes that are my concerns. So long as American anticommunism increases the danger of nuclear war, I believe that one must hesitate about echoing the anti-Communist chorus and, as a matter of personal dignity, avoid the self-righteous and moralistic indignation that, among its other evil consequences, cuts many American intellectuals off from the intellectuals of Japan, Latin America, and even Western Europe, where the spectrum of opinion on the left is wider, if often unsophisticated. I trust it is clear that I am not arguing for a double standard in judging countries within and without the Communist orbits. To deceive oneself about communism is no help to anyone, especially to people who are trying to moderate contemporary American fanaticism and whose efforts may at any time be undercut by unexpected Communist moves.

The American Sociological Association's symposium was devoted to social science research on problems of war and peace. I suppose I have already implied my skepticism concerning what research, at least in the narrower sense, can accomplish. The large institutional and popular pressures within America, its allies, and its adversaries, are not readily miniaturized for better understanding, and in any case, the gap between what we already know in our best selves and what we actually accomplish is so enormous that research often seems an altogether too slow and peripheral enterprise. We are dealing with political questions and we need to look for political support. Generals in the "Federal" tradition, such as Eisenhower, are of . . . the greatest importance, and I keep looking for alliances in the Pentagon with military men who are conservative enough to prefer traditional old-style (sufficiently terrible) wars to new-style nuclear experiments in altering environments. I also wish it were possible to find conservative businessmen who want to save the country as a going concern and who are not so timid as to prefer to save their illusions or their reputations. And of course no matter how pessimistic one is concerning the political impact of a small number of intellectuals or the research they might do, the dangers are so enormous that we must exploit that chance even against what common sense might warn us about the possibilities of influence. And moreover, in the long run it is people like ourselves who are more likely than conservative military or business leaders to help Americans to find a moral equivalent for war.

We are all familiar with the need for such an equivalent. But let me call your attention to just one illustration which comes from my lifelong habit of reading the letters to the editor in the daily press and the news weeklies. One phrase comes up over and over in these columns like a chant, namely that the writer is "sick and tired" of something or other. White Southerners say that they are "sick and tired" of being pushed around by Negro agitators or the northern press or the federal government. Jingos say that they are "sick and tired" of Castro or Khrushchev or the United Nations. More rarely, the oppressed say it about their oppressors, when things have lifted a little and they can afford to be sick and tired. But in general it seems to me that the warlike in the United States are the sick and tired ones, who find their own lives insufficiently preoccupying and who, in ways Professor Osgood describes, project their difficulties on the agreed-upon enemy, the Communists abroad and at home. I do think that social science can contribute to a better understanding of what people mean when they say that they are sick and tired. More difficult, but still not out of the range of possibilities, is the ability of an inventive social science to discover alternative agendas which may make people less "sick" if more agreeably and good-humoredly tired. It may even be that the exhausting enterprise of sending men to the moon and the planets will turn out to be a transitional vehicle for Federal and Confederate energies.

The Nylon War
(1951)

Today—August 1, 1951—the Nylon War enters upon the third month since the United States began all-out bombing of the Soviet Union with consumers' goods, and it seems time to take a retrospective look. Behind the initial raid of June 1 were years of secret and complex preparations, and an idea of disarming simplicity: that if allowed to sample the riches of America, the Russian people would not long tolerate masters who gave them tanks and spies instead of vacuum cleaners and beauty parlors. The Russian rulers would thereupon be forced to turn out consumers' goods, or face mass discontent on an increasing scale.

The Nylon War was conceived by an army colonel—we shall call him "Y"—whose name cannot yet be revealed. Working with secret funds which the Central Intelligence Agency had found itself unable to spend, Y organized shortly after World War II the so-called "Bar Harbor Project," the nucleus of which, some five years later, became "Operation Abundance," or, as the press soon dubbed it, the "Nylon War." After experiments with rockets and balloons, it was concluded that only cargo planes—navigating, it was hoped, above the range of Russian radar—could successfully deliver the many billion dollars' worth of consumer goods it was planned to send. Nevertheless, when Y and his group first broached their plans to a few selected congressional leaders in the winter of 1948 they were dismissed as hopelessly academic. America had neither the goods nor the planes nor the politics to begin such an undertaking. But in the fall of 1950, with the country bogged down in a seemingly endless small-scale war in Korea, Y's hopes revived. For one thing, the cargo planes needed for the job were beginning to become available. Moreover, a certain amount of overordering by the armed services, panicky over Korea, had created a stockpile of consumer goods. More important, the Administration, having locked up all known and many suspected Communists in one of the old camps for Japanese aliens, had still not convinced the country that it was sufficiently anti-Soviet, though at the same time many Americans wanted peace but did not dare admit it. A plan which, in fact and in presentation, took attention away from alleged Far Eastern bungling, and which was both violently anti-Soviet and pro-peace, appeared to offer the possibility of restoring the Administration's tottering position in the country.

This is not the place to recount the political maneuverings that preceded Truman's success in securing a two-billion-dollar initial appropriation from Congress, nor the Potomac maneuverings that led to the recruitment of top-flight production and merchandising talent from civilian life. Our story begins with Truman going before Congress to secure authority to "bring the benefits of American technology to less fortunate nations" by round-the-clock bombing, the day after the news of the first raids hit the American public.

The planners of the Bar Harbor Project had staked American prestige, their professional futures, and the lives of six thousand airmen on the belief that the Soviets would not know of these first flights nor meet them with armed resistance. When the opening missions were accomplished without incident, permitting Truman to make his appeal, Washington was immensely relieved; but when the second wave of planes met with no resistance either, Washington was baffled. It was at first assumed that the Soviet radar network had again simply failed to spot the high-flying planes—cruising at 48,000 feet and self-protected from radar by some still presumably secret device. We now know that what actually happened was a division of opinion in the Kremlin—we can piece the story together from intelligence reports and from clues in *Pravda*. A faction, led by foreign-trade chief Mikoyan, maintained that the scheme was a huge hoax, designed to stampede Russia into a crusade against a fairy tale—and so to make her the laughing stock of the world. He counseled, wait and see. And, indeed, it *was* a fairy tale for secret-police boss Beria, who argued that the raids had never taken place, but that reports of them had been faked by some Social Democratic East Germans who had somehow gotten access to the communications networks. When this idea was exploded, Beria counseled shooting the planes down, on the ground that they were simply a screen spying out plants for an atomic attack. Stalin himself believed with repentant economist Varga that American capitalism had reached so critical a point that only through forcible gifts overseas could the Wall Street ruling clique hope to maintain its profits and dominance. Coupled with these divisions of opinion, which stalemated action, was the fear in some quarters that America might welcome attacks on its errand-of-mercy planes as a pretext for the war of extermination openly preached by some only mildly rebuked American leaders.

At any rate, the confusion in the Politburo was more than mirrored by the confusion in the target cities caused by the baptismal raids. Over 600 C-54s streamed high over Rostov, and another 200 over Vladivostok, dropped their cargoes, and headed back to their bases in the Middle East and Japan. By today's standard these initial forays were small-scale—200,000 pairs of nylon hose, 4,000,000 packs of cigarettes, 35,000 Toni wave kits, 20,000 yo-yos, 10,000 wrist watches, and a number of odds and ends from PX overstock. Yet this was more than enough to provoke frenzied rioting as the inhabitants scrambled for a share. Within a few hours after the first parcels had fallen, the roads into the target cities were jammed. Roadblocks had to be thrown up around the cities, and communications with the outside were severed. The fast-spreading rumors of largesse from above were branded "criminally insane," and their source traced to machinations of the recently purged "homeless cosmopolitan Simeon Osnavitch (Rosenblum)."

But the propaganda of the deed proved stronger than the propaganda of the word. As Odessa, Yakutsk, Smolensk, and other cities became targets of aggressive generosity, as Soviet housewives saw with their own eyes American stoves, refrigerators, clothing, and toys, the Kremlin was forced to change its line and, ignoring earlier denials, to give the raids full but negative publicity. David Zaslavsky's article in the June 10 *Izvestia* heralded the new approach. Entitled "The Mad Dogs of Imperialism Foam at the Mouth," he saw the airlift as harbinger of America's economic collapse. "Unable because of the valiant resistance of the peace-loving democracies to conquer foreign markets, America's Fascist plutocracy is now reduced to giving away goods. . . ." Taking another line, *Red Star* argued that to accept American consumer goods would make stalwart Russians as decadent as rich New Yorkers.

However, the Russian people who could get access, either directly or through the black market that soon arose, to American goods seemed not to fear decadence. Again, there was a change of line. Falling back on a trick learned during Lend-Lease, it was claimed that the goods were Russian-made, and *Pravda* on June 14 stated that the Toni wave kit had been invented by Pavlov before World War I. However, Colonel Y's staff had anticipated this altogether routine reaction. On June 17, the target cities of that day—Kiev, Stalingrad, Magnitogorsk—received their wares wrapped in large cartoons of Stalin bending over, in a somewhat undignified pose, to pick up a dropped Ansco camera. This forced still another switch of line. On June 20, Beria went on the air to announce that the Americans were sending over goods poisoned by atomic radiation, and all papers and broadcasts carried scare stories about people who had died from using Revlon or Schick shavers. And indeed booby traps (planted by the MVD) succeeded in killing a number of over-eager citizens. For a while, this permitted specially recruited Party members to gather up the goods and take them to headquarters for alleged deradiation.

But here something unexpected occurred. We know from a few people who managed to escape to the West that a number of Party elements themselves because disaffected. Asked to turn in all American goods, they held on to some possessions secretly—there was a brisk underground trade in fake Russian labels. Sometimes wives, having gotten used to the comforts of Tampax and other disappearing items, would hide them from their more ascetic husbands; children of Party members cached pogo sticks and even tricycles. Thus it came about that when Party members were ordered to join "decontamination" squads the depots were re-entered at night and portable items taken. By the beginning of July, all attempts to deceive the people had only made matters worse; things were getting out of hand.

Faring badly in the "war," the Kremlin turned to diplomacy. On July 5 at Lake Success, Malik described the airlift as "an outrage reminiscent of Hitlerite aggression" and, invoking Article 39 of the UN Charter, he called on the Security Council to halt the "shameful depredations of the American warmongers." Austin replied that "these gifts are no more or less than a new-fashioned application of ancient principles," and the Russian resolution was defeated, 9–2. The next step occurred in Washington, when Ambassador Panyushkin handed Secretary Acheson a sharply worded note warning that "should these present outrages continue, the U.S.S.R. will have no recourse but to reply in kind."

Seattle was the first American city to learn the meaning of the Soviet warning as on July 15, a hundred Russian heavy bombers (presumably from bases in the Kuriles) left behind them 15,000 tins of caviar, 500 fur coats, and 80,000 copies of Stalin's speeches on the minorities question. When the Russian planes came, followed in by American jets, many were apprehensive, but as the counterattack had been anticipated it proved possible to prevent incidents in the air and panic on the ground. Since then, Butte, Minneapolis, Buffalo, and Moscow, Idaho, have been added to the list of America's front-line cities. But in quantity and quality the counteroffensive has been unimpressive. Searing vodka, badly styled mink coats (the only really selling item), undependable cigarette lighters—these betray a sad lack of know-how in production and merchandising. In an editorial, "Worse than Lend-Lease," the New York *Daily News* has charged that the Nylon War gives the Soviets free lessons in the secrets of America's success, but truly conservative papers like the *Herald-Tribune* see the comparative showing of Americans and Russians as a world demonstration of the superiority of free enterprise.

It is clear, at any rate, that free enterprise has not suffered much of a jolt—nor, indeed, has the mounting inflation been much reduced—by the Russian campaign. To be sure, the massive air-borne shipments of caviar have made luxury grocers fear inventory losses, and Portugal, heavily dependent on the American anchovy market, has been worried. But these pinpricks are nothing to what is now becoming evident on the Russian side—namely the imminent collapse of the economy. For the homeland of centralized economic planning is experiencing its own form of want in the midst of plenty. Soviet consumers, given a free choice between shoddy domestic merchandise and air-lift items, want nothing to do with the former and in a score of fields Russian goods go unwanted as the potential buyer dreams of soon owning an American version. Soviet housewives, eager to keep up with American-supplied "Joneses," pester their local stores, often to the point of creating local shortages—indeed, the American refrigerators have created demands, not only for electricity, but also for many foods which can now be stored (and hoarded).

Much of this disruption is the result of careful planning by the Bar Harbor Project's Division of Economic Dislocation. The Division, for example, early began studies of Russian power distribution, and saw to the landing of 60-cycle radios, shavers, toasters, milking machines, in 60-cycle areas; 25-cycle appliances in 25-cycle areas, and so on, especially with an eye to areas of power shortage or competition with critical industries. In co-operation with GE, methods were worked out by which the Russian donees could plug their appliances, with appropriate transformers, directly into high-voltage or street power lines; thus simply shutting off house current could not save the Russian utilities from overload. Similarly, drawing on the American monopolistic practice of tie-in sales, goods were dropped whose use demanded other items in short supply—oil ranges, for instance, were dropped throughout the Baku fields. Of course, mistakes were made, and in one or two cases bottlenecks in the Russian economy were relieved, as when some containers were salvaged to repair a tin shortage of which the planners had not been advised.

But it is not only on the production end that the raids have been disruptive. Last Friday's raid on Moscow—when 22,000 tons of goods were dropped—may be taken as an illustration. For the first time General Vandenberg's airmen tackled—and successfully solved—the knotty engineering problem of dropping jeeps (complete with 150 gallons of gasoline and directions in simple Russian). So skillfully was the job done that half the three hundred vehicles parachuted down landed directly on the Kremlin's doorstep—in the center of Red Square. The raid was given wide advance publicity through the Voice and leaflets and when the great day came Moscow's factories were deserted as people fought for roof-top perches; in addition, an estimated 250,000 collective farmers swarmed into the city. In fact, as people drift from place to place hoping that their ship may fly in, the phrase "rootless cosmopolite" at last assumes real meaning. Economists, talking learnedly of "multipliers," calculate that Russian output is dropping 3 per cent a month.

The Kremlin has reacted in the only way it knows, by a series of purges. Serge Churnik, erstwhile head of the cigarette trust, is on trial for "deliberate wrecking and economic treason." Bureaucrats live in terror lest their region or their industry be next disrupted by the American bombardment, and they waver between inactivity and frantic Stakhanovite shows of activity. These human tragedies testify to the growing fear in the Politburo concerning the long-run consequences of the American offensive. The tangible proofs of American prosperity, ingenuity, and generosity can no longer be gainsaid; and the new official line that Wall Street is bleeding America white in order to create scarcity and raise prices at home, while "believed," has little impact against the ever mounting volume, and fascinating variety, of goods and rumors of goods. Can the capitalistic gluttons of privilege be such bad fellows if we, the Russians, are aided by them to enjoy luxuries previously reserved for the dachas of novelists and plant managers? In an article in *New Statesman and Nation*, Geoffrey Gorer has recently contended that the airlift serves to revive primitive Russian "orality," and that the image of America can no longer be that of a leering Uncle Sam or top-hatted banker but must soon become amiably matronly. It is thoughts along this line that most worry the Politburo although, of course, the MVD sees to it that only a tiny fraction of the mounting skepticism expresses itself openly or even in whispered jokes. But what is the MVD to do about a resolution of the All-Workers Congress of Tiflis that "Marxist-Leninist-Stalinist democracy demands that party cadres install officials who can cope with the mounting crisis"?

Translated into plain talk, this means that the Russian people, without saying so in as many words, are now putting a price on their collaboration with the regime. The price—"goods instead of guns." For Russia's industrial plant, harassed by the rapidly growing impact of Operation Abundance, cannot supply both, let alone carry on the counteroffensive against America. Intelligence reports speak of scheduled production cutbacks varying from 25 per cent on tanks to 75 per cent on artillery; it is symptomatic that washing machines, designed to compete with the American Bendixes which are being dropped in ever increasing numbers, will soon start rolling off the assembly lines of the great Red October Tank Works—after its former manager had been shot for asserting that conversion to peacetime production could not be achieved in less than two years.

Meanwhile, diplomatic moves are under way—so, at least, the Alsop brothers report—to liquidate the Nylon War. It is obvious why the Russian leaders are prepared to make very considerable concessions in the satellite countries, in China, and in Indo-China in order to regain the strategic initiative in their domestic affairs. But on the American side the willingness of many to listen to Russian overtures is based on the success, rather than the failure, of the campaign. One sees a repetition of 1940 as the Washington *Times-Herald* and the *Daily Compass* join hands in attacking Operation Abundance, the former calling it "an international WPA," the latter arguing "you can't fight ideas with goods." Addressing the Stanford Alumni Club of Los Angeles, Herbert Hoover spoke for millions in observing that the monthly cost of the airlift has already exceeded the entire federal budget for the year 1839. Still another tack has been taken by senators who want the airlift to continue, but with different targets; some, insisting that charity begins at home, have wanted free goods landed on their districts; others have supported the claims of Japan, the Philippines, or Franco. Still others fear that many of the air-lift items could be reconverted in some way for use by the Russian war machine; they are especially opposed to the jeep delivery program, despite reports it is wreaking havoc with the

Russian road system as well as with the gasoline supply. And the House Committee on Un-American Activities has charged that trade secrets are being delivered to Russian spies by Red homosexual officials and professors disguised as plane pilots.

These are the obvious enemies, and against them stand some obvious friends of the Nylon War. Both AFL and CIO, now in their eighth round of wage increases, vigorously support the program, though it is rumored that the Railroad Brotherhoods have done so only in return for a fact-finding board's support of a fourteen-hour week. Farmers have become reconciled by the promise that bulk agricultural products will soon move over the aerial transmission belt—in part to encourage the wanderings of Russian farmers. The business community is divided, with the CED, Juan Trippe, and Baruch leading the supporters of the airlift.[1] But it would be a mistake to assume that support of Operation Abundance springs only from hopes of material gain. The renewed fight against oppression and want, the excitement of following the raids in maps and betting pools, the ridiculousness of the Russian response—all these things have made many millions of Americans less anxious than they have been since the days in October 1950 when it seemed as if the Korean War would be quickly concluded.

Indeed, it is just this loss of tension which has given rise to much of the covert opposition to the Nylon War, as distinguished from the overt opposition already discussed. On the one hand, certain leaders are frightened that the Russian dictatorship may indeed be overthrown—as Colonel Y in his more optimistic moments had ventured to hope. This is thought to raise the possibility of all sorts of chaotic movements developing in Central and Eastern Europe, and even further west—Franco, for instance, feels threatened at the loss of his "enemy," and has offered to act as mediator in the Nylon War. On the other hand, it has become increasingly difficult for American politicians to frighten the American public about Russia: the once-feared monolith now appears

---

[1] It goes without saying that there are many fights within pressure groups as to *what* the airlift shall carry—and ideological considerations are not confined to the Soviet side. Thus, the Committee against Juvenile Delinquency has registered strong protests against sending comic books. More serious issues revolve around the Planned Parenthood League's campaign to get contraceptives included in the air-lift items. In addition to humanitarian arguments, the claim is made that this will reverse the demographic trend now so favorable to Russia; the League's slogan is "Give them the tools and they will do the job." Walter Lippmann predicts a Rome-Moscow axis if the League should win out.

as almost a joke, with its crude poster-and-caviar reprisals, its riots over stockings, soap, Ronsons, and other gadgets which Americans regard in matter-of-fact fashion. The sharp drop in war sentiment in the United States has resulted in psychological and even actual unemployment for a number of people.

What do the coming months hold? It is significant that this depends almost entirely on the outcome of the American domestic struggle: the Nylon War has altered the whole power-complex which, as the Korean War dragged on, still heavily favored Russia. It is now Russia, not America, whose resources are overcommitted, whose alliances are overstrained. In fact, Mao's visit to Moscow at the end of July seems to have been attended with apprehension lest he ask America to cut Red China in on Operation Abundance—at a price, of course. The possibility that this may redound to the credit of the Truman Administration in the 1952 campaign is not the least of the nightmares haunting many Americans, and at this writing it is impossible to predict whether the opponents of the program will win out.

Meanwhile, Operation Abundance marches on, solving technical problems of incredible complexity. The latest move is the perfection of an ordering system whereby Russians can "vote" for the commodities they most want, according to a point system, by the use of radio-sending equipment, battery-run, with which we have provided them. The commodities available will be described over the Voice of America—now for the first time having something to "sell"—by Sears Roebuck-type catalogues, and by dropped samples in the case of soft goods. The method making it impossible for the Russian government effectively to jam this two-way communication of distributor and consumer is still the great secret of the Nylon War.

EPILOGUE (1962)

The unfictional character of much science fiction (though the genre as a whole has become the repository of a good deal of genuinely satiric or utopian thought) is one of many indications of the disorientation from which many people suffer, the terrible bewilderment about what is going on in the modern world. When "The Nylon War" was first published, I began to get letters and telephone calls asking me if the "war" (whose fictitious date had then been passed) had actually gotten under way! People have asked for references to the New York *Times* or periodical literature where they could catch up on these events. I was reminded of the "Invasion from Mars" broadcast analyzed in the book of that name by Hadley Cantril and of the still unresolved disquiet about flying saucers. That my tale could be taken for literal fact was a sign of the remoteness of the inquirers from the current of what was probably so. The mass media that, like the typical newsreel, parade events without historical or other context, give them a discreteness and lack of structure that make it easier to picture the enemy of the moment as devoid of human qualities. Indeed, I have had a letter from a man in Sydney, New South Wales, asking me for further references on the Nylon War on the assumption that it has occurred and also asking whether *Common Cause* (where the article first appeared) is not (as charged by a local representative of the United States Information Service), a "Commie magazine" in which case presumably the article itself, if not the "war," would be "Commie propaganda." So humorless and fearful an American representative abroad is, I would hope, not characteristic. But it seems clear that satire is too playful and perhaps too snobbish a mode, save in cartoon form, to combat the combination of fright and self-righteousness of many Americans, who would accept the *fait accompli* of a Nylon War if the authorities ordered it, but who could not otherwise possibly grasp a world they never made.

Both in England and in the United States several movie makers have been interested in making a film of "The Nylon War." A few years ago one British effort got bogged down, apparently because they had shifted the locale to Yugoslavia and this ran afoul both of recent events and of British foreign policy. More recently an American producer bought the rights to the idea—but then discovered to his dismay that the Russians were no longer so short of consumer goods but were themselves sending out technical-aid missions to far poorer countries.

Since "The Nylon War" was written, my interest—nay, preoccupation—with the interrelation of disarmament, foreign policy, and domestic policy has become still more intense. I have attended many conferences, and have read and written many memoranda on these matters. But I still haven't encountered many fruitful discussions that simultaneously analyze both American and Soviet (and now also Chinese) social character and social structure as these affect the possibilities of a *modus vivendi*. People who understand the Soviet Union tend to believe that in a disarmed world communism would indeed win out, as the Communists themselves profess to believe. Not only does this give the Communists too much credit and America and other Western countries too little, but it assumes that "tomorrow is already here" not only in the quite evident fact that one country can destroy the world unilaterally, but also in the not yet evident idea that one country can rule the world from one place unilaterally (George Kennan, a sober student at once of American and Soviet bureaucracy, doesn't think this can be done). In this state of barely avowed defeatism, the covert American fear that the cold war will come to an end has, if anything, increased since the period in 1948-49 when I was working on "The Nylon War." At the same time, it is far more widely recognized now than it was before Stalin's death that in many ways the Soviet Union has become, like the United States, a status quo power, with a strong residual dynamism whose strengths and weaknesses are hidden by ideological cant and dogma. The importance of Marxist-Leninist ideology in the minds of Soviet leaders is less, it would seem, in turning them into driving fanatics out to conquer the world than in distorting their perceptions of day-to-day events and their image of the future.[2]

Whatever its crudities as morality and satire, there is still one viable lesson in "The Nylon War," concerning the possibilities of unilateralism. (I refer here to unilateral initiatives in the sense in which Charles Osgood uses the term, often mistakenly confused with unilateral disarmament.) In trying to mitigate the cold war, we need not always either negotiate explicitly or respond at those points of obvious tension where both adversaries are locked in conflict that they cannot break out of because of domestic veto groups or intransigent allies. It is sometimes possible to end the stalemate by seeking fresh ground, which is not necessarily less safe even in conventional military terms. For example, one could maintain for the time being a relatively invulnerable deterrent (such as the Polaris submarine provides) while withdrawing from bases that are provocative and vulnerable militarily and may entangle us with allies who have an interest in maintaining international tensions. I believe that with ingenuity and courage one might discover measures, not dependent upon immediate Communist reciprocation, that would render the United States less dangerous to itself and others and commit us somewhat less firmly to the political, economic, and psychological dynamism of the arms race.[3]

[2] I do not say this dogmatically, for Soviet policy is unstable as indeed is America's, and of course not entirely unaffected by our own actions and those of other powers and would-be powers.

[3] Cf. Charles E. Osgood, "Graduated Unilateral Initiatives for Peace," in Quincy Wright, William M. Evan, and Morton Deutsch, *Preventing World War III: Some Proposals* (Simon and Schuster, 1962), pp. 161–77; see also Arthur Waskow on possible American initiatives in Council for Correspondence *Newsletter*, July 1962.

The release of energies in areas other than the arms race could serve to give Americans a sense of vitality and flexibility in our society, and thus make it less difficult to negotiate an agreement with the Soviet Union that, for domestic reasons, we would have to dress up as not weakening our posture—that word that expresses the *rigor mortis* of the mindlessly energetic—in any way. Let us suppose that the United States and the Soviet Union were competitively—or, even more improbably, jointly—engaged in intensive efforts to assist at once Chinese and Indian industrialization—would we not then feel less passive, less worried, and, as a total society, less disarmed? And would we not then be better able to give up the false and delusive security of our deterrents without falling back either on the Maginot Line of the budget or on the Maginot Line of military sufficiency?

Clearly enough, the Chinese now are obdurate, and overtures that might once have moderated their fanaticism will no longer suffice. My point here, however, does not depend on the political feasibility, either domestically or internationally, of one or another particular proposal; rather I aim to emphasize more generally that steps toward disarmament need not be taken in the field of disarmament itself. If I am right that articulate Americans suffer from a sense of doom about our own society which leads in turn to frozen thinking about alternatives, then it follows that a wise administration would not go before a suspicious Congress with only a test ban in hand, but would at the same time present other measures which would make our country stronger internationally, and still others that would make clear to Soviet leaders that we were really intending by the test ban to reduce tension, and not simply to save money or to hold our lead in weaponry—we would simultaneously announce, for instance, that we were halting all cooperation by American firms in the rearmament of West Germany and make clear our disapproval of such rearmament by whatever measures of economic and political pressure we could bring to bear; in that case, the violent protests of Adenauer, Strauss, and other German leaders would help convince the Soviet Union, the Germans, the Poles, and our own citizens that we really meant business. This is the kind of many-sided policy that I associate on the one hand with unilateralism, for the policy could be pursued even in the face of a frozen foe, in the hope of unfreezing him, and on the other hand with the possibility of negotiating particular steps that might then give rise to other steps.

While there are millions of doggedly defeatist Americans who hang on desperately to what they have got, though this is a sure way to lose both it and themselves, there are, I hope, others whose imagination and generosity and historical understanding can in co-operation with like-minded men everywhere discover not only moral equivalents for war but also economic equivalents for the arms race and political equivalents for the use and threat of force in the drive to implement one's ideals and protect one's other interests at home and abroad.

Some Observations on the Limits of Totalitarian Power
(1952)

Twenty and even ten years ago, it was an important intellectual task (and one in which, in a small way, I participated) to point out to Americans of good will that the Soviet and Nazi systems were not simply transitory stages, nor a kind of throwback to the South American way—that they were, in fact, new forms of social organization, more omnivorous than even the most brutal of earlier dictatorships. At that time, there were many influential people who were willing to see the Nazis as a menace but insisted that the Bolsheviks were a hope. And even today one can find individuals who have no inkling of the terror state—people who, for instance, blame "the" Germans for not throwing Hitler out or for compromising themselves by joining Nazi party or other organizations, or who attribute Soviet behavior to the alleged submissiveness of the Russian character or trace it back to Czarist despotism and expansionism and whatnot. Yet it seems to me that now the task of intellectual and moral awakening has been pretty well performed, and stands even in danger of being overperformed; in pursuit of the few remaining "liberals who haven't learned," groups such as this [the American Committee on Cultural Freedom] may mistake the temper of the country at large, misdeploy their energies, and, paradoxically, serve complacency in the very act of trying to destroy complacency.

Intellectual communication, in this as in other cases, cannot avoid the ambiguities arising from the differing attitudes in the American audience at large. I know that I will be misunderstood. For one thing, those who have suffered directly at the hands of the totalitarians, and who can undoubtedly find many audiences where complacency still rules—where, for example, the Soviet Union is still sneakingly regarded as somehow on the right track as against "capitalist exploitation"—such people may feel that I take too lightly the domestic well-wishers of the

Soviet Union, or the lethargic. No one likes being robbed of a well-earned agenda.

Yet I cannot help but feel that the telling of atrocity stories—undoubtedly true stories—may have ambivalent consequences and, after a time, may harm the very cause in hand. Let me give as an illustration the way in which many liberals today, in government service or in academic life, repeat tales of loyalty-probe incompetence or injustice, of school-board and trustee confusion between liberals and "Reds," of stupid FBI questions, and so on. Such tales are meant to arouse us against the dangers of domestic reaction, but they have frequently the consequence of leading a government employee to burn back issues of *The New Masses,* of a faculty to drop *The Communist Manifesto* from its reading list, of a student to fear getting involved with even Americans for Democratic Action lest it prejudice his possibilities for employment. Then such tales are in turn spread, to justify still further concessions to an alleged need to conform to the prevailing climate of opinion . . .

Now I want to suggest that something of the same sort may occur if we begin, after greatly underestimating, greatly to overestimate the capacity of totalitarianism to restructure human personality. During the last war, I talked with people who were concerned with the plans for occupying Germany at war's end. Most assumed that there would be not only physical but organizational chaos and that it was necessary to have skilled civil affairs officers to take over tasks that the Germans, broken by Hitler and the war, could not assume for themselves. I felt that this was unduly patronizing of a great and gifted people, capable of spontaneous organization and of settling affairs with the Nazis if the occupying powers merely held the ring and supplied some necessities of life. I think we can make the same mistake—for I believe it was a mistake—about the Soviet Union and its satellites, and fail to see that even the terror is not omnipotent to destroy all bonds of organization among its victims.

Similarly, I think we can become so fascinated with the malevolence of Stalinism that we may tend to overestimate its efficiency in achieving its horrible ends; and we may mistake blundering compulsions or even accidents of "the system" for conspiratorial genius. Overinterpretation is the besetting sin of intellectuals anyway, and even when, with Hannah Arendt, we rightly point to the need to cast traditional rationalities aside in comprehending totalitarianism, we may subtly succumb to the appeal of an evil mystery; there is a long tradition of making Satan attractive in spite of ourselves. And the more practical danger of this is that we may, again reacting from underestimation,[1] misjudge not so much the aims as the power of the enemy and be unduly cowed or unduly aggressive as a result.

Consequently, I want to open up a discussion of some of the defenses people have against totalitarianism. Not that these defenses—I shall discuss apathy, corruption, free enterprise, crime, and so on—threaten the security system of the Soviets; that system is a new social invention and there are as few defenses against annihilation by it as against annihilation by atom bombs. Indeed, in some ways totalitarianism is actually strengthened by these partial defenses people are able to raise against it, which make it possible for many people to compromise with the system as a whole. But at least a few European thinkers may be perplexed by the readiness of Americans, lacking firsthand experience of people's capacity to resist, to assume that totalitarianism possesses the kind of psychological pressure system pictured by Orwell in that sadistic but symptomatic book *1984*: here is a fantasy of omnipotent totalitarian impressiveness which I think may itself, among those who admire efficiency and have little faith in man, be an appeal of totalitarianism for those outside its present reach.

For we must distinguish, first of all, between the appeals of totalitarianism when it is out of power and its appeals when in power; my concern here is mainly with the latter. Out of power, totalitarianism competes like any other party, only more so: it can be all things to all men, attracting the idealist by its promise to reform society, to clean out the swindlers; attracting the disoriented and bewildered by its simplistic "explanations" of their misery and of their world, and by promising to get rid of seeming anarchy by enforcing social co-operation; and

---

[1] I have had some fairly extended experience of this. I remember in 1931 talking with American engineers in the Soviet Union who thought the Russians too incompetent in the mechanical arts ever to build tractors, let alone planes; they failed, as it seemed to me, to realize how the huge friction of Soviet incompetence could be partly overcome by the even huger burning up of human resources if one cared not at all about them. Likewise, when some seemed complacent about the Chinese Communists on the ground that "you could never organize the unbelligerent Chinese for aggressive war," I felt that this left out of account the awful weapon of systematic terror and utter ruthlessness about killing one's "own" people that is Moscow's first export to its satellites and "national" Communist parties.

attracting the sadist in the way the Berkeley study of the "Authoritarian Personality" has documented. (In the Moslem countries and the Far East, the Communists do not need even this much of an armory: a promise to drive out the foreign devils while promising Western-style commodities to everyone may be almost enough.) Most large-scale societies will offer a spectrum of people available for the high-minded, middle-minded, and low-minded aspects of totalitarian politics, though probably a crisis is necessary to convert their organization into a fighting revolutionary party with a real hope of capturing power. That is, the fact that totalitarianism has captured a country doesn't tell us as much as some observers have supposed about the character of its total population; the mass base necessary can be far less than a majority and it can include people of profoundly nontotalitarian personalities who have been fooled—to whom the appeal has not been a very deep-going one.[2]

When the latter wake up to the fact that the God they followed has failed them, it is of course too late to change deities. For many years it seemed to me that the Soviet Union was more dangerous in this respect than the Nazis, let alone the Fascists in Spain and Italy, because the latter were so clearly corrupt that they could not help but disillusion their idealists rapidly. Thus, during the Nazi regime, while the concentration camps were more or less hidden, the power and pelf struggles within the Nazi echelons were not: Hitler might remain for some unsullied, but hardly the party bums and barons of lesser magnitude, struggling to build up private empires of business and espionage. The ideological trappings fell away speedily enough. To be sure, there remained some fanatics, especially perhaps in the SS, savagely incorruptible. But many Germans who were drawn to the Nazis precisely by their claim to eliminate corruption were quickly enlightened when they saw the even greater corruption introduced. As against this, the Communists have seemed more incorruptible—a kind of Cromwellian type, hard-bitten and ascetic—thus perhaps retaining ideological impressiveness as well as gaining physical oppressiveness even after being installed

[2] What I have said here needs to be qualified by an understanding of the less conscious motives which attract people to a totalitarian party. The Nazis, for example, were not really all things to all men; they gave the wink to some men that, for instance, their legality was merely window dressing, and the latter could use the window dressing to satisfy their conscious inhibitions against what at bottom drew them to the party. See, for example, Erik H. Erikson's discussion of "Hitler's Imagery and German Youth," in *Childhood and Society* (Norton, 1950), pp. 284–315.

in power. And certainly that impressiveness remains even today for many of those outside the system. Inside, however, there is some evidence—and of course only tantalizingly little—that corruption, blackmarketing, crime, and juggling of figures are widespread; presumably this makes it hard for the idealistic young to be overimpressed with the system's ethical rightness. To be sure, we have had such "training" in contempt for bourgeois comfort-seeking and the dangers of the desire for wealth, that if a Communist is desirous not of wealth but of power he can more readily appear idealistic; perhaps we should learn that the *auri sacra fames*, the cursed hunger for gold, is not half so dangerous to the human race as the ascetic drive for power—a point recently remade by Eric Hoffer in *The True Believer*. Indeed, anyone who claims he wishes to eliminate vice utterly is declaring a very dangerous and antihuman heresy—one all too prevalent, I might add, in today's municipal and national politics in this country. We must teach ourselves, and the young, to distinguish between genuine idealism and arrogant, curdled indignation against behavior which falls short of some monastic image of virtue.

More generally, I have long thought that we need to re-evaluate the role of corruption in a society, with less emphasis on its obviously malign features and more on its power as an antidote to fanaticism. Barrington Moore in *Soviet Politics*, and Margaret Mead in *Soviet Attitudes Toward Authority* present materials documenting the Soviet campaign against the corrupting tendencies introduced into the system by friendship and family feeling—some of Mead's quotations could have come from Bishop Baxter or other Puritan divines, and others from American civil service reformers. While Kravchenko shows how one must at once betray friends in the Soviet regime when they fall under state suspicion —and here, too, the Soviets are more tyrannous than the Nazis who expected friends to intercede with the Gestapo—it would appear that such human ties have never been completely fragmented, whether by Puritanism,[3] industrialism, or their savagely sudden combination in Bolshevism. Actually, people have had to defend themselves against the Soviet system's high demands for performance by building personal cliques, by favoritism, by cultivating cronies; thus, an informal network

[3] While I think that there are many revealing analogies between theocratic Calvinism in its heyday and Stalinism, I do not think the similarities should be pressed too far; among many other differences, the Puritans—in any case, far less powerful—believed in law.

has continued to operate alongside the formal one, whose extraordinary expectations can in fact be met only in this way. (Similarly, Petrov points out that no amount of indoctrination has persuaded the Russian people to like and admire spies and informers, or to extirpate from their own reactions the profoundly human emotion of pity.)

To be sure, corruption does not always and inevitably work as a solvent for ideological claims. Hannah Arendt, returning from Germany last year, described the way in which many middle-class, educated Germans, in order to justify to themselves within their rigid code the compromises they made with the Nazi system, had to exalt that system ideologically; they were trapped by complicity as they would not have been had they been more cynical. Incidentally, their wives, who had to hunt for subsistence on the black market, were probably better off in this respect—they did the needful things to keep going, while allowing their husbands to remain deceived in their older morality. And it could at least be argued that women—as the Bachofen-Fromm interpretation of the Oedipus trilogy would indicate—are more immune than men to impersonal and abstract ideals; they are more conservative in the good and in the bad sense—more "realistic."

I am not, it should be clear, discussing what are called resistance movements, but rather what might be called resistance quiescences. I am talking about the quieter modes of resistance to totalitarianism, not so much in practical life as in mental obeisance, in refusal to internalize the system's ethical norms. I am, moreover, quite unable to say what *proportion* of people, either under the Nazi regime or the Soviet, succumbed or managed to defend themselves in this way; I cannot assign quantitative weights to one mode or the other. It is one of our difficulties as intellectuals that we cannot easily assign such weights. We are likely to overestimate symbolic behavior that appears to give deference to totalitarian power. And the testimony of intellectuals who once believed in totalitarianism and have now fled it is further indication as to the dangers of a totalitarian regime for the emotional life of people like ourselves: ours is in many ways the most exposed position since overt obedience to mere power is least habitual, and since we need—whatever our rational beliefs about men's irrationality—to justify and integrate our behavior in some fashion, perhaps especially so when we ourselves are wholesalers or retailers of ideology.

Gunnar Myrdal, when he visited this country, commented on the "protective community" of the Negroes and of lower-class people generally who, vis-à-vis the whites and the authorities, "ain't seen nothing or nobody"; long training has made them adept in duplicity, evasion, and sly sabotage. (A similar phenomenon exists in Italian peasant communities, under the name of *"la omertà."*) True, this kind of protective community breaks down on occasion, even under the relatively mild pressures and promises of white or official society; the Soviets have much more violent and fearsome methods. Moreover, the Soviet secret police are facing a population most of which is new to urban life, ways and byways: industrialization always stirs the melting pot and throws strange peoples together who have little understanding of or sympathy for each other, or whose suspicion of each other can be easily aroused. Whereas the workers of Hamburg were already accustomed to the industrial revolution and its problems and prospects of social interaction, the Soviet Union is in a sense one vast labor camp where social organization has to start pretty much from scratch.[4] Even so, I think it likely that there are protective communities in Russian farms and factories, which punish Stakhanovites and cope with spies.

In a brilliant article in *The Reporter*, Lionel Trilling has delineated the antisocial, antisocietal bent of a great deal of American literature: Huck Finn escaping the well-meant civilizing clutches of the Widow Douglas is a good illustration of his theme. But we may raise the question whether such escapes—if not to the open spaces then to a protective community or an underground institution like a blind pig or a whorehouse—are not to be found in all the major cultures which have any complex institutions at all, and possibly even in the simplest cultures if we only knew where to look for them. We must never underestimate the ability of human beings to dramatize, to play roles, to behave in ways that seem contradictory only if we do not appreciate

[4] There is no space here to go into the analogous problem of the concentration camps themselves. Kogon's and David Rousset's accounts would seem to indicate that in these camps some prisoner rule developed, and much corruption (reminiscent of the kangaroo courts in the worst American jails), with various groups of prisoners fighting among themselves, and with guard allies, for hegemony. When I raised this problem at the Committee's meeting, Hannah Arendt insisted that the camps described by Kogon and Rousset were exceptions, and that in most no such prisoner ingenuities and defenses developed. Reliable evidence is hard to come by; see, however, Theodore Abel, "The Sociology of Concentration Camps" in December, 1951, *Social Forces*, vol. 30, pp. 150–55, which offers some support for my own position; and see, also, David P. Boder, *I Did Not Interview the Dead* (University of Illinois Press, 1949).

the changes in scene and audience. A friend of mine, Mark Benney, riding a train with peasants in Nazi Germany, was struck by their impassivity of feature. When he and another stranger, a Nazi, got off the train, he could feel behind him a sudden relaxation of facial and postural tensions, and looking back he saw people who were, in a sense, not at all the same people.[5]

By the block system and the other machinery of a police terror, the Soviets can cut off many of the traditional underground institutions, and make others too hazardous for all but a few heroes. But even in such a case, human ingenuity is not completely helpless. Overfulfillment—literal obedience to extravagant Soviet demands—can be another form of sabotage; I have heard tell of one group of Moscow cynics who would go to meetings and joyfully accuse all and sundry of deviationism as a sure way to break up the party. All fanatical movements, I would suggest, are as threatened by the real or pretended deviations in the direction of perfect obedience as by the underground. Beyond all this, there remains the escape into the self, the escape of withdrawal, of what Kris and Leites have termed "privatization." The Soviet press, by its attacks on the practice, gives evidence that depoliticization tendencies are strong, and one would expect people to develop ritualized ways of responding to political exhortations without inner conviction.

In my 1931 visit to the Soviet Union, I talked with students who had decided to go into medicine or engineering, rather than journalism or writing, as more protected, less polemical and sensitive areas; doubtless, many of them were sadly fooled when, in the purges, they found themselves accused of sabotage and wrecking, or even theoretical deviations based on their seemingly unideological decisions. Ever since then, I have sought to find out whether young people were able to choose army careers, or skilled labor, as ways of avoiding such dangers; I have found some evidence that such escapes are extremely unlikely, since bright boys are already spotted in high school and compelled as well as bribed to develop their talents and deploy them; they cannot hide their light under a bushel.

[5] In a letter, Norman Birnbaum has suggested that the peasants' uneasiness was prepolitical—due to their natural reserve with urban people (city slickers) not of their kind. But he also points out that if this were the case it would not change the fundamental fact: the ability of people to be "two-faced" and to practice social concealment on the basis of minimal cues.

One of the reasons why young people are willing to assume dangerous responsibilities is of course that the rewards of success in managerial posts are very great. It has become obvious that Soviet managers are no longer held, as in the earlier years of the regime, to ascetic standards of living. It is possible that, among the abler cadres, an entrepreneurial risk-taking attitude toward life is encouraged, which makes the prospect of becoming a factory manager with access to women, *dachas*, power, and glory worth taking the risk that it won't last, and may even be succeeded by exile and still grimmer fates—a psychology which bears some resemblance to that occasionally found among professional soldiers for whom battles mean promotions as well as deadly dangers.

But monetary rewards have their own logic. The loose change in people's pockets tends to encourage free enterprise or, as it is known in the Soviet Union, the black market. The black market also enters when managers scrounge for goods in order to fulfill production quotas and so remain managers. And business as usual, like other forms of corruption, is a wonderful "charm" against ideologies, useful particularly because of its own ordinarily unideological character. Under the Nazis, both in Germany and in the occupied countries, business was often almost an unconscious sabotage of the regime: people in pursuit of their private ends violated the public rules without, so to speak, intending any resistance. They did not have to be heroes, any more than the scofflaws were who drank under American prohibition, or the fellow who wants to make a fast buck in the Western war economies. Guenter Reimann, in his book *The Vampire Economy*, tells as a characteristic story the answer to a question as to what a permit from a Party member for a certain commodity would cost: "Well, it all depends on what kind of a Party member you have to deal with. If he no longer believes in National Socialism, it will cost you a hundred marks. If he still does, five hundred marks. But if he is a fanatic, you will have to pay a thousand marks."[6]

[6] Dr. Arendt in her rebuttal criticized the relevance of this and similar incidents on the ground that they occurred prior to Germany's entry into World War II—prior, that is, to the descent of the iron curtain which protected and facilitated complete totalitarianism. Without the slightest doubt, the Nazis grew ever more ferocious as the war progressed—thus, mass genocide did not really get under way until then; nevertheless, just because of the iron curtain, it is all the more necessary to examine whether the system did ever become efficiently monolithic even when all possible restraints of a humanitarian or public-relations sort disappeared. Cf. Trevor-Roper's *The Last Days of Hitler* (2nd ed., The Macmillan Company, 1950).

In the past, we have tended to interpret such signs of passive resistance in terms of our hope for an eventual overthrow of the system from within; we have been like the Marxists who thought contradictions would bring capitalism down. Now we know that it takes more to destroy a system than its own contradictions, and we have been apt to go to the other extreme and assume that the system, therefore, since it didn't collapse, was all-seeing and all-powerful over the minds of men. Two errors common to the social sciences have worked together to this end. The first error, as just indicated, is to imagine social systems as monolithic, and as needing to be relatively efficient to remain in power. Actually, systems roll on, as people do, despite glaring defects and "impossible" behavior. We have created an imaginary image of what it takes for an institution to keep going; in fact, it can go on with little support and less efficiency. One reason for this mirage we have is that when a revolution does occur, we explain it as a matter of course by pointing to the defects of the previous system—and we fall here into the error of supposing that what happened *had* to happen. Barring relatively accidental factors, the system might well have gone on for a long while. (Incidentally, this same historicist error is an element in the overestimation of the power of totalitarian appeals; we assume, for example, that these appeals were responsible for Hitler's victory in Germany as if that victory were a foregone conclusion and not a series of reversible choice-points.) Social scientists, having logical minds and being efficient themselves—even when they sing the praises of irrationality—seldom take a sufficiently perspectivistic view of a society to see it as rolling along in spite of all the things which should bring it to a stop. In this error, of course, they do not stand alone; most of us tend to overinterpret the behavior of others, especially perhaps when we are menaced by them.

The second error, which is perhaps historically older, is more formidable. It assumes that men can be readily manipulated and controlled, either as the earlier Utopians thought in pursuit of some greatly uplifted state, or as the more recent anti-Utopians such as Huxley and Orwell have thought, in pursuit of vulgarity and beastliness. (Orwell, to be sure, exempts his proles from the ravages of ideology.) Social science is concerned with prediction, with categorizing human beings and social systems. So it has perhaps a professional bias toward cutting men down to the size of the categories, and not allowing them to play the multiplicity of roles, with the multiplicity of emotional responses, that we constantly show ourselves capable of. Thus we run into a paradox. On the one hand, we think men can be adjusted into some Brave New World because of fundamental human plasticity and flexibility, while on the other hand we do not see that men's ability precisely to fit, part-time, into such a world is what saves them from having to fit into it as total personalities. We have assumed—and in this of course we reflect our own cultural attitudes—that people must be co-operative in order to co-operate, whereas throughout history people have co-operated because to do so made realistic sense, because certain conditions were met, and not because of the psychological appeal of co-operation per se. We have, under the pressure of recent events, reacted against the older view of writers like Sumner that people and cultures can hardly be changed at all toward the view that they can not only be changed but can be easily destroyed.

Ever since the rise of the bourgeoisie and of public opinion and mass politics, people have been afraid of the seeming chaos created by the open fight of special interest groups. The fight is open because there is a press and because each group tries both to solidify its own members and to recruit others by universalizing its appeals. In the contemporary world, there are many influential men who believe that this war of vested interests, occurring within the framework of a democratic society, will endanger consensus and disrupt the entire social fabric. Totalitarianism, in fact, makes an appeal, less to people's special interests as, let us say, workers, than to their fear of all competing interests, including even their own as these are organized by lobbies and pressure groups. Having an image of society as it ought to be, as orderly and co-operative, they tend to welcome, especially of course when the going gets rough, a system which promises to eliminate all social classes and other vested interests which impede co-operation. Thus, on the one hand they are frightened by the ideal of a pluralistic, somewhat disorderly, and highly competitive society—still the best ideal in the business, in my opinion—while on the other hand, their view of men as plastic allows them to suppose that the totalitarians will change all that and transform men into automatically socialized creatures like the ants. When we put matters this way, we can see that there may be grandiose fantasies at the bottom of the fears of people like Orwell, deeply repressed fantasies of human omnipotence such as Hannah Arendt has traced in the totalitarians themselves.

For me, the most striking conclusion to be drawn from the state of Germany today, from the stories of the refugees from behind the Iron Curtain, even from the present behavior of former concentration camp inmates, is precisely how hard it is permanently to destroy most people psychologically. Once the terror is removed, they appear to snap back, ravaged as in any illness, but capable of extraordinary recuperative efforts. In extreme situations such as Dr. Bettelheim has described, people sink to almost incredible abysses or more rarely rise to incredible heights; but if they survive at all, they exhibit an astonishing capacity to wipe away those nightmares.

As the concept of social harmony and integration has misled us as to the amount of disorganization a going society can stand, so I believe that the concept of psychological integration has misled us as to the amount of disintegration and inconsistency of response that an individual can stand. Even in our society, we tell lies to ourselves and others all day long; we are split personalities; yet, with a minimum amount of support from the system, we manage to keep going. All our days we give hostages to history and fortune, and yet are able to call on self-renewing aspects of the ever filled cup of life.

A certain immunity to ideologies seems to me to be spreading in the world, if not as fast as totalitarianism, at least in its wake. This immunity is far from perfect, even in its own terms. Totalitarianism can appeal to cynics in their cynicism just as much as to idealists in their idealism. An ideology can be fashioned out of anti-ideology, as totalitarian parties have been fashioned out of an anti-party program. And a world is certainly ill-omened in which we must fear the enthusiasm of the young, and prefer their apathy, because we have learned (a hundred and fifty years after Burke) to fear ideas in politics.

We simply do not know whether, over a series of generations, it is possible to rob people even of the freedom of their apathy. Very likely people need at least some ability to communicate disaffection if they are not to conclude that only they alone are out of step. And privatization implies accepting the given regime as part of the order of nature, not to be fought by the likes of oneself—only in that way can terrible guilt feelings be avoided.[7] There comes to mind the story of a German anti-Nazi who, shortly after Hitler's coming, had taken a job as stenographer to an SS committee. Everything went well for a while; his con-

[7] We must be careful in evaluating evidence here. A group of people near Frankfurt remarked to Everett Hughes, when he had won their confidence, *"Unter Hitler war Es doch besser."* This did not mean they had been or were still Nazis, but just the opposite, namely that they were making an unideological judgment, immune as well to Occupation, to democracy, as to Nazism.

victions remained unshaken, and he continued old Socialist associations. But then one day he had a paralysis of his right arm; he could not move it at all. He went to a psychiatrist, who came quickly to the source of the paralysis, namely that the stenographer could not resign himself to the constant Heil Hitler salutes.

And, indeed, many of the defenses I have discussed are little better than forms of paralysis which, by their presence, evidence the resistance men put up against seemingly implacable destinies. I would prefer to see men fighting back through paralysis than succumbing through active incorporation of the enemy. But this is hardly an optimum way to live one's life, and we cannot be—even apart from the danger to ourselves—unmoved by the plight of those now living and dying under Communist regimes. All we can do while we seek ways to bring those regimes down without war is to find our way to a more robust view of man's potentialities, not only for evil, about which we have heard and learned so much, not only for heroism, about which we have also learned, but also for sheer unheroic cussed resistance to totalitarian efforts to make a new man of him.

The Cold War and the West:
Answers Given in a
Partisan Review Symposium
(1962)

1. What is your opinion of the position of the West in the cold war? Has the West been winning, losing, or holding its own? If you think it has been losing, or is likely to lose in the future, to what do you attribute this? Which features of the social and economic system prevailing in the West generally, and in the United States in particular, account for failures in coping with Soviet communism?

As I have said before, in many ways the very preoccupation in our country with "winning" or "losing" the cold war with the Soviet Union is a distraction from the deeper problems of an unevenly affluent society.

Writing these comments in Japan, I am reminded of the enormous impact of Western values as well as Western techniques even in countries and among social strata that are often considered (and sometimes profess to be) "anti-American": in most of the less developed countries of the world, including the Soviet Union, our vices as well as our accomplishments (including among the latter our effort to provide relatively open encouragement to talent through a widespread system of public education) are imitated in spite of periodic nativist resistance. If we do not in a game of mutual terror destroy ourselves in nuclear war, or bury ourselves underground literally and culturally in the frustrations that the cold war intensifies, we can permit ourselves to realize the extent to which the West is very much a going concern. And yet, especially in the United States, we are persuaded by illusions of omnipotence, by demogogic pressures on our leadership, and by belligerent mass media, that we have suffered one defeat after another (Cuba, Laos, South Vietnam—you name the next one) and that we must stop this process of apparent attrition by "standing firm" in the revolutionary world. . . .

2. To what degree is it desirable and possible for the United States so to reorient its policies so as to identify with the movements and leaders of change throughout the world, instead of supporting the opponents of radical social reform, as the United States has tended to do in the past? Do you think the present Administration is making any decisive change in American policy in this respect?

There is a kind of unwittingly shared agreement between many Americans and Communists on many vital issues. Both tend to identify radical social reform with communism. Indeed, not a few nationalist leaders of former colonial countries, on being called Communists and treated like Communists by Americans, may in fact conclude that that's what they will have to be if they must choose. Beginning as non-Communists in search of some versions of freedom but not willing to be anti-Communists, they may be drawn into the Communist bloc from lack of any other place to turn. Both Communist and American reactionaries tend to see the world as polarized between two sharply opposed camps, whereas it is in the interest of the whole world, as well as of the nuclear powers, to encourage the development of as many variants of socialism as possible. Unfortunately many American public and private men do not even understand that there are many variants of "capitalism" but regard the mixed economy of the United States as capitalist in some conventional sense. A similar stereotyping blinds them to the actual existence of a number of forms of communism: in the U.S.S.R., in Poland, in China, in Yugoslavia, perhaps in Cuba. If every movement of radical social change or even of protest is interpreted as Communist, then the growing domestic hysteria that we are "losing the cold war" is bound to increase. This hysteria will certainly produce administration policies that are alternately truculent and conciliatory, leading in the latter case to right-wing charges of "appeasement" and in the former perhaps to the increased power of Khrushchev's domestic and Chinese enemies to undermine his policy of "peaceful coexistence." Or more accurately, the inconsistencies in our policy make it difficult—it would never be easy—for the Soviet leaders to understand our intentions and to act in ways less threatening and dangerous to peace.

I believe that the present Administration took office with hope of making a change: while in the Senate, President Kennedy had identified himself with Indian and Algerian hopes, and neither he nor his immediate advisors were inclined to lump all "un-American" or even anti-American regimes together as Communists or as equally beyond the pale of human encounter and discourse. So, too, new ambassadors were appointed in Latin America and elsewhere in the hope of getting outside the small circle of conservative politicians, military men, and businessmen within which American emissaries had tended to become entombed, misled, and comforted. But at the very same time, the hope of some others in the Administration to fight the cold war in a more streamlined, ascetic, and "hard" way led to the growth of new illusions about the possibility of contact with or creation of antiguerrilla forces on the American side, analogous to the illusions of the French, who, defeated in Indo-China, retired to Algeria in the vain hope of applying Mao Tse-tung's guerrilla tactics among a basically hostile and anti-colonial population. Though the cosmopolitan Allen Dulles has been replaced by the parochial John McCone, it seems fair to say that the new Administration is more cosmopolitan than its predecessor, and its difficulties in dealing with the leaders of change throughout the world do not stem from vested business interests or provincial prejudices. Still, it is extremely difficult for well-educated, successful, and logical men to understand the angry, inchoate, illogical radical leaders of the new countries or the popular attitudes that underlie the radical mood of the non-Western intelligentsia—an intelligentsia that obstinately refuses to grasp either the good intentions of the United States or the bad intentions of the U.S.S.R. And in some of our embassies there is enough legacy of McCarthyism (including people who simply aren't there) and fear of vested interests and monistic thinking back home to make officials wary of too eagerly seeking contact with radical groups of students and workers and other potential leaders; not only would they be criticized for this at home, they would be criticized by fellow officials in the embassies (who now of course include operatives from the various intelligence services) and by conservatives like those Japanese businessmen who, along with Americans of like mind, tried to prevent the appointment of Ambassador Reischauer to Japan, on the ground, among others, that he could speak Japanese too well. Even so, I believe that the Administration possesses the intellectual and moral capacity to become more receptive abroad, provided that it can gain the leeway on the domestic front that it can find only by combatting the radical right rather than seeking itself to move onto rightist ground—an illusory operation since the right can always go still further right and will.

3. Does the position of democratic socialism have any relevance, in the short or long run, to the cold war (not only in Europe and in the underdeveloped areas but in America as well)?

By implication I have already indicated my hope that a variety of democratic socialisms can be encouraged in the world as alternatives to traditionally exploitative developments in both capitalism and communism. The former would seem clearly inappropriate and unlikely in the underdeveloped areas; the latter appeals to many intellectuals in those areas as a way to power and purpose when they cannot discover less violent and fanatical modes of achieving collective national goals. And in the overdeveloped countries, such as our own, it would seem essential to define new Utopian goals that do not depend on the cold war as an imperative for our national existence. In quest of these goals, what is best and most humane in democratic socialism must be rescued from the Communist label and subjected to reformation and reinterpretation. The national economy must be organized in such a way that neither disarmament nor automation are costs borne by a few displaced workers, businessmen or stockholders. And the reinterpretation must tackle problems of social organization and mass culture.

4. What are we defending in the West? Are the intellectual values and freedoms and the political and civil liberties we all affirm inseparable from the West's existing political and social institutions?

I do believe that private property—and I don't mean large corporate property—furnishes direct and indirect support for civil liberties and cultural freedom. Private property enables some men to be independent of bureaucratic and organizational pressures. The opportunity to start a small business, whether it be a publishing house, a magazine, a shoe store, or a construction company, is a genuine freedom. Moreover this freedom, by preventing monolithic control of employment, makes possible pluralistic centers of power and hence of opinion. (In the present cultural climate, private property also has far less benign aspects in encouraging surly aggressiveness and greed, and it is a task of enormous proportions—as I need hardly say—to envisage how one might separate those aspects of property that nourish the human spirit from those that corrupt it.)

Moreover, I believe strongly in the importance for civil liberties of an independent judiciary and of a bar not wholly committed to the defense of the ideological and economic status quo. A pluralistic pattern for academic organization is also a support for freedom; one could only wish that our public and parochial secondary schools could develop the traditions of freedom preserved in our best universities, private and public. And while most Americans are cynical about politicians, I am not: there is much courage and disinterestedness among our best senators and congressmen. Each congressman is in effect a "small businessman"; and while our political system is obviously out of joint in many ways, a few courageous men in office remind us of how greatly it protects political and civil liberty.

Yet institutional forms are moribund if not tied to individual attitudes. If people feel impotent and hapless, elections are only a source for bad jokes. If professors retreat from large questions to safely specialized ones, they will neither test nor defend their own civil liberties or those of others. If we do not feel that we can control our destinies either from day to day or in the long run, freedom becomes an empty word, another shell in the cold war. The cold war needs to be brought under control primarily because it can lead to catastrophe. But it has the ancillary danger that, while it lasts, the defense and reinterpretation of freedom are made far more difficult, as illustrated by the young egocentric chauvinists who call themselves the Young Americans for Freedom. Even the possibility for safely attacking unfreedom and repression in the Communist countries requires a peaceful world, that is, a world not faced with the threat of nuclear war, hence one where political and ideological conflict can be a source for growth. Those traditions in the West that make for openness and fluidity, for spontaneity and vigor in persons and in institutions, can under stress become frozen as part of the defensive armor of "the American way of life."

5. What has been the effect of the cold war on political thought and speculation in the Western world?

It is rare that anything human is an unmixed evil, and even the cold war has had some beneficent effect upon political thought. It has led many intellectuals to re-examine the values of their own culture, including its popular variant, as against an earlier xenophilia. The danger here, however, is that of moving from complaint to complacency. To some degree, moreover, the cold war has facilitated making American political thought more cosmopolitan, and even French thought has become less provincial: the Western world has been drawn more closely together. Nevertheless, the preoccupation with power has meant some concentration upon the more, rather than the less, troublesome countries; and political thought has often lost its closet quality but also its detachment, historical scope, and intellectual generosity.

I think on the whole it must be said that the cold war has been one factor in increasing the tendency to narrow, if sometimes productive, specialization among young people in academic life. On the one hand, the large questions seem politically unsafe; and on the other and perhaps even more important hand, they seem unanswerable. When governments have power to exterminate the globe, it is not surprising that anti-Utopian novels, like *1984*, are popular, while utopian political thought about a more hopeful future nearly disappears. These developments have occurred at the same time that research has become a large, often vigorous, and well-equipped area in which to make a career. All this of course is most marked in the United States; elsewhere, speculation remains less unfashionable—though it may often be arid because unlinked to any empirical context. Above all, the cold war is a distraction from serious thought about man's condition on the planet. Novelists, poets, and prophets who are concerned with man's condition find themselves at home in the private and the unpolitical. Political thought tends to become the province of men who are often very intelligent, well-informed, and crisp, but seldom speculative, contemplative, or compassionate.

Among the public at large the effect of the cold war on thinking has been to reduce it to a series of fallacious historical analogies. We are consistently warned against "Munich," for instance, forgetting that there is not much danger of appeasing Khrushchev, who has no influential American constituency, while blinding ourselves to the actual appeasement of Adenauer and De Gaulle, Chiang Kai-Shek and other dictators who are tied to us by military assistance programs. By reference to Pearl Harbor we are periodically reminded of the dangers of surprise attack; and the flight of the U-2 was defended as a precaution against such an attack when that flight may well have caused the Russians to fear we knew where their "soft" missile bases lay and hence to fear surprise attack on their side, thus exacerbating the arms race and threatening our own security. So, too, the widely prevalent idea among many serious and dedicated men that we "have died for our ideals before" transfers a pre-nuclear morality into an era when the nature of death is radically transformed by nuclear weapons. Hence the rethinking that is required is prevented by these false analogies which the cold war renders at once emotionally patriotic and intellectually convenient.

The preoccupation with big power politics narrows our view of human experience and possibility. In the never ending task of understanding man's nature, a preliterate tribe in the South Pacific may teach unexpectedly much, while the study of Soviet society, important as I myself believe this to be, may have surprising limitations. The cold war tends to turn all roads to understanding into a superhighway on which only big, fast, nonstop cars travel.

6. What are the objectives of the East and West? Are they ulti-

mately negotiable? If the answer is yes, what are the chances of nuclear disarmament. And if some form of such disarmament were achieved, what would the West's prospects be in the ensuing political, economic, and ideological competition? If the answer is no, do you think the advance of communism can be stopped without nuclear conflict?

We live in a transitional time, still dependent on balance of power diplomacy, even while seeking to move into a world order less dominated by force, that is, by the force of a few big powers and of rival elites within those powers. It seems to me conceivable that the issues at stake between Soviet and American national interests are in principle negotiable, in which stability in Eastern Europe, which the Soviet Union desperately wants, is traded for some sort of moving but partly stabilized settlement in the Middle East, Africa, and Latin America, which we desperately need. I think I recognize all the enormous and protracted problems of any negotiation with the Communist powers, and the infinite patience and persistence necessary in seeking out common interests and in persuading our adversaries that we share some aims even while differing on others. We ourselves will find it difficult to do this if we are irrevocably committed to believing that all immediate Soviet objectives are simply gambits in a campaign for world domination; and it seems to me the task of American policy to explore the possibility that the residual ideological dynamism in Soviet Communism does not entirely foreclose the possibility of interim, partial agreements whose result would be to curb the ambitious and the incautious both in the Soviet Union and in the United States. If by "East" one means the Soviet Union, I believe agreement is made still more difficult by the fact that each of the two great powers has allies who profit from heightened tension. But Communist China is another story entirely and here I am not sanguine even in principle, for the ideology and fanaticism of the Chinese have not been dimmed by history or thawed by Western contact.

However that may be, lack of faith within America in the attractiveness, political acumen, and economic viability of our society in a situation of disarmament leads to the belief that in a disarmed world Communism would win out. Such a view, while common on both sides of the Iron Curtain, does not take account of the many defeats Communism has suffered through its own arrogances and stupidities, which run counter to the nationalism, pride, and desire of many of the new countries, and the slow awakening of many people everywhere to Communist belligerence, thought-control, and imperialism. It is urgently important for us to show that the American economy is capable of disarmament while maintaining full employment, and it would seem in the interest of big business as well as of the whole society to make very concrete studies as to the reallocation of resources and, where necessary, of whole industries. A vigorous Western program of internal development, coupled with aid to the new countries, might eventually drive home the lesson that there is more than one route to industrialization and modernization, and that new routes, scarcely dreamed of as yet, remain to be invented. When many intellectuals in the underdeveloped countries now turn to communism, they do so in part because they feel it is the only way of overcoming vested interests and age-old corruptions; some indeed are attracted precisely by the apparent purity of Chinese communism. Yet on the whole I believe that men turn to totalitarian "solutions" out of desperation, when less oppressive alternatives seem unavailable. Generosity, openness, spontaneity, and pluralism in the American tradition have a greater appeal—sometimes to the very same people who also are tempted by communism and who are in doubt both as to what they seek and as to what they are. In a disarmed world, the United States would appear less threatening to such countries as Japan, where not even conservatives have forgotten Hiroshima, and perhaps the Peace Corps could eventually be seen for what it is—a mission developed out of the best American traditions—and not as a cold-war instrument. The military-industrial complex about which President Eisenhower warned in his farewell address would no longer weigh on the American economy and the American spirit; and resourcefulness might be forthcoming to achieve full employment free of the combined spur and soporific of the permanent war economy. Thus both domestic and international prospects could become less oppressive, and America might once more seek to be a hope for the world, not only a defender but a discoverer.

I can even imagine a world in which the United States and the Soviet Union, as two great powers with much to save, would seek to co-operate in the industrialization of Red China—though I find it much harder to imagine Red China's compliance with any such plan. Even now, however, in the UN and elsewhere, the United States and the Soviet Union have sometimes tacitly co-operated toward the stability, brittle as it is, of the status quo.

7. Do you think the issues at stake in the cold war so decisive as to be worth a nuclear war?

We learned the art of total war from the Nazis and bettered them at it. Today millions of Americans are so lacking in compassion and good sense that they accept the policy that requires that, after our country has been devastated, our missiles and bombers will proceed to destroy the enemy's country (hopefully, in the mad "capitalist" dream of the neutron bomb, leaving property intact). Those who advocate so-called tactical nuclear weapons of a counterforce sort avoid this savagery but impair the important line that divides conventionally terrible war from genocide. Frequently those who ask whether "the issues at stake in the cold war [are] so decisive as to be worth a nuclear war" have made wholly insufficient efforts to explore non-nuclear alternatives to strengthening the position of democracy and freedom in the world. When some assume that recovery from nuclear war will not be much more difficult than Japanese recovery after World War II, such thinking fails to grasp the tragic elements in that recovery or the extent to which it depended on the undestroyed parts of Japan and help from America. Even more, such thinking completely misses the immeasurable differences between even the mass bombings to which people became accustomed over a period of many months and the inconceivable damage to civilized life among the shattered and scattered survivors of the callousness and complacency that found no way out save nuclear war. . . .

I have never been convinced that totalitarian governments are here to stay, whatever their own boasts or the fears of their enemies, and I share the concern of George Kennan and many others for finding ways of combatting totalitarian government without resort to totalitarian weapons. I believe that, if in spite of all we manage to survive the next years without war, the want of imagination and ingenuity among ourselves that makes slogans like "Red or dead" attractive will be replaced by a fresher, less menacing vision of the human enterprise.

SECTION II

Abundance for What?

Preface

Given a disciplined and literate labor force, modern factory organization, automation, quality control, credit facilities, and a modicum of managerial ability, high productivity looks surprisingly easy. I say "surprisingly" because even now we barely realize how truly productive modern industry can be, if there is flexible planning to assure markets and supplies, including an adequate supply of technically trained people.

The case of Japan makes it clear that natural resources are no longer necessary for high productivity. The postwar boom in once ravaged countries like Japan, Yugoslavia, Germany, and France makes us ask what these various economies were doing before the war that made them turn out so relatively little? Once a society realizes that its national budget is not simply an extrapolation from a household budget—and a petty bourgeois one at that—high growth rates seem possible under a variety of political labels, in industry if not on the farm. It would seem that national ideology is less important in organizing production as such than in helping to shape the pre-industrial world, especially the educational and cultural background for the moral and intellectual disciplines that propel economic advance and make it seem worthwhile. (Several essays in the next section deal with this matter.)

Once the techniques of industrialization have been invented, shown to be effective, and rendered transportable, it is no longer necessary for newly developing societies to go through the miseries of the firstcomers, whether one thinks of the industrial revolution in Great Britain or of the wildly and cruelly forced pace of industrialization in Stalin's Russia. I agree with Seymour Melman in *The Peace Race* that, in a disarmed world, America's excess capacity could be put to use mitigating the pains of transition for the large part of the world that is poor.

The considerable minority of Americans who are still poor have tended to drop out of the political and cultural spotlight. Indeed, as Stimson Bullitt has pointed out in *To Be a Politician*, the economically depressed in today's America are a disorganized minority, living in scattered pockets of poverty, kept down by the sheer weight of the relatively affluent middle majority, and thus not available to support political leaders who can mobilize them in pursuit of their long-run economic interest. The patrician reformers who once devoted themselves to these "masses," and to some degree still do, have become even more concerned with foreign policy or with racial rather than economic equality. Slums and levels of misery exist in the United States that European countries with lower per capita levels of living would not tolerate. The momentum of distributive justice has been halted, only partly in order to focus on a much greater and still more implacable burden of misery in the rest of the globe; and little has been done to develop the kind of economic and educational plans that might help relocate and employ the undereducated rural and urban poor (who are often Negroes). In "A Career Drama in a Middle-aged Farmer," I set forth a vignette of one of the many millions of Americans who didn't make it; a man who, but for the Second World War, might never have left the state of virtual peonage in which he lived on a Missouri farm.[1]

For the past twenty years I have mistakenly assumed that what might be termed military Keynesianism had "solved" the problem of assuring reasonably full employment. This politically salutary and noncontroversial medicine for the economy, however, seems to be encountering the same sort of difficulties that some of the new drugs encounter when resistant strains of bugs get used to them. For the shift in military procurement away from heavy hardware toward the research and development of small-scale and non-mass-produced devices, along with the continuing automation of production itself, makes it possible greatly to increase defense spending without appreciably absorbing the pool of unemployed.[2] Hence we find an increasing demand for highly specialized scientists and technicians (as can be seen, for example, by perusing

[1] In "Some Observations on Interviewing in a State Mental Hospital," *Bulletin of the Menninger Clinic*, Vol. 23, No. 1, January, 1959, pp. 7–19, not included here, there are references to similarly rejected persons who turn up in the wards of our big state mental hospitals—wards where, among other places, we have hidden the people who belie the youthful, smiling, radiant, and glamorous faces in our advertisements that purport to show what an American ought to look like.

[2] See Gerard Piel, "Can Our Economy Stand Disarmament?" *The Atlantic Monthly*, September 1962, pp. 35–40. (Phi Beta Kappa Address at Harvard, June 11, 1962.)

the advertisements for personnel in any issue of *Scientific American*), while the demand for semiskilled and to some degree for what used to be called skilled labor has diminished.

Once it becomes harder to sell goods than to make them, the nature of both work and leisure undergoes changes—changes discussed at length in *The Lonely Crowd*. On the side of leisure and consumption, there is the compulsion to prove oneself a good, normal American by acquiring what Howard Roseborough and I, in "Careers and Consumer Behavior," refer to as the standard package of consumer goods. We try to outline there the relation between the life cycle and the ability to consume, taking account of the demands on one's domestic economy at various stages on life's way. "Leisure and Work in Post-Industrial Society" explores the paradoxical distribution of leisure and work, so that those with the most exciting work tend to have the least leisure, while those whose work is boring are deluged with more leisure than their lives can endure. In another essay, "Work and Leisure: Fusion or Polarity?" (with Warner Bloomberg, Jr.), this theme is explored with reference to the factory worker as his situation has changed in the last hundred years, and especially as it now exists in the unionized and relatively well-paid industries.

Careful readers of this article will see, perhaps, that the authors do not regard the industrial worker as quite so alienated as Paul Goodman, Erich Fromm, and C. Wright Mills have pictured him. Goodman, for example, in *Growing Up Absurd*, describes a garage mechanic who does not care to work on a Cadillac tail fin or fender because he knows it's all junk anyhow, a symbol of the corruption of the whole society. My own impression is that, while many workers may feel this, many others are still a long way from such detachment: they take the world much more for granted, are psychologically more "adjusted" and politically less adventurous than the concept of alienation might predict. Such workers enjoy the hedonistic fruits of the "system" and suffer its deprivations less than intellectual onlookers often suppose; and their bitterness is mixed with sufficient hope and good humor to make a focussed indignation unlikely.[3]

[3] For fuller discussion, see Robert S. Weiss and Riesman, "Social Problems and Disorganization in the World of Work," in Robert A. Nisbet, ed., *Contemporary Social Problems* (Harcourt, Brace & World, Inc., 1961), pp. 459–514. See also my essay written with Eric Larrabee, "Company Town Pastoral: the Role of Business in 'Executive Suite,'" *Mass Culture: The Popular Arts in America*, Bernard Rosenberg, ed. (The Free Press), pp. 325–37.

In an essay in *Individualism Reconsidered* ("Recreation and the Recreationists") I recommended the establishment in the federal government of an Office of Recreation, charged with making plans for greatly increased recreational facilities and personnel, once disarmament and underemployment freed resources for this purpose; and I argued that in a severe recession "it may turn out that a 'Play Progress Administration' rather than a WPA [Works Progress Administration] will be necessary to spend the money fast enough." When I make such suggestions, and in general when I discuss leisure, I often encounter the attitude that the subject is not quite serious—and certainly not a solid topic for research. We are still work-minded in our view of what constitutes a proper subject for research, even though people will agree that our general attitudes are greatly shaped by our leisure, our sociability, and our behavior as consumers.

I have encountered these attitudes especially in connection with a study of sociability, primarily at parties, which several of us began at the University of Chicago in 1955 under a grant from the National Institute of Mental Health. One essay coming out of that work is reprinted here: "Sociability, Permissiveness and Equality: a Preliminary Formulation," in which my collaborators were Robert J. Potter and Jeanne Watson. This deals with some of the consequences for the style and pacing of middle-class sociability of the loss of earlier conventions. We discuss some of the not always happy consequences of the effort of people to be casual and not to push themselves or each other around, and suggest some of the dilemmas for host and guest created by these new styles. But we proceed on the basis of very limited evidence and what we say is tentative and exploratory.

In "Some Issues in the Future of Leisure," Robert S. Weiss and I cope once again with the social management of leisure (and its relation to work), this time in terms of generational differences. Professor Weiss, as a member of the Survey Research Center at the University of Michigan, directed national surveys on how people define work, what it means to them, and what they get out of it. In this essay we draw on this research but engage primarily in speculation.

The changes in the relationship between work and leisure have been influential in the growth of suburbs and the migration of more and more middle- and even working-class people out of the central city. The view of the suburb that appears in "The Suburban Dislocation" and "Flight and Search in the New Suburbs" has been sharply challenged by a former student at Chicago, Herbert J. Gans, who has been a participant-observer in Park Forest, Illinois; in the West End of Boston (now undergoing redevelopment); and in Levittown, New Jersey. (In Park Forest and Levittown he was on the spot at the beginning of development, with access to both tenants and homeowners and planners and officials.) Gans observes that the attack launched against the suburbs by urban-bred intellectuals is often a disguised attack on the values of the nonintellectual world, particularly those of the lower-middle class —values more visible in the new suburbs than in the crowded tenements of the city. And Gans contends that people like myself should not project large esthetic and political judgments onto people in the first stages of emancipation from poverty and crowding, people who are often feeling for the first time that they have a real stake in society.[4]

I would be less uneasy about Gans's qualified and discriminating relativism if I could feel more confident about the prospects of American life as a whole. The suburbs represent both a liberation and a scattering of human energies and potentialities. And I believe that in a long life, inevitably beset by loneliness and loss, the densities and facilities of the city provide higher horizons and greater opportunities. It is conceivable that in the future great cultural variety may be possible in the suburbs even if the cities disintegrate; and I am aware that most residents of the city are, in Gans's phrase, "urban villagers" who draw hardly at all on its resources. I can leave the question open, but not without anxiety.

Similar issues arise with respect to the article Eric Larrabee and I wrote on the auto. Here, too, our attitude is that of lovers of the city who fear its strangulation by the private car. Yet we would have to admit that the car has made much possible in our own and our friends' lives and has to some extent compensated for the decentralization to suburb and exurb. Plainly neither Larrabee nor I share the fascination with cars that has come to be part of American folklore, especially among men. But the trouble is that the car is not simply a plaything or hobby; it is the creator of a set of dynamic and intractable institutions that are virtually out of social control. This is true of the individual driver who, as our paper suggests, is in but not of the stream of traffic

[4] See, e.g., his essay, "The Effects of the Move from City to Suburb," in Leonard J. Duhl, ed., *The Urban Condition: People and Policy in the Metropolis* (New York: Basic Books, 1963); and *The Urban Villagers: Group and Class in the Life of Italian-Americans* (Glencoe, Ill: The Free Press, 1962).

so that his conduct is not judicialized. And it is true of drivers as a class who act as a lobby on the entire culture.

The essay that gives this book its title was originally written as a contribution to a symposium, mostly of economists, in which the Committee for Economic Development asked individuals to discuss what they regarded as the major problems of economic development in the United States in the years ahead. I should add that I have no particularly original blueprint myself for an answer to the question, Abundance for what? Within the United States and the other countries of relative abundance we are far from even beginning to decide what we would do with the surplus if we were able to plan for a better existence.

Such questions do not appear to trouble the selected college seniors of 1955 whose interviews I report in the essay, "The Found Generation." These college students impressed me when I read their interviews (as such students have done in person) as extremely decent, lacking for the most part in greed or malice, tolerant, urbane, and friendly. Yet, given the fact that this was a privileged group, what struck me were their limitations as well as their good qualities: their general coolness, comfortable acceptance of the world, and unreflecting naïveté, disguised as realism and sobriety, about the dilemmas of existence. As I try to make clear in my essay, the older generation is in no position to point the finger of scorn, for its own values bear examination even less. And the college seniors of 1955 are not the seniors of 1963: the latter seem at once more awake and more anxious, more dissatisfied and more involved.[5]

With a few exceptions the interviews reported on in "The Found Generation" were all with young men, and a survey of the general

[5] I say this with hesitation because I have no comparable empirical survey; indeed quick scrutiny of questionnaires gather by *The Intercollegian*, the YMCA magazine, asking students in 1962 such questions as what they would live and die for, indicates in the main a picture not greatly different from that in "The Found Generation." My sense of change comes about from talking to Peace Corps volunteers, and to students active in the sit-in movement or concerned with disarmament; but cf. the general tenor of two essays by Kenneth Keniston, "Alienation and the Decline of Utopia," *The American Scholar*, Vol. XXIX, No. 2, Spring 1960, pp. 1–40; and "Social Change and Youth in America," *Daedalus*, Vol. XCI, Winter 1962, pp. 145–72. It should be recognized that the sample of youth both Mr. Keniston and I are talking about is an extremely limited one, including the more gifted, the more educated, and, on the whole, the more privileged in terms of background.

literature on youth will show, I believe, that most of it is concerned with young men. (So much is this tacit bias the case that David Potter has recently argued that discussions of American character, including my own, are really discussions of male character.[6]) In "Some Continuities and Discontinuities in the Education of Women," I try to say something about what the opportunities and hazards of abundance have been for college-educated women, and how their situation has changed since the feminist movement of an earlier day. Indeed I see the residential college as presuburban, just as the Oxford colleges may have provided a model for suburban development in both England and, later, this country.

At the University of Chicago in 1958 I gave a series of lectures under the title, "The American Future," in which I discussed a number of the issues considered in the essays in this section. The final lecture was "The Search for Challenge," which, like the others, was tape-recorded. Paul Goodman, in one of his recent essays, has ridiculed the idea of building artificial mountains and ski trails as a "moral equivalent" for anybody (I suggest it in the lecture only for the young), and I recognize that my proposals, here as elsewhere, are far from matching my critical diagnoses.

"The Search for Challenge," written before the Peace Corps, proposes something like it: a civilian corps analogous to the Civilian Conservation Corps during the Great Depression. An idea for which there seemed little chance in the Eisenhower period has since blossomed, thanks to the response to Kennedy's campaign speech at Ann Arbor and to the dedication of Sargent Shriver and his staff. There are virtuous as well as vicious circles in history; one good idea can lead to another, one "impossible" proposal to another, until our very idea of what is possible changes. History keeps catching up with us, and in seeking to anticipate the future, our critical faculties are among the few assets that stand between us and what Veblen called "the *vis a tergo* of brute causation."

What in *The Lonely Crowd* are spoken of as the veto groups in American life are immensely strong, so strong that it is astonishing when anything gets accomplished over alert and well-organized opposition. The veto groups represent not only interests, in the old-fashioned sense of economic blocs, which could conceivably be persuaded or

[6] American Women and The American Character," *Stetson University Bulletin*, Vol. LXII, No. 1, January 1962, pp. 1–22.

bought off in building a new program for our domestic life, but also vested ideologies, set and sometimes curdled ways of seeing the world —and these, it seems to me, backed by all the rhetorical momentum of the cold war, are even stronger than they were a dozen years ago. Even so, intellectuals in America would be wrong to use these obstacles as an excuse for not thinking about a better future. Such a future may never come into being in America, but it might in some other country; and hopefully, in the world that lies ahead, every man's patriotism will be planetary.

Careers and Consumer Behavior
(WITH HOWARD ROSEBOROUGH, 1955)

We have in this paper availed ourselves, perhaps too freely, of Professor Lincoln Clark's encouragement to present a congeries of questions, impressions, and more or less educated guesses concerning the life cycle of consumption in America—a large order. Following anthropological practice in monographs, where the life cycle is described from birth to death, we shall proceed chronologically, from the child as consumer-trainee to the young and not-so-young adult, the old, and the decedent. The members of preliterate tribes, however, cannot usually be said to have careers; and careers, in the sense of a life plan wrapped around an occupation, complicate consumption and lead us into the bewildering variety of social-class consumption patterns. Moreover, tribes are not supposed to change (at any rate, the ethnographer is there for only a moment of history), while we have had in mind throughout our work the historical issues of what is changing in career styles and consumption styles. Since we cannot write a symphonic score and introduce these many themes concurrently, this paper demands of its audience that they keep more than one idea in mind at a time.

I

In the summer of 1954, the Kroger Food Foundation made an experiment. They turned several dozen pre-teen boys and girls loose in a supermarket, telling them they could have twenty items free, without any limits on what they chose. (According to the sponsors, the idea was based on the rather fantastic suggestion of a "world's fair for children" in *The Lonely Crowd*, a proposal as to how consumer free choice might be developed.) Recorders, human and mechanical, observed the proceedings and a group of social scientists are now examining the results. What was immediately evident, however, was that the children, in addition to picking up watermelon and pop for immediate consumption, filled their carts with the very sorts of things their mothers might have taken, such as sacks of flour and meats and vegetables. They did not select—perhaps in that setting they did not feel quite entitled to—the cameras and other toys which the supermarket, as a one-floor department store, carries in addition to groceries, nor did they pick as much candy and ice cream as had been predicted.[1] It would seem as if anticipatory socialization[2] had occurred, in which these children had been trained, at home and by the media (perhaps at school, too, in the "junior home economics" of a book like *Let's Go Shopping*), to view themselves as prospective householders and to take an adult role. (We don't mean to imply that this socialization was the result of deliberate parental or societal decision—many of the parents would no doubt have been surprised to see how "well" the children behaved when on their away-from-home good behavior.)

At the same time, it may be likely that the parents of these children were involved in what we might term "retroactive socialization," in that meals reflected children's tastes as influenced by the media and each other, with breakfast cereals or Coca-Cola serving both age groups (much as many comic books do). For today, it is our belief, a general lowering of barriers is going on: between the age grades, between the sexes, between regions of the country, and between social classes, with the prospect in view of a fairly uniform middle-majority life style becoming a major American theme with variations.

The *theme*, a set of goods and services including such household items as furniture, radios, television, refrigerator, and standard brands in food and clothing, shows a considerable uniformity throughout American society: it encompasses the (steadily rising) national standard of living. Some seek to level up to it, and some level down, with the

[1] Boys bought slightly fewer, but more expensive, items than girls—a sign perhaps of the future "male" shopper, extravagant but narrow, as if overdetailed or sparing purchasing of household items were "women's work." Boys, of course, would be less likely than girls to identify with their mothers in the role of shopper.

[2] This concept owes much to Robert K. Merton's formulations; cf. his article with Alice S. Kitt, "Contributions to the Theory of Reference-Group Behavior," in R. K. Merton and Paul F. Lazarsfeld (eds.), *Continuities in Social Research: Studies in the Scope and Method of "The American Soldier"* (Glencoe, Ill.: The Free Press, 1950), pp. 87–89. We may think of anticipatory socialization as a kind of psychological hope-and-fear chest the individual accumulates as he imaginatively transcends his membership group.

result that quality differences are minor, and expense-concealing rather than class-revealing. The *variations* include both embroideries and elaborations on this standard package and, more importantly, the setting given this package by the home and neighborhood; the neighborhood in turn involves such class-bound services as schools, churches, clubs, and civic amenities. While possession of the standard package, the theme items, carries membership in the broad band of the American middle class, the variations identify one as the possessor of a specific life style, localized by region, subclass, ethnic group, and occupation. Social mobility in America is made easier by the ability of the family, through minor variations (in terms of expense and complexity), to adapt the standard package to a new peer group—much as one can buy parts that will make one's Ford look much like a Mercury.

In childhood and adolescence, one builds the standard package into one's anticipations, and the young married couple will expedite its acquisition—at first, or ordinarily, in an apartment. But by young adulthood anticipation begins to assume, at least in the white-collar strata, a more specific form, for the husband's occupational peers and superiors, and to a lesser extent the wife's neighbors and friends, provide models for what the family's style will be at the peak of the husband's career; it is here, of course, that variations enter. Meanwhile, as the husband advances in his career and as children arrive, the package will be moved, probably geographically, possibly socially, nearer to the community that symbolizes his final occupational status. As we shall see, this destiny is compressed for the skilled worker; it may be protracted until late middle age for the corporate vice-president. Even so, parts of the "dwelling complex"—the schools, clubs, cars, plus inconspicuous elaborations of the standard package—will be acquired in anticipation of the career peak.

This is not the only cycle for consumer behavior: we propose the hypothesis that it is increasingly typical. There are, of course, many Americans even today who have made money faster than they could possibly anticipate; their resocialization does not begin until after they are rich, and often it is painful.[3] Others have their anticipations so

[3] Some political consequences of this painfulness are suggested in D. Riesman and N. Glazer, "The Intellectuals and the Discontented Classes," *Partisan Review*, XXII (January–February 1955), 47–72; also in *The Radical Right* (New York; Doubleday, 1963).

structured by their subculture as virtually to eliminate discontinuities and discretionary areas; for an example, we can refer to a study, which is in some ways the antithesis to the Kroger experiment, by the social psychologist Manford Kuhn.

Kuhn asked a group of Amish and of matched non-Amish children in Iowa what gifts they would most want to have. The "American" children wanted toys: dolls, electric trains, and so on (these being things, of course, their parents expect them to want). The Amish children, rigorously brought up on first-class farms and, save for baseball, not allowed to share in the general youth culture, wanted such things as a team and wagon, an oven, a tractor. Though eleven or twelve years old, they already saw themselves as grownups; indeed, only by anticipatory socialization that deprived them of what many Americans would consider a normal childhood, could the Amish youngsters be kept "to home," safe from the seductions of the urban and secular world. Moreover, for them as for their parents, useful producers' goods such as handsome tractors and barns moderated the consumption asceticism of the sect, and permitted reward of the faithful in fine equipment useful if not essential in agricultural success. Indeed, only in a rural area can children enjoy and use adult equipment in quite this way, in which increasing access to the world of work becomes, like Tom Sawyer's fence, a kind of eventful fair whose pleasures only pall with time; but by then the Amish are mostly hooked, unprepared in tertiary skill or in energizing consumer passions to enter the middle-majority market. They are ready in turn to become unyielding Amish parents, relatively unaffected by retroactive socialization and hence compelling their children to imitate them unequivocally; the age-grade barriers remain firm, and the children, short of occasional instances of revolt, must accept the adult world on adult terms.

The Amish are, we suggest, an exception to many of the generalizations one might develop about the careers of Americans as consumers. But before we leave them aside, we should underline the point about their expensive farm equipment, in order to foreshadow our discussion of "conspicuous production," a kind of corporate consumption in which the energies displaced from individual consumption by sumptuary rules are channeled into impressive or luxurious or stagey ways of doing business. Early observers noticed that American farmers tended to overmechanize, as contemporary observers might notice that American manufacturers may tend to oversplurge on new plants and machine tools, and perhaps the Amish have been ever so slightly of this world in this so-easily rationalized area of producers' vanity.[4]

II

Anticipatory socialization (or what some social psychologists prefer to call role-taking in the sense of playing at a role in fantasy) occurs at all ages and in all areas. It occurs, of course, in all cultures, but what is striking about American life is that people are prepared for roles their parents have not played, indeed, that no one yet has played: they are prepared, in terms of motivation and social skill (a large component of "know-how"), for jobs not yet invented and for consumption of goods not yet on the market. (If children are to surpass their parents, both the job market and the goods market *must* expand.) It would appear that the children in the Kroger food-store experiment had learned at home about the basic food necessities, and also to distinguish secular shopping days from ceremonial gift occasions, and it would seem in general that what they learn from their parents is a kind of basic set of domestic arrangements: foods as "necessities," furniture as a quantitative rather than stylistic concept, and the "need" for such durable home furnishings as stoves, refrigerators, and television sets. In contrast, what they learn from their peers is a set of styles and moods of consumption, "affective" consumption beyond and around the basic domestic items.[5]

We can, quite speculatively, connect this progression with Eliot Freidson's observation that children from kindergarten years through the second grade prefer contact with the media in company with their families; in practice this means that in early years they prefer television to going to the movies or reading comic books. The nature of much television advertising—foods, soaps, cars, refrigerators, furniture, brand-name clothes, even beer and cigarettes—educates the child, as well as his parents, in what goes with what in the "domestic economy" of the average American; he also learns what his parents think about all this. By the sixth grade, the children prefer the movies, and their own

[4] Manford H. Kuhn, "Factors in Personality: Socio-cultural Determinants as Seen through the Amish," in Francis L. K. Hsu (ed.), *Aspects of Culture and Personality* (New York: Abelard-Schumann, Inc., 1954). We need not stop to encompass the irony of the Amana Society, whose handsome freezers and refrigerators, products of co-operative asceticism, may often be the prime adornments of an urban housewife's ménage.

[5] Cf. the stages set forth in Jean Piaget *et al.*, *Moral Judgment of the Child*, trans. Marjorie Gabain (Glencoe, Ill.: The Free Press, 1948).

company while viewing them. The movies introduce them to a larger and more complex world of affects and relations, of styles and skills—a new or modified context for the possessions advertised in the other media.[6] Likewise, the jobs these children will begin to hold in adolescence will ordinarily be in the tertiary areas—soda-jerking, baby-sitting, delivering goods and telegrams, camp counseling, waiting on table, and so on—rather than in the primary or secondary areas. This is consonant with our general picture of adolescence as a time of gregarious, consumption-oriented activity, as a time of sports, music, dancing, dating. The school system itself increasingly comes to terms with this youth culture by seeking to turn out teen-agers "adjusted to life" in terms of citizenship and consumption rather than mathematics and welding; in part, of course, this represents a triumph of liberal-arts abundance over traditional and technological demands, while in part it represents a breaking down of the barriers between school and not-school.[7] Indeed, the school itself, like other "tertiary" buildings (bars, resorts, and plants and offices of companies engaged in "conspicuous production"), is frequently more modern than the home: it prepares one for the ranch house, for the relaxed style.

We may restate this in Parsonian terms.[8] The child learns at home, with assistance from the media (principally television), the goal-directed elements of consumption; of course he also acts as an opinion leader, influencing his parents, for instance, away from any notion that water, as compared with pop or a cola drink or Koolade, is a potable substance for children. He learns from his peers (with assistance from the movies) the expressive elements in consumption, the affective embroidery about the basic package that he takes as given in the home. He learns in school something of the adaptive functions of consumption; he becomes prepared to take his place in neighborhood affairs by courses in civics or in home economics, and by the general group-oriented atmosphere of the newer schools. However, he probably learns

[6] Cf. Eliot Freidson, "The Relation of the Social Situation of Contact to the Media of Mass Communication," *Public Opinion Quarterly*, XVII (1953), 230–38.
[7] See further, D. Riesman, "Teachers Amid Changing Expectations," *Harvard Educational Review*, XXIV (Spring 1954), 106–17.
[8] Especially, T. Parsons, R. F. Bales, and E. A. Shils, *Working Papers in the Theory of Action* (Glencoe, Ill.: The Free Press, 1953), chap. iii; also Parsons, "The Integration of Economic and Sociological Theory," The Alfred Marshall Lectures, Cambridge, England, 1953 (unpublished).

much less than formerly about what (continuing to paraphrase Parsons) we might define as integrative purchasing, including the allocation of savings to insurance and other investments. Katona's evidence that, in all strata, life insurance amounts to 3–4 per cent of income[9] would seem to indicate that people are not taught to save the way they are taught to spend; if Janet A. Fisher could repeat in a decade her study of age-graded patterns of spending and saving,[10] we might expect to find saving and investment less prevalent than today in the younger age groups, and static "zero saving" (as against dissaving) less prevalent than today even among those over sixty-five. As something amounting to tenure (seniority in the lower ranks, tacit mutual protection against discharge in the upper) spreads to the non-academic population, people will look increasingly to their employers rather than to their own efforts for financial security in old age, and consumption will increasingly move toward making life now, comfortable and "well-rounded." (Even the serious-minded young, for whom well-roundedness in the conventional sense is not an ideal, are not concerned with the distant future in terms of goal-directed investment in their own careers and nest eggs, but rather in terms of the state of the world in general or of its underprivileged portions, near and far.)

Something of this sort, we suggest, forms the social-psychological background of installment buying, not among the traditionally "improvident" hand-to-mouth, or television-set-to-bedroom, lower strata, but among the middle classes who would in earlier days have saved up for durable goods. Marriage itself, so to speak, is now bought on the installment plan, following the "anticipatory socialization" of going steady from the seventh grade on: people are marrying younger than ever, without waiting until the man is settled in his career, much less until the woman has a dowry. And, once married, even though wage equalization brings high starting incomes, the young adults are trained to spend up to and beyond them in rapidly accumulating the full package

[9] George Katona, *Psychological Analysis of Economic Behavior* (New York: McGraw-Hill Book Co., Inc., 1951), p. 105.
[10] "Income, Spending, and Saving Patterns of Consumer Units in Different Age Groups," in *Studies in Income and Wealth* (New York: National Bureau of Economic Research, 1952), XV, 77–102. As against this, we must set the rise in savings of the most recent years, and also perhaps the education in saving given many by the GI Bill's nest-egg provisions. Cf. also James Duesenberry's works, especially *Income, Saving and the Theory of Consumer Behavior* (Cambridge, Mass.: Harvard University Press, 1949).

they have in general learned to consider basic. As Marvin Sussman shows, the parents on both sides will help out if they can (they do not want to lose their young so young), by tactful gifts in money, in kind, and in services such as baby-sitting.[11] New items and revisions of older models can be gleaned from *House Beautiful, Better Homes and Gardens, American Home,* and other service magazines that, as Lloyd Warner found, are widely read in the middle and even the lower strata.[12]

These and other media, it goes without saying, have enormously accelerated the transmission of fashions between the classes, the regions, and the age grades. Dr. Harriet Moore of Social Research, Inc., informs us that the average anticipated life of living- and dining-room furniture has shrunk from twelve to seven years within the last two decades. As Americans live longer, their possessions (from grandfather watches to refrigerators) would seem to succumb to obsolescence faster. In more general terms, the immediate indulgence that was once a lower-class characteristic, in comparison with the delayed and calculated future-oriented saving of the middle class, has now infiltrated the middle class so that increased income increments are spent rather than saved—and, indeed, dissaved through installment buying. We might speculate that the child who has been somewhat permissively brought up, who has had a hand in family consumer choice, who has earned and spent substantial sums in the teen-age period of ersatz grown-up culture, will as a young married person assume as a right many of the items that for his parents were delayed and planned-for luxuries. The capital equipment for domesticity with which such a person starts out must now be, for millions of people, very substantial; it is paid for during the early years of marriage, as well as maintained and expanded by "do-it-yourself" activities in leisure from the paid job; there is little saved up with which to educate the new generation or to protect the old from inclement weather; indeed, an air conditioner may soon be added to the standard package.

The teen-ager's electric shaver, his jalopy or classy convertible, the young couple's washing machine and dryer—there is in some of these purchases an element of *rites de passage,* a sort of self-declared initia-

[11] Marvin B. Sussman, "The Help Pattern in the Middle-Class Family," *American Sociological Review,* XVIII (February 1953), 22–28.

[12] See table of magazine reading in W. L. Warner and P. S. Lunt, *The Social Life of a Modern Community* ("Yankee City Series," Vol. I; New Haven: Yale University Press, 1941).

tion in a culture that has notoriously not systematized the age grades. Parents can no longer, with the drop in barriers, raise their children on a lower standard of living than their own, or see them start out in marriage at a markedly lower status—any more than those rare women who still have servants can keep them on a cheaper diet than their own. By the same token, children rebelling against their parents seldom abandon the standard package, but rather reject some of the parental variations on it; even a few such modifications are enough to alter the style or *Gestalt*.

Evidence for the breakdown of generational differences is less easy to come by than evidence for the breakdown of regional ones. Russell Lynes recently discovered, in talking with Sears Roebuck officials, that they no longer put out regional catalogues and that, in furniture, there are almost identical tastes in all sections of the country, so that if a certain sofa covering is chosen by 50 per cent of the purchasers in New England it will hit 49 per cent in the Southwest and 52 per cent in Oregon. Likewise, Eric Larrabee has recently observed that pizza dishes have spread to Midwest towns that have never seen an Italian; an ethnic homogenization of taste must of course accompany the regional one.

III

A number of studies, including those of Kuznets on the shares of the upper-income groups and those published in *Fortune's* series on the Great American Market,[13] indicate the increasing pace of homogenization of possessions between the top ranks of factory workers (notably where there is more than one employed person per spending unit) and the lower ranks of the professional, managerial, and entrepreneurial people. A study done by S. Stansfeld Sargent in Ventura, California, indicates that the "dwelling complex" of a skilled worker will not differ in any obvious way from that of an air-plant physicist—even life-style differences seemed minimal.[14] To be sure, those parts of California where everyone is new may be a special case, but we do believe that

[13] S. Kuznets, *Shares of Upper Income Groups in Income and Saving* (New York: National Bureau of Economic Research, 1953); the Editors of *Fortune*, *The Changing American Market* (New York: Hanover House, 1955).
[14] S. S. Sargent, "Class and Class Consciousness in a California Town," *Social Problems*, I (June 1953), 22–27.

the differences between the social and occupational strata are coming more and more to lie primarily in consumer attitudes, not in consumer behavior or the objects bought at any given moment; more precisely, the attitudes influence behavior only when the whole life cycle is taken into account. To a degree, for the office and factory workers, the "poverty cycle" that B. Seebohm Rowntree found in York, England, a half century ago[15] still holds, though at a far higher level: an early peak is reached, followed by a plateau and a slow decline—modified, to be sure, by the secular rise in real income, especially among factory workers.[16] However, Warner Bloomberg, Jr., a thoughtful participant-observer of factory life, has commented on differential meanings of the cycle for men and for their wives. He points out that the young man, before marriage, has been well supplied with funds, often living at home: "he may well indulge in tailor-make suits, expensive whiskies, and high-priced restaurants if they also are not high falutin' . . . always more object- than experience-oriented, with fun correlated with expenditure of money, even in sex—the more high-priced the woman, the better she must be."

"This period," he continues, "is usually brief, ending as soon as he marries, though the emphasis on recreation as a highly valued activity remains: that is, he will continue to want to have his sports, his nights with the boys for cards and drinks, his dancing, etc. However, he must now acquire the capital goods of a home or apartment to be furnished (he already has a car). Over a period of time he becomes more and more engrossed and expert in the 'consumption' of these hard commodities and the recreation-orientation slowly subsides under the pressure of family obligations and the nagging of his wife. But once the most difficult period, financially, of the marriage is over, the emphasis on recreation returns, especially travel, sports, and the like, although those who acquire homes (and the number has been increasing at a fantastic rate) are forever involved in the purchase, repair, and replacement of the hard goods of the domicile and of the car—involved as

[15] B. S. Rowntree, *Poverty: A Study of Town Life* (2nd ed., New York: Longmans, Green and Company, Inc., 1922).

[16] In their valuable paper, "Savings and the Income Distributions," Dorothy S. Brady and Rose D. Freidman emphasize, as Katona's work also does, the importance of the reference group for a relativistic income analysis: if real income rises for "everyone," everyone will think himself no better off and will not save new increments. *Studies in Income and Wealth* (National Bureau of Economic Research, 1947), X, 247–64.

buyers and users (and stealers, we might add) of tools, since 'do it yourself' has been part of their occupational culture for a long time."[17]

While, for the men, graduation from (or early leaving of) high school brings liberation, even if followed by the gradual constrictions of domesticity, for the girls the end of high school is viewed with real distress, for it means the end of the pleasant round of dates and opening of the unromantic prospect of early marriage (in this stratum, the seamy side of marriage cannot be hidden from the young). While in an earlier day all they expected of marriage was a pay check, a home in repair, and a spouse who behaved himself, they now have learned—anticipatory socialization again—to look forward to wider alternatives; for one thing, they can protect themselves by their own jobs from having to marry the first man who asks them (nor are they, with contraception, so likely to have to marry because pregnant). "More often than not," Bloomberg observes, "the girls who cry at night as graduation approaches have been introduced to a vague but compelling notion of a richer life, mainly through the mass media and the high schools. More than any others in the working class, they are experience-oriented rather than object-oriented. The men, still in the main occupied vocationally by thing-centered jobs and avocationally by the traditional skills of the hunter or the ball player or the homebuilder, are a big drag on the largely unformulated desire of these girls to build into their lives some *expertise* in consumership which, by an emphasis on experience, could provide the variety and alternation in routines which they believe to be enriching.[18] Travel comes the closest to doing this for both of them, and the working people are getting to be great travelers as time and money permit."[19] No wonder that travel agents have begun to be aware of the guidance function they control; a group of them, re-

[17] Statement in a letter to the authors.

[18] Owing to these attitudes, working-class girls often have an easier time attaining white-collar jobs and lower-middle class status than their male compeers do, and their ability to pass their aspirations on to their sons has been a continuing dynamic in the American drive for upward mobility. Mark Benney also reminds us of the "concealed" mobility the lower-class girl may have in affairs with men of higher social position—after which the girls are never quite lower class again. Moreover, he has noticed how continuously working girls give each other gifts—at showers and like occasions—and comments that gift buying, in all classes, tends to be the most socially sensitive form of consumption, analogous to the money girls persuade their boy friends to spend on them.

[19] *Ibid.*

cently organized for adult education at the downtown branch of the University of Chicago, met with Reuel Denney to discuss the emotional aura in which people increasingly were buying their way, often on the installment plan, "from here to eternity." Travel becomes a recurrent second honeymoon, a compensation for the disillusion built into the first by the contrasting expectations of the worker and his bride; and no doubt the home itself, as the man works his evenings and weekends around it, also reflects these tensions and some "built-in" compensations for them.

To return to the life cycle of the educated strata: here it is not contrasting expectations drawn from the youth culture, but the role of the corporation or other large employer in dictating a specific style of life, that creates adult tensions between the spouses. At one level, brilliantly portrayed by William H. Whyte, Jr.,[20] are the wives of management who cannot drive Cadillacs because the fuddy-duddy president drives a Buick; a little lower down are the wives who must hear their husbands groan on returning from a business trip because the latter must conceal the fact that they live much better "abroad," on the expense account, than their wives can afford to at home, on a mere salary. Still more unhappy are the wives of the Negro school principals described by a student in a recent seminar: These principals are required by their position to live in a large house and to drive a good car (though not too large and too good) but their salaries have not kept pace and they have had to take outside jobs; since these (dairy farmer, trucker, redcap, bellhop, bartender, gas station attendant, and so on) are too lowly for school principals to hold, they must do so under an assumed name and in a neighboring community. The strain on both spouses, caught in a status conflict and in a series of concealments, can well be imagined.

In general, we believe that, despite the foreshortening of time perspectives in all social classes, the middle-managerial groups still take a good deal longer than the working classes to acquire the full domestic package; and they also, again unlike the working classes, cut down on the size and housekeeping demands of this package as they age. Thus, a study done under Everett Hughes in Chicago indicated that the middle-class person usually begins his adult life in an apartment, where he may live for the first several years of marriage; then in his late twenties

[20] See William H. Whyte, Jr., *Is Anybody Listening?* (New York: Simon and Schuster, Inc., 1952).

or early thirties he buys a house (and the neighborhood to go with it) in which to raise his children; after the children have grown and flown, the house becomes a heavy burden, and the bereft couple move back to an apartment, though of a different cast, so that the cycle does not quite end where it began. (In Chicago, he is perhaps also more likely than the working-class person to move because Negroes have "invaded" his neighborhood, for he clings less tenaciously to real estate, including "his" church, and more tenaciously to the values of nonviolence.) Though people when they buy their homes are not fully conscious of the likelihood they will stay in them at most for two decades, the general pattern in their milieu certainly casts its shadow before.

While a house cycle of some sort may be characteristic of the middle class as a whole, at least in large cities, ambivalence about putting down "roots" is especially characteristic of the younger executive groups that Whyte has studied for *Fortune*. He notices that they would engender criticism by premature purchase of an overimpressive ménage (even if a private income, rather than a bet on future advance, could sustain the cost), and that their careers would also be jeopardized by overcommitment to a particular peer group and neighborhood, which might tie them too closely to people whose careers may not prove commensurate with their own. On the other hand, Charlie Grey is invited by his boss to migrate to a fashionable suburb and to join an expensive country club before he feels quite ready to swing it (though the boss has decided, in a self-fulfilling prophecy, that he *is* ready for the move); accepting, he passes the point of no return.

In terms of family life, this means that, while the husband is to some extent stabilized by his career line within or among firms in a given field or set of fields, his wife and children must be prepared for moves and for the domesticity of transiency, though with only limited knowledge of, let alone satisfactions from, the occupational culture that imposes these requirements. As W. H. Whyte has observed, a man's move up is almost always also a geographic move, and if the wife is not to redo her hair and replan her life while she packs, she must subtly anticipate the promotions her husband may or may not get, while not antagonizing the current peers or baiting the current superiors who see in the consumption field no less than in the office the margins that distance them from their prospective successors. In the new locale, the children (whose own life cycle may not jibe comfortably with this) will attend a slightly different school, the parents join a slightly different club, meanwhile rearranging the standard package in the home so that old objects carried by the moving van will combine into a new *Gestalt*.

Those among us who pull up stakes with difficulty should not, of course, read our own malaise into the transients for whom schools and the army have already provided anticipatory experience. Moreover, in the middle strata of which we are talking, the growing interregional uniformity of the country, doubtless in part the product of mobility and migration, and of the effective system for distributing goods and services, makes moving easier financially and psychologically.

To be sure, there remain millions of people, not only Amish, who do not buy the standard package, much less transport it, either because they fall far below the $4000–$7500 per year range that *Fortune* speaks of as the Great American Market, or because they have not been trained to want it. Thus, there certainly remain in less free-floating parts of the country many working-class folk who will use increments of income to buy real estate, not for living only, but for social security, and who will reject many of the amenities in and around the standard package as irrelevant. That is, people in the working class do not see the home as an expendable consumer good but as an investment for old age—something like the West Room into which the Irish peasant retires when his heir takes over the farm. Likewise, workers may buy happenstance items that, in a different combination, form part of the middle-class standard package, but these items will reflect special earning-power bonanzas and may even be compensations, as the Negro Buick or Cadillac sometimes is, for inability to buy the standard package as an entity and an identity.

At the other end of the social scale, the upper end, the standard middle-majority package operates as a different sort of pressure: not as an aspiration, not as something one prepares for in imagination or in childhood paradigms, but as a limitation, as a kind of sumptuary guide. Contrary to the situation described by Veblen, it does not seem to us to be the members of the upper class who dictate life styles, which then filter down; these residuary legatees of the past are influenced as much as they influence, and the location of style leadership, like other leadership, is ramified and, to our mind, obscure. The upper Bohemians have a hand in it, as avocational counselors, just as the upper middlebrows have a hand in diffusing high style to the general population through the mass media. The upper-class youngster in school wears blue jeans and drives an old car; on graduation he wears Uncle Sam's jeans; save in a few enclaves, he avoids high fashion. If he enters the corporate hierarchy, it is, as already pointed out, his official rather than his genealogical rank that will determine the make of car he drives. (As for the academic hierarchy, we recall the profuse apologies of an instructor at a Kansas college for driving a Lincoln—he explained he had got it cheap; and in Cambridge were heard many wry comments on a colleague who drove a red Jaguar.) On the whole, in a tug-of-war between the occupational culture and the social-class-and-kinfolk culture, the former is likely to win out. The father of one of the authors, a consulting internist, felt compelled to appear for consultations in patients' homes in a car at least the equal of the doctor's who called him in, much as he disliked display; he ironically referred to the car as his "delivery wagon." (In his own office, where other colleagues would be less embarrassed, he could afford shabbiness.) In one of our Kansas City interviews, a housewife bitterly and repeatedly complained about her husband's air-conditioned Cadillac, which he insisted was necessary for selling trips. One investigator recounted the violent objection of a group of clerks in a large city bank when management insisted on their wearing white collars; though many of them had originally come into the bank because of its genteel white-collar aspects, they felt envious both of the salaries and the shirts worn by the working class and if they could not have the one, at least wanted the comfort and economy of the other!

As we have just said, the upper-class person entering on an occupation will have to be careful not to carry with him his class consumption patterns. This is not easy for him since some of these patterns are bred in the bone, so to speak, in his accent and the way he looks and carries his body. But he must make the effort because of the still far-from-evaporated cultural defensiveness of the middle-class businessman, for whom a Harvard accent is not only a doubtful idiosyncrasy but an aggressive one. Provided he conforms in the office, the upper-class businessman may find a hobby on which his excess income may be spent without rivalry-creating inflation of his life style; that is, he will early buy the standard package in one of its more elaborate and expense-concealing variations and then look around for something to collect—a cause or charity, possibly—or have more children and educate them better than the average for the class, or even save something. But, in general, the standard package operates here as a restriction on gaudiness, in part because the older sorts of conspicuously flamboyant objects (footmen, for instance) are no longer made, and in part because equalitarian ideologies influence people to level down as well as to level up.

The main, and not insignificant, difference is that the upper-class person will carry the standard package lightly, expand it more quickly, and renew or discard it more ruthlessly, whereas the person of lesser income and less assured position will strain under the load and be toppled by unemployment, serious illness, or miscalculation.

IV

Everett Hughes has described (in conversation) a company that brought in its Harvard Business School graduates too soon for its own industry position. Individuals have even less leeway for miscalculation in seeking status through consumption, and they have far less chance of recourse to government to bail them out, unless they have gone the way of whole strata that possess political leverage. Despite the extent of childhood training for consumption, there are some omissions—how to buy a house, for instance, is seldom discussed. Professor Bossard in his studies of family life has stated that the children reflect the influence of their parents when they are in turn parents, and act as they think their parents would have.[21] This often works, but by no means always; we may recall Crevel, in Balzac's *La Cousine Bette,* who, having admired when young the mansion of his employer and dreamed of a house just like that, when he did become rich "with eyes closed and purse open he went straight to Grindot [the same architect]," an architect then completely forgotten. "So," Balzac writes, "dead glory lives on, supported by retrospective admiration." More usual, in America, will be the case where the parents' home pattern is not opulent enough for the children, or relevant to altered moral climates; this largest of durables is in some ways least attended to (in terms of such problems as are admirably spelled out by Robert Woods Kennedy in *The House and the Art of Its Design*).[22] Like the hobby-boat builder described in *Time* whose boat could not be got out the door of the shack in which he built it, some home buyers may not allow enough room for all the developments of their married life. Some failures in anticipation they can repair by their own carpentry, but some may involve the neighborhood, the school, the possibilities of transport, and they may find them-

[21] J. H. S. Bossard, *The Sociology of Child Development* (New York: Harper & Bros., 1954).

[22] New York: Reinhold Publishing Corp., 1953. Cf. also R. J. Neutra, *Survival Through Design* (New York: Oxford University Press, 1954).

selves overinvested and overcapitalized when they should be able to pull up stakes.

It is true, as we have already noted,[23] that the young married protoexecutives in the Park Forests of America become very adept at pulling up stakes, and at being at home everywhere and nowhere. They learn to adapt to the neighborhood and to adapt the neighborhood to themselves, and this is made possible by the very existence of the standard package, items of which can be bought or serviced or transported anywhere. It is rather like a theater in the round, or omnipurpose stage, or like those two-piece outfits advertised in *Seventeen* or *Charm* or *Mademoiselle* that can be modified to fit almost any occasion. But it is also true that these young people who have invested so much capital in a style of life (including, as a major element in style, their marriage to each other) have withdrawn a certain modicum of their energies from their careers as such. They have done this, in the first place, along with the rest of the population, by not working such long hours; the whole suburban package depends, in large measure, on the two-day weekend. In the second place, they have rearranged somewhat the career commitments both of the husband and the wife. The latter agrees to earn money only to support the family in the manner to which it has, in anticipation, become accustomed; she enters the labor market to bring home a new car, a new room, a vacation canoeing in Minnesota, but not to "have a career" in the sense of seeking status and satisfaction in advancement on the job and in enlarged work horizons. The former, the husband, agrees to earn enough money to keep the standard package away from the repossessors, and, since the standard package grows in size as new products come on the market or old ones develop new angles (as cars have done), to keep up with its elaborations. For this, he needs merely to get on a seniority ladder—and a recent survey of young people made by the Social Research Service of Michigan State College indicated that they think seniority the fairest way of distributing promotions. That is, seniority plus fringe benefits from the wife's working will keep the family up with the rising standard of living.

But beyond that the husband need not go, and in fact may be discouraged from going by his wife. Russell Lynes, in "What Has Succeeded Success,"[24] discusses the results of a survey of women college

---

[23] Citing W. H. Whyte, Jr., "The Transients," in *The Organization Man* (New York: Doubleday Anchor, 1956).

[24] *Mademoiselle*, September, 1954, p. 101.

students and recent graduates. Typical is the comment of a University of Texas girl: "I think definitely that a job should not consume your life. It should be one in which you are interested and which enables you to live a well-rounded life." Says another: "I want my husband to be ambitious but not dangerously so"; and still another: "I don't want him to have such a high executive position that it would ruin his health or personal relationships with his friends or family." Presumably, too, she would not want him to have so high a personal standard of living as to put strains on friends or family.

We may conclude that the American economy is poised between the ease with which people move from one income gradient to a higher one along well-worn and hence anticipated steps, and the frictions that family and friendship create for the markedly mobile individual. In a recent article on the strains on kinship which mobility creates—the old problem of the "poor relation"—LeMasters describes a family that got rich quick during the war as the result of the boom in building; they moved to a nice suburb and traded in an old Plymouth on a new Buick, and their children, entering a new and wealthier high school, helped educate them to their new fortunes, while the parents' siblings were left far behind.[25] The author does not observe that the shift from Plymouth to Buick is not only one of price but perhaps even more one of style: the Chrysler line, as recent market researches tend to show, appeals to the sedate and stable, while the General Motors line appeals to the more ambitious and flashy; thus, the move to Buick is not quite the same, on the average, as the move to, say, De Soto. (The Ford line is again something else: a "hot" engine for the young people of all ages, a vehicle perhaps for maleness rather than mobility.) General Motors and Chrysler devotees are, in other words, like Republicans and Democrats, partly accidental aggregates and partly prisoners of different self-images. (We suggest that the devotees of Consumers Union are perhaps like the political "independents" in such a constellation, who make it a point to look at the machine and not at the Briggs or Fisher personality!) But at the same time, as this instance implies, there may be shifts of identity in the course of the life cycle; we can imagine this builder ending up with a Mercury convertible after having dowered his children with Oldsmobiles and Buicks, to show himself that he is still quick on the uptake.

[25] E. E. LeMasters, "Social Class Mobility and Family Integration," *Marriage and Family Living*, XVI (1954), 226–32.

V

There is a lack of any thoroughgoing histories of the careers of individuals as consumers in which one might align in parallel columns the job history, the family history, and the consumer history, and relate these in turn to general cultural developments that link the life cycle with the cycle of the husband's industry or with the social fate of his ethnic and other identities. Talking recently with a group of young German industrialists, one of the authors was told of a frequent practice among middle-aged executives who feared they might be slipping: they would sink their savings into a baronial mansion, buy a Mercedes-Benz, and otherwise move into a new stratosphere of luxury, in a desperate hope either to salvage their careers or to compensate for feared occupational downgrading; they could do this in part because among contemporary Germans thrift has become even less conceivable than for Americans, and they might as well go out in a blaze of glory. On the other hand, the University of Chicago's research among older people in Kansas City has turned up a few elderly individuals who cannot bring themselves to live out their lives on an annuity basis: intellectually they know "you can't take it with you," but emotionally they cannot adjust to the altered value of the dollar and are too old either to learn carpentry or to appreciate paying carpenters for an hour's work what they once learned to regard as a good day's wage. We do not know whether such people loom large in George Katona's surveys; what is striking to us is how rare is this provincial reaction, as against the many people whose lifelong anticipatory socialization prepares them to spend now what they have now, and more besides. One of our Kansas City respondents, whose existence had been wrapped up in her daughters' social life, when asked what she did when the daughters married and moved away, said that she slept more—and redecorated the living room. Still another became more active in church work—and redecorated the vestry.[26] As such women get still older, it will be interesting to see what, if any, arrangements they make for caskets and grave lots; Robert Habenstein, making a study of the career of the funeral director, has observed a growing vogue for caskets which cradle the dead on cushions, as well as for hearses which do not jolt the body—though on the

[26] These examples are taken from Irwin Deutscher's unpublished study of "Husband-Wife Relations in Middle Age," based on long interviews with parents whose children have left home.

whole there is evidence that, despite the revival of churchgoing, the standard of dying has hardly kept pace with the standard of living.[27]

VI

Having now followed the individual from childhood to the grave, we would like in these concluding remarks to touch on the specter of uniformity, both in careers and in consumer behavior, that specter which haunts so much of our, and European, thinking about America. At the outset, it should be clear that whatever uniformities do exist are at least in part defenses against the no less prevalent instabilities of the life cycle. Thus, the rising standard of living inevitably alters the character of the neighborhoods in which people live; neither restrictive covenants nor landscaping can bring permanence. Usually, the only way to stay figuratively in the same place is to keep moving. This is true on the career side too: the more people seek security in large, pension-bestowing organizations, the more likely they are to be shunted around the country, or at least to have to be emotionally prepared for such moves; this is because the large organization, providing for its own future, does so by diversification, decentralization, and a large research and development program, including executive development.

The new suburbs to which people in such organizations move are heavily age-graded. Levittown outside Philadelphia, for instance, has few children over fifteen and few adults over forty-five.[28] A householder in this situation is not likely to plant trees to shade his prospective great-grandchildren. (Such uniformities of instability are only in small degree the product of atomic threats and insecurities.) The shifts in the labor force implicit in what we have said mean that parents cannot plan their children's specific careers any more than they can plan their living rooms. At most, they can head them toward a range of careers within a broad middle-class spectrum of permissibility, and they do this by sending them to school and college and seeking to instill the motivations currently in demand.

What is left of the old-family upper class is an exception to all this. A number of these families possess summer estates—private arboreta— with homes for all the children, homes that upper-middle-class children,

[27] "The Career of the Funeral Director" (Ph.D. dissertation, University of Chicago, 1954).
[28] E. D. Baltzell, "Urbanization in Lower Bucks County," *Social Problems*, II (1954), 40.

brought up on the contemporary standard package in vacations, might consider shabby. Likewise, Charles C. McArthur, studying the career plans of Harvard students, discovered that those, and only those, from upper-class homes and the "St. Grottlesex" preparatory schools knew what they were going to be—and became it: they followed in their fathers' or uncles' footsteps as lawyers, doctors, trustees; they carried these occupations almost as inherited occupations, and often against their personal preferences.[29]

In general then, the upper-class person is prepared for what lies ahead because of a certain constriction of choice and aspiration. By contrast, McArthur's research shows that the mobile upper-middle-class boy's career aims are apt to be vague: his aptitudes predict what will become of him occupationally better than any statements he makes. He hasn't been there, in terms of a parental model; what he wants is to achieve and maintain a certain style of life, within the range of his limitations and capacities. In much the same way, he is prepared to become a consumer of the standard package as this may have developed up to the time when he is ready to enter the market: there will be a kind of ecumenical freedom about his consumption, not bound to sectarian or parental dogma.

Indeed, one of the few restrictions on the consumption of the mobile person is the resistance of the upper class to the *arrivistes* by exercise of the strategy of conspicuous underconsumption; in this way the already arrived attempt to impose their own limits on those who would become their peers. So it occasionally happens that a man of working-class or lower-middle-class origins who has risen fast to the possibility of splendor, and hopes by splendor retroactively to compensate for his origins and the frustrations of his rise, discovers soon after he has begun flamboyant spending that this devoutly longed-for goal is now looked down upon. Anticipatory socialization has played a trick upon him: he rose from the working class by learning to postpone gratifications, but the working class taught him what gratifications to seek; now these, when he at last "deserves" them by striking oil or the FHA, are once more denied him. He may as a result spend part of his fortune supporting politicians who attack snobs, the elite, Easterners, and Harvard

[29] C. C. McArthur, "Long-Term Validity of the Stong Interest Test in Two Subcultures," *Journal of Applied Psychology*, XXXVIII (1954), 346–53; also, McArthur and Lucia B. Stevens, "The Validation of Expressed Interests As Compared with Inventory Interests: A 14-Year Follow-up," *Journal of Applied Psychology*, XXXIX (1955), 184–89.

men generally; and this is especially likely when so many people have made money so fast that he is not a lone Great Gatsby seeking admission to an established Society, but finds many of his new peers in the same boat as he, capable of extrapolating the tycoon pattern decades after the demise of Newport, Bar Harbor, and Tuxedo Park.

For such people—whatever uniformities there may be in the beholder's eye—there are real choices to be made both in career and consumption; inheritance, far from foreshadowing the way, merely indicates what is not to be done, not to be bought.

In any event, we must disabuse ourselves of the common notion that mass production, in the contemporary sense, is responsible for consumer uniformity. A dozen decades ago, Alexis de Tocqueville observed the American preoccupation with comfort, as well as occasional revivals of "fanatical spiritualism" in protest against it. He wrote:

> In democratic society the sensuality of the public has taken a moderate and tranquil course, to which all are bound to conform: it is as difficult to depart from the common rule by one's vices as by one's virtues. Rich men who live amid democratic nations are therefore more intent on providing for their smallest wants than for their extraordinary enjoyments; they gratify a number of petty desires without indulging in any great irregularities of passion; thus they are more apt to become enervated than debauched.[30]

This was long before people had cars with automatic steering!

Thus it seems that it was only in the Gilded Age that enormous disparities—between a Hearstian castle and a hovel—existed in American consumption; indeed, as we have become relatively emancipated both from grinding poverty and grinding inhibition, and as, in the same development, we mix work and play, youth and age, and the sexes, we lack the resources as well as the limits that would make "great irregularities of passion" seem appealing; only in our entertainers, including our political figures, do we look for these—many of them seem living substitutes for a historical novel. Tocqueville was writing, we are inclined to think, less about an extant America pictured in reportorial detail and more about an ideal-typical "America," an abstraction based on his imagination of what society would look like where egalitarian tendencies predominated. This involved him in the danger that we, his successors, also face: of standardizing our image of standardization to

[30] A. de Tocqueville, *Democracy in America*, ed. Phillips Bradley, (New York: Alfred A. Knopf, Inc., 1945), II, p. 132; see also pp. 105, 128-29, 134-35.

fit our constructed type; and Americans, trained in adaptability, may also co-operate with their interpreters. While we agree with Tocqueville that great irregularities, whether for good or evil, tend to be weeded out, does it follow that the great middle belt is thereby made more uniform?

We must notice, first of all, that the flexible and adaptive uniformity of this belt, to the degree it exists, is a departure from the traditionalism of the two social extremes. For instance, the lower-class diet, in its regional and ethnic enclaves, is highly standardized. In most countries, peasant customs quaint to the observer are uniforms to the observed. When this "standard package" crumbles in the revolutions of taste brought about by the media and mobility (and the anticipatory socializations these bring in their wake), the first consequences are distressing; W. J. Cash speaks of "the thin jazziness which seems to be the necessary concomitant of industrialization everywhere";[31] and the Delta-born Negro, making $100 a week at Inland Steel in Chicago, may seek to imitate at once the Negro rich as pictured in *Ebony* and his memory of Snopes-like planters of a generation ago. In seeking to be "quality," he will hardly study *Consumer Reports* but will leave one standardization to pursue another; his children, however, may be free to make somewhat more discriminating choices.

The traditionalism of the residual upper class has, of course, never imposed peasant monotony on its members, and even the occupational monotony of careers already referred to exists as a pattern to rebel against. On the consumption side, Richard Coleman's study of Kansas City society indicates that there is a considerable number of sets—the horsey set, the music-and-culture set, the civic-minded set, and so on—all of which overlap in terms of families, neighborhoods, and occupations but subdivide in terms of friends pursuing a wide gamut of leisure interests, vacationing in different spots and in different ways, and welcoming by virtue of similarity of interest newcomers, properly introduced, brought to Kansas City by expanding and decentralizing commerce and industry. Very possibly, this is a way of saying that Kansas City has no true upper class, in the sense of a stratum with a markedly non-middle-class life style; in the much larger city of Baltimore, it is our impression that Society is far more inaccessible and tightly knit, with proper grooves for consumption more deeply cut: thus, stables seem to

[31] W. J. Cash, *The Mind of the South* (New York: Doubleday Anchor Books, 1954), p. 293.

be staples. But this would only tend to confirm our judgment that the rising middle class engulfs the old upper class, modifying its idiosyncrasies while giving its young people the much wider range of middle-class styles of life among which to choose.

With this preface, let us take one more look at our "standard package" of middle-class consumer items. For each family, the items have a somewhat different history, once we go beyond the increasing group that comes with the house or apartment as part of a complex: this coffee table is ancestral, that mat on the wall collegiate, and the new cover on the Sears borax sofa was glimpsed in a *Harper's Bazaar* read at the hairdresser's. More important, each of these items, and each area in and around the house, is differentially tinged with affect: for some the kitchen may be the center of drama, for others the garden, for still others the rumpus room. The standard package allows for both expansiveness and expressiveness, even while (to return to our Parsonian metaphors) it represents one's integration into the society and allows, once it is bought and paid for, further goal-directed moves in preparation for an open-ended future.

Even so, it can be argued that these differences within the frame of the standard package are fairly marginal; it is in the leisure area beyond the package, for which the package is only a home base, that greater differences exist. No single leisure pursuit (if we except television-viewing) enlists as much as half the population, including auto travel during vacations, which, according to A.A.A. estimates, brought 66,000,000 Americans onto the highways last year. Spectator sports such as baseball appealed to about 10 per cent of the population in 1952, movies and drive-ins to about 35 per cent, fishing and hunting to many millions, but to no majority, even of males. (These percentages must be compared with the much higher ones reported by Katona for nonconsumer behavior, such as the 80 per cent who own some life insurance.) Lyman Bryson, in *The Next America*,[32] has described the millions of new enthusiasts for the arts, and Reuel Denney in a penetrating essay has suggested how the hi-fi passion of American scientists allows them to identify at once with the gadgeteering do-it-yourself impulse and with imported elements of high culture, thus modifying both.[33] Denney writes:

[32] Harper & Bros., 1952.
[33] See "The Scientific Corps—A Sixth Estate?" *Confluence*, III (1954), 220–29. This paper as a whole draws heavily on the bibliography concerning leisure compiled by Professor Denney as well as on many specific suggestions by him.

The scientist modifies class conformist consumption of gadgets by setting forth in his consumption pattern a gadget quite his own. The scientist, oriented more toward things than persons, finds a "thing" to become passionate about which has the delicate qualities of a human organism and the function of conveying one of the greatest of the human arts. The scientist puts pressure into his social life because of his "social distance" at work from his clients among workers and consumers, and from the preoccupations of his co-elite among the industrial managers [for whom the scientist and his technical adjuncts are often counters in a game of conspicuous corporate consumption]. The scientist seeks clear and simple symbols of consumption because, being highly mobile, he shares with the executive class rapid geographical and class moves through regions of disparate styles of consumption. The scientist . . . seeks to display consumption in items that are less invidious than distinctive. In this sense, he has an ascetic morality of consumption.[34]

Nevertheless, Denney concludes, the scientist's "occupational progress seems to have been faster than his ability to define himself outside his work."[35] The advertising man who is so often the scientist's enemy within a company has probably had more influence even on the latter's leisure and consumption than his own corps has had.

Studies of consumer purchases of durables indicate that each new addition to the standard package has taken less prelude time to reach peak sales, and the same is probably true of industrial capital goods. The organizational revolution in communications and advertising is in large measure responsible for this: Americans can hardly escape "consumer literacy" even if of a more rhetorical sort than *Consumer Reports* teaches. As the early enthusiasm of the newly literate vanishes, and as the standard package becomes standard operating procedure for the middle millions, can we continue to look mainly to our large organizations for inventive spending of the surplus, whether on big, glamorous bombers or bomb plants, on big, glamorous superhighways, or on the increasingly standardized elements of conspicuous corporate production? We doubt it. The scientist who has given us our model of the hi-fi fan—so much so that this equipment can now also be bought as part of the standard package—may be looked to for other pioneering in the arts of consumption and leisure.

[34] *Ibid.*
[35] *Ibid.*

A Career Drama in a Middle-aged Farmer
(1953)

Recent work with the Kansas City Study of Middle-Age and Aging has directed my attention to the crises in the lives of certain men who are forced to sudden awareness that they are far behind the expectations normal for their age-grade. Thus, I have observed a number of graduate students in social science come to the age of thirty and suffer a "nervous breakdown" at the prospect of having to leave the university and take up a career as an independent intellectual entrepreneur in a small college or research project. Hanging out a shingle becomes for such students a much more decisive separation from the "extended family" of the graduate school than it was to leave home for school, or even for the Army.

What makes this step so inordinately difficult is that these young men are, due to war service or similar interruptions, older than others who have just gained their doctorates and are starting out on their own: hence they feel more is expected of them and that they will be less protected in a continuation of the student role. (Indeed, every large university contains a periphery of aging students who cannot bring themselves to sever the tie that binds.) The person who is a boy when expected to be a man can find ways of postponing realization of this, but certain rather vaguely delineated dates, such as the age of thirty or thirty-five, or the attainment of a doctoral degree, may penetrate his defenses; despite the absence of formalized age-grades and initiation rites, individuals in the United States are of course not entirely on their own in determining when they should be doing what.

Sociological generalization on these matters is difficult: We know all too little about perceptions of age, beyond adolescence, or about the sorts of dates and events that, in different groups and social strata, stimulate defensiveness or awareness. Nor do we know much about changes in these dimensions, for instance whether young women, if they become aware that the average age at marriage is dropping, face any earlier that traditional panic of becoming old maids, or whether young men, aware only vaguely of bureaucratization in American life, re-arrange the traditional dates at which one is expected to be independent.

These were some of the considerations I was pondering when I had the opportunity to act as a consultant in the case of a psychiatric patient at a veterans' hospital, a forty-four-year-old farmer who appeared to be caught in such a crisis of aging. When I returned from a conference with the patient and later with therapists and social workers who had directed his course in the hospital for the two weeks since his admission, I made some informal notes for my own use and for the confidential scrutiny of my colleagues in the Kansas City Study. Since these notes (which, it should be observed, slight the extensive discussion of the patient's medical history and somatic complaints) reflect a sociologist's preoccupations, their lacunae as well as their specific contents may be of interest to clinicians; in what follows, I have merely made a few further alterations to insure safeguarding the patient's identity and, without modifying the somewhat telegraphic style of my original report, to elucidate several of those shorthand expressions by which social scientists communicate with themselves and each other.

The case of Harold Ackley had been worked up by an enterprising psychiatric team: there were reports from the psychiatric section chief, the internist, the social worker, one of the nurses, and several of the psychiatric residents—all of whom had managed to establish some rapport with this shy and withdrawn man; my comments are largely based on their data and conclusions, supplemented by my own brief observation of him.

Ackley was born on a Kentucky hill farm, one of eight children, the second of five brothers. He went through grade school, exhibiting neither unusual proficiency nor unusual deficiency. Save for his war experience, he has lived all his life as a subordinate member of a family-farm enterprise. Four of the eight have left the farm; one brother, younger than Ackley, and said to be the father's favorite, has the original farm with his wife; the father rents two quarter-sections, a large farm for those parts, and runs the farm aided by the oldest brother, by Ackley, by a younger brother, and by a crippled sister who keeps house. Two sisters have married and moved away. The mother died when Ackley was about ten. He never mentions her.

The social participation of the Ackley stay-at-homes has never been great. They went to church in the past, but seem now to have dropped out. Once a week they go to the neighboring small town, stand about, attend an auction—Ackley's favorite recreation—and come back. Occasionally they take the crippled sister to a meeting of other cripples in a nearby town; they much resent having to do this.

The father makes all purchases and decisions; as perceived by the patient, he is still vigorous and patriarchal. He recently bought a $3000 hay baler, much to the fury of the brothers, who felt this was extravagant, as they could readily bring hay in by hand. Ackley himself is not paid any cash for his work, but gets an occasional handout for tobacco or clothes. The older brother appears to Ackley as fearless and upstanding; he argues with the father, throws his weight around, and upbraids the patient, who is afraid of him. The younger brother makes no claims.

For many years prior to World War II, Ackley had dreamed of leaving this farm, where his father dominated him and his older brother frightened him. But he had never been out of the county, never seen a farm superior to his father's, never had the courage and resource and imagination needed to make the break. He had no friends and had never dated a girl. When the war came, it seemed to him that he could make a dash for freedom, and, though exempt as a farm laborer, he enlisted in the Army in 1942.

This move, however, did not seem to have been entirely voluntary, for Ackley was apparently kidded by brothers and neighbors about his draft status, and urged by them to enlist. And it is my impression, hard to support with so inarticulate a man, that he harbored a dim awareness that his life was a serflike one, unbecoming to a man.

(I am acquainted with a Vermont hill family whose second son, a corpulent boy of twenty who bears the sad nickname of Piggy and who has never left the environs of his village, claimed his farm deferment to avoid the draft. His older brother, whom the war turned into a cosmopolite, sending him to Archangel and the Mediterranean, pleaded with him to enlist; so did his neighbors and agemates. But this youngster, who has always been afraid to ride on a bus to a nearby town, stubbornly refused—and thus lost what many who know him thought his last chance to escape the "isolation ward" of a back-country farm.)

While for perhaps most of the young men whom it seizes, or who seize it, the Army serves as a catapult to thrust them away from home, it does not appear to have had this consequence for Ackley—nor for some of the graduate students I have encountered who, after fighting through severe campaigns in Europe or the Pacific, return to the university as if they had only dreamt they were away. Ackley seemed aware of this: he told his doctors that the Army had been his hope of change, but implied that it had not worked out that way.

His army experiences emancipated him only briefly. To be sure, he three times had intercourse with prostitutes (the first time in his life he had been out with a woman), and he said this had changed him. How? It had made him less shy with girls. But since he had never had a date since his return, this "change" does not seem very great. What did he do in the Army? Kitchen police mostly; no combat; a correspondence course in Diesel engine maintenance. He found it no less irksome than the farm and after three years could think of nothing better than to return to the farm.

In the Army he had fallen off a truck (in boyhood he had fallen off a horse, and thought perhaps his difficulties stemmed from that). Because his back hurt, he went to a doctor nearby—apparently a chiropractor—who found an inflamed prostate and gave him massages, sent him on to a quack who gave him massage and medicine. He felt better and returned to the farm. But life at the farm went even less pleasantly for him than before he went away. His brother seemed bossier, his father critical of him. Ackley decided he was losing his memory; he kept mislaying tools and not recalling where they were. Driving a tractor, he could be happy all day alone; but working around the barn, as he used to like to do, made him edgy and fearful when his older brother was near. Finally, one day he left the farm and went to the nearest Veterans Administration hospital.

Why had he come? He told the doctors vague stories of backache, but since they could find nothing tangible to account for it they put him on the admitting psychosomatic ward and talked with him for two weeks. Very soon, the backache story dropped away; he said something about a pension—somebody had told him he could get a pension; but then that dropped, and he came to talk more and more about his desire to get away from the family farm and the hope that the doctors and nurses could somehow help him make the break.

The clinical findings showed a slightly but not seriously enlarged prostate, a partial deafness in one ear, a "low normal" intelligence but great forgetfulness; thus he could not remember a list of numbers longer than seven. Since he was withdrawn on the ward, did not interact with anyone, but simply stood watching others interact—as if the ward activities were a daily auction—a tentative diagnosis of schizophrenia was made. I was one of those who pointed out that, if he were "schizophrenic," so were quite a few of the less successful, less advanced farmers in this country; indeed, the whole tribe of Ackley stay-at-homes seemed not so sharply different from this one who had come to get help.

When I first visited Ackley my immediate feeling was: here is the prisoner, called before the warden. He had the close-cropped hair, the fatigues, the constrained look of a prisoner; if he had had a cap, he would have stood and twisted it. He was stocky, sunburned, shy and timid. He showed affect only when he said that, if he returned to the farm, he would probably never leave it again—his family would talk him out of it; he had no confidence he could stand up to their pleas. Could they get along without him? They were managing now—they had when he was in service. Could he get along without them? Could he try it for six months, returning to the hospital if it didn't work out? I discovered from Ackley that he had never seen a large dairy farm or indeed any sort of farm other than the hill sort like his father's, or less extensive ones. He simply did not know what varieties of farm jobs were available for such as he, feared that if he mislaid a tool he would be fired by some surly boss, and since he would end up at home, he might as well go back there, or better still, stay in the hospital where it was so much more pleasant than home, where people were friendly, did not bark at him, did not kid him. (When he went to town now, he said, people didn't speak to him—not that he had any feeling of being persecuted; he was just ignored. This seemed to be hardly less true of his whole family.)

Ackley expressed himself with forcefulness rare for him in declaring that he had come to the hospital in the hope of getting away from home. It seemed evident to me that he was dimly aware that his father, hale as he was, would not live forever, and that when the father died, Ackley might be at the mercy of the older brother—indeed, since the farm was rented, there might be minimal assurance of continuity. Or the father might leave whatever rights he had to the favorite son. I thought of Everett Hughes's interest in which brother gets the farm when under conditions of nonprimogeniture; Ackley "by rights" should have had a claim, but clearly he could not conceive running a farm, even a small one, on his own—his father handled all market transactions, indeed all the money. (Professor Hughes has observed that, in some farming communities, the son who is most likely to inherit the farm is the one—very rarely the oldest—who is around thirty when his father begins to think about retiring: the son will still be on the premises, fully equipped as a farmer but not too independent, and prepared to shelter his father in his declining years; in the absence of primogeniture or fixed custom, families are unaware how often this pattern repeats itself, but think of the decision as to who inherits the property and who gets a share to be paid off in cash as peculiarly their own.)

Ackley expressed confidence that, if he should obtain another job, and if then his family wrote him urging him to come back home, he could withstand the pressure: it was only in their physical presence that he felt weak. All of this taken together seemed to indicate that that he had some dim awareness of facing a career crisis. He was getting to the point in years where it would become inconceivable to him to leave the farm—it was now or never. As already indicated, he expressed some sense of not living as a man should; very likely the Army had strengthened this sense, by giving him the same uniform, the same privileges, as others who were not so radically different from him, yet had homes of their own, received wages, and did not depend for very life on their father's bounty.

When, after my visit with him, Ackley was led out through the ward, the men on their bunks did not greet him; though he had been there as long as they, it appeared that he was still a stranger, even if one makes allowances for the withdrawn and limited participation of many of his wardmates. At the same time, he obviously expected no response from them. Although he had stated that he enjoyed auctions more than anything else, yet he never bid and just watched; on the ward, too, he never "bid." (He also stated that his family at home listens to Grand Old Opry—not too isolated for this refraction of their "own" culture; he could not name any other radio favorite of the Ackleys'.)

After my "interview" with Ackley, I had the opportunity to discuss his case with the psychiatric team. I cannot say enough for the humanity and patience of this group, who were moved by his plight and were endlessly understanding in trying to draw him out and to help him to help himself. It was felt that he had only three choices: to become a chronic patient, to return home (and remain a chronic dependent), or to find another farm, not too radically different from home but more benevolent and less stressful and taxing. It was amusing to hear one psychiatrist from Central Europe say he didn't see how Ackley could possibly hold a job other than on the family farm—he had exalted notions of American efficiency (as of course many Americans do), whereas an Iowa-born doctor and I agreed that Ackley was hardly more incompetent than many farmhands and herdsmen, and that in a time of farm labor shortage he almost surely could get and keep a job. I added that the state agricultural colleges were increasingly turning out young men who had taken courses in human relations, who would perhaps not be as rough on Ackley as the latter feared, being influenced both by their education and by the labor shortage. (We were all inclined to doubt whether Ackley could exist independently in a city, no matter how lowly the job; perhaps we accepted too readily Ackley's own feeling of being a displaced person from the farm.)

It was the general consensus of the group that, if Ackley decided that he did want to take a try at a farm job, the social worker should seek to turn one up for him near the hospital (which does not itself run a farm)—a place where he could go protected by the understanding that he was going for a six-months' trial, able to return to the hospital at any time. Meanwhile, it was recommended that he spend some time on an open group-therapy ward where he would be encouraged toward independence, helped by his fellows as well as the therapists toward solidifying his belief that a man should stand on his own feet. In this discussion, it appeared to me that the high value put on independence not only expressed the value judgments of the staff but those of Ackley himself: it was for this that, in his inarticulate way, he had come to the hospital in the first place. It would have been possible to tell him that he had best go back "where he came from," to the family farm, and to adjust him to this course by reminding him that not everyone has to have an independent career, or to be a hero; in this way, his feelings of having failed in life would have been assuaged rather than made use of to demand of him more active participation in his own fate.

Quite conceivably some anthropologists would regard these implicit decisions in favor of independence as ethnocentric, as premised on American individualism and careerism; they might have stressed as equally important the quasi-peasant values of the remote Kentucky hills. Unfortunately for this program, Ackley had "seen Paree"; he had also now had the experience of pyschiatric concern in a hospital. Doubtless, if his first try at more independent outside living failed, his psychiatric team would reconsider, and might confer with him about the alternative of going home; in that sense, the decision would always remain up to Ackley, awed as he might momentarily be by the hospital personnel. Indeed, it would seem that one great problem of the hospital staff was to get across to him that they were not bosses like his father and older brother, or the Army noncommissioned officers; on the whole, I felt they had managed to convey something of this.

And this brings me to another way of looking at the drama of his career, less in terms of his own "vital statistics" and more in terms of the general societal developments which happened to coincide with his own life-cycle. One of these was of course the war itself. The war, moreover, had speeded up the processes of change in farming techniques which were perhaps symbolized for him by his father's purchase of a hay baler; his own wartime course in Diesel engines would hardly suffice to prepare him for the sort of skilled entrepreneurship now demanded of the farm operator. Finally, the war had enormously accelerated the spread of psychiatric thinking: the fact that Ackley could come "for free" to a VA hospital, that he could after a *pro forma* discussion of backache come out immediately with his real grievances, and that these would be understood and taken seriously by thoughtful and ingenious therapists (able to stop, look, and listen despite their own career problems and the waiting army of cases)—these, too, were signs of the secular changes that were contemporaneous with the aging process in the individual himself. Full employment was another such change, coupled with the greater willingness of college-trained farmers to cooperate with a hospital's social worker.

In general, as I have indicated elsewhere,[1] I believe we must look for such questions of timing and coincidence in seeking to understand the undemarcated steps by which a man ages psychologically, or interrupts his "career of aging" as Ackley did by enlisting, thus achieving his first, if abortive, taste of freedom. And we must not omit to consider the changes in the public image and suction power of different professions which appeal to people who are or want to be on the move. Ackley, I would guess, would never have gone directly to consult a social worker, let alone a sociologist interested in geriatrics, nor would either of these have been likely to enter his horizon. Medicine provided, so to speak, an opening gambit, legitimizing his quest for supportive treatment in his career problem; doctors (that is, men and women in white coats)

[1] See "Some Clinical and Cultural Aspects of Aging," *Am. J. Soc.* 59: pp. 379–83, Jan. 1954, reprinted in *Individualism Reconsidered* (The Free Press, 1954; Doubleday Anchor, 1955).

could talk with him fairly freely, once the conversational openings of backache and prostate had been gotten out of the way. Their world was so remote from his that he could enter activities, such as group-therapy sessions, on their say-so which would otherwise have been closed to him by his own culture and his own inhibitions. From a sociological perspective, many contacts of doctor and patient may involve a mobility factor for the latter (as Jurgen Ruesch, Martin Loeb, and their coworkers have observed in their investigations of social aspects of illness), and sometimes for the former as well. More generally still, transference and countertransference may be regarded (as Ruesch and Bateson do in *Communication: The Social Matrix of Psychiatry*) as processes of mutual acculturation.

Contrary to what is often thought, the aged were not necessarily better off when such processes were slower and more unconscious, and in a pre-industrial peasant culture Ackley as he grew older would not necessarily have fared better. Speaking of the treatment of the old among the French peasantry, Charles Fourier wrote in 1808 in *Social Destinies*, that because they have no function they "are neglected, importuned, secretly railed at, and often harried to the grave . . . reproached every hour with their useless existence." World War II, among its many other, mostly evil consequences, managed to bring very different psychiatric attitudes into the near-peasant world of Harold Ackley, and to open up new areas of interpretation and expectation in the conference rooms of the Veterans Administration.

Work and Leisure: Fusion or Polarity?
(WITH WARNER BLOOMBERG, JR., 1957)

As if reflecting the gulf which widened between work and leisure with the rise of the factory, there has been some tendency to regard leisure as not quite a serious topic.[1] Only occasionally does a student of factory life note the consequence of divergent leisure patterns for the forms of industrial relations.[2] We know of nothing for contemporary workers comparable to William F. Whyte's *Street Corner Society*—an incredibly conscientious and sensitive "time-study" of the seldom interrupted leisure of the unemployed "corner boys" in a Boston slum. In the present situation, where specialist students of industry and of leisure seldom meet, we have decided to concentrate on our own speculations and on our limited personal experiences. The latter (which we don't dignify as "research") are almost entirely confined to the Midwest.

Each of us has argued in earlier writings that (1) leisure must provide meanings and satisfactions, even challenges, which work no longer

[1] Thus, while noting that leisure can be of crucial importance, R. F. Tregold (*Human Relations in Modern Industry* [New York: International Universities Press, 1950]), devotes but three pages to it (cf. pp. 70–72), while C. H. Lawshe et al. (*Psychology of Industrial Relations* [New York: McGraw-Hill, 1953], pp. 50–53) sees leisure rather narrowly in terms of its effects on productivity. Conversely, many books on leisure (e.g., Martin and Esther Neumeyer, *Leisure and Recreation* [New York: A. S. Barnes, 1947]) make only tangential contact with work as setting the time, energy, and often compensatory nature of play. A greater sense of the dialectic between work and leisure can be found in Foster Rhea Dulles, *America Learns to Play* (New York: D. Appleton-Century, 1940), and notably in Johan Huizinga, *Homo Ludens* (Boston: Beacon Press, 1955).

[2] Thus Alvin Gouldner (*Patterns of Industrial Bureaucracy* [Glencoe, Ill.: The Free Press, 1954]) observes that miners and millworkers behave differently among each other and with supervisors and sees these patterns refracted in their behavior off the job. Elton Mayo, of course, devoted passionate attention to the reveries and off-the-job worries which the Hawthorne Plant workers brought from their often underprivileged and less than cosmopolitan homes.

furnishes for many, both because of changes in the nature of work and in our nature; (2) work and leisure are becoming increasingly indistinct—reminiscent in some ways of the pre-industrial age—with interpersonal relations growing in importance in both; (3) factory workers at play are coming increasingly to behave like the general American population, raising the question whether their widely shared roles as consumers (a word we use very broadly to connote nonwork spheres) do not influence their outlook at least as much as their segregated roles as producers. In what follows, we propose to qualify some of these ideas.

THE CENTRALITY OF WORK

At the beginning of the industrial revolution, Adam Smith was so impressed with the stultifying nature of factory life that he hoped the hours away from work might somehow strengthen those qualities of character he regarded as essentially human. Marx went much further in seeing the factory as the ambush of brutishness, so terrible that it might engender a rational revolt against itself. No doubt, both men overlooked elements of passivity and boredom in the peasant's life, the yeoman's life, to which they could still look back. Quite possibly they missed elements of creativity, disguised in tricks of the trade or sabotage or group solidarity, in the factories of their times—though the day was still a long way off when time-study departments would assume that two-and-a-half of the eight hours in a steel mill would admittedly be nonproductive, with many workers managing to import into the factory ever larger bits and pieces of their nonwork games and reveries.

Despite such shadings of the bleak picture which has come down to us, it seems fair to generalize that industrialism in England and America came with such speed as to force into the mills people of an essentially rural tradition, unprepared for the shift, so that their merriment became pushed to the fringes of life, hardly more by the arduousness of the factory itself than by the inroads of Puritan uplift. These "fringe benefits" were the remnants of night and Sunday—with the tavern and the church shifting from a village or parish setting to an urban one.[3]

[3] The L. S. Ayres department store in Indianapolis made the discovery that when it gave its employees Monday off (rather than a shifting weekday) many more went to church Sunday, for they could use the following day to rest up and catch up; undoubtedly, the present phenomenal rise in church attendance among Americans owes a good deal to the shorter work week and two-day weekend.

They included occasional "seasons" of unemployment, and the increasingly rare holidays (Everett C. Hughes reminds us that in the Catholic Rhineland the first strikes were occasioned by Protestant ironmasters' cutting down the very large number of saints' days and other holidays characteristic of pre-industrial Europe).

Some workers responded to the exhausting demands of the workplace by a heroic effort to build up a counterlife outside the plant—for instance, through the Mechanics' Associations which thrived in mid-nineteenth-century America among workers newly introduced to print and the scientific outlook. Some retired into a close-knit family life and to home-improvement rather than self-improvement, here aided by the tradition of "do-it-yourself" carried over from the countryside or from the handicrafter's household and abetted by leakage of factory tools and materials. In the smaller towns and cities, there remained access to hunting and fishing in slack seasons, and gardening one's own or some unclaimed patch of land in the summer—all this regarded more as work to supplement the meager earnings than as a chosen hobby or relaxation.

Where no other escape existed, the factory workers tended, like sailors, to fall back on the common denominator of the male sex as defining their leisure: gambling, fighting, whoring. This common denominator was especially important because the factory, almost everywhere it appeared, threw together men of different regional and ethnic traditions, and thus made even more difficult the creation of a new and more appropriate urban and industrial pattern of life and leisure. The emerging industrial culture made work central to a man's image of himself, and yet almost entirely separate both from his past and from the meager resources he had left over outside of work. Men became habituated to the factory, as children to school, but this "second nature" never overtook them completely nor turned them into enthusiastic addicts of monotony.

No wonder that a counterattack soon began against the central place of work on the simplest level of demanding shorter hours, with men choosing to take part of their increasing productivity in the form of time off rather than of an increase in real income. It is part of the same demand that men, not themselves close to retirement and thus not faced with its financial and psychological hazards, press for ever earlier retirement "so that a man can do all those things in life you can't do while you're working." Among steelworkers we have found in conversation that employees from twenty-five to fifty-five almost unanimously advocate retirement commencing at fifty-five or earlier, blithely dismissing the inevitable economic questions with assertions that they will be able to "make out" and expectations that better stipends for the retired are just around the political corner.[4]

At a certain point, however, workers seem to want to buy leisure inside rather than outside the plant. No doubt this in part reflects still operative conventions as to a proper working day, conventions built into transportation, bookkeeping, and shift patterns. And in part men may fear to have too much time outside—time perhaps on which their wives could make demands.[5] They may, like many of us in the business and professional strata, prefer to complain at home of their hard day's work while secretly profiting from its frivolities. At any rate, the unions in many advanced companies no longer spend all their energies resenting management abuses and encroachments, but can protect the processes of communication and interpersonal relationships in the plant (many grievers and shop stewards have become a kind of maintenance crew for sociability and gossip networks), and supervisory practices are forced to become more nearly commensurate with leisure-tinted images of what a proper workplace should be like. Many companies have taken the initiative on this front, moving for this as well as other reasons to pleasant suburbs, or to that Great American Suburb of the Southwest, thus luring employees out of the mills and offices designed in the pre-Raymond Loewy era.[6] Of course, there remain depressed industries and

[4] Warren Peterson in a study of Kansas City schoolteachers found also this growing demand for early retirement, expressing boredom and defeatism about work as much as any specific desires for postwork leisure activities. (Unpublished doctoral dissertation, Department of Sociology, University of Chicago, 1956.) Many old-timers, however, both in schoolteaching and in the mills, continue to resist retirement, their grumpy habituation to work being the only structure their lives have. Cf. Eugene A. Friedmann and Robert J. Havighurst, *The Meaning of Work and Retirement* (Chicago: University of Chicago Press, 1954).

[5] See also "Leisure and Work in Postindustrial Society," p. 162.

[6] Cf. E. L. Ullman, "Amenities as a Factor in Regional Growth," *Geographic Review*, XLIV (1954), p. 119. Among less mobile or redecoratable industries there is some resurgence today of management-sponsored recreation programs, which received a big boost during the "progressive management" movement of the 1920s. Indeed, what was worth a couple of chapters three decades ago (e.g., Lee K. Frankel and Alexander Fleisher, *The Human Factor in Industry* [New York: Macmillan, 1920], Chaps. 9 and 10) has now become a specialty for submanagers (e.g., Jackson M. Anderson, *Industrial Recreation* [New York: McGraw-Hill, 1955])—and one in which unions are beginning to stake out their own claims.

service trades which cannot afford the high overheads and mechanization of these new style-setters of "conspicuous production."

When Puritanism hit Merrie England, it had the effect, intensified by the subsequent industrial revolution, of pushing a larger and larger middle-class wedge between the Anglican gentry and the not yet Methodized workers, thus preserving only at the top and bottom of society certain pre-industrial pastimes and values. In this country, however, the middle-class wedge expanded until it embraced nearly the whole population, and the unaffected residues of older strata (as in the South) are small and uninfluential. Yet it is implicit in what we have said that the leisure which was once a fringe benefit now threatens to push work itself closer to the fringes of consciousness and significance. In many facets of our national life, the anti-Puritan revolution seems to be almost accomplished (to be sure, among American workers Puritanism's hold, for ethnic and other reasons, was never complete).

Thus, the new situation confronts us with questions to which our own past is almost irrelevant, and the experience of less bountiful countries not much help either. We must ask, for instance, whether it is conceivable that, in a culture built on the industrial system, we can and should regard our still obligated work energies as mere payment for our consumer hedonism. Would we be happy if we attained a good racket, in which we never had to extend ourselves or never had to come into contact with any productive activity of men (other than voyeuristic contact through conducted tours of automatic factories)? It should be possible to give some empirical substance to speculation here through studies of standby musicians, pipefitters, railroad firemen, and others who get paid for not working, especially after they can no longer coast on motives of revenge against management and "the system." As we were once unprepared for the factory, are we now not at least as unprepared for "the life of Riley," when it becomes no longer a dream but a barrier we have broken through?

Management and the workers both go on pretending that we needn't answer such questions. Management says that workers have lost the will to do an honest day's work, have lost ambition and the taste for workmanship. Workers argue that management wants to squeeze and speed them for the end of greater profits—not seeing the ideological unease their apparent indolence creates in a supervisory force itself no longer unequivocally committed to work-mindedness. None of this makes very much sense: it is using the rhetoric of the past to obscure the present, let alone the future. Fromm in *The Sane Society*, and

Percival and Paul Goodman in *Communitas*, believe that radical reconstructions of the work process are necessary before it can be humanized and enlivened. The latter touch on the difficult problem of periodicity—of how to alternate challenge and routine—a problem that will increase in importance as work flows become stabilized with automation, full employment, and a permanent war economy. In part, of course, these are matters beyond our limited assignment in this volume, but we cannot look at leisure without inquiring about its relation to work: is it escape, counterpoise, or possibly the managing partner, with work now the sleeping one?

WORK AND LEISURE IN THE LIFE CYCLE

We know all too well some of the less amiable ways in which training for both work and leisure takes place in school—that pre-industrial waiting room to which our high productivity, our youth-centeredness, and many other forces consign the young. It is here, *inter alia,* that the future factory worker learns to define tasks set by authority as a test of his individual skill at evasion and of group co-operativeness in setting easily accessible norms and in punishing rate-busters. It is here that aspirations are whetted for consumption goods—and often blunted for other potential or historical goals. Creativity may sometimes find an outlet in hot-rodding—a craft that may also serve the young factory worker as a subliminal protest against the monopolization of skilled jobs in the plant by the older men and against the middle-class mores and functional inefficiencies built into the vehicle by Detroit. Even while one is still in high school, part-time jobs may provide the wherewithal for a car, and also set the later life pattern of part-time service jobs held in addition to the steady but meaningless factory job in order to bring additional income in for the sake of a higher standard of living. The car, of course, also serves an as aid to sexual adventuring and general free-spending, which the young and unattached factory worker can today readily afford, what with the compression of ranks and the decline of older patterns of apprenticeship. What liquor was for an older, rougher, and more impoverished generation, gasoline (plus some liquor, too, of course) is for the contemporary young worker. He can also afford, though paying a token room and board to his mother, expensive (though not elegant) dates, trips, and tailor-made suits.

But marriage comes early in the life cycle of the industrial worker, and the costs that the paycheck, little higher than before the wedding, must meet jump steadily with the acquisition of a family and a household.[7] Hot-rodding is then likely to cease, and the worker will settle into a family car which he carefully maintains in its original form for the sake of its trade-in value—though he may take it for repairs to a friend who has retained the practiced ability to tinker with automobiles as an adult leisure specialty. Or he may drive to work in a clunker to which he devotes as little attention as possible so long as it runs. At this point, his house rather than his car is likely to claim his attention. Even half a century ago, according to Frederick Winslow Taylor's account of "Schmidt," the unreflective Dutchman whom he taught a better way of loading pig iron, this worker "upon wages of $1.15 a day . . . had succeeded in buying a small plot of ground . . . and was engaged in putting up the walls of a little house for himself in the morning before starting to work and at night after leaving."[8] It seems likely that Schmidt's model was not an urban bourgeois but rather a well-to-do peasant, the farm-boy newly come to the city, or the small-town artisan. This model is still alive among many factory workers today. They buy homes because they have never resigned themselves to the role of tenant and because they want a house and land as a bit of old-age security (including the security of activity).

Especially since World War II, many young married workers have kept mortgages low by living in tarpaper shacks or trailers or basements while accumulating above or around them what in four or five years will be at least a "decent," if not inspiring, shelter—not jerry-built but with little regard for the symbolic values real estate agents find or invent in dwellings. One of us has been engaged in this process in a working-class suburb of Gary, Indiana, to which subsequent settlers have come to build more imposing homes with bigger mortgages and some symbols of status, such as stone facing (which in such a Veblenian neighborhood must be justified by reference to insulating qualities and ease of maintenance and, in moments of honesty, the pacification of a style-conscious and insistent wife). But these later arrivals are not trying to catch up with any middle-class Joneses, having deliberately moved to an area where middle-class people are conspicuous by their absence and

[7] Marvin Sussman has gathered data on how, in middle-class families, the parents help the young married couple to get started by tactful gifts of furniture and funds; in the working class, capital resources of this sort scarcely exist. "The Help Pattern in the Middle Class Family," *American Sociological Review*, XVIII (February 1953), 22–28.

[8] *Scientific Management* (New York: Harper, 1911), pp. 43–44.

where they can get more land and a lower tax rate. For the men, at least, the primary fulfillment provided by the house is not dissimilar to that of the car: it is the tangible possession, with the feel of ownership or of "thingmanship."

While possessions and children are being accumulated, the steps in the ladder of plant seniority are likely to seem particularly slow and frustrating, and the ex-teen-ager who casually hired in may begin to wonder about some entrepreneurial activity which might allow escape from the plant altogether if it pays off (and minimally allow mitigating the pressure of his installment payments). He may spend his weekends repairing TV rather than looking at it, or (like some of the workers described in Charles Walker's *Steeltown*) driving a cab or truck for hauling, or servicing cars at a gas station rather than driving aimlessly about. This period may be the low point of his preoccupation with leisure within as well as outside the plant, for he may make a play for advancement or upgrading.

Only a good deal later will he have risen high enough in the pay-skill hierarchy, paid off enough of his investment in the hard goods of domesticity, and given his children, in the language of the labor movement, "a childhood for every child," so that he can resume the extensive and intensive preoccupation with leisure of his own adolescence and youth. At this point there may be a renewed interest in how much fun one can have at work. This is what in all probability one is going to be doing for the rest of one's days; one has what it takes, and one might as well enjoy it. For those numerous workers who love to eat and travel, rising standards of living and a plateau of obligations at this point usually mean more of the same traditional and conventional fare and faring: a classier motel, a more expensive steak (cooked as before). The children and grandchildren are enabled to enjoy expensive play equipment—bicycles, sports gear, camping.

Yet, for many, a fundamental dissatisfaction remains which one of us has called the "tradition of failure": the conviction of many older workers, including those who have nice homes, expensive cars, and children in college, that success in life is achieved only by men who manage to get out of the mill by the routes of small business, politics, or "some other good racket." America has taught them that the best things in life are not free. They are close enough to production and profits to know that the things are there for the asking—and to their unions to know how to ask. But they are also too Americanized to look favorably on mill work, no matter whether their standard of living is the envy of the lower ranks of the white-collar world.

LEISURE CLASS AND MASS

By the same token, it becomes increasingly difficult to distinguish their leisure from that of the rest of the country. Even worker suburbs *are* suburbs—very different (as Clark Kerr has seen in another connection) from the monolithic mining towns, lumber camps, or urban districts which encapsulate a distinctive working-class style and labor ideology. It is a commonplace that the mass consumption goods and the mass media tend to blur class lines, and tend, moreover, not only to foster filtering down of leisure-class patterns from the taste leaders at the top but also to promote uniformities from below. Thus, the casual garb of the worker off the job tends to merge with the "sincere" and unaffected garb of the office worker—and their wives may both read *McCall's* at the same beauty parlor.

Yet there remain certain distinctions. One of these may be summarized by noting that the worker, as a parvenu, tends to have a more unequivocal relation to consumer goods than do people who have had a longer exposure to them. One of us supervised a study which illustrates the point. Working-class and middle-class parents were interviewed concerning their attitudes toward TV: for the former, this was an extrapolation of radio and the movies, and an indubitably good *thing* in a world of things, whereas for many middle-class parents TV presented a problem in self-definition, as well as in its possibly harmful effects on children.[9] The working class, for all that some of its attitudes resemble those of the idle rich of a generation ago, is still a long distance away from the plight of those who, bored by possessions, begin to collect ideas, diseases, or (as in Louis Kronenberger's witty novel, *Grand Right and Left*) people.

This adherence to the tangible, then, characterizes working-class leisure activities in a wide gamut: the garden harvest which, like the fishing catch, can be counted and weighed; the travel mileages and car horsepowers which can be compared; and sex (whether marital or not), drinking, sports, and betting, which are all felt as essentially palpable. To be sure, we do not want to exaggerate, after the fashion of D. H. Lawrence and other romantics, the lack of abstraction, nuance, and shadings of taste among factory workers. We know that even where the objects are the same, the meanings we assume to be attached to them

---

[9] Cf. Margarete Midas, "Without TV," *American Quarterly*, III (1951), 152–66.

are of course attached only to their human possessors and that there is great variety here. For a Mississippi-born Negro to own a car may be a pleasure only those who have experienced Jim Crow transportation can realize, and his Buick, bought on time in St. Louis or Detroit, may be not only a triumph over caste restrictions but also over a life without possessions—even repossessions. In contrast, the same car in the hands of a semiskilled high school graduate of high intelligence, a man who is filled with frustration and unspent energy as he leaves the plant and drives like mad through homebound traffic, may signify a still further resignation to a fate beyond his control within and outside the factory.

Beyond that, it is our impression that the simplicities of working-class leisure are under pressure not only from the tastes of the better educated strata as class consciousness and cultural encapsulation decline, but also from what we might term the feminizing of leisure. To be sure, this has not yet won much recognition in the all-male world of the factory, where the talk among the mill hands, like their horseplay, defends a cherished masculine preserve, resembling the talk of a military post, a lodge, a poolroom, or an all-male convention. Likewise, whenever the worker finds himself among other men in the working-class suburb or established working-class section of the metropolis, he can either talk shop or continue the other rather uninvolved talk—sports or sex or automobile talk—of the shop. So, too, a strike gives him the chance to choose, free of domestic prior commitment, between painting the garage or going fishing. However, as we know, the factory itself is increasingly invaded by women, no longer always segregated in separate departments. And we have also seen how the decor of the plant tends to become softer and less rugged, so that a foundry today often looks like a light industry of a generation ago.

More important still, in the outside world feminine influences are clearly increasing, as marriages, following the middle-class mode, become more companionate and less patriarchal; often the teen-age daughter first "brings up" her mother and then, in conspiracy with the latter, goes to work on Dad. Here again the situation of the factory worker today is reminiscent in certain respects of that of the nineteenth-century capitalist whose wife dragged him reluctantly toward "culture" and away from his "materialistic" preoccupations. The plant continues to be a refuge for those men who either cannot or do not want to acquire the sorts of "feminine" sensitivity and aspirations which go with more abstract forms of work and recreation. But such men, much as they may set the tone in mining or logging camp or open hearth, are seldom in the majority in a plant, and it follows that in-plant sociability does not always exclude (as it does, by tacit convention, on a hunting trip)[10] those leisure roles that involve women, including discussions of house-building and maintenance, movies and TV shows, home cooking (with trading of ethnic recipes), flower raising, and so on. Here, too, of course, the emphasis is on the tangible, but the ambit of domestic relationships involving the objects is wider.

Other changes within the factory, present and impending, point in the same direction. No longer does factory work concentrate attention on objects directly, on the hardness of the materials. Increasingly, apart from the maintenance and transportation crews, the production employees are engaged in communicating with each other concerning what the equipment is doing, and maintaining the proper relationships between intricately co-ordinated machines. Work itself becomes more abstract, more complex, more intellectual—hence, in the specialized sense of this paper, less "masculine." The physical feel for the work which allowed an old-time furnace tender to tell from a glance at a peephole if the heat was of proper quality gives way to the practiced utilization of instruments such as the spectroscope, and eventually to an electronic control system which provides on charts and dials a numerical and graphic overview of the whole production process. (All this is quite apart from the actual decline of manufacturing labor as a proportion of a work force increasingly engaged in the tertiary trades, including the servicing of each other's leisure.)

Such developments imply that the class line in the plant, presently attenuated, is likely to become even less clear-cut. Even now, the jobs of many production-line workers would allow them to wear shirts and ties, perhaps protected by lablike smocks, and their pay would allow them access to the nicer cafeterias, rather than eating at a canteen or sitting on a machine or stool to open their lunch boxes and their thermoses. The dirt and noise and smell now associated with the production floor are as likely to disappear from the factory of the future as the shabby locker room and nondescript plant uniform of the blue-collar man. For a while, loyalties and traditions will make for friction if the worker tries to dress up in the plant and "act middle class." But we have already spoken of the decline of violence and of the general softening of manners (save in international relations and on TV!): as

[10] Cf. Gregory F. Stone, "American Sports: Play and Dis-Play," *Chicago Review*, IX (1955), pp. 83–100.

production-floor work becomes increasingly safe and comfortable, brawling within or outside the plant falls progressively into disrepute. Unlike the situation in Europe or South America, there is virtually no aristocracy to provide models for the working class which contrast sharply with general middle-class norms; indeed, such once aristocratic sports as breeding pedigreed dogs, sailing, and horseback riding have come to be widespread among industrial workers as well as white-collar employees. And we should again remind the reader that this is a two-way traffic, so that lower-class manners are softening while the upper social strata complain of a loss of refinement, and their children wear blue jeans.

A PAUL BUNYAN OF THE SUPERMARKETS?

In a justly famous essay, Leo Lowenthal traced a decline in biographies of "heroes of production" in *The Saturday Evening Post* and a rise in biographies of "heroes of consumption" such as movie and sports celebrities; and even when magnates and statesmen are now discussed, he observed that it is their personalities and their nonwork activities that are commented on:[11] leisure gives status to work, rather than the other way around. Likewise, it is our impression that there has been a change in heroes within the working-class community. A generation ago these were production heroes who brought their prestige with them out of the mill—supercraftsmen like the old hammer-forge operators who could control the massive power of their tools to crack the crystal on a watch without damaging the works, and physical giants who could lift more than anyone else in the plant and win more fights in front of the tavern. As part of the same setting, the big steel mills and metal-working plants were the most impressive aspect of the workers' communities, dwarfing even the cathedrals built by the massed savings of the various ethnic enclaves.

Today, in contrast, though the mills and the oil-cracking plants are still impressive, industry no longer favors River Rouge-type displays of concentrated power but rather dispersed one-story plants no more imposing than one of the new suburban shopping centers. For competing symbols of glamour, workers have access to their own consumer hard

[11] See Lowenthal, "Biographies in Popular Magazines," *Radio Research, 1942–1943*, Paul F. Lazarsfeld and Frank Stanton, eds. (New York: Duell, Sloan and Pearce, 1944), p. 507.

goods, to the big screens of Hollywood and the small ones of TV. By the same token, the worker today can bring status into the plant from the bright and various world outside—from his extravagant hunting or extensive traveling, as well as from his activities in the union or in local politics. Within the plant, the general upgrading of industrial workers, the bureaucratization of wage rates and promotions (and union control or influence over these), and the development of finer gradations so that the top men are not so clearly distinguishable from the rest, de-emphasize the place of status won within as against status won outside. Elton Mayo, writing a generation ago of the factory as a restorative and stabilizer for clique members against the disruptions of the surrounding anomic neighborhoods, could hardly have anticipated the degree to which the factory, despite the continuing growth of its ancillary services to workers and their communities, would lose its position of emotional dominance as the workers' Americanization and often pat sophistication in leisure-time affairs proceeded.

This shift is part of a larger one in the forms by which the drive for social mobility is expressed. At one time, one gained status only from one's place on the land and from the nexus of kin which related one to the land. The factory accompanied a change to more portable forms of status, yet it was itself at first tied to a particular place by the need for water power or coal or transport, and the work-group was anchored within the plant to stationary machinery. Commensurately, one rose in status by climbing the occupational ladder within the plant, meanwhile consolidating one's position in the town through family alliances, an impressive house, and visible civic and parochial activities. Today, as we have seen, the factory is free of close "ecological" ties to real estate and can move in search of amenities defined as such in a national inherently portable system of consumer values. Under these conditions, the younger workers, high school trained, become quickly impatient with their slow progress within the plant hierarchy—but this hierarchy is no longer the only one they see in front of them. In nonwork activities, they already have more experience and expertise than many senior men; and in these, "around end" as it were, they look for roads to a more personal as well as more portable kind of status. A mill hand today may feel he has it made if, for example, he can afford winter as well as summer vacations. His leisure-time specialties may bring him income or prestige or both. If he takes a hand in local politics, it may be less out of class-conscious ideology or out of a desire to leave the mill for an easier life, and more because he now has time for the great game of politics, as well as the know-how to profit from its incidental perquisites. If he moves from the old working-class part of the city to a suburb on its perimeter, he is again freeing himself from the need to have access to many factory gates, counting on his car and his union to provide him with a job within a reasonable orbit; in his new suburb, he will be judged as it were "horizontally" by his style of life rather than "vertically" by his occupation.

In this new perspective, leisure, which was once a residual compensation for the tribulations of work, may become what workers recover from at work (as children recover from vacations at school)! Fred H. Blum quotes a worker as saying: "The routine keeps your mind well grounded . . . and makes you a stable citizen."[12] Work may appear as a last remnant of rootedness, of "grounding," in a world of such mobility that goals, including the nature of status itself, are being continuously redefined in experiences away from work.

Were he alive today, Veblen would almost surely feel disheartened at this prospect; it would seem to him as if the rationalities of production had been defeated by the irrationalities of consumption and leisure so that even skilled workers, his favorite cadre, had joined the apostles of wastemanship rather than workmanship. Yet he might also conclude that the older form of the drive for status—the source of meaning for many, but of suffering for most—had lost something of its imperative quality. No doubt, this replacement is partly fatalistic, reflecting growing rigidities in the social and political structure of a garrison state, but does it not also reflect a greater maturity, a greater mobility of the imagination? (No doubt also, before we look too far ahead, we must remember the enormous distance still to go toward equalization: to move, for instance, from the noisy tenements of Chicago's Black Belt, with its population swollen by postwar waves of immigration from the Delta and other rural and small-town areas of the Illinois Central's South, to the neat well-off, well-kept homes of craft-conscious German and Swedish workers in Milwaukee is to change worlds. Yet these worlds even now communicate with one another, and all American experience, all industrial experience, shows the fabulous speeds with which social distances can be annihilated or reduced to marginal and even nostalgic tokens.)

Let us assume, beyond continuing equalizations along the lines here

[12] *Toward a Democratic Work Process* (New York: Harper, 1953), p. 97.

intimated—between the social classes, between men and women, young and old, rural and urban—the continued full employment and prosperity on which, to a considerable extent, they rest, and that this will continue to put unionized factory workers above even our changing definitions of poverty. Let us assume, too, that we continue to opt for increased productivity as well as increased time off. Does this presently visible potentiality of "nonwork" for variety and mobility—in home building, domestic handicrafts, travel, organizational activity, sports, spectatorship, and even part-time entrepreneurship—provide an infinitely expandable package deal for the satisfying expenditure of time and energy and for the attainment of an adequate identity? Or are we coming to an era when workers have all the housing they care for, and can no longer pour energies into home building? When possessions no longer lure them, when travel palls? No doubt, adult educators look eagerly and hopefully at the prospect—for they are in the business of selling intangibles for which the market is totally elastic. Yet how many workers are going to read this volume, concerned as it is with their prospects?

The future seems "impossible," whichever way we look at it. Leisure marches on, while understanding of its import escapes these reporters, and invention and design of its opportunities escape all of us.

Leisure and Work in Postindustrial Society
(1958)

To the rest of the world, the American has characteristically appeared as someone who cannot stand being idle or alone, someone who rushes about, whether in work or play, and is preternaturally restless. Tocqueville for instance observed, "No men are less addicted to reverie than the citizens of a democracy."[1] Like Tocqueville, Lewis Mumford, in his remarkable book, *The Transformations of Man*,[2] discusses these changes from Old World to New World life, suggesting that the Americans, released by social and geographic space from age-old limits and norms, have exhibited from the beginning an exuberance and vitality, a romantic strenuousness, that in their respective ways Emerson and Whitman represented and celebrated.

I

At the present time, two processes are going on simultaneously. On the one hand, a decline of exuberance is just barely noticeable in America, making itself felt particularly among the more highly educated and the well-to-do in a loss of appetite for work and perhaps even for leisure. On the other hand, the spread of industrialization and of the mass media are bringing both the residual pockets of traditionalism within this country and the great areas of it outside into a more "American" pattern. Whatever a nation's political or religious ideology, mass

[1] *Democracy in America*, Phillips Bradley edition (New York: Knopf, 1945), vol. 2, p. 208. Tocqueville had in mind the contrast with the members of an aristocratic society who had a smaller portion of discontent because people knew their place and, whether resignedly or not, remained in it; his view anticipated that of Durkheim.
[2] New York: Harper, 1956.

culture continues to spread, even ahead of industrialization, bringing the disruption of old ways and the lure of a new hedonism (as most dramatically seen in the cargo cults of the Pacific islanders which combine a nativist revival with the belief that the white man's goods can be obtained, without the white man himself, by appropriate rituals[3]).

I recently saw a documentary film focused on a family living in the hills of Tennessee in the 1930s—a family with many children and many dogs, eking out a bare existence. Despite efforts to insure minimal schooling, knowledge of the outside world scarcely percolated. Today, many of the very Tennessee shacks where, before the coming of the TVA, life resembled that in other peasant and pre-industrial cultures, are equipped with television aerials that now bring in not only the local boys who made good with a guitar, like Elvis Presley, but all the insignia of making good which pass as currency in the nation at large: cars, clothes, washers (which are often put on the front porch), and general styles of life and leisure. Some of the farms even in this area have become nearly as overmechanized, and hence engaged in "conspicuous production," as in the richer agricultural areas of the North; horses and mules are disappearing, and the South is catching up with the rest of the country in per capita ownership of automobiles.

Indeed, Southerners coming North, white or Negro, Caribbean or native, have replaced the immigrants from Southern Europe as fodder, not for the machines of production so much as for those of consumption; for coming from a pre-industrial culture they lack sales resistance, let alone consumer sophistication: entering, if not the high-wage economy, at least the high-credit one, they are being "processed" as consumers, while escaping, because of their late arrival, some of the drill and exhausting hours that met earlier pre-industrial cadres entering the work force of industrial society.

They enter a society which has over the past eighty years taken in the form of leisure or free time approximately a third of the gains in productivity which industrialism and organization have achieved. (The average work week now hovers around forty hours, as contrasted with seventy hours in 1850 and, in many industries and on the farms, nearly as much as that as late as 1920.) When the Bantu who works, let us say, in Johannesburg, has attained an increment over his old standard of

[3] Cf., e.g., Margaret Mead, *New Lives for Old* (New York: William Morrow, 1955); also Daniel Lerner, *The Passing of Traditional Society* (Glencoe, Ill.: The Free Press, 1958).

living, he is likely to quit and return to the reservation; few of these Americans have a reservation to return to[4]; consequently, the Americans remain rather steadily at work while having time enough left on their hands for learning how to spend money in accordance with, and just beyond, their new wages. (There still remain in America more or less permanently underprivileged enclaves, principally among the old, the infirm, and among the less agile and mobile Negroes and poor whites.)

Those who have recently been released from underprivilege by mass production and mass leisure have gained, along with an often meaningless political vote, an often influential voice in the direction of consumption and hence of production. It is, for instance, the very millions whom Henry Ford helped release from drudgery who eventually defeated his ascetic and still rural canons of taste; it is they who like borax furniture or jukebox culture; their aesthetic is akin to that of all deracinated peasants whose folk culture crumbles at the first exposure to mass-produced commodities.[5]

[4] To be sure, something analogous to a reservation exists in our urban and rural slums to which migrants come and in which they seek, despite pressures and temptations, to preserve enclaves of traditionalism. Conversely, even in Africa, the reservation, though geographically more stable, proves fragile in the face of the inducements and pressures of industrialism and urbanization.

[5] The consequences of this overexposure, in the short and in the long run, are complex and are the themes of passionate debate (cf. the contributions to *Mass Culture* and especially Clement Greenberg's article, "Work and Leisure under Industrialism" in that volume). While I agree with Lyman Bryson that it is not right to judge a culture by its peaks of art and artisanship alone but that one must also judge it in terms of the total quality of its life [cf. *The Next America* (New York: Harper, 1950)], Bryson is readier than I to sacrifice the peaks of aristocratic attainment to the pleateaus of popular contentment, in part because perhaps we differ on how long the latter can last without the former.

Certainly, the role of the artist changes when his patrons are no longer the few but the many. In a traditional society with a small elite, he is ancillary to the elite: they patronize him and he serves them, and he may remain unaffected by the attitudes and desires of the mass of the people—save as these furnish folk themes for his music or imagery. Even if patronized, he moves among those who count, whereas today the successful artist may be rich and famous and still not feel he knows anybody who counts. Artists and intellectuals in our time have a choice of constituencies: they may try to serve the traditional elite of culture and taste or the mass of people who for the first time in history have money enough to become patrons. This dilemma has driven some artists toward willful efforts to

II

As many thoughtful people have recognized, our society offers little in the way of re-education for those who have been torn away from their traditional culture and suddenly exposed to all the blandishments of mass culture—even the churches which follow the hillbillies to the city often make use of the same "hard sell" that the advertisers and politicians do. In the past, the relatively voluntary nature of the immigration to this country, and the belief in progress of natives and immigrants alike, have tended to blind us to the casualties of transplantation. There are a few exceptions. For example, in the 1930s I admired the Rust brothers, inventors of the cotton picker, who hesitated to market their invention because they were worried about technological unemployment among southern workers. (They were as unconvinced of the gospel of automatic technological progress as were the members of the Advisory Committee which recommended under Oppenheimer's leadership against proceeding with the H-bomb.) It is ironical to reflect that this invention came along just in time to save some southern fields from utter desertion—not only because Negroes and poor whites were

---

stave off mass understanding, whether by obscurities, sadism directed toward the audience, or serious attitudes which are unpopular. The results of this have not always been bad for art—on the contrary—but they do curtail some of the possibilities for the artist by making obscurities sometimes seem attractive per se. Conversely, such artists as, let us say, the typical jazz musician who plays popular, feel that they have sold out to the largest purse; the same occurs with painters who go commercial. Sometimes artists are thrown back upon their fellow artists as the only ones who understand this dilemma, but this does not always save an artist from being caught in the enormous machinery for disseminating his work if it catches hold. Indeed, if popular taste were utterly debased, then what is "high" and "low" could be clearly differentiated; but we have a situation of an infinite series of minute gradations in which it is not easy to say what is high-brow and upper-middle-brow and so on; thus, the Book-of-the-Month Club may circulate a very good book at times. As a result, the climate for the most intensive achievements of art and intellect has a good deal of smog in it: the artist does not necessarily starve but may be all too well patronized without giving him any sense that he has a genuine audience. Moreover, in an age of plenty, it may require more conviction for an artist to remain poor than when all but a few were poor. (I have profited from the discussion of these issues in Nathan Glazer's, "Technology, Mass Culture, and High Culture," a paper delivered at the American Sociological Society meetings, August 1958).

leaving for the cities in the North but also because the cotton-picking machine, as a form of conspicuous production, frees its operator from work which has long been considered dirty work and thus raises the status of the operator: it is the counterpart on the production side of today's Tennessee shack, electrified and gadget-filled. Even so, I think that the Rusts' scruples were well taken: people should not be ruthlessly torn away even from their incapacities and given the industrial bends: this country is rich enough and inventive enough to make social provision for a moratorium and retraining in those instances where uprooting is inescapable.

For many people today, the sudden onrush of leisure is a version of technological unemployment: their education has not prepared them for it and the creation of new wants at their expense moves faster than their ability to order and assimilate these wants.[6]

III

In the mercantilist era, and even today in the countries of grinding poverty, the creation of new wants has been a first step toward a better life and wider horizons of choice. But in the United States today, the belief that one cannot stop invention, cannot stop technological progress, has itself become a tradition, indeed a form of realistic insanity, or what C. Wright Mills calls "crackpot realism." Although adult Americans, contrary to European impression, are not dazzled by machines as such—but simply want to have those appurtenances that betoken an appropriate style of life—we are nevertheless half-willing

[6] Since the writing of this paper, John Kenneth Galbraith's *The Affluent Society* (Boston: Houghton Mifflin Company, 1958) has appeared. With superb understanding, Professor Galbraith shows how the fear of economic insecurity which haunts Americans makes us the victims of our own productive processes—processes which create and then supply the "wants" as well as the leisure we choose because we don't want the wants that much. Galbraith also shows that the very primacy given to full production and full employment in the United States robs the economy of the flexibility that would permit diverting some of the surplus to wiping out the residual but stubborn poverty in this country and to making a dent on the vast and apparently increasing poverty of the nonindustrialized world. And Galbraith sketches some of the political and ideological reasons why high production has become a goal, not only for dairy cows, but for human beings—a goal which is now shared by liberals and conservatives and, almost by definition, by economists.

slaves of the machine process. Even big business, thanks to the antitrust laws and to the potential competition of small business, does not quite have sufficient control of the market to plan to its own liking the sequence of applied technology. A fortiori, it seems inconceivable to Americans that we could reduce the aggression our technology keeps up against our traditions and the texture of our lives—and we can always use the competition of the Russians to counter any tendency within ourselves to relax the rate of growth or to question the belief in growth as a value per se.

To be sure, the optimism of the booster was once much stronger in America than it is now. The ideal of Manifest Destiny, which took us across the continent and held the South bound to the Union in the Civil War, infects now only those perpetually adolescent males who are eager to conquer space or the planet Venus.[7] But the booster psychology has for so long been built into our culture and into our patterns of individual and group achievement that we tend to take for granted the notion that growth in population, in assets, in national income, is inevitable if not always desirable. Imagine the outcry, for instance, and not only from Catholics, against any suggestion that people be encouraged in this country to practice birth control, let us say, by removing the tax concession for child dependents or by instituting a sales tax on children's toys and clothes, or even by pointing out forcefully to people some of the less happy consequences of an exploding population.[8] For most Americans still believe that the future can take care of itself, or at any rate that we are not required to do anything to make it easier, less crowded, less full of friction, for our descendants.

In other words, we have become a conservative country, despite our world-wide reputation for seeking novelty, in that we are unable to envisage alternative futures for ourselves.

[7] The space age is not a safety valve for the luxury economy and for our overflowing energies. Although the comparison is often made, I believe there is a real difference between our space age and the exploration of this continent in the fifteenth and sixteenth centuries; at that time Europe was cramped and bound in all kinds of traditional constraints, and could find in colonization an opening for its growing population, its growing energies, its growing rationalism; the best use of the space frontier today would be to deflect our weapons—we can bombard Venus rather than each other.

[8] For a better grasp of some of these problems, I am indebted to the writings of John R. Platt, Harrison Brown, and Richard L. Meier.

IV

So, too, it has been until recent years in the field of leisure time—so much so that my collaborators and I in *The Lonely Crowd* took it for granted that it was impossible to reverse the trend toward automation; we assumed that the current efforts to make work more meaningful—which by and large succeeded only in making it more time-consuming and gregarious but not more challenging—might as well be given up, with the meaning of life to be sought henceforth in the creative use of leisure. We failed to see, in the famous Marxist phrase, that "quantity changes into quality" and that there would come a point where additional increments of leisure would prove more stultifying than satisfying and that the mass of men would be incapable of absorbing any more.

In pre-industrial cultures leisure is scarcely a burden or a "problem" because it is built into the ritual and ground plan of life for which people are conditioned in childhood; often they possess a relatively timeless attitude toward events. Likewise, the tiny leisure classes of the past would sometimes be able to absorb what seems like an overdose of leisure because they lived in an era when work itself was thought demeaning and when free citizens engaged in physical and intellectual self-cultivation and in the arts of war and government—they, so to speak, exercised their leisure on behalf of the whole society. During this era, which lasted throughout most of history, it was inconceivable that the mass of men could support a large and growing leisure class, let alone join such a class themselves. Yet today we live in such a world. The rich and leisured are no longer drastically set apart, but seek for the sake of their souls as well as their public relations to work with relative sobriety and consume with relative modesty and inconspicuousness; thus, they no longer set an example for either good or ill.[9]

At the present time, the closest thing we have to the traditional ideology of the leisure class is a group of artists and intellectuals who regard their work as play and their play as work. For such people, and for the larger group of professional people whom we shall discuss later,

---

[9] It is however a very different story when one views the rich, not in their individual capacity, but in their collective capacity, whether corporate or national. For discussion of America's wealth as a barrier in our relations with other nations, see my Introduction to Daniel Lerner's book, *op. cit.*, and "Human Relations and National Boundaries," *Comprendre*, 1958.

work frequently provides the central focus of life without necessarily being compartmentalized from the rest of life either by its drudgery and severity or by its precariousness. . . .

V

An informal poll of a union local (conducted by James Carper) found that the leaders did want a shorter work week whereas the rank and file did not. This was interpreted as suggesting that the leaders, better educated and more enterprising, feel cramped for time to do everything they want to—to read more books, to see more of their families, to take more adult education courses. Such men already had many hobbies, including being union leaders. But the less active members (no doubt including many who might tell the union leaders that they "lack time to go to meetings") had no similar feeling of wanting the days to be longer. Such men, asked what they would do with an extra day, sometimes say, "sleep"; others could use it in hunting season—and already did so, to the dismay of the foreman. . . .

In a study by Nancy Morse and Robert Weiss, some 80 per cent of industrial workers stated that they, in effect, kept on working for lack of alternatives, not for positive satisfactions. These workers were asked whether they would go on working even if there were no financial need to do so, and they said they would, although also indicating that the job itself (and in many cases any job they could imagine) was boring and without meaning in its own terms. This clinging to the job is not simply a legacy of the Puritan ethic: it is rather a legacy of industrialism itself, of the old structures it has destroyed and the new structures it has created. Nor is it merely the feeling of shame in not having a job that is involved (although this is certainly an element). Work may not be an active presence in the life of American workers, but its absence would be an active absence. Or, more accurately, it is not so much *work* that would be missed as having a job: it doesn't have to be, and should preferably not be, hard work, nor need it even be gregarious work, but rather the self-definition (these data refer only to male workers) that comes from holding a job and the punctuations of life provided by regular employment. These workers, in other words, are too intelligent and too well educated to accept the routine of most factory work, while being still a long way away from the education of the artist or intellectual who can in some measure create his own work with a minimum of outside structuring.[10]

Such considerations concerning the limits of leisure suggest that it might be easier to make leisure more meaningful if one at the same time could make work more demanding. When work itself is infiltrated with leisure (as it is today in many jobs where the time-study man has been stymied), leisure may lose its savor, often becoming not much more than a continuation outside the plant of the sociability and inanity that go on within the plant. In this situation, I believe that we cannot take advantage of what remains of our pre-industrial heritage to make leisure more creative, individually and socially, if work is not creative too. And not only have we lost the folk and peasant traditions: we are rapidly losing those which have developed under industrialism itself—whether of the John Henry variety or of the free-swearing, free-swinging construction engineer who gets roads and dams built: such legends hold little allure in an opulent society, even when building continues at a rapid pace. It is from the Soviet Union that the story comes of a mill foreman who, though complaining of his pay, says he "must be content with the 'thrill of producing something anyway.'"[11] Though he may have been speaking in part for the record, there is no doubt that production remains exciting for many where industrialism is the unfinished business of a rising power. Americans, however, cannot artificially recreate that atmosphere; we cannot make factory or other industrial and commercial work over on the model of army basic training or campcraft just to make it hard (though in fact many workers do enjoy making a game of output, for instance, working up the line on an assembly line, in order to establish control and dramatize their

[10] Many of the workers in the Morse-Weiss study harbor the vague hope of some day having a small business of their own, such as a gas station or television-repair shop. So too the practice of moonlighting or holding two jobs testifies not only to the continuing inflation of consumer wants and of the corresponding prices, but also to the fact that many factory workers are like the Russian peasants who were drafted into the collective farms: they give a minimum quantum of their work to the factory as the peasants did to the farms, and save up their real energies for the "private plots" of their work outside. Cf. Ely Chinoy, *Automobile Workers and the American Dream* (New York: Doubleday, 1955), and Charles R. Walker and Robert H. Guest, *The Man on the Assembly Line* (Cambridge, Mass.: Harvard University Press, 1952).

[11] See Max Frankel, the New York *Times*, September 21, 1957, p. 3, col. 1.

activity). One alternative is to redesign our factories with an eye to the educational or challenging quality of each job, following the example set by some industrial units which have eliminated assembly lines and are giving workers larger units to assemble, or what is sometimes termed job enlargement. The march of specialization, which had originally been based on steam production but has in our day become an end in itself with its own dynamic and momentum, could thereby be reversed.[12] Undoubtedly, work flows could be redesigned to maximize the demands on the worker's intelligence, while retaining present advances in making work quiet, free of dirt, and relatively unstrenuous. . . .[13]

VI

The hopes I had put on leisure (in *The Lonely Crowd*) reflect, I suppose, my despair about the possibility of making work in modern society more meaningful and more demanding for the mass of men—a need that has come upon us so rapidly that the taste of abundance we have had in the past now threatens to turn into a glut.

My despair on this score, I must add, was not greatly alleviated by the feeling in a group of union leaders in one of the more open-minded unions that it was impossible to get either unions or management in the least interested in making work more humanly satisfying. I hoped the union leaders might co-operate with management in, so to speak, turning the engineers around, and forcing them to design men back into their machines rather than out of them. As the discussion with the union officials continued, it became clearer to me that the workers

---

[12] See, e.g., Peter Drucker, *Concept of the Corporation* (New York: Harper, 1946), and the brilliant discussion by Daniel Bell, *Work and Its Discontents: The Cult of Efficiency in America* (Boston: Beacon Press, 1956).

To be sure, there would always be a question whether the work was being complicated only by the energy of the work force to create a plot for the daily drama of life or because the total configuration had been reorganized so that the work and the workers were seen as a single product. Assuredly, such reorganization, like anything else, could become a gimmick of management but it need not do so.

[13] Nelson Foote tells me of a case in Detroit some years ago where workers through their union insisted on their right to sing at work against the objections of a puritanical management. I am indebted to Mr. Foote, and particularly to his unpublished paper on "Stultification at Work," for illumination concerning the themes discussed in this paper.

themselves were too much of this same school of engineering thought really to believe in the reorganization of industry.[14]

In this perspective, the rebellion of workers against modern industry is usually mere rebellion, mere goofing off. Many are quite prepared to go on wildcat strikes (Daniel Bell notes that in 1954–55 there were forty such in just one Westinghouse plant in East Pittsburgh); they are quite prepared to deceive the time-study man and to catch forty winks on the night shift, and otherwise to sabotage full production while still "making out" in terms of the group's norms—being in this like students who might cheat on exams or cut classes but could not conceive of reorganization of the curriculum or of asking for heavier assignments. The great victory of modern industry is that even its victims, the bored workers, cannot imagine any other way of organizing work, now that the tradition of the early-nineteenth-century Luddites, who smashed machines, has disappeared with the general acceptance of progress. We must thus think of restriction of output and other sabotage of production as symptoms.[15]

Furthermore, the resentment that manifests itself in these symptoms helps engender a vicious circle, since it confirms the opinion of management that workers must be disciplined by bringing them together in

[14] It may be asked (and was) whether we can reverse our technical impetus and the trend toward automation without losing the very source of our leisure and our high productivity. In my opinion, we are already far past the point where we must be bound by such alternatives. In the great world of impoverished people with a very low life expectancy and the annual income of, let us say, an Indonesian villager, the question would answer itself: many people would be willing to sacrifice much for the greater amenity and ease of life Americans have. But if in America the changes I am recommending would make industry less productive, which I doubt, I think many of us would be willing to pay the price of working harder and having less so that we might have a more meaningful life at work. In fact, however, we have no evidence it would lower our over-all productivity to redesign our industrial pattern. Instead, I am convinced that ideology dominates factory and machine design to such an extent that we have a dream or myth of efficiency whose long-run cumulative costs are enormous in the sabotage and resentment of the work force, in boredom, in absenteeism, and so on. Engineers still act as if workers were as undisciplined and inefficient a group as they were before mass education and before industrialism—and by so doing they make our industry less productive than it might be even in its own terms.

[15] For an understanding of how to look for and interpret such symptoms in a whole society or subculture, I am indebted to the work of Erich Fromm.

great factories and subjecting them to the relentless pressure of assembly lines—as against the possibility, for instance, that work could be decentralized so that workers would not have to commute long distances and could proceed more at their own pace and place.[16] In the high-wage industries given over to "conspicuous production," management has the resources to be concerned with the amenities of work—the group harmony, the decor, the cafeteria and other ancillary services—and to make provision for the worker's leisure, such as bowling teams, golf courses, and adult education courses too; in fact, a whole range of extracurricular pleasures and benefits. Sometimes these benefits include profit-sharing, but they are much less likely to include decision-sharing, for of course managers object less to giving away money, especially money that would otherwise go to stockholders or to the government in taxes, than to giving away power and prestige and freedom of action to workers whose unionized demands reflect merely their discontent and scarcely at all any desires for reconstruction.[17]

It is obvious in addition that managers are not free to reorganize their plants in order to provide their workers with a more satisfying work environment, if this might risk higher costs, unless their competitors are prepared to go along. Yet competition is not the whole story, for the situation is hardly better and is often worse in nationalized industries in Great Britain and Western Europe generally, while the situation of industrial workers in the Soviet Union today reminds one of the worst excesses of the Victorian era and the earlier days of the industrial revolution in the West. Managers of whatever ideological stripe seek to measure themselves against a single, unidimensional standard by which

[16] Cf. Daniel Bell, *Work and Its Discontents, supra;* also "The Evasion of Work" in *Work and the Welfare Age,* L.P.E. Papers #4, July 1956, pages 23–30.

[17] What is General Motors to make, for instance, of some of the UAW locals' demands which are being presented in the current negotiations as these pages go to press, e.g., that the scores of World Series and other baseball games be announced at the end of each inning over the public address system or that motor scooters be furnished for union committeemen, or that workers be allowed to buy GM products at 40 per cent off! Another demand, that schedules be adjusted to allow employees wanting to go deer hunting to take time off (as in fact many do anyway), has a pre-industrial ring to it but hardly betokens a new rearrangement of work and leisure. See *Time,* June 9, 1958, page 84.

Lest I be misunderstood, let me make clear that I am not recommending arduousness per se, nor do I object at all to the steps workers and unions have taken to make life pleasanter and less exhausting.

they can judge performance and thus are drawn to simplified work routines and an unremitting drive for maximum output. To open the possible consideration of factories as making not only things but also men, and as providing not only comfort and pay but also challenge and education, this would itself be a challenge to the way we have assimilated technology for the last three hundred years; and it would compel us to search for more Gestaltist and amorphous standards, in which we were no longer so clear as to what is process and what is product. There have, to be sure, been paternalistic employers (such as the Lowell mills in the 1840s or the Pullman plant a half century ago) concerned with the education and uplift of their operatives—often to the eventual resentment and unionization of the latter (who felt it was enough to have to work for the bosses without imitating their preferred inhibitions). But these were efforts to compensate outside the plant for the dehumanization regarded as inevitable within. What I am asking for now are explorations in reorganizing work itself so that man can live humanely on as well as off the job.

VII

The work of the managers themselves, of course, striving to get out production in the face of technical and human obstacles, is seldom boring, although if the product itself is socially valueless, a point may be reached where work upon it, despite technical challenges, is felt as stultifying. Indeed, one could argue that the great disparities of privilege today are in the realm of the nature of work rather than in the nature of compensation: it has proved easier partially to equalize the latter through high-wage and tax policies than to begin at all on the former, which would require still greater readjustments. In that brilliant precursor of much contemporary science fiction, Aldous Huxley's *Brave New World,* the lower cadres are given over to fairly undiluted hedonism while serious work and thought are reserved for the ruling "Alphas." Likewise, a recent science-fiction story once more illuminates the issue (it is my impression that science fiction is almost the only genuinely subversive new literature in wide circulation today[18]): this

[18] Regrettably, few women appear to read science fiction and thus they fail to connect with a literature which at its best satirizes the additive and mechanistic quality of life; the world of technology remains a very "male" world and women rarely penetrate the technological fantasy to see the political fantasy which is on occasion at work underneath.

is a story by Frederick Pohl called "The Midas Plague" which pictures a society in which the upper classes are privileged by being allowed to spend less time and zeal in enforced consumption; they are permitted to live in smaller houses and to keep busy fewer robots in performing services for them.[19] Their ration points—rations to extend rather than to limit consumption—are fewer; their cars are smaller; the things and gadgets that surround them are less oppressive. Best of all, they are allowed to work at work rather than having to spend four or five days a week simply as voracious consumers. That is, as one rises in the status system by excelling at consumership, one is allowed a larger and larger scope for what Veblen called the instinct of workmanship.

As already indicated, the world presented in "The Midas Plague," as in so much science fiction, is all too little a fiction. For, if we except a number of farmers and skilled workers, such as tool- and diemakers, it is the professional and executive groups who at present have the most demanding and interesting work and for whom, at least until retirement, leisure is least a time to kill. A survey by *Fortune* in 1957 showed that top executives, despite giving the appearance of being relaxed and of taking it easy as our mores demand, work an average of sixty hours a week or more. In many other fields, the leisure revolution has increased the demands on those who service the leisure of others or who have charge of keeping the economy and the society, or considerable segments of it, from falling apart. High civil servants and diplomats probably work as hard or harder than ever. The same is true of a good many teachers and professors who are presumably training others to spend their leisure wisely! . . .

In our egalitarian society, however, it would be surprising if the attitude of the masses did not influence the classes (there are of course also influences running the other way). As I remarked at the outset, I have the impression that a general decline is occurring in the zest for work, a decline which is affecting even those professional and intellectual groups whose complaint to their wives that they are overworked has often in the past been a way of concealing the fact that their work interested them rather more than did their wives. For example, there is some slight evidence that application lists to medical school are no

[19] "The Midas Plague," in *The Case against Tomorrow* (New York: Ballantine Books, 1957). I am indebted to Eric Larrabee for a reference to this story and for conversations concerning matters touched on in this paper.

longer so full, a decline which is attributed to the belief among young people that medical education is too arduous and takes too long before one is stabilized on a plateau of suburban life and domesticity. Similar tendencies would appear to be affecting those already in medical school. Howard S. Becker and Blanche Geer report (from the study of medical education at the University of Kansas being carried out under the direction of Professor Everett C. Hughes) that the teaching faculty complains that the students are no longer as interested in the more theoretical or scientific aspects of medicine: three quarters of them are married, and, instead of sitting around waiting for night duty or talking about their work, they are eager to go home, help the wife get dinner, and relax with television.

Likewise, there is evidence that young men in the big law firms, although they still work harder than most of their clients, do not glory in putting in night work and weekend hours as they once did. And several architects have told me that similar changes are showing up even in this field, which is famous for the enthusiasm of its devotees and the zest for work built up during *charettes* at architectural school. (Possibly, this may reflect in part the loss of the enthusiasm of the crusade on behalf of "modern" and the routinization of what had once been an esoteric creed.)

If such tendencies are showing up in the professions to which, in the past, men have been most devoted, it is not surprising that they should also be appearing in large-scale business enterprise. Though top executives may work as hard as ever—in part perhaps because, being trained in an earlier day, they can hardly help doing so—their subordinates are somewhat less work-minded. The recruiters who visit college campuses in order to sign up promising seniors or graduate students for large corporations have frequently noted that the students appear at least as interested in the fringe benefits as in the nature of the work itself; I would myself interpret this to signify that they have given up the notion that the work itself can be exciting and have an outlook which is not so very different from that of the typical labor-union member: they want and expect more but not so very much more than the latter.

The movement to the suburbs is of course a factor in these developments, especially now that young men move to the suburbs not only for the sake of their wives and young children and the latter's schooling but also for their own sake. It is hard, for example, for a scientific laboratory to maintain a nighttime climate of intense intellectual enthusiasm when its professional cadres are scattered over many suburbs and when the five-day week has become increasingly standard throughout American life (outside of a few universities which cling to the older five-and-a-half-day pattern). The sport-shirted relaxed suburban culture presents a standing reproach to the professional man who works at night and Saturdays instead of mowing the lawn, helping the Little League baseball team, and joining in neighborly low-pressure sociability. The suburbs continue the pattern of the fraternity house in making it hard for an individual to be a ratebuster or an isolate.

It is difficult to form a just estimate of the extent and scope of these changes. It is not new for the older generation to bewail the indolence of the young, and there is a tendency for the latter to maintain much of the older ethic screened by a new semantics and an altered ideology. Moreover, Americans in earlier periods were not uniformly work-minded. In Horace Greeley's account of his famous trip West in 1859 (which ended in his interviewing Brigham Young), he commented with disgust on the many squatters on Kansas homesteads who, in contrast to the industrious Mormons, sat around improvidently, building decent shelter neither for themselves nor for their stock (they sound a bit like Erskine Caldwell types).[20] Similarly, the correspondence of railroad managers in the last century (and railroad managers were perhaps the most professional managerial groups, as they were in charge of the largest enterprises) is full of complaints about the lack of labor discipline; this is one reason that the Chinese were brought in to work on the transcontinental roads. There were, it is evident, many backsliders in the earlier era from the all-pervading gospel of work, and the frontier, like many city slums, harbored a number of drifters.[21] Today, in contrast, the gospel of work is far less tenacious and overbearing, but at the same time the labor force as a whole is postindustrial in the

[20] Eric Hoffer has written that people who remember the "real" pioneers describe them in terms which resemble our picture of the Okies. "The Role of the Undesirables," *Harper's*, December 1952.

[21] Even if proportionally there has been only a slight shift in the number of people who have no zest for work or shirk it, the social accent has shifted. It is clear from Leo Lowenthal's article on the change from heroes of production to heroes of consumption that even when men at work are pictured today in the mass media, what is emphasized is less their work than their golf score, their weekend behavior, their family life—and this emphasis must feed back to the men themselves and give them an image of how they ought to behave.

sense of having lost much of its pre-industrial resistance to the clock and to factory discipline generally.[22]

VIII

So far, I have largely been discussing the uneven distribution of leisure in terms of differential attitudes toward work in different occupational groups. In comparison with the achievements of our occupational sociology, however, we have little comparable information concerning the sociology of leisure. For instance, we have very few inventories of how leisure is actually spent (apart from fairly complete information concerning exposure to the mass media). Pitirim Sorokin before World War II[23] and more recently Albert J. Reiss, Jr.,[24] have tried to get people to keep diaries which would include accounts of their day-by-day use of leisure time; but these suffer from faulty memory and stereotyping (people often say, "one day is just like another," and report accordingly) as well as from omissions of fights and other improper activities. A more systematic study than most, by Alfred Clarke, found that radio and TV listening were the top two activities for both upper and lower prestige groups, followed by studying in the upper group

[22] It would be interesting to know to what extent this change is a result of a general speeding up in the pace of life which seems to accompany urbanization and industrialization. I am told, for example, that the music of Bach and Mozart is played today some 10 per cent faster than the original tempo (the pitch is also higher). And it may be that the mass media, with their swift movement, help to expedite the rhythms of our contemporary life at work as well as at play. In this connection, Warner Bloomberg, Jr., has observed that factory workers in Gary sometimes have a hard time keeping their productivity down to the agreed-upon norms: they are apt to forget themselves and, without half trying, turn out too much (perhaps a little like the experience we may often have on a thruway of finding ourselves going faster than we had intended to). It would seem as if our society —in comparison with subsistence cultures—is geared to an interlacing of high-paced work and leisure; it gives that impression of speed-up still to visitors from abroad.

[23] Pitirim A. Sorokin and Clarence Q. Berger, *Time-Budgets of Human Behavior* (Cambridge, Mass.: Harvard University Press, 1939).

[24] Albert J. Reiss, Jr., "Rural-Urban and Social Status Differences in Interpersonal Contacts." Paper delivered at the American Sociological Society meetings, August 1958.

and do-it-yourself activities in the lower.[25] The latter spend much more time just driving around, as well as polishing the car; they also spend much more time in taverns. Only in the upper group do people go out to parties, as against simply dropping in on a neighbor to look at TV or chat in the kitchen; and going to meetings is also largely confined to the upper group. In both groups, commercial recreation outside the home, such as going to the movies, plays little part. This and other, more impressionistic studies point to the conclusion that the busier people, the professionals and executives and better-educated groups generally, also lead a more active life in their time away from work; as the saying goes, they work hard and play hard. In Reiss's study, for example, there turned up a surgeon at a leading hospital who went to Mass every morning, then to the hospital, then to attend to his private practice; he belonged to about every community organization, and he and his wife entertained three or four nights a week. Contrastingly, at the other end of the social scale, the unemployed as we know from several studies have in a psychological sense no leisure time at all; they, and the underprivileged generally, do not belong to voluntary associations (churches and unions are an occasional exception); they live what is often a shorter life on a slower timetable.

At the same time, as I have indicated above, it is among the less privileged groups relatively new to leisure and consumption that the zest for possessions retains something of its pristine energy. Consumership which is complex if not jaded among the better-educated strata seems to be relatively unequivocal among those recently released from poverty and constriction of choice (although since the recession began, some of the latter may feel that they have been too ready victims for advertising and salesmanship and easy credit). With very little hope of making work more meaningful, these people look to their leisure time and consumership for the satisfactions and pride previously denied them by the social order. . . .

IX

Even the most confident economists cannot adequately picture a society which could readily stow away the goods likely to descend upon us in the next fifteen years (assuming only a modest rise in annual

[25] Alfred C. Clarke, "Leisure and Levels of Occupational Prestige," *American Sociological Review*, vol. 21 (1956), pp. 301–7; see also Robert J. Havighurst, "The Leisure Activities of the Middle-Aged," *American Journal of Sociology*, vol. 63 (1957), pp. 152–62.

productivity), with any really sizable drop in defense expenditures. People who are forced by the recession or by fear of their neighbors' envy or by their own misgivings to postpone for a year the purchase of a new car may discover that a new car every three years instead of every two is quite satisfactory. And once they have two cars, a swimming pool and a boat, and summer and winter vacations, what then?

Increasingly, as we all know, the motivation researchers are being pressed to answer these questions, and to discover what the public does not yet know that it "wants." Just as we are lowering our water table by ever-deeper artesian wells and in general digging ever deeper for other treasures of the earth, so we are sinking deeper and deeper wells into people in the hope of coming upon "motives" which can power the economy or some particular sector of it. I am suggesting that such digging, such forcing emotions to externalize themselves, cannot continue much longer without man running dry.

Even now, some of the surplus whose existence presents us with such questions is being absorbed in the very process of its creation by what I have termed the "conspicuous production" of our big corporations, acting as junior partners of the welfare state and absorbing all sorts of ancillary services for their own members and their own communities.[26]

Defense expenditures loom so large in our political as well as economic horizon because they do offer an easy and seemingly feasible way out by creating goods which do not themselves create other goods. (They are "multipliers" only in a Keynesian sense.) I would contend that expenditures which serve no real social imperative, other than propping up the economy or subduing the sibling rivalry of the armed services, will eventually produce wasteful by-products to slow that economy down in a tangle of vested inefficiencies, excessively conspicuous production, lowered work morale, and lack of purpose and genuine inventiveness.[27] The word "to soldier" means "to loaf" and conscription

[26] As Professor Galbraith makes abundantly clear in his book (*supra*, note 6), these corporations along with their employees are actually senior partners, with the State and its subdivisions in contrast living shabbily as a very junior partner in a period of inflation. See *The Affluent Society*, ch. 14, 18, and elsewhere.

[27] Discussion-period question: "Isn't there a good deal of cynicism or debunking among workers concerning the product they are making?" Answer: "You are right that the problem of meaning in work lies not only in its intellectual or physical gamesmanship but in its relevance to the total social context. Thus, one could make work in an aircraft plant or missile

gives training in soldiering to a large proportion of the future work force (despite islands of asceticism in the Strategic Air Command or the air-borne "brushfire" infantry). For a time, men will go on producing because they have got the habit, but the habit is not contagious. Men will scarcely go on producing as mere items in a multiplier effect or conscripts in an endless cold war, nor will they greatly extend themselves to earn more money which they are increasingly bored with spending. To be sure, many workers have little objection to getting paid without earning it by traditional standards of effortfulness. And while those standards are usually irrelevant in a society of advanced technology and high expenditures on research and development, there are certainly many parts of the economy, notably in the service trades, whose gross inefficiency we only conceal from ourselves by contrasting America with pre-industrial societies or with those possessing far less adequate resources of men and machines—if we compare ourselves with the West Germans, for instance, or with the Canadians, the advance in our economy since 1946, great as it is in absolute terms, is unimpressive. The pockets of efficiency in our society are visible and made more so by the myth that we are efficient; hence, the evidence of disintegration and incompetence that is all around us strikes us as temporary or aberrant.

X

Correspondingly, some of our desires have been made highly visible by advertising and market research and lead to equally visible results such as good cars and, intermittently, good roads to drive them over. But other desires, which require co-operation to be effective, are often lamely organized and all but invisible. Thus, while some of us have a missionary zeal for learning, which we regard as the basis of later leisure as well as later employment, we have not been helped even by the

plant more intriguing without in all dimensions making it more meaningful. Of course it does not prove that something is a good product because it gets bought. Cynicism among advertising men comes out of the feeling that the work they do, although creative in many ways—artistic, imaginative, ingenious in terms of research methods—is not meaningful or is actually harmful, so that they don't enjoy it. Surely this is the feeling of many intellectuals, whose work, although demanding and challenging, is not worthwhile. We must proceed on both fronts: to make the work more invigorating and pleasant in its own terms, that is, in terms of technical operations, and in terms of its bearing on what adds to human growth and development."

push of sputnik to get a bill for school construction past the same Congress which eagerly voted federal money for highways (in part, no doubt, because the annual maintenance of schools falls upon a local tax base which grows constantly more inadequate while the maintenance of highways can be more easily financed from gasoline and registration taxes).[28] Other services, not so clearly "a good thing" as secondary and university education, are even more lacking in organized institutional forms which would permit the channeling of our surplus in ways which would improve the quality and texture of daily life. For example, even the great demand for scenic beauty (anemically reflected in the new highways) cannot make itself politically felt in preserving the countryside against roadside slums and metropolitan expansion, while men of wealth who could buy up whole counties and give them to the nation as a national park are lacking. It is extraordinary how little we have anticipated the problems of the bountiful future, other than to fall back on remedies which did not work in the less bountiful past, such as individualism, thrift, hard work, and enterprise on the one side, or harmony, togetherness, and friendliness on the other. Meanwhile, we stave off the fear of satiation in part by scanning the technological horizon for new goods that we will all learn to want, in part by the delaying tactic of a semiplanned recession, and, as already indicated, in part by the endless race of armaments.

That race has its cultural as well as Keynesian dynamic: as poll data show, a majority or large plurality of Americans expect war, though perhaps in a rather abstract way—war is one of those extrapolations from the past; like technological progress, we find it hard to resist. And, on the one hand, the threat of war is one factor in discouraging long-term plans, while, on the other hand, the continuation of the cold war provides a sort of alternative to planning. Thus, there tends to be a state of suspended animation in the discussion concerning the quality of life a rich society should strive for; social inventiveness tends to be channeled into the defense of past gains rather than into ideas for a better proportionality between leisure and work. Like soldiers off duty, "as you were," we subsist in default of more humane hopes.

But I should add that no other society has ever been in the same position as ours, of coming close to fulfilling the age-old dream of free-

---

[28] On this point, as on so many others of this paper, Professor Galbraith's discussion adds clarity and perspective. See *The Affluent Society*, chs. 11, 13, 22, 25, and *passim*.

dom from want, the dream of plenty. And I want to repeat that millions of Americans, perhaps still the great majority, find sufficient vitality in pursuit of that dream: the trip to the end of the consumer rainbow retains its magic for the previously deprived. Yet, by concentrating all energies on preserving freedom from want and pressing for consumer satiation at ever more opulent levels, we jeopardize this achievement in a world where there are many more poor nations than rich ones and in which there are many more desires, even among ourselves, for things other than abundance.

Some Issues in the Future of Leisure
(WITH ROBERT S. WEISS, 1961)

We want in this article to explore some of the problems in the use of the leisure that technological and organizational development have brought within our reach. Primarily, we shall be concerned with the consequences for the industrial worker of the new phase of the industrial revolution in which the level of productivity for mass-produced articles is almost independent of the input of human energy, and leisure consequently is available to just those men who might once have found themselves condemned to endless days in the plant. Secondarily, we shall be concerned with the consequences for members of the professional and managerial stratum of a shift in our cultural climate by which work seems to have lost some of its centrality, although the hours of work demanded of professionals and managers, and the psychic arduousness of their tasks have declined little, if at all.

WORK AND LEISURE FOR THE INDUSTRIAL WORKERS

It is a political and economic problem to ensure that leisure be the consequence of technological developments, and not simply unemployment. This first, and basic, problem is far from solved. Wage protection alone is not the answer, although Galbraith has cogently argued[1] for maintaining the purchasing power of the unemployed at almost the level they realized while employed. Such a measure fails to give to men the structuring of the day, the feeling of personal adequacy, and the relatedness to society that only work provides for most adult male Americans. It is true that if industrial workers are asked in a survey why a job is important, they tend to respond with matter-of-fact phrases like "You have to work to eat," or "That's the way the society works."

[1] John Kenneth Galbraith, *The Affluent Society* (Boston: Houghton-Mifflin, 1958).

Yet these conventional remarks cover the fact that for most of them holding down a job is necessary to a sense of responsible and respectable adulthood.[2] Not only do they feel that it is a man's role, in a timeworn phrase, "to bring home the bacon," but a sizable minority of them believe that marriage is important because it provides a man with a family for whom he may work.[3] (A paradoxical reversal of the image of the man trapped into marriage and a life of servitude.) To be sure, there are exceptions in those groups and communities that have adapted to widespread, endemic unemployment. Young single men awaiting military service are often at a disadvantage in seeking employment; occasionally, having dropped out of school, they may seek to prove their manliness by what is ironically called juvenile delinquency. So, too, those discriminated against in the job market, such as Negroes and Puerto Ricans in Harlem, may find other patterns of masculinity.

In a society where most men work, the job furnishes a metronome-like capacity to keep in order one's routine of waking and sleeping, time on and time off, life on and life off the job. As surveys show, however, only a minority of industrial workers have any interest in the jobs themselves: it would be amazing to find a job so satisfying that a man would be anxious to continue with it after the day is over. Occasionally a skilled machinist will take pride in his ability to turn out a blueprinted piece, or in his ingenuity in outwitting the time-study man, but these accomplishments seldom suffice to sustain his interest during a long day spent setting and nursing a turret lathe. Moreover, as Robert Dubin has argued, not even the community that springs up on the shop floor is of great moment to the production worker,[4] although his membership in it and liking for it may be essential in permitting him to get through the day.[5] His relations with his fellows are neither deep nor

[2] Material on the functions of work is based on a study by R. S. Weiss and R. L. Kahn, supported by a grant from the Institute of Labor and Industrial Relations, The University of Michigan—Wayne State University. See also R. S. Weiss and R. L. Kahn, "Definitions of Work and Occupation," *Social Problems,* 8 (Fall 1960), pp. 142–51.

[3] Based on unpublished results of a survey conducted by the Survey Research Center, University of Michigan, 1953.

[4] Robert Dubin, "Industrial Workers' Worlds: A Study of the Central Life Interests of Industrial Workers," *Social Problems* (January 1956), pp. 131–42.

[5] Donald Roy, "Banana Time," *Human Organization,* Volume 18, No. 4 (Winter 1959–60), pp. 158–68.

necessarily permanent. No matter how friendly the work group to which he belongs, the industrial worker is unlikely to stay on a job simply because of his group membership; instead, he is likely to assume that his next job will furnish him with an equally good group of men to work with. Save in the form of car pools, work contacts are almost never carried off the job. (Not that this is necessarily regrettable: contacts off the job may be regarded as all the more refreshing because they differ or appear to differ from those on the job.)

Given the lack of intrinsic interest in work, it is not surprising that during the last century the lower ranks of industrial and office workers have taken part of the gains of productivity in the form of time off rather than in the form of increased pay. Up to a certain point, this drive to reduce hours is a drive also to increase one's chances to be human: but when waking time outside of work comes to equal or exceed waking time at work, the marginal utility of further free time or unpaid time may come into question. Even so, the drive to reduce hours continues. Perhaps it is partly maintained by the sheer momentum of the revolution by which the working class has become the new leisure class; partly by the growing cynicism regarding the intrinsic worth of any work, which is noted by Paul Goodman in *Growing Up Absurd*;[6] and partly by the high hopes of what a holiday may bring, which is to be found among those who, like many workers as well as many school children, are thoroughly bored with what they normally do; and justified always by the need to spread the work as a response to automation. Indeed, in the light of the purposes a job serves, reduction in the hours spent at work does not require any redefinition of the importance of work: so long as one has a job, requiring some substantial fraction of time, work has met its most important requirement for the industrial worker. Yet when free time is empty and resembles a temporary layoff more than it does an anticipated weekend, men begin to be restless; many complain that the day is filled by small tasks requested by their wives. Continued reduction of the work week may yet come to mean for many men, not so much that they will give a disliked employer even less for more, but that they will again have gotten more free time than they know what to do with.

One development, of course, anticipated by Veblen, has postponed this day of reckoning; namely, that the free time is time to expose

[6] Paul Goodman, *Growing Up Absurd* (New York: Random House, 1960).

oneself to all the stimuli for acquiring new consumer tastes, which in turn require new sources of income. Certainly increased leisure does not reduce financial need, and, where the six-hour day has been introduced, many men have taken on second jobs.[7] The unions are sharply opposed to the practice, on ideological grounds, since it defeats the aim of a reduced work week for members, and on practical grounds, since it means there are then fewer jobs to go around. Yet the practice is insidious, and in union circles it is whispered that even union officials have taken on second jobs as real estate agents or bartenders or cab drivers. The most obvious explanation, and the one offered by union officials, is that the men are "money-hungry" and no doubt the increasing rain of commercial appeals on all members of the family encourages a creeping inflation of desires. But this is an insufficient explanation. These same men would object violently to working on holidays such as the Fourth of July, let alone Christmas, irrespective of double- or triple-time wages. Few of them, we would guess, would be willing to work seven days without a break, and most would object to having weekdays off instead of Saturday and Sunday. Rather, what has happened is that they have free time that is not clearly earmarked for leisure. It is as though their jobs suddenly turned from full time to three-quarter time, and they must decide whether to loaf in that extra quarter time available or to go out and earn some money. And, given not only the desire for newer cars or refrigerators, but the indebtedness resulting from previous purchases, many members of this group could hardly help feeling that they had no right to work only part-time when, with only a little enterprise, they can find a second job which will bring them up to full-time. Nor are members of this group likely to catch up. There is a built-in cumulativeness about many consumer goods: a house can always be added to or improved; a car is a standing invitation to travel and to evenings out on the town; a television set, an invitational mirror of the good life.

It is hard to see any way out of this spiral in the distribution of leisure to industrial workers. Given incomes inadequate to aspirations, and aggressive selling through the mass media and elsewhere, with resulting indebtedness, is it likely that the individual who is in debt will accept a thirty-hour or a twenty-hour week without looking for another

[7] Harvey Swados, "Less Work—Less Leisure," in *Mass Leisure*, Eric Larrabee and Rolf Meyersohn eds. (Glencoe, Illinois: The Free Press, 1958), pp. 353–63.

job? What indeed are the alternatives for him? He has now more time than necessary to recuperate from work's pressures or compensate for its demands: increase in the amount of leisure means that not only will there be more time for compensatory activities—to the extent that this is a primary function of leisure—but that there will be less need for such activities. Thus, recuperation from work's pressures as a rationale for the use of leisure time may no longer loom so large. Even if recuperation remains important, a man may decide that another job of a very different sort is just as "recreational" as one more evening spent bowling or looking at television or driving about.

An ironic commentary on the pressure toward a reduction in the work week is provided by a study in which industrial workers were asked what they would do if they had an extra hour a day; most of them responded: "Sleep."[8] While for a few this may bespeak an overfull life, and for others a general irritation with a nettling or silly question, the answer seems to us to symbolize the lack of interests and resources that could give point to the leisure time that is now available. A study of the impact of the four-day week in a situation where it was too unpredictably scheduled to permit other employment on the additional day off, indicates that this additional day was less of a boon for the workers than they had originally anticipated.[9] The extra day off was not a day off for the children, so there was an empty house during school hours; nor was it a day off for the wife, so there was housecleaning and vacuuming, with the man in the way. In this plant, a small aircraft manufacturing company in southern California, the four-day week was scheduled for one week out of four. Though originally looked forward to with high hopes, it was soon disliked: television, loafing, ball games, all these were felt to be weekend activities, and fell flat during the work week. One wonders whether, even in California, this reflects residual Puritanism, analogous to the feeling that it is wicked to go to the movies in the morning. It certainly does reflect the social or festive nature of much valued leisure, as well as the difficulty in developing a program for the use of a sizable increase in leisure time when other members of the family and the community are not equally free.

When we talk of programming, in fact, we come to a characteristic

[8] Reported by Rolf Meyersohn.
[9] Rolf Meyersohn, "Some Consequences of Changing Work and Leisure Routines," paper presented to the Fourth Congress of Sociology, Section on Leisure, Milan-Stresa, Italy, September 1959.

which seems most common within working-class groups: the lack of the middle-class pattern of postponed gratification and planning ahead, if not actual contempt for it. Only a few of these men use increased leisure to prepare themselves for higher vocational tasks. Only a few turn out for union meetings, and fewer still evidence any interest in improving the lot of the occupational group to which they belong or in taking a hand in the decisions that may affect them in the future. So, too, Great Books courses or union education programs seem to attract few workers. This relative indifference has not always been the case: in the period before the Civil War, energetic workmen, in a burst of enthusiasm for science and literacy, created and attended the Mechanics Institutes. Presently our educational system tends to siphon off from the working class the more literate and ambitious, while at the same time there is lacking in this country for the most part the level of intensive secondary education that, in countries like Denmark or Japan, leads many workers to become active, lifelong readers. Furthermore, the ideological appeals that drive some workers in a country like Yugoslavia to pursue educational and agitational tasks have largely vanished from what is no longer a labor movement but a (somewhat shrinking) labor vested interest.

In this situation, most industrial workers appear to fall back on their families as the enclave within which leisure is to be spent. The long drive on Sunday, with its combination of aimlessness and togetherness, is traditional in this group. Leisure time away from the family, "with the boys," is defined as time for blowing off steam and is limited to what is thought to be physiologically and psychologically necessary. Of course, this is not the whole story. Many workers cultivate fairly expensive and time-consuming hobbies, such as hunting. Some attend art classes for adults, and a handful may join the predominately middle-class groups devoted to amateur music. A very few take part in voluntary associational activities; by and large these are staffed by the upper social strata.

It is discomfitting to reflect on the complexity and scope of the programs that would be required to overcome this legacy of passivity and aimlessness. What sort of adult-education program could meet these workers halfway in helping them plan their leisure in terms of lifelong opportunities? What sort of change of perspective on the world and the self is required before muted and barely realized dissatisfactions can become a lever for individual development?

At the level of the society the problems are no less grave. Where the recreationist works for the public rather than the private sector, he has as little leverage at his disposal as the city planner has. One of us recently had the chance to observe the enormous resistance that developed in a small Vermont community to a recreation leader's idea that the town should build a swimming pool, rather than some monument, as a war memorial: the project was fought by the town's elders as frivolous and a waste of money, in spite of the fact that the nearby rivers had become too polluted for swimming. Only great civic effort finally carried the project through, and now "everyone" can see what a boon it is to children and their parents, to farmers and workers after a hot day, and to otherwise idle teen-agers, who can display themselves on the high dives, or, if they swim well enough, make a little money and gain some sense of responsibility from helping act as lifeguards around the pool. One consequence of the political weakness of public recreation is a tendency to overideologize particular leisure-time activities, exaggerating their importance and their potential contribution to individual character and the fabric of society. The President's campaign for physical fitness as a way of beating the Russians is an illustration. College sports may have suffered in the same way; it has repeatedly been shown, in novels and in the newspapers, that football or basketball do not inevitably build character. Yet it is hard to see how social forms adequate to the new leisure can be developed without an ideology that will mobilize people and strengthen the power of the few groups who are now concerned with the preservation of wilderness areas, the setting aside of land in our sprawling metropolitan belts for the play of adults and children, and the general release of resources other than commercial ones for experimentation and research in the field of leisure.

In comparison with the organizational forms developed for the integration of effort at work, there barely exist the social forms within which the energies of leisure might be developed or even illustrated. Yet this whole observation evokes the image of the Boy Scouts or the YMCA, and the whole paradox of planning for the use of what is an uncommitted part of one's life. Leisure is supposed to be informal, spontaneous, and unplanned,[10] and is often defined as unobligated time, not only free of the job but free of social or civic obligations, moonlighting, or more or less requisite do-it-yourself activities. One re-

[10] See, in this connection, "Sociability, Permissiveness, and Equality," p. 196; and, also by Riesman, Robert J. Potter and Jeanne Watson, "The Vanishing Host," in *Human Organization,* Volume 19, No. 1 (Spring 1960), pp. 17–27.

sult of this outlook, however, is to discourage whatever planning is possible (except, perhaps, in terms of the family, not always the optimal unit for leisure when one thinks of the development of its individual members). When we confront such problems, we are inclined to think that significant changes in the organization of leisure are not likely to come in the absence of changes in the whole society: in its work, its political forms, and its cultural style.

LEISURE IN THE BUSINESS AND PROFESSIONAL STRATA

As we have indicated at the outset, young business and professional people cannot by and large look forward to a decreasing work week or decreasing work day; nevertheless, it is our impression that there is a relative decline in the emotional loading of on-the-job and off-the-job activities.[11] Less and less do men in these strata behave as though, in Margaret Mead's terms, "Leisure must be earned by work and good works . . . (and) . . . while it is enjoyed it must be seen in a context of future work and good works."[12] Instead, leisure becomes an opportunity for what are being defined as the really important tasks of life: care for home and family, service to the community, exploration and gratification of the self. Thus, while work is losing its hold on the time of the industrial worker, it is moderating its demands on the interest and dedication of the business and professional person. In fact, the familism of these latter strata comes more and more to resemble that of the industrial worker.

Even so, there are still very large differences in different occupations with respect to the centrality of work. Top managers, as surveys and stories make clear, can still work sixty- and seventy-hour weeks without feeling too remorseful about neglect of domesticity. In contrast, physicians, college instructors, and schoolteachers may work equally long hours but without quite so good a conscience about their neglect of their families and themselves. It is in these latter groups that one sees developing a more complex concept of what one might do with one's

[11] See, on the future aspirations of college students, David Riesman, "The College Student In an Age of Organization," *Chicago Review*, Vol. 12, No. 3 (Autumn 1958), pp. 50–68.
[12] Margaret Mead, "The Pattern of Leisure in Contemporary American Culture," in *Mass Leisure*, Eric Larrabee and Rolf Meyersohn, eds. (Glencoe, Illinois: The Free Press, 1958), pp. 10–15.

life, a concept that requires that individuals achieve self-realization as well as a certain position in the community. Attention to the family and to the community tend to become elements of this new aim, though perhaps insufficient in themselves. What is clear is that the individual who has only his work is thought to be one-sided, possibly sick, and certainly unfortunate. Similar attitudes may be spreading in the ranks of middle management, where junior executives may realize that they are not indispensable and that, in an increasingly complex and bureaucratic society, they may be fools to drive themselves only in order to achieve a moderately greater income and vastly greater responsibilities.

But these tendencies are only incipient, and most business and professional men view their work in terms of a career rather than a job, and depend on their work, not only to structure their day and to provide a minimal sense of adequacy, but for a sense that they are living up to their potentialities and their education. In business and in many professions it is very difficult to prevent the invasion of leisure by the requirements of one's career. For example, cocktail parties may be necessary to cement work relationships; evening courses and summer seminars may be necessary to "keep up," let alone advance; and the full briefcase carried home at night tends to accompany professional and managerial responsibilities.

Undoubtedly, the middle-class person is likely to have many greater resources for using his generally smaller quotient of leisure. He possesses the financial and intellectual resources for complex hobbycraft equipment, for attending lectures and concerts and art museums, for skin-diving and skiing, and for reading nonfiction (while his wife reads novels). He may also be prepared to invest time in the development of new skills because, despite the growth of fun morality, he is likely to retain a belief in long-range planning, and distant goals. Furthermore, unlike the industrial worker, he is likely to look for activities in which he may make new friends with similar interests, just as his sociability is more formal and less likely to be confined to the family. Yet these class differences should not be exaggerated. There are a great many businessmen who find no leisure activity of great interest although they, unlike the industrial worker, are apt to find their work engrossing. Many of these regard leisure as time to be spent with one's family, time which is dull, obligatory, but nevertheless important. This becomes all too clear when these men are forcibly retired and when, despite ample financial resources, they sometimes go to pieces much as do the unemployed. Many of them feel that release from work leaves a void, one not easily filled by recreational activities. A few manage to substitute voluntary unpaid work in civic and charitable affairs, but most lack the ability or flexibility or contacts to do this.[13]

There is also an ideology of anti-planning in these strata, corresponding to the ideology of anti-planning among working-class men. But, whereas the latter ideology opposes too intense planning for one's self, the former ideology opposes permitting one's life to be planned by others (except within the often very tightly planned organizations of which they are members); hence many in these strata would hardly welcome a government-sponsored program of planning for leisure such as we have mentioned above in connection with the industrial workers. Yet these men are often victims of poor phasing of the boon of leisure during their life cycle. Had this phasing been planned it would have become apparent that leisure can be packaged in a great many ways: late entrance into the labor force, permitting longer education, or more time for decision about future occupation; shorter days on the job, permitting second jobs, serious commitment to voluntary organizations, longer commuting ranges, or a great deal of time regularly spent around the house; longer weekends, permitting excursions, or an extra day spent entirely at home; longer vacations, permitting travel, or the alternation of an educational period with a work period; early partial retirement, permitting an individual to begin devoting himself to a new activity, a new occupation, or a new relationship to or rejection of the world where things are going on.

Very likely, people have different rhythms or personal "seasons" of work and nonwork which they should learn early in life and to which they should seek to adapt their careers. It seems likely to us that retirement will come ever earlier, certainly for the working class and probably for the executive class, as productivity marches on and as higher education spreads and suitable positions have to be found for presumptive members of the meritocracy.[14]

[13] See the comments on the retired in Alan Harrington, *Life in the Crystal Palace* (New York: Knopf, 1959).

[14] Morris Janowitz, in a personal communication, predicts that as the society becomes more affluent, and there is increasing recognition of the elements contributing to the "good life," there will be more pressure for early retirement from those in industrial work. This will arise not from economic considerations, but in order to permit them time to "get something out of life" after years of unrewarding work.

Of course, among the well-to-do, Veblenian motivations are not extinct, and the piling up of consumer goods (and playing the stock market as a form of moonlighting) still absorbs much energy. But for younger business and professional people who have always been reasonably comfortable and well fixed, the acquiring of possessions seldom becomes a mania, and the acquisition of cars, new homes, and *objets d'art* cannot fill even the residual leisure. One symptom of the restlessness that this occasions is the uneasy flirtation being carried on, in some of these groups, with the ascetic ideology of national purpose.[15] Durkheim long ago noted that nationalism is the religion appropriate to the modern state, and increasingly political action organizations appear to be enlisting the free energies of the emotionally underemployed.[16] It has been observed many times that race riots are more common in the summer, primarily because people are out-of-doors and have nothing else to do. (Not that they decide to organize a race riot, but they become interested in what is going on, and go down to see, and things go on from there.) Southern picket lines in Little Rock and New Orleans appear to be made up in large part of housewives whose children are no longer young enough to be all-absorbing, and who are seeking to discover, in the process of its defense, a "way of life" that permits them to use their leisure in marches, telephone harassment of opponents, and meetings with comrades which provide a sense of personal worth and belongingness. When leisure is absorbed in this way, one can only wish momentarily that television, ordinarily the greatest single occupant of leisure time, could draw these people back to the Westerns and other melodramas.

In the best of our college students we see a use of leisure that is often admirable: instead of the fraternity make-work of an earlier day, there is serious concern with current issues, with reading and companion-

---

[15] Several years ago one of us (D.R.) got a letter out of the blue from a group of business and professional men in a small Midwestern community who asked about the John Birch Society because they wanted to devote themselves to the fight against communism. Upon receiving the reply that in their whole state there were probably no more than a dozen Communists, half of them likely FBI agents, and that there were a number of less exciting but more worthwhile tasks to be accomplished in their local community, they terminated the correspondence.

[16] For its description of the way in which the well-to-do who would like to be considered natives in Santa Barbara, California, have joined the John Birch Society, see John D. Weaver, "Santa Barbara: Dilemma in Paradise," *Holiday*, 29 (June 1961), pp. 82–86.

ship, and often a strong interest in music, drama, literature, and nature. We need only compare these students, products of affluence, intelligence and civility, with many of their parents to see that the future of leisure is not merely a dangerous abyss. The first well-to-do generation, whether in this country or elsewhere, often spends its leisure as it spends its riches (if it does not hoard both) with self-defeating aimlessness. We have seen new Americans, released from the poverty of peasant backgrounds, go on a buying spree and end up possessed by their possessions—nostalgically still hungering for a vanished good life after the manner of Gatsby in Fitzgerald's novel. Having just escaped from poverty, they are not yet ready to escape from freedom. And then we have seen their children, often to the third and fourth generation, wonder what to do when the simplicity of the older goals has been destroyed and their meaninglessness revealed by experience and by contemporary social criticism.

Yet, today, we find among the best of our students many who do not think of themselves as an ascribed elite or even an ambitiously achieving one: they are democratically oriented and they are capable of solidarity and social concern. In fact they *are* an elite, but one which by its nature, may show the way for others. The students may represent a pattern that will flourish, one that will break down the boundaries between work and leisure without getting rid of either.

Sociability, Permissiveness, and Equality

A PRELIMINARY FORMULATION

(WITH ROBERT J. POTTER AND JEANNE WATSON, 1960)

For the past three years, a group of us at the University of Chicago has been studying the sociology of sociability (profiting, of course, from Simmel's brilliant paper on that topic[1]), primarily by participant observation of parties given by young, middle-class, urban adults;[2] but also by interviewing people concerning their experiences of sociability, and by examining ethnographic and other cross-cultural materials concerning the sociability of other times and places. In this paper, we generalize from our data in order to present some of the problems created for sociability by the decline in formality and the growth of an equalitarian ethos in America.

Learning to Observe Sociability

The participants in sociability whom we observed (outside of the elite) might be self-conscious as individuals, but they were seldom conscious of the patterns their behavior followed, of the leadership developed in sociable interaction (other than the all too obvious "life of the party"), or of the phases through which parties pass (other than those which conclude by people passing out). We had to discover from observation, rather than from interviewing participants, what divisions of labor exist in sociable groups, what types of leadership emerge, and what "products" there might be for participants as individuals or for the group itself. We had to learn for ourselves that it is possible to

[1] Georg Simmel, "Sociability (An Example of Pure, or Formal Sociability)," in *The Sociology of Georg Simmel*, edited and translated by Kurt Wolff (Glencoe, Ill., The Free Press, 1950), pp. 40–57.

[2] These and other descriptive data will be presented in forthcoming publications resulting from our studies of sociability.

take sociable behavior seriously, to regard it as no more aimless and random than Freud thought dreams to be.³

Both in observing parties and in interpreting them, we have moved back and forth between the group and the individual, always with an eye on the ways in which the group allows an individual to define himself, to defend himself, to discover himself, to align himself—ways which are not necessarily therapeutically relevant for him as a total person, but which are interpersonally and situationally relevant for him as a sociable, or potentially sociable, person. We have also kept an eye on the group as a group: on its preferred forms, on the flow of its behavior over time (within the party and between parties), and on the roles allotted to members. We trained ourselves to record these forms as best we might, while recognizing that much that occurs even at a fairly small party would escape the observer, or would escape us because we were observers.

Finally, we have regarded sociability as an art form, bringing forth a product which is partly verbal, partly choreographic or stylized and ritualized action—a product for which the producers are also the consumers, the performers also the audience. And we have not shied away from becoming critics of this artistry.

The Context for Sociability

While the standards for our criticism have been refined by our research, they do not spring directly from it, but rather from our previous thinking about personal autonomy and the relationship between an individual and his society.⁴ Sociability, like other forms of interaction,

---

³ Understandably, our efforts to make a serious study of sociability encountered resistance, both from colleagues and from "subjects." The serious ethical problems involved are not shelved by announcing to the guests at a party that one is observing them, for the real issue is the extent to which social scientists have a responsibility not to invade private life, even when given formal permission—especially when the cultural consequences of converting the latent into the manifest are not always happy (as can be seen, for instance, in the dehydrating effect psychoanalysis has sometimes had on parent-child relations). For a sensitive discussion of analagous dilemmas, see John R. Seeley, R. Alexander Sim, and Elizabeth W. Loosley, *Crestwood Heights: A Study of the Culture of Suburban Life* (New York, Basic Books, 1956).

⁴ See Nelson N. Foote and Leonard S. Cottrell, Jr., *Identity and Interpersonal Competence* (Chicago, University of Chicago Press, 1955); David Riesman, with Reuel Denney and Nathan Glazer, *The Lonely Crowd* (New Haven, Yale University Press, 1950); and *Individualism Reconsidered* (Glencoe, Ill., The Free Press, 1954).

has never been independent of its social context. No group exists without having its hegemonies influenced and its tasks set by the relationships which its members have beyond the group. Simmel pictured a salon society which made strenuous efforts to insulate itself from the contaminations of the worlds of competition, lust, and violence. Yet to the extent that subtle and complex rules are used by a leisure-class group to define and delimit what is permitted in sociability, it is likely that only those born to the rules of the group, or groomed early to assimilate them, can take part in its social affairs. This, as C. Wright Mills argues, makes sociability useful as a device for excluding lower-status persons and hence providing an upper-class forum for attitude-sharing and decision-making.[5] In this perspective, at least in the American context of self-salesmanship, exclusionary salons aiming at the kind of insulation and playfulness Simmel described run the risk of becoming exploited by their very efforts to keep out potential exploiters and "contaminating" topics.

We see sociability at its best as serving more than the functions of maintenance and repair—that is, of controlling anomie and providing an interlude for work-driven people or a forum which may serve their work, status, or self-esteem—although these are not negligible functions. In addition, we see sociability as lending drama to life, intensifying reality—and not only the reality of the relationships affirmed in sociability but those which exist, independent of the group, in the outer world. Much sociability, as we shall see, feeds upon itself; and this, despite its apparent freedom from inhibition and restraint, gives it a closet quality, intimate, at times festive, but still lacking the *élan* and aliveness that come of linking the sociable group to the larger society and the cosmos.[6] Such linking, if continuous, would be ponderous

[5] C. Wright Mills, Introduction to Thorstein Veblen, *The Theory of the Leisure Class* (New York: New American Library, Mentor Edition, 1953); p. xvi.

In many studies of small-town social structure, the country club looms as the locus of power. No doubt this mixture of play and power is very American, yet we wonder, considering the chronic threat to Simmel's "pure" sociability from sexual commerce and the commerce of self-salesmanship, whether he meant to eschew rather than describe the sociability of his day. Alternatively, too strenuous avoiding of outside contamination may engender a salon sociability too precious and fragile to be enjoyable.

[6] Arthur Miller has criticized contemporary playwriting from just such a perspective, insisting that the greatest plays are those which connect the

and would make work of sociability, or a lesson in civics. But in the groups we observed it seemed to us that people, in avoiding the big issues, made themselves smaller than need be[7]—that they were being obedient to an ethos of spontaneity, permissiveness, and equality, without full awareness of the constraints forced upon them by these contemporary American emancipations.

Work Groups Versus Play Groups

Early in our research, we turned for guidance to investigations of the interaction of work groups, task groups in laboratories, therapy groups in hospitals, classroom groups, and gangs on street corners. Such studies imply that there is no clear definitional boundary by which one might say that *this* is a purposive, task-oriented group whose sociability is ancillary to the task, and that *that* is a sociable, nonpurposive one. Rather, the theoretical clarification offered in George C. Homans, *The Human Group*,[8] suggests that groups forced to interact by a task tend to develop "static" interaction of an affective sort which sometimes facilitates and sometimes frustrates the achievement of the task. Conversely, an "unemployed" group like that portrayed in *Street Corner Society*,[9] with few if any clear-cut and tangible objectives, seems to develop over time a structure of leadership and even an agenda that makes it behave in some ways like a task group.

Nevertheless, thanks to many ingenious researches, interaction in a laboratory task group, complex as it is, seems today more readily analyzed than that in a sociable group of similar size. The task focuses the attention of the group, defines what is ancillary to itself, and thus facilitates the work of the observer. Robert F. Bales, for instance, is able to observe the emergence of leaders who are "idea men," oriented to the task in hand, and also of emotional or mood leaders, who help dis-

---

grist of personal affairs with the realm of justice and injustice outside the bedroom and the living room. See especially *Shadows of the Gods* (New York: Harper, 1958).

[7] We refer here primarily to our "population"—not conceivably a sample —of eighty parties among urban, Midwest, middle-class professional and academic groups, largely in the age-range of twenty-five to thirty-five. For purposes of contrast and, in effect, historical comparison, we made use of observations of 10 parties of more or less upper-class seaboard groups in the age-range of forty-five and up.

[8] New York: Harcourt, Brace, 1950.

[9] William F. Whyte, *Street Corner Society*, 2nd ed. (Chicago: University of Chicago Press, 1956).

sipate the tensions created by the task and by the idea man.[10] To be sure, Bales measures the movement of a group not only toward or away from a task, but in directions irrelevant to the task—but the task still bounds the group's attention, and its completion ends the span or episode in question. Sociability, in contrast, is interstitial and amorphous; when people leave, it is not necessarily over; and what appears to be a group may in fact be fragmented. The closest analogue to a task leader is the host, but his task may be accomplished before the guests arrive—in selecting them, setting the stage, providing food and drink—and other leaders may develop who set the mood, draw others out, or perform. Thus, in observing sociability we learned to note not only what people said and did, but what effect their actions had in leading on to the following episode or phase. Yet in trying to capture the qualities generated by a particular event, we were aware that the event, and the group in which it occurred, had a history, usually including previous sociable contacts, which preceded us and which helped give context to any single encounter (whereas most laboratory groups have individual but not group histories and must develop a group culture *de novo*).

Thus, our quest led us away from the laboratory and work-group studies and toward the field. Accounts of the interaction among, for example, crowds or children at camp indicate the importance of contagion in establishing patterns of activity and mood.[11] At a party, too, contagion is one of the processes by which people establish consensus about what they shall do to "have fun." Thus, if one person has a hard-luck story to tell, someone else will have worse luck; if one makes a brilliant, somewhat malicious observation, another has an equivalent,

[10] See, for example, Robert F. Bales and Philip E. Slater, "Role Differentiation in Small Decision-Making Groups," pp. 259–306; in *Family, Socialization and Interaction Process*, edited by Talcott Parsons and Robert F. Bales (Glencoe, Ill., The Free Press, 1955). Also useful for us has been the thinking of W. R. Bion and his notion of therapy groups as doing "work" and as engaging in "fight-and-flight" behavior; see his "Group Dynamics: A Re-View," pp. 440–47; in *New Directions in Psycho-Analysis*, edited by Melanie Klein, Paula Heimann, and R. E. Money-Kyrle (New York, Basic Books, 1955). See also Dorothy Stock and Herbert A. Thelen, *Emotional Dynamics and Group Culture* (New York: New York University Press, 1958), in which therapy groups are seen as developing a structure out of what the authors term emotional "valencies."

[11] See Norman Polansky, Ronald Lippitt, and Fritz Redl, "An Investigation of Behavioral Contagion in Groups," *Human Relations* (1950) 3:319–48.

perhaps more malicious one; and if one person is festive and gay, others may respond on that level too. For contagion to occur, guests must be well matched: one person must be able to pick up the cues of another, and then respond at the same level. Without this minimum degree of matching, the party is likely to fail.

Limits of Our Observations

When we began our research we did not seek a rigorous definition of sociability. We were satisfied to say that sociability is the interaction which occurs between people who have come together to enjoy each others' company; or between people who are trying to enjoy each others' company because they have been brought together. Thus defined, sociability may be found at the luncheon table, the *Kaffee-Klatsch,* or the family dinner table; it occurs on railroad trains, in dormitories, and on the job. Yet it seemed to us that the small invitational party could be taken as the prototype of sociability. We have not tried to say how large or small a party may be, nor to define it in other respects, but have simply sought to observe and understand a selection of small parties to which our staff members could get access. To help place our party observations in context, we have observed and recorded sociability in luncheon settings, in dormitories, at resorts, and on trains, concentrating particularly on the sociability of young adults. We were interested, in a very broad way, in mental health among young adults, and in the possibility that they might use sociable situations as opportunities for exploring and defining their individual identities. Also, we were interested in looking at groups for whom styles of sociable behavior were as yet undefined—at people for whom sociability presents itself as both a problem and an opportunity rather than as a routine, a part of a job, or refreshment from a job (as it might be among some older, more established persons).

To be sure, groups and styles tend to perpetuate themselves:[12] people come together by force of habitually having done so; or they are thrown together by school, occupational, or other ties and opt for a

[12] However, we must not overestimate the degree of perpetuation where no large framework, such as is provided, for example, by Rotary or the PTA, can carry a group through schisms and dry seasons. A careful study in a small New England town showed that groups formed for sociability alone had an average life span of about a year. See John W. Riley, Jr., *Dynamics of Non-Family Leisure in a New England Town, 1857–1935,* unpublished doctoral dissertation, Harvard University, 1937.

group form rather than an aggregate or a queue; or they have inherited or hope to acquire a tradition of reciprocal entertaining. When the sociable grouping is inherited, it has much of the "given" quality of the family or of larger kin-based groupings and hence resembles the nucleations out of which larger and more directly purposive human groups have arisen. To the person born into such a group, it is simply *there*, a fragment of the timeless and seamless web of human intercourse.

VARIATIONS IN SOCIABLE STYLE

Is Sociability Vanishing?

A frequent theme among critics of America is an alleged decline of conversation, in comparison with Europe and with an earlier America innocent of television, games, cars, and other distractions. Neither in our limited orbit of observations nor in our wider orbit of reading did we find any evidence of this; on the contrary, the indications are that more Americans are being more sociable than at any earlier time.[13] Americans have more time on their hands, care more about human relations outside the immediate family, and are more mobile both physically and emotionally than hitherto. Teen-agers attend the movies, not to avoid conversation entirely, but as the focus for a date and a topic for talk; likewise, television lurks in the corner, not as an alternative to conversation among adults, but rather as a kind of urban weather, providing common conversational coin.[14] While undoubtedly there are many strata, new to formal parties and wary of them, where organized games provide a cloak for, or defense against, personal contact, in the groups we studied both games and the mass media were seen as routes toward contact and conversation. Thus, studying the luncheon sociability of a group of law students,[15] we noted that television tidbits (what Margaret Mead has called "quiz-bits") provided a ready opener

[13] Compare the Riley thesis, footnote 12; see also Gerhard E. Lenski, "Social Participation and Status Crystallization," *Amer. Sociological Rev.* (1956) 21:458–464.

[14] See the amusing article by William K. Zinsser, "Out Where the Tall Antennas Grow," *Harper's*, April 1956, pp. 36–37. Zinsser reported that his Iowa in-laws, through watching "Omnibus" and other serious shows, had acquired more highbrow items to talk about than he, as a supposedly sophisticated nonviewer from New York City.

[15] This study was reported by Kenneth D. Feigenbaum, "Sociable Groups as Pre-political Behavior," in *PROD* (Production, Research, Organization, and Design) (1959) 2:29–31.

for talk while the group was getting acquainted; later, more personal topics could partly replace the public, parasocial items.[16] So, too, among some of the groups we studied, games such as bridge or activities such as folk singing were seen as legitimate alternatives to conversation, but not as the one-and-only version of being together; indeed, at some of the parties, struggles would go on as to which version should have hegemony at any given time.

Sociable Resources

Sociable interaction may be viewed as the development of sociable resources; and value judgments about particular forms of sociability often spring from value judgments about resources. In more settled cultures, there may be widespread agreements which define acceptable sociable resources. There was a time in Great Britain, for example, when one's accent and bearing ticketed one as having attended schools within a certain range, and as being familiar with a certain reading list, viewing list, and visiting list; and socially mobile newcomers sought to adapt themselves to this pre-existing repertory. In such a society people may then develop eccentricities of interest or manner—novelties beyond the standard repertory—just as in the stuffier parts of American society people often depend on professional entertainers or party-enliveners like Elsa Maxwell.

In contrast, in all but a few circles of America one cannot count on a uniform subsoil of sociable resource: one must prospect for hidden resources, hoping to find a match[17] which will permit the conversation to move rapidly away from the familiar to a level which combines surprise and mutual understanding; and yet which will avoid the tactlessness of reminding people of what they may regard as deficiencies of education, reading, or taste. Topics are seldom taboo per se (the ban on politics or religion still holds in some strata, but not in those under our observation), but neither are topics easily given per se by the very

---

[16] See Donald Horton and Richard R. Wohl, "Mass Communication and Para-Social Interaction," *Psychiatry* (1956) 19:215–29; and also Donald Horton and Anselm Strauss, "Interaction in Audience-Participation Shows," *Amer. J. Sociology* (1957) 62:579–87.

[17] We do not mean agreement, but rather the discovery of common concerns with common or contrasting perspectives. People can match on a play they have all seen and then, finding that they have not in fact "seen" the same play, can match on that very discrepancy, on playgoing in general, on the state of the drama and of the cosmos.

nature of those present. They may, in fact, more readily be given by the nature of those absent, as when women alone feel free to talk about domesticities and men alone to tell dirty stories or talk of sports or the stock market; or GIs about officers, students about teachers, Negroes about whites (and in the South, vice versa), and so on.

Thus to bring strangers together at a party does not necessarily bring sociable equipment into play; without adept prospecting, they remain impalpable to each other; or, more likely, the mystery and novelty which one might offer to another is lost in the catalogue of job, residence, and family. But prospecting takes time—although Americans (as many foreign observers, including Kurt Lewin, have noted) can often move quickly from a standing start into the high gear of relatively intimate sharing. Notoriously, they are able to do so in chance encounters, as in taverns or on trains, where they can unburden themselves to strangers whom, hopefully or inevitably, they will never see again.[18]

One paradox of sociability, however, is that if people bring too much in the way of resources, and often if they come with too high expectations of a good time, they will simply clog traffic and defeat themselves.[19] Although at a party more people can talk at once than at a meeting,[20] there is still a question of bringing in everybody's shop—yet

[18] The deftness in this sort of quick encounter reflects the freedom of courtship, in which young people must try to size each other up as whole personalities, only marginally assisted by parental and other adult restrictions. It also, in large strata, reflects the freedom of salesmanship, in which people are constantly buying and selling personalities in quasi-commercial dealings, and must make quick judgments of others' qualities and vulnerabilities.

[19] They may also defeat themselves by coming with no expectation and no chance to change style and pace from the workaday world. The fact that people seldom dress for dinner, but frequently come directly from work, having fought traffic en route; that they do not live the leisurely lives that permit anticipations to luxuriate; that the settings are casual rather than formally festive—all this creates a problem of transitions, of the recovery from the "bends" of work, which the cocktail was invented to resolve (the drearier the party prospect ahead, the more likely a cocktail en route!).

[20] The processes by which a work group controls the allocation of speaking time are discussed in Robert F. Bales, Fred L. Strodtbeck, Theodore M. Mills, and Mary E. Roseborough, "Channels of Communication in Small Groups," *Amer. Sociological Rev.* (1951) 16:461–68. Also relevant is Fred L. Strodtbeck, Rita M. James, and Charles Hawkins, "Social Status and Jury Deliberations," *Amer. Sociological Rev.* (1957) 22:713–19; and

one man's enthusiasm is another's boredom. Thus efforts tend to be made, in the trajectory of a party, successfully to define it in ways which meet both group and individual desiderata. In the groups we studied, there was often an "after-party party" in which those whose requirements had not been met continued to seek them, or to continue for a longer time qualities generated by what had gone before.

While we did not interview people on the doorstep of a party as to what they expected (which might well have affected what then would have transpired), we did conclude from postparty interviews that there were at least three different qualities which made for "a good party." One was intimacy, the discovery of closeness with another person or persons; a second was festivity, or a general gaiety, abandon, hoopla; a third was solidarity, the reaffirmation of personal ties and group identity. This last involves primarily the sharing of group norms, group antagonisms, and group loyalties, whereas intimacy tends to differentiate the self, to emphasize its uniqueness and its qualitative independence from the group.

Obviously, the expectations of party-goers as to which of these qualities they think appropriate will be influenced by the occasion or season of the year—for example, New Year's Eve—by their own age and experience, and by what has occurred before in this particular circle. Often an effort to repeat a notably good party fails, although or because all the ingredients appear to be the same. For, while at least a superficial solidarity comes easily in the groups we studied, neither intimacy nor festivity do: these are more fragile moods, readily destroyed by trying too hard and relentlessly to achieve them. Indeed, both qualities were often most valued when least expected—when an ordinary affair became extraordinary.

The Insecurity of Expectations

If in the older regimen there was danger in the overprepared and overstilted party, with its hierarchically defined relationships and constricted agenda, there is in the new regimen, with its relative freedom from precedent and lack of shared traditions, the opposite danger of the underprepared and underorganized affair. On one occasion, a young instructor and his wife gave an after-dinner party, asking people to "drop

---

Robert F. Bales and Edgar F. Borgatta, "Size of Group as a Factor in the Interaction Profile," pp. 379–96; in *Small Groups*, edited by A. P. Hare, Edgar F. Borgatta, and Robert F. Bales (New York: Knopf, 1955).

in around nine." Since the invitations were casual and the responses noncommittal, the hosts did not know how many to expect, or when to expect them. With a handful of friends, they waited (a bit like a Charlie Chaplin movie) from ten to one, when finally a group arrived. In the meantime, the hosts' embarrassment had been communicated to the earlier guests, for whom, however, the size of the party was immaterial, and who resented the late arrivals for altering the rhythm of the party and for making it awkward for them to leave at an hour of their own choosing. Even then, the hosts were unsure whether still others might not show up; and, like the early guests, they found it hard to shift emotional gears to take account of the expectations of the new arrivals. In a setting where the rule is to have no formal rules and where one is supposed to be casually prepared for any eventuality, the hosts' security proved too fragile to bear up easily under the fun-morality of the group.

On another occasion, two young career women gave a large party which, what with friends bringing friends, became much larger than anticipated. Some guests thought they had been invited to a small dinner party and were dismayed by the long period of waiting and sparring with strangers which preceded a late dinner; others did not know dinner was to be served, and came late, having already eaten. Food was buffet-style, but its coming was never clearly announced, so that many guests were not sure when to begin eating. Many guests were at loose ends; they huddled together with others whom they already knew, helped themselves to the delicious food, and, in the absence of introductions, ignored the other and unfamiliar cliques. One group gathered around a record player and filled in the empty spaces with records of folk music, loudly played. The hostesses were immersed in problems of serving the food and repeatedly sending out for more to drink; they had no time for their guests until dinner was over. By then it seemed that the party could continue under its own steam; so one hostess joined the party by retreating to a distant part of the apartment where there was quiet music and she could dance with her date; and the other left the party altogether to meet her date elsewhere. The guests settled down to various forms of having fun—dancing, singing, dramatics, and flirtation. When they got tired they went home, leaving the distressed hostesses with an immense task of cleaning up afterward.

The freedom, the lack of stagecraft and formality, in the party just described might have been a stimulating if strange interlude for someone accustomed to more ceremonious and plotted occasions—even the too noisy music might have struck one of E. M. Forster's heroines as exotic. Conversely, a few of the same young professional people who attended this party enjoyed a very ceremonious holiday party at the home of a distinguished and elderly gentlewoman who received her guests formally and served mulled wine with an almost liturgical flair.[21] Such an occasion, too, were the mood not right, could fail dismally, a punctured balloon; but the sprightliness of the hostess, the antique beauty of her home, the known traditions of the event—all novelties to some of the more upwardly-mobile guests—encouraged the gushers and subdued (although it did not silence) the cynics.

The diverse national, ethnic, and class origins of many of our subjects, their mobility and motility, along with other "urban anxieties," introduce special problems with regard to sociable style. Sociability is neither immune nor deaf to the individualized needs and proclivities of participants and hence is often victim to idiosyncratic desires that are not socialized. Yet, many such affects, in the hands of skillful fellow participants, could serve to power a party, to make it resonant and meaningful. At one small dinner party, for example, a man, driven by the need to dominate, would have turned the affair into a monologue-seminar, but was restrained by two guests who, although previously unknown to one another, joined forces to maintain a certain balance, while a perceptive, quiet hostess kept the encounter from becoming too polemical and strained.[22] Without this energetic guest, however, the party might have been anemic; as it was, the arguments had spirit, and the coalition formed to restrain the stronger party led to liking and sharing between the two strangers. At another small party, a young married woman was determined to prove she was not "just a housewife," but an intellectual too; this led her to invade the separate circle the men had formed (as they too often and so unsociably did in the groups we observed).[23] Her move coincided with a feeling among several of

[21] Asked where she had learned the tradition of entertaining, this hostess was at first at a loss, then said, "Well, you just *know*, you live it," indicating how close this competence is to general life style and that learning it is not a formal process.

[22] Cross-cultural factors were involved: the would-be lion was a German refugee, a little like the charming, self-indulgent figure in Randall Jarrell's *Pictures from an Institution* (New York: Knopf, 1954). European-style heckling and polemics would not vitiate sociability for him as it would for many Americans of comparable position.

[23] It seems that the more frequently occurring exclusion of the absent by scapegoating or conspiritorial gossip is less destructive than the exclusion implicit in male-female segregation at parties.

the men that they shouldn't again congregate and talk shop; they joined the other women, who had resented both their own isolation (at least some had; others found it comfortable) and the issue made of it by the woman who had deserted them. A general redistribution of the sexes occurred, and most of the women were relieved not once again to have to talk their own domestic "shop," while some of the men discovered or were reminded that sex differences do after all lend savor to sociability—and not merely of an openly sexy or flirtatious cast. In both parties, given the lack of prescriptive rules and the limits which responsive participants were able to impose, the impatience of individuals, their unwillingness to wait indefinitely or to be a passive container for an endless sociable process, eventuated in giving life to encounters.

Each of these illustrations provides evidence of ways in which increasing demands for sensitivity to others and the acceptance of responsibility by guests can be seen as resting the issue of the outcome of a party in a widely distributed leadership among the participants. To the extent that people enter a party without fully formed expectations, without commitment to convention or to personal strategic plans, they are free to be spontaneous and to respond to the moods of others present. Thus, in the best case, minimal organization and planning may be requisite: the group, responsive to itself, can be left to itself.[24] But this decentralization, this reliance on spontaneity, can itself become a compulsion: like many valuable things in life, if it is pursued too directly, too ideologically, it can be dissipated by the very effort to find it. Or, once established, spontaneous festivity may go "too far," without limits, much as children may play more and more violently until only tears can bring their excitement again under control.[25] We are not suggesting that such contagious spasms are necessarily bad, but only that a minority of persons can take over a kind of demagogic leadership in a leaderless party and disrupt the occasion for the majority, and even for themselves.

[24] At some parties the host or hostess denies obvious conversational topics to the guests, such as shoptalk or juicy gossip, in an effort to encourage them to more stimulating conversation. If the host does not make a game of the denial, the result is to block bridges to richer fields. See, in general, Riesman, Potter, and Watson, "The Vanishing Host," *Human Organization* (1960) 19:17–27.

[25] For this and other characteristics of contagion among children, see Polansky, Lippitt, and Redl, footnote 11.

THE RELAXATION OF STANDARDS

The Shifting Burden of Demand

As we have indicated, the ethic of performance or achievement is relaxed in modern sociability. As compared with the spheres of work, sex, and sports, there are no clear standards as to what constitutes adequate performance; instead, sociability is thought of as a sphere of relaxation, where you come as you are and do as you please. Yet, there are expectations that people will "have fun," which place subtle demands on those who feel responsible for living up to them. But who is responsible? Apparently, not the host, and not the sociable leaders either. In equalitarian principle, everybody. Thus, by comparison with traditional etiquette in sociability,[26] the ambiguity of modern valuations of performance creates a mixture of added demands on the less competent guests and reduces demands on those of greater competence and experience.

The model of sociability here, at its best, would seem to be that of a jam session moving through space as well as time, in which individual runs take off from, and return to, the combo's own rhythms, in which leadership is almost wholly decentralized or invisible, and in which players know each other well enough to respond to subtle cues. It is, to be sure, very cool jazz, seemingly uninvolved and resilient, unrehearsed and as the spirit moves—a beat beat. Or, to use another analogy, it is a kind of theater-in-the-round in which the property men wander on and off stage, the audience exchanges with the players, no make-up is worn, and the script gives the barest minimum of direction.

Much of the show of "front" that formerly went into party-giving,[27]

---

[26] For a historical survey of sociable styles and settings, see René Fueloep-Miller, "The Social Role of Conversation," *Autonomous Groups Bull* (1957) 12:4–11.

[27] Erving Goffman's treatment of the nature of front has been stimulating to our work. See, for instance, "The Nature of Deference and Demeanor," *Amer. Anthropologist* (1956) 58:473–502. Much earlier, Thorstein Veblen, in *The Theory of the Leisure Class* (see footnote 5), spoke of the shabby interior and commonplace home life that existed behind the elegant front of the nineteenth-century family, and made the interesting point that this distinct separation gave rise to much of the middle-class demand for privacy. Now front and back are less distinct, with the economy of the kitchen merged with the extravagance of the parlor, and there is less value put on privacy.

as into housekeeping, has simply been discarded and, almost as a counterfoil to the growing complexities of public and corporate life, party-giving has been simplified. Increasingly, parties are given on the spur of the moment, with little planning of the guest list and little distinction between guest and host. Certain peripheral necessities of providing place and time still fall to the host, but elaborate preparations for a party, if too showy, may be felt as putting competitive pressure on the guests and hence unsociable; it is more casual and less pressureful to perform some staging activities after the guests arrive, and to defer to them by acting the servant role.[28]

By the same token, the lowering of the threshhold of what is expected at parties makes it harder for people to refuse invitations. They cannot stay away, for instance, with the excuse that they lack "proper" clothes—nor that they lack a "proper" line, for the older imperative, especially for young women, that they become quick and tireless talkers, has become greatly attenuated.[29] People can, of course, still say of themselves that they "hate parties"—and, in fact, interviews with some highly

[28] This, of course, is only one of the many changes in style of life brought about by the relative disappearance of servants in middle-class homes—a decline resulting not only from cost and unavailability but from the very ethos of equality we are describing, which makes people uncomfortable to have someone present who is not a potential participant. With the linking of kitchen-and-pantry with living-room-and-dining-room, the house itself is no longer a stage for sociability, with front and back—as, of course, is very clear at an outdoor barbecue. The disappearance of servants, with their expectations for style and their coaching of their masters, in itself encourages informality in dress and decor; the gourmet shelf in the supermarket, along with Clementine Paddleford's column in the newspaper and *Woman's Day*, has taken the place of the chef, but nothing has replaced the butler and maid.

[29] Our subjects—and we have observations on the sociability of some 750 people—were not in that segment of the mobile and half-educated who confess not knowing how to be sociable and take lessons or even correspondence courses from the many Arthur Murray-like instructors who have sprung up in large cities. On the contrary, many of our subjects—almost all of them college graduates—were in the difficult position of being anxious about their social behavior and yet unable to admit either that they had deficiencies or that it mattered, especially since what matters most is to be natural and sincere. Had we been able to observe them while they were still in high school, we might have found a greater readiness to escape from sociability into dancing and games, or to enter it with the avowed aim of learning the ropes.

poised and attractive young women in their early twenties brought forth with surprising frequency the report that previously they had hated and feared parties, even to the point of becoming physically ill rather than attend. But for people beyond the crises of adolescence, the protest seems to be more against making the effort to get to a party than against the party itself; and, of course, if they really want to escape from having to interact with their friends, the relative lack of distinction between the roles of host and guest makes it possible for them to busy themselves with providing others with food and drink; or to escape to the kitchen to wash the dishes.

There is a tendency to overlook the extent to which leadership and invention are required at a party—as elsewhere in the national life; people tend to believe that they can diminish the hosting function without a corresponding increase in the demands put on the guest. And while the elimination of many formalities almost certainly reduces the total demand, the host is robbed by these developments of his sense of the legitimacy of a strong leadership. The very fact that guests are often asked to bring their own food or liquor,[30] and thus to share one traditional function of the host, accompanies the shift to the collective group of decisions concerning the nature and destiny of the party—whether, for instance, it is to develop the intimacy of pairs, the community of small groups, or the festivity of larger groups. But at the same time, guests feel that it would be presumptuous to take active command: to lead when one is not in the concert master's seat requires at once remarkable tact and the concealment of its exercise; thus, to cope with an emergency created by a disruptive member may call for empathy with the feelings and expectations of many people.

At conventions and other large gatherings where strangers meet, Americans have developed notorious devices for getting acquainted and onto a first-name basis—wearing big name plates, having people rise and introduce themselves, and engaging in mixers of various sorts which make Jim Farleys of even the most forgetful. The groups we looked at

[30] In the hard-pressed groups to which a large part of our attention was confined, it would have been difficult to manage parties otherwise. We observed only a few parties in several of the various martini belts of America, where, of course, the host provided the liquor. But even impoverished graduate students and young professional people prefer hard liquor to beer and soft drinks, for liquor has become an essential solvent for sociability, and a party can hardly be expected to cost less than $1.50 per person, not counting baby-sitters.

would have regarded all such baggage as vulgar, and were in any case too small to justify these devices. Yet they did not seem to have adequate alternatives, for introductions were frequently minimal or omitted altogether. And the rise of cocktail parties and decline of dinners, along with informal furniture and small living rooms that provide few avenues of escape from forced sociability, often left guests overdependent on one or two people whom they knew. With each guest on his own, with informality the order or disorder of the day, guests were not apt to feel responsibility for one another.

In fact, in some circles there was as little guesting as there was hosting, and the solidarity of the group was affirmed by the very freedom members felt to leave it temporarily. Thus, in some of the orbits we studied it was not inappropriate for a guest to fall asleep, or to pick up and read a magazine; he needed to be only intermittently "there," and withdrawals and lapses of attention were not felt as criticism or deprivation by others.

Similarly, there would seem to be a decline in the role of "lion" at a party and a commensurate but less visible decline in the role of "lamb." People who assume that everyone should participate actively and equally in the enjoyment of a party are unwilling to listen to a performer, however entertaining and enlivening he may be. No one person is encouraged or even permitted to hold center stage for very long—unless the party has reached such a state of famine that people can only sit and stare at each other, in which case they will be eager to exploit any available lion, however tedious he may be. There is a distaste for distinction, and all but the most obtuse and solipsistic learn that parties, like games, require fair play, with everybody—except, maybe, a few shy womenfolk—having a turn.

There is a danger that unaccented sociability may suffer from a kind of entropy, running down through lack of inputs of sociable energy, and reaching the point, in the absence of any euphoric group feeling, of being indistinguishable from a group of people who just happen to be in a room together—a room which is certainly not the old-fashioned parlor, or even the middle-class living room, but rather a combination "family room," kitchen, bedroom, and veranda. This is especially true if the people see each other regularly, thus minimizing the likelihood of surprise and mutual discovery. Indeed, while in principle such discovery even among long-married couples is unbounded, continued exploration requires both great intimacy and great intensity, and the latter quality, at least, is lacking in these parties of familiars who see each other on a low-pressure, old-shoe basis. In referring to this pattern as the "familial"[31] style in sociability, we have in mind a family model which is homey and comfortable, more maternal and accepting than patriarchal and demanding.

But to carry this style outside the family and the home may mean, as already indicated, that the residual responsibility of seeing to the minima of sociability may go by default. It is more likely, however, in our observation of these laissez-faire groups, that someone, usually a woman, takes up the slack and furnishes the background of hosting which allows others to be informal and irresponsible, often without awareness of the unofficious and unostentatious assistance they "consume."[32] In such cases, the equalitarian ethos does not prevent a certain exploitation of some party-goers by others. And one of the most important aspects of the role of the host—drawing out the sociable contribution of silent members—does not get performed. The few tape recordings we have indicate that, even at the most easygoing and relaxed parties, there are almost invariably a few nonparticipants—much as in the task-groups studied by Bales and others—some of whom might have been stimulated and encouraged by sensitive hosts or fellow guests, with a net addition to total resources for sociability. Certainly few parents would deny the positive value of freedom to be silent, if one wishes, in the family home, but in sociability it is another matter.

However, as everyone surely knows, not all silences are alike. People gather on sociable occasions from all sorts of motives and with all sorts of expectations: so diverse is the traffic even among otherwise likeminded people that it is astonishing that any consensus can be generated at all. There are people who are silent because they are tired; because in sociability they are expressing the passive or receptive rather than active or domineering aspects of themselves; because they would rather let a spouse perform (in a setting where, owing to the number of people or the heat of the topics or the absence of a host, the air is crowded); because they fear to make fools of themselves, or are bored, or lack the kind of presence that gives weight to what they are starting to formu-

[31] See Jeanne Watson, "A Formal Analysis of Sociable Interaction," *Sociometry* (1958) 21:269–80.

[32] Many of the larger relations between American individualism and collective responsibility have this same quality: thus, "free enterprise" depends on a host of services which the community provides and which businessmen are often ignorant of, or antagonistic toward, until they have to manage without them.

late. There are kinds of silent listening which are so empathic and active as to be as evocative as any words; there are kinds which are impenetrable; there are kinds which appear as criticism to vulnerable talkers. The old-fashioned sort of hostess, offering tea but no real sympathy, usually makes matters worse; it is only the unobtrusively gifted one who can so manage topics and the ecology of seating as to create maximum opportunity for people to choose whether to talk or not. Without such assistance, the shy may go home with the sense that once again they have not contributed, and thus add to the vicious circle of their self-exclusion, while others may go home with the sense of again having talked too much, of having taken up too much room, and of having lost the opportunity to relate to new people or new aspects of familiar people.

These hangover feelings point up a paradox in the familial style in sociability. By virtue of the very fact that everyone's contribution is accepted, and that indeed everyone is accepted whether he contributes or not, people are very often made uneasy as to whether their performance is really adequate. They are caught in a conspiracy of acceptant silence, like children in a progressive school that does not give out grades—children who know that out in the "real world" things are different and people are graded.[33] Not able to shed entirely their feelings of the relevance of criteria of performance, even in low-pressure sociability, they may build up a vague feeling of dissatisfaction—sometimes to the point of seeking in a psychiatric relation the kind of candid evaluation and detached appraisal their warm and professedly candid friends may perhaps not be giving them.

The Cult of Sincerity

These changes in the ethos of party-giving and party-receiving have been accompanied by analogous changes in the forms of selfhood one presents at a party. If one looks at the photographs of successful men

[33] However, increasingly a man is never fired for not doing the job. Rather, he is allowed to resign. One of us recently encountered an executive in a benevolent company who suffered from analogous misgivings: "Everyone is so nice to me," he said, "and so pleasantly refuses to criticize my work, that I sometimes wonder whether I am about to be promoted or fired!" Another executive in a similar company complained at the endless round of conferences among executives which occurred because lack of a clear hierarchy made necessary a great deal of interaction to keep people in place.

today, whether leaders in industry or in the professions, one is struck by their presence; they are commanding people, very much *there*, big, self-possessed, poised. They may dress, in the modern fashion, inconspicuously, but their clothes still serve as a frame for their personal qualities —qualities, of course, which are enhanced by the cumulative halo of their positions. Contrastingly, the young adults we have observed are often notable, not for their presence, but for their "absence"; they may be Bohemian, but they are rarely flamboyant; they seek to be, or resign themselves to being, inconspicuous; they often sit or slouch in a way which may reduce rather than enhance their "thereness." It would not be quite correct to say these young people lack poise; rather they possess poise of a different sort, less stiff, perhaps more sensitive, than that of earlier generations, but undoubtedly less easy in command positions.

Perhaps the "absence" of these young people is an appropriate presentation of self for one who must live and work in an administered, as against an earlier competitive, society. To be sure, this style of "absence" is incompatible with the European-formed image of the bureaucrat: neat, formal, meticulous, rule-oriented, and white-collar-pinched. The style rejects both meanness and elegance. Its devotees did not attend college to secure specific technical training, nor to become "collegiate" in the old-fashioned sporty sense, but rather to begin preparations for gradual mobility into professional and semiprofessional positions, usually after a further round of graduate training. In the process, ethnic and other idiosyncratic edges are rounded, but the outcome is not a polished personality but an affable, casual, adaptable one, suitable to the loose-jointed articulation and heavy job turnover in the expanding organizations of an affluent society; the organizations are already there, demanding incumbents rather than innovators.[34]

Competition among individuals, however, has not been done away with; there are better and worse jobs, faster and slower movements. Commitment either to groups or to the organization has not replaced rivalry. Even so, in the family and in social life there is a search for qualities of solidarity that are as yet only incipient in the world of work. The style of "absence" and the search for sincerity are ways of rejecting egocentric claims. The young people we are describing differ from their parents, who maintained a protective front before society; they aim to be open, not closed and defensive; and they avoid behavior

[34] See William H. Whyte, Jr., *The Organization Man* (New York, Doubleday Anchor, 1956); and "The Found Generation," p. 309.

that would result in their being labeled as posers. Correspondingly, they are quite gullible in the face of mass-media performers whose carefully contrived absence—a front that looks like a back—convinces them they are seeing the "real" Godfrey, or Elvis, or James Dean. The great debunkers of the first half of the twentieth century appear to have done their work well, for anyone is willing to believe that public figures, no matter how much prestige they have, are in truth simple homebodies. So much is this true that modern young adults refuse to believe in their own potential for greatness—using as proof their facile interpretations of Freud. Although there is much truth in these attitudes, there is the further truth that absence, when it is self-conscious, as we have often found it to be in our observation of parties, is a front too. In this sense, absence, personalization, and sincerity seem not only to be defensive mechanisms, but also to be egocentric and irresponsible.[35]

In sociability, dedication to the values of sincerity and spontaneity may, in fact, impose strict constraints upon the individual. The most serious of these is the prohibition in many small and insulated groups against any person's presenting himself in a new or unfamiliar light; each must always appear to be just as he has always been. We observed compulsions in parties which kept a shoemaker to his last, whether this took the generic form of women talking about their children or the specialized form of holding individuals to their previous type-casting or sociable roles. In some of the groups we studied, the "comic" person was always forced to be funny: people expected this, and he did himself, and resigned himself to it, though weary of the role; so, too, the beautiful girl was always forced to be beautiful, held to her sex-role by a suit of armor. Despite the ethos of spontaneity and naturalness, people could seldom change their styles in a given group; they could only sulk and withdraw.

A different kind of constraint upon sociability is the frequent prohibition against display of personal achievement. We have observed roommates and friends in camp and college who share with each other sociably many seemingly intimate details of their lives, such as their conversations with their analysts, their feelings of weakness, and, of course, their encounters with the opposite sex, but who make modest efforts to conceal conspicuous achievements in fields that matter for

[35] Compare the portrait of "Henry Friend" in David Riesman and Nathan Glazer, *Faces in the Crowd* (New Haven, Yale University Press, 1952).

others in the group, or mention them only in passing, without elaboration. Those who violate these tacit norms, as, for example, the girl whose entire conversation (with other girls) dwells on the irresistible appeal she has for men, are shunned and disliked. Herein may lie the technique of interaction whereby the peer group discourages achievement orientations—a girl such as this is forced to nurture her achievements in isolation, in fantasy or revery, hence to become more and more deviant and out of touch with her peers. We are reminded of S. N. Eisenstadt's description of how, in some societies, youth groups serve to make a bridge between the family, with its collective front vis-à-vis the world and its unconditional acceptance of all members, and the general society, with its individualistic roles and its emphasis on performance and achievement.[36] As Eisenstadt observes, fraternities in college have some of the aspects of an age grade; and some of the sociable groups we have been describing can be seen as informal post-collegiate continuations of that fraternity.[37]

Observers of our own society have noted that some of the socializing functions of the nuclear family of earlier eras have been taken over by various peer groups. Perhaps the peer group is a more appropriate socializing agency for young people who must learn to exist (and enjoy it) in a rationally organized administrative bureaucracy. Many modern organizations which require that candidates for recruitment should have gone to college are, in effect, recognizing the college as an appropriate socializing agency—the requirement is obviously not an informational or educational one, since other means of education are not recognized, and, moreover, many colleges have little effect on students in this respect.

And yet it is not enough to say that the sociable style we have been describing is governed by peer-group norms. To be sure, this tells us part of what we need to know. So, too, does the fact that much of the

[36] *From Generation to Generation: Age-Grades and the Social Structure* (Glencoe, Ill., The Free Press, 1956).

[37] However, the fraternal orders such as the Masons and Elks emphasize formal rituals and put a fair amount of emphasis on achievement—although no doubt the regulars around a clubhouse may become a group of familiars like those we have been describing. It is perhaps because of the ritual and formality, increasingly eschewed in American life, that these orders appear to be declining in importance, even though other voluntary associations with an activist and sociable purpose are not. Certainly, the college-educated, who are especially the carriers of the informal mode, are not interested in lodge membership.

more constricted sociability that we have observed occurred among relatively privileged young adults—college students, graduate students, and recent graduates who have spent more time on the development of privately meaningful intellectual and personal identities than on the creation of sociable "fronts" which could serve as resources for public play. For some of these people, sociable styles will change as they move out of the period of preparation for life and into a period of established occupational and recreational patterns. But we do not think that the ethos of low-pressure sociability is confined to a stage in the life cycle; rather, we think that the sociable styles of younger adults may bespeak more general shifts in middle-class values, and particularly the growth of a present-oriented hedonism among those very classes which in the earlier stages of industrialization were oriented toward the future, toward distant goals and delayed gratification.[38] People formerly gave parties either because it was expected of them or because they hoped for some distant reward: social acceptance, return engagements, marriage chances for their children, and so on. Of course, this still happens. But today people believe often enough that they can win such goals without working so hard and postponing so long; or they regard the goals themselves as frothy or factitious; or their whole outlook has altered, and the goal that matters is that of having fun—on which the verdict cannot be put off to the far distant future. Thus, at some parties the host simply cannot bear the postponements involved in the role of being host: he makes inadequate preparations, and then tries to join the guests and to become, as it were, a guest at his own party. To some extent, of course, a host must exude enjoyment and not be too obviously hard-working lest he spoil others' pleasure. By the same token, many guests enjoy taking the role of the host—it may make for greater intimacy as well as greater equality to move into the kitchen, to help introduce and circulate guests. This sort of temporary role reversal can be characteristic of some sociability, adding to its flexibility and its contrast to ordinary patterns of interaction.

The "Gemeinschaft" Style

Relaxation of the future-orientation and of the traditional structure of host and guests advances other values than spontaneity and freedom of movement. There is also the desire to establish a solidary group, reaffirming its close-knit quality by the warmth of the atmosphere

[38] In considering such matters, we have been stimulated by Erik H. Erikson, *Childhood and Society* (New York, Norton, 1950).

created. In contrast to an older, primarily European model of sociability, where people seek to shine as individuals, to be brilliant and clever, the newer model is more communal—not antiperformance but antiindividualistic. It does not reject brilliant contributions so long as they do not flaunt themselves and can be integrated with overriding collective purposes, such as defining the group, defaming its enemies, and revealing commonalities of human experience. But it does tend to reject the soloist,[39] the perennial performer, much as it deprecates the too central, too active host. It is as if both egoistic and altruistic attitudes, in Durkheim's sense, had become somewhat attenuated, with sociability increasingly serving to affirm mechanical solidarity among people whose working lives are specialized and compartmentalized. In this respect, sociability becomes an aspect of the holistic and integrative attempts, outside the sphere of work, to restore community on more simple and direct terms.[40] The mechanical solidarity that seems so characteristic of this sociable style resembles that of smaller communities in simpler societies where, as a result of the limited alternatives given by a homogeneous life-experience, differentiation is minimal. Sociability, particularly in the very small parties where we observed this model in force, appears to move toward what Robert K. Merton calls "value-homophily"[41] through the medium of parallel experience of a single activity —for example, singing songs.

The increase of this type of sociability among people whose working lives are becoming more specialized and compartmentalized—for example, young professionals—leads to the speculation that there may be a complementarity between a desire for mechanical solidarity in sociability and the organic solidarity of workaday lives, a counterbalance effect. Lacking longitudinal data, we might nevertheless conclude that men are ineptly socialized for life in a society of interdependent specialists

[39] One of our informants stated that he gave up playing the guitar at parties, even though this is an accepted form of integrating activity, because he found it singled him out too much and made it difficult for him to sink back into a more anonymous and freer role.

[40] For thoughtful consideration of these more generic issues, see Robert A. Nisbet, *The Quest for Community* (New York, Oxford University Press, 1953).

[41] See Paul F. Lazarsfeld and Robert K. Merton, "Friendship as Social Process: A Substantive and Methodological Analysis," pp. 24 ff.; in *Freedom and Control in Modern Society*, edited by Morroe Berger, Theodore Abel, and Charles H. Page (New York, D. Van Nostrand, 1954).

and compartments; that the sociable group is an arena for the continuance of the mechanical solidarity of relatively undifferentiated family and other primary groups. In this respect the sociable group is a "primary" group serving throughout life to take up imbalances encountered in less flexible institutions.

The Ban on the Vicarious

Mass entertainment in America has been dominated for a long time by the mode of documentary realism.[42] Even historical costume dramas hire academic experts to get every detail correct. This realism is more than a stage convention: it is a form of equalitarianism, as if the journalist or script writer is saying to his audience: "You can see as well as I that there is nothing fancy here, nothing contrived." Movies may present improbable-looking people, but they are "real," their measurements recorded and publicized.[43] "You Are There" is the title of a justly famous television documentary. (Yet of course these entertainments do not merely reflect people to themselves as they are, but take them outside of themselves, at least occasionally. And the style of documentary realism, though regnant, is challenged by entertainers who are undeniably fantastic—indeed, even the mass media seem to be on the threshold of an era of freighted symbolism.)

This ever present realism has its impact on children who early become too precocious for *Just So Stories* and fairy tales; over the media and at home, as well as at school, they subsist on here-and-now stories. What strikes us about most of the middle-class parties we have studied is their similar here-and-now character, with little planning and little anticipation. Likewise, parties are seldom regarded as experiences to be enjoyed retrospectively, as part of one's emotional subsoil. When we interviewed people about a party which had occurred a few days earlier, it was remarkable to us how barren of recollections they were. They tended to categorize the affair as "good" or "bad," but they had obviously not assimilated and reflected on the occasion either privately or with

---

[42] For discussion of this mode, its variants, and its esthetic limitations, see Reuel Denney, *The Astonished Muse* (Chicago, University of Chicago Press, 1957).

[43] Needless to say, a like realism prevails in social research, which proceeds on the premise that no operation which cannot be repeated by any Ph.D. is scientific.

friends—much less in a diary.[44] An occasional party was memorable, not because it was "fun" and easeful at the time, but because it opened a window on another time, another place—as in the instance of the holiday party referred to above, a party designed as a ritual, not a relaxation.

We are not recommending a return to ritual. Our society is not one which depends on an oral tradition, carefully preserved in primary groups and handed down from elders to children. Anyone who doubts that the loss of etiquette brings liberation should read Nicolson's account of the forms of frozen politeness encountered, for instance, at a Persian court.[45] But, as always happens, a social advance—in our case toward a more open, more fluid society—brings new problems, unforeseen ones, in its wake. A middle class no longer oriented entirely toward the future has developed, in the absence of a feudal class oriented toward the past; but in the sociable and personal styles we have been describing, both past and future have so disappeared from view as to dull the pleasures of the here-and-now.

In the case of do-it-yourself around the house, home craftsmen are able to follow a professional model, or even buy a kit with instructions. But as sociability becomes more participative and equalitarian, do-it-yourself proceeds without models. Guests do not learn from other guests artistic ways of recounting experience, because of the rule that everyone can talk, play, or somehow get into the act: there is a tacit ban on efforts to provide novel interpretations of idiosyncratic or shared experience—although there is no ban on reiterating legends and self-justifications which are already staples of a group's ethos. Likewise, there is a tacit ban, even stronger, on discussing one's private or political hopes for the long-run future—any topic which is too remote from the everyday would seem to claim too much. In the absence of models and of an audience which can respond to and appreciate one who takes them beyond themselves, the parties we have studied are bare of sustained flights of imagination or of language in any way out of the ordinary—and this is among educated people who have read many books

[44] One informant described her disappointment with friends who were unable or unwilling to discuss a movie or play or party after the event—they turned immediately, without a moment's unwinding, to the humdrum of housewifery ("I wonder if the kids are in bed yet").

[45] Harold Nicolson, *Good Behaviour: Being a Study of Certain Types of Civility* (Garden City, N.Y., Doubleday, 1956).

out of the ordinary and may even like modern poetry. In getting rid of pressure on each other to shine, they have permitted themselves to become drab.

Of course, this puts matters too generally. We have observed only a few parties among the established elite—among men and women of large affairs. On such occasions, people do shine. If they have recently come back from Ghana, they say so, and are encouraged to "perform" about it. Conversational "runs" are longer, competition for the floor more intense. Sometimes there is a depressing ban on the everyday, and only "public faces in public places" are paraded: only the vicarious is allowed, only what is "out there"—although for some of the participants "out there" is not far from home. People sometimes make speeches at each other; they are too stagy, too "unnatural." But at their best these parties link the personal and the global, the past, the present, and the future; in the course of an evening, both private and public will have their turn and may be integrated with each other. Verbal grace is not eschewed; indeed, in some groups—as among many British intellectuals —it can become an end in itself. The men at these affairs do not feel the need (again, in the best case) to establish their reputation for practicality: they have risen "above" that, and can afford to be charming amateur conversationalists.

In the middle class, however, capacity for transcending the here-and-now by means of vicarious participation in the world "out there" seems to be largely absent. At a number of parties, especially among such disadvantaged groups as graduate students, any effort at long runs or cadenzas was cut down to size, and the parties ended in a welter of sporadic nihilistic comments. Nihilism can, of course, be lively, but in these groups it had become a monotone, long since gone flat—a uniform of nonconformity, providing in-group acceptance at the price of unremitting out-group denigration. In the anti-authoritarian atmosphere, no leader could arise to alter this, but only to reaffirm and renew it. By the very nature of sociability, there is nothing analogous to parliamentary procedure by which the rules can be changed: they can only be broken and new ones built up tacitly and inchoately. Thus, while the people we studied were aware that the rules of the game, in Piaget's sense, lay within their power, and were not given from outside, they were, unlike the children Piaget studied,[46] not members of a common subculture

[46] Jean Piaget, *The Moral Judgment of the Child* (Glencoe, Ill., The Free Press, 1948).

but carriers of a quite wide array of subcultures, democratically hesitant to impose standards even of evaluation of behavior, let alone party practice. Under these conditions, permissiveness is not enough, any more than, in another context, love is enough.[47] As Nelson Foote has pointed out, people need coaching to learn new games;[48] and they also need specific hosting or coaching to discover new styles in sociability.

We have been curious about sex roles in sociability, wondering whether it is possible to identify either men or women as the current spokesmen for enlarging sociable horizons. Men have been forced out of the vicarious and into the documentary by the demand for technical exactitude and clarity and the pressure against self-dramatization involved in so much of their schooling. They no longer learn the arts of rhetoric in the academy (the debating team hews to the documentary), but the techniques of manipulation in the laboratory. Despite—and in part because of—all the emphasis on communication in the society, they seldom learn to communicate what is special, precious, and not immediate. Even in going steady, they are sometimes able to avoid the need for more than phatic noises, and their movie models are often young men whose inarticulateness is intended to convey sincerity, pain, and even profundity.

Young women, less task-ridden, are somewhat freer in these matters: they are permitted more fantasy, and, indeed, may associate fantasy and frivolity with being "feminine." They read more novels and thus add to the range of vicarious experience—even if those novels often drag them back to the here-and-now, it is somebody else's here-and-now. They talk more on the telephone, and perhaps talk more in general—in part, because they cannot escape, as boys can, into hobbies and hotrods and sports. At the lower cultural levels, they expose themselves to soap opera, an index of what is missing in their lives and of their dream of becoming an audience for boys or a particular boy; and in all strata their empathy and vicariousness in dyadic relations helps compensate for the boys' deficiencies.

But by the same token, many women, even in the middle class, in

[47] Compare Bruno Bettelheim, *Love Is Not Enough;* (Glencoe, Ill., The Free Press, 1950). To be sure, there is a semantic issue here, and if we define "love" as Erich Fromm does in *The Art of Loving* (New York, Harper, 1957), it is by definition enough.
[48] In private conversation.

the terms of Herta Herzog's article on soap opera listeners,[49] exist too much "on borrowed experience" to bring much of their own, direct or vicarious, to sociability—except, perhaps, for a ready ear. Too often they resign themselves to, or retreat into, discussion with other wives at a party of matters which are very much here-and-now, such as recipes and children's diseases. In talking with us about their sociability, they frequently look back with longing at their college years—the opportunities to form close friendships, and the introduction to the big world "out there." But these years which are used—at least by some—for imaginative and intellectual endeavor seem to have little relationship to the career of mother and housewife;[50] bound to a model of femininity which emphasizes raising children and condemns career women for leaving the home, these women sometimes act as if any imaginative departure from the work of the house would be a violation of the marriage contract. They miss the big world, but cannot use their menfolk to keep them in touch; they feel uncomfortably confined, despite having their own cars and often, save when the children are very young, their own jobs.[51]

As for middle-class men, the very technological developments which once required automatonlike performance now mean that they are freer than ever to be "impractical," freer to be articulate, even in some ways to be "unnatural." The greater permissiveness so evident in the loss of traditional sociable forms extends also to them. But they have taken advantage of it to loosen their neckties more than their tongues, to relax the way they stand and sit rather than the way their imaginations work. We have already mentioned parties where the rule that anything goes is extended to include silence, or even sleep—an absurd extension which so weakens demands and expectations that in some parties nothing goes, and guests and indistinguishable hosts sit and look at each other. While such expectations do increase the demand that everyone be responsive

[49] Herta Herzog, "On Borrowed Experience," *Studies in Philosophy and Social Science* (1941) 9:65–94.

[50] See Nevitt Sanford, editor, "Personality Development During the College Years," *J. Social Issues* (1956) 12:3–68.

[51] If they are not lucky in their own husbands, they cannot, in the circles we studied, form friendships (rather than having affairs) with other women's husbands. This fact reflects Puritan traditions less than it reflects the very conversational lacunae we have been describing. In these groups, sex is a conversational filler—when at a loss for something to talk about, one may flirt or put in a sexual reference or two.

to the desires of everyone else, this demand may equalize anxieties when things do not go well.[52]

It is noteworthy, in this connection, how seldom the party-goers in our observation went anticipating a good time. No doubt, they feared to be disappointed, and had long got over "childish" enthusiasms which might be short-lived. But expectations here, as elsewhere in social life, tend to be self-confirming, and if everyone goes to a party without expecting to enjoy themselves, then the party can often do little more—despite drink—than confirm the prevailing mood. So often, this is set at the very beginning, and as sensitive people respond to the going topics of talk, and the mode of talking about them, they never discover the other things which they might conceivably talk about under a different leadership. That is one reason why parties which start out with a nihilistic and denigrating attitude toward the world can seldom strike any other note: people respond as they are responded to, and after a while the mold is set for the evening. To strike another note would imply a criticism of the one already given, and is thus avoided or, if presented, drowned out.

More and more, our observations have led us to conclude that sociability remains inadequate without the guidance of leaders sensitive not only to a group's mood but to things and values outside the group, to the possibility of participating vicariously in experiences not directly accessible. An overequalitarian ethos has the same effect on sociability as on the schools: by denying differences of skill and motivation, it compresses all into a limited range of possibility. Sociability, an art like any other, cannot be learned if the participants deny that there is anything to learn—and if, to strengthen the force of their denial, they turn personal "absence" into the virtues of sincerity and artlessness. Sociability, like much contemporary fiction, can serve to insulate people against the larger world—not, in this case, the reader and his book, but the quasi-primary group and its defenses. Of course, people need defenses, and they need escapes from society too; yet sociability can be at its best only when it links society, through choice of topics, through energy and resource, to the sociable group of adult men and women.

[52] The very phrase, often used, "Things didn't go well," is revealing: Dorothy D. Lee has called attention to the great use of passive and "thingified" expressions in American as compared with English usage, in "Symbolization and Value," in her book, *Freedom and Culture* (Englewood Cliffs, N.J., Prentice-Hall, 1958); pp. 78–88.

The Suburban Dislocation
(1957)

Among aristocratic nations, as families remain for centuries in the same condition, often on the same spot, all generations become, as it were, contemporaneous. A man almost always knows his forefathers and respects them; he thinks he already sees his remote descendants and he loves them. . . . As the classes of an aristocratic people are strongly marked and permanent, each of them is regarded by its own members as a sort of lesser country, more tangible and more cherished than the country at large. As in aristocratic communities all the citizens occupy fixed positions, one above another, the result is that each of them always sees a man above himself whose patronage is necessary to him, and below himself another man whose co-operation he may claim. Men living in aristocratic ages are therefore almost always closely attached to something placed out of their own sphere, and they are often disposed to forget themselves. It is true that in these ages the notion of human fellowship is faint and that men seldom think of sacrificing themselves for mankind; but they often sacrifice themselves for other men. In democratic times, on the contrary, when the duties of each individual to the race are much more clear, devoted service to any one man becomes more rare; the bond of human affection is extended, but it is relaxed.

Among democratic nations new families are constantly springing up, others are constantly falling away, and all that remain change their condition; the woof of time is every instant broken and the track of generations effaced . . . the interest of man is confined to those in close propinquity to himself.

Alexis de Tocqueville,
Democracy in America

The suburbs have become so characteristic of life "among democratic nations" that some of our most acute social observers in the post-World War II years have seen in them the shape of the egalitarian future. William H. Whyte, Jr., in his *Fortune* series on "The Transients" has emphasized the poignancy of the relaxed yet inescapable bonds in the new suburbs, notably Park Forest.[1] Others, too, have been struck by a kind of massification of men in Levittown and other housing developments such as was once postulated for the endless residential blocks of the cities created by the industrial revolution.[2] Even in a Canadian suburb, where one might expect slightly more hierarchical traces, a team of social scientists has found "the track of generations" barely visible.[3] In the light of these commentaries, the emphasis on status in *Middletown, Yankee City, Elmtown*, or the New York suburb which marks for Charlie Gray in Marquand's novel the point of no return—this emphasis on graded ranks seems almost archaic. In contrast, the new suburbanite appears to suffer less from exclusion than from a surfeit of inclusions.[4]

Yet this is impression, based on a few soundings in a few perhaps strategic and surely highly visible locations. We know very little about the relatively settled suburbs, especially those leapfrogged by the waves of post-World War II growth; and so far as I can see we know almost nothing about the suburbs (old or new) surrounding the smaller cities. The new developments which have altered the physical and moral landscape so strikingly may betoken a trend or a blind alley. They may fascinate us owing to our contemporary fears for the loss of liberty and individuality; and intellectuals, seldom unambivalent about the suburbs

[1] *Fortune* (May, June, July, August 1953); also *The Organization Man* (New York: Simon & Schuster, and Doubleday Anchor, 1956), part VII. See, also, an unpublished master's thesis on Park Forest by Herbert Gans done in the Department of Sociology, University of Chicago.

[2] Compare Frederick Lewis Allen, "The Big Change in Suburbia," *Harper's Magazine* (June 1954), pp. 21–28, and (July 1954), pp. 47–53; and H. Henderson, "The Mass-Produced Suburbs," *Ibid.* (November 1953), pp. 25–32, and (December 1953), pp. 80–86.

[3] See John R. Seeley, R. Alexander Sim, and E. W. Loosley, *Crestwood Heights: The Culture of Suburban Life* (New York: Basic Books, 1956); and the discussion by William Newman, "America in Subtopia," *Dissent*, Vol. 4 (1957), pp. 255–66.

[4] As in the witty but unrevealing novel of exurbia, Max Shulman's *Rally Round the Flag, Boys!* (New York: Doubleday & Company, 1957); see, also, the slight topographical variations in exurbanite status dissected by A. C. Spectorsky, *The Exurbanites* (New York and Philadelphia: J. B. Lippincott Co., 1955).

—whether or not they make them their own domiciles—may generalize from them too readily to middle-class life and leisure as a whole.

Such considerations led me to a review of what sociologists have recently written, at their most empirical, about cities, suburbs, and the urban-rural fringe. Much of this work is based on census data or on such repeated explorations as the University of Michigan's Detroit Area Survey or the Metropolitan St. Louis Survey. Such studies tend to put a brake on extrapolative generalization. They indicate, for example, the presence of urban elements in rural areas, and vice versa.[5] The city is not necessarily the seat of urbanism, and the suburban way differs from the city way only at the polarities of each and is based on variables not entirely dependent on ecology or visible from a helicopter.[6] Hence these investigations do support the common-sense observation that can find suburban styles in many cities and urban ones in many suburbs; that an urban fringe is growing which is neither country nor city nor quite bedroom suburb in the older mode.

If this is so, then it means that the differences which divide Americans today depend less and less on where one lives, what one does, or who one is in terms of lineage, but more and more it depends on style and social character. Of course, some self-selection will occur toward places to live and toward occupations—especially between the two sectors of our "dual economy" I shall describe later. However the sorting at any given time reflects chance and idiosyncrasy and scarcely predicts the life cycle of individuals.[7] Occasional studies of suburban voting and a few intimations concerning suburban worship shed tangential

[5] See Albert Reiss, Jr., "An Analysis of Urban Phenomena," in Robert M. Fisher, Ed., *The Metropolis in Modern Life* (New York: Doubleday & Company, 1955), pp. 41–49; Morris Janowitz, *The Community Press in an Urban Setting* (Glencoe, Ill.: The Free Press, 1952).

[6] See, for observant commentary, Gregory P. Stone, "City Shoppers and Urban Identification: Observations on the Social Psychology of City Life," *American Journal of Sociology*, Vol. 60 (1954), pp. 36–45; also Wendell Bell and Marion D. Boat, "Urban Neighborhood and Informal Social Relations," *Ibid.* Vol. 62 (1957), pp. 391–98, and references there cited; Sylvia Fleis Fava, "Suburbanism as a Way of Life," *American Sociological Review*, Vol. 21 (1956), pp. 34–37.

[7] See the forthcoming book of G. E. Swanson and D. N. Miller in which they distinguish within the city of Detroit and within the middle-income strata between "entrepreneurial," (inner-directed) and "bureaucratic" (other-directed) families.

light on such major questions of attitude. On the whole, however, it seems fair to say that empirical investigations—including those recently done on problems of zoning, planning, and recreational needs; on the location of industry and the journey to work; and on problems of suburban and regional administration—scarcely connect with the kinds of writing cited at the outset. Thus, we cannot link nation-wide data on changes in metropolitan areas with Whyte's descriptions of how Park Forest feels toward its pro tem inhabitants. This is the characteristic situation in sociology today—that research in the macrocosmic and in the microcosmic scarcely connect, scarcely inform each other.[8] At any rate, this is my excuse, or my opportunity, for dealing in this paper with quite general themes only illustratively and sporadically pinned down in empirical research: I speak for a point of view—at best for a seasoned subjectivity.

The other day I went back to read that remarkable book, *Communitas: Means of Livelihood and Ways of Life*, by Percival and Paul Goodman.[9] This book includes a commentary on utopian community planning in the past and some suggestions as to potential utopias within the American scene of our day. It makes strange and disturbing reading now on at least two grounds. In the first place, it is easy to forget how much enthusiasm there was, during and immediately after World War II, for creative planning and reorganization of communal life, both here and in Europe. Ten years later, the air is sodden—as if a fallout over intellectual life had already occurred—the cold war absorbs much of our political energy; and we struggle, not to plan, but even to register what is happening to our fantastically expanding economy, population, and metropolitan malaise.[10] In the second place, it is curious how

[8] I may, of course, be unaware of important work in this area—work, for instance, of the scope of G. A. Lundberg, and others, *Leisure: A Suburban Study* (New York: Columbia University Press, 1934).

[9] Chicago: University of Chicago Press, 1947; Vintage Books, 1960; cf. my discussion in "Some Observations on Community Plans and Utopia," *Yale Law Journal*, 1957. Reprinted in *Individualism Reconsidered* (Glencoe, Ill.: The Free Press, 1954).

[10] The countries of Western Europe do not appear to be greatly in advance of America in these respects, but instead to be trying to enjoy with prosperity our new problems as well as their traditional ones—a far cry from, for example, the radically reconstitutive hopes expressed in the French Resistance press during the German Occupation. Cf., e.g., the interesting book

many of the Goodmans' then utopian suggestions have been incorporated into our lives, ten years later, without planning and with fundamental change coming about interstitially only. We have come much closer to approximating their first ironical plan for a city of efficient consumption, although our shopping centers are suburban rather than urban: Certainly our advertising is more "efficient" now than in prewar times, and our waste more exuberant.[11] Their second plan, for the decentralization of work and life, has come about in some measure: through turning the home into a do-it-yourself workshop, through some degree of suburbanization of industry, and through greater labor mobility; but the quality of this plan, aimed at minimizing central political and economic control and at making work and leisure more meaningful, seems further away than ever. Their third plan, which aimed at a subsistence economy for security on top of which a luxury economy would be reared, has come about in an utterly paradoxical form. We have now a dual economy; one part is luxurious, pays high wages, lives in handsome plants, and generally engages in "conspicuous production"; the other part lives as if on another continent, paying low wages, not practicing Harvard Business School techniques, and seldom financing itself out of retained profits and quick depreciation accounts. The Goodmans' third plan was intended to minimize government regulation and private price-administered regulation. Our dual economy, however, depends on continued war preparation, suitable tax and credit policies, and agreement between labor and management in the high-wage economy to let the consumer, and sometimes the stockholder, pay the costs of private socialism and creeping inflation.[12] Yet the consumer also benefits from the dual economy if he works for the high-wage, managerial side of it, or if, while working for the underprivileged economy, he can somehow use the former as leverage or

---

by Karl Bednarik, *The Young Worker of To-day: A New Type*, Renée Tupholme, Translator (Glencoe, Ill.: The Free Press, 1956); and see also recent articles in *Encounter* on "This New England" and "The Younger Generation" of the Welfare State.

[11] We buy more services than the Goodmans allowed for, which lowers our efficiency in production and distribution—and absorbs what would otherwise be a labor surplus.

[12] I am indebted to Eric Larrabee for stimulating discussions of the "dual economy." The concept is analogous to that of the dual state described by Ernest Frankel for Nazi Germany and resembles the contrast of controlled, *i.e.*, abundant, and free, *i.e.*, pinched, sectors in a totalitarian economy.

"host" for raising his own income without the corresponding in-plant efficiencies and extra-plant responsibilities of the managerial side. Moreover, as Whyte makes clear in *The Organization Man*, the new neatly assembled suburbs, with their handsome school plants and their neighborly fraternalism, are the consumption side of the managerial economy, valuing a similar "social ethic" and suffering from a similar lack of ultimate goals. Likewise, the residual but still immense slums to be found in both country and city are the domestic or consumer side of the low-wage, non-expense-account economy.[13]

This latter economy lacks the subsistence security at which the Goodmans aimed—rather, it remains the principal arena in which one is allowed to fail or to make a very fast buck. And the luxury economy exercises a ceaseless pull, both in its styles of production and in the spread of these, via the expense account, into so-called private life.[14] Thus, private life gets further and further from even the possibilities of a subsistence minimum. At least it does so apart from the possibility, conceivable but unlikely, of a Savonarola-type revolt against high standards of living and dying and the economic and social structure that accompanies these.

Perhaps the most significant difference between the Goodmans' book and the present state of the American experience and imagination is that the latter are encased in an additive or extrapolative mode of perception. When we have a problem, we have a standard remedy: more. We add a road, a wing to a school, a new department or government agency. Seldom do we rearrange the givens so that they become takens into a new configuration—as was done, for notable examples, in the Tennessee Valley Authority and the Marshall Plan. This is not merely the old American formula of "bigger and better" or the old American optimism, now in any case considerably attenuated. Rather, it is some-

[13] To be sure, there live in the slums Negroes and other migrant groups who have jobs in the high-wage economy but have not yet had a chance to adopt, at least in residential pattern and usually also in family style of life, the suburban concomitants. And the slums also contain many elderly people, only rarely at work in the high-wage economy, whose skills and tastes antedate the spread of the dual economy both on the production and the consumption side.

[14] The lower-wage economy has its expense accounts, too, and being mostly small business and small government, these have often more gravy if less finesse than those in the luxury economy; but they are confined to the boss and his nephews and friends: they are not institutionalized.

thing which goes deeper into the way Americans structure their very image of physical and social reality. In his essay, "What is American about America?" John Kouwenhoven gives many illustrations of the additive principle: from the land-grant section to the reiterative beat of jazz, the roll of film, the highway grid of our cities, the added stories of the skyscraper or high-rise apartment, our soap-opera serials, our assembly lines.[15] Dorothy Lee, on the basis of linguistic studies, has shown the lilt and drive of analogous tendencies in the changing patterns of American English.[16]

One could argue that these are no more than minor American variants of Western dualism and the decimal system and other similar categories which govern our perception and communication. But America is today, as in Tocqueville's time, freer for better or worse of alternative perceptions rooted in feudal or ecclesiastical history—even the South is being rapidly colonized. Moreover, for a variety of reasons, planning has become almost a specialty of the large corporations which are committed to the additive principle by the very nature of their annual balance sheets, tax returns, and inventories—just as government agencies can seldom plan for more than one or two years by the nature of our budget and electoral systems. While federal expenditures and hence capital investment are held on a plateau by past wars and the present strife of the services, and while states and local governmental units seek to keep up with yesterday, big business has at least some opportunity to look ahead in terms of capital spending and, where financially backed foresight has monopolistic support, as with Bell Telephone and General Electric, even to look further than the next annual report.

Forecasting, however, is almost always wrong, in part because it is confined to certain parts of the society; it assumes that other things will stay the same—they never do. In earlier generations, when America was an underdeveloped country, the limits of prophecy could always be set by reference to England or some other fully industrialized and urbanized place, but now we have become an overdeveloped country and have outrun our models. (We use the Soviet Union in this capacity whenever they will oblige.) Thus, we turn to our own past for a model and go on extrapolating. For instance, it seems generally to be assumed by business planners—some government officials are less sanguine—that

[15] *The Beer Can on the Highway* (Doubleday, 1961).
[16] "Freedom, Spontaneity and Limit in American Linguistic Usage," *Explorations*, Vol. 6 (1956), pp. 6–14.

a larger population will produce and consume proportionately more than a smaller one despite the friction its very size may create and the possible loss of much of its potential productivity through inadequate schooling and low morale. The inadequate schooling will reflect, *inter alia*, the much smaller energy for foresight that civic and educational institutions typically have, in comparison with the huge self-financing corporations, which often would as soon set staff men to work on forecasting and a thousand other things as raise dividends and pay more taxes.

At any rate, with these few exceptions, there would seem to be in this country, considering the increased ability to plan given by more subtle techniques in the social sciences,[17] a recklessness on the part of the whole society not much different in temper from the way millions of individual families have decided to plunge now, pay later: to finance on credit a shaky structure of personal plans and possessions which no insurance can protect against the mischances of illness, separation, untimely death—quite apart from socially induced disaster.[18] This absence of personal planning, this foreshortening of individual time-

[17] Such a phrase, in a paper of this length, must do duty for an elaborate dialectic. While I am not one of those sanguine social scientists who believes that, if only our "industry" had atomic amounts of money, we could solve the planners' problems, I do feel that "survival through design" can be carried much further with the aid of our somewhat better understanding of how to discover what people "need" and can learn to want. Thus, social science has helped us to realize the hidden values even in slums and hence to temper rashness in erasing them; it has also tempered the ethnocentrism of planners and other officials—sometimes to the point of reducing them to weathervanes. For an interesting example of the use of social science thinking by an architect, cf. Robert Woods Kennedy, *The House and the Art of Its Design* (New York: Reinhold Publishing Corp., 1953).

[18] The surveys of consumer finances and purchases by George Katona and his colleagues of the Survey Research Center document the relation between purchases and private optimism. See the discussions in the several volumes of *Consumer Behavior*, edited by Lincoln Clark and published by New York University Press.

In comparison with willingness to spend on consumer goods, people today are somewhat less willing to spend on their children's education, let alone to save for it: they expect the state or other scholarship aid to do that. This is one reason why college tuition has not risen in proportion to the ability of some families to pay and many to borrow (nor are many students willing to give up having a car in order to pay more tuition). In this case, too, families look to society or its agencies to take care of the future while they live up to and beyond their incomes now.

perspectives, is sometimes attributed to the fear of war and the bomb, but in my opinion such a fear can only be a very small part of the explanation. For one thing, in the Midwest, people who never give the hydrogen bomb a second thought, or Europe or Asia a second thought either, live quite as much in the immediate present as do people who live on either seaboard with a somewhat greater awareness that they are part of an unsettled and warlike planet. It is not so much fear of the future—including the fear of inflation, which often rationalizes present extravagance—that forces people to live for the present. Instead it is in some ways a lack of fear: a loss of the older anxieties about credit, about spending, about enjoyment. The democratization of consumer values has made people refuse to put up any longer with what they regard as arbitrary deprivations, whether in old-model cars, homes, or styles of life in general—this is behavior familiar enough in all the newly rising "democratic nations."

A parallelism of individual and social behavior—in which the recklessness of families is reduplicated in state and nation—is not essential: there can be a prodigal society based on thrifty citizens, and vise versa, for institutions and elites mediate between the largest whole and the motives of individuals. But democracy means that individuals influence institutions and, in time, may reshape them according to their hearts' desire. And, as already stated, radically alternative ways of life which might evoke different desires are strikingly absent from the visual and psychological landscape of America. This is why we see parodies of the Goodmans' and other utopias rather than serious attempts, on a scale comparable in our time to Radburne in the 1920s, to experiment with new forms.[19]

There are, fortunately, counter tendencies: Victor Gruen's plan for Fort Worth, Mies van der Rohe's plan for the Gratiot Area in Detroit are examples.[20] But I found a recent summary of such plans by Catherine Bauer in the *Architectural Forum* depressing when I realized that most of the work described originated in the 1920s at the *Bauhaus* or was the achievement of a few aging visionaries like Frank Lloyd

[19] Most fictional utopias have themselves become, either anti-Utopias like *1984* or parodies in the form of science fiction (as in the work of Ray Bradbury or Frederik Pohl).
[20] Cf. Gruen, "How to Handle this Chaos of Congestion, this Anarchy of Scatteration," *Architectural Forum* (September 1956), pp. 130–35; also "The Miesian Superblock," *Ibid.* (March 1957), pp. 129–33.

Wright.[21] Not that I object to the *Bauhaus*: I think that the Weimar period was one of the great creative bursts of Western history. Rather, I am troubled because its emissaries, though they have some disciples, are not self-renewing and the problems of scale and quality of life are much greater now. We expect more of life than did our parents and grandparents—more, even, than freedom from want and the standard consumer durables. Our very abundance has increased the scope of our expectations. . . .

Having said this, I must immediately qualify it by pointing out that, for millions of suburbanites, their post-World War II experience has been prosperous and open far beyond their depression-born expectations. For them, the suburbs have been one vast supermarket, abundantly and conveniently stocked with approved yet often variegated choices. The children are less of a worry there than on city streets; the neighbors often more friendly than those city folk who "keep themselves to themselves"; life in general is more relaxed. . . . Life on credit has worked out well for many such homeowners, allowing them to have their children young and in circumstances far better than those in which they themselves grew up. Whatever the outsider might say about the risks blithely taken, with no allowance made for personal or social setbacks, or about the anemic quality of the relaxed life or its complacency, he would have to admit that such first-generation suburbanites have found the taste of abundance pleasant and, for the younger ones with wages rising faster than prices, not notably problematic.

This subjective attitude does not, however, alter the fact that, among such suburban dwellers and in general in our society, we are witnessing a tremendous but tacit revolt against industrialism. It is a very different sort of revolt from either that of the machine smashers of the early nineteenth century or that of the various anti-industrial sects—socialist, anarchist, agrarian, etc.—of an earlier day. Large manufacturing industry is increasingly moving to the luxury side of the dual economy, and back-breaking toil and harsh physical conditions are vanishing (except in industrialized farming and the service trades) with the coming of electricity, full employment, unions, and personnel men. But the luxury, which is often used to make the work more gregarious and less of an ef-

[21] Catherine Bauer, "First Job: Control New-City Sprawl," *Ibid.* (September 1956), pp. 105–12.

fort, is seldom used to make it less monotonous.[22] Naturally, men treat their work as delinquents treat school (though schools are less likely than plants to pioneer the partial truancy of the four-day week, escaping and sabotaging when they can). Managers and foremen try in vain to restore the "old school spirit" to their employees and, failing, seek through automation and quality control to make up for the deliquescence of the "instinct of workmanship" once so painfully built into the labor force. Observers of factory life have repeatedly pointed out that status within the plant is no longer gained by hard work and craftsmanship, but rather by one's consumer skills outside. Men dream, not of rising in the factory, but of starting a small business such as a motel, gas station, or TV repair shop in the shabby and open-shop underside of our dual economy.[23] For youngsters from subsistence farms, for hillbillies, and southern Negroes, a Detroit or Gary factory is still glamorous or at least a liberation from drastic poverty and insecurity; but for second- and third-generation factory workers, it no longer holds much meaning other than as a (hopefully temporary) source of funds and fringe benefits.

To be sure, there is a new industrialism of electronics, plastics, aviation, and so on, that retains a certain appeal that the older industries have so largely lost. However, the new firms, increasingly located in suburbs or where people want to live—California and the Southwest, and Florida—speed the movement out of heavy industry and merge factory and suburban life in a blend Patrick Geddes would probably disown. But we see in these industries precisely the form that the revolt against industrialism has taken today, namely to partially incorporate the "enemy" so that industrialism is not compartmentalized but rather, in muted form, spreads into all parts of the culture. This is, of course, what happens in so many social struggles: one defeats the enemy by becoming more like him.

[22] Cf. Peter Drucker's discussion of job enlargement and related measures in *Concept of the Corporation* (New York: Harper & Brothers, 1946). Union leaders who once were in the forefront of the drive to make work less exhausting—often an extrapolative matter of lowering hours, slowing the assembly line, lessening dirt and noise—have seldom moved into the more difficult area of making it less uncreative.

[23] Cf., e.g., Ely Chinoy, *Automobile Workers and the American Dream* (Garden City, N.Y.: Doubleday & Company, 1955), and, on older patterns of work morality, Eugene A. Friedmann and Robert J. Havighurst, *The Meaning of Work and Retirement* (Chicago: University of Chicago Press, 1954).

Let me pursue this further by looking at what is happening to the older form of industrial and commercial metropolis. When, a few years ago, I studied interviews done with several hundred college seniors at twenty representative universities,[24] asking them what they would like or expect to be doing in fifteen years, I was struck by the fact that the great majority planned to live in the suburbs. There were few who recognized some incompatibility between focus on suburban life and focus on big-city ambitions (for instance, a senior who wanted to go into advertising, yet not live in or near New York). Those who hailed originally from the suburbs suffered from no disenchantment and wanted to return to them—often to the same one—while both city-bred and small-town boys also preferred the suburbs. I assume that some of the latter in an earlier day would have wanted to leave Main Street behind and make their mark in the big city, whatever lingering agrarian fears and suspicions of it they still harbored. The city today, for many, spells crime, dirt, and race tensions, more than it does culture and opportunity. While some people still escape from the small town to the city, even more people are escaping from the city to the suburbs.

The successful book and movie, *The Man in the Gray Flannel Suit*, dramatizes these values quite explicitly. The hero chooses unromantic suburban cosiness, with (in the movie version) a not altogether inspiring wife and progeny, in preference to a high-pressure but potentially exciting business opportunity.[25] The head of the business is portrayed as having destroyed his family life and as virtually alienated from all human contact. Very likely, some of his junior executives would describe the company as a "mink-lined rattrap," thus explaining and justifying their withdrawal of affect from the work itself, while recognizing that they are still competitive. A recent survey presents fragmentary evidence that managers are less satisfied with their work even than unskilled workers, and it is conceivable that the middle-class occupations in general will soon be regarded as sources of funds and of periodic contacts and activity, much as the working-class occupations are now largely regarded.[26] If work loses its centrality, then the place where it is done

---

[24] See "The Found Generation," p. 309.

[25] There is an equivalent rejection of a wartime love affair with an Italian girl. The business in question is broadcasting—typical for the luxury economy and far removed from traditional industrialism.

[26] See Nancy C. Morse and Robert S. Weiss, "The Function and Meaning of Work and the Job," *American Sociological Review*, Vol. 20

also comes to matter less, and the access to variety in work that the central city provides may also come to matter less. Indeed, so much is this the case already that advertising for engineers in *Scientific America* and in trade journals looks more and more like the vacation advertising in *Holiday*. Minneapolis-Honeywell offers seasons and skiing as a counterlure to the aircraft and electronic suburbs of the Far West.[27] In this regimen, white-collar and blue-collar move toward one another, as each group now emphasizes consumership.

This [consumption-oriented] life is increasingly focused on the suburbs, which, since World War II, have grown so in quantity as to change their quality. Although upper-class and upper-middle-class people have lived in the suburbs of our great cities since the 1880s or earlier, the cities before World War II still retained their hegemony: they engrossed commercial, industrial, and cultural power. The city represented the division and specialization not only of labor but of attitude and opinion: by discovering like-minded people in the city, one developed a new style, a new little magazine, a new architecture. The city, that is, provided a "critical mass" which made possible new combinations—criminal and fantastic ones as well as stimulating and productive ones. Today, however, with the continual loss to the suburbs of the elite and the enterprising, the cities remain big enough for juveniles to form delinquent subcultures, but barely differentiated enough to support cultural and educational activities at a level appropriate to our abundant economy. The elite, moreover, tend to associate with like-income neighbors rather than with like-minded civic leaders, thus dispersing their potential for leadership beyond township boundaries. Ironically, these people sometimes choose to live in communities that might be almost too manageable if millions of others did not simultaneously make the same choice.[28]

(1955), pp. 191–98. It should be noted that many men in the professions (the study included only men) and many in sales express great satisfaction with their work.

[27] An occasional ad is more work-minded and will feature opportunities for responsibility and creativity along with the suburban fringe benefits.

[28] This is somewhat analogous to fad behavior, for individuals no longer live in suburbs as, so to speak, statistical isolates, but live there with recognition of the suburban style as theirs and their country's. Cf. Rolf Meyersohn and Elihu Katz, "Notes on a Natural History of a Fad," *American Journal of Sociology*, Vol. 62, No. 6 (1957), pp. 594–601.

Indeed, the suburbs are no longer simply bedroom communities but increasingly absorb the energies of the men as well as the women and children. The men, that is, are not simply being good providers while still attached to the values of the industrial system: they are seekers after the good life in the suburbs on their own account. Early marriage and the rise in the birth rate are so many rivulets of individual, only barely self-conscious protest against the values inherited from industrialism and the low-birth-rate middle-class metropolis—so many decisions to prefer companionship in the present to some distant goal, and so many mortgages of the future in the benevolent shadow of the luxury economy and its escalator of slow inflation, promotion, and protection. Whereas men once identified themselves with commerce and industry—with its power, its abstractions, its achievements—and forced women to remain identified with domesticity—save for those women who broke through the barrier and became man-imitating career girls—now, as many observers have pointed out, a growing homogenization of roles is occurring. Women take jobs to support the suburban menage periodically while men take part in its work (do-it-yourself), its civic activities (Parent-Teachers Association, and so on), and its spirit. Rather than delegating religion to their womenfolk, men go to church in increasing numbers, occasionally as in an earlier day to be respectable or to climb socially, and occasionally out of a genuine religious call, but more typically because the church, like the high school and the country club, has become a center for the family as a social and civic unit.

All this brings with it an increasing decentralization of leisure. Just as the suburban churches tend, within the boundaries of the "three faiths," to an amiable syncretism, ignoring doctrinal or liturgical differences, so, too, the other leisure activities of the suburbs tend to reduce the specialized differentiations possible in a metropolis. What I mean here can be illustrated with reference to music. A metropolis has enough music lovers to organize highly differentiated groups: Mozart lovers may split off from Bach lovers and would never encounter lovers of Wagner, while in the suburbs the music lovers—if they are to support communal activities at all—must in some measure homogenize their tastes and hence create a local market for "classical music." Indeed, they will be exposed to a good deal of community pressure to support the musical activities of their friends in return for having their own enterprises supported. The same holds, *parri passu*, for the other arts—just as it does for the differentiation of specialty stores, churches, and museums found in a large city. By the same token, the suburban activist can feel that his own contribution matters, as he would be likely to feel in the big city only when he is very rich, very active, or very influential. People brought up in the suburbs may not realize what they are missing, and they may relate their emotional ties entirely to their locality, not going downtown to shop or to visit friends or to go to the theater.[29]

Suburbs differ, of course, in what they make available, and so, as we noted at the outset, do central cities; thus, Morris Janowitz showed that many people who, to the visitor's eye, live in Chicago actually live in a small neighborhood that might as well be a suburb.[30] Moreover, central cities are increasingly influenced by suburban styles of life: people trained to a surburban attachment to their cars drive downtown even when good and commodious public transportation is available, and often they wear the casual dress of the suburbs when they do.

The suburban dweller believes, in fact, that he has the best of both worlds. In the interviews with college seniors I referred to earlier, in which such stress was placed on suburban domesticity, many students also emphasized their wish not to lose the cultural amenities they had enjoyed in college.[31] Some of these amenities will certainly be distributed in the suburb though frequently in diluted doses: piped in through television and radio and high-fidelity sets; the suburb may even support a theater group and, in a few cases, amateur chamber music; the local high school will provide entertainment of a sort, as well as facilities for adult education.

However, as the radii lengthen on which people move away from the city—as they must with the crowding of the suburbs leading to the jump to the exurbs—people either learn as in California to drive great distances for dinner or confine themselves to their immediate environs: the central city as a meeting place disappears—a process which has

[29] I am indebted to unpublished work on the performing arts in the suburbs done by Philip Ennis at the Bureau of Applied Social Research of Columbia University.

[30] *The Community Press in an Urban Setting, op. cit.* (note 5 *supra*).

[31] Colleges themselves make the same claim that the suburbs do. I recently had occasion to go through a large number of college catalogues as well as the descriptions colleges give in brief compass in the *College Board Handbook;* all but the huge urban universities did their best to present themselves as near the advantages of a large city, but far enough away for suburban safety and charm. (Correspondingly, some teen-agers, raised in safe suburbs, find glamour in going downtown, at least for a time.)

gone further in Los Angeles and Chicago than in Boston or New York. The neighbors make up little circles based—as William H. Whyte, Jr., showed for Park Forest—largely on propinquity.

The decentralization of leisure in the suburbs goes further than this, however, as the home itself, rather than the neighborhood, becomes the chief gathering place for the family—either in the "family room" with its games, its TV, its informality, or outdoors around the barbecue. And while there are values in this of family closeness and "togetherness," there is also a loss of differentiation as the parents play pals to their children and the latter, while gaining a superficial precocity, lose the possibility of wider contacts. At worst, there is a tendency for family talk and activity to seek the lowest common denominator in terms of age and interest.

Some of these matters are illustrated by an interview with a housewife who had recently bought a house in one of the wealthier suburbs north of Chicago. Her husband had been transferred to Chicago from a southern city and had been encouraged by his company to buy a large house for entertaining customers. Customers, however, seldom came since the husband was on the road much of the time. The wife and three children hardly ever went downtown—they had no Chicago contacts anyway—and after making sporadic efforts to make the rounds of theater and musical activities in the suburbs and to make friends there, they found themselves more and more often staying home, eating outdoors in good weather and looking at TV in bad. Observing that "there is not much formal entertaining back and forth," the wife feared she was almost losing her conversational skills; yet she felt that her family had been pulled closer together by the shared activities, in which the husband joined on weekends, around the home. After listening to her list and discuss the friends made at church and golf, it became evident that her immediate environment just missed providing her with people close enough to her in taste and interest for intimate ties to develop.

One interview, of course, proves little, and many factors are obviously involved in choice of friends; suburban location in an older, nonhomogeneous suburb is only one of them. I recall obtaining such interviews in Kansas City, too, among people who had lived there all their lives and had potential access to wide strata in the metropolitan area. Nevertheless, there seems to me to be a tendency in the suburbs, though not a pronounced one, to lose the human differentiations which have made great cities in the past the centers of rapid intellectual and cultural advance. The suburb is like a fraternity house at a small college—or the "close propinquity" to which Tocqueville referred—in which like-mindedness reverberates upon itself as the potentially various selves within each of us do not get evoked or recognized. For people who move to the suburb to live when adult, of course, matters are different than among those who never knew another milieu. And, to be sure, creative human contact need not be face to face but can often be vicarious, through print or other mediated channels. Certainly, highly differentiated human beings have grown up in locales which gave them minimal support. Moreover, though the nonneighborly seldom seek the suburbs,[32] a few doubtless manage to survive there. Ease of movement, in any case, permits periodic access to others, although as these others themselves scatter to the suburbs, this process becomes more difficult.

Indeed, at least until each of us has his own helicopter or rocket, this pattern of life requires us to spend a great deal of time in automobiles, overcoming decentralization—but driving is itself a terribly decentralized activity, allowing at best for car-pool sociability, and at worst mitigated by the quiz-bits, frequent commercials, and flatulent music of AM radio. As compared with the older suburbanites who commuted by train and read the paper, did homework, or even read a book, the present and increasing tendency to travel to work by car seems vacuous and solipsistic.[33] Whereas in pre-industrial cultures and in the lower classes in industrial society, people sometimes just hang on a corner or sit vacantly, it is striking that in a society which offers many alternatives, people will consent to drive vacantly but not refreshingly—woe betide the careless or unspry pedestrian or bicyclist who gets in the way of industrial workers pouring out of the factory parking lots or white-collar workers coming home on a thruway. The human waste here is most important, but the waste of resources and land, the highways which eat space as railroad yards even in St. Louis or Chicago never did, are not negligible even in a huge rich country.[34]

[82] Cf. Sylvia Fleis Fava, "Contrasts in Neighboring: New York City and a Suburban County," in William Dobriner, Ed., *Suburban Community* (New York: G. P. Putnam's Sons, 1958).

[83] To be sure, driving may offer some commuters a change of pace and a chance to be alone.

[84] A few superhighways have been designed to refresh the traveler and increase his sense of visual possibility as well as to speed him on his way; the Taconic State Parkway in New York is a fine example.

Where the husband goes off with the car to work—and often, in the vicious circle created by the car, there is no other way for him to travel—the wife is frequently either privatized at home or to escape isolation must take a job which will help support her own car. Whereas the rental courts of developments like Park Forest provide companionship for the stranded wives—companionship which, given the homogeneity of age and sex, is sometimes oppressive—other suburbs are so built and so psychologically "unsociometric" as to limit neighboring and leave many women to the company of Mary Margaret McBride and Arthur Godfrey. Indeed, in a few instances of interviewing in the morning in new suburbs south of Chicago, I have been struck by the eagerness of the housewives to talk to somebody (and not only to a man!) who is not a salesman—once they can be weaned away from the TV that amuses them as a kind of vicarious baby sitter. It is not only the visiting intellectual who finds the lives of these women empty, their associations fragmentary.[35] The women themselves, if at all sensitive or well educated, complain of having their contacts limited to their young children and to a few other housewives in the same boat. And, as a result of efforts to understand the extraordinary philoprogenitiveness of the suburban middle classes (a theme I return to below), I have come to entertain the suspicion that, once started on having children, these women continue in some part out of a fear of the emptiness of life without children and of the problems they would face of relating themselves to their menfolk without the static, the noise, the pleasures, the "problems" that the presence of children provides.

The children themselves, in fact, before they get access to a car, are captives of their suburb, save for those families where the housewives surrender continuity in their own lives to chauffeur their children to lessons, doctors, and other services that could be reached via public transport in the city. In the suburban public schools, the young are captives, too, dependent on whatever art and science and general liveliness their particular school happens to have—again contrast the metropolis, with its choice of high schools, as most notably in New York.[36]

[35] See Donald Horton and R. Richard Wohl, "Mass Communication and Para-Social Interaction: Observations on Intimacy at a Distance," *Psychiatry*, Vol. 19 (1956), pp. 215-29.

[36] I doubt if even the most superior schools of Scarsdale or Winnetka are as good in the arts as the High School of Music and Art, or in science as the Bronx High School of Science—or at least this was so when New York City was not yet a slum for the southern and Caribbean migrants. The suburban

Let me stress again that the themes I am discussing are peculiar neither to the United States nor to the twentieth century. Just as cities are older than industry so are suburbs. It is the democratization and extension of the phenomena I am describing, and the resultant constriction of alternatives, which give them a new and cumulative quality. The modern suburb is the product of the car, the five-day week, and the "bankers' hours" of the masses. As hours drop further, we can anticipate that still fewer families with children will willingly live in the city. Exceptions would be cities like Minneapolis, where the inhabitants can focus their leisure around their cottages on nearby lakes. But the same developments which have reduced hours for those white-collar and factory workers who do not go in for moonlighting or extra jobs have in turn put additional pressure on the still limited leisure of certain professional groups. These latter, in one way or another, cater to those whose enhanced income and leisure time allows them greatly to increase their consumption of services. People, that is, can now afford both the time and money for better medical care, more professional advice (therapeutic and otherwise), additional schooling, and so on. And the professions and service trades that supply these wants do not benefit from automation. Thus, the very developments that have increased the leisure of the masses have greatly reduced that of certain of the classes: doctors, civil servants, teachers, school and college administrators, and some groups of managers and intellectuals work almost as long hours as steelworkers did in the nineteenth century. While some of these cadres, notably the doctors, have enough of a monopoly position to earn high incomes in partial revenge for being overworked, others, notably the civil servants and teachers, are poorly paid both in money and time. It is these groups who are becoming the victims of the anti-industrial or leisure revolution.[37]

Yet these victims, too, live in the suburbs where they are exposed to the styles of life of neighbors with at least equal incomes and a far easier schedule—neighbors, moreover, who need never bring work home at

---

schools, of course, can hardly cope with the crowding their very advantages have brought about—just as the suburbs, to which people go to escape the city's dirt, suffer from a water shortage and may shortly not be able to wash away their own dirt.

[37] Cf. the comments on an "administrative depression" among white-collar workers in Harvey Wheeler, "Danger Signal in the Political System," *Dissent*, Vol. 4 (1957), pp. 298–310.

night. This developing pattern of uneven distribution of leisure has not been channeled into political slogans. We do not hear cries for the doctors of the world to unite and throw off their patients (a good many of whom have no better or more socially mobile ways to spend their time than by absorbing doctors' time!). Few today would begrudge the masses their claims both on the landscape and on services; but few have asked what this portends for the leisure of the servicers. Even now, school superintendents sometimes poignantly say they should never have gotten married and had children, for they must continuously serve other families and other children. Nor can such a group partially make it up to their families through the status and ease that money can buy as, for example, do busy surgeons or top executives. Ministers and rabbis, too, are victims of the suburban style in belongingness; and they are likewise unprotected by celibacy from having their own families wish they were in some other line of work.

How do people feel who live in the suburbs without the comforts and indulgences the ads tell them they ought to have—and not only the ads, but the "propaganda of the deed" of their neighbors and their neighbors' children? Visitors to the metropolis have often been struck by the contrast of Gold Coast and slum, of majesty and misery. Suburban contrasts in housing and decor appear less stark; majesty rides less high and misery less low. Yet, just because the suburb doesn't present poverty and deprivation as a given, the less self-evident lack of privileges must sometimes rankle and smolder. This is true even though some middle-class suburbanites, weary of the time on their hands, no doubt envy the doctor his busy rounds and his unquestioned usefulness.

Thus it would seem that a polarization is occurring between those who are dispensable to their jobs, and who therefore have a lot of time off, and those who, precisely as a result of this development, have no time off. A hundred years ago, doctors took it easy. In those days few could afford their services or were educated enough to recognize and discover symptoms; today illness is felt to be arbitrary, not one of the givens of life. A hundred years ago, civil servants took it easy: their jobs were sometimes sinecures for impecunious writers. Today city and suburban officials, planners, highway engineers, and National Park personnel struggle in vain to cope with the problems created by mobile masses of Americans. The struggle is similar to that of a permissive mother with a brood of willful, well-fed, and not wholly socialized children. In the novels of Trollope and other nineteenth-century novelists we glimpse a vanished world in which professional people led a leisurely existence. Today this is available only to those who can turn a deaf ear to importunate clients and customers, to colleaguial pressures, and to their own ambitions.

Of course, I have minimized in this account the fact that doctors and other professionals are often among the happy few who enjoy their work. They like the constellation of activities they perform; they find their colleagues and sometimes their clients stimulating; in the best case, they regard their work as play, with the freedom and creativity of the best play. We cannot speak of "overwork" where the task and the pace are freely chosen—even if there are included some inevitable marginal increments of boredom and compulsion.[38] Yet we must also recognize both that many intellectuals and professional people have entered their careers under some compulsion—even though their horizons are wider than those of most farmers and factory workers—and that the developments here discussed have sometimes trapped them beyond the point of no return. Their image of the career may have been formed on an older, less harassed model. Furthermore, they may have chosen their careers, in part at least, out of such factors as a distate for business and industry and ethical, ideological, or snobbish scruples against big business rather than out of a positive pleasure in, for example, scientific work. They may find themselves, then, in a quasi-big business of their own, but with few of the protections big business can give. They may retain the illusion of setting their own pace whereas in actuality the traffic sets it for them. In rejecting industry and commerce, only to be plunged right back into it as is the case with many professors and physicians, they resemble the suburbanite who flees the city and has it catch up with him.

The University of Chicago's Center for the Study of Leisure has been conducting studies of limited scope in several Chicago suburbs in an effort, *inter alia*, to see what happens to people who leave the city for the suburbs in terms of new commitments and new demands. We have also done a very inconclusive study of how people in the city spend their weekends. We have the impression that the suburbanite, tied to his house as the doctor is to his practice, may actually be less

[38] We must recall that, although play is by definition more freely chosen than work, it has also marginal compulsions: to finish the rubber, the sociable evening, the set of tennis—even, for many of us, the novel.

likely to take off for a weekend in the country than the urban dweller whose janitor can look after his apartment and even the cat. Indeed, it is the city people, freed by industrialism from long hours of grinding work, who (along, of course, with an ample supply of untied suburbanites) make up a large proportion of the outboard population of our lakes and rivers and of the thirty-five million fishermen—more than twice the number of those urban sportsmen, the bowlers. Although air conditioning makes even the most humid and dirty city potentially habitable, people can't wait to leave town on weekends and during the summer, even though in many parts of the country it means spewing the city into the countryside and fighting with like-minded crowds for space on roads, lakes, and at motels.[39]

As I have indicated, I believe that snobbery and imitation of the rich play a declining part in this exodus to the suburbs and that the quiet revolt against the city and industrialism plays an increasing part. I would argue that there is often less "front" in the new suburbs than in equivalent sections of a metropolis, and less pressure for a lace-curtain life concealing back-stage scrimping and meanness than there once was. People do not usually learn the idea of a garden suburb either from British models or Mumford or Clarence Stein: The idea, in its uncomplicated forms, is an omnipresent dream, carrying overtones of the Bible, peasant life and folk imagery. The urban wish for contact with nature has been crystallized for many Americans around the habits of the British gentry and their middle-class imitators. But, more modest than the aspidistra-lovers of the London suburbs, we prefer not to give fancy names to our own "villas" but to let this dumb show be done for us by the realtors. In the Chicago area, for instance, a great many suburbs have either "Park" or "Forest" in their names, and two of them have both! Furthermore, social mobility means that many, perhaps most urban dwellers will have suburban relatives or friends. The mass production of suburbs, especially in the postwar years, has made them accessible

[39] It is, however, striking how much of this movement, though largely "private" and unorganized and unideological, is determined by fashion—in this respect, resembling residential location itself. On warm winter days Central Park and its rowboats are often nearly deserted, as is Jackson Park in Chicago; likewise, the Atlantic beaches such as Coney Island in their off-season magnificence are as unpopulated as the Labrador coast. People feel it is arbitrary to be cooped up in the city on a summer weekend in some measure because they partially accept the definitions of "living it up" provided by the media and conversation.

to almost everyone. Only in the rural and impoverished parts of the South and Great Plains farming regions are we likely to find many people who do not know anybody who lives in a suburb and have never had occasion to visit one. Beyond that, the vicarious socialization of Americans into the experiences of consumption they are about to have is the continuous task of the mass media. Many of these, and at a variety of income levels, are devoted to expounding the suburban way of life directly in ads and features; other media are indirect vehicles for suburban styles in the homes pictured in stories, the sport shirts worn, and the idols of consumption portrayed.[40] The whole American ethos, which once revolved about the dialectic of pure country versus wicked but exciting city, seems to me now aerated by the suburban outlook. This produces an homogenization of both city and country, but without full integration.

While on the whole the lower-middle- and middle-income suburbs sponsor the relaxed life, there is one area where they impose an imperative which many city dwellers have not met, namely that of having some sort of garden—less as a cultural amenity than as a minimum contribution to civic decency: a kind of compulsory outdoor housekeeping. Indeed, in the study of gardening in two Chicago suburbs conducted by our Center for the Study of Leisure[41] we gained the impression that garden clubs were not extremely active in either one (though we have found very active and prestigeful clubs on the North Shore); garden clubs are much more characteristic of older communities, where they represent a familiar activity of some of the established families, rather than of the new suburbs, where gardening must compete with many other hobbies and activities, both outdoor and indoor. We found in Fairlawn, a new developer's suburb, for example, that to many housewives the garden was simply one more chore. It represented neither a contrast with the asphalt jungle of the city, nor a pleasure in

[40] Cf. Leo Lowenthal, "Biographies in Popular Magazines," in P. F. Lazarsfeld and Frank Stanton, Eds., *Radio Research*, 1942–43 (New York: Duell, Sloane & Pearce).

[41] For a report on this study, see Robin Jackson and Rolf Meyersohn, "The Social Patterning of Leisure," address to the Annual Institute of the Society for Social Research, Chicago, May 30, 1957. I also draw in this paper on a study under the direction of Donald Horton (with the assistance of Robin Jackson) which is concerned with the conflict in styles of leisure in one of the North Shore suburbs, and with the ways in which the institutions of the suburb, particularly the high school, become the foci of that conflict.

growing things, nor a rage for order. It was rather a tax imposed by neighborhood consciousness—the neighbors often being interpreted as more concerned and censorious than they, for the most part, were. Thus we find that many people who have moved newly to the suburbs to escape the city come without awareness of the constraints they will find—or mistakenly interpret—in the suburb. They meet pressures of the very sort they had thought to leave behind, though altered in form and impact.

One of these pressures, already adverted to, is the metropolis itself; its traffic, its ethnic minorities, and its tax rates tend to catch up with them. The waves of succession within the city proper do not halt at its boundaries, and many old and established suburbs are finding themselves cut in two by freeways and by the new kinds of people they bring. In this situation, some of the old kinds of people are among those tempted to become exurbanites, putting the ever approaching city another few miles away and hoping to solve the dilemma of distance versus intimacy by a superhighway.

However, in this quandary the emphasis on superhighways—and on supercars which require them—takes on much of the lunatic quality of an arms race. As highways get bigger and better, they invite more cars, destroy what undeveloped and unschematized country (or central city) remains, and require still more highways in an unending spiral.[42]

People have been drilled by industrialism in the values of efficiency —narrowly defined in terms of speed, performance, and a kind of streamlined look. Thus, even when they flee from the cities and the style of life industrialism has brought about, they cannot change the style of thought which sees the solution to ribbon developments in stretching them still further until our East and West coasts threaten to become continuous roadside slums.

What is true of the planning, or lack of it, of our road-centered culture as a whole is also true of domestic architecture. Efficiency here

[42] Highway engineers resemble guided-missile engineers in an understandable irritation with the tiresome "human factor" which is bound to produce accidents—and every effort has typically been made to reduce the functions of individual drivers or soldiers, thus making them more bored and more accident-prone.
Lewis Mumford has been pointing these things out for so long that he resembles the hero in Wells's story, "The Country of the Blind," who comes close to wishing he could share the visual defects of his fellow-men, for it would be more comfortable that way for everybody.

is less stark—and consequently often less attractive—since it must compete with traditional definitions of a suburban free-standing home. But, as many architects have pointed out, the interiors are highly modern in the sense of mechanization. Indeed, one reason why husbands have been willing to become domesticated is that they have been promoted from dishwashers to operators of dishwashers. Similarly, they use power mowers to give crew cuts to handkerchief-sized lawns and pierce their wives' and neighbors' ears with the screams of high-fidelity music. The open plan of the very newest ranch-style homes puts the TV set on a swivel in the center. Here it can be seen from all parts of the house so that urban news, fashions, gossip, and jokes can circulate in the home throughout the daily cycle of the members of the family. But all these improvements are bought at the expense of space for the individual whose bedroom in the suburban development is often smaller than in city tenements. This is especially true, as Albert Roland of *Household* magazine has pointed out to me, of the newest suburban homes. These have both a family room and a living room. The latter, like the old parlor, is used only for state occasions; the family room is big enough for games, the TV, an inside barbecue, and general clutter.

Nor does the lawn or backyard provide a bounteous free space in most of the new developments. In comparison with the size and cost of the house, plots are small (much as they have traditionally been in midwestern cities where people wanted to avoid the row house but not to be too far from their next-door neighbors). Moreover, the fact that there is both a front and a backyard—the latter being, in many developments, the "family room" and the former the "parlor"—means that what space there is becomes divided. And just as the homes have no interstitial spaces, no nooks and crannies, so the lots have no texture taken individually or together.[43] I keep asking myself what the lots will look like when the explosion of our population doubles the numbers in the suburban hegira without, in all probability, increasing proportionately the services that our new expectations crave. Will houses and lots get smaller when people can no longer spread further afield? People have

[43] It would seem as if Americans, gaining some of the feelings towards the city and its works and ways that Thoreau had, have succeeded in blending his values with those of Carnegie. However, as indicated earlier, they are far from having Andrew Carnegie's concern for hard work, wealth, and thrift—let alone his self-taught passion for literacy—but they do have his interest in serving an image of efficiency, modified by Dale Carnegie's concern for gregarious friendliness.

been moving to the suburbs in many cases in pursuit of an inchoate dream of spaciousness. They have looked for a release from urban tensions, from crowded and ugly schools, from indoors. And ordinarily this release has more than compensated for losses in urban qualities which are difficult to sense or describe—qualities of possibility, often, rather than of actual use.[44] What will occur when the urban qualities have been dissipated, while the suburban ones elude all but the rich?

Such questions assume, as I have here been doing, that Americans have ceased being socially inventive outside the corporate or military spheres. They assume that we will not discover the governmental or voluntary channels either to give many people alternative satisfactions to large families or to create forms of life and livelihood appropriate to another age of population expansion—this time with no frontiers left. Certainly there is now a kind of private inventiveness in the suburbs among people who, having lost "the track of generations" and traditional standards of judgment and taste, are somehow managing, with ambivalent aid from the media, to create new forms and styles. The leaders of Park Forest and several other new communities, surrounded by others as green as they, often managed to develop some communal decencies and controls; in that sense, the town-meeting spirit is far from moribund. It is easy to see the negative and ironical features of the suburbs —harder to see emergent crystallizations.

But one trouble is that the suburbs, like the families within them, can scarcely control their own immediate environs, let alone the larger metropolitan and national orbits that impinge on them and decide their eventual atmosphere. And here is where the suburbanites' immense liking for Ike is portentous. It expresses the wish of so many of the college seniors mentioned above that civics and the Community Chest replace politics; it expresses the hope, built into the very structure of credit and the additive-extrapolative style of thought, that nothing serious will occur, that everything will go on as before. And it expresses this hope, of course, at the very moment when private decisions—irresponsibly influenced—to buy or not to buy, to propagate or not to propagate, store up our destinies (quite apart from the similar activities of the rest of our small planet). . . .

[44] Anselm Strauss has been engaged in a study of the informal tone or aura of cities, their images of themselves; I have profited from conversations with him about city life.

In the days of Lincoln Steffens and later, people emphasized the "shame of the cities," and in the 1920s major novelists emphasized the constraints of small-town and occasionally of small-suburban life. Today, the comparable worry, in the books dealing with the suburbs, is conformity—*Point of No Return*, with its concern for place and competition, strikes a somewhat older note; writers point to the uniformity of the ranch style, the ever present television antennae, the lamp, if not the crack, in the picture window—which usually provides a view of the nearly treeless street, the cars, and someone else's picture window. Actually, uniformity and conformity are quite different matters (as George Simmel has observed in his essay on "Fashion"[45]). The former may dictate to men only in inessentials, whereas the latter involves some psychological mechanism. And the conformity of the new suburbs is, in some important ways, far less stringent than that of the old; if it is not quite the case that "anything goes," lots of things do go which once would, if known, have brought ostracism. If one does not seek to force the new suburbanite back across the ethnic tracks he has just crossed, he is quite tolerant, even bland. If he is political at all—rather than parochially civic-minded, tending to a "garden" which includes the local schools and waterworks—he is apt to be an Eisenhower Republican, seldom informed, rarely angry, and only spasmodically partisan.

No, what is missing in suburbia, even where the quality of life has not overtly deteriorated, is not the result of claustrophobic conformity to others' sanctions. Rather, there would seem to be an aimlessness, a pervasive low-keyed unpleasure. This cannot be described in terms of traditional sorrows but is one on which many observers of the American scene have commented. For millions of people, work no longer provides a central focus for life; and the breadwinner is no longer the chief protagonist in the family saga—just as Saturday night no longer provides a central focus for festivity. In fact, the decentralization of leisure in the suburbs is not only spatial but temporal, as evenings from Thursday through Sunday are oriented to play rather than work and are not individually accented or collectively celebrated.[46]

[45] The essay, which originally appeared in *International Quarterly*, Vol. 10 (1904), pp. 130–55, is reprinted in *American Journal of Sociology*, Vol. 62, No. 6 (1957), pp. 541–58.

[46] I sometimes consider the drive-in movie the archetypical symbol of decentralization where people go to the theater not in stalls which permit circulation of elites but in cars which keep the family or the dating couple together with no sense of the audience or any shared experience outside the sedan.

At the same time, leisure has not picked up the slack—as, in earlier writings, I was too sanguine that it might. Whatever balances of work and play might have been possible for pre-industrial man, postindustrial man is keyed, as I remarked earlier, to greater expectations. He has learned more "needs" and cannot in any case reconstitute the institutions industrialism destroyed. It is almost inconceivable, for example, to imagine a reconstitution of the folk arts which everywhere—in Nigeria as in New Orleans, in Damascus as in Tennessee—prove fragile in the face of mass-produced music and imagery. In *Communitas* the Goodmans devoted much ingenuity to suggesting how, in their New Commune, work could be made more varied and interesting: by job rotation on a grand scale, by alternating supervision and apprenticeship, by scrutiny of all work in terms of means as well as ends. But automation as presently interpreted moves us yet further away from such a re-examination of work routines, even though, were our values different, it could provide an opportunity for eliminating monotonous work and bringing far more variety and spark into it.

I recently had the opportunity to talk about the future of leisure with some thoughtful union leaders and adult educators. They were looking forward, in dismay as much as in hope, to a far shorter working week and a less demanding working day. They were asking specialists on leisure how these vacua of time and energy could be filled with more creativity and less boredom. They were saddling leisure with the burden which indeed it did carry for a small minority of the leisure class in some aristocratic eras—the burden of supporting life's total commitment and significance. Suggestions were made for better adult education courses, even for sabbaticals for everybody or short periods of residence in an Aspen-like setting. And one leader spoke of efforts to link workers possessing underused craft skills with groups such as nursery schools possessing substandard facilities—groups which could benefit greatly from the energies and capabilities of people who would in their free time build jungle gyms, chairs, or other needed equipment. But it was clear from the tone of the meeting that these notions, valuable as they were, could not even claim the status of palliatives. It was not only that they could not (given workers as they are) compete with commercial recreation or polishing the car, but also that they did not provide the "moral equivalent of work." We can see in the bored teenagers who don't like school, and are already sated with sex unmitigated by love, what leisure is like for most people when life lacks the accent and structure given it by work—not simply stand-by "work" but some effortful and periodically challenging activity.

In the studies of unemployed men made during the Great Depression, the observation of the demoralizing nature of being without work was often made, but it was sometimes assumed that this was mostly a matter of status and of poverty which forced the unemployed man to hang uselessly about the house. And in the studies of men who have retired, the same theme recurs. They are demoralized because the job gave status and income, and also because they grew up in a work-minded era and were not prepared for the age of leisure. I myself had thought that when a whole generation had been reared which was not driven to work by the agreed-upon motives of hunger and gain—often unconsciously driven because work-mindedness was instilled, so to speak, with mother's bottle feeding on schedule—such people could retire more comfortably than the elderly now do because they would have been preparing for it all life long. Presently, however, I am inclined to believe that work is still necessary because our inventiveness has not found ways of relating masses of men to creative activity or to each other outside of work. Though the artist, of whatever sort and for whom there is no real division between work and play, indicates what may someday be possible, even the artist, whatever his ideology of *l'art pour l'art*, needs usually to feel he is being of some use—if only in acting out a counterpoint to Philistine utilitarianism.

With these considerations in mind, I suggested to the union leaders that if work were more demanding (without being, other than occasionally, totally exhausting) leisure would present slightly less unmanageable prospects. If men, instead of standing at a row of dials or on an assembly line, could have the freedom of the plant that maintenance men have, and their opportunity to set their own schedules; if they could work under pressure at times, without being charged with rate-busting, they might then leave their work without feeling resentful of industrialism, only to pepper away at deer with elephant rifles, or to seek a second job sometimes allowing independence from a boss without diminishing monotony. I stressed this because of my belief that the boundaries which once separated our problems from each other (as other boundaries separated city from country, men from women, middle class from lower class, sociology from politics, and economics from anthropology) have been disappearing, along with many forms of parochialism and isolationism.

City planners are, of course, among the few people who are forced to know this already, try as some of them do to act like highway engineers or efficiency experts. Some of them know that the motives which once gave structure to both work and leisure, and the interchanges and journeys between them, have also been disappearing, even though millions of people, shorn of other rationales for activity, still go after money. At present they do this not in the form of capital but in the form of consumer goods. Our new middle-class large families are, in part, an effort to fill this gap. Similarly, our suburbs are an effort to build a life not based on work but instead on the family and on voluntary associations. It is surely an advance to prefer children to capital gains, and suburban *Gemütlichkeit* to urban pavements (though, as British planners discovered in building the New Towns and as writers for the *Architectural Review* have insisted, there were values concealed in the most seemingly depressed urban conglomerations which were lost in the move to the more hygienic and aseptic planned communities—much as farmers for a long time failed to realize that worms and other "varmint" were essential to a well-nourished soil). But the advances cannot be consolidated unless they are made on a broader front; otherwise, people may quickly oscillate again toward such apparent security as industrialism gave them. Faced with the mounting depreciations of the crowded suburbs and aware of their own powerlessness, they may turn to strong authority which promises to clean up the already foreseeable mess. Even now, drivers in a traffic jam, frustrated by each other's presence, are not the most amiable of men. This, despite the fact that, once on the move again, it is largely the sense of moving rather than anything they actively do or enjoy which gives them pleasure and release.

One of the findings of our gardening study comes to mind here, and it may serve as a coda to these adumbrations. I have remarked above on the tendency for families in the new suburb of Fairlawn to assume that their nieghbors, who were in fact quite tolerant, were putting pressure on them to have not merely a passable garden but a good one. Actually, the neighbors' visual sense was not that highly developed, nor their emulative sense either. They were tolerant of each other's gardens as of each other's life in general. I asked myself then what was the source of the extensive misinterpretation which led to such comments as the following by a Fairlawn housewife. She described to the interviewer an ambitious plan for a rose garden and large beds of flowers all around the house as follows:

> I really hate gardening; we both do. My husband never plays golf any more and we do nothing all weekend but work in the garden. I mean work.

I recalled analogous comments made by students who were working allegedly to prepare for an exam which their intelligence told them they could not easily fail; I recalled other such comments by business and professional men who created anxieties in their work in order to give it drama and bite. I realized that, since we are not really attached to anything we are doing, we look for spurs when life no longer automatically provides them. Perhaps the housewife just quoted cannot make herself (or her spouse) work at all without picturing dire consequences for failure. Or perhaps she has in this case simply projected her own moralism or malice into her neighbors—possibly also as a part of an internal family argument with an indifferent or indolent husband. Games, the arts, conversation are all activities which have institutionalized short bursts of effort as the price both of pleasure and performance. The suburbs, however, in seeking to take the place of the city, provide insufficient comparable agendas, and housewives such as those we saw who gardened with neither pleasure nor skill still clung to the demand that neighbors and nature seemed to make.

I have lost any sanguinity that they will learn better simply by sticking it out; they may only get more bored, more destructive. Their pleasure in flowers, or in the arrangements of nature, cannot be very intense if they put up, as they seem ready enough to do, with the visual blight of so much of our suburbscape, the roads that take them there, the cars they drive in. I am not speaking of "taste," in the sense of high taste, but rather of the quality with which visual experience is assimilated. And I am certainly not speaking of the uniformity of the Levittowns as such. The row houses in Baltimore or Philadelphia are often handsome in ways which our suburbs, varied in a studied fashion, fail to achieve. In the course of the industrial revolution and the rise of the middle classes, both elite taste and traditional taste decline. Today, despite frequent improvement in advertising and magazine layout, in interior decoration, and in corporate and public building, the sense for visual imagery of Americans remains stunted, and the children of the suburbs grow up accepting the neat, the new, the shiny, but with minimal awareness of vista, proportion, or independent critical judgment of the look of life around them.

THE SUBURBAN DISLOCATION

Writing ten years ago about the Goodmans' book, I was up against the perennial planners' problem: how to get from here to there, when "here" is the omnipresent educator, the agent of socialization. Yet, as makers of goods and ideas know, Americans are almost too ready to abandon one thing for another, provided they are persuaded by the media or friends that the other is somehow "better" or, preferably, "the best," along a dimension which is already given. To be sure, the range of such persuasion is not terribly wide, and it is wider of course in inessentials or externals, though the last ten years have seen radical changes in food habits, men's clothes, child rearing, and other (one might suppose) tenacious things. More problematic is the persuasion itself. When mobilized for the planners' good ends it is frequently self-defeating because it almost inevitably uses the given means such as appeals to snobbery or to a fake efficiency. Yet the fear of this problem, with its practical and ethical dilemmas, seems to me at present to have intimidated thinking about what the good ends are. Thus, even if people could be persuaded, there is nothing to persuade them of. Plans, as history occasionally shows, have their own persuasive power, particularly in unexpected historical junctures. Many Americans will soon discover the loss of urban and suburban texture and might then be ready to do something, were a model available. The social processes I have touched upon in this paper are moving people into the service trades and professions and out of industry and farming. We need to find meaningful work for the displaced ones rather than locating still more of them in selling, public relations, and looking after each other. The country can "use" poets, painters, planners, and prophets in virtually unlimited amounts. With poets in recent years the country has not done too badly; with painters—despite all I have said about visual blight and the country of the blind—not too badly, either. But planners and prophets?

Flight and Search in the New Suburbs
(1959)

Recently, in a doctoral dissertation done in the Sociology Department at Berkeley, Bennett Berger described a working-class suburb south of San Francisco which differs radically from the image most of us probably have of "the suburbs." In the first place, the people there were Democratic voters when they lived in the city and are Democratic voters now. In the second place, they have no aspirations toward social mobility and no particular interest in neighboring and local activities or in most forms of suburban participation. In the third place, they live near their work in a nearby Ford plant. They are not commuters in the traditional sense, and indeed are nearer their work in terms of time than most city workers are. In sum, they have not noticeably altered their style of life as the result of their shift of residence. They are glad to have better homes and more room, but they have not become suburbanites in the social-psychological sense. One can find neighborhoods in many large cities where people live not so differently.

What puzzled the author of this dissertation was the difference between the suburb he studied and the image of the suburb that appears in much recent writing. The latter is the image we are all familiar with (and to which I myself have contributed): an image of mass-produced houses with picture windows and handkerchief-sized lawns, of endless neighboring across the lawns, of social anxiety and conformity, of transiency and overorganization. Since suburbs in fact differ from each other, probably quite as much as central cities do, it is worth stopping for a moment to ask ourselves why this image exists—why, for example, many people who attack conformity do so in stereotyped terms. I think that several elements can be sorted out. For one thing, we educated middle-class Americans have become extraordinarily self-conscious about ourselves in recent years, even more so than was the traditional American who wondered what was this new man, this American, and read anything which could shed light on the question. Since reality is complicated, intractable, and often opaque, we tend to jump at statements about ourselves even when these are negative in order to give structure to our experience, while at the same time (much as with language itself) our concepts serve to divorce us from that experience. In the second place, these tendencies, which have always existed, have been speeded up in recent years by the enormous industry of the mass media which must constantly find new ideas to purvey, and which have short-circuited the traditional filtering down of ideas from academic and intellectual centers. We can follow an interpretation of the suburbs from an article in *Fortune* to an article in the *American Journal of Sociology* to an article in *Harper's* to a best-selling book like John Keats's *The Crack in the Picture Window* to an article in *Life* magazine or a TV drama—all in a matter of a couple of years—much in the way in which a few poets, who have been reading their poems to jazz in San Francisco for quite a few years, suddenly have become the symbol of the "beat generation" and are imitated almost before they really exist.

Furthermore, some of the most visible new suburbs have also been the most accessible, such as the Levittowns of the forties on Long Island or of the fifties in Pennsylvania, and Park Forest, south of Chicago. These developments are untypical in any representative sense: I am sure, for instance, that they are more civic-minded, better planned, and better managed than the suburban scatterations that Robert Wood describes in his book, *Suburbia*. If new developments such as Park Forest are not typical, are they then in some way representative? Are they the shape of the future? I must say that I feel very unsure about these matters. When I read Berger's thesis, for instance, I am struck by the fact, to which he himself doesn't pay much attention, that many of the workers in the suburb he studies came from the South. This alone would make for differences with another workers' suburb inhabited by, let us say, Italians who have moved out of Boston, or Poles who have moved out of Buffalo. Homogenization proceeds at very uneven rates in these different ethnic groups and strata. And this is in spite of all superficial similarities and standardizations which are often mistakenly taken by people as indices of inner similarity as well.

This last mistake is a very puzzling one, if one reflects on it. Do people assume that all Catholic priests are alike because they all wear a uniform? Or do they assume that the people who lived in the eighteenth century in the row houses of Philadelphia or Baltimore or Beacon Hill were alike? Could it be that the focus or external similarities as symbols of conformity is a purposeful deflection of the real issue, which is whether people think and feel alike—so that the self-styled nonconformist can feel he is being different because, for example, he wears a beard or a beret or paints his house an odd color or, until recent years at least, drives a foreign car? I would suggest that the very fact that people can engage in these marginal games of difference is evidence that, in some ways, there is less strict and stern conformity in or out of the suburbs than there was in an earlier generation, but by the same token this very freedom creates its own problems in ways Erich Fromm has pointed out, and its own factitious as well as more genuine efforts at resolution.

For a better grasp of these matters, we need to go beyond the handful of suburbs which have been intensively studied on the one side, and the large-scale efforts to generalize, such as my own, on the other side. We need many people with the pertinacity of Samuel Lubell to go tramping the streets and ringing the doorbells and looking in the picture windows—and the old mullioned windows as well—in all the great variety of suburbs that there are. But now let me put these standard cautions aside, and try to ask in general what it is that people are fleeing from or leaving when they opt for the suburbs.

Land and gentility have, we know, a traditional connection in the West—as compared, for instance, to the situation, as I understand it, in China before the Communists, where the landlords moved to the city as soon as they could afford it, although they kept a place on the land. The British gentry, of course, kept close ties to the land, and even in their crowded, urbanized island, still do. People began to move out of the center of Philadelphia or Boston to avoid noise and dirt as early as the eighteenth century. But the suburban movement did not really get underway in this country until the turn of the nineteenth century—at the point in our history when urbanization and industrialization, and particularly immigration of "new kinds of people," were giving the older Americans a feeling that their Jeffersonian country was disappearing. The desire for a little place in the country with its own little plot of land became, under these conditions, not only a return to British gentry patterns, but also an effort to recapture an image of an earlier America as a counterweight to the immigrant-crowded and apparently immigrant-corrupted city. Industrialization was seen by many Americans as "the machine in the garden" that would inevitably destroy their pastoral dream. But the dream dies hard. The individual freestanding house, with its front lawn and back lawn, the houses with their artfully variegated decor, the often pastiche Georgian of Gothic railway stations, all testify to the desire to re-create an America that one had perhaps known in one's youth, or that one wishes one had known and tries to live up to.

We virtually cut off immigration from Europe in the 1920s as one of the more regressive features of this dream, but it was, of course, not possible to cut off internal immigration from the poor whites and the poor Negroes of the South and from Puerto Rico and Mexico. And though, of course, the Negroes are among the very earliest arrivals and oldest Americans, their pressure in many northern cities has been feeding the flight to the suburbs in the postwar years, for they bring in not so much the "un-American" ways of Europe as the non-middle-class ways of the impoverished.

But I am not suggesting that new people entering the city at the bottom are driving out old people at the top in any simple way. Indeed, the old rules of ethnic succession, developed by sociologists of an earlier generation, no longer seem to hold. And undoubtedly there are economic factors of rentals and taxes and deferred maintenance which play a part in all this. Beyond, however, realistic considerations, there remains the fact that our cities have become less uninhabitable for middle-class people than they often were in the late nineteenth century. The city of Philadelphia, for instance, in which I grew up as a child, is much more a place of hope than it was in the 1920s, or when Lincoln Steffens described it earlier as "corrupt and contented." Urban renewal was, in fact, one of the few spending programs, other than armaments, to which the Eisenhower administration was not allergic, and it is astonishing how much has been done in this respect in the last ten years. But on the whole, educated middle-class people have not been lured back to the city, but have continued to avoid it.

One element here, which is relatively new, I think, is a complex and subtle relation between democratic values and exclusionary practices. In the late nineteenth and early twentieth century, although many well-to-do people left the city because they wanted fresh air, many others remained, or at least kept their town houses there. In a highly stratified society in which people at the top feel secure about their position and people at the bottom know their place and lack the autos and the spending money to get out of their place, cities can crowd together the Gold Coast and the slum, or as in the typical southern city, the Negro and the white, without explosive friction and resentment on either side. The rich are protected from the poor by the latter's self-restraint and by the former's servants and relative monopoly of the higher levels of schooling. The poor are protected from the rich by the hope that their children, if they behave themselves, may make the grade some day, or at least one step toward it. To be sure, this didn't always work, and the slums bred crime and delinquent protest. Nevertheless, awareness of this threat from below was only periodic, and many of the rich kept their town houses or apartments in the city even when they began, in the 1880s and thereafter, to move part-time to the suburbs for fresh air and a pastoral setting.

Today, it goes without saying that all this has quite changed. The children of the poor do not stay in place. The news that they don't is publicized in reports of crime waves and juvenile delinquency, and by the fact that they flaunt on alien turf their leather jackets, cars and motorcycles, and generally disturbing ways. Furthermore, the children of the rich are not immune to the values thus spread from below, and the parents of the children of the rich, or at least the moderately rich, are not well defended from their children's own demands. I recall a case that recently came up in one of the better Westchester suburbs. A high school boy of good middle-class family had been dressing like a hood. His parents, pleased and perhaps tempted by this sign of masculinity, remonstrated only mildly with him. One night he and a friend of his, similarly dressed in a leather jacket and all the fixings, went with their dates into a bar in the local village. They asked for Cokes, but before they could be served, the bartender grabbed them and threw them violently out on the sidewalk, saying he didn't want "that kind" in there. The boy of whom I am speaking was much shaken and slightly hurt, and his parents were furious. They asked the chief of police to prosecute the bartender for assault. The chief refused, saying that his men were trying to protect the community against hoodlums and, if their child dressed as one, he should expect no different treatment. I suggest that this story illustrates the ambivalence of many parents today, and their need to protect themselves against their children's temptations toward downward mobility, not by their own stern and impressive rules, but by moving to a community where the high price of real estate will keep down the numbers of the wrong sort of people and where the schools will be in the hands or under the control of educated parents like themselves. And this becomes all the more important precisely because, in our mobile society, parents can no longer protect the social and financial position of their own children through ties of lineage and sheer nepotism, let alone by inheritance. The best they can do, and they know this, is to give their children a good education—this is the only capital equipment they can really count on—and then hope that the educational system will locate their children not necessarily near home but in some comparable position.

Thus, the task of the schools as sorting agents becomes ever more important and the suburb is seen consequently as an enclave within which one can be quite democratic because a certain minimum exclusion is worked automatically by zoning and the realtors. Likewise, in college, young people are much more democratic than they used to be, much readier to go around with people on the basis of their personal qualities and without regard to conventional status, but this is possible only because a certain amount of exclusion is worked by the admissions committee, or at least by the image which the college presents to the minds of high school youngsters, their teachers and guidance people.

Hence, one of the things people are fleeing when they leave the city is the need either to reject people who are less well educated than themselves, or to accept them with all that implies for their children's education and future placement in the society. If I am right, then the suburbs, which are often criticized for their one-class homogeneity, may actually permit a good deal more mixing than people would allow themselves, in fact, though not in theory, in the metropolis. But of course, in this field too there are great differences.

So far, I have talked about the image of pastoral life in the suburb as against the city—the latter seen as the locale of alien folk, of violence and of threat to one's children's education and social placement. But I think something still more fundamental is also at work in this country, namely, a general rejection of the commercial and industrial revolution of the eighteenth and nineteenth centuries. . . . So much is this the case that when industry follows its workers out to suburbs, as it is doing more and more, it builds plants which are indistinguishable from the new suburban schools or supermarkets, and which look as little as possible like the industrial enclaves or constellations of an earlier day. Though we still live *by* industry and commerce, we no longer live *for* them . . . Electricity, trucking, telephones, and other forms of industrial and commercial decentralization have made it no longer necessary to bring together in a single market or in a single plant or industrial complex as many different skills and trades as a big city encompasses. And the city has come to stand in our minds for the market, for impersonality, for great ambitions and risks and great failures and losses—for that boom and bust world, hectic and driving, that still is very much the picture of America in the rest of the world, but on which we ourselves, and again I am speaking of the young and especially the college-educated, are increasingly soured.

How do I know this? I am not sure it is so. I have looked at the attitudes toward work that turn up in national sample surveys . . . Young people are tending to avoid those occupations that make great demands or that require central business-district location and to prefer those that make modest, though not at all inaudible, demands, provide some interest and camaraderie, and permit a suburban location. There are many exceptions to this, particularly perhaps in the South and among previously deprived groups, but that is the general, although still tentative picture that I get.

I might add that to many among the older generation, all this seems like a bad sign, and younger people are denounced as security-minded, afraid of hard work, and having the other symptoms of softness that Admiral Rickover so enjoys denouncing. I regard such criticisms as one-sided. In the period of the metropolis, the period of industrialism, people strove for often shallow rewards which went in the end not to them, but to the capital equipment of the system to which they subordinated themselves. Young people today are seldom willing to do this. They want more in their lives, especially more in the way of personal relations. The only capital equipment to which they will devote themselves is their children, which they are having sooner and in larger numbers than anyone has expected—one reason, of course, they have had to move to the suburbs is to find room.

But such considerations turn my attention away from why people are leaving the city to what they are leaving it for.[1] What is it that they are looking for, particularly in the new suburbs? Once the pressures are off for survival on a new continent, once people have built themselves a relatively productive economy, and a not too unstable polity, other long-repressed human needs have an opportunity to be invented. And certainly one of the needs which the suburbs make visible is the need for primary groups and kinship ties—for some sort of face-to-face relatedness to people.

[1] It should be pointed out that many people are not leaving the city for the suburbs, but are leaving old suburbs for new suburbs: the suburbs now house so substantial a proportion of Americans as to be almost self-generated.

The more impersonal the big world looks, the more organized and elaborate and difficult, the more there occurs a phenomenon which, in the totalitarian countries, has been labeled the "inner emigration": the withdrawal by people of emotional attachments to the large goals of the state or other corporate body and the search for ties in a small trusted group where, it is felt, one can "be oneself." Robert Gutman, who has been studying suburban communities in northern New Jersey, tells me that when people move to such a community, they almost invariably assume that it is, in fact, a community, that there exist networks of human relations into which they can be invited and where they can "belong." Their experience in this respect is perhaps not so different from the feeling of the college freshman who goes away to a residential college from a high school which doesn't send a big delegation to his college: he is apt to arrive with an image of what college life ought to be like, an image that, of course, includes friendships and activities, as well as work and studies. It may look to him when he gets there (maybe depending on the chances which locate him in one entry of a dorm rather than another) as if everybody else belongs while he is out of it. The others may strike him as reserved, particularly if he comes East from the Middle or Far West. He may then turn to sports and activities as a way of finding a niche for himself in a new and disturbing milieu.

It is just this experience, I am suggesting, this hope of finding ties to other people with whom one can be friends, that many college-educated people look for in the suburb—and of course their college and high school training often serves them in good stead in giving them leads as to how to go about meeting others. It is the wife on whom these pressures bear most strongly, for the husband still has his ties at work, even though these do not suffice to make a social life for him. The wife is thus a kind of social ambassador in the suburb (and she, in turn, may have small children and dogs to help her).

But it sometimes happens around the fringes of our metropolitan areas that there is no real community; rather, the Mixmaster of the auto has scattered people in every direction with the result that there are no easily marked roads to friendship and relatedness. Professor Samuel Stouffer made studies of New England communities, many of them suburban, and found that the patterns of leadership and neighboring vary enormously as one moves from one community to another, depending on historical and local factors. One community will be relatively monolithic: there will be somebody in charge, and everyone will know who it is. And there will be a church one can join as a slow but sure way of access to people and activities. Other communities seem utterly fragmented. They tend to leave all responsibility to outside agencies, sometimes, for instance, in order to avoid controversy between old and new residents, or between old and new ethnic groups. People may circulate in narrow orbits of kinfolk—as some Italians who have moved out to Boston suburbs go back to the West End for recreation and sociability. In still other communities, civic-minded men and women, eager to have an impact on their immediate environment (perhaps in part because they feel impotent in the larger metropolitan or national environment), will be actively concerned with the schools and roads, the zoning assessments, and other aspects of communal life—and ready to welcome fellow workers who are, in turn, eager, as I have said, to discover something to which they can belong and to which they can devote themselves.

What I am suggesting is that the very amorphousness of many suburban communities leads to social pressures of two sorts. On the one hand, people are amenable to pressure because they are in a new situation and want to belong to something—a little like freshmen in orientation week. And, on the other hand, anybody who wants to get anything done, any organization built or financed, has to put on pressure because he cannot rely on traditional and well-worked-out channels. Indeed, in many new suburbs, community organizations which had been built up over generations in the city have had to be re-created over night—much as the immigrants to this country had to create institutions such as churches which were part of the landscape in the old country, and taken for granted. The governmental organizations large enough to cope with the problems of the suburbs scarcely exist, and everything that gets done has to be done, so to speak, by hand.

Sometimes it seems to me that what people are seeking in the suburbs is a kind of pre-industrial incompetence and inefficiency. Certainly one thing that is striking about American life in general is the contrast between areas of tidiness and managerial skill and a kind of underside of messiness and makeshift. For example, one will find a gleaming new shopping center in a suburb, a consumer's paradise, brilliantly designed, fronting on a highway where the traffic in and out of the supermarket is a threat to life if not to sanity, and surrounded by used car lots, hot dog stands, and jerry-built motels. Similarly, if one visits the stunning and expensive Technical Center built by General Motors near Detroit, one is struck by the fact that, once outside this technocratic island, one is back in the typical traffic and roadside morass of the urban fringe, when only a little more money and effort would have provided a setting for the Center in better keeping with its needs and aims. It almost looks as if every victory of efficiency and planning, design and taste, in America was won at the expense of an underside of disarray—a little reminiscent of one of the earliest of planned suburbs, the town of Pullman, south of Chicago, which was surrounded outside the company limits by taverns, whore houses, union lodges, and store front churches, all catering to needs which Pullman himself had either ignored or deprecated. (Similarly, Mr. Wood points out in *Suburbia: Its People and Its Problems* that the more exclusive the suburb, the more likely it is that a nearby nonexclusive suburb will grow up, populated by the people whom one has excluded—and leading, possibly, to a further effort at escape by moving out to a still un-bulldozered exurb.)

Of course such contrasts exist in every country, and if we compare America with the poorer countries of the planet, America certainly appears to be one great glorious suburb, at once efficient and well-ordered, with the contrasts that strike and sometimes dismay us fading in crosscultural perspective. My hunch is that the contrast also exists within ourselves. It represents, as I have suggested, our reaction against industrialism, and its demands for skill, professional ability, and foresight. While we were building our industrial society, we seemed to accept the demands put upon us, but now, with that task over, the negative aspects of our ambivalence can come into view. Our country has been rich enough to afford much waste, or at least it has acted on that premise, and always derided efforts at conservation. Moreover, there has been room enough to make a mess and move on, or tear it all down and start over.

Many people have achieved, in the suburbs, a face-to-face community and a domesticity which give meaning to life even while, in some degree, also oppressing them. And we must recognize, of course, that they have not totally rejected the industrial revolution, but rather have incorporated it in part, in the way that revolutions always have incorporated part of what they are fighting against. The husband who works a forty-hour week or less comes home from his job to use a basement lathe, a Polaroid camera, or a power mower. His wife, who has made the kitchen coterminous with the family room, and thus restored an almost peasant pattern, has, of course, mechanized the kitchen thoroughly, and the supermarket has half processed what she eats (fearing to process it further because, as the cake-mix people have discovered, housewives tend to feel guilty if all effort is removed and they are not making any of the motions that their grandmothers did). Moreover, in many suburbs organization creeps back in the complex schedulings that must be arranged if husband and wife and their growing children are to lead their independent lives without each having his own independent bus company! And it often turns out that many of the women put into their civic activities as much managerial know-how as any professional —indeed, Professor Stouffer, in his study of communities in New England, concluded that members of the League of Women Voters were able to give his interviewers the best picture of the actual government of the communities, better even than they could get from the old-time newspaper editors and reporters.

Yet, as quite a few commentators have observed, the localism that is achieved in this way looks scarcely viable for the future when there will be more people, less room, and perhaps less leeway between the organized and efficient and the parochial and purposefully antique. Many college towns have a high concentration of gifted, intelligent, and attractive people. But for many kinds of stimulation, one must go to New York or Chicago or San Francisco or some other metropolis. If one is looking for highly specialized relationships, just as if one is looking for a specialty shop, one needs both a greater density and a greater diversity than even the most attractive suburb offers.

Some of this becomes evident when one starts to examine the sociability in some of the newer suburbs. Certain kinds of traditional middle-class strain are missing from suburban encounters: there is, for instance, little effort to impress people with one's wealth or lineage or other attributes of social status. The general tone, on the contrary, is low-pressure, informal, homey. Indeed, what seems to have happened is that these sociable groups have re-created the family, the primary face-to-face group, with a vengeance. In putting down roots in the suburb, many young adults have tended to immobilize themselves. Just as the young person has to leave home, has to make a break from his family in order to develop and grow up, so also it would seem not unreasonable to be fearful lest these quasi-families of the suburb provide a new, if gentle and tolerant, captivity.

There is also, as I have already implied, a great danger that dedication to the *civic* affairs of the suburb will be at the expense of the *political* affairs of city, state, nation, and planet. This is not necessarily so: since the busier people get more done and since those who belong to some committees have others added unto them, it will often happen that those who meet their parochial obligations will not neglect their planetary ones. But there will be others, surely, caught up in the endless tasks of localism, and the pressureful pleasures of the face-to-face group, who might have made a contribution to large affairs. In the well-to-do suburbs on the North Shore of Chicago, one can find busy and capable executives dedicating themselves to what appear to be relatively trivial issues: whether dogs should be leashed or not, the problem of parking in the main street of the village, the recurrent issues of zoning, and the by no means trivial, but almost wholly absorptive issues of the schools. If one talks to these men, many of course would not agree that they are sacrificing national interests to provincial ones, because, in fact, they don't believe they can make a dent on the national scene. And this is true of some of the most important men. For instance, even big businessmen often feel quite helpless when asked to do something about urban renewal—even though, in fact, as the experience in New Haven, Philadelphia, Pittsburgh, or Cincinnati shows, they can be extraordinarily effective when a group gets together. Such individuals, out of a combination of modesty and ignorance, and as a way also of keeping out of the more complex and controversial distant matters, may still enjoy the feeling of being active in a local setting.

And I expect this tendency will increase as businessmen, better educated in better colleges than ever before, become increasingly weary of making money or of the game of business itself as they reach relatively more secure positions, and look both for challenge and for a feeling of accomplishment to the community around them. Indeed, as large business becomes more and more decentralized, such a policy is being encouraged among plant managers. Many in suburban locations find themselves both invited and pushed into assuming local civic responsibilities. While only a very few businessmen go to Washington to serve for a term, a very large number serve on a continuous part-time basis, on the finance committee of the school board, or helping manage the community drive.

In my judgment, the gardens of the suburbs remain at the mercy of fallout, as the little patches of efficiency and good management remain at the mercy of sprawl and chaotic decentralization. I am not for giving up gardens, but I feel that the judgment that one is impotent in large affairs is self-confirming and self-defeating, and that a dialectic between the garden and the wilderness, the suburb and the asphalt jungle, is essential. There is, as various people have pointed out, no place to hide.

Autos in America
(WITH ERIC LARRABEE, 1956)

I

So far as we know, though he lived until 1929, Thorstein Veblen never owned a car. During his years at Stanford, he drove an old mare, as lovingly described by R. L. Duffus in *The Innocents at Cedro*. Veblen, of course, was a functionalist, a believer in engineering, and a hater of show and waste. Probably he would have thought any kind of car needless, just as he thought furniture mostly needless and washed dishes, after they had accumulated for a few days, by turning a hose on them. But it would be interesting to know what he would make of the role played by the automobile in America today.

Perhaps he would not quite have agreed with the late Justice Brandeis, who used to speak angrily of the way in which the auto gave the workingman a false sense of power, which he then dissipated on the streets. Brandeis felt that power should be earned through activity, through character, not by pressing the accelerator. He was a Southerner, however, and shared many of the Southern Agrarians' views toward industrialism—he hated Detroit as a symbol of all he thought wrong with America; his attitudes in this resembled Gandhi's. Veblen, on the other hand, admired industry and, having started life as a farmer, had few agrarian illusions; he would not have begrudged power to the workingman. He would only have hated to see him seduced, as Veblen would surely have seen the buyer of current cars to be, by glamour.

To find a car today that Veblen would not have despised, one would have to go to the civilian Jeep or perhaps the Volkswagen. He would doubtless be dissatisfied with the Willys station wagon for making too many concessions to the human propensity for surrounding useful objects with symbolic overtones, or to that even more human tendency to let means to an end become ends in themselves. He would find at present that even *Consumer Reports*, long a Veblenian stronghold, was beginning to abandon functionalism in its criticism of commodities, so that an Oldsmobile or a hydramatic transmission—for all the waste of gas—can now enter its pages without being condemned out-of-hand.

Nor could he attribute these departures from a strict functionalism simply to the chicanery of auto makers; for he would have to observe that those few companies that have survived—out of the estimated fifteen hundred that, since 1893, have attempted to produce trade-marked models—were those that learned to obey the whim of the consumer rather than the Johanssen gauges of the engineer. True, the industry has succeeded in bureaucratizing the consumer's whim, an archetypical Detroit achievement that will be one of our chief concerns in these pages. But the engineer has had to take second place to the designer and the market researcher, while the auto itself has come more and more to conceal its ancestry in surface transport and to engross a panoply of hitherto unrelated images—of a living room, a jukebox, a jet plane, or even (in certain hard-top models) a bathroom.

Henry Ford, unconscious Veblenite that he was, held out as long as he could. His Model T sold for as low as $290 in 1924, when the number of cars on the scene varied greatly in performance and price, some of them selling for fifteen times as much. These prices reflected the separation of American classes, as well as other disparities—between country and city with their diverse clearances and road conditions; between men mechanically adept, and women, mechanically prissy; between the Stutz-Bearcatted, coon-coated young and their sedate parents, driving Marmons and Pierce-Arrows; or between doctors wedded to their air-cooled Franklins and salesmen who swore by their sturdy Studebakers. Ford made no effort to accommodate such variety through style or color, let alone appeal to the small minority who wanted and could afford, a generation ago, something more than transport per se.

His son, Edsel, reared regardless of parental disapproval in contact with Grosse Pointe luxuries, tried to persuade him to abandon the Model T and compete with Bodies by Fisher, but for a long time without success. The elder Ford insisted with Veblenian severity on putting technology first; he preferred to hang around the shop or pass the time with his oddball buddies rather than in an office with industrial designers or students of consumer behavior. (There is a story of Edsel bringing a new and gaudy Lincoln to Dearborn, and his father walking by it without a word.) Old Henry, moreover, had as little love for trim and whim in the plant itself as in the car. He despised the white-collar worker or, for that matter, any appearance of methodical management. He preferred creating deliberate confusion to letting his trusted subordinates forget their dependence on his own intuition, and he never lost his cagey rural mistrust of bookkeepers and banks. These two he also linked with Wall Street, which he fought and detested, and he would be as aghast today to see his firm's stock on the market as to see his family's foundation investing in the social sciences.

Yet history, which he had called "bunk," caught up with him before he died. It was partly his own doing. As the great innovator of the assembly line and the five-dollar-a-day wage, he was instrumental in creating an economy far too bounteous to be satisfied with the Model T. Like other Puritans, Ford himself was willing to reject the givens of history only on the side of production; on the side of consumption he had no talent, no appetites, no emulative envy. For his customers, however, as now in many underdeveloped countries, the automobile was the very symbol of an end to sumptuary traditions, a statement that things need not always be as they are. Machinery, seldom the neutral agent it is commonly said to be, redefines aspirations as rapidly as it absorbs them; and Ford's unending stream of inexpensive cars released exactly those demands that he had tried to stifle. The possession of a personal power plant under standing orders not only diffused a sense of infinite industrial potentiality; it made compulsory all the roads and auxiliary services that have since homogenized the auto market, bringing the country to the town, penalizing the idiosyncratic vehicle, and admitting women and children to the act of purchase that had previously been a male prerogative.

As Ford's star declined, the one left shining was that of his exact antithesis: William C. Durant, the financier who had founded General Motors; a manipulator and organizer noted for his ignorance of engineering; and a model of the Captain of Industry whom both Ford and Veblen feared and hated. Since he could control his galaxy of companies only by means of paper, Durant needed the rational accounting methods that Ford did without; and, though no engineer, he could hire such engineers as Alfred Sloan and Walter Chrysler. While his two personal regimes collapsed, Durant left in GM an organization capable of responding to consumer pressure and of granting increased authority to the department then innocently known as Art and Color. Though one would have expected the depression of 1929 to save Ford from the gaudier GM line, even the workman on relief insisted on having a car, so that 38 million were sold in the ten years after 1929, 10 million more than in the previous decade; and during this same period, though some of the fancy machines in the high-price range gave up the ghost, the former low-price cars (including Ford's reluctant Models A and V-8) themselves became fancier—a process which, as we shall see, has continued since World War II.

Today, despite the prominence granted to past and present presidents of GM, the dominant position in controlling the car as a physical object is neither that of mechanic nor money-man, but of designer. As cars became easier to make than to sell, their shape and color became major sales points with the inevitable result that power passed from the engineers to what Detroit calls the Styling Section. This institution— GM's involves 12 studios and 850 persons—is the personal creation of Harley Earl, a vice president of GM and the first industrial designer to attain that rank, who established the principle that "appearance sells cars" as GM policy. Beginning with the 1927 LaSalle, Earl can claim to have designed a total of 32 million automobiles; more than any other individual, he is responsible for the auto's present apotheosis as a piece of wildly imaginative metallic sculpture.[1] To take only one example of his commanding status, when he decided on a wraparound windshield for the 1954 models, he got it—in spite of the uncertainty of engineers that it could be mass-produced, in spite of the image distortion it produces at the sides, and in spite of the fact that turning it out required fabulous waste and virtual command of the country's laminated-glass facilities.

To be sure, even today a social archaeologist could find legacies of Ford and Veblen. For one thing, a covert hunger for visible and tangible engineering is reasserted in the sports cars and their imitators, in the tachometers of a Jaguar or the boast of Chevrolet's Corvette to have "instrumentation as complete as a light plane's." For another, while the image of the GM line is set by the Buick or to some extent by the Cadillac, the image of the Ford line is still set by the Ford, the cheapest car, to such a degree that, in interviews made in 1953 for the Chicago Tribune's study of the auto market, people spoke of the Mercury and even the Lincoln as a bigger Ford, where they would never speak of the Buick or Pontiac as a bigger Chevrolet.[2] Moreover, even today Ford is willing to advertise itself in terms of mechanical "features" (as in a

---

[1] See Jane Fiske Mitarachi, "Harley Earl and His Product: the Styling Section," *Industrial Design*, October 1955; an issue devoted wholly to "Design in Detroit."

[2] "Automobiles—What They Mean to Americans," A Study for the Chicago *Tribune* by Social Research, Inc., pp. 50, 53, 55, 57.

double-page spread in July 1956), despite the extensive consumer research that demonstrates the American driver's desire to be treated as a passenger on a moving sofa.

Subsequently Ford has also conducted market research with the aim of developing the "optimum" personality for a new car in the middle price range, since the Company wishes to fill the competitive gap in the market which accounts, with postwar prosperity, for better than half of all car sales. Also, it was discovered that Ford owners do not graduate upward in the Company line but think of the Mercury as more suitable for the flaming-youth trade than for the reliably rising bourgeois. Perhaps, under the impact of this research, the Ford engineers will finally give way to the designers whose job it is to translate private whim into public property. But naming the new car the Edsel, apparently by managerial fiat, represents a defeat for market research and a victory for Detroit's apparently invincible parochialism. Henry J. Kaiser was the last great individualist to enter the auto business and dare stamp his name on a car (before that, the last "named" car seems to have been the Rockne), and his example is not encouraging. However such an assertive and sentimental decision was arrived at, it seems to have been made in defiance of every indication that the name Edsel is meaningless to most Americans, who could be expected to respond more readily to the connotation of elegance in some such name as Pageant, Jupiter, or Sabre.

II

We have already had an illuminating case history of design in the past few years' experience of the Chrysler Corporation. Chrysler had always been engineer-controlled and noted for economy—Plymouth has been a taxi driver's favorite—and at the same time it had suffered from premature streamlining with the Airflow model of the 1934 De Soto, just as Studebaker has recently suffered for its innovations in design, only to find them taken up by other companies in the irreversible process of homogenization. By 1950, in any event, Chrysler was falling behind, and it called in the market-research firm of McCann-Erickson to tell it what was the trouble.[3]

[3] Plymouth, parenthetically, had earlier experimented in the use of semi- or pseudopsychological advertising, a field pioneered by the late Henry G. Weaver of GM.

The interviews showed that people thought of the Chrysler line as well engineered and sedate, an image that strongly appealed to a declining portion of the population but not to the new generations allied to the outgoing life, the two-level ranch house, and the two-tone car. Chrysler therefore took the big gamble of abandoning its shrinking group of fans and taking out after the GM pacesetters. Of course, it hoped not to lose its original following in seeking a new one; every designer's ideal is after all a car with so many built-in appeals that anyone can shape it in the image of his private dream. But Virgil Exner, Chrysler's director of styling, was given a virtually free hand in 1952 to design the 1955 "Forward Look"—though it may not be entirely ironic that in this abortive chase after GM it is the rear end of Chrysler cars that one frequently sees emphasized in ads!

What Exner did, as other designers had done before him, was to build into the car a set of compensations for a variety of social strata, age groups, and even competing whims within the individual. (Exner is himself the product of conflicting experience: he left GM to work with Raymond Loewy on the first postwar Studebaker.) Customers can rarely be consistent about their wants; that is, they are more likely to express a pious disapproval of excess chrome and horsepower than to make purchases accordingly, and they are more fond of flirting with a desire than embracing it. Few can really want to pilot a jet plane, but many can safely sample the jet-age aura by having a design "based on" the Sabrejet—as the '56 Plymouth, in a double-page ad, stands silhouetted in front of an air-borne F-86, or as a Ford stands next to a Thunderbird, which in turn echoes a guided missile. So, too, the consumer can be in tune with the future through his dashboard, which looks like an intergalactic control panel, and with his youthful past through the hardtop, which reminds him of roadsters and convertibles (a *real* convertible, like a real mistress, would be problematical). So, too, several companies now emphasize safety, often in the same sentence with praise for engines of fantastically dangerous capabilities—"New 225 or 210 horsepower safety surge V-8 . . . for more safety in passing and hill-climbing" (Mercury); "second-saving acceleration for safer passing . . . puts more safety and fun in your driving" (Chevrolet).

With all these internalized and overlapping attractions, there is little left for the salesman to do but mediate between the actualities of the car and moribund minority preferences in the customer. Here one of the present writers can speak from recent experience. When he reluctantly decided to turn in an early Plymouth station wagon for a new model, being an unreconstructed Chrysler type, he was dismayed by the loss of the old square back and its replacement by flaring fins. The salesman noticed this and remarked that the fins helped locate the rear of the car in backing, a rationalization he must have hit on for quieting the Veblenian conscience of some customers since it was quite without factual basis (a more reasonable excuse, e.g., that the fins help to distinguish new models from old, would have been unseemly at the point-of-sale).

Market-research interviews suggest that the sales pitch often serves this useful purpose, soothing the customer in his self-indulgence by calling attention to features other than those in which he is most interested. People do seem to want both the crazy whimsicality of the Detroit package and an image of themselves as sensible, just as the first-time Cadillac buyer, made uneasy by his own motives, wants to be reassured by statistics about the car's economical gas consumption. Indeed, a great deal of advertising, contrary to what one might expect, is read after rather than before the car is bought, and serves to repersuade the reader that he has been wise and practical; Cadillac is well aware of this, and its ads constantly pat the owner on the back for his good taste and rationality.

Of course cars today, in the neon-lit supermarkets of the bootleg lot, can also be bought on impulse, and are meant to be. This shift to high-turnover retailing is made possible not only by raised living standards and confidence in meeting time payments over thirty months (not long ago it was twenty-two months), but also by the fact that the cars are so much alike, and on the whole such well-built standard products, that a customer does not gain significantly by deliberation. The old-line dealer, with the cornucopia of the assembly line upended over his head, has been forced to make way for the super-salesmanship of the new-style huckster who has little overhead but advertising. Though the customer's saving may be slight, what with the "pack" and inflated credit terms, he no longer sees the excuse for a conventional markup when he has largely sold himself the car, with an assist from the designer on the basis of the gamut of appeals built into it.

But this buyer's security, as we have implied, is gained through a lowered range of choice. The difference between Caddy and Chevy is much less than it was in the 1920s; instead of lowering the price of low-price cars, as Henry Ford always wanted to do, more and more is built into them. Instead of keeping Chevrolet where it was, and allowing people as they made more money to get either a newer Chevrolet or a Pontiac or an Oldsmobile, Chevrolet itself moves up the ladder, becoming longer, flossier, and generally less functional. In a similar way the mass media also devote their revenues not to lowering costs but to beefing up the product, with wider screens for the movies and, for magazines like *Life*, ever more elaborate projects of four-color cultural diffusion. The automobile industry seems to have been merely more knowing and systematic in its effort to become a kind of moving platform of this American inflation, lifting as it is lifted, and carrying us all to heights of comfort and luxury quite beyond our other accoutrements, such as doctoring or schools.

III

People are fond of their cars; they like to talk about them—something that comes out very clearly in interviews—but their affection for any one in particular rarely reaches enough intensity to become long-term. We find such attachments only among those groups that are not on the escalator of mobility—the Bohemians who boast their deviant vehicles as symbols of not caring, the few antiquarians of cars (a bit like the jazz fans who will hear only Dixieland), and the declining elite whose Daimlers and Duesenbergs have a timeless look about them. Impermanence of value and appearance is what suits the auto to a prosperity ethic, as we have said, and it is in turn dependent on that most essential of Detroit devices, the model change.

For if an automobile is to be traded in before it breaks down, it must have a sufficiently brassy allure to survive several bouts of ownership. Its design cannot be too virginal or take itself too seriously—it must appear airy and whimsical as well as solid and substantial; it must have the "reversible" quality of a game as well as the forward march of real life; it must have, as it were, one foot in reality and one foot out. Only in the "class" ads is the car a passport to palaces and playgrounds; elsewhere, neither owners nor designers have anything to gain from arbitrarily fixed levels of distinction. Better an auto should look temporary, with the shapes of models before and after it, year by year, stretching to the horizon, than look, like a Rolls or a Bentley, as though it stood for a terminal (or ancestral) point in time and career.[4]

---

[4] In "What is American about America?" (in *The Beer Can on the Highway*, Doubleday, 1961), John Kouwenhoven discusses the characteristic additive pattern of our gridiron city plans, quarter sections, jazz, skyscrapers, comic strips, and so on; the new car models, one coming after another, have a similarly satisfying regularity of march.

The forced obsolescence of annual change, change not of engineering advance but of design and advertising gimmicks, carried mass production a step further than Ford had brought it. Henry Senior seems to have been attracted by the idea of an all-plastic car, made out of soya beans and other renewable resources, so that it could be used up and thrown away; but not by the idea of selling new cars both to people without cars and people without new gadgets—people whose old but still useful cars could then be disposed of in backward colonial pockets, within and outside the country, as TV sets can now be sold in Canada.[5] Something similar is happening at last in the housing market, with the FHA attempting to encourage trade-ins and the inhabitants of the new suburbs buying houses as they would once have rented—with the intention of moving in a few years, regarding their mortgage payments as rent, and keeping an eye open for the new model house with the more fully equipped kitchen or the extra bedroom demanded by a new sibling rival.

We cannot emphasize too strongly that the annual model change has thus opened up production decisively to nonengineering concerns —to innovation oriented around design and style, like the cyclic variations of fashion in clothes.[6] But it has served even more importantly to "bureaucratize whim," if we may now define the phrase, by subjecting fancy to periodicity—the periodicity of the tax return, the annual inventory, or in domestic planning the yearly decision (possibly conjoined with the purchase of a car) as to where to go on vacation. The regularity of the choice precludes all but a small degree of disconnected whimsy. George Katona and his colleagues of the University of Michigan's Survey Research Center are even able (though within limits) to predict who will buy cars in a given year on the basis of a questionnaire concerning consumer finances and family hopes: people buy cars when they feel that next year will be as good as, or better than this, so that the demand curve is psychologically a fairly malleable one,

---

[5] The annual model change also accustomed the industry to constant retooling, so that in World War II it was able to shift over to bombers and tanks more rapidly than anticipated. Once again, GM showed greater facility than Ford, whose Willow Run plant managers were compelled to plead with the Air Corps to "freeze" the B-24.

[6] On the other hand, as Peter F. Drucker reminds us, cars are not sold by appearance alone so much as by a total image in which design plays a part related to function and price, especially "real" price (based on second- and thirdhand sales) as opposed to list price.

assuming that the limits of saturation are yet to be explored. To that extent, what is good for GM is good for the United States, and vice versa.

Whim can be called bureaucratized in so far as maker and buyer conspire to channel it within mutually manageable limits, preferably those, like fashion and unlike engineering, that are resistant to irreverent iconoclasts like the elder Ford. The effect of limited room for maneuver is most evident on the dealers, who clearly feel caught between the customer who sells himself if he smells prosperity around the corner and the manufacturer who has done his best, three years ahead of time, to prefigure the hundreds of technicolor-and-box-top configurations the customer will want. In their lachrymose outburst to Congressional investigators, these normally Republican free-enterprisers begged for governmental controls and even price support, their love of *laissez-faire*, like that of most businessmen, being quite platonic. If and when the dealers catch up with the unions and secure the equivalent of a guaranteed annual wage, yet another bureaucratizing pressure will have made the reliable anticipation of consumer preference more exigent than ever.

In general, one might say that the victory of designers has indicated that no one else can agree what a car is supposed to look like—even its own ancestors, as the case of Chrysler shows, can influence it less than its competitors. Packaging predominates over product. It would be an extraordinary thing, were it not commonplace, that a piece of hard goods weighing two tons and costing several thousand dollars should enter the realm of fashion with the facility of commodities much less costly and less intended to be useful. The resulting freedom of form has led to what many, including the authors, regard as the bloated design of the postwar cars, their often vulgar profiles, and their moody changes in relationship of driver to road—getting rid of gear shifts and other connections to reality, including the wheel, now that power steering is upon us.[7]

The designers, as we have indicated, seek to please everybody (and every motive within everybody) with these same metallic mobiles. Variations are left, except at the jalopy and Jaguar extremes, to accessories

---

[7] For those who must drive in dense traffic, however, like cab drivers and suburban mothers, the lowering of strain soon seems a necessity. Columbia University's Institute for the Study of Human Variation finds a similar justification for superhighways. See *Automobile Facts*, XV, No. 5 (June, 1956), 1, 4–5.

that escape the untutored eye and not to the enormous status gap that once separated the cars of rich and poor.[8] Even though the car has long since become a traditional manifesto of self-definition—almost as effective as accent, house, or clothes—the gradients of its prestige system have been so flattened that a basic similarity can simultaneously attest one's democratic impulse. The effect is one of blurred boundaries between individuals, classes, products, and sexes. Not only do cars come to look like one another, and like other things, but other things come to look like cars, so that we need not be surprised at the proliferation of Cadillac V-emblems on refrigerators, or a recent ad in which a model carrying a two-tone TV set is herself wearing a two-tone dress.

It is easy, of course, to overinterpret the motives of individual car owners, even those for whom polishing their cars has become a Sunday ritual as devoutly practiced as a leisure activity can be. But we think it is evident nonetheless that Detroit has successfully learned to exploit its customers' fragile and usually unspoken desires, their latent capacities for fashion and symbolism. Admittedly the manufacturers begin with an object that offers the intrinsic appeal of freedom—for adolescents, from parental planning and supervision; for the Negro, from Jim Crow; for married people, from their spouses; for a single woman, from the need for male escorts.[9] If one of the attractions of the Western is the cowboy's liberty to ride off into the sunset, leaving responsibility and complexity behind, the car, which doesn't even require saddling, is even handier. But what seems remarkable to us is how this invitation to masculine getaway has been retained at the same time that the trend from monotone to technicolor and from hard to soft, rounded lines appeals to the feminine. A similar trend in men's clothing, toward a mixture of the sporty and colorful, may be part of a wider process.

[8] So small were the differences on some lines between 1955 and 1956 models that the auto columns of daily papers showed readers how to differentiate them, much as a philately column might deal with differently watermarked stamps (see Cleveland Press, September 23, 1955, p. 20). Life also provided a lavishly colored chart (January 30, 1956). For purposes of illustration, Jay Doblin of the Illinois Institute of Technology has had prepared a set of slides in which the two-tone pattern of one make is superimposed on the silhouette of another, with utterly confusing effects on any but the most fanatic car watcher.

[9] One of our associates observes that for many men the woman who has her own car seems less accessible, has control of the steering, and is therefore sexier. If true, this augurs a decline in women-driver jokes.

Needless to add, homogenization, with its merging of tastes from the several social strata, raises problems as well as solves them. For, if we have uniform tastes, where will we get models for next year? Formerly the Big Three took care of this by letting the small independents (especially Nash and Studebaker) do their pioneering for them or, on occasion, as with Chrysler, pioneering themselves. (Studebaker-Packard still claims, in a recent ad, to be "small enough and *flexible* enough to bring you the newest and best advances *now*—months and years before the rest of the industry.") But now that the Big Three look so much alike, both like themselves and like each other—and even permissible variants like the station wagon look neither like their prewar half-timbered Tudor incarnations nor their relatively functional postwar stage, but more like a Chris-Craft—Detroit has had to start deliberately creating its own minority cars. The Corvette, the Thunderbird, the Continental Mark II, and the Golden Hawk serve both to lend prestige to the line and to provide cars of the future that can readily be disowned if the future turns up somewhere else. That is to say, these experiments are intended to sound out consumer taste, perhaps to lead it, without committing the major lines—they are spies in enemy country.

European cars, which are models for some of these "American" experiments, can of course exercise a similar function. But we suspect that they will do so decreasingly as American taste backfires and takes on a defiant-minority prestige, like Jantzen bathing suits on the Riviera, in Europe. (The Hillman Minx has already gone two-tone.) There is some evidence for this, including the implication of a recent article in *Encounter,* called "I Dream of Motor-cars," by the British artist Andrew Forge, who expresses his admiration for American willingness to design a car as though it were something else, as opposed to the British stuffiness of making cars that merely look like cars. What a curious cycle it would be if GM followed MG which in turn followed GM!

There is a further sense in which a minority is essential to the auto industry, inasmuch as a fashion, once it is accepted by everybody, is no longer a fashion but is on its way out. A fashion requires a label— the "New Look" in clothes or defense policy, "rock and roll" in popular music, "behavioral science" in Academia. But if the label takes hold, then everything and its brother tries to crowd in on the success, and the label inevitably loses its distinctive meaning and attractiveness. The ground is then prepared for a sudden reversal of fashion, when a small group hitherto protected from the majority is discovered and labeled, and the process starts over. (We might add at this point that some interesting research has shown that those who own minority cars, such as the Studebaker, are likely to know other owners of the same make personally; they need close-in support, while those who own the major makes can draw support from the general environment.)

And one might even argue that the fashion cycle in auto design must sooner or later reverse itself, despite the desire of the industry to plan ahead for a series of minor model changes in the same direction, year after year. There are still objective limits on the governance of whim in automobiles as compared with, let us say, books or paintings. For instance, the silhouette can hardly be lowered further except (as in some new models) by reducing the diameter of the wheels. Cars are in this like dresses, which can only go up or down so far, in terms of hem or decolletage, and where there are, as Alfred Kroeber and Jane Richardson have shown in their history of these changes, long-term pendular movements of lowering and heightening, on which the year-to-year fashions play minor modifications.[10]

Cars, for a while, can get wider and longer and lower, but when the limits are reached an abrupt change must set in, or some other part of the car must become the focal point of "progress." (Paradoxically, people have been getting taller while cars and ceilings have been getting lower!) So too with the secular increase in horsepower, 15 per cent between 1955 and 1956, which has already reached, some engineers are rash enough to claim, a virtual limit. And the makers of the new Continental believe that the limits of what they term "informal" taste have likewise been approached, and that sooner or later customers will begin to move away from the rounded, the gaudy, the borax, in search of "formal" elegance through restraint in line and color.[11] When such changes come, they may say less about the *Zeitgeist* than they appear to, and more about the "Brownian movement" of fashion per se.

The problem remains, moreover, of where minority tastes are to come from in a country where the range of choice is wider for many than

[10] Jane Richardson and A. L. Kroeber, "Three Centuries of Women's Dress Fashions: A Quantitative Analysis," *Anthropological Record* V (1940), 112–50.

[11] The Continental experiment has been illuminating, since it was always possible that a car of such overt snob appeal would appeal only to upper Bohemians who could afford the snobbery but not the cash, whereas the new rich apparently still prefer a Caddy whose vulgarity matches their own.

it has ever been, yet the number of significant alternatives is actually small. We are struck, for one thing, with the relative lack of revolt among young people against the cars of their parents. They seem not to want the ostentatiously casual and sloganized jalopy of an earlier day, nor do they usually want hot rods; they don't mind driving their parents' Buick and wouldn't be too unhappy with one of their own. In many cities, if not in a megacity like New York, no high school girl will go to a dance in a cab, or allow her own or her date's parents to drive her; the boy must have a car—and, what with dating beginning in the early teens, this causes more heartburn than any other social bottleneck. Yet it seems to stimulate no challenge to the adult hierarchy of styles and habits.

Though the car has for many years been a decisive counter in adolescent life, young people now seem more sedate and set in their car tastes; they also, again with minor exceptions, drive less recklessly—going steady as they are at fifteen, and marrying at twenty or twenty-two, they are driving steady too; and increasingly getting driving instruction as a part of their formal education. At the same time, whatever innovations have come from the hot-rod minority have been closely screened by Detroit, so that these become a part of the process of homogenization—or "restriction by partial incorporation," to use Harold Lasswell's phrase—in which the rebels and those they rebel against can come to terms, say, in a high-powered Oldsmobile hardtop that has gearing and carburetion taken from the drag-race fanciers, but about as much relation to a teen-ager's car of the 1930s as an automobile has to a bicycle. While they can still modify the cars they get, the young can hardly represent the shape of the future, as long as cars continue to represent youthfulness as part of their panoply of symbolisms.

Where else are we to turn? Actually it is not impossible, by avoiding turnpikes and main highways, to find minority car cultures in the United States. One such is that of the Mennonites in northeastern Indiana: they typically drive twenty-year-old black Plymouth sedans. (Those who still drive black buggies are serviced by a Chicago manufacturer who, according to Everett C. Hughes, knows in detail the varying specifications, the shades of blackness, of the different ascetic and unworldly sects.) But cars require too much capital equipment to be made for a dwindling poor minority or even a dwindling aristocracy, which is in any event better served by Rolls Royces of whatever vintage. When their prewar cars wear out, the Mennonites will have no choice but to gulp and go democratic, buying Buicks and Chevrolets like everyone else, reassuring themselves that they have no control in the matter or that the vulgarities of the damned are equally deplorable.

Indeed, to protest too much is often as vulgar as the most vulgar of cars, especially when a system of status-grading invites the ploy of underplaying and penalizes those who take it too seriously. A characteristic anecdote of the present period is that of the aspiring Hollywood actor who sweats over the decision of what car to buy in order to impress his producer, only to discover that the latter drives a 1942 Lincoln. When a car has become that important as a positive or negative symbol, it has gained a functional autonomy of motives, much like that which one psychiatrist has observed among adolescent boys; believing it wrong to start dating until they have cars, they then become so involved in the care and upkeep of the machines that they have little time left for their dates (a theme implicit in some of the scenes of *Rebel without a Cause*).[12] Hollywood, too, can hardly provide us with models when it is so imitative itself.

Looking elsewhere—as, for example, to modern architecture, with its own wraparound windows, low lines, and push-button mechanisms—we are less likely to find one-way influences than the reflection of general tendencies, like the cult of effortlessness, in several aspects of the culture at once. Since people who want automatic steering, windows, and seat adjusters often use their cars to go to and from eighteen holes of golf, it can hardly be that they can't stand the effort (even the increasing numbers who go from tee to tee in a golf cart periodically swing their arms). More probably they enjoy that phenomenon which Professor Robert Spier of the University of Missouri has termed "overdesign," the building into a mechanism of more features than it requires in order to function. One can find this in the super-rifles with which people hunt varmint, or the supercameras with which they hunt banal exposures, or the fantastic fishing equipment for teasing perch—or, indeed, wherever in this abundant culture one looks, including the pastiche overdesign of our colleges. The result has been to remove the car driver farther and farther from the engine, from the outdoors, and from the feel of the road, just as the king-size filter cigarette separates the smoker from his tobacco, or the superhighway eliminates any connection between the people on it and the local landscape or life, whether messy or quaint.

[12] J. Hyman Weiland, "The Adolescent and the Automobile," *Chicago Review*, IX, 3 (Fall 1955), 61–64.

There are nonetheless among these general tendencies certain ascetic and Veblenian motifs—as, again, in modern architecture—which we would be rash to reject as irrelevant to car design. After all, the hot rodders did challenge Detroit, and, while their forays were absorbed and contained, the motives of their revolt remain unassuaged. (Today, one of the few gambits remaining to them is to strip a car of ornament and paint it black, presumably in memory of the late James Dean.) There is a constant undercurrent of American admiration for the lean and mean that has come to the surface in such items as Carl Sandburg's outburst against our "fat-dripping prosperity," the prevalence of guilt at being overweight revealed by calorie-reduced foods, Russell Lynes's raising of the question: "What's So Good about Good Times?" and the momentary willingness of the relatively Spartan Army to attack the overbudgeted Air Force. It seems to us, moreover, that as Americans become accustomed to luxury it will lose some of its glamour, and that eventually cars that restore to us a sense of reality and functionalism may find at least a modest market. Affection for the Model T, with its adaptability to home repair, is not entirely a matter of nostalgia.

Naturally such cars will not appeal to the Negro for whom the bulbous Detroit product is his first victory over Jim Crow trains and buses, not to mention a substitute for decent housing; nor will they appeal to the factory worker to whom the car offers freedom not only to change jobs and drive to a plant fifty miles away but also to compete with the foreman for status satisfactions that the job does not provide. But such cars may appeal to the many for whom "do-it-yourself" is a luxurious necessity, an approved opportunity to escape from onerous white-collar consumption patterns into semi-Bohemian self-reliance, or those who found in the postwar station wagon a welcome ally (the first all-steel exemplar, brought out by Plymouth in 1949, was half expected not to sell; it surprised everyone by rising in popularity to the point where hardtops are challenged by the station wagon and nearly every company is making one). While it may be true, as Mr. Ralph Hansen of the Monsanto Chemical Company contends, that the ascetic modern house is mainly a masculine preference, which most older women with a taste for the frilly, the chintzy, and the comfy usually manage to defeat, we doubt that this is true among the college-educated younger generation, where it is the women who are the style leaders on behalf of modern architecture (if there is a sex difference in taste) and restraint is a weapon brought to bear by the upper-educated against the *nouveaux riches*, as Veblen in his irony foresaw.

Once the turn comes, if it does come, it will of course be the new fashion and almost everyone will accept it; but we must not over-extrapolate such changes to indicate a revolution in American manners and motives. What the German sociologist Georg Simmel has to say about fluctuations in his great essay on fashion—in this instance, of clothes—is revealing, though here he is speaking of the swing toward extravagance rather than away from it:

> Fashion furnishes a departure . . . which is always looked upon as proper. No matter how extravagant the form or appearance . . . as long as it is fashionable, it is protected against those painful reflections which the individual otherwise experiences when he becomes the object of attention. All concerted actions are characterized by the loss of this feeling of shame . . . It is one of the strangest social-psychological phenomena, that many fashions tolerate breaches of modesty which, if suggested to the individual alone, would be angrily repudiated . . . Fashion also is one of the forms by the aid of which men seek to save their inner freedom all the more completely by sacrificing externals to enslavement by the general public.[13]

Fashion, in other words, protects us from full awareness of how tasteless we might appear if we stood alone, and also protects our private judgment beneath our outer conformity. The message of the car is not an invitation to involvement; it says, like the famous Pillsbury ad, "Why not? and, if eventually, why not now?" in the effort to minimize the customer's anxieties in his purchase. Some anxieties among some of us inevitably remain, but they may have less to do with the marketing of cars than with the consequences to society of making car possession a new kind of citizenship. At some time or other all of us must realize how crazy our auto-oriented culture must look to a visitor from elsewhere, and it is to the aspects of this culture other than the look and feel of cars that we now turn.

IV

Many of us know, or suspect, how heavily our postwar prosperity, above its cushion of defense spending, rests on the twin supports of new cars and new suburbs; in fact, the latter depend primarily on the

[13] Georg Simmel, "Fashion," *International Quarterly*, X (1904), 147. We are indebted for this reference to Professor Kurt H. Wolff of Ohio State University.

former. The leisure life of these suburbs is inconceivable without the car, and the two-car garage is spreading even in the tract houses of the mass-produced suburbs—freeing the wives for sociability, shopping, and chauffeuring of children.[14] In this connection one should think not only of the new suburbs ringing the old cities but also of those parts of the country that may be regarded as suburban to the urban East. The car not only enhances the freedom of people to move west and southwest (and to Florida) but helps shape the image of the good life that these suburban states symbolize, a life in which at work or play one always has one's car beside one as a potential escape mechanism.

Increasingly, the same considerations have come into play in the urban use of cars as well, to the defeat and demoralization of mass-transit planning and finance.[15] Mark Benney, questioning his fellow clerks at the Chicago Federal Reserve Bank as to why they invariably drove downtown, with all the congestion and trouble of parking, when they could just as easily ride comfortable commuter trains, discovered this same motive of the imaginary getaway. They would answer that perhaps they might get sick, or their wives might, and they'd have to leave in a hurry. They seemed to have a sort of claustrophobia which was alleviated by having the space of one's own car around one—even in a traffic jam, in which one could sit and complain: why don't "they" do something about it?

So politically dominant is the automobile, in fact, that cities and states will tax and tear themselves apart in the effort to "do something" about traffic, but only through measures that facilitate (in effect, increase) the flow of vehicles, never reduce it.[16] The result of each new

[14] "Going our separate ways, we've never been so close," reads an ad for used Chevrolets, which pictures a family threesome affectionately grilling hamburgers in front of a double carport. "No doubt you already realize that the family with two cars gets twice as many chores completed. Completed quickly, so there is far more *leisure* time to enjoy *together*." Life, May 21, 1956.

[15] See Margy Ellin Meyerson, "Implications of Sociological Research for Urban Passenger Transportation Policy," Proceedings of the Thirty-fourth Annual Meeting of the Highway Research Board, January 1955.

[16] One of two proposals to relieve "the steadily worsening traffic congestion" presented to the mayor of New York City by his traffic commissioner was to "penalize pedestrians who interfered with traffic flow," the New York *Times*, September 23, 1955. For a mordant comment on such measures and their consequences, see David Cort, "Our Strangling Highways," *The Nation*, April 28, 1956.

palliative parkway is only to relieve some roads at the expense of others, inducing more people to drive more cars in an endless vicious circle. Astonishingly, this class engineering—for the suburbs, at the expense of the urbs—is rarely protested by those whom it disprofits. Aside from schools, highways are the only collective product not to be condemned as creeping socialism, or damned by nonusers (and the residual carless, privileged or poor) as offering no benefit to them.

And the car at the same time is demanding, impractical, and murderous. The possibility of cancer caused by cigarette smoking occasioned the manufacturers greater difficulty—and a more serious setback to their stocks—than the actual casualties of the road have caused the car companies. A recent survey showed that at least one fifth of the population over the age of twenty-one had been in an accident in which someone was hurt; yet unless a local outcry about this is being made in the press, or by a politician like former Governor Ribicoff of Connecticut, it is not taken very seriously. The grudging interest of manufacturers in safety devices seems intended mainly as compensatory sales appeal to the security-minded. We should add, especially in view of the evidence that only a small percentage of car owners voluntarily install seat belts or other self-evidently desirable equipment, that we regard most discussions of auto casualties and auto safety as a kind of titillation like horror comics, or the news stories of rail and plane accidents, or civil defense.[17]

Both the present writers have recently had all-too-personal illustrations of this. One of us, while attending army maneuvers in Louisiana as a correspondent, was involved in a head-on collision with a civilian car (driven by an intoxicated salesman of moonshine liquor) which had headed directly into the wrong lane of a two-lane highway. On his return from a field hospital that evening the press section of maneuver headquarters in a mock ceremony awarded him a "simulated Purple Heart," which was thought by nearly all concerned (the recipient included) to be a friendly and humorous gesture. It was none the less the effect of this incident to serve as a safety valve, to socialize the closeness

[17] Characteristically they are illustrated by lighthearted little drawings or photographs of dummies, not real people, smashed up in cars. A case in point is the annual summary of accident data published by the Travelers Insurance Companies under the title *Misguided Missiles,* in which cartoons by Chon Day serve to draw the sting of the statistics ("Is it anyone we know?" asks the wife from the back seat, as her husband peers under the car at the body they have just run over).

of injury so that it need not define the auto as a menace or become part of a cumulative roster of indignation against the auto as an institution. Many accidents must be attended by a similar amnesia.

Our second example occurred when the other writer was shepherding a group of five children to the movies at a local art theater. Afterward the group came out of the theater and crossed the street, only to be nearly run down by a drunk and wildly aggressive driver who drove right into the crowd, which scattered for its life while he collided with a parked car. He would have driven off, shouting abuse, if some of us had not intervened; we managed to get him to a nearby police station, where he refused to take an alcohol test; he told the police he had had a fight with his wife, and he seemed to be taking this out on the car and the public. Next morning in emergency court the writer and his children appeared, along with two policemen, to testify against the driver on a charge of reckless driving. The man could not believe it was not we whose car had been damaged, and he kept insisting to the judge that he would pay for repairs. This seemed to be all that concerned the state's attorney, who lectured us for not crossing at a traffic light. No official but the disgusted policemen cared that the defendant had been drunk and a highway menace; without even hearing their testimony, other than to ask about damage to the other car, the judge dismissed the charges.

No doubt some readers have witnessed similar scenes, and many observers have been impressed with the brutality and solipsism that the car allows the driver. Margaret Mead, in *Male and Female,* has commented on the way in which Americans use objects to intervene in their relationships with one another: one might think of card games in this way, or cigarettes, or Christmas cards. The driver of a car is completely surrounded by a nonsocial object, isolated from physical contact with others and yet completely dependent on and related to them, even when he isn't playing bumper tag. The traffic is a stream in which he can immerse himself without getting wet, so to speak. It is a group in which there are no sanctions that can effectively socialize him (though there are rewards of approval and self-approval, as we shall later see, for good performance), and he enjoys the right to snarl at other drivers while making the same independent decisions as to speed and direction that they in turn resent. A far cry from Thoreau, whose creative anarchism hurt no one.

A recent study of tourists on US Highway 30 through Nebraska, by the anthropologist Jack Roberts and his associates, indicates that these drivers are seldom aware of the countryside through which they travel, unless it is defined as "scenic," in which case they may stop for thirty seconds or so to take it in. When they do stop, they often get out of their cars too groggy and punch-drunk to walk, having for no urgent reason driven without a break from Chicago or the West Coast; their interchange with the roadside service people—gas-station attendants, motel-keepers, etc.—is perfunctory; and back they get into their moving tube, in which they never can or do neglect a roadside sign, and receive more impressions of print than of anything else.[18]

One might compare the driver's decision-making process, moreover, with that of the airline pilot, whose complete control of his vehicle has been very differently institutionalized. It often happens that people get on board his plane and he taxies out to the runway, only to decide at the last moment that the plane or the weather is not fit to fly. If it were only his own life he would probably take chances, since he would be subject to taunts about his honor or he would think that the noise he heard wasn't really serious. But he is responsible for the property, the lives of others, and for the company's reputation. He has judicialized himself and thereby destroyed the earlier image of the pilot as a wild and erratic fellow. The auto driver, on the other hand, has had no such judicial experience; he is oblivious as an individual to the death and damage he deals out as a class; and he considers traffic violations, somewhat like drinking during Prohibition, as licensed misbehavior. He is not an institution and no judicial process has taken hold of him.

And yet this is only part of the story. There remain judicious drivers, and already scattered elements of a highway ethic are appearing in which "bad" driving incurs searing disapproval: one thinks, for example, of how the drivers of semitrailers manage to deflect potential hatreds of their monstrous impediments to joyriding by showing their skill and by observing elaborate courtesies. At the same time, there is a camaraderie of the road in which some of the car's gloss of roving masculinity rubs off on those who service it, so that their impersonal relationship to the driver can yet be highly sociable and they may lavish infinite pains on polishing his windshield in spite (or perhaps because) of the

[18] John M. Roberts, Robert M. Kozelka, Mary L. Kiehl, and Thomas M. Newman, "The Small Highway Business on U.S. 30 in Nebraska," *Economic Geography*, XXXII, No. 2 (April 1956), 139-52.

fact that they are never tipped. Garage mechanics, similarly, have promoted themselves to prestigeful repute by taking advantage of the felt need for their competence to relax and develop latent abilities as conversationalists and "characters."

The car culture, as such, can furthermore serve as an autonomous and cosmopolitan influence on the communities that it nets together. Thus, merchants along a highway traversing many states may form a trade association in which their parochial interests are transcended by a common one in keeping the traveler on the route as long as possible. Thus do shopping centers tend to acknowledge their higher loyalty to the highway by staying open on Sunday, in defiance of local blue laws. The roadside stores and services form a sort of intranational PX. Just as the oil companies have recognized the long-term advantage of standardized facilities, to exploit the driver's longing for the familiar and predictable, thus also have the proprietors of eating and sleeping establishments progressively been compelled to upgrade provincial standards of sufficiency to the preset national levels of Duncan Hines or Quality Courts United, all of which, in spite of its effect on what W. H. Auden has called our "anonymous countryside littered with heterogeneous *Dreck*," cannot be considered a total loss. And, too, it is precisely when one thinks of the ribbonlike roadside slums—not only of the man-made rural ugliness but of the endless aesthetic atrocity of our cities—that the auto itself seems least anomalous. However it may offend the aesthete or functionalist, against its partially self-created landscape it looks clean and neat, a thing of beauty and even of sense.

What we are suggesting here is that the impact on the driver of belonging to the automobile culture should not be underrated. While the car is both a source and an outlet of violence, it has simultaneously been a force for the softening of life and a reducing of violence among American adult males.[19] Warner Bloomberg, Jr., has observed that many Gary steelworkers, when they marry and settle down, can no longer find the time and money for hot rodding; they have to accept a new Chevrolet or a secondhand Pontiac as a utility wagon, since their income is going into new babies and home equipment, and their time into do-it-yourself around the house. As a result, the car is for the factory worker what lace curtains are for his wife. Driving to and from work in his chromed and polished divan, he is less likely than heretofore to

[19] For the argument that violence *has* declined, see Daniel Bell in *Fortune*, January 1955.

get into brawls or spend Saturday night in a bar. The car is, as it were, a decompression chamber in which he avoids the bends and the benders in making a transition from the all-male, working-class atmosphere of the plant to the mixed company and middle-class atmosphere of the suburban home, with its middle-class leisure pursuits of travel and gardening, and its violence piped in vicariously through television.

And here again we can see that the car, in its reciprocal relationships to individuals both helps to homogenize the social strata and the sexes and to represent in its appearance the degree to which this homogenization has progressed. Where its future seems to us less clear and far more demanding of general reflection is in the emerging array of institutional decisions made urgent by the car's impact on urban and suburban planning. To date, the car has revolutionized patterns of land use faster than theoretical conceptions of social time and distance have evolved to keep up with it, with the result that it bears many of the marks of an institution out of control, intractable to previous disciplines and impervious to moralizing. To be sure, it does have the beneficent effect of forcing choices (such as the eradication of urban blight) that might be further postponed, and it has stimulated the rapid and extemporized maturing of such seldom-promising devices as the shopping center, the motel, and the drive-in theater.

It is in fact our suspicion, current appearances to the contrary, that the automobile may eventually be the savior of the American city, since it has restored to the decadent downtown centers their lost potentialities for uniqueness—in this case, the potentiality of the auto's absence. The future of the city, that is, may lie in barring the car from a central core of concentrated facilities, so as to increase both its accessibility and attractiveness.[20] For the city-bred, it is disconcerting to discover how difficult it is in many parts of the country (especially the Far West) to go for a walk without being harassed by continual offers of a lift. It is perhaps symptomatic that even now a major appeal of living on Manhattan Island is freedom from the car, and though in this New York is atypical it may also be filling its traditional role of pioneer in new

[20] Not to mention value. Fort Worth's mile-square pedestrian enclave, with its access roads and six garages, would release to commercial use space that is presently worth $30 to $40 million. It is the work of Victor Gruen & Associates, designers of the inventive Northland shopping center in Detroit. See *Architectural Forum, the Magazine of Building,* May 1956, pp. 146–55.

avenues of consumption.[21] It was appropriately in New York that there occurred the stand of embattled housewives against the destruction of their children's play space in Central Park to make way for a parking lot—an early and successful defiance of the omnipotent auto (and its agent, Robert Moses) that should someday find a place in history!

V

Let us in conclusion go back for a moment to Veblen and Henry Ford. "It was not accidental," as Christy Borth of the Automobile Manufacturers Association has said, "that most of the pioneers in this field of endeavor were from the farms and the small towns of the land. They knew, by bitter experience, the grinding drudgery and the appalling loneliness which were all too much the most characteristic attributes of rural life in America. . . ."[22] Ford himself, in his reaction to that drudgery and loneliness, became a man obsessed by time. As a boy, he repaired watches; as an advertiser, he chased speed records with Barney Oldfield; as a billionaire, he collected the past and put it in his museum at Dearborn; and, as a manufacturer, he came to understand that cost is a function of time and so to pace the assembly line, shaving seconds off the productive process—indeed, he was one of the first to understand that production *is* a process, as Veblen also understood, rather than merely the attempt to make things, let alone money. Yet his imagination was unequal to a world in which consumption would also be a process, the world he had himself helped create, a world that can afford to preserve under museum glass its memories of the pinched, utilitarian sparseness he sprang from and never quite escaped.

Today, however, the automobile is teaching its owners to consume and its producers to produce for a context in which the limitations of historical scarcity and meanness no longer apply. It is a kind of self-contained education in abundance. Very possibly the promises of an era of endless abundance are spurious; we may be unjustly extrapolating from the symptoms of boom prosperity. It may be that Detroit is

[21] For an example of the urban logic, see John Lardner, "The Case for Living Here," the New York *Times Magazine*, April 29, 1956, p. 12. "New York's traffic crisis is fed by out-of-towners, including suburbanites, who are so fatuous as to bring automobiles into New York and to drive and park them there. The vast majority of New Yorkers are too intelligent and too considerate to use private cars in Manhattan . . ." *Ibid.*, p. 44.

[22] Address to Centennial of Engineering, Chicago, September 8, 1952.

more wedded to cars than their buyers are, and will be unable to diversify successfully, despite Ford's missiles and GM's Frigidaires and Diesels; and it may even be that the increasing capitalization of the industry will require new cars to come out every six months, while consumers, though willing to make extraordinary adaptations, will be unable to keep up with this. But we are already having arduous difficulties in assimilating the incipient abundance that is already upon us. If we are to prepare for the possibility that abundance may increase, we will need all the experience with the improbable, or even the impossible, that we can get.

POSTSCRIPT: DECEMBER 1957

We wrote the foregoing pages two years ago, just after the 1956 models had come out. We wrote before the first returns were in from the Chrysler line's gamble in plunging into styling rather than solid engineering as the principal basis for appeal: a gamble which brought them up from 13 per cent of the market to 20 per cent, drawing into their orbit many who would previously have bought GM products, and no doubt some "new voters" who might have bought Mercury (or, presently, Edsel) while at the same time alienating, though not always losing, the staid types who wanted the security of good workmanship rather than the flamboyance of fins. We wrote also, of course, before the Edsel made its overadvertised debut: a car in search of a character that would indicate at once its novelty, its sibling relation to the rest of the Ford line, and its "status personality" in competition with the hot-engine, lace-curtain mélange of GM and Chrysler's "medium-price" cars.[23] We wrote before both the Volkswagen and American Motors' Rambler had counterattacked in favor of small cars, leaving GM and Ford to send out feelers from their European satellites, while their executives sat around cursing Mr. Romney of American Motors almost as severely and as insanely as they had attacked Walter Reuther in the summer of 1957 for his salutary plea to lower, or at least stabilize, the price of cars.[24]

[23] For fuller discussion of the extensive market research involved, see Eric Larrabee, "The Edsel and How It Got That Way," *Harper's Magazine* (September 1957), pp. 67–73.
[24] The violent response of the auto makers to the Reuther proposals; the instinctive and unvarying assumption that they must all be propaganda and a trick; the moralistic attacks on him for creating inflation in the first place —these morbid and frozen posturings resembled all too closely the nearly

Plainly enough, even before sputnik, the leading auto makers were uneasy as they faced the 1958 model season. With dual headlight assemblies they had cleverly managed the front-end obsolescence of every car on the road, much as fins had managed a rear-end obsolescence. Raising prices in a falling market, they had retooled even more heavily, advertised even more lavishly than usual. They had cultivated their dealers, seeking to keep up the profit margins of those small businessmen (small, but often quickly wealthy) who, in so many small communities, form part of the solid Republican cadre, opposing those policies of increased government spending and lowered trade barriers that might keep them afloat a while longer.[25] And yet, the companies were terribly worried beneath their façade of prosperity, like people who have drunk too much too long and are waiting for the hangover or the ulcer. Pressure was being put on the market researchers to tell the designers what, in the future, people "really" wanted in a car, and it was even beginning to percolate into some Detroit offices that the customers might care less about cars (as illustrated by the lack of excitement over the Edsel) than they had appeared to care.

Sputnik heightened all this. While nearly every propagandist, for nearly every cause good or bad, hitched his wagon to that star, there were many for whom sputnik evoked the underlying asceticism we have discussed above—evoked, that is, the repressed ambivalence about the gaudier aspects of prosperity. To understand this, we must see the car market as reflecting the country's own economic and social development in which millions of previously underprivileged people have been making enough money to become neophyte consumers, while smaller numbers of people have now had money enough to become more sophisticated, "tasteful" consumers. Market research seldom has a chance to follow people in this trajectory over time,[26] so that efforts to study consumer preferences can hardly help concentrating on the general growth of the market for large cars, and extrapolating from this growth, while

---

simultaneous rejections by American officialdom, in and out of the State and Defense Departments, of Soviet proposals for a reduction of tensions in the cold war and a halt to the testing of nuclear weapons.

[25] It is interesting how one falls into the trap of saying "solid Republican" (one never says "solid revolutionary") when in fact the paradoxes of Republicanism today, whether "modern" or "ancient," are as porous as any outdated yet fanatical ideology can possibly be.

[26] For some preliminary discussion, cf. "Careers and Consumer Behavior," p. 113.

neglecting those buyers, small in numbers but growing, who were beginning to find in things other than cars, and activities other than driving, their ties to self and society. It seems usual in history that decline in a culture or an area has set in before the peak of its visibility and power, and so it may be with the extravagant automobile in America.

Already one can see the effects of the auto manufacturers' provincial inability to learn from others who have had experience in industrializing fashion. Detroit, ignoring the rationale for cyclic variation and the role of minority taste-makers, persists in the assumption that model must follow model in a single-track, linear progression, with no imaginable replacement for a given style but more, *ad nauseam*, of the same. Confronted with a situation somewhat similar to that of the French dressmaking industry after World War II, with an excess of facilities and a threatened loss of leadership, it has been unable to bring forward anyone with the courage and inventiveness of the late Christian Dior, who launched an excessively long and full skirt in the fall of 1947, completely counter to the going trend, and thus gave work to the idle mills of Lyon and Saint-Etienne at the same time that he restored the lost initiative to Paris. The lesson should be clear by now that mass taste no less than class taste is subject to satiety, and that any business enterprise dependent on style must maintain a watchful and sympathetic espionage over the impulses of intellectuals and other deviants. It is often an unhappy side effect of market research, however, to confirm the manufacturer in his "democratic" refusal to discriminate among his customers and thus deprive him of interpretive tools for coping with a drop in sales, so that among his few potential responses to the current sag is a Neanderthal fury against friend and foe alike.

We might raise the question, for example, why the auto makers could not have protected themselves against this decline by riding at once the majority trend toward the gaudy and the minority trend against it, by seriously putting out two lines of cars. Why, for instance, could not the first Plymouth postwar station wagons, which found a market precisely because of their form-follows-function appeal, have been kept in production rather than turned into a sedan-cum-backporch—much as many handsome colonial and Georgian houses in this country were fitted with false fronts, big-pane windows, etc., to conform to the vulgarities of post-Civil War taste? One reason why not lies in the curious fact that even the minority's taste, willy-nilly, is influenced by the visual scene created by the majority: there are only a few whose vision of what a car should look like and feel like can hold out against the massive impact of forced obsolescence. In this, as in other aspects of life, we become corrupted by the seemingly inevitable, the given. At best, we transfer our desire for a visual aesthetic to other realms, consigning the auto to the featureless majority, and thinking it more important to have beauty in our book jackets, our ties, our living rooms, our gardens.[27]

Indeed, one speaks too crudely in identifying majority and minority as persons, instead of tendencies within persons. We doubt if there are Volkswagen yearnings in the new-rich southern ex-farmer working in a Louisiana oil refinery, or even in his children—any more than there are such yearnings in the oil-rich of Saudi Arabia. But we suspect that there are such yearnings in many whose "status personality" remains adapted to the cars of the Big Three so long as things in life go well with them and no criticisms of their taste reach them from sources they respect. At the first rumblings of depression, however, impulse buying of cars takes a sharp drop: the fact, previously repressed, that the old car is good enough—and even good enough for me—becomes more salient; and sputnik for some furnishes still another rearrangement of "needs" and socially influenced perceptions.

But if the "minority" taste within individuals is repressed, that within the auto industry itself appears to be even more repressed. The provincialism of Detroit, referred to above, can hardly be overestimated —this, despite the managerial sophistication brought to GM by Alfred Sloan and to Ford by the grandchildren of Old Henry and their GM-trained associates. We doubt, for example, if it occurred to any high-level people in the Ford Motor Company or their rivals elsewhere that it was a tragic social waste—if a company imperative—to spend a quarter billion just to add one more boxy car to the country's range of models. (In some market-research interviews concerning the Edsel, before its release, respondents did ask why there was need for a new car, but they readily accepted the explanation that Ford needed a car in the medium-price range.) Philanthropic as the Ford family is, in its Sun-

[27] Actually, an increasing number of Americans satisfy both tendencies by a first car which is big, a second which is European or Rambler style. And the Volkswagen and other European car makers quite consciously cultivate this second-car market, which allows the owner to have the status as well as the roadability of two worlds. (One of us was recently met at a convention by an educator in a brand-new Mercury of the gaudiest sort, and then told "If I'd known what you were like, I'd have brought our Renault.")

day best, its weekday considerations would hardly have included the question as to whether the country might not have better uses for the money and skill and energy that went into the Edsel. (Again, the analogy with national politics is striking: post-Sputnik, few ask whether there are alternative uses of American energy to a mad missile race with the Russians.)

To make two sets of cars at once—one to appeal to the majority, and the other to hold open the door of the future for a minority—would of course require an ability, rare in American life at any level, to operate with conviction and enthusiasm at two levels simultaneously. Can one imagine the Chrysler ads simultaneously flaunting the "Forward Look" and the nostalgic look? Or GM's TV personalities pushing the Chevrolet and the Opel in alternate commercials? The very sincerity of American businessmen and professional people, which makes it necessary for us to believe wholeheartedly in what we are doing (and gives a good conscience to many life insurance salesmen and a bad one to a few vocal admen), also makes it difficult for us to throw ourselves in our corporate capacities in two directions at once. Americans want unconditional surrender whether they fight a war or seek a market; and lack, for the most part, the flexibility to conduct limited warfare for limited aims.

Thus, we come back to what we have emphasized above, namely the desire to build into every car an inescapable appeal to every whim within the Great American Market, and into the advertising and sales pitches a rationalization to hold down repressed ambivalences. Chrysler could not rest secure, as a stock-owned company, with a shrinking share of the market prior to 1955, along with a hope that trends would change: they had seen Henry Ford try this by main force in the twenties and lose out to General Motors.[28] Nor could they, as we have just argued, subdivide and compete with themselves, taking the risk of diminishing the market share of each car in the Chrysler line without attracting the attention and taste leadership that might result from a total commitment to novelty. Such innovations have to be insulated by being located in Europe (it is rumored that Chrysler is now also con-

---

[28] Perhaps the industry has also drawn premature conclusions from the failure of the revived Lincoln Continental. In the text above, we suggested that this car might be too expensive for the highbrow, too highbrow for the new rich. We should have added that any car costing $10,000 is vulgar and conspicuous per se, irrespective of ascetic styling, and therefore could not even appeal greatly to the old rich.

sidering importing a foreign car as a hedge against itself), just as only from countries outside the United States have forcible incentives come to compete with the interservice rivalry and its consequences for frenzied armament.[29]

In drawing these gloomy parallels between Detroit and the Pentagon, we are seeking to emphasize the built-in instabilities of competition among oligopolies. Having taken out after GM, there is no easy road back for Chrysler to its one-time devoted clientele. The Edsel is, in the same system, a plea for brand loyalty to Ford: stay with us, even if you rise above us. GM is much too big to follow anybody or to experiment with wide extremes: within the industry it can neither lead nor follow, even while defining the popular taste by its own majority vote. How hard it is to imagine another way of marketing autos, having them, for instance, sold only on order, for cash, after the buyer has had a chance to wait until his own tastes caught up with his impulses! With a whole economy geared to the auto, on what else would we spend our surplus productivity, our surplus energy, were the car suddenly taken away as a central prop? We are no more ready for such a shift than for sudden disarmament.

[29] The Navy, lacking a big stake in strategic bombing and missiles, was once the Chrysler of the Armed Three, backing sobriety and even diplomacy; more recently, it has conceded to the nuclear doctrine of SAC in return for being allowed to build big carriers, thus maintaining the principle of "competition" at the expense of any strategic alternative to self-destruction.

Abundance for What?
(1957)

I was one of those quasi-Keynesians who became convinced, shortly after we entered the Second World War, that great depressions were most unlikely in the American future; as I occasionally overstated matters to my economist friends: "John Taber may be able to bring on a depression by the main force of his stupidity, but it is most unlikely the country and even the Republicans would allow this." My conviction was based, less on confidence in the Keynesian armamentarium as politically feasible medicine, than on the surmise that the war had taught Americans the lesson that wars cure depressions and are, as conducted extraterritorially, less unpleasant: not a lesson to be learned in school or pulpit or even to be explicitly stated to oneself (save perhaps in lower-class male circles), but rather a tacit agreement that government can control depression, if need be, by war and preparation for war. (There is some fragmentary evidence from surveys of public opinion that in the period from 1949 to 1956 more Americans have expected a major war than a major depression in the years ahead.)

It should be clear that I am not talking about the "merchants of death." Such companies as Du Pont are much too frightened—and too responsible—to influence policy in favor of military rather than diplomatic preparations; and even the direct military producers would throw their weight in favor of "their" arm of the services out of patriotism rather than profits. Domestic support for American military spending is popular, despite the outcry against high taxes, in part because it has the tacit backing of people who recognize the support it gives the economy, or their fair city; in an era when corruption is less and less a vehicle for government spending (despite what is said later about highways), this is the new, often relatively disinterested pork-barrel, periodically supported by the U.S.S.R. and its allies.

To be sure, there are many influential taxpayers, whether in the Taber mold or the more sophisticated Humphrey mold, who do not like government spending, even for defense: Old-fashioned pre-Keynesians, ready to equate the morality of private with that of governmental budgets, they cannot accept what must seem to them the sleight of hand by which an economist like Sumner Slichter defends allopathic doses of inflation as a disagreeable remedy for worse diseases. They were not brought up to approve of waste, either in their own family, their own company, or their own country—and they are patriotic enough, and insular enough, to believe that what is good in the one realm is good also in the others. And they may even sense, from the base line of their limitations, a certain lunacy in military spending anyway: they may feel that the amount the services can spend in competition with each other is almost as limitless as what could be spent on civil defense if we really took seriously the mutuality of threat implicit in our own and Soviet military policies. They may have come to realize that, while most American military men are (to my mind, quite astonishingly) deferential to important businessmen, there are some dedicated members of a warrior caste who—as in all militarized countries—have contempt for business caution, business "selfishness," and business lack of political foresight.[1]

Businessmen of this stripe, moreover, have convictions: they are not shaken by the equally strong convictions of diplomats, politicians, or military men. They know a dollar is a dollar—or ought to be. Their own past, and their image of America's past, supports them.

Such businessmen, however influential the positions they hold, are not a very large group, although they probably exceed in number the "modern Republican," or Committee on Economic Development, or Keynes-influenced managerial businessmen (who read, rather than simply purchase or advertise in, *Fortune* or *Business Week*). Their power comes in large part from their control of the nostalgic rhetoric of an earlier, thriftier America—a rhetoric to which many small businessmen and small-town professional men (including state committeemen and congressmen) almost automatically respond. Nevertheless, the majority of businessmen, I suspect, do not unequivocally share the traditional convictions they think they hold: they are perfectly willing to join the ritualistic outcry against high taxes and government spending, but

[1] Conversely, both in the American Army and Navy, there have been many leading men in the cold-war years who have had a keener sense of the madness of an arms race than many bellicose civilians: they have not had to show their manliness, or their patriotism or political purity, by gestures of jingoism.

their hearts are not always in it, especially of course if there is a jolt in the rate of economic expansion; such businessmen are like most of us in being able to coexist with apparently incompatible opinions, and with firmness of tone screening willingness to be unorthodox. Correspondingly, whatever temporary extravagances they may allow the local Chamber of Commerce or the NAM to perpetrate on their alleged behalf, they are too public-relations-minded to dare to be accused of undermining prosperity or sabotaging national defense and the national interest (as, let us say, the energetic Alsop brothers define the national interest). Many of them are accustomed, in their corporate capacity, to pay money in order to prevent a row or even criticism: money to their workers, to their civic associations, to their fellow executives. Running their businesses (and often their personal lives, too), like increasing numbers of other white-collar Americans, on the buy now, pay later, basis (greatly modified, however, by retained depreciation and dividends, and by federal tax policy), they realize in spite of their comptrollers that "it's only money," and are reluctant Keynesians whatever their theoretical adherence.[2]

America has been, since Jacksonian times and earlier, a country in which the creditor class, and the creditor-minded, were a minority, and moderately slow inflation was hence politically popular. But only recently has the combination of alluring advertising, easy credit, and the loss of sumptuary restraints brought millions of consumers into the debtor class. One short-range consequence is that the moral basis of a George Humphrey is not widely shared in the planning of families and other future expenditures of the electorate at large, outside the business class; the electorate has no platform from which to be really indignant at government debt, government spending.[3]

[2] Attitudes toward Sewell Avery are a good test for business thinking. While some businessmen may still admire the saltiness and tenacity of Avery's character, very few admire his public relations or his hoarding attitude toward capital and fear of the future. And Montgomery Ward has now joined Sears, Roebuck in a managerial outlook favoring expansion as against stability.

[3] Intimations as to the factors of buoyancy and anxiousness that enter into purchase plans in the expanding "discretionary" area turn up in the periodic surveys of consumer finances and purchases conducted by George Katona and his colleagues at the Survey Research Center for the Federal Reserve Board. (Less is known about the often comparable factors that enter into business investment decisions, though the McGraw-Hill surveys and the work of Franco Modigliani and others are illuminating.)

They may, to be sure, assail the government, projectively, for "bad habits" they will not give up in their own case, but they will in the end be ambivalent, seeing in the government the insurer of their own perilous course—a course which assumes that no one in their family will be seriously ill (beyond what Blue Cross or their corporate employer covers) or crazy, and that close to full employment will continue as before. It was a straw in the nonagricultural wind when a reporter in the town of Anaheim, California—a town dependent on new and war-supported industry (and Disneyland)—inquired as to what residents might do in the case of a depression; the latter were all, in good suburban style, mortgaged thirty or more months ahead for cars, furniture, etc., as well as for their homes. One man replied:

> No one is worried, because there's a theory in town that if anything slips up the government will declare a moratorium on all debts. No one knows who started the rumor, but these kids really think it's true. The government would *have* to do something like that, they say to me, because otherwise this whole place might be a shambles overnight.[4]

It is only a step from this outlook to assume that the government would be forced to stockpile cars.

What are some of the long-range implications of these versions of political economy? One is an orientation toward tangibles—toward what the military call "hardware." We have to consume, or stockpile, some *thing*. Yet, as many people at the same time recognize, there can be a surfeit of things: it is only for intangibles, and the people producing them, that markets are truly insatiable. We are coasting psychologically on the remaining gaps and deficiencies in the ever rising "standard package" of consumer goods but, beyond that, we have very few goals, either individually or socially. Those Americans who attain, let us say, 25 per cent or even 50 per cent more income in stable dollars can quickly learn ways to spend it but if faced with 250 per cent they cannot easily and rapidly learn new wants. The level and style of living of a well-to-do businessman at the turn of the century, with his large house, his many servants, his stable, *objets d'art*, and caretakers (and sometimes courtesans)—this is not for them. Their corporation or institution can live this way (what I like to call "conspicuous production"), and they can benefit from its expense accounts, including a

[4] See Bruce Bliven, Jr., "The Golden Age of Buy Now, Pay Later," *The Reporter*, May 3, 1956, p. 21.

Canadian chalet or Florida yacht. But many in the younger generation of reasonably well-off Americans are not drivingly or basically materialistic: invidiousness in taste or acquisition is not their style. Contrary to the image envious non-Americans often have, ferocious desire for things for their own sake is declining, let alone desire for money or land for its own sake. Rather, Americans resent being deprived of the things they are supposed to have, and advertising tempts us with the halo of association rather than with the objects per se.

Thus, I suggest that there is a tendency for people, once accustomed to upper-middle-class norms, to lose zest for bounteous spending on consumer goods. This tendency remains hidden from us by the fact that, even in this stratum, there are still modest expansions under way, along the moving escalator of an inflation which is at once monetary and material; moreover, the look of asceticism, whether in Mies van der Rohe houses or foreign cars, is still a minority desire, hence expensive. More important, the zeal of the previously underprivileged to make up for lost time brings into the market for gaudy consumption more millions than education presently removes (of course, only in part) from the market. And enormous expenditures for research and development of new, or seemingly new, products, along with ever larger advertising budgets, have helped postpone the specter of satiation. Finally, I would admit that, as the country gets more tangled and crowded with unrestricted growth of population and urban sprawl, many upper-middle-income families will pay large sums simply to keep at their present level of amenity and space and sanitation.

Nevertheless, the basic stockpile on which our society's dynamism has rested—the stockpile of new and exhilarating wants—seems to me badly depleted. (I say this knowing that alarmists have thought this periodically—Milton Friedman reminds me that in 1908 people thought the limit on autos had been reached; and I learn from George Katona's surveys of consumer expectations for the Federal Reserve Board that most Americans, asked what they would want if they had the money to buy it, can come up with desires: a newer or another car, another room, a Deepfreeze, air conditioning. But, after all that, then what?) The rate of increase expected in the next years in the Gross National Product exceeds what the country could readily absorb, given any really sizable drop in defense expenditures; we have no adequate plans for substitute goals, or the political channels for securing understanding and support for the process of developing such plans.

Indeed, as Gerhard Colm's article, "Economic Implications of Disarmament,"⁵ suggests, it is hard to forecast how we will deploy our rising productivity even without reducing defense expenditures. He sees education as absorbing much the largest part of the surplus, highways and other transport facilities next, along with public works in general, hospitals, and water conservation. Education is, of course, one of the intangibles for which the demand curve is nearly completely flexible—but we do not have as a cultural goal the ethos of "each one, teach one," nor do our educators have a utopian vision of a humane education around which to build new curricula for adults and young people alike. Nor do we as yet have a culture in which the desire for quality in urban and rural landscape justifies conservation not only of a few natural grandeurs and historical mementos, but of the textures (and aesthetic values generally) which have been built over generations into whole regions and cities. Thus, when I recently suggested that New Orleans, for instance, be made a national park, with its homes inhabited by subsidized families (much as bear or deer are "subsidized" to live in Yellowstone), I was thought to be joking.

But, of course, I want to conserve not only precious urban and rural "prospects" (to use the old English term), but also the core of all our still viable metropolises: conserve them, not for the auto, but from the auto (as in Victor Gruen's plan for Fort Worth). Urban renewal is fabulously costly and, if done with enough taste and vision to keep people coming to the city even if they have a choice of locale, can certainly absorb much of our productivity in the next twenty years; but again, what is lacking is not only the willingness to tax and spend for such collective purposes—purposes that will outlive any one of us—but also the kind of political and cultural organization to accomplish anything like so radical a change with no apparent crisis to make our "needs" visible and dramatic. That is, we appear to be in a trap in which we may become weary of the goods we have learned to miss not having, without having learned other than inchoately what we are missing when we do have them—let alone having learned how to institutionalize acquisition of such values as the complexity and beauty of certain cities, and the simplicity and quiet of certain countrysides, or their proper relation.

What are the economic consequences of this wantlessness? I rather doubt if we shall stockpile cars: the auto industry lacks the gerrymandered political base of the farmers and their ideology of small family-scale business. We are, however, already stockpiling highways, with

⁵ *Illinois Business Review*, 14 (July 1957), pp. 6–8.

little regard for the consequences in the amenity of both city and country life the thruways will have. Highways—unlike schools, public and private health, nonobvious scenery, or nonslum redevelopment—are not controversial—though the carless poor and bulldozed rich might wish they were; they disperse much patronage, and speed and efficiency of movement do have an aesthetic appeal to which Americans respond, though the appeal is buttressed by "economic" arguments. Even so, the new federal highway program will spend in fifteen years around 60 per cent of what our military establishment spends in one. There will be a multiplier effect in this program, of course, filtering through contractors, makers of road-building equipment, of bridges, concrete, and lumber. But defense contracts are geared into the whole manufacturing economy in a way that road-building contracts could never be. I doubt if road-building can take up the impending slack due to the cheapening costs of total destruction, and I cannot conceive of an economy as rich as ours supported by public works alone, on any scale now contemplated, any more than pyramid-building could sop up a Gross National Product which will soon be $500 billion. . . .[6]

So the question comes back to what we want. For the present, though, as already implied, with perhaps diminishing enthusiasm filtering down from the elite, we unequivocally want to have good cars and good roads to drive them over. What else do we want as unequivocally? We want healthy babies and suburban homes to put them in, and we want an increasing variety of services (including education). We seem increasingly to look in our family life for some of the satisfactions missing in our economic and general social life. But I repeat: there are few channels, political or economic, for translating these as yet undefined shades of feeling into a program which could give us alternatives both to spending for defense and to spending for spending's sake.

No society has ever been in this position before, or anywhere near it, and thus the dream of plenty has remained unsullied. Indeed pleasure in possessions has been for many people throughout history partly shored up by the surrounding backdrop of general poverty. At the present time some smaller countries are in much the same boat as the

[6] If not pyramids at home, Aswan Dams abroad? Congressional and general American experience with Point IV and its successor programs does not make me sanguine, especially as the newly industrialized and still xenophobic South turns increasingly away from its traditional internationalism. Great and courageous political leadership might conceivably change this, but few signs of it appear in either party.

United States—these include Switzerland, West Germany, and several Scandinavian nations, which have the highest or close to the highest suicide rates in the world; these countries have solved many social problems which in the United States still have much (but still insufficient) psychological mileage in them. Likewise, if we cannot look to the experience of other times and other countries for models for the American future, we can also not discover much wisdom in earlier prophets of abundance, for very few of them foresaw the actual cornucopia of even so modestly efficient an industrial plant as ours.[7] Edward Bellamy's *Looking Backward*, for instance, which had an enormous impact in the Gilded Era, envisaged an amiable and genteel level of living, long since attained in amount throughout a large middle-income belt, though scarcely touched in inner peace and spaciousness. Even the most devoted apostles of capitalism in previous generations scarcely foresaw that it would soon outrun its most optimistic boosters (though Schumpeter did grasp this)—while its enemies, like Karl Marx, who realized capitalism's power to subdue all earlier traditional levels of production and consumption, could not foresee its chastened managerial form nor indeed its bounteous exploitability. . . .

I think we fear the future's opacity, and try not to pierce it with concrete plans. The terrifying prospect of atomic and biological annihilation has been one factor in this foreshortening, but for most Americans it is not a very important (not nearly important enough) cloud on anticipation. What we fear to face is more than total destruction: it is total meaninglessness; and it is my contention that we may bring about the former, in some part because the latter inhibits our alternatives to what I have here depicted as our sub rosa military Keynesianism; and, perhaps more important, our future as a country is not inviting or challenging enough to mobilize our attention and our energies.

Since I began this paper, the sputnik has shot into the sky and shown that there is life in the old armaments race, the old comparisons, yet. Democratic leaders have been attacking Republican budget-mindedness. They are like coaches whose athletes have broken training and lost a game. But the motivations which give vitality to an economy cannot for long endure on a merely sporting or collegiate basis

[7] As any serious businessman knows, American efficiency is a legend which exists because other countries are either even more inefficient or have fewer cushions against waste; much of our productivity now gets eaten up by friction—some of which, as in much featherbedding, is based on fear of productivity itself.

—though one could well argue that the United States in two world wars postponed reckoning with aims which transcended levels of welfare and justice which the social thought of previous generations had proposed. We have seldom bothered to stockpile hopes, not for a rainy but for a sunny day.

There are those who would argue that people do not discover new values and meanings in prosperous times, but only in times of oppression, of war or other crisis; that at such a time, men must fall back on basic cultural imperatives or rediscover values that had been repressed during the good times. I am not sure this is historically correct: crisis evokes meanness as well as creativity; more important, "crisis" is itself a conception, a product of our conceptions, not a Kantian a priori proposition. The age of abundance has its grandeurs and miseries which are both like and unlike those of any other age, and the searching of aims and discovery of motives appropriate to our new forms of peril and opportunity, along with the discovery of ways to institutionalize our collective aspirations, seems to me the fundamental economic and meta-economic task.

The Found Generation
(1956)

It is not easy to say when one generation ends and another begins (as Karl Mannheim noted in his essay on "The Problem of the Generations"), for people are not produced in batches, as are pancakes, but are born continuously. And it is only in certain countries and in certain epochs that historical events, as unconsciously transmitted through parents to their children, lead to a generational gap rather than a smooth and silent succession—a gap across which the young cannot easily talk to the old who grew up in a different world. Obviously, moreover, even the most drastic changes fail to break the continuity in every family, and there will always be members of any current generation who resemble their ancestors more than they resemble their peers.

Still, we have certain conventions, as illustrated in silver weddings, twenty-fifth reunions—and twenty-fifth anniversaries of magazines, colleges, and corporations; these make sure that people with a normal life span will have some occasions for an intellectual sabbatical or day of reflection. What for others, however, is a sabbatical occasion is for me, as a social scientist, a regular preoccupation with discontinuities in attitudes and values, both between "my" generation and its predecessors and successors. I have become a reader of college class reports, which permit the comparison at least of college "generations" with their rapid turnover, as well as make it possible to follow shifts in the attitudes and career patterns of the same generation at five-year or ten-year intervals.

To be sure, there are flaws in such a procedure, among them the fact that the regional and social-class base of a college does not remain constant: one might find great changes which said more about the "career" of the college—for instance, its loss of religious tone, or its wider geographic base—than about changes in the values of comparable individuals. We know, moreover, that not everyone responds to the appeals of the class secretary to get his report in; and if he does, he may respond in a very perfunctory way with little more data than "name, rank, and serial number"; the nonrespondents are very likely the less successful, but they may also include those who despise old-grad nostalgia and ceremonies.

If I put aside such misgivings, I can find a certain coherence of values uniting those who were graduated from the major Ivy League colleges between, say, 1920 and 1946. (I shall touch later upon certain differences.) Thus, in the Yale 1946 report, *Decade of Decision,* which has just appeared, one gets an impression of men who remember the Great Depression, who attended college in a wartime era of transition, and whose impetus and drive reflect these origins.[1] In contrast with this, however, it is at least arguable that the men just graduating, whose parents experienced the Depression but who were themselves growing up as the economy improved—men, moreover, many of whose parents, rigidly raised, shifted to a more permissive child-rearing—that these men would belong to a different psychological generation from any comparably large body of previous college graduates. While as a teacher I have had some impression that this may be the case, I have hesitated to trust my impression, since I know I am getting older while my students are not, and that I may not be free of old-grad nostalgia myself.

Thus, I welcomed the opportunity to study 183 *Time*-commissioned interviews of seniors in last year's graduating class—interviews asking the student respondent what he expected his life to be like in fifteen years, i.e., 1970.[2] Perhaps since so much of that life seemed to be concerned

[1] I owe to Professor Richard D. Schwartz of the Yale department of sociology, a member of this class and an author of its report, helpful comments concerning the nonrespondents. I am also indebted to Professor Reuel Denney for discussion of Dartmouth class reports.

[2] *Time* wrote a letter to the deans of twenty colleges, including Harvard, Princeton, Notre Dame, Williams, Dartmouth, Georgia Tech, the Universities of Houston, Michigan and Wisconsin. They were asked to find a student, preferably a graduate student, who would do ten interviews, and sent an illustrative interview with a Princeton senior. Regrettably, we do not know how the respondents (or, for that matter, the interviewers) were selected. In what they did, they followed a variety of forms or no form; thus, at Ohio State the interviewees tended to respond in terms of what the planet would be like in fifteen years (mostly science-fiction extrapolations) rather than of what they would be like. So, too, the interviews vary from long and searching ones at Stanford or Columbia to perfunctory paraphrase at some of the schools. There is a like difference between those colleges where the respondents appear to be talking "for the record," rather piously, and those where the discourse, or the report of it, seems more spontaneous. In each case, the interviewees declared themselves, after the interview was over, willing to let their names be used. I am indebted to the promotion department of *Time* for making this material available.

with hunting and fishing, golf, boating, and puttering, *Time* turned the interviews over to our Center for the Study of Leisure at the University of Chicago. Our first reaction to the material—I speak here for myself and for Robin Jackson, who independently studied the interviews—was that it was too unreliable to take seriously. Nevertheless, a picture of the Class of 1955 emerged which was congruent with other data—a picture which contrasts sharply, I believe, with what would have been obtained from seniors in the same colleges twenty-five years ago.

Twenty-five years ago, of course, the Great Depression had been under way for two years, forcing many who were graduated then to drop plans for further training, others to take refuge in graduate school against the uninviting job market. But it was not only the Depression that made students of the Class of 1931 feel uncertain about the future (in contrast to the relative certainty felt by college graduates today); it was ambition also. Many of us wanted to make our mark, and were not sure how high we would get. Our class had no floor under it, and by and large did not want a ceiling—indeed, in our generation a number of wellborn men whose floor seemed all too solid chose, in many different ways, to test their ability to live without a floor: they beachcombed (although not so drastically as George Orwell in *Down and Out in Paris and London*); or they became anthropologists, labor organizers, or cold-water-flat artists and poets; and a number became that bright combination of adventure and responsibility, the foreign correspondent. Such men often wanted to lose the self they had inherited and romantically to create a new one out of whole cloth.

Most aspirations pursued by our class, and by classes of the same era at Princeton, Yale, Dartmouth, and other colleges concerning which I have scraps of evidence, were more conventional: to make much money, to rise high in the government, to become a doctor, lawyer, merchant or chief. Since the first jobs we got were often makeshifts or didn't appear to lead anywhere, we changed jobs frequently. In a rough estimate, I would say that at least 40 per cent of us in the Class of 1931 have actually changed occupations at least once, not counting war service. There are, naturally, a great many exceptions: men who went into medicine were captured in all but a few cases by the severe system of rehazing and resocializing the student in the medical apprenticeship (but we should recognize that a man who has shifted from internal medicine and private practice to epidemiology and the Public Health Service has actually made a drastic shift of self-definition); men who went into their fathers' businesses and stayed there; men who are teaching school or practicing law or architecture without infidelity to their first love.

One reason so many of us shifted jobs was that we didn't know ourselves very well, and we knew the world even less well. As Charles McArthur of the Harvard Psychological Clinic has observed, many of the upper-middle-class boys at Harvard in the late 1930s did not know what they wanted to become but only where they wanted to land—up. The route had to be surveyed as they proceeded. Upper-class boys, in contrast, knew what they were expected to become—lawyers, bankers, trustees—but may have tired later of that inherited role and switched into something closer to their repressed desires.[3] In line with these findings, a number of us became critical of our values as we went along. I recall two friends who left Wall Street, where they were doing nicely, one to run a mattress factory for the unemployed, and the other to develop a ranch in the West and get into local politics. Quite apart from depression and taxes—though as part of the same world that brought the latter as a homeopathic remedy for the former—some of our generation concluded that money isn't everything. I remember in college snorting a bit sarcastically at those of my classmates who said that they were going to make a million before they were forty and then retire and "live." But the astonishing thing is how many did something not so dissimilar: they left a profitable job in New York—the mecca for so many then at Harvard and other New England colleges—to find "the good life" in some other work and some other part of the forest. We shall see in contrast to this that hardly any of the Class of 1955 would ever want to live in New York in order to make a million, or in any other big city. "No life in the ulcer belt for me," as one of them says, explaining why: although he plans to enter advertising, he will stay away from New York despite his realization that most big firms have their head offices there.

The same uncertainties that led to changes in occupation and aspiration also seem to me to have been a factor, along with the obvious economic hazard, in the relatively late marriages of so many of our generation. Many of us were searchers, not sure of the type of family life we wanted. Many did not want to be tied down. Nor would it have occurred to us to have our wives support us through graduate

[3] Charles McArthur and Lucia Beth Stevens, "The Validation of Expressed Interests as Compared with Inventoried Interests: A Fourteen-year Follow-up," *The Journal of Applied Psychology*, XXXIX (1955), 184–189.

school, as is so common today among the young. And, indeed, if we think of the Class of 1931 at Radcliffe or Smith, Bryn Mawr or Skidmore,[4] we realize that these young women were often ambitious too: they wanted careers, and not simply an intermittent series of low-level jobs that would help support four or five children and the suburban life the children "deserved." Those of us who did marry before or soon after graduation were often the well-to-do boys who seemed clearly headed down the ancestral occupational paths; and not a few changed wives as well as jobs—perhaps marrying the Mary Monahans that the George Apley family tradition had first forbidden.

World War II served some in these uncommitted groups as a switching point allowing the formation of new affiliations. Coming after ten years of doubt or underemployment, it permitted us to discover the potentialities we were often unaware of, to find new confidence and see new parts of the country. It served, of course, for many noncollege men in the same way, and California—the great American suburb, which many saw for the first time during the war—still gains light industry and population as a result. Others obviously were affected in other ways: some became better at what they already were—notably so the doctors, who beefed if the war wasn't arranged for their postgraduate benefit; or, sadly, still others were cut off or, though still living, remained lost. Coming back from the war into an expanding economy (so different from some of the post-World War I economies) we were able to confirm experiences which had only been potential; age might, with equal prosperity, have brought much of this, but the war speeded things up and gave us, I think, more differentiated fates.

Going over our class reports, that recount this at five-year intervals, I have detected a tendency to emphasize increasingly the nonvocational aspects of our lives: the family and hobbies and, markedly, the fabulous array of philanthropic and civic activities into which we have been drawn. It is hard to think of a disease or a civic bane that one of us hasn't "taken" and become a vice-president of! Many of us have, we report, moved to the suburbs for the benefit of the children, or even become exurbanites for the sake of a better family life. Still, we bring these things up because we have done well enough vocationally to afford these concessions to the rest of life. Were we without drive, men without readiness to sacrifice the nonwork sides of life, we would not seek

[4] I am indebted to Mrs. Doris B. Shartle for the Skidmore twenty-fifth anniversary report.

the high and demanding posts in business, government, and the arts which so many of our class and neighboring classes do hold in far above average trajectories of energetic mobility (even taking account of our inheritances of opportunity). In reading the reports, moreover, I get the impression that our class, though it may no longer have as many Frank Merriwell ambitions, is by no means ready to retire, even if it could financially afford to do so. (Some of the Class of 1955 talk in the *Time* interviews of the retirement plans in the companies they are going to enter.) Our class still has wants which are unfulfilled, not for things—which it owns in a measure to gladden *The New Yorker* advertisers of gifts for the man who has everything—but rather for meaning and purpose. George Weller defined us, in his novel of Harvard, as coming to college "not to eat, not for love, but only gliding" (an observation Emerson once made of snakes in Concord); we have done a lot of gliding but, unlike snakes, we want to understand what we have endured.

If, then, in this perspective upon ourselves (a perspective which may be too "projective"), we look at the *Time* interviews, we are struck by the knowingness of the present college generation: they come to college to eat, to love (and often to get married), but certainly not to glide. Although they enter a far more prosperous and secure world in economic terms, they appear in more of a hurry—not from a driving ambition which, as we shall see, not many have, but because they have already made up their minds as to exactly who they are and exactly where they want to go on the superhighway of their chosen corporation or profession.

Each knows, understandably enough, the branch of military service he is entering. (At Michigan, for example, the students speak of the "deal" they have in the guided missiles branch of the Army or the personnel section of the Marines or a reserve branch.) No one voices objection to service on political grounds or as a pacifist; and only two complain of the interruption to their careers; a great many see the period of military service as a kind of postgraduate training, helpful to their careers. In any case, such service is a fact of life to be casually accepted and gotten over with. War as a possible interference is scarcely contemplated by these rather optimistic men, and not anticipated by any but a few—largely Catholics for whom world communism is more of an omnipresent menace than it is for most of the respondents. Nor is there anything opaque for the majority about their careers: they know the type of professional office or large corporation they want; and most who are going into business (which includes many who have majored in engineering or chemistry and are going to business school after that) prefer the salaried life of the large corporation. As one Princeton senior says:

> Let's face it, I'll be on salary, not making capital gains, even at 36. . . . Why struggle on my own, when I can enjoy the big psychological income of being a member of a big outfit?

And he points out that he doesn't have the brass his father had to be a lone wolf—a comparison a number of them make, in almost every case with detached admiration for the old man's toughness, but with hardly any despondency for not living up to him as a model.

As another young man says, speaking of the large corporation in general:

> They try to do what's best for you and best for them—if they see you'd do better in one department than in another, they transfer you. . . . There's no back-stabbing and politics like there is in a small firm. Your worth is recognized.

The notion that the company might also recognize negative worth, failure, just doesn't come up; it is the company's role to develop and train, never to threaten or fire. This, indeed, is part of the benevolent world these men foresee and will perhaps help create as a self-confirming prophecy. As one of them remarks:

> I've always believed that if you are honest and sincere and can convince other people that you are, you'll get ahead, and I don't think I'll find out that I am wrong when I get out in the business world.

This is an understandable outlook, especially in view of the experience these men have had of being courted by large corporations. One Michigan senior tells the interviewer:

> One nice thing about it is you don't really have to go out looking for a job—they come around looking for you!

In Stephen Potter's handbook of gamesmanship, he has a ploy to floor any generalizer, namely, "What of the South?"—a question you can ask in any country, for whether in Italy or France, China or the United States, the South is almost always another country, sometimes another colony. So it is that in these interviews, some of the Southerners, including Texans, seem more eager for the big money, and more willing

the more striking since it is my impression that the interviewers tried to get "representative men," who were often big men on campus (a strategy which seems to have failed totally at Harvard, where the respondents—some of them prospective doctors—include neither the intellectual nor the social elite who would, I suspect, have avoided or kidded the whole "deal").[5]

This relative subordination of career ambition goes together with the fact that for most of the respondents the girl they are to marry is already picked out in fact or fancy, and the style of life the family will lead is foreshadowed with clarity. Some sound rather psychological about it (like a Harvard man, already engaged, who declares: "Well, it's supposed to be psychologically bad for the middle child if you have three, so I suppose we'll have four"). Others are as uncomplex as the Michigan engineering student who says that he and his girl have "talked some about a family, and we're agreed that we'd like a pretty fair-sized one—maybe four or five kids. We're both fairly easygoing and a lot of noise wouldn't bother us."

One Princeton senior is so very explicit that I first thought he must be pulling the interviewer's leg, but that was because I happened to

[5] At the University of Denver, the interviewer got a more Bohemian and unconventional range of respondents. They include an actor, aggressively individualistic, who says he's willing to live in "a room which is yours and nobody else's"; a man who wants to produce plays (but not live in New York); a man who proclaims himself a Taft Republican, who's going into nuclear engineering because that's the future; and a girl who wants to become a missionary. Oberlin also presents a contrast, with one man who wants to be a foreign correspondent; another who plans to become an agronomist for missions to underdeveloped lands; one wants to be a philosopher; and several are going into psychology (one of whom aims at becoming a dean of students). In general, the Oberlin seniors are outspokenly idealistic and prepared to accept modest incomes.

Nevertheless, taking the interviews as a whole, it seems probable that many of the more interesting students were either left out or sounded more "normal" in their interviews than they might under less stilted conditions. Only three women got into this jumbled sample: the comments of one form a curious obbligato to the image the men have of the kind of wife they want. She is a Wisconsin senior who says that she's afraid of "that nice little pattern that everyone wants to fit into; the cheery little marriage and the husband working to get ahead in his job, the wife being a clubwoman and helping her husband to advance. . . . Beating the pattern is the hardest thing of all, and I'm not much for fighting. It would be a lot easier just to go off to Africa or somewhere and live there. . . . It isn't that I want to be an odd-ball. I like odd-balls but I wouldn't want to be one."

read his interview first and didn't realize that it only highlighted a norm. He is going into law, and he declares:

> I'll belong to all the associations you can think of—Elks, V.F.W.'s, Boy Scouts and Boys' Clubs, Y.M.C.A., American Legion, etc. It will keep me away from home a lot. But my wife [a purely hypothetical wife] won't mind. She'll be vivacious and easy with people. And she will belong to everything in sight too—especially the League of Women Voters. I won't marry her until I'm twenty-eight, and so when I'm thirty-six we will have only two of the four children I hope for eventually. We'll be living in an upper-middle-class home costing about $20,000 by then, in a suburban fringe. . . . We'll have two Fords or Chevvies when I'm thirty-six, so we can both keep up the busy schedule we'll have. But in addition to this public social life, we'll have private friends who don't even live around Toledo—friends with whom we can be completely natural and relaxed. That's where Princeton friends will be very important.

To members of an older generation, this may sound like a young man on the make who wants contacts. But that is a small part of it: the civic-minded life, the gregarious life, is at once felt as an obligation, seen as professionally useful, and anticipated as a pleasure and an end in itself. The wife is an indispensable auxiliary to this life which, even if it is a very outgoing, two-car life, is still centered in the backyard bosom of the family. This is an element in the resentment which appears again and again in the interviews toward the (almost purely hypothetical) career girl. One Harvard man says about the sort of girl he wants to marry:

> She shouldn't be submissive, she can be independent on little things, but the big decisions will have to go my way . . . the marriage must be the most important thing that ever happened to her.

Another says what many feel:

> My wife can work if she wants when we are first married, but she shouldn't work when we have children.

At the same time, they don't want a stay-at-home wife; they want a presentable date who, as we have seen, will be active in community affairs; she must be college-bred, she must understand her husband and know how to bring up children. There are contradictions lurking here; as one Harvard man says:

> I want someone who would stay home and take care of the children, but on the other hand I want someone who can stimulate me intellectually, and I don't know if those things are compatible ... if a woman goes to Radcliffe and takes up economics, she isn't learning how to bring up children.

In order to see what kind of mother their girl will make, a number of men say they will take a hard look at the girl's mother, to see what kind of a model mother she is—a rather awesome theme for those of us in the Class of 1931 who have eligible daughters and hopelessly impractical wives.

One Princeton senior is more graphic than most about all this. He says:

> Life will not be a burden for me at thirty-five [How old and tired he makes that august age sound!] because I will be securely anchored in my family. My main emotional ties will center in my wife and family—remember, I hope for five children. Yes, I can describe my wife [again, quite a hypothetical person]. She will be the Grace Kelly, camel's-hair-coat type. Feet on the ground, and not an empty shell or a fake. Although an Ivy League type, she will also be centered in the home, a housewife. Perhaps at forty-five, with the children grown up, she will go in for hospital work and so on. ... And improving herself culturally and thus bringing a deeper sense of culture into our home will be one of her main interests in fifteen years.

And then he concludes: "... in fifteen years I look forward to a constant level of happiness."

It is this vision of life on a plateau that perhaps most distinguishes the Class of 1955 from that of 1931. We who were graduated twenty-five years ago found our way by trial and error—and I emphasize the error as well as the trial—to many of the values and styles of life the Class of 1955 already begins with. We were, as I have suggested, more immature in many ways, and by the same token we expected to change and to be changed by our work and our experiences. The Class of 1955, judging by these interviews and forgetting their unreliability, would appear to expect to go on successfully adapting as they have already done, but not to change in any fundamental way, save that the family will take the place of the fraternity. The girls in question, however, may find it harder to stay on the plateau—or if they're *that* good, they may not want these boys;[6] after all, Grace Kelly has had a career and has married a prince.

But there is very little evidence in the interviews that the respondents have had to struggle for anything they want—or have wanted anything that would cost them a struggle. Some of the things they have surrendered are surely baubles. Thus, I have the impression that hardly anybody seeks swank or social distinction, and this seems not merely an artifact of the interview but an expression of the prevailing democratic ethos. A number who themselves went to prep school say they will send their children to public school. The suburb they aim for is regarded as the scenic backdrop for the happy family, not the locale of mobility as in *Point of No Return*. As I have implied, they have very few dreams, these young men; they dream of neither conventional prestige and social éclat nor, in general, of unconventional accomplishments. A fortune which can be passed on to children would be one sort of accomplishment, but very few of these seniors look for even modest capital accumulation; the capital is, as it were, society's, built into the schools and suburban developments and Blue Cross plans and corporate reserves. A floor is under these men, a low ceiling over them (analogous to the ranch-type houses in which they will live, in contrast to the high-ceilinged Victorian home), and these provide a narrow and "constant level of happiness." As one Harvard senior declares, explaining why he had dropped his plan to pursue the strenuousness of a medical career: "I think contentment is the main thing."

Do they see the political future as a possible interference with having all utilities "laid on," as the British would say? They were all asked about the political future—a boring topic for most of them. I am sure few know or care who is our Ambassador to France, and, save for a few Catholic nationalists already referred to, they expect peace within the country and with the Soviet powers. Their political views are decent

[6] In 1954, *Mademoiselle* magazine sent out questionnaires to women undergraduates at a number of colleges, and also to a few graduates. I had an opportunity to examine these, and the picture they present is not different from that presented by the men: they, too, want the well-rounded life, suburban and family-centered (but, like the men in the *Time* interviews, near enough to a big city for cultural advantages—it isn't clear who will populate the city), and fear ambition in themselves and their prospective spouses. Russell Lynes, in "What Has Succeeded Success?" (*Mademoiselle*, September 1954), discusses these interviews perceptively, pointing out how demanding and strenuous the goals of well-roundedness and contentment can become, and what effort it takes to be "cool."

and, in a nonpolitical sense, liberal; the Southerners are generally opposed to segregation, and are optimistic that it will cease to be a problem as the older generation dies out. They like Ike; and in a certain complacency, a fondness for golf (which many in our generation thought an old man's game) and the outdoors, they are like Ike. For most of them, save for a few who are going into law and want to dabble in politics, the national and international political scene holds neither fear nor fascination.[7]

This doesn't mean they aren't civic-minded; they are very much so. Whereas quite a few of our generation moved to the suburbs, at least allegedly on the children's account, while resenting the life of a commuter, the Class of 1955 has an emotional attachment to the suburb and sees it as far more than a spawning bed. As one Michigan student says:

> I'm definitely interested in community activities. More than anything, I'd like to work with the youth of the community, especially in athletics. . . . When I say I'm interested in community activities, that doesn't mean politics. I'm not interested in politics whatsoever, and I never will be! I hate to say anything against politicians, but they just waste too much time. . . . I want to live my own life, not a public life.

The suburb appears to be an extension of private life: its P.T.A.s, its Little League baseball, and in some cases its general cultural level—these the Class of 1955 wants to take on as its proper responsibilities. This goes for religion, too; as one civic-minded Cal Tech senior says:

> I think that I will be going to church. . . . It is good for a whole family to do things together; more or less builds unity.

Indeed, it would perhaps be as correct to say that private life is the domestic intensification of the suburb, as we can see in the remarks of a Harvard senior:

> I'd like six kids. I don't know why I say that—it just seems like a minimum production goal. I like kids and I've done a lot of work with them. . . . I like group life and family life and I

[7] One Harvard man of top academic standing, who is going into law, says: "I suppose as I become more allied with the business world and with business associates I'll tend to shed my Democratic preferences." This is not said cynically or bitterly, but as part of an image of a relaxed, suburban future.

want to have a home filled with inner richness. Nothing is as human as a child.

A world populated by the men who appear in these interviews, and by the girls they almost without exception have in mind—the bachelor's freedom is a vanishing theme—would be a decent world; nobody in it would blow up or blow it up. If we ourselves manage to live the next fifteen years in such a world, we may count our bland blessings, though some of us of 1931 may not regret that we lived for our first fifteen years after graduation in a world of passion and turmoil which many of us experienced as such, whether it touched us closely or at one remove.

Afterthought: When I presented the foregoing observations to the Class of 1931 and to their wives and college-age children, I set going something of a cross-generational argument in which the "younger generation" felt a need to explain their apparent security-proneness and members of my own generation to berate them for it; to berate them even for not revolting against us—and then to berate ourselves for being so mild and nice as not to produce revolt. Indeed, as I have indicated, the Class of 1955 is at peace with its parents in so far as the *Time* interviews shed light on the matter. They may regard their fathers as tougher men than they (perhaps we are not as tough as we appear), but they do not regard them as Philistines to be overcome by fight or flight, but rather as helpful and even exemplary older siblings. On the other hand, judging from our discussions in Cambridge, parents worry that life has been made too easy for their children, that they do not crave eminence or seek excellence, that they are almost too well rounded. In this particular sequence of the generations, as so often in the history of this country, the self-made person finds that—at least in the absence of powerful Puritan traditions—he cannot reproduce his kind.

But it is, of course, much too early to predict to what degree the Class of 1955, with all its considerable realism, will succeed in finding the good life so many now look forward to. Perhaps unjustifiably extrapolating from the interviews, they appear to have encountered few moral and psychological hardships; school and college have been for many an extension of the nest rather than a traumatic initiation outside its protections. Military service still lies ahead of most of them, and after that the suburb with (as William Whyte of *Fortune* has indicated in many articles[8]) its subtle pressures for smooth performance in personal relations. Moreover, the job may not turn out as promised, either in terms of what it will buy or of what strains in family life it may involve. Just as many of us in the Class of 1931 could not tell what we were like until war experience revealed us to ourselves, so obviously we cannot know in advance what demands will be made on our children or how in the light of their experience they will interpret them. Conceivably, they will have to face an existence which at forty-five, with the children grown and flown, the job ceilinged and routine, the hobbies long since explored, will bring a quiet crisis of meaning—somewhat like that of some members of an older generation who cannot, being work-driven, face retiring at sixty-five or seventy. But such a notion is probably ethnocentric to our generation, as it stares into the opaqueness of another age-culture; and I guess our curiosity will have to wait until the Class of 1955 tells us, in more artistic and dramatic ways than through brief interviews, what it feels like to belong, by birth rather than individual effort, to an economy (though it be a war economy) of abundance.

[8] I have learned much from Whyte's book, *The Organization Man*, describing the junior-executive life on and off the job; see, also, his *Fortune* article on "The Class of '49," June 1949, the argument of which is largely congruent with my own. Whyte (in correspondence) observes one interesting difference between the Class of 1949 and that of 1955, namely that the former chose the big corporation reluctantly, out of a Depression-bred insecurity, and fearing for their individuality, whereas the Class of 1955 does not, for the most part, feel the need to make a choice.

Some Continuities and Discontinuities in the Education of Women
(1956)

When I was a student at Harvard Law School and first became acquainted with Bennington, the college represented for me many of the values that were then nearly invisible in the Law School or at Harvard generally: an interest in modern theater, dance, and music; a concern with art rather than art history; a preoccupation with creative writing as well as with literary history and the Kittredge type of analysis. Since I had been one of a small group at Harvard College who regretted the loss of the Baker Workshop in drama, and the absence (presently repaired by amateur efforts) of any facilities for stagecraft; since I preferred Martha Graham to the Russian Ballet and Stravinsky to Wagner, Bennington struck me as idyllic: a new departure. The girls I knew in the first groups who went there appeared to take wise advantage of its freedom to develop their gifts, especially in the arts, and not notably to miss either city life or coeducation.

Today we are all of us, the young included, older and wiser, and in recent visits to Bennington and other women's colleges I have realized that the old, easy enthusiasms no longer hold sway. The utopian colony becomes incorporated into the general cultural advance—just as *Life* or TV brings modern art to the millions—and the members of the colony look over the now porous walls and wonder what in the "world" they are missing, such as casual, daily contact with men or with metropolitan life. The *élan* of experimentation understandably leaches away, and moderate sacrifices that were once gladly made now become irksome. People even look back to the "good old days" of a mere two decades ago, because it has become harder to imagine a future radically different from the present.

I have sketched a few lines in the background of my personal life cycle as the prelude to examining certain changes in the "life cycle" of higher education for women; the "continuities and discontinuities" my title refers to are those in the lives of individuals, rather than in the traditions of educational institutions themselves. Then, in the latter part of my talk, I shall turn to the more general problem of the ways in which young people who go to college at present find themselves in radically new milieux as against recreating on the college level the cultural patterns of the home, the high school, and the suburb. In general, my bias is in favor of presenting students with creative discontinuities as they pass through the stages of formal education, though I believe I am not blind to the dilemmas young men as well as young women face when, after an exciting education, they feel trapped in the routines of livelihood and getting through the day. In other words, I share John Dewey's faith that education should put pressure on life, as well as vice versa.

In a study a few years ago, Mirra Komarovsky showed, in quantified detail, that even if one holds income constant girls still go to college nearer home than boys; they are kept on a tighter leash—and perhaps in many families (and to the girls themselves) their education isn't thought to matter quite so much as the boys'.[1] And of course when these girls get married—and we know now from many surveys (notably Ernest Havemann and Patricia Salter West's *They Went to College*) that college girls, unless they are Catholics, do get married about as regularly, and no more often, than noncollege girls—they will again be on the leash of their husband's career, moving when he does, whatever this may mean for their own plans. Against either the first or the second of these leashes, there seems to me today to be very little protest by the girls themselves.

Let me elaborate. The headmaster of a fashionable girls' private day school in a midwestern city tells me he has a hard time persuading his brightest seniors to apply to one of the first-rate Ivy League colleges, even in those few cases where their mothers have attended such a college. He can even dangle a Radcliffe or Smith or Bryn Mawr scholarship before such a girl without getting her to choose this opportunity for development rather than the nearby state university or such good but not quite so demanding schools as Knox, DePauw, Beloit, or Colorado College. The girls' parents don't want them to become dis-

[1] This work is reviewed in her book, *Women in the Modern World: Their Education and Their Dilemmas* (Boston, Mass.: Little, Brown, 1954).

satisfied with the Midwest or to travel so far; the girls themselves, though highly gifted, don't care enough to put up a fight.

Another example. Suppose I took a poll of girls in college today, and asked them, if they had to choose, would they rather be Gertrude Stein or have a family in some pleasant, unchallenging suburb, married to a nice guy? Wouldn't they overwhelmingly choose the latter? And would they not also make the same choice if, eliminating eccentricity and homeliness, we substituted Marguerite Higgins? Indeed, we need not guess here, for there is much empirical evidence we can draw upon. There is the high attrition rate at the girls' colleges, in which as many as a third or more who start as freshmen do not finish: they marry (and may continue schooling at their husband's base of operations), or they transfer to a coed school where they may hope sooner to marry, or they just quit and take a job. It's very much a bird in hand—or rather, bird in nest—philosophy, in spite of good statistical probability that they could graduate and still find a husband. (If I sound unsympathetic here to husbands and homes, I don't mean to, but it will take me a while to develop the whole context of my argument.)

If the romance of far-flung but possibly unmarried careers attracts few college women, it should also be noted that the images held as to the ideal spouse have departed quite widely from the dreams of romantic love that were popular a generation ago. A study of the values sought by both sexes at the University of Michigan today indicates that the qualities are those we associate with good, "natural" human relations rather than with razzle-dazzle or rating-dating.[2] Good looks matter somewhat less than good humor; emotional maturity, dependability, well-roundedness matter more than glamour—leading Professor Blood to forecast "the stabilization of American college marriages about a norm of equalitarian companionship" (p. 45).

[2] Robert O. Blood, Jr., "Uniformities and Diversities in Campus Dating Preferences," *Journal of Marriage and Family Living*, vol. 18, 1956; pp. 37–45. By the same token, it should be emphasized that, while I speak here of women, the differences in values between them and young men are not so great. Margaret Mead has called my attention to a recent study of the image of the scientist among high school students: not only do the girls not want to marry scientists (other than physicians), who are viewed as careless of their leisure and their families, but the boys don't want to be scientists themselves, which they associate with baldness, glasses, and no home life. (I am indebted to Dr. Mead for discussions of this whole set of questions, in print and in person.)

even to desert the big corporation and the suburb in its pursuit. One senior at Georgia Tech tells the interviewer:

> Fifteen years from now—well, I'm pretty ambitious and I think that I'll be with a progressive company at Burlington. Maybe I'll be a division director making—say—$25,000 a year.

This is a modest aim enough, but large in comparison with the others who expect to be making $15,000 or $18,000 at most to support the four children and the two cars, the club dues and church contributions, the vacations in Europe and Bermuda, and the small boat on the lake. He continues:

> And I'll probably be working in the Southeastern states since the trend is definitely toward the elimination of the Eastern mills. But South and Central America are going to move up as textile areas . . . if I do get overseas I think I would enjoy it.

Another Georgia Tech student wants both to write a big novel about the Civil War—he says he thinks there's still a big market for all the magnolia stuff—and to make a lot of money on his father's Mississippi Delta farm. A Texas boy at Princeton is going into the oil and gas business with his father. To this group I should add a Notre Dame boy from Pittsburgh who expects to make big money practicing law, in part because he can count on the influence of his father, a probate judge; and another Catholic, son of an oil and gas producer, a Harvard senior, who says, "Christ, I'd live in Nome, Alaska, if there was money there."

These are the exceptions, however, the immoderates, who want neither the fringe benefit nor the fringe suburb. Their idiosyncrasy is evident in the fact that they say more about their careers and less about their prospective wives and families than most. Rather than looking to a large corporation to advance them if they deserve it, they want to find a situation to which *they* make a difference—a situation small enough for them to make an impact on it. They want a ladder, not an escalator.

Most of them, however, as I have indicated, think of themselves as too mature—and perhaps of the economy as too mature as well—to be that interested in self-advancement. The career they want is to find the good life, for which their corporation or profession serves as the good provider. These men already know they won't be president—they wouldn't want the job with its unpredictable demands, its presumptive big-city locale, its disruption of family and recreational life. This is all

Less carefully gathered but more revealing of total orientations were the questionnaires that *Mademoiselle* magazine sent out in 1954 to women undergraduates at a number of leading colleges and universities, and also to a few recent graduates. Feminism was clearly rejected by virtually all of these girls: they wanted not only marriage but the kind of marriage just indicated—sober, suburban, intellectually and emotionally alive but not in any way earth-moving or earth-shaking. And while they were willing and even eager to travel, it was as tourists, not as foreign correspondents or expatriates or even anthropologists. In locale, appurtenances, and opportunities, if not in emotional tone, the home they want appears not to be so very different from the one in which they grew up.

Yet there is one vitally important difference: these young women want to have jobs: before marriage, before the children come, and after the children have grown. Whereas in an earlier day, a small handful of feminists wanted careers and the vast majority of "femininists" wanted homes, today the entire college generation wants, not a career, but a job as a supplement to marriage. Working wives have, in fact, increased tremendously since World War II, helping overcome the shortage of labor in our full-employment society (at the very time when the children of the low-birthrate Great Depression years are entering the labor force—a labor force which must support an increasing number of old people kept alive by modern medicine and the present wave of children given life by the new valuation put on marriage and the family). Married women are even helping put an end to the famous schoolteacher shortage. Through these jobs, few of them lucrative and hardly any of them eminent, college-educated women contribute to meeting the costs of a standard of living which pushes ever higher, thus making it possible for them to raise three or four children in middle-class circumstance with not much assistance from accumulated or inherited capital.

Moreover, the job gives the intelligent housewife the feeling that she is not being cloistered in domesticity; she can move in an orbit wider than the backyard and the neighborhood. But very few of these working women seek to expand the constrictions still surrounding the employment of women in the professions and in business: they are at work, not for the sake of the work itself, nor for the sake of rising to intellectual or financial heights thereby (nor, indeed, as every union official knows, for the sake of labor solidarity), but rather for the needed supplement to family income and the sought respite from isolation.[3]

What I have just said must, however, be interpreted in the light of the gains which the feminist generation permanently won for working wives—gains which reduce the need for such wives to battle ferociously for decent minima of recognition and treatment; with the passing of the cruder inequalities, it is no longer so exciting simply to achieve the status of a woman doctor or even woman engineer. And, as Mirra Komarovsky points out in correspondence, women today refer to callings as "jobs" which, in a less privileged time, they would have regarded as "careers"; this holds true, for example, of their work as schoolteachers, social workers, researchers, and so on; and the semantic change probably also reflects today's more general vogue of understatement of claims and ambitions.

Even so, the whole development must be very hard on women of the feminist era who are teaching in the women's colleges today, and finding only rarely among their students a devotion to Chaucer or microbiology or professional (as against amateur) artistic competence. They must feel that the still somewhat greater luxury girls have, to pursue courses which are not directly vocational, is being thrown away in pursuit of the vocationalism of domesticity itself—on courses in child psychology, consumer economics, human relations, and perhaps civics—even when the vocationalism of the secretarial or other minor league jobs to be sought on graduation does not intrude. They must also feel that their students are humbly submitting all too soon to the imagined demands of the personality market, which would make any eccentric intellectual enthusiasms a handicap with both boys and girls—submitting to the mandate of well-roundedness as much in the intellectual as in the physical sphere.

I think, for instance, of a college girl of my acquaintance who, like some of an earlier generation, is a balletomane but who, having the choice between studying with a fine teacher during the summer or teaching dance herself at a summer camp not passionately devoted to the arts, preferred the latter; there, her personal claims to distinction

[3] In *The Lonely Crowd*, we suggested a four-hour day at work as one way of relieving the "privatization" of young housewives who could not take responsible care of their children and yet put in an eight-hour day. Some department stores, school systems with perennial "substitutes," and clerical offices are doing this now, but not nearly enough to absorb the sad underemployment of many women who could be at work while their children are at school, but now are confined to the company of TV.

were muffled in service, and she felt she was being of use rather than narcissistic. Money was not involved here, any more than it is in a great many of the jobs which college and high school students seek, often in preference to idiosyncratic personal development. And while I would defend the choice this particular girl made over the snobbery that sometimes attends art as such, I am troubled when I see the same choice so regularly being made by many of the most spirited young women of a whole generation.

It used to be, of course, that only a few exceptional women went to college, while today the women's colleges as well as the coeducational ones have been swamped by girls who did not make a courageous and somewhat individual choice to go to college and who have no markedly unique aims to be furthered by an education. A bit earlier, the wealthy and well-connected among these girls would simply have "come out," while the less well off would have helped mother and waited for callers. If anyone doubts that college for this great majority represents some emancipation, let him recall Tocqueville's comments about the relative vacuousness of the American girls he met on his trip up the Hudson to Albany: these were "accomplished" young ladies who spoke bad French and forced him to listen to their lachrymose songs with piano accompaniment—ladies who were the products, not of colleges, which then did not admit women, but of small local academies. The aims of the founders of Mount Holyoke and Russell Sage, or of Oberlin and Cornell, were not at all to produce pallid imitations of salon types—and, obviously enough, the great state universities, when they began admitting women, sought to co-opt them into the same intellectual world as men, even though the women might do more and better work in English, and the men in math and engineering. (The normal schools, virtually for girls only, were part of a different social movement.)

In fact, higher education for women from the earliest days down to the founding of Sarah Lawrence and Bennington seems frequently to have struck profounder notes of emancipation and innovation than higher education for men, which has often been satisfied to imitate British, or occasionally German, models, or to imitate itself; I think one can argue that this is true even in the South, where Sweetbriar and Randolph-Macon, the Women's College of the University of North Carolina, and even Stephens College, however frilly, horsy and magnolia-scented they may seem from afar, put pressure on their southern students for more intellectuality and independence than was favored by the southern traditions of the virtuous lady. The women's colleges could afford their greater experimentalism—not financially, sadly enough, for they are always meagerly endowed (after the male old grad has taken care of his own undergraduate alma mater)—in part because, as I have remarked, only the more enterprising girls formerly went to college; in part because girls and their careers have been thought to matter less; and in part because those who taught at a girls' college have been themselves somewhat less apt to be careerists in terms of their academic disciplines and more apt to be concerned with wider educational and intellectual goals. I should like to stress that it is not simply because women have been, in terms of power, a minority group that they have been more venturesome academically: there is nothing in the least pioneering about such Negro universities as Fisk or Dillard or Howard, nor so far as I know about the Jewish university, Brandeis. (Indeed, Diana Trilling once made the observation that, as long as women felt inferior to men, they ought to get an education at least as bad, in order to think they are not being discriminated against; this was her argument in favor of Radcliffe—an argument which, judging by present admission pressures, is still a very powerful one! It was also her argument against Lynn White, Jr.'s thesis in *Educating Our Daughters* that women ought to have an education tailored to their special capacities and their presumptive roles in contemporary society.)

Yet today it is my impression that the women's colleges, though still outstanding, no longer provide an education markedly better than the Ivy League colleges for men (as I believe they did twenty years ago, before the freshman year at Amherst became as demanding and experimental as it is today), and, as innovators, share the honors with such good colleges as Antioch, Swarthmore, Reed, and Chicago. As in so many other sectors of our national life, the floor under the education of women has been greatly raised—with more women in college by far than ever before—while the ceiling has risen but slightly. The bluestocking era (whose savor we can recapture in Henry James's *The Bostonians*) is over, probably for good—an era in which a very few girls were ambitious to compete with men professionally and were prepared, if need be, to sacrifice marriage (if not sexuality itself) on the altar of distinction in their chosen fields. At the same time, we can be grateful that the "accomplished lady" era, which lasted from the time of Tocqueville's visit down nearly to our day, is over also: most debutantes now attend college and squeeze their round of parties into a brief season, nor do they believe that the capstone of their education will be a touristy tour of European capitals—or even a junior year abroad. An amalgamation has occurred, in which some of the outlook of the bluestocking has permeated the college-educated group quite generally, while the home-and-marriage aspirations both of the debs and of the great majority have influenced what was once the small feminist avant-garde.

What this means is that very few women today, in the middle and upper classes, move from their families of orientation to their families of procreation with the earlier all too easy continuities—easy in the sense that choice of role and even choice of marriage partner, were limited by tradition and by the fact that the educators of these young women were themselves mostly women in the home and in the secondary schools. Thus women are much less of a captive audience than they once were, and they can hardly help in their college education being exposed to wider and more differentiated perspectives.[4]

At the same time, I believe that the virtual elimination of the feminist stance as an alternative has somewhat constricted the choices—hence, the discontinuities—once available to a very small minority. For marriage has become much more imperative for women (no less so for men) than it was in the nineteenth century, when failure to marry was regarded as a social disadvantage and sometimes a personal tragedy but not necessarily as a quasi-perversion. This is all the more the case since high social-class position is no longer a protection for idiosyncratic choices by women (as it remains in France where being an aristocrat counts for more than being a woman, allowing a wide leeway even in a country which—judging by Simone de Beauvoir's *The Second Sex* and other less eloquent testimony—has a Catholic impatience with feminism among the less exalted).

Yet this development must be appreciated for its emancipating as well as its constricting features. Feminism provided an alternative model for some women, whether they actually followed it or kept it in

[4] This differentiation is achieved today in many women's colleges by staffing the faculty very largely with men—a policy, defensible in its own terms, which aggravates the miserably great discrimination which still operates against the woman professor. I need hardly add that I believe that the education of men would greatly profit if they were more exposed to gifted and sensitive women professors at the highest levels—and perhaps had more men teachers in the primary grades; the change in values which such a policy might help to promote would benefit both sexes.

mind as a vicarious possibility against male oppression; but, as Margaret Mead and others have pointed out, it was itself often a subtle form of male dominance: it assumed that a name on the door was more important than the "trivia" of motherhood and homemaking, and it could lead to a sterile form of careerism which men themselves are today beginning to reject—and, for greater numbers, to a feeling that their roles as housewives were by definition narrow and inferior.[5] In my own scheme of values, no one should be asked to sacrifice family life to ends outside himself—often idealistic ends in the sense that they redound to the community, not the individual, even though the latter may appear to be selfish in pursuing his career. I can respect as well as understand the motives which lead the present generation of college-educated men and women to choose what their middle-class parents would have regarded as large families, as an option for an immortality which you can take with you every day, as against one which is more inscrutable and remote.

Even so, if today one meets the survivors of the unmarried feminist generation, one is struck by their frequent sanguine vitality: in pursuing their careers, they knew they were giving up some good things for other good things—but not the essence of life itself or personal identity. Young college women today, it is my impression, feel that they can fulfill themselves *only* in marriage and child-rearing, and an exciting career is not really an escape route even from the prospects of a dull and trying marriage (Catholic women, whose menfolk are still somewhat less inclined to want college graduates for wives, do have the alternative of becoming nuns). Thus, not particular marriages, but marriage in general as a monolithic and unarguable premise, has become an ideological weight for women to bear—and, with hardly less imperative force, for men as well.

But this, as already indicated, does not mean that college women after marriage are satisfied to be "merely" housewives, no matter how severely and unself-indulgently they interpret the demands of motherhood. For instance, studies of Vassar alumnae by Nevitt Sanford, Mervin B. Freedman, and others reveal the disquietude of many that

[5] In an unpublished paper, "Male and Female in *The Lonely Crowd*," Professor Walter Weisskopf argues that the spread among men of empathy and "other-direction" is in part a protest against the "maleness" of large-scale industrial society, with its abstraction and artificiality—a protest which leaves many women confused either when they seek to imitate men or to become what men want of them.

they have not lived up to the potentialities their education encouraged —a malaise foreshadowed by the attitude changes among undergraduates as they lose some of the certainties that protect many freshmen. Bearing in mind Theodore Newcomb's pioneering investigation of attitude changes at Bennington itself—in which he noted the way in which the more conservative students took on the liberal and emancipating values of the dominant campus culture—I would expect that Bennington alumnae would also often feel they had, as it were, let their education down as they returned, not entirely contentedly, to the family fold or married, let us say, a Williams boy of lesser rebelliousness.[6]

This situation has, in fact, led to a number of proposals for cutting women's education down, so to speak, to the presently available "ecological" possibilities. It is said that when educated women stake so much on marriage, they will insist on marrying interesting and intellectual men, and that there aren't enough such men to go round, when one takes account of the probabilities that many of them will pick (or be picked by) the quite carefully unintellectual girls. Sometimes this view —that women's aspirations should be phased to what at any given time men are willing to accept—leads to opposition to the topflight women's colleges, or to the co-ed experimental colleges, as giving women too high hopes for a stimulating life. Sometimes the view leads to suggestions for a more "feminine" curriculum for women, which would cultivate their empathy rather than their acumen, removing them presumably from the orbits of mind in which they would be tempted beyond the qualities desirable in a modern housewife, hostess, and mother. While I agree both with some authorities (e.g., Erich Fromm, Margaret Mead) and with the vulgar that there *are* over-all tendencies toward difference between men and women that are not entirely the product of culture and its patriarchal heritage,[7] I do not think these nuances of difference should be used to force either men or

[6] I don't mean to imply that today's Bennington graduates are Madame Bovarys married to Philistine men: the men, as I have tried to make clear, are catching up fast. But there remain great differences of region and class on this score [some of which I note briefly in my introduction to *Crestwood Heights*, p. 506].

[7] In the first chapter of my book on Veblen, I try to indicate some of the "masculine" and "feminine" aspects of the thought of a man who himself did a great deal to elaborate the historical consequences of male domination. See *Thorstein Veblen: A Critical Interpretation* (New York: Scribner's, 1953).

women into a statistically normative mold—men should no more be confined to abstractions than women to the earthy and concrete. Nor is such a program likely to make women more satisfied with themselves, or men with them. As one of Bennington's most perceptive recent graduates points out, in discussing feminism and, *inter alia*, Mirra Komarovsky's work, such a forcible division of labor would tend to exclude men from all nonlogical family affairs; she continues:

> Some of the consciously "feminine" women of our own day show what the anti-feminist reality can be: they will not demand to be heard in conversations on politics, and no one can accuse them of being intellectual or of trying to compete with men. Somehow, though, the conversation is always quickly turned from politics to natural childbirth. Any man who felt uncomfortable might have difficulty in understanding it—that is, if he *could* feel anything or could escape from his omnipresent abstractions; annoyed, he might be told that he was envying the feminine capacity to produce life naturally. We can see that "feminine" goals serve the will just as readily as any others, but often with more hostility and less honesty.[8]

Quite apart from such ironic consequences, it seems to me that most educational programs that have sought to tailor the curriculum to the probable future needs of the student have imposed needless sacrifices on the latter, because the future went somewhere else. Very few people even fifteen years ago predicted the current situation in America, and the most "realistic" education often turned out to be the most irrelevant. Take, for instance the Negro colleges like Tuskegee which said to their students: "There's no chance for Negro engineers, Negro technicians and professionals in a dozen fields where they would be in the same pyramid with whites; so we've got to turn out Negro mechanics, artisans, and agriculturists, for which there will always be a market." What happened? Today one finds many places that would like to hire a Negro anesthetist or engineer or psychologist, but not enough Negroes took chances a generation ago on an "impractical" education to be available for these places which now unexpectedly exist: hence, the sound practical earlier judgment turns out to be self-confirming, like so much work in the field of vocational guidance. The Tuskegee policy might make sense of sorts in a very poor and "underdeveloped" country, which can spare only a small number of people and pitiful re-

---

[8] Sonya Rudikoff, "Feminism Reconsidered," *Hudson Review*, vol. 9; 1956; pp. 178–198 at pp. 193–194.

sources for higher education; but in an immensely rich country like our own the shape of the future is much more open, and the undisclosed range of alternatives open to the society should, a fortiori, be open to each individual within it.

Indeed, many of these alternatives will, with general social change, force themselves on the individual whether he wishes or no, and whether he is prepared or no—just as some Negroes today who were trained morally as well as intellectually only to hold semiskilled factory jobs are faced with the threat of automation and its demand for different and more mobile skills. Discontinuities would seem inevitable in American society even if we should eventually learn to value stability as well as expansion, and learn also to make the risks of change for individuals somewhat less traumatic. Thus, an education which seeks to avoid discontent by avoiding discontinuity between college and life is actually maladaptive as well as patronizing. We all need, above all, what Gregory Bateson terms deutero-learning, or learning to learn.

Beyond such pragmatic considerations—though these, too, have their evident ethical implications—it seems to me to be an essential human freedom to be able, in existentialist terms, to *choose oneself*; and discontinuity in education and experience is necessary to allow us to discover some of our potential selves. It is morally wrong to insist that one's sex must predetermine one's vocation or even one's style of life; on this point, the feminists were entirely right (and should not be too harshly blamed for assuming, as any oppressed minority is apt to, that the right vocation and style were to be found in the ways of their oppressors, rather than in possibilities that transcended both the oppressor and the oppressed). Even if one assumes that there are "feminine" gifts, these should not dictate the choices of women who possess those gifts, let alone of women who possess "masculine" gifts (since, as in any typology, we are dealing with overlapping traits, there will always be women more "masculine" than most men, and vice versa). It is a part of freedom to be able to decide the vocational outcome of one's gifts—anything else is conscription—and this means that people must have the right, as it may appear from the outside, to throw away their gifts. (We don't doubt that a girl has the right to deny collective use of her beautiful body, but we do sometimes doubt that the possessor of a "beautiful mind" has as much right to keep it to himself, provided he harms no one.)

This point is so important that it is worth digressing for a moment to indicate the part that vocational guidance plays in this process. Increasingly, and not only in the Army, people take vocational inventories and tests (such as the Strong Vocational Interest Inventory) as the basis for deciding on a career. To the degree that this frees them from parental and other insistence that they do something prestigeful for which they are quite unqualified by talent or interest, this guidance is liberating—as when it convinces a Philistine businessman that a son has no talent for accounting, but a great gift for the plastic arts, or an exigent Jewish mother that her child should not "go for doctor" but would be quite capable and happy selling life insurance. Likewise, such guidance may help surmount peer pressures and seductions, persuading the football star that he should pick his college in terms of his potential abilities as a physiologist, not as a physical ed. major. But increasingly, it appears to me, the students who take these tests do so not only to find an objective support against pressures that would thwart or warp them, but also to discover what they ought to do. They assume that the judgment of tests which seldom go into any real depth is truer than their own preference, and out of fear to be whimsical or irrational they submit to a kind of voluntary selective service.[9]

And what I have said about vocational guidance for careers holds, as already implied, for that more general sort of guidance which tells young women what they ought as young women to feel and do. It may liberate the daughters of unquestioningly intellectual parents to learn that they need not have careers or look down on domesticity out of intellectual or social-aesthetic snobbery. But for most daughters it means, as I have said, to limit the alternatives which are actually going to be available to them. This is clearest in terms of presently foreseeable contingencies. The country is full of widows and divorcees, and of

---

[9] One of the facets of education about which least appears to be known is the influence on young men of their period of military service. To what extent does the anticipation of this already cast its shadow over ambition and hope? To what extent does it serve to homogenize the young by throwing them on each other with little adult excellence which offers alternative models? I do know that for many rural and other educationally less privileged youth, the armed services—even apart from the now defunct GI Bill—were profoundly educational in giving them a sense of possibility, and nothing else could so effectively have pried open their constricted prior orbits. But what of the more privileged—does the Army help inculcate patience with mediocrity, with endless waiting, with living in the immediate present? Or does it make men impatient with these things? The only thing I am fairly sure of is that it does not indoctrinate men with the martial spirit or a love of glory!

women bereft of their children in early middle life; it is also not so empty of women who conclude they made a bad bet in staking everything on marriage, but are now stuck with children and no way of earning more than wages for unskilled work, or of enjoying work enough to compensate for temporary dislocation and emptiness. For such contingencies of life as these, which must now seem very remote to a Bennington undergraduate, I think the best preparation comes with the awakening of the possibility that intellectual and artistic interests can help make life livable even under difficult personal circumstance. To evoke these interests is no disservice to girls (or to boys), but as much an insurance for an open future as an adequate counseling program or other training in the arts of living.[10]

To be sure, I haven't quite answered the argument that women with developed intellectual powers are going to find themselves unhappy in the marriages they cannot help making. One cannot answer this argument from society's point of view alone, by insisting that if girls adapt themselves to what they estimate boys at any given historical moment will want, we shall all—including the children of such unions—grow gradually stupider, especially since we are not turning out *heterae* or geisha girls to entertain and "socialize" the men. But I do feel that it is not only society at large which is the loser if the ferment provided by women of high and potentially unsatisfied aspirations is damped down, but the women themselves. I doubt if an intelligent woman married to a man of limited horizons is worse off for having gone to Bennington or Vassar—and if *he* feels inferior and hence worse off because she did, he has after all many compensations in his work and with "the boys." I am hopeful that an education can be given women which will prepare them for the highest and best eventualities of marriage and/or career while also helping sustain them if it turns out that family life alone does not prove wholly absorbing.

In these last remarks, I have, as often happens, in effect fallen into the trap of practicality of those whose arguments I was opposing. For

[10] This was written before I had an opportunity to study the searching criticisms of some approaches to "contingency education" in Florence R. Kluckhohn's "American Women and American Values," in *Facing the Future's Risks*, Lyman Bryson, ed. (New York: Harper, 1952). This article, and Mrs. Kluckhohn's chapters in *Patterns for Modern Living*, O. H. Mowrer, ed. (Chicago: The Delphian Society, 1952), pp. 25–140, give historical and cross-cultural perspective to themes discussed in my own address.

in fact (as I said to those in the discussion period after my lecture who worried about my "intellectual ivory tower" approach to education) I don't believe in using life as a club over education—I prefer John Dewey's view that education can more appropriately be a club over life. With the image of the continuities of preliterate and folk societies in mind, many people today want to abolish the distinction between school and life, and while this orientation has done much to get rid of indefensibly stuffy academicism, it has also tended to blur creative discontinuities. It deprecates human beings to assume that they stop learning when they are through school, and that they must in school be prepared for everything they may encounter thereafter. And this educational philosophy has come upon us just at the time when the young people themselves, as I indicated at the outset, are seeking to anticipate the future in many different ways: by early job-taking, early marriage, early child-bearing—and early mortgages for household consumer goods.

The media have, I think, had a good deal to do with this anticipation: the ten-year-old, reading *Life* and looking at television, knows much more about the UN, or astronomy, or psychology, than ten-year-olds did in an earlier day. And the media, along with general permissiveness and the parental worries about children's social relations, encourage early dating, so that precocity rules here, too, and one finds in the suburbs many teen-age children already bored with parties, elaborate dances, and even with sex.[11] Obviously, the War did a good deal to set ahead our timetables for living, but it is not entirely responsible for the cult of immediacy which chafes against all postponement and breaks down—in a fashion quite contrary to that of some preliterate tribes (as described in S. N. Eisenstadt's survey, *From Generation to Generation: Age-Grades and the Social Structure*)—the boundaries which separated age-grades from one another.

And this brings me back to my starting point and the curious paradox that while in some ways young people are less sheltered than hitherto—and bear in mind that I am talking entirely about the college-educated and not about the working class—they may also be somewhat less likely to leave home in the metaphorical sense; rather, they may move from one more or less comfortable nest to another. (Please note that I am turning at this point away from the theme of women's education to the more universal problems which are shared by men and women in

---

[11] It would be a not uncommon mistake to think this is a peculiarly American phenomenon, but we deal here with the postindustrial world.

the better-educated strata.) The prohibition against incest has origins lost in prehistory, but it seems to me highly probable that, among other functions, it was and remains a way of dealing with the human dialectic between wishing for adventure and wishing for home. We are, in psychoanalytic theory, as in biblical myths, driven from home, driven from the womb (but such a doctrine does not explain its own discoverers, or any discoverers). As Fromm has said, we face the problem of metaphorical incest in human relations, even where people do not dream— or only dream—of sexual relations with close kin. The boy and girl who marry after going steady since they met in the fifth grade may continually discover novelty in each other, but I have my doubts— especially since our school friends are so very apt to come from the same social and geographical area as ourselves. There is an "incest" of the parish, as well as of the home—as those primitive tribes "recognize" where all marriages must be with members of outgroups.

It may seem strange that I speak in this fashion about a society in which people move, on the average, once in five years, and where most of our social observers worry about rootlessness rather than about overattachment to home. Their worries are not groundless; in fact, it may be that overreaction to rootlessness is one of the principal reasons for the often desperate clinging to what in our society of abundant choice is often a kind of *ersatz* rootedness, like the religiosity which brings so many people to the suburban churches today because "it's a good thing for the children" or because it's a good thing for religion. Thus, both things—traumatic mobility and impoverishing refusals to move—are happening at once, with different emphases in different parts of the social structure: if semiliterate Negroes are leaving the Delta for the quick and caustic literacies of Chicago's Bronzeville, and if workers are moving to what were once white-collar suburbs, it is also true that among the upper middle class some young people are stopping short of their full potentials for diversity of confrontations.

Take, for example, the much discussed practice of going steady, which, to some in my generation, sometimes appears as a kind of group insurance scheme, worthy but unadventurous (to others, who also misunderstand it, including some Catholic priests, it appears as sanctioned promiscuity). Going steady is not new; it has existed among rural and "poor but honest" urban youth for decades; it is only new among the elite of the Ivy League who would a generation ago have as seldom confessed to going steady as to a nonpatronizing attachment to "the governor" or "the old lady." No one should think that the loss of the old stag line and its cruelties should be mourned—nor the loss of the crudities on the one side and innocences on the other that the double standard often implied. And we should be aware that going steady sometimes brings young people to a real awakening and a genuine concern for each other with a commensurate moderation of peer-group pressures; we should not begrudge such pairs their new-found seriousness. It may also be suggested that going steady can, in some settings, give boys greater ease and freedom vis-à-vis each other, with fears of homosexuality muted and with the steady relation as a kind of anchor. Nevertheless, once the pattern of going steady becomes dominant, and nearly everyone in some high schools and colleges is, or is supposed to be, pinned, the choices available to the remainder shrink and many of them, too, will get pinned as the only way out, making it still more difficult to play the field, or not to play, or to feel justified in idiosyncrasy. I have in mind, for another example of potential constriction, the new suburbs where young couples have reacted to transiency of residence by limiting their friendships and civic activities to the particular suburb in which they live at the moment—indeed, we see here that the pattern of going steady, which permits shifts only consecutively, is recreated among the young marrieds.

People may move around a lot, in other words, without leaving "home"—as everyone knows who has observed Americans abroad. Certainly, when I recently studied a group of nearly two hundred interviews with college seniors, mostly men, I concluded that they had not in any profound sense left home in coming to college, nor would they necessarily do so in entering the well-marked first stages they anticipated in business or the professions.[12] . . . I have referred earlier to the fact that girls are likely to move in a narrower orbit than boys, and they lack whatever break the Army provides; moreover, as Talcott Parsons and Mirra Komarovsky and others have shown, girls are more tied to their mothers than boys to the parent of either sex, and in that way may be less prepared to start a new family and new life than the boys.

How can we reconcile this lack of productive discontinuity with the seemingly enhanced worldliness of the young? It would seem as if home and world had become in some fashion amalgamated, so that home is far from being a nest in the traditional sense: it is rather a nodule in a complex network of communications; moreover, the parents and children are not as differentiated from each other as was true in an earlier

[12] See "The Found Generation," pp. oo–oo.

day when parents married later and behaved in a more reserved way vis-à-vis children. Thus, the young are rapidly sophisticated in the home, and the boundaries of home and world are less firm; parents do not—fearing to be overprotective—hang on to their children but, as already stated, energetically facilitate their social contacts outside the home (often beyond what the children prefer or profit from). Likewise, the high school, with its social studies and its elaborate extracurricular life, its fraternities and sororities, anticipates at least the externalia of college, also reducing discontinuity. And when, as many educators plan, we have community colleges everywhere, a large proportion of young people will even attend college under the same auspices as their high schools, with the same people, and, in all too many cases, at the same intellectually undemanding pace;[13] there will be even less discontinuity.

It is, I realize, stretching the concept of "home" quite far to ask it to cover both the dormitory where the children sleep and the school—often in competition with the home—where they play and work. Perhaps the situation is coming to resemble that of a kibbutz or collective settlement where home-and-school are merged into a single local environment for which all children born there are captives. The young people are not kept out of the world during a chrysalis stage; rather, from the age where they can first look at TV or participate in adult gatherings, they are as it were innoculated with the world in doses large enough to make still more massive doses seem quite uncalled for. The girls I spoke of at the beginning who stayed near home to go to college have not felt oppressed: they are not capable of being either homesick or sick of home, and they do not know that they have a problem of leaving home.

This is perhaps among the reasons why we have not had in this country a youth movement of the German form, in which parental pressures and scholastic mentors were thrown off and young people sought to establish ties with the opposite sex, with "life," and with general movements of thought. It did not take a youth movement for our young people to reject many of the differentiations which an older culture valued—our high schools and colleges have long had a generalized amateur flavor about them, in which the students judge each other

[13] Some junior or community colleges act as transfer points, sorting out those capable of profiting from a first-rate four-year college and sending them on—a policy which of course requires that the top colleges remain willing to accept transfers. It goes without saying, moreover, that many "junior" colleges are more alive than their "seniors."

not as specialists but as whole personalities, and thus maintain a group spirit and affective ties which in other countries, as Professor Eisenstadt has noted, were only rebelliously achieved under the aegis of an elaborate ideology. And, indeed, why should young Americans become *Wandervogel* when their parents allow them the use of the family car (or their own) as soon as the law allows?

I discussed some of their matters, insofar as they might bear on educational policy, at a conference at Vassar called by the student curriculum committee. On the panel with me was Professor Everett Hunt of Swarthmore, who described his school's honors system in which for the last two years selected students pursue a course of study often more independent—and of higher quality—than is prevalent at many graduate schools. He observed, however, that some Swarthmore students were inclined to reject the program as involving undemocratic distinctions, harsh on those not admitted to honors work, and in some degree confining those who did such work almost exclusively to small seminars among each other. A number of the Vassar students appeared to share these misgivings—indeed, I was led to inquire of them whether they would pick the hockey team or the madrigal group without regard to skill (by lot?), lest the good players and singers be undemocratically deprived of the chance to mix with the bad ones.[14] Apart from what I regard as a fallacious definition of democracy, there is in this reaction something of great importance for our understanding of the relation between the world and the parish in education. For among the most sensitive students today are some whose wish to anticipate the future includes a fear lest their associations in school and college be *too* parochial, in not including enough people from across the tracks. This sometimes leads them to the seemingly parodoxical decision not to go away to boarding school "where all the kids will be middle class," but instead to attend the local high school (which in fact is likely, if it includes a socio-economic cross-section, to be highly stratified). They act as if

[14] In a discussion of this theme at a conference on Utilization of Human Resources, John Gardner, President of the Carnegie Corporation, made the useful comment that in a society which values grades as a measure of total performance it is understandable that those who can't play hockey or sing feel less excluded than those termed "stupid"—a verdict even "femininist" girls don't know how to endure. In schools where they are taken seriously (as, despite teacher complaints, they are by most middle-class families), grades often become the "money" of the system, by which academic values are all too simply rendered comparable.

their later life could not possibly bring them into contact with all sorts of people—just as in their nearly unanimous option for steady dating they act as if they would never again have a chance for intimacy with a single person. And, since the confrontation with "alien tribes" from other social strata is often stereotypical, they actually meet less idiosyncrasy and creative discontinuity than they would in a program with more apparent homogeneity of students—for what is noteworthy about the gifted (even in the middle class) is that they are different from each other.

On second thought, what I have just said should be restated as a question, not an assertion, for until we know better what we mean by "gifted" and how to enlarge our notion of what we mean and then how to select it, young people may justifiably remain skeptical about the varieties they will meet at a selective school or college.[15] And, just because our confrontations are so generally with our preconceptions of others, we may not know how to experience the differences that are actually there when the surface appears homogeneous.

The fears I have been discussing of being too sheltered, too parochial, are especially strong among some of the more thoughtful students at the women's colleges. They often maintain what I regard as a myth about the proper mix for an educational institution, namely that it should be lifelike in its quasi-parliamentary representation of both sexes and all conditions, even if this means cutting down the actual variety open to particular students who might recognize and profit from variety. One might think that the artificial injection of the big world into the home we have been describing would make young people feel less isolated from broad contact during their college years. After all, they have "met" Marlon Brando, and read Françoise Sagan at fifteen, and I doubt if in all the Ivy League one could today find so much as a bus load of girls so spinsterish as to be shocked at a dirty word or an intoxicated and indecent boy. Yet life holds its lure and makes its glib

[15] A study of public high schools in Illinois which James Coleman of the Sociology Department of the University of Chicago has undertaken aims to uncover some of the factors associated with pluralistic as against monolithic value-systems in the student culture. Preliminary examination of yearbooks and other records indicates that there is wide variation in the degree to which high schools of similar ethnic and social-class composition distribute the honors—athletic, academic, musical, social, etc.—which are valued; and hence either limit or enlarge both the definitions of what is important among young people and the opportunities to pursue it.

and unexamined claims even on people whose life expectancy is beyond threescore and ten.[16]

Many of my fellow educators put all this down to American anti-intellectualism and long for the undisputed hegemony of the curriculum. For my part, despite my conviction that many students now shortchange themselves in overanticipating the future, I am not wholly grieved that the curriculum has to compete with the extracurriculum. Indeed, in the better colleges today, the curriculum is more enticing than it was a couple of decades ago, and does not suffer the kind of mindless rejection which was then common; the "gentleman's C" which was once the passport to our own inchoate youth movement is nearly gone. And on the other hand it may be an advance if at the women's colleges the curriculum no longer finds perhaps quite the same sort of docile and overconscientious acceptance by the "good girls" that it once did. We have seen that the curriculum has to defend itself, in the first instance, by showing some connection with life—life now rather than life later; and while this leads to much restriction of intellectual orbit, it is also an opportunity for imaginative redefinition.

As a teacher, I have found undergraduates often amazingly willing to accept novel connections of things and people with one another, even if these transcend or contradict their images of contemporary life. As one instance, the movement for general education would seem to be supported by the growing feeling of young people that they want what Erich Fromm terms "relatedness" rather than bits and pieces in their lives. As another instance, the American Studies programs have appeal, and so do interdisciplinary courses such as the one in culture and personality that I have taken part in at Chicago. Strikingly enough, the classics at some few schools have had an extraordinary revival—no longer simply as a status-bound accomplishment, but as an effort to grasp the values of another epoch, in some ways like our own; in pattern, these are "Mediterranean Area Studies," like the other area programs which are popular. And who would have thought thirty years ago that theology and religion courses would have such an impact on some campuses as is the case at present, along with a widened interest in myth and ritual? To some, both these trends may appear simply as evasions of the hard

---

[16] Undoubtedly, fear of atomic disaster helps speed up young people's timetables, and gives them a sense of urgency. But such feelings, in my judgment, would exist today in our culture, if less powerfully, quite apart from international menaces; indeed, the latter often serve as useful rationalizations for a lack of inner steadiness.

economic and political questions of today, and no doubt this is partly true. Yet the very search for these more private areas of meaning indicates a willingness to reject life as given, and points to an effort to make something new of it.

On the extracurricular side, we find many analogous developments. The musical culture and skills of the Bennington undergraduate today would surprise not only Tocqueville but the student's grandmother. Student glee clubs are not any longer satisfied to sing "glee" type songs, or vintage musical comedy; they prefer madrigals or Bach chorales, or maybe a Benjamin Britten opera; and the traveling quartets that play on college campuses have audiences of far wider sympathies than was conceivable a generation ago. It is the same in all the arts, in sculpture and ceramics, architecture and painting. And let me emphasize that these cultural concerns are not simply carried by the womenfolk; in the general loosening of roles I have been discussing, they are coming to be men's business as well. Moreover, as I have implied, they are not any more the affair of the upper classes only, but a domain in which great numbers of the college educated are convinced they can find, not status merely (though this is no doubt one of the motives), but meaning, enjoyment, and connectedness.

Again, I must stress that the relation between Bach or Bartok and contemporary life is oblique; it does not stare one in the face, but has to be discovered, as the Italians of the period of the Renaissance had to discover the purport for them of the Greek heritage. For many of those who play chamber music, including jazz, or sing madrigals, one aspect of meaning is relatedness with others through the medium of music; for culture today is largely something shared, rather than something enjoyed solipsistically. Another aspect may be the search for quality as such, in the face of many temptations to mediocrity.

Young people are often apathetic toward their elders' preoccupations, but seldom cynical. Underneath their defenses, they are eager to be shown—shown meanings, connections and ultra-individual purposes. Save for those who want to get into medical school, bucking for grades, with its contamination of the curriculum, seems to me less overpowering—and at the other extreme many girls are less zealous to get nothing higher than B's to prove they are not *too* bright. Likewise, the campus big wheel today seems not to have everything his or her way: people don't go out for the college paper any more at the better schools simply to get their names into print, nor die a thousand deaths for Wellesley on the hockey field. The young are less gullible consumers of the standard fare of the academic disciplines, or of the extracurricular legends, than they once were—they are perhaps slightly more gullible about what life requires of them now, this minute, but gullible in part because they know, and care to know, more than they once did about the adult nonpolitical world.

As I have said, I do not wholly regret the pressure this development puts on the curriculum. Our culture is much better off if the good things in it are kept good by having to compete with the dross.[17]

As to what "good" is, in curricular terms, I am not fanatical about content: it can be general education or something else which serves to inspire the faculty with a conviction of intellectual advance, while retaining high standards of excellence. What I want for young people is that they shall, in leaving the orbit of home and parish, somewhere be exposed to excellence, and the form here is perhaps more important than the content. Thus, when I sit with the dogmatists of general education, my memory recurs (with that tendency to autobiography we can at best control and not wholly escape in thinking about education) to a course I had with C. K. Webster in British diplomatic history during the regimes of Castlereagh and Canning. While I have forgotten the details, I got a sense in that course of craftsmanship that made a profound impression; I learned how a fine historian went devotedly through mountains of documents—and enjoyed it; and this was a significant part of my general education.

Dwight Chapman, a member of the Psychology Department at Vassar, who attended the conference I have referred to, wrote me at its close a letter along similar lines, from which I quote with his permission:

> I was wondering out loud, you remember, what we have to offer to take the place of bygone securities that used to let students dare to escape the lonely crowd and enjoy freedom. Now I think I know of one thing—and I wonder if you'd agree that perhaps you have one form of it at Chicago?
> Here's the notion: I was struck toward the end of the Saturday-

[17] For similar reasons, I wish business careers offered competition for academic personnel on bases other than salary and perquisites. I'd like to see universities have to become more interesting and alive as educative institutions for their faculties by having harder competition from creative men in business—today, as things are, if a university can pay enough it can recruit a large proportion of the men who want an opportunity to be creative in an encouraging milieu.

morning session with how many people seemed to be agreeing that a student grows up best in college if he gradually takes on additional little bits of liberty and responsibility—in titrated doses. Well, wouldn't an anthropologist have fun making a rag rug of that idea! Because, what are the cultures in which people do a lot of rapid maturing? Certainly not the ones in which the young pass gradually, ambiguously, and puzzlingly into adulthood, but rather the ones that set a time when things change radically and that mark out that time with a good, unmistakable puberty-rite.

The British system was able to celebrate such a rite between public school and college (and the German one between *Gymnasium* and university). All of a sudden you went from lockstep to liberty—and expected to—and were publicly identified as one of the elite who had deliberately accepted that commitment. Contemporary American colleges don't dare celebrate the rite, because they still have some of the school's work to do. But *an* answer is to set up a crucial ritual somewhere between lower and upper college—to say, so to speak, all right, you've been at college two years now, and school is over; now either go to college or go home. And I take it that the Chicago qualifying exams for upper college are just that. (An improvement might be to tattoo upper-college folk—but I'll settle for something short of the full anthropological analogy.)

I can enjoy technical arguments about whether to start with the Great Books or the Great Headlines; but a corollary of my thesis is that it may matter less whether a college is Bennington or St. John's; and that what does matter is that it be vociferously identified as something Out of This World. Then, when you go there, you are tattooed, and you *do* have a front tooth knocked out, and your lips are pierced for platters. And because you're that queer, you're more than half free to educate yourself instead of going to college, like everyone else.

Only in some such way will we manage, in my judgment as in his, to keep under control this curious worldly parochialism of the young I have been seeking to describe. I believe, as I have said, that people do not only desire the womb, the nest, the family; rather, they want—enough of them to have kept man going—to leave the womb and the home: novelty is as imperative as security; discovery as much a human "need" as stability. Whereas a few girls at Bryn Mawr, Vassar, or Mount Holyoke a generation ago were striving, along with equally career-minded and ambitious boys, to pass the point of no return and to leave a mark on the planet, the boys themselves have today in large part changed their aims: as we have seen, they want the good life—a life in which the girls have a definite place—even at the expense of the famous or successful life. They have seen the shallowness of many of the goals to which they once sacrificed domestic and private happiness—whether these goals were financial or political—and when the corporate economy has taken over the duty of being the good provider for all but the families of teachers, social workers, and clergymen, is it surprising that the girls these young men marry find the bargain an attractive one, and the sacrifices it requires unimportant? The image of togetherness presented in a Doubleday Christmas ad (1956) is revealing: the wife is sitting upright next to her young daughter in a matching T-shirt, while the young husband is lying next to her: all are reading, and all under the same lamp. In the summer they may all be fishing, or working in the garden. If the feminist style has disappeared, some of its accoutrements remain: college men today want wives who can read, and who are capable of understanding them and the world they both live in. College remains the principal opportunity for developing this panoply of permitted talents, and making them appear to be worth cultivating.

Perhaps I speak only for my own generation in thinking that nonetheless there is something missing here, in the mature and in many ways advantageous life plan laid out by many thoughtful college students of today. With more choices than were ever available for so many before, there is a subtle constriction at the edges—where the immoderate begins. "Togetherness" is a fine ideal, not to be scorned by the malicious, or defended against by the overintellectual, but its very value depends on a continuing dialectic with apartness. And college provides the best and most nearly justified opportunity I know for apartness—one not likely to recur for many until much later in life—for apartness from "life" and from the role definitions provided by even such quite loose garments as our sexual and ethnic identities. If only I could convince the young people I know that "life" will catch up with them even if they try to escape it! But no, they are like grubs convinced *they* will never be butterflies, and hence unable to take full advantage of being a grub. As Erik Erikson says, the young need a moratorium, if they only knew it.

The Search for Challenge
(1958)

I want to discuss the problem of discovering challenge in what Galbraith calls the "affluent society," challenge when the older challenges based on the subsistent society and the struggle for sheer survival are no longer imperative. One of the perspectives I want to use is cross-cultural, and we shall look at an anthropological example. Another is historical, and we shall look at ourselves as we were in an earlier day—this, too, is cross-cultural. The third perspective is genetic, in which I shall ask what sorts of challenges are requisite at what stages of one's own life cycle. This is a vast topic. I don't bring to it the erudition of a Toynbee or an Alfred Kroeber, but on the contrary I shall bring to it some observations and free associations in the hope of stimulating further thinking.

Periodically throughout Western history, men have imagined that collective as well as individual life could be better, or at least less bad. In times of chaos and of war they dreamed of social stability and hierarchy, as Plato did in *The Republic*, or as Sir Thomas More did in his *Utopia*. Myths of heaven refracted the popular weariness of toil, short life, illness, and social disorganization. Periodically, too, men could be mobilized for revolt against plainly oppressive conditions, once these conditions had lightened enough to make them seem less than divinely given. For the ills that have plagued man have been such nightmares that men at all but the lowest levels of brutishness could grasp the possibility of being less badly off, once they *were* less badly off. Today, however, we are faced with a paradox: the United States and a few other rich countries have caught up with many Utopian ideals while at the same time literal belief in heaven has almost vanished. In this country people suffer less from nightmarish misery than from the more subtle disorders previously buried by the harsh struggle for existence.

We can see an analogue to this development in the short career of psychoanalytic therapy, which is about sixty years old. When Freud began, patients came to him who were suffering from hysteria, from paralyzed arms, from inability to talk, from obvious symptoms. By helping them internalize what they had externalized, that is, what they had (so to speak) thrown into an arm, it was relatively easy, even speedy, to cure them. Today, in contrast, one sees such cases only, for instance in this country, among immigrant Poles in Pittsburgh or among rural Southerners in West Virginia. Many therapists go through their entire lives without ever seeing such a case. People come to analysis today who do not suffer from an external subsistence problem, from a paralysis. Their limbs work and their sexual organs work, but somehow life doesn't live up to its billing for them; they carry on an unrepressed interior dialogue, but it bores them. Often, I might add, all they do is include the analyst in the dialogue and bore him. They need, usually without knowing it, a new vision and not merely a new way of talking about themselves; in fact, most patients today talk very freely indeed about the things that in Freud's day would have been considered private and intimate.[1]

Yet, as we all know, most of the rest of the world would trade places any day with the rich American and trade its miseries for his neuroses. An ironic instance are the Manus, whom Margaret Mead revisited several years ago, twenty-five years after her first field trip in 1928. When she had first been there, the Manus had been a Stone Age people; then had come World War II, and their island had been a staging area for American troops. When she arrived, the Manus had just finished throwing out a Catholic mission because the mission was trying to get them to adjust slowly to the ways of the West, whereas they wanted to take over the distance to modernity in one big jump. They thought the white people in the mission were patronizing them, holding out on them, trying to ration the blessings of industrial society. You can imag-

[1] A number of people have taken exception to this position and to the similar outlook of Allen Wheelis in *The Quest for Identity*. They insist that their own therapeutic experience shows that the old-fashioned neuroses are far from vanishing; that sexual problems are still exigent, and nearly ubiquitous; that merely the forms of repression and defense have changed. To these criticisms, I have been inclined to reply that all "geologic" strata exist simultaneously in the United States; that different therapists have different clienteles, and evoke different aspects of the same clientele; that all problems, sexual and existential, are of course interrelated, but that there are some people for whom the problem of meaning is more significant even than the problem of sex; and that the question of the distribution of these several strata and symptomatologies remains an empirical and open one.

ine the position of the mission which was saying in effect, "It isn't just so wonderful to be Westernized, and take it easy." For the Manus the effort to act like Americans was a heroic challenge; one, in fact, which produced a revolutionary leader, Paliau, a man of enormous strength and determination. For him, it was a new religion to become Americanized.

The Manus, like many South Pacific peoples, had had their craze of cargo cults in which traditional objects had been thrown in the ocean in the fond belief that planes or boats would come, piled high with the white man's goods, if only the Manus would propitiate the cargo by appropriate action. Even where the cargo cult does not take such open and violent form, it exists. Daniel Lerner, in *The Passing of Traditional Society*, discusses interviews which were done a few years ago in seven countries of the Middle East. In these, the theme that life in America is more modern and, hence, better comes up again and again; whatever the political hostilities toward America, one finds this lure among Egyptians and Syrians and others who are, politically and ideologically, violently antagonistic to America, yet admire it. The dream of America —the dream of plenty—is shared by people at all levels, and it is also rejected on religious and traditional grounds by many who are obviously influenced by it. The conflicts are only about the rate of speed with which one should move to plenty and the mode, and the Malthusian handicaps and how they are to be overcome, and the values to be reintegrated by doing so. And all this is new and exciting to peoples to whom it happens, but it is not new to the West—we have had it.

In fact, we can today in some considerable degree measure the backwardness of a social class or a nation by the extent to which America provides it with a model of Utopia. For the intellectuals of Europe and of India, for instance, America is more to be feared than admired, distrusted than copied. The collapse of the image of America as a vision of Jeffersonian equality and of orderly democracy has been rapid and is not merely the result of Communist propaganda. One factor is the shutting off of immigration after the First World War, which doused the hopes of millions of South Europeans and Levantines that they might find a personal Utopia in the United States; and in these interviews of Professor Lerner one finds this also coming up again and again—people from Syria or Turkey who have uncles in America and who would like to come here and can't.

The more vociferous Americans themselves, moreover, in desperate search for a self-justifying ideology, have been tempted to identify *the*

American way with their own tendentious misinterpretations of our economy as one of free enterprise or to boast of American technological virtuosity or of the workingman's standard of living. This last might appear to appeal to workingmen in some places, but it does not appeal to the elites whose own frustrated materialism is all too well acted out on their behalf by strident Americans.

I have in the last years talked to a good many non-Americans who are visiting this country in the hope of hastening the economic development of their own land, and they have gone home again with an ambivalent feeling: can they reduce poverty, cut the birth rate, start cumulative economic growth, all without arriving at the American destiny —that is, arriving at the place we are now, from which the next steps are opaque—once the novelty wears off?

I would be giving the wrong impression if I were understood to contend that there is no utopianism in present-day America. There are first of all many conservative people who find in the American past an adequate image for the future: they contend that if only we balanced our budgets, spanked our kids, worked hard and uncomplainingly, tore down all the teachers colleges—all would be well. And there are many others who find in the huge distance we still have to travel toward economic, and especially toward racial, equality enough challenge for their lifetimes—and in a sense it is enough. Likewise, the effort of the Communist bloc to overtake America has given still other Americans of both major parties the feeling that with a little discipline and locker-room talk, along with better scouting and recruiting for scientists, all will be recouped. Perhaps the major benefit thus provided for Americans is the renewed conviction that there is a game and that winning it can give meaning to life. In my opinion none of these, not even the generous one of getting rid of the residues of inequality, is sufficient to mobilize social energies to take the next obscure steps in American life that would bring us a measure of international security and more adequate social goals for an age of plenty.

In this situation many of the most sensitive and truly disinterested young people have given up the larger societal goals to pursue what I might call the utopianism of private life. It is in the family first of all, and beyond that in the circle of friends and neighbors, that one looks for Jeffersonian simplicity, an idyll of decency, generosity, and sensibility. Much of the confusion in current discussion is due to failure to distinguish between the high quality of these personal goals of young people and the low quality of our social aims. That is, if one is looking at the texture of individual life in America, this country is harboring, despite all surrounding miasmas, extraordinarily fine enclaves whose tone, though not ascetic, has something in common with the outlook of Utopian colonies in the last century, or with Hopi pueblos, or with the spirit of some of our great nineteenth-century dissidents, whether Melville or Whitman, William James or Bellamy. In many past epochs of cultural greatness the dichotomy between an avant-garde few and the brutalized many was taken for granted and would occasionally perpetuate itself for long periods. But in the United States today the contrast between the private utopianism that I have spoken of and the widespread low level of vision in the general population, especially vis-à-vis political activities, seems to my mind both less tolerable and less viable for the long term. With the growth of interdependence within and among nations, private virtues do not become public vices but may become almost irrelevant—isolated families at the mercy of fall-out. I don't expect every young person to take part in the development of a more inclusive Utopia than "familism," but I would like to see a better proportion achieved between private and public visions; indeed, I believe that private life would be enriched if the two spheres were both more forcefully cultivated.[2]

When I spent a summer in the Soviet Union twenty-seven years ago, I met many eager young Communists who had enthusiastically junked all private aims in the communal enterprise of "building socialism." Amid a Philistine culture made desolate with slogans, they *were* building socialism in an all too literal sense, i.e., they were building dams, railroads, factories, and machine tractor stations and Communist party apparatus. They brought to their work the zeal of pioneers and, as a blueprint for their own activities, the model of American industrial

[2] A number of students took these comments to mean that I was opposed to painters, writers, composers, and other artists—or was asking of them a dedication to "agitprop" activities. Of course not. People don't have unlimited energies and have to make choices reflecting their own idiosyncratic temperaments and gifts. I don't want to see a good artist become a poor politician—or vice versa (any more than I want to see a good engineer become a bad physicist because "pure" science has greater prestige). However, I believe that many artistically inclined people shun political discussion when it could actually enliven them, and shun it out of misunderstanding, fashion, and fear. Moreover, I think there are occasions when the sense of solidarity should help us overcome our more characteristic isolation on issues—such as the current arms race—when all life and hence all art is threatened.

achievement. At the Stalingrad tractor plant, then barely beginning to produce, I saw fanatical young Stakhanovites (and I suppose the term "Stakhanovite" is unknown to many undergraduates today; that is a kind of Russian version of an Eagle Scout) working with tremendous zeal in the midst of a mass of sullen peasants, new to industry and by no means reconciled to its restrictions. I had gone over with a group of American students, some of whom found this spectacle in contrast to the America of the Depression marvelously exhilarating. It was a battle with simple rules and clear goals, or so it seemed, and, in fact, the reports from Stalingrad in *Pravda* and *Izvestia* were couched in the language of battle—so many tractors had been turned out that week on the Stalingrad front, or there were so many defeats in the battle for electrification, and so on. I thought then, and I still think now, that the tasks confronting Americans are more exhilarating but also more problematical. It would be child's play for us to build the Turk-Sib Railway or the Dneprostroi Dam, although, as I shall indicate later, every child should have this opportunity. We have to make our own model of the future as we go, in a situation which is new historically.

It is at this point that the Communists have done us an immense and possibly fatal disservice by so largely discrediting secular Utopias at the very time when religion no longer offers an illuminating otherworldly Utopia but has become to a great extent an adjunct to private life. While it is helpful for people to realize that fanaticism in pursuit of Utopian goals is a danger, allowing people to express their worst impulses while defeating their best hopes, the reaction among contemporary non-Communist intellectuals has gone much too far. Today the most influential Utopian writings are satiric anti-Utopias such as *Brave New World* or *1984*, which extrapolate, in the former case largely from the United States and in the latter largely from the Soviet Union, to their visions of a more total despair.[3]

[3] A number of critics have objected to the very term "Utopia"; as one colleague succinctly put it, "The only Utopia I am willing to think about at this moment is the society which develops people who will not need Utopias." There is a lot of semantic confusion between "Utopia" and "ideology"; I use the former term (in Karl Mannheim's sense) to mean a viable and conceivable society, not an intellectual swindle for True Believers. I think one needs goals based on the truth about man's nature and about society and that these goals have to be more than piecemeal and *ad hoc*, but I won't quarrel with people who would prefer to call this a vision rather than a Utopia.

The Poles and for a time the Hungarians who rose against the terror could express in the writings of students and intellectuals a kind of minimum-decency platform—humane and sensible, but Utopian only in contrast to Stalinism. They have been like hysterics recovering from paralysis in the early days of psychoanalysis; and as the hysterics, once cured, could continue to operate on the moral capital of Victorianism, so these Polish and Hungarian revisionists can draw on the moral capital of prewar Social Democracy; hence can project into the future their recall of the slightly less gruesome past, just as heaven is often the retroactive image of a childhood Eden.

As I have said, however, we Americans have caught up with our future at the very historical moment when the Communist example has done much to dampen Utopian thinking; such thinking, I need hardly say, is never easy. All literature shows that writers can more readily picture terrors than delights. For one thing, as Margaret Mead has pointed out, we can all empathize with terrors, whereas delights, if they go beyond platitude, differentiate us. (Contrary to Tolstoy's epigram, all happy families are not alike.) I have been struck with how difficult it is for people—even storytellers and artists—to imagine nonexistent things: to imagine, for instance, nonexistent animals, they can only put parts together which are already available and come up with a centaur or a unicorn, much as science fiction for the most part is more science than fiction. Now that we can draw on the world storehouse of cultures through our knowledge of anthropology and history, we can in imagination make unicorns, i.e., fit pieces of culture together, but we find it hard to invent new ones.

And yet on the whole, social science, while enabling us to draw on a far wider spectrum of human experience than any one culture has ever had available to it, may have contributed to the decline of Utopian thinking. To free themselves from moralism and the kind of shallow evolutionism one can find in Herbert Spencer, social scientists in our time largely have eschewed either looking at evolution or engaging in prophecy. Somebody asked me recently whether sociologists weren't "do-gooders" and I said I was afraid that that was a thing of the past. The most frequent device for saving thought and conscience here is to say that the social scientist when he makes proposals for change, rather than presenting limited alternatives to a powerful decision-maker, is simply a citizen. As a scientist that is not his business. And science increasingly has become his business, and a business carried on in a businesslike way, making measurements and keeping up with the literature. Utopianism reappears in disguised forms, to be sure, as for instance in the belief that if vaster sums were spent on the sciences, prediction and control could take the place of prophecy; there is also the narrower Utopian hope that if each subdivision of science pursues its private aims, some later ecumenical movement may reunite the scattered findings within a grand scheme. (The very largeness of the branches of social science in so vast a country as this means that men can live their whole intellectual lives within the boundaries of a single subdiscipline.) Moreover, as more and more people go to college and more and more people teach those who go to college, intellectuals are increasingly becoming attached to universities; this is a trend which may have ambivalent consequences in the light of the experience of the past that many of the most seminal ideas have come from outside the academy. And social science, like other intellectual activities, has been steadily democratized, in the sense that its concepts and findings are regarded as valid only if they can be taught to any competent graduate student. Thus, analysis of social wholes, entire cultures, which remains something of an art, is not a game at which any number can play, and it tends to be deprecated and hence postponed until that quite distant and hardly foreseeable day when it can be handled in terms available to anybody. Thinking, that is, about a whole society is not something that can readily be democratized. And as for Utopian thinking, most of us after childhood form categorical images of our society and, while aided by images of hell we can imagine things being worse, we cannot imagine them being significantly better.

In addition, although the first explorations into social science often made men hopeful, as they made Condorcet or Marx hopeful (although not Malthus), later immersion tends to make people less hopeful, for it destroys the illusion that the masses have noble dreams that the capitalists or the bureaucrats repress. It shows how immense and how far-reaching are the changes in men's hopes and desires that would be necessary for the creation of a better world: we do not stand outside the portals of heaven only because some vested interests bar the way. And market research is frequently interpreted in such a way as to confirm the status quo; it makes, when conducted by politicians, things that might be worth doing "politically impossible." Let me take a trivial illustration: we go to people for instance and ask them if they would like a small car, and they say "no," or they say "yes" in such a way as to mean "no." Then we proceed to make many big cars, thus changing the visual landscape and people's expectations of what a car looks like and thus prove that people don't like small cars. Even so, a change in circumstances, let us say a slight recession, can show how evanescent was the earlier preference, especially among educated people who, having gone to college, have opinions and tastes which fluctuate more rapidly than do those of people of lesser learning. And, of course, market and public opinion research often can serve, if well done, to show that people no longer believe what they are supposed to believe and this can be emancipating.[4]

Nevertheless, it seems to me that over-all the effect on us of our increasing knowledge of man is to curb radical departures of thought in the social sphere, less I think because of McCarthyite opposition than because we ourselves want to feel we are sensible, calm, well-organized people. The great achievement of the physical sciences, in my judgment, is not their ability to codify and measure—this is a detail, though important—but their ability to go beyond common or even uncommon sense to hold ideas—like the concept of the wavicle—which are paradoxical or contradictory and which bear no relation to daily sense experience. (It would be better, on second thought, to speak not of daily sense experience but rather of our cultural and linguistic codification of reality: those categorical imperatives which result from our specific and historical way of seeing as well as from perspectives framed by the human condition as such.)

Young children are somewhat less firm in their control of and by the established ways of seeing reality, and I want now to turn from the general and cross-cultural problem I have been discussing, of how one finds or how one fails to find a new vision, to the genetic one, that is, to see what forms of challenge can be expected in the different ages of

[4] A good many students in discussion took the position that social science, at least under present conditions, could never be emancipating, but only manipulative. The dangers of manipulation are real enough, particularly if one is thinking of the long-run climate of opinion and of the indirect effects of living in that climate; but I feel that there is a great tendency to exaggerate the power of "the hidden persuaders" to influence people in making short-run choices. This fear of the power of the Madison Avenue adman to put really important things over on us (and not merely relatively inconsequential choices among consumer goods, or among nearly identical political personalities) seems to me a highbrow version of demagogically inspired fears that the bankers or the Jews or some other small conspiratorial group pull the strings behind all events. In any case, defeatism about the potentialities of social science for nonmanipulative ends tends to be self-confirming and to leave this as yet quite awkward tool to work only on behalf of the status quo.

man from childhood to maturity. Observers of children's play, such as Piaget and Erik Erikson, have commented on children's desire for mastery, the integrative quality of much play. The studies of these men lend some support to the belief that children at certain stages of development can be freer in their aesthetic sensibility and their formation of concepts than in earlier more literal, and later more conventional stages. Other students of childhood (notably Ernest Schachtel in his paper, "On Memory and Childhood Amnesia") have noted the ability of great artists, such as Proust or Paul Klee, to recapture the codifications of childhood without going crazy: ability, that is, to retranslate the freedom and imagination of childhood into adult terms. Percival and Paul Goodman have shown that kind of freedom and imagination in *Communitas*, where they employ the traditions of Utopian thinking and the customs of other cultures to create several kinds of social and architectural designs for the future of America. In fact, they employ the model of children's play in much of their discussion. But I don't know any case where a researcher has systematically asked children before their teens to depict the sort of world they would like to live in, that they would find exhilarating, or has invented a game which would call on their conceivable abilities for making cultural kaleidoscopes. (We have, of course, games which children play which simulate the adult world as it is, such as Monopoly; and *Mad* Magazine recently suggested that children might also play other adult games, for instance, "alimony"—player who reaches Reno first wins—"draft dodger," and "make-out"—in which boy chases girl. Here once more the macabre is easier to evoke than the Utopian.)

Moving on now from children to adults, I want to mention one example of approaching Utopia through the techniques of social science —an example that, I fear, shows how little these techniques can contribute at present. I have in mind a study done at the University of Michigan for the Michigan Bell Telephone Company in which a group of articulate adults were invited to let their imaginations roam free and to tell trained interviewers what sort of things they would like to see in the "world of tomorrow." Out of 126 interviews, mainly with well-educated respondents, there were, in fact, few suggestions that were at all visionary. Respondents want a machine which will bring them the morning newspaper from the doorstep. They want conveyor-belt highways and drive-in supermarkets and automatic car controls. They want a personal air-conditioning unit inside their clothes. (This reminded me of Aldous Huxley's novel *Antic Hay*.) Or they want a machine which will bring them any sight, sound, smell, or climate they choose without having to go out to find it. They want to be able to bring back fond memories at will and to erase annoyances at will. One wants a device to look a doctor over without going to his office, another a device to make it easy to complain to a supercilious salesperson, or another a gadget to allow one safely and anonymously to bawl out somebody. One wistfully asks, and here is one of the few quasi-political suggestions, for some means of making suggestions to the legislative government (that's his term), and still another says, "I want to be able to visit relatives and friends without missing church." One wants "more variety in my daily living—a surprise every day."

If such wishes can be called Utopian at all, they are once more very private; they are seldom connected with any plan for the development of the individual's powers, let alone any plan for society more extensive than that of the person who wanted whole cities covered with plastic to keep out the weather. Many of the suggestions represent what I have sometimes called the cult of effortlessness. I speak of it as a cult, for I don't believe that most Americans not presently overworked seek this nirvana with steady passion. But it is striking that in the interviews, and perhaps reflecting their relaxed form, no one seems to wish for obstacles, for challenges, for things that take time and require effort.[5]

Children assuredly are seldom like that unless they are sick: they are often a problem for parents and other adults, and for people who have to enforce parietal rules too, because they have energy to burn. To some extent, children fall back on the nearly universal culture of games, for which they need only modest equipment and a modest tradition which they fondly elaborate. At the December 1957 American Anthropological meetings I saw films from New Guinea showing children at play—they kicked balls, climbed trees, imitated adult ceremonies, including a complete funeral with a dead chicken as corpse. They also slid down mountains on homemade sleds, not on snow (this was in the tropics) but on sand or grass. And as I watched them I recalled my

[5] Much could be said about these interviews and how their lack of dialectical bite may have contributed to the banality of the responses. It would, of course, take a great deal of ingenuity and imagination to discover how one might evoke the almost atrophied power of ordinarily unreflective people to think about a better society—in other words, to make the situation real for them so as to stimulate their fantasy. The Goodmans' book, *Communitas*, by presenting models and the drawings to accompany them, does move in this direction.

experience when I lived a few years ago in Kansas City. My home was near a park where gangs of young people from well-to-do homes would gather in their parents' cars at night in search of, as it seemed to me, nonexistent mountains. With much screeching of voices and brakes, they would tear around in their parents' Buicks and Oldsmobiles at eighty miles an hour. In the movie *Rebel without a Cause* comfortable California teen-agers sought even more desperate challenge than merely driving too fast, as if they had to initiate each other in the absence of more formal initiation rites. What is left in such children of the Utopian impulse is soured and is only negative; all that is open for them is the road ahead. Such young people hang suspended between the traditional games of children and those which war and work and some new and some old kinds of play provide for adults.

It is hard to imagine a culture like ours suddenly turning every adolescent into an artist who finds challenge in creative exploration, although some hot rodders seem to me to be sculptors in metal and inventors as well, whose "cars of tomorrow" have sometimes been imitated by Detroit. Considering the emphasis currently put on sports, it is surprising how small is the proportion of high school students who actively engage in them; there are, I would surmise, as many drop-outs from the athletic program as from the academic one. The community and the coaches alike interest themselves for the most part in the valuable players of team sports and only a few high schools have adequate teaching and equipment outside the squads for the major sports. The Y and the Boy Scouts do ancillary and often important work, but often the slow and awkward boys have little encouragement, and the girls none at all.

No doubt extremely inventive children could find other alternatives, but when I was in Kansas City I kept thinking that it made a difference that there were no nearby mountains where these young people could go skiing or climbing and fulfill in that way the desire of young people to test and extend themselves, the recurrent romanticism and individualistic utopianism of the young. I am quite sure that if mountains were plunked down near Kansas City, many of these high school youngsters would go there to ski and climb. Of course they would not have invented the idea, but the mountain would still create its own demands on them once the idea existed. We all know young people who look as if under ordinary conditions they couldn't walk a step if they could drive, yet go to Aspen or Wisconsin or Vermont on weekends and spend a day or two in often bitter cold weather schussing down mountains. It seems to me that as a social policy for full employment the country might build other things than armaments and superhighways and might move mountains to Kansas City for the youth of that city and other such cities to tackle!

Moreover, I believe that building the mountains, and the ski trails and firebreaks to go with them, would provide another challenge for these young people. Many parents today try to discipline and harden their children with chores or paper routes, but in our society the young, always sensitive in such matters, are quick to realize that the work they are asked to do is after all not really necessary but could be done with machines. The experience the psychoanalyst Allen Wheelis describes so movingly in his book, *The Quest for Identity,* of being forced by his father in the South to cut the grass with a razor blade all one summer as an exercise for the will—such an occurrence seems impossible today. Yet the testing that parents and adults no longer provide, the children seek; can it now be provided institutionally? That is, can we think of any organized way of locating snowy mountains needing to be cleared as well as skied down, any way of connecting the young person with others in the way that the age grades of a primitive tribe connect him and get him to go through initiation rites together with other young people? Such a rite tells the young person, "Now you're a man, no question about it." Compulsory military service seems to me a remote analogy for some young people in wartime, and even during peace. But save for a brief spell of basic training, compulsory military service seems to me to be training in nonwork and more or less impatient time-killing. Although some privileged young men do enter the Army with the thought of experiencing a common democratic fate, the military situation today is so anomalous that most recruits don't enter service with any zeal or any spirit save resignation, or at best the hope for some relevant training. Moreover, the avoiding of service raises moral dilemmas just as service itself does. For the privileged who are studying physics or clinical psychology or something else of presumptive usefulness, there must always be the question whether their motives for choosing this career are contaminated by draft dodging, just as they may feel they married the girl for the same reason. Is there any meaningful as well as moral equivalent for basic training which could be applicable to all and to women as well as to men?

One partial answer has received insufficient attention, partly because it was blotted out by World War II and the ensuing full employment, and partly because we are careless of small social experiments although not of small scientific ones: I am referring to a variation of the CCC camps ("CCC" stands for "Civilian Conservation Corps"). The CCC was one of the many improvised relief measures, like the WPA, but its aim was conservation of lands and forest—and, as a by-product, people. Young men out of work and in need could enlist and go to camp in the country where they would clear trails, install soil conservation ponds, build firebreaks, and so on.[6]

Many privileged young people have a desire for this kind of experience, as manifested in Quaker work camps, at Antioch, and in other ways. And there was founded in Vermont during the Depression a variation, for such boys, of the CCC camp, called Camp William James. Its founders were Dorothy Thompson, Eugen Rosenstock-Huessy, a Dartmouth professor, and a few other people who felt that the CCC experience should not be limited to the desperately poor. It attracted Dartmouth students and Bennington girls and others whose needs were psychological rather than alimentary. Camp William James was an appropriate name, for James was passionately concerned with the moral tone of the elite who were his students at Harvard and eager to find in the moral life forms of discipline other than the juvenile hunting of men and beasts he despised in Theodore Roosevelt and would have distrusted in Hemingway. I never had the good fortune to attend Camp William James, but I have known a number of people whose lives have been deeply affected by their experience there. Some of these people today look back on that experience as a naïve

[6] As it turned out, there were a few people in my audience who had been in the CCC; and some of these attacked my notion on the ground that the commanders of the CCC had often been anything but educationally minded, but instead noncom types who could only regret that no actual war was going on, and who ran their units with as much militaristic highhandedness as they dared. Unquestionably, the leadership of such a project would make all the difference; there is no activity that cannot become stultifying or an excuse for sadism or moral inertia. As I sought to make plain in the discussion, I suggested CCC camps, not as an unequivocally noble experiment, but rather as an illustration of a mode of thinking about the conservation of people and places. (Since presenting my paper, I have discovered that Senator Hubert H. Humphrey has proposed a reconstitution of the CCC; see his excellent article, "A Plan to Save Trees, Land, and Boys," *Harper's Magazine,* January 1959, pp. 53–57.) And of course my discussion of mountains was intended to be similarly metaphorical and suggestive: I am sure one could think of a better solution for Kansas City's young people than building a mountain in nearby Lawrence—the real problem is to find work that taxes and discovers their powers.

and nostalgic venture, a ruralistic oasis for a Mary McCarthy to satirize; they recount how ridiculous they were as amateur trail clearers or well-intentioned emissaries to unenlightened Vermont villagers. Indeed the fear to be thought naïve today, or a do-gooder, has been in many ways as corrupting as fears in an earlier day to be thought evil-minded or agnostic—correspondingly, I know it is far harder to interest college students in a work program than it is to interest high school students, and it is harder to interest high school students than eighth graders. But my point here is not to denounce the skepticism of the young today, which has many positive aspects, but rather to indicate how hard it makes their task of finding challenge in the work of conservation and, in general, in fighting for and against nature.

One enormous advantage of a period of some sort of compulsory service, foreseen by Bellamy, beyond the advantage to the young people of having their energies made use of rather than dissipated, lies in the possibility of justifying through this service future periods of voluntary paid unemployment. Most of us, once out of college, never have another chance for a moratorium during which we can reflect on our course and perhaps reshape it, getting such additional training as may be requisite. (And incidently, as colleges get better and harder to get into, they become less of a moratorium, too, and courses can interfere with one's education.) I am thinking not only of the millions of young people who are trapped in their careers, and of the older people, too, who cannot afford the risks of change, including many housewives with children, who are captives of their own families. I am thinking also of the many people who would welcome a change from their particular specialty (a change which I have myself enjoyed). The only way in which, for instance, many academic people, many doctors, many engineers can change jobs at present is to become administrators. They are seldom able to switch to an entirely different specialty which requires extensive preparation. But if such people had in their youth contributed to a kind of social insurance fund, they would then be both morally and financially free to live for an equivalent period on the labor of others and have this period in which to retrain themselves for some other activity. Possibly if they would loaf for a time they might purge themselves of the dream of effortlessness; at any rate, they could try another form of life without undue hazard for themselves or their families.

Perhaps you will see what I am getting at here—namely, that each particular stage of life requires its own particular forms of tradition and change, challenge and surcease. In the dialectic between specialization and wholeness, people should be encouraged not so much to change jobs, which Americans do all the time, as to change the very forms of work. In the last great war, that is, in World War II, an extraordinary number of Americans discovered gifts that they had for all sorts of activities, and many returned dissatisfied with old occupations and prepared to risk entering new ones. Here the GI Bill is a model of what I am looking for—it justified retraining at public expense for millions of men who had been introduced during the war to new experiences and opportunities which they would never have thought they were capable of. What I am seeking, in other words, is the basis for a GI Bill for everyone—women as well as men—not as a handout but as a right earned through arduous service as youngsters.

Let me refer in this connection to those management training programs in which men are taken out of middle management positions and sent for a period to a university, not to study techniques or a specialty, but to obtain a liberal education. I visited some years ago the most exemplary of such programs, that of the Bell Telephone Company at the University of Pennsylvania, where a number of men, some twenty in all, were there for a year in one of the most uncompromisingly humanistic programs one could find in any liberal arts college. Many of the men there had not been to college, or worse, had been to a narrow-minded engineering school. They were suddenly faced with a program equivalent to two or three years of the most avant-garde intellectual fare—plunged into reading Joyce, hearing Bartok and Hindemith, studying cultural anthropology, and reading Lewis Mumford. It amazed them, as well as their teachers, that they could in the majority of cases rise to the challenge, rise to the point of discovering interests and capacities in themselves they had not been aware of. Like college students, or like some college students, they would stay up most of the night reading and discussing an assigned book and plaguing themselves with its obscurities. No group I have talked to was more alive and responsive than these men.

If we examine these instances, we see some of the problems of creating challenge when the natural environment no longer forces us to struggle. In the first place, there is a group, there is support for the work and for the temporary miseries and agonies found in the work. It asks too much of people today, I think, to expect them to find these challenges alone. In the second place, there is an assignment—a norm is set by the group. The norm is set outside oneself, so that one is not running alone around an unmeasured track to an unknown destination. In the third place, there are models provided in the books themselves and in the mentors who are lecturing or coming to the group from the outside. All these things are concessions to human frailty. Most of us have to make a game of work, to set deadlines for ourselves, to put ourselves into situations, as a skier does, from which it will take exertion and skill to get through and extricate ourselves. Indeed many of the important choices in life are those we make to create conditions in which we develop under something like forced draft, and for many of you I imagine that the choice of college was such a choice. In fact, college provides at its best the closest thing we have to an initiation, one in which the cultural heritage is not so much stamped onto the bodies of the young, as transmitted to their minds and senses. Of course it happens in high school too; there is no definite date for the initiation when we begin to accept responsibility for making the culture a part of ourselves. Some of us, of course, accept more of the culture than others. This, unlike my notion of Camp William James, is a more selective service which is at once obligatory and an opportunity.

In this connection I would like to mention a notion which I once discussed with a group at Antioch—that students during some part of their college life be locked up in the library alone with books, and adequate food and drink, for a week at a time. Though I think some might go "stir crazy" in the absence of audio-visual aids and chatter and study dates, still I would like to see the experiment tried. For I regard the arts as capable of providing many of us with tasks more than sufficient to challenge us, even were our industry and farming and commerce to become more nearly automatic. In the library, and in the whole experience of becoming part of the process of cultural transmission, one discovers one's own mountain, one's magic mountain, which one creates as one climbs it. In this perspective we can view a curriculum, whether of the traditional studies or of the less usual ones, as a series of ranges set down in Chicago, Kansas City, Columbus or anywhere else by the work and imagination of earlier generations as well as the present one.

If books were the only such vehicle, many young people would, of course, be entirely excluded—either because of lack of native talent for literacy or, more usually, because the reading of books somehow got involved with struggles against parents or other adult figures. The same is true of the language of numbers—not because there is anything inherently difficult about it, but because learning arithmetic or algebra has gotten involved with wishes to be taken care of by others or to make life hard for others or for oneself in all sorts of complex ways, or for girls to define their femininity by letting men read the timetable for them. The learning of music also may have its blockages, but it is usually outside the formal curriculum and often thus provides a second challenge for some young people, one increasingly made use of in our own day with the immense growth of group singing and playing. As with the authors of books, so with the composers of musical scores, though they may have been dead two or three hundred years, their spirit is kept alive, their imagination, their sense for form, by being bred into the fingers and bones and voices of the young amateur. Of course, as I have already implied, there are children who are forced, let us say, to practice piano and they respond by learning-blocks. But there is a difference between those subjects one has to learn and the arts one generally learns out of inclination. Thus, while any subject, any discipline, can become an arena for struggle between adults and children, the arts are relatively free, as compared with the academic program, of the kind of misplaced parental vanity which wants the child to do well.

I realize fully that the better and more exciting graduate and professional training becomes, the greater are the demands put on later life to live up to expectations. A first-rate college often seeks to make us dissatisfied with what we do later. What I am driving at here, is that, provided each stage of life offers challenge and as we therefore grow to meet the challenge, we demand challenge in the next stage. I have heard good prep schools criticized because colleges aren't as good as the best prep schools, and now I am saying that colleges are sometimes criticized as breeding discontented intellectuals who are too good for this world, whether "this world" is the graduate school to which they go on or a career in business or the professions. But I would be much happier if more colleges put more of this kind of pressure on later life to live up to college; that is, if more people got out of college who insisted that the world live up to the expectations created by college. I think one reason such insistence is muted is that people, once in a job and in a marriage, have no financial leeway to make a radical break and therefore the criticisms they might otherwise make simply don't occur to them; and this again goes back to my thought that if one had a period of compulsory service doing such work as building mountains, one could then later in life have a claim on society on the basis of that service. Now, actually, our society is rich enough so that we don't need that basis, we don't need it, that is, economically, although we do need it psychologically or politically. Today, if people find their job undemanding, their temptation is not to seek for a demanding job or to struggle politically for a world in which jobs are more demanding and more interesting and in which industry and the professions do less in the way of stockpiling talent than they now do. Rather I think people flee into what I have called the utopianism of private life, of domesticity. One trouble with this is that it puts too much of a burden on domesticity.

To return to the beginning, it comes as a surprise to Americans that when we are faced with plenty we still find problems no less grave. It still takes nine months to produce a baby; it still takes time to develop anything worthwhile, whether this be a painting or a friendship or a talent or an interest. Walt Whitman wrote: "It is provided in the essence of things that from any fruition of success, no matter what, shall come forth something to make a greater struggle necessary."

SECTION III

Abundance for Whom?

Preface

The essays in this section, like those in the previous one, deal with the growth of abundance and its uneven spread. But the focus here is also on scarcity.

The first essay, like my book on Veblen, was an effort to relate Veblen's ideas to each other and to his milieu. In both I combined textual analysis of his writings with reading whatever I could find, and talking with whomever I could buttonhole, about the man himself. (Veblen ordered all his correspondence and possessions destroyed—hardly any of his letters have been made public—and his last wish was that there should be no biography or even a tombstone to recall him, a wish that reminds us of another ailing son of a strong-willed father: Kafka.) In the essay I offer some tentative suggestions about Veblen's character structure and the relation this bore to his choice of profession, of intellectual weapons such as irony, and of topics. My concern here is with the background of his theories and some of their consequences for American intellectual history, rather than with their correctness.

In 1960, seven years after its first publication, my book on Veblen was to be brought out in a paperback edition. Staughton Lynd, a historian with whom I had worked on the original publication, joined me in writing a new preface and correcting what seemed, in retrospect, a too ready dismissal of Veblen's relevance to the economic and political scene in the United States today. After three recessions since the Korean War, despite a high plateau of defense expenditures, Veblen's mordant sense of the wastefulness of capitalism struck us as not inappropriate. The new preface also gave us an opportunity to do a greater measure of justice to the Populist and Progressive traditions in American life, traditions whose crudities and exaggerations have been overemphasized in recent scholarship. Finally the rise—or should one say the fall?—of the Beats reminds us of the extent to which Veblen was a forerunner of the Beat writers, choosing poverty, unassertiveness, unkemptness, and Bohemianism—that is, the resigned Bohemianism of today rather than the exuberant version of the 1920s.

Still I doubt that the Beats will take up Veblen. He was an economist who employed tortuous syntax to say both complicated and simple things. He addressed himself only peripherally to the problems of personal relations and private life. And the lessons taught in *The Theory of the Leisure Class* have been learned so well that students who read Veblen today are apt to conclude they already know what he is saying, and to put him aside impatiently for saying it in too roundabout a fashion. I would be happy if the two essays in this volume could send some readers back to Veblen. He has a good deal to say about the fetters that prevent us from attaining abundance, the rivalries and gentilities that make abundance purse-proud and envious, and the very present danger that excess productivity may destroy itself through the wars that he regarded in a characteristic oversimplification as the sport of latter-day knights seeking markets and a crusader's glory.

The last two essays in this section reflect my interest in interviews done in seven Middle Eastern countries on behalf of the Bureau of Applied Social Research at Columbia University—interviews dealing with the respondents' exposure to the mass media and their attitudes toward progress, their own nations, and other nations, especially America.[1]

"Self and Society: Reflections on Some Turks in Transition," which I wrote with Daniel Lerner, is based on the interviews he conducted in Turkey, which I read in translation. It is included here because of its bearing on major concerns of this volume, among others, the problems of interviewing dealt with in Section IV. This essay, like the one that follows on "The Oral Tradition, the Written Word, and the Screen Image," deals with the ambivalence of American attitudes toward those societies that are strenuously pursuing consumer values that no longer appeal to our own most sensitive spirits. I suppose one might say that in our attitude toward the developing Turkish society, Lerner and I take the position Herbert Gans takes toward the suburbanites among whom he has lived: we may not share their values, but we are hesitant to patronize them, let alone to judge them. If others want the affluence we have, it ill becomes us to say it isn't worth it.

[1] For a full account see Daniel Lerner with the collaboration of Lucille W. Pevsner, *The Passing of Traditional Society: Modernizing the Middle-East* (The Free Press, 1958).

When I prepared the address to Antioch College students that is the final essay in this section, however, I was less hesitant to defend the sort of culture that is built on the printed word as against what I refer to as the "postliterate" culture built on the new electronic media. In the course of the ceremonies at the dedication of the Kettering Library, I was only half joking when I proposed that students at colleges like Antioch be encouraged to endure a "retreat" in the library, removed from the distractions a society provides in which all modes of literacy coexist.

This essay is an attempt, all too abbreviated, to construct a typology of societies in terms of the forms of communication, suggesting (in part on the basis of the Middle Eastern material) that societies that move directly from the nonliterate to the postliterate, largely skipping the stage of print, will end up rather different from societies like ours in which the printed book was one of the first mass-produced products.

I do not think of myself as an unreconstructed foe of the newer media, any more than I think of myself as a foe of the suburbs or the auto. It is a question of proportion and balance, of place in the life cycle and of historical development. I think a culture can be the richer for the newer media, but only if they do not sweep all else before them.

The Social and Psychological Setting of Veblen's Economic Theory

(1953)

In Veblen's own critique of other economists—and a major portion of his theory is just that—he relied securely on quasi-Marxist simplicities concerning causation. Other economists got that way because they were members of or sycophants of the kept classes, aristocratically disdainful of the actualities of production. Their theories, if they were classicists, were superstructural in the sense of being both above and behind the battle, for Veblen was one of the pioneers in the use of the cultural-lag concept which has done so much to confuse the understanding of the relations between technology and society. If they were *American* classicists, such as (in Veblen's view) J. B. Clark, they were likely to couple a pallid reformism with their fine-spun technicalities, offering palliatives at the level of pecuniary theory for evils rooted in the very divorce of the pecuniary culture from its industrial base. And this reformism Veblen saw as a leisure-class product, along with female philanthropy, the arts and crafts movement, social work, and vegetarianism —the archaic by-products of the sheltered life of the better-off and the better-educated strata whose menial and hence life-giving work was done for them by others. Reformism was archaic because it was pre-evolutionary, pre-Darwinian; for Veblen, "A.D." meant "After Darwin." His emphasis on the datedness of economic theory—a charge to which Americans are especially sensitive since we like to be progressive and up-to-date—led Veblen to express recurrent hopes for the "younger generation" of economists, whom he wanted to make less literate and theoretical, less parasitic and less sanguine, less refined and more machine-minded. For Veblen as for Rousseau, what was young was not so likely to be corrupted and spoiled.

Veblen, however, never explained why some economists, himself included, were historically minded and literate in spite of being "younger." He admired Sombart and borrowed much from him; he had good words to say for Schmoller; and he attacked the German historical school only for not being completely free of chauvinism and reformism; for Karl Marx, in his role as economic historian and not in his role as prophet, Veblen had a good deal of sympathy. In his efforts to make economics a historically relativistic science, in his refusal to "take the current situation for granted as a permanent state of things," Veblen contributed to economic history rather than to economics proper, granted that his morganatic anthropology was a kind of history, a Just So story of stages in a universal unilinear human destiny. And perhaps it can be said that Veblen's unremitting warfare with what he called "the guild of theoretical economists" opened up possibilities for a more historical or anthropological economics which later students, more cautious and less given to economistic explanations, have been exploiting.

I

But how, drawing from Veblen, are we to explain him? In my book on Veblen,[1] I made a very tentative effort to show how his theories reflect the conflict between his harsh, intrepid, and technologically adept father and his Bible-reading, softer, and whimsical mother. Take, for example, his view that in the matriarchal past life was at its best, but that modern man is simply nostalgic if he dwells on this, for modern man must adapt to the discipline of the machine, its cold, impersonal calculus, or go under. Might we not say that this outlook, like analogous lost paradises, reflects the coexistence in his mind of periods of his own life: the earliest childhood, dominated by his mother, and the succeeding harsher if more productive phases, dominated by his father? Plainly, neither such a theory nor such a family constellation is idiosyncratic to Veblen; such families, indeed, peer out at us from Victorian portraits and memoirs—and, in fact, justify themselves by reference to ideologies of masculine work-mindedness and domination of nature, of masculine mathematics and calculation. Yet such correspondences between family and ideology, while fruitful for speculation, are not explanatory: they illustrate compatibilities but do not show why some children of ascetic fathers, like Samuel Butler, rebelled to become antagonists of the machine and admirers of luxury, while others, like Veblen, rhapsodized their fathers and defended their coldness, ascet-

[1] *Thorstein Veblen: A Critical Interpretation* (New York: Charles Scribner's Sons, 1960), paper edition.

icism, and solemnity. In fact, a closer look at Veblen, while it shows the father portrayed as the philosopher-king of the future, the engineer, also shows the father attacked in the son's muted praise for "idle curiosity" and muted contempt for pragmatism—contempt expressed also in his unceasing and successful effort to make a failure of his own career.

Veblen's father, though notably progressive in his use of farm machinery and interest in science, never learned English; Rolvaag's statement is applicable to him: "We have become strangers—strangers to the people we forsook and strangers to the people we came to."[2] But Veblen's Norwegian heritage is important not only because it made him a marginal man, linguistically and intellectually cosmopolitan, socially awkward, and emotionally expatriate, but also because of certain specific values he seems to have acquired as a youngster. Blegen notes the fact that the Norwegian immigrants could not understand competitive sports and games. Recalling Schumpeter's observation that for the entrepreneur "economic action becomes akin to sport,"[3] it would seem plausible to connect Veblen's fear and distrust of the entrepreneur with his Norse peasant's sort of Puritanism which rejected sport.[4] Indeed, Rolvaag's novels show how the Norwegian immigrants viewed plays and dances as sinful; their ministers urged them to hold fast to their racial traits and not to emulate American ways. While Veblen emancipated himself from this piety in certain respects, sexually and theologically for instance, he remained in many ways a seventeenth-century sort of Puritan protesting against the more commercially minded and urbanized Yankee Puritans whose faith seemed to him as watered as their stock, whose expenditures appeared as wasteful as their wars and their agronomy, and whose Anglo-Saxon ideal of sport struck him as a form of juvenile delinquency.

Staughton Lynd, who has collaborated with me in the study of Veblen's background, has observed that Simon Patten was born on better, richer land than that of Veblen's parents—and Patten of course went on to emphasize American abundance and consumption whereas Veb-

[2] Quoted in Theodore Blegen, *Grass Roots History*, p. 113.
[3] *The Theory of Economic Development*, p. 93.
[4] A genealogy of the Veblen family indicates that most of Thorstein's siblings married other Norwegian-Americans (judging from names, and the names given children) and apparently remained in rural areas; one brother, and his favorite nephew Oswald, entered academic life. Only in the next generation would there appear to have been widespread assimilation to American middle-class norms.

len, ever fearful of scarcity, remained an ascetic and aesthetic enemy of consumption, above an efficient subsistence minimum. (Patten had studied in Germany and been impressed by *Gemütlichkeit*, by how well the Germans made use of their leisure.) Veblen did not feel, with Willa Cather, that "it took more intelligence to spend money than to make it,"[5] but rather that getting and spending were both frivolous pecuniary diversions from modern man's essential problem: habituation to the machine and its relentless logic. In turning in his own career from philology and Kantian philosophy to economics, he was not only converted, as his first wife later declared, by Bellamy's *Looking Backward*, but also seems to have wanted to immerse himself in the study of livelihood. But perhaps at the same time he was attracted as well as repelled by the almost philological intricacy the science of economics, in comparison with other social sciences, was beginning to attain.[6]

This last point is important, for it introduces us to the fact that Veblen did not remain a Populist or a Bellamy nationalist: he outgrew both movements in part. Thus, while a good deal of his economics may be interpreted as a farm boy's stubborn empiricism—a show-me attitude toward theory and refinement, a dislike of classics and the classical, a fear of art and artfulness, a chronic suspicion of lawyers and financiers —Veblen is neither a Bryan nor a Dreiser. Soon after moving to Chicago in 1892, he ended his concern with agricultural economics and the price of wheat and began his lifelong preoccupation with the most subtle market and monopoly tactics of business enterprise. He was thoroughly aware that the future, not only of the United States but of the planet, lay with industry and not, by any fond hope, with the rural, the tribal, the fundamentalist. Though proud throughout his life of his Scandinavian ancestry, and happier with farmers and Wobbly workers than with professors who could not chop a tree, make furniture, or saddle a horse, he nevertheless identified himself with the international

[5] *One of Ours*, p. 102.

[6] To be sure, in Veblen's America economics was still often taught by divines and other amateurs, but Veblen, a gifted linguist, was familiar with the work being done on the Continent. On coming to Chicago, he translated Ferdinand Lassalle's polemical *Science and the Workingman,* and in the *Journal of Political Economy* he reviewed scholarly as well as socialist European economic literature. These reviews—some of them reprinted in *The Place of Science in Modern Civilization and Other Essays*—exhibit Veblen's skill in handling complex Marshallian types of argument in economic theory.

world of scholarship and only on occasion with the more folksy and destructive vulgarities of Populism.[7] Indeed, as a self-proclaimed matter-of-fact scientist, he was able to conceal from himself (and from many of his readers) the extent of his animus against the rich and the scholastics who neither toiled nor spun—save for spinning theories to justify their idleness and prestige. Through science he could sublimate his alienations and harness his hostility.

II

He came late to economics, as he came late to the English language and the genteel tradition, to cities, and, in a way, to America. And this, too, is not idiosyncratic but reflects an era in which it was very difficult for the underprivileged young to get higher education, although it was also an era in which professors, secure in their own status, enjoyed polishing and bringing along those rare ethnics—a Veblen, a Bernard Berenson, a Morris Cohen, an Alvin Johnson—who did manage to get access to them. The zeal and enthusiasm of these newcomers for the classical culture was thus stimulated and preserved (as compared with the situation today in which professors and students, no longer so different from each other, are cool, sharing know-how rather than isolated excitement). The very backwardness of America then held certain advantages for the pioneers of scholarship who, even if like Veblen they turned hostile to classicism, came as individuals to a library with the same passion that whole nations have come to literacy when the printing press is first introduced. I should add, moreover, that but for this backwardness I doubt if we would be taking Veblen very seriously today; he stands out among turn-of-the-century thinkers in this country as he would hardly do in an international conspectus that took account of his great contemporaries on the European continent.

To return to Veblen as a late-comer: Trained initially in philosophy,

[7] Neither Veblen's idealized engineer nor his footloose Wobbly hero has much in common with the masterful, muscular hero of Jack London's *The Iron Heel*. During the First World War, Veblen, though ferociously anti-German, was concerned about how international scholarship might be preserved through American aid. In this man of multiple and wavering identities, a concern for scholarship and especially economics—if not for particular scholars and economists—remained an abiding concern even when he became a left-wing journalist on *The Dial*.

the field in which he took his doctorate with a thesis on Kant, he turned his critical intelligence and linguistic acuity onto what he termed the "received homilies" of economic theory; his papers on Clark, Marx, Böhm-Bawerk, and others are magnificent forays in criticism. Often unaware of what he had learned from the men he attacked, he tested their theories for both internal consistency and relevance, not to "the economy" in the narrower sense in which that sphere is the province of a special breed of men called economists but to "the economy" in the broader sense which includes all human use of resources, political and cultural, tangible and intangible. By bringing the state of the industrial arts into the discussion of market relations, he forced attention to the cultural and technological prerequisites which many theorists of marginal utility had taken for granted. Likewise, he insisted on bringing into technical academic discussion the usages of the common man. Thus, in a review of Irving Fisher's *Capital and Income*, he argued that "capital" can be defined only by empirical observation of how businessmen use the term—there is no point in a more refined definition. Indeed, the study of economics becomes the study of businessmen's habits of thought; changes in businessmen's linguistic usage, therefore, reflect changes in what they do. Here the outsider speaks—or, in terms of his own theory (see *Imperial Germany and the Industrial Revolution*), the late-comer who takes over modernity without the encrustations of habit, sport, and dilettantism. In this and other papers, he stresses that price, interest, value, and other categories are conventions, not given in the nature of things or in human nature but through the institutional processes and social learnings we would today summarize as culture.

III

Moreover, like many outsiders and late-comers—including some of the most significant minds of the nineteenth century—Veblen employed the search for economic origins as a way of discrediting capitalism's claim to be sacrosanct and traditional, as well as the claim of particular capitalists to be innovators and contributors to welfare. In regard to the latter, when he did not charge them with usurpation and sabotage, he observed that they lazily engrossed the community's common stock of industrial understanding: they stole not so much surplus labor (a metaphysical concept Veblen derided) as a racial inheritance of instinctive workmanship (Veblen's racism was metaphysical, too, as he sometimes admitted). Concerning the former, Veblen pointed to the historically late entrance of substantial capital assets upon a population already somewhat crowded by the growing scarcity of land, giving rise to the exceptional and unstable phenomenon of modern capitalism—a parvenu likes to pretend he has always been there. But the "assets," Veblen insisted (in line with single-tax thinking), are such only because the institutions so define them; thus when metals came into use, flint-beds were no longer assets, and in general "the maker's productivity in the case was but a function of the immaterial technological equipment at his command, and that in its turn was the slow spiritual distillate of the community's time-long experience and initiative."[8]

While Veblen was simply one of a number of nineteenth-century thinkers who, by ennobling earlier ages or submerged classes, challenged the capitalists' own lately attained patents of nobility, he was distinctly stimulating and original in his emphasis on the insubstantiality of capital, not only in terms of its historical uniqueness in its contemporary form but also in terms of its resting on interpersonal expectations and understandings much more than on plants and tools. Under Veblen's analysis the impressive physical apparatus of industrialism is separated from the interpersonal racketeering, the "intangible assets," the absentee ownership, the salesmanship and propaganda—all the vendible imponderables that truly dominate the business culture and constitute specifically modern "capital." His awareness of the role of propaganda, of confidence and confidence men, of "good will," is sophisticated and links him with such political scientists as Harold Lasswell or such sociological economists as Pareto or Schumpeter, rather than with the classical or, for the most part, the institutional economists either then or now. Just as he saw socialism as grounded in large part on emulation, he saw capitalism resting on Kwakiutl-like motives of waste and display and on the airy romance of unstable hopes rather than on the solid substance of land, labor, and equipment. Indeed, one can trace anticipations in Veblen of Keynes's and Schumpeter's theories of crisis. And Veblen also anticipated their sense of the precariousness of future prosperity and the historically limited nature of the capitalist world of the nineteenth century.

[8] "On the Nature of Capital," in *The Place of Science in Modern Civilization*, p. 339.

IV

He got there, however, I suggest, in part by the skeptical farm boy's route of distrusting the words, the promises, of city slickers, while being fascinated by them. His father, who had lost his first farm to a shrewd claimant, had been a man of very few words—and those in Norwegian; Veblen's own style is a conscious parody of the prolixity, pedantry, and legalism of the half-educated country lawyer or deacon. His distrust, moreover, is not only that of the farm boy who can never quite accept the reality of things beyond the palpable necessities of life but also a quite far-reaching distrust rooted in his character structure—a fear of being caught, made a fool of, taken in. This is one reason he was never willing to commit himself to a cause, a movement, a colleague, or a woman. All obligations seemed unstable to him. He was so ready to see the role of expectations in society in part because he himself was so fearful lest anything be expected of him; his whole academic career may be viewed as a sidling out of commitments, and his unfactual attitude toward getting the facts and unscientific attitude toward himself as a mere scientist may be seen as efforts to escape from amorphousness and to relate himself to something solid, if not to somebody. His crusade to get theory "down to earth" was thus in part the argument with himself of a refugee from the farm.

This fear of constraint and commitment, coupled with a fear of the freedom that would result from their absence, is one of the most distinctive themes of Veblen's character structure, visible in his writings as well as in other behavior. His writings, for example, have as a formal matter no principle of flow, of organization; they are endlessly repetitive in the large and in detail; sentences have style but little structure. Moreover, as we have seen, Veblen insisted on man's subordination to the machine, to the slow evolutionary drift of things, while at the same time he identified with the Wobblies, the less bemused portions of the underlying population, the masterless men who bowed to no authority save logic and to no rule save the slide rule. This ambivalence we can relate once more to his parents, who thought him bright, expected much of him, but gave him little warmth—and these parents in turn provide a link with the tight patriarchal family and the no less tight ethnic group—a group who supported the postdoctoral Veblen while he loafed and read, read and loafed, because as a traditional culture they accepted the responsibility even for such kin as were deviants. And on the other side, we can relate Veblen's character structure to his choice of field, for I suggest that economics then, with its undefined boundaries and unmathematical, more or less speculative, often historical methods, attracted those who feared constraint, much as sociology and anthropology have more recently done. That is, economics may have appeared to Veblen to mix agreeable proportions of intricacy and openness, methodology and topicality. Veblen broke down the boundaries of economics even further: his very fluid definition led him to subtitle *The Theory of the Leisure Class* "An Economic Study of Institutions." The state of the art allowed him not to be cabined by his chosen discipline; and his eloquent pleas for opening it up to new areas of investigation—business practice, anthropology, psychology, as well as politics—have helped create such cadres of no longer quite marginal but also not wholly free men and women as the economic historians of today.

V

All this only brings us to another paradox in Veblen's relation to his *Zeitgeist*, if this term can still be used. The psychology he went to school with, so to speak, was that of Peirce, James, and Dewey—a psychology that stressed, as indeed Kant's did, man's selective perception and active organization of the world, his adaptation of it to him, rather than his mere passive response to hedonistic drives. Again and again, Veblen states that man is an agent, an actor, shaping the institutions which in turn shape him; moreover, his concept of idle curiosity is a sort of instinctual basis for autonomy. He had some sympathy for Lester Ward, who drew humane implications from Darwinism; he was friendly with W. I. Thomas, who stressed the subjective nature of social life;[9] he even saw in animism a projection of the human will. And yet, because as already indicated he was afraid of his own fear of constraint,

[9] I have relied heavily, for information on Veblen's life and times, on Joseph Dorfman, *Thorstein Veblen and His America*. I am also indebted to a conversation with Professor Max Fisch concerning Veblen and Peirce. Since my address was written, an interesting essay has appeared comparing Veblen and William James: Lewis Feuer, "Thorstein Veblen: the Metaphysics of the Interned Immigrant," *American Quarterly*, V (1953), 99–112. Feuer, somewhat less sympathetic to James and more to Veblen than I am, stresses that Veblen was too close to a precarious personal existence to afford James's middle-class optimism about the human will.

afraid too of the freedom he regarded, as his father might have, as soft and sentimental, he resisted the implications of his psychological affiliations for his economics. For him, Darwinism came as a discovery of mankind's submergence in blind, cumulative drift over which it would be naïve and vain to seek control. In counseling adaptation to the machine, he urged on men a ferocious surrender to the existent, even at the cost of distorting instincts which Veblen thought had been shaped for all time in a savage past. And in his aggressive scientism, no less deterministic than that of Comte and St. Simon and more so in some ways than that of Engels, he urged his fellow economists to give up their personal wishes for amelioration and to bind themselves, in fraternal anonymity, to become consultants for industrial managers, statisticians for project engineers (shall I say "policy scientists"?). In a famous passage, he criticizes Marx and his followers:

> The neo-Hegelian romantic, Marxian standpoint was wholly personal, whereas the evolutionistic—it may be called Darwinian— standpoint is wholly impersonal. . . . The romantic (Marxian) sequence of theory is essentially an intellectual sequence, and it is therefore of a teleological character. . . . On the other hand, in the Darwinian scheme of thought . . . the sequence is controlled by nothing but the *vis a tergo* of brute causation, and is essentially mechanical. The neo-Hegelian (Marxian) scheme of development is drawn in the image of the struggling ambitious human spirit: that of Darwinian evolution is of the nature of a mechanical process.[10]

Indeed, I think William Graham Sumner, hard-boiled at least on the surface, had more influence on Veblen than his gentle colleague, John Dewey, with his, at least on the surface, more hopeful view of man. In making his choice among "influences"—and it will be seen that I myself see men as having some leeway in choosing their influences rather than simply succumbing to tropisms—Veblen may have been picking his father over his mother, his enemies over his friends, his need to be restrained over his fear of restraint. Beyond that, a certain personal passivity and shyness may have been at work which made him dislike any theory or custom that gave renown to individuals or brought them into the limelight. Veblen, having early handed in his resignation to life and being in many ways a very dependent person, seems to have

[10] "The Socialist Economics of Karl Marx and his Followers: II," in *The Place of Science in Modern Civilization*, pp. 436–37.

felt that the "struggling ambitious human spirit" could neither found a scientific system nor change the world, even though, as in many fatalist schemes, this discovery heartened him to espouse, with a very personal style, the claims of impersonality and, with a very unexpedient life, the mandates of expedient adaptation and determinism.

VI

Such psychological explanations, however, leave me somewhat unsatisfied, not only because I know all too little about the details of Veblen's parentage and childhood but also because I know all too well that men of very different background espoused quite similar views of the economy—while of course other farm boys, such as Alvin Johnson, differed from Veblen. Nevertheless, we must ask how Veblen happened to select, among available careers and themes, the particular contradictions that he made his own. The question is in principle answerable even though others could achieve outcomes similar in general, though never in detail, from different motives and, of course, follow him for again different motives. And if we then ask why so intelligent a man as Veblen did not go farther, why he failed in so many ways appreciably to transcend his age, we are once more brought back sharply to his biography. We see, for instance, that his country-boy late-comer skepticism and bitterness had its opposite side in a certain gullibility. He was overimpressed by the very captains of industry he derided. He gave them more power to do damage, as saboteurs of production and Goliaths of consumption, than they actually possessed; their personalities and even their success impressed him, in his shy, resigned failure, despite his Darwinist defense. Their values impressed him even more. In making the canon of efficiency the standard for judging all social life, he was able to demolish much Victorian cant and pretense, but by the use of a Philistine weapon borrowed from businessmen. Veblen contended that businessmen were unbusinesslike, though only by insisting that they were single-mindedly in pursuit of profits rather than production; this very single-mindedness, though some of the robber barons came close to it, was for most of them an unachieved ideal. In his own attempt to be single-minded, Veblen would have very little quarrel with the businessman today who wants government to be run like General Motors: if technocracy was a caricature of his gospel, it was not without his co-operation. Even the businessman who depises art, culture, and philanthropy finds something of an ally in Veblen, whose hatred for all archaic, inefficient, untechnological pursuits has at times a very militant quality. Believing himself a critic of his culture, he fell into some of its most characteristic nineteenth-century crudities and self-deceptions.

Even more striking, perhaps, is Veblen's unconscious acceptance of nineteenth-century rationalistic individualism. Veblen never seriously concerned himself with the problem of social solidarity: he assumed that men, once freed of the imposed incubus of pecuniary rivalry, would work together in obedience both to their instincts and to their self-evident subsistence needs. While he spoke occasionally of the "parental bent" as a kind of instinct of social solicitude, he more typically took it for granted that "masterless men" would find in engineering mandates a sufficient basis for co-operation. During the same era that Durkheim and Freud, Brooks Adams and Sorel, Max Weber and Pareto were in one or another way preoccupied with centrifugal tendencies in modern society, Veblen saw the role of leaders and elites as sheer unnecessary swindle and expense. His preconceptions concerning human relations were those of a market economy—impersonal, rationalistic, calculable. Here again, Veblen is the very "American" efficiency expert, and paradoxically one who is attacking orthodox economics for its reliance on premises of hedonism and rationality. All of us suffer from the illusion that we are outside what we are criticizing.

To be sure, all this needs to be qualified by recalling once again that Veblen kept a kind of ikon corner for the impractical and the "un-American," the inefficient, the unbusinesslike, and the irrelevant, in the form of his concept of "idle curiosity." He called it an instinct, to give it a biological base beyond criticism—and obviously biology is the true nobility, coming first before all learned parvenus. But under idle curiosity he smuggled the university and research, his own vested interest and the one he cared most about. While everywhere else his mentality is that of the engineer or accountant, the Puritan and debunker, the person who has no truck with frills, frivolity, and nonsense—a mentality that drew him at once to the Bolsheviks in 1919— his design for the universities, and hence by implication even for economics, is impractical and indeed remains an attractive dream for many of us who are harassed by demanding students, repetitive committees, administrative chores, and foundation benevolence; we may be grateful here, as with other thinkers, for a certain lack of consistency.

VII

One more paradox and we are done. For reasons partly indicated, Veblen failed to account for modern capitalism in its specifically American variant—he gave the captains too much power, saw credit only as collusive and collapsible, and otherwise overestimated the destructive elements in the system; his asceticism prevented him from seeing that waste and luxury can play a constructive role in both production and consumption.[11] In my judgment, he is a poor, if often amusing and provocative, guide to America.[12] But he really comes into his own when taken as a guide to the economics of underdeveloped countries—"underdeveloped" being our not wholly satisfactory semantic substitute for "backward." By simplifying and empiricizing economics, by putting it back into its cultural context and rejecting partial equilibrium analyses, by teaching us that every society draws on motives which are left over from previous epochs, he introduces an essential curriculum for Point Four missionaries. The new theorists of economic development, working where there is only a rudimentary market and not even a semblance of entrepreneurial ideology, may find Veblen's anthropological econom-

[11] After the meeting, Mrs. Edna Macmahon of Vassar College told me of the following incident, which occurred when she was a student of Veblen's: After a New School lecture, a pretty girl (a species usually able to overcome Veblen's defenses) presented Veblen with a gold clasp to substitute for the safety pin with which he attached his pocket watch to his clothes. Veblen declared, pulling out his pin, that it had true beauty, which he would not exchange for anything: that it could be bought at any five and ten, six for five cents; that the pin did not damage his clothes; finally, that if the girl could not grasp the functional aesthetics of the pin, she had learned nothing from the course!

[12] For this judgment, I was gently chided by Professor Willson Coates of the University of Rochester and others who felt that to criticize Veblen in terms of developments since his time was unjust. The problem, of course, would not arise had Veblen not sought to transcend his times, both critically and prophetically; indeed, were he not to some degree original, there would be no point in seeking to understand him as an individual rather than simply as a type. It may well be that I expect too much illumination from Veblen, of a sort he is not equipped to give, and in this paper insufficiently stress his accomplishments. However, since many still move in evaluating contemporary America within the ambit of Veblen's rhetoric, it is important to emphasize that Veblen's America, to the extent it ever existed, predeceased him—while, to name a profounder guide, Tocqueville's America is in some ways more ours than his.

ics, with its iteration of the interrelatedness of everything, good and even inspiring reading. Someday we may be able to trace a United States Technical Assistance project in aid of Javanese home industry (tied to matrilineal descent lines) to a set of ideas inspired originally by Veblen's own encounter with a magisterial father and with a society which, for much of his life, insisted on defining him as impractical, even at times subversive, but mostly not good for much. And that would be the final ironic verdict on a man whose great discovery, in his own eyes, was the vanity of any human effort to oppose "the *vis a tergo* of brute causation."

The Relevance of Thorstein Veblen
(WITH STAUGHTON LYND, 1960)

The interpretation of Veblen offered in these pages emphasizes above all the ambiguity, even the internal contradictions, of his thought. Inconsistency, as Emerson said, need not be altogether a defect: it may reflect a complex and honest mind working on inherently difficult problems. Yet we remain more critical of Veblen than do a good many of those who have written centennial interpretations of his work and influence; this is in some measure because we attempt to view his writings as a whole, where contradictions are most in evidence, rather than taking them book by book or theme by theme. Moreover, we attempt to link the man and the work, not in order to diminish or explain away the latter, but to try to make sense of its incompatibilities. Thus, for example, it remains a problem for us why Veblen invoked over and over again the virtues of small-scale neighborly life among peasants and savages, while at the same time praising the industrial technology which worked in his view toward ever-increasing centralization. So, too, we must ask what he intended in attacking the psychology of classical economics for assuming men to be passive, while at the same time he mocked at reformers as tinkering busybodies. And, since war and preparation for war preoccupy us as these pages are being written, we also want to ask what kind of radical was the Veblen who, although strongly against war, supported American entry into the First World War, when La Follette, Debs, and Randolph Bourne, along with many other brave and farsighted men, opposed it?

Veblen was a reserved and idiosyncratic person, who expressed, in a language all his own, attitudes toward American society which were then novel and are today still unconventional (it follows that, as one's judgments of America shift, so will one's reaction to Veblen himself). His wordplay, his thought, and his personality were for him means of concealment as well as of expression, and each can become a barrier to the reader seeking rapport with the writer. Henry Adams, unlike

Veblen in so many ways, was like him in the obsessive impersonality with which he referred to himself, as in the famous third-person manner of his *Autobiography*. Both men, seemingly, felt inwardly crushed and suffocated by the Gilded Age of late nineteenth-century America: a world, as Adams wrote, in which a sensitive man could not bear to live without a shudder. And this led both men to hesitate in expressing their feelings. Yet these feelings leaked out, and were among the many influences pressing toward a climate in which educated people today feel free—sometimes virtually compelled!—to open themselves up, to express themselves, to be sincere and direct. Many people who have grown up in this more permissive milieu find it hard to be sympathetic with Veblen's indirection and irony; although they might bear easily with myth and symbolism in poetry and tale, they are impatient with an economist who doesn't come right out with what he thinks.

More assertive men than Veblen reacted to him in his own time with a similar impatience. Thus, H. L. Mencken said that Veblen's language often merely clothed the obvious in sonorous prolixity. He was right up to a point: Veblen was at times trapped within his self-defensive apparatus, and he repeated himself interminably, burying an unforgettable phrase—and the trenchant idea behind it—in wordy exegesis. Viewed, however, with less impatience and with sympathy for a man who could not believe that anybody was listening, Veblen's style strikes us, after many readings, as brilliant and inventive—a genuine contribution to American polemical and scholarly prose.

But it is a mixture of strangeness and simplicity in Veblen's intellectual framework that probably inhibits and confuses his would-be readers even more than do the complexities of his personality or the style he used as a mask. Because key Veblenian terms like "instinct," "institution" and "barbarian" are in common use, we are overready to assume we understand the special sense in which Veblen used them. In fact, it would almost be better to consider his terminology as one does Plato's *hubris* and *nemesis*, or Machiavelli's *virtù* and *fortuna*: words which because of their strangeness are rightly suspected to clothe unfamiliar meanings. Veblen, for all his claim to derive only commonsense conclusions from merely everyday words, in fact relied on an anthropology, an economics, a psychology, and a philosophy which are superseded or out of fashion today. Posing as the king's jester or the village idiot, he was actually encyclopedic in his learning, and original, not as a researcher in the modern sense, but as an "armchair theorist" who made an extraordinary synthesis from derived materials.

What were these materials? In economics, Veblen followed the German "historical school" of Schmoller and Sombart, which emphasized the development of economic systems and institutions, rather than the mathematical interplay of economic interests within a capitalist system assumed to be eternal. In philosophy, Veblen was a disciple of Kant, taking from him especially the notion that men look out on their experience with preconceived interpretative categories. Owing to his admiration for Darwin and his insistence on evolutionary method in every field of knowledge, Veblen distrusted Hegel's developmental logic as non-empirical and goal-directed ("teleological"). In fact, in his distrust of any romantic, Hegelian view of man and history, any utopian image based on a not merely biological understanding of man's essential nature, Veblen was very much in the Anglo-American tradition of hard-headed empiricism, more narrowly pragmatic than John Dewey or William James.

Yet at the same time his psychology was largely shaped by these two men, one of whom (Dewey) was a contemporary of his at the University of Chicago. James and Dewey insisted that human nature was active, unfolding, and whole. Veblen, from this same point of view, never tired of accusing his fellow economists of retaining a conception of the human mind as merely passive and receptive, propelled by discrete external events, at a time when psychology had left this view behind. However, Veblen relied also on the concept of "instinct," which hardly seems holistic or purposive to us; nor did he link it with "impulse," as Dewey was later to do in *Human Nature and Conduct*: there were elements of reductionism in Veblen's thought, partly as a way of reminding himself that he was "scientific" and not nonsensically metaphysical, partly perhaps also reflecting his deep personal passivity and despair. (Freud, who handled the biological concepts of the instincts more inventively, also selected among current concepts of science those compatible with his more active pessimism.)

Anthropology was the one major field on which Veblen drew without at the same time feeling called on to reform it. It was a new discipline and, as he saw it, wholly and beneficially under the influence of Darwinian method. This anthropology which he knew and trusted conceived that all mankind had evolved through a definite sequence of social systems; and that the primitive mind, characterized by an "animism" which considered all things to be living and goal-directed, likewise evolved by regular stages toward science and secularism. Veblen's own schema of social evolution involved two essential stages. The first, "savagery," was for him peaceful, co-operative, and good. The second, "barbarism," was competitive, warlike, and spiritually oriented to personal rather than communal achievement, hence (as Veblen saw it) to a falsely teleological rendering of external reality. All this Veblen elaborated in great detail, and correlated with definite stages in the development of technology, in his conception the dynamic, causal factor. The daring and satirical twist which Veblen gave to the then common anthropological assumptions lay in his bland assertion that modern society was, in its essential tone, only a latter-day barbarism.

In this distinction between a peaceful, industrious, co-operative "savagery," and an aggressive, parasitical, competitive "barbarism," Veblen knitted together the intellectual strands which he inherited. The contrast between "savagery" and "barbarism" was for him a contrast of cultural atmospheres, of ways of getting a living, of personality types, of outlooks on the world. And this perception of bellicosity and peaceableness as fundamental themes of history and social psychology should not be confused with the conceptual machinery Veblen employed to express it. It is not particularly important whether a peaceful, harmonious society really existed at the dawn of history, or is only a hope cast in the form of a fictive past, like the "state of nature" of Locke and Rousseau. What matters is that Veblen's sense of the central problems of American society, when stripped down to this quintessential contrast of two ways of life, has enduring truth. To view modern civilization as still barbaric at its core seems less funny today than to those who laughed in 1899 (at the end of the "splendid little war" with Spain) at *The Theory of the Leisure Class.*

Veblen's black-and-white juxtaposition of "savagery" and "barbarism" was in good part derived from the Populist atmosphere of the Middle West in the post-Civil War decades (Veblen was twenty in 1877). The historian Richard Hofstadter has brilliantly characterized the "folklore of Populism": the mélange of inarticulate major premises which held together the strongest popular movement in American history. Populists believed in a golden age of peace and happiness in the past; the natural harmony of society if uncorrupted by power and money; a "dualistic version of social struggles"; and a "conspiracy theory of history."[1] One does not have to read many pages of Veblen to find each of these themes not merely present, but central to his thought.

The "captains of industry" Veblen satirized—the stock manipulators,

[1] *The Age of Reform: From Bryan to FDR* (New York, 1956), p. 62.

bankers, and other assorted robber barons who had come to pelf and power after the Civil War—were creating widespread apprehension, not only among the impoverished wheat and cotton farmers who flocked to the Populist party, but also among the business and professional men of the "old" middle classes who led the Progressive movement. To compare the barons, as Veblen did, with the feudal lords of the Middle Ages, or to attack "Wall Street" as a conspiracy, as the Populists did, may strike us today as wild exaggeration; to understand these responses, we must put ourselves back into a period when speculators "under cover of night and cloud" (in Veblen's repeated phrase) made and unmade prosperity, and when industrialists could sneer "The public be damned!" and "Ain't I got the power?" By their tastes as well as their tactics, moreover, the *nouveaux riches* invited comparison with feudalism. They built castles; laid out towns for their own sort (like Tuxedo Park near New York City, which imported a village of Slavic workmen to make its roads, and one of Italians to tend its lawns); bought paintings and founded the D.A.R.; discovered family coats-of-arms and read Sir Walter Scott. Others beside Veblen spoke of a "new feudalism"; and the first illustrator of *A Connecticut Yankee in King Arthur's Court* put the faces of contemporary businessmen and politicians on Mark Twain's armored knights; so, too, in *Huckleberry Finn*, Twain paid his respects to the Gilded Age (his own phrase) by naming his small-time shysters "Duke" and "King." Exploring opposite extremes of language—the one colloquial, the other a parody of academese—Twain and Veblen restated the Jeffersonian antithesis of the yeoman's simple and co-operative style of life versus the aristocratic pretensions and corrupt and warlike values of the well-to-do.

Populism no doubt oversimplified Jefferson's own outlook—one so complex that one can find in his letters precedent for a wide variety of positions. Moreover, Richard Hofstadter, Oscar Handlin, and other historians have recently emphasized that, while Populism raised for the first time as public issues the great themes of modern American reform —such as the graduated income tax, government regulation of monopolies, direct election of senators, government subsidization of farm surpluses—it also fostered darker currents of popular social attitudes: racism and isolationism, and a quasi-paranoid and demagogic cast of thought. Much recent writing has tended to emphasize these darker currents, as contrasted to the more hopeful ones, not only in American Populism, but also in many popular revolutionary movements; modern totalitarianism has made many non-Communist intellectuals uneasy about any forms of political militancy, with its inevitable exaggerations, its dangers for intellectual and artistic cultivation, its potential threat to an orderly, sober, and constitutional democracy. But we can see (especially clearly, perhaps, after eight years of the Eisenhower regime) that political moderation is not a lasting or creative quiescence; that an age of reform looks better than an age of stagnation; that the end of ideology could betoken the end of ideas. While there are undoubted linkages of content and form between, let us say, the elder La Follette and the late Senator McCarthy, there are also enormous differences of tone, buoyancy, and context. The gentle, yet shrewd, humanity of Senator George Norris is somehow missing from our contemporary picture of the demagogic and mean-spirited side of Populism.[2] All this has been well stated by C. Vann Woodward, who argues that while the Populists were occasionally anti-Semitic, this was seldom a salient theme, and quite negligible in comparison with frequent courageous advocacy in the South of solidarity between whites and Negroes.[3]

Veblen's future impact on our thought will probably depend less on his specialized contributions than on the outcome of this debate about

[2] It may be objected that La Follette and Norris were "Progressives," not "Populists." This distinction has been made by Oscar Handlin and other historians, and there is certainly a difference of tone between the middle-class, controlled kind of reform (which Woodrow Wilson himself typified) and the Populist mass movement, the "rising sea of discontent," as so many genteel writers of the time called it. Yet the elements of continuity between Populism and Progressivism are extremely strong. In his autobiography, La Follette wrote of the Granger Movement swirling around him when he was a boy. The states which pioneered in the Progressive reforms of women's suffrage or initiative, referendum and recall, which gave heavy votes to La Follette in 1924 and sent Norris, Borah, Wheeler, and like-minded men to the Senate, were almost without exception west of the Mississippi. Populists and Progressives were alike, moreover, in their resentment not only against the robber barons at the top of society, who were forcing society away from a Jeffersonian and Jacksonian ideal, but also against the new "inferior" immigrants who were coming in at the bottom and who, in their way, seemed to be subverting white, Anglo-Saxon values. Thus, if a Populist like Tom Watson turned in the end to racism, Progressives in the era of Theodore Roosevelt and Wilson turned to a "white man's burden" imperialism.

[3] See "The Populist Heritage and the Intellectual," *The American Scholar*, XXIX (Winter, 1950–1960), 55–72. Woodward adds that when the Populist program failed, many Populist leaders themselves turned sour and rancorous, only then using racism as a form of attack on the status quo.

Populism and about political radicalism generally. For it is a measure of Veblen's strength as a social critic that no rounded judgment of his work can be made that is not also a judgment of American society, now as well as then. If, as the antagonists of Populism assert, the evils perceived by the Populists were more imaginary than real, and in any case irrelevant today, and if the fear to be naïve becomes a stronger political motive than indignation at cruelty and injustice, then the inclination will be to stress the psychological sources of both Populism and Veblenism at the expense of (rather than in clarification of) their substantive content. A quite different approach will follow if one agrees, as we are inclined to do now, with William Dean Howells' summary of the Populist impulse (in his introduction to Hamlin Garland's *Main-Travelled Roads*): "They feel that something is wrong, and they know the wrong is not theirs." Undoubtedly the Populists, including Veblen, oversimplified the wrong, and regarded the wrongdoers with a Philistine and at times vindictive hatred. But in reading Veblen we must never forget that he lived and wrote at a time when Americans, both on the land and in the cities, could and did starve to death; when homeless men wandered the roads without hope of public succor; and when the newly rich and complacent lived a far more Philistine life than their humanitarian critics, condemning those who failed not only to terrible poverty but to guilt for not having "made it" when, according to doctrine, anyone could.

In contrast to his alienated Populist tone stands Veblen's attitude toward the First World War. When he left academic life to join Wilson's war government it marked a startling departure from his customary ironic skepticism toward efforts at reform. His book *The Nature of Peace* wavers between an unusually exposed plea for intelligent peacemaking and the more familiar claim to be attempting nothing more than "a systematic knowledge of things as they are."[4] In no other work does Veblen stray so often and so far from the naturalism he shared with novelists like Stephen Crane and Frank Norris: what Parrington calls "a pessimistic realism that sets man in a mechanical world."[5] Here is an inconsistency which calls not so much for analysis or satire, as for pondering by all those who seek to combine social analysis with personal action for social change.

[4] *An Inquiry into the Nature of Peace and the Terms of its Perpetuation* (New York, 1919), vii.
[5] *Main Currents in American Thought*, III (New York, 1930), xii.

The dichotomy between peaceful "savagery" and predatory "barbarism" appears in Veblen's war writing as a contrast between the Allies and the Central Powers. Veblen's attitude toward peace and war, like that of Woodrow Wilson, embraced two powerful sentiments. One was a horror of war as such, a tendency to believe that no provocation could be sufficient excuse to unleash the holocaust. Wilson expressed this view most notably in his "peace without victory" speech of January 1917, delivered just at the time Veblen was composing *The Nature of Peace*. In that book, however, Veblen was already straining forward to the new attitude adopted by Wilson in his war message of April: the conviction that autocratic governments could not be trusted to make a lasting negotiated peace, hence that war must be pressed on to victory "to make the world safe for democracy."

In hindsight, or even in the perspective of the many radicals who at the time refused to go along with Wilson, Veblen's identification of the Allies and the United States with democracy seems curious—as no doubt the phrase "free world," used indiscriminately to refer to the anti-Communist coalition of our day, will seem a generation hence, provided that the very antithesis allows a new generation to grow up. Before the war, Veblen plainly regarded American capitalists as latter-day barbarians; how is it that he suddenly sees the Germans as the real barbarians? How is it that the skeptical student of propaganda, who was later to dub advertising "creative psychiatry," fell so unguardedly for the anti-German war propaganda of the Allies and the Yankee Easterners whom Veblen had previously mistrusted?

Do we deal here with the frequent phenomenon that the more suspicious a person is, the more gullible he can become? Suppressing and hence keeping unclarified his own radicalism, Veblen imagined that he could transpose into the conflict between the Allies and the Central Powers his dichotomy between peaceful habits and institutions ("savagery") and warlike and predatory ones ("barbarism"). And, concluding in terms now quite familiar to us (as we fight the cold war with Maginot Line slogans about Munich and appeasement) that Germany's dynastic state was not only evil and oppressive in itself, but inherently expansionist and impossible to treat with, Veblen came to justify war itself, chafing as angrily as Theodore Roosevelt at Wilson's effort to mediate rather than fight.

When Wilson did declare war, Veblen came for the duration to persuade himself that Wilson might go so far as basically to modify American capitalism in the interest of winning the war and making a lasting peace. Veblen did not realize that Wilson's anti-German moralism was not so sharp as his own, nor could he be aware of how tormented Wilson felt the very night before he asked Congress to declare war. So, too, Veblen's hopes for Wilson as a revolutionary blinded him to evidence to the contrary, such as Wilson's antagonistic attitude toward labor, toward Debs, and toward Mexican uprisings against American investments and dollar diplomacy there. (Such self-deception was to find devotees among Franklin Roosevelt's admirers in the Second World War and, *pari passu*, in the cold war.)

Ironically, we know today that Wilson's pronouncement of the famous Fourteen Points in January 1918, was in good part brought on by the Russian Bolsheviks, who published the secret Allied treaties and sent forth to the world the slogan of "no annexation and no indemnities."[6] Yet the Bolshevik slogans were themselves borrowed from the speeches of Wilson; and in this complicated interplay of appearance and reality, the sources of Veblen's later hatred of Wilson and angry pro-Bolshevism are to be found.

Thus, in the Veblen of 1914–17, we meet a man whose mind was not the "hard clear prism" Dos Passos spoke of, whose stance was not the unwavering hostility to the status quo in all its aspects which is so often attributed to him. Rather this is a Veblen whose judgment was quickly questioned by scholarship, as in other cases it was rendered obsolete by events.[7]

None of this, however, is said in a spirit of debunking Veblen. Few are the saints who utterly escape the temptation to join their nation in a moral crusade against an obvious international wrongdoer! And, to the extent that we have succeeded in overcoming the contamination of nationalism within ourselves, so that we can look with appropriate horror at the policy of deterrence and see through the fanatical rationalizations with which moral men justify it, we are in debt to that more fully human side of Veblen that saw war as the health of the dynastic (or, as we would say, garrison) state, and saw peace as the health of mankind. Beyond that, Veblen had a sense of the ways in which technology could be married to nationalism for war-making pur-

[6] Cf. the authoritative and enlightening discussion by George F. Kennan, *Russia Leaves the War* (Princeton, 1956), Chapters VII, XII.

[7] Thus ten years after America's entrance into the war, Sidney B. Fay was writing in *The Origins of the World War* (New York, 1927), II, 522: "Germany did not plot a European War, did not want one, and made genuine, though too belated, efforts to avert one."

poses, and of the contribution of the "underlying population" to a war-like animus, so that while he is far from a complete guide to the present world conflict, he is a good preliminary one. Like other Midwesterners of a later generation—we think of Wendell Willkie, George Kennan, Harold Stassen, Glenway Wescott, among many very unlike men—he found his way to an intellectually cosmopolitan outlook.

In view of all this, it is remarkable that Veblen has found no place in the mainstream of socialist thought, in America or abroad. The key themes of *The Theory of the Leisure Class* were first presented by Veblen in the context of socialist theory, as an attempt to deal with the failure of Marx's prediction of increasing material misery among the industrial proletariat. In one of his earliest essays, "Some Neglected Points in the Theory of Socialism" (1891), Veblen forcefully advanced the thesis of relative deprivation and in this connection introduced the conception (although not yet the term) of conspicuous consumption:

> The existing system does not make, and does not tend to make, the industrious poor poorer, as measured absolutely in terms of livelihood; but it does tend to make them relatively poorer, in their own eyes, as measured in terms of comparative economic importance, and, curious as it may seem at first sight, this is what seems to count.

Veblen saw that the increase of well-being among industrial workers has led to their bourgeoisification through their leisure-time activities. He saw that the leisure class in modern Western societies extends almost to the very bottom, including all those who "keep up appearances." He argues, in this early work, that the motive of envy among workingmen may be strong enough to bring on a socialist transformation.

In *The Theory of the Leisure Class*, this notion of defeating the devil by his own devices no longer satisfies Veblen. He has begun to develop his most original conception: that the psychological discipline of factory work will train men to think matter-of-factly rather than subjectively, to place emulation and aggression second to the impersonal needs of the communal technology. In this hope were fused many other Veblenian motifs, and in particular his contention that work was not (as the "received economics" postulated) naturally distasteful to man.

The opaque discipline of modern machine-tending, Veblen argues, can act as a solvent on institutions grounded in animistic and self-centered thinking. The impact of the machine Veblen conceived to be largely negative: its effect on the workingman's thought would be toward nihilism. In *The Theory of Business Enterprise* he wrote:

> There is little indication of a constructive movement toward any specific arrangement to take the place of the institution whose existence is threatened. There is a loosening of the bonds, a weakening of conviction as to the full truth and beauty of the received domestic institutions, without much of a consensus as to what is to be done about it, if anything. In this, as at other junctures of a similar kind, the mechanically employed classes, trained to matter-of-fact habits of thought, show a notable lack of spontaneity in the construction of new myths or conventions, as well as in the reconstruction of the old.

But Veblen—and this brings us to the center of his thought—was not dismayed, as for example Tocqueville or Durkheim were dismayed, by the attrition of the going cultural consensus, because he had faith in the a-cultural or biological man who would thereby be set free.

In the introduction to *The Theory of the Leisure Class* and in the chapter on "The Conservation of Archaic Traits," Veblen gives us his revised picture of man in the state of nature. This was the peaceful, primitive Ur-society which he thought he found in such contemporary groups as the Eskimo and the Pueblo Indians, in pre-Christian Scandinavia as portrayed in the Icelandic sagas, and indeed throughout the folklore and archaeological remains of earliest man.

> They are small groups and of a simple (archaic) structure; they are commonly peaceful and sedentary; they are poor; and individual ownership is not a dominant feature of their economic system. . . . Indeed, the most notable trait common to members of such communities is a certain amiable inefficiency when confronted with force or fraud.

Enormously influenced by Darwinism, Veblen saw this putative Golden Age as the social environment in which the generic traits of human nature had been biologically selected and fixed. Thus he thought he had a scientific basis for hope: that the mélange of predatory institutions brought in by nomadic barbarians, and in the saddle since, was but a cultural crust which could be scraped away, leaving man as he was biologically meant to be, a creature on the whole willing to live and let live.

This core conception of *The Theory of the Leisure Class* has serious flaws. Veblen was aware of some of them. He knew that the archaic communal life to which, in his view, man was by nature suited, was small-scale and local, while the modern industrial discipline is far-flung and expansive. In a note to *Imperial Germany and the Industrial Revolution*, he observed that the "small-scale, half anarchistic, neighborhood plan of society would be enforceable only within such territorial bounds as would be covered by the habitual range of neighborly contact," but,

> In the course of time, though it appears to have occupied several thousand years of slow but scarcely broken advance, their excessive efficiency in the mechanic arts pushed the North-European peoples out of that state of culture answering to their natural bent. And ever since they so passed the technological limit of tolerance of that archaic scheme of use and wont they have been restlessly casting back for some workable compromise that would permit their ideal of "local self-government" by neighborly common sense to live somehow in the shadow of the large-scale coercive rule that killed it.

In the same book Veblen described how a pre-industrial society like Germany could appropriate the industrial arts and, far from being transformed by them, use them for its pre-existing, that is barbarian, purposes. He did not seem to see that a man conditioned by the cumulative fakery of the leisure-class world, where all was personalized and distorted, might be impervious to the cause-and-effect logic underlying the machine technology, and simply use his factory job as a source of the wherewithal to sustain an emulative life. Nor did he quite appreciate how factory work confines the purposeful bent which can make labor a delight, how, in contrast to all that James and Dewey taught, it permits the emotional engagement of only a fraction of the self.

What is the relevance of Veblen today? His social science was in large part a gloss on then current agrarian attitudes; and where it broke new ground, as in his concept of the discipline of factory work, it leaves many questions unasked.

What survives is an attitude, not a doctrine. Veblen's legacy is the bleak and pungent quality of his belief that the social atmosphere of modern capitalism is in every way hostile to a peaceful, co-operative life. As an immigrant's son (he could not speak fluent English till well on in college) as well as a radical, Veblen was doubly alienated from his society. His detachment, both from the powers-that-be and the reform movements, made possible a thorough commitment to fundamental things.

These qualities remind one of Thoreau, although Veblen is even more bitter, withdrawn, and passive. No one now bothers with Thoreau's theories, such as the notion of "correspondence" between the biological and mental worlds; and in a hundred years, if the interpretation here advanced is correct, few will remember "the instinct of workmanship" or the contrast of "savagery" and "barbarism." Veblen's social psychology will outlive its terminology, his Populist critique its time-bound enemies.

Veblen, like Thoreau, turned back to the enduring qualities of nature and life itself, and arraigned American society as their betrayer. The cabins in the woods which both men frequented are a kind of symbol of this attitude. The fondness for nature and the natural, the rejection of all cant and hypocrisy, the "inner emigration," and in Veblen's case the unaggressive unkemptness and relaxed sexual attitudes—all these would seem to link the attitudes of these men to those of our contemporary Beats, or to the J. D. Salinger characters for whom also a cabin in the woods becomes a symbol of incorruptibility. But the differences are as profound. Neither Veblen nor Thoreau sought escape from the political conflicts of their time, but instead took risks for what they believed in. Both men were disciplined workers who never dreamed that messy behavior would provide an alibi for messy work. And while both men shared a post-Enlightenment distrust of the ravages and ridiculousness of which the human, and perhaps especially the academic, intellect is capable, neither man praised mindlessness nor was fundamentally anti-intellectual—surely not the Veblen who remained a lifelong scholar and devotee of "idle curiosity." If they rejected aspects of their world, it was with the hope of changing them.

And yet it is at this point that the tragic fate of both men becomes most clear. Being, like so many Americans, clearer about "freedom from" than "freedom to," they tended in their bitterness and isolation to become solitary rebels; both men hurt and spurned the companionship they might have had. Escaping from fierce constraint, they distrusted all given authority, all given institutions: they sought (in Thoreau's words) "hard bottom and rocks in place, which we can call reality, and say, This is, and no mistake; and then begin."[8]

We must indeed begin there—begin by seeing reality clear. But further steps, even toward the grasp of reality, require communal sup-

[8] Cf. the similar rejection of institutions by Allen Wheelis, a psychoanalyst influenced by Veblen, in *The Quest for Identity* (1958).

port, and this in turn depends on a human solidarity that neither Veblen nor Thoreau rejected, but that neither could call forth in self or other. Veblen was driven by his epoch to associate solidarity with "savagery," that is, with a prehistoric peaceable tribe. However, quite rejecting folksiness and sentimentality, Veblen also insisted that man must make his peace with the machine; much like C. P. Snow in his lectures on *The Two Cultures and the Scientific Revolution*, Veblen was sensitive to the snobbery and subtle inhumanity hidden in literary hostility to technology and to the modern world. Admiring both the matter-of-fact skepticism he believed industrial man to possess and the amiable, unassertive humanity he attributed to pre-industrial man, Veblen was unable in his own life or in his work to bridge the two cultures, or to envisage a post-industrial world that might be both abundant and fraternal.

Much as Freud saw the advance of civilization as a trap in which man's libidinal and aggressive instincts become turned against himself, so Veblen saw the increase of human productivity as the very source of exploitation and waste: he has few suggestions as to how economic abundance, the fruit of the workmanship of the race, can be used to join men in fraternal solidarity rather than to divide them in emulation and war. With a pessimism characteristic of him, but far rarer in his day than in ours, he wrote:

> History records more frequent and more spectacular instances of the triumph of imbecile institutions over life and culture than of peoples who have, by force of instinctive insight, saved themselves alive out of a desperately precarious institutional situation, such, for instance, as now faces the peoples of Christendom.

Self and Society:
Reflection on Some Turks in Transition
(WITH DANIEL LERNER, c. 1956)

I speak of the relation of the self to *culture* rather than to *society* because there is useful ambiguity which attends the meaning of the word culture. It is the word by which we refer not only to a people's achieved work of intellect and imagination but also to its mere assumptions and unformulated valuations, to its habits, its manners, and its superstitions. The modern self is characterized by certain powers of indignant perception which, turned upon this conscious portion of culture, have made it accessible to conscious thought. . . . Men began to recognize the existence of prisons that were not built of stone, nor even of social restrictions and economic disabilities. They learned to see that they might be immured not only by the overt force of society but by a coercion in some ways more frightful because it involved their own acquiesence. The newly conceived coercive force required of each prisoner that he sign his own *lettre de cachet*, for it had established its prisons in the family life, in the professions, in the image of respectability, in the ideas of faith and duty, in (so the poets said) the very language itself. The modern self, like Little Dorrit, was born in a prison. It assumed its nature and fate the moment it perceived, named, and denounced its oppressor.

And by this act it brought into being not only itself but also the idea of culture as a living thing with a fate of its own, with the possibility, and the necessity, of its own redemption.

The Opposing Self, Lionel Trilling

In the fall of 1950, three hundred long, exploratory interviews were conducted in Turkey by native interviewers trained by a researcher from Columbia University's Bureau of Applied Social Research. The respondents were selected to overrepresent listeners and potential listeners to the Voice of America; thus, three men were interviewed for every woman, urbanites were overchosen, as were upper-income groups. In some villages, the interviewers had difficulty finding anybody who would talk to them, but in general, as in the six other Middle Eastern countries in which similar work was done, it proved possible to reach people at all levels of the social structure, and at virtually all levels of self-awareness. The interest of the Voice of America, which financed the original fieldwork and extensive analysis,[1] in securing some feedback from its broadcasts turned out to provide a record, as fascinating as it is complex, of a country in which the old prisons of the self are in process of being shattered, while the existence of new prisons, products of liberation, is only dimly recognized.

To be sure, the "modern" Turk, like the experts of the Voice, is unambiguously in favor of Progress, of the growth of public opinion and facilities and receptivities of mass communications. In fact, for purposes of our work, "modern" was defined in terms of media exposure, as were the other categories—"traditional" at the opposite extreme, and "transitional," an intermediate type as the term implies. Whereas 33 per cent of the "traditional" Turks in the sample pictured themselves as unhappy, only 15 per cent of those classified as modern did so; and nearly two thirds of the former felt sad or angry about the last piece of news they heard, as against 39 per cent of the former. In fact, these figures understate the difference in the fatalism-optimism dimension of the moderns and the traditionals; the latter have the peasant's despair; the former, a Rotarian bounce.[2]

---

[1] Costs of the follow-up fieldwork and reanalysis of the data were borne by the Center for International Studies, Massachusetts Institute of Technology.

[2] Kemal Ataturk's effectiveness and the absence of an internal Communist threat may be partly responsible for the relatively euphoric reactions of the modern, cosmopolitan Turk to modernity. Quite different is the attitude of a physician, member of the "old" middle class in a Southeast Asian country, who has become a leading political figure and backer of industrialization for his nation. One of us recently met him at a conference on economic development and asked why he was interested in acquiring for his countrymen the techniques which would upset the values he held precious and the social stratum of lawyers, merchants, politicians—mostly quite untechnologically oriented—to which his own family belonged. He replied resignedly that he and his class had no choice in the matter: once the masses had seen Hollywood movies (or their Indian counterparts) and had realized the existence of other ways of life for folk such as themselves, it became a

A key to this difference turned up in the reactions to questions which asked the respondents what they would do if they were President of Turkey, or the editor of a newspaper, and where they would like to live if they could not live in their present locality. Such questions struck the traditional Turk as sacrilegious or senseless: he could not conceive of himself as living anywhere else or being anyone else. When pressed, a number said they would rather commit suicide than live anywhere else (the modern Turk had an easy Eden in Istanbul, Paris, or New York). And a characteristic traditional Turk's reaction to the question about the presidency was: "My God! How can you ask such a thing? How can I . . . I cannot . . . president of Turkey . . . master of the whole world!"

In all probability, these "rooted" individuals (to use a "modern" term —individual—which applies to them only with qualifications) underestimate their actual flexibility when confronted with a new physical setting. Someone steeped in the ethnographic literature of the Zuni or the Navaho might have been startled to see these Indians as GIs in World War II—the former carrying prayer-sticks yet shooting and sometimes even drinking in the all-American way. The very concreteness of the tradition-bound person, his paucity of abstract images of self and society, his relative freedom from ideological projections, may have the consequence that new physical settings, however disquieting and unprepared for, have an immediacy of impact that they lack for a person whose mind has traveled ahead of him, so that any physical encounter is a *déjà vu*.[3]

---

race between the Communists and his own group as to which would arrive first with the most factories, the most Cadillacs. For the modern Turk, however, the competition that spurs the incentive toward change is international, not intranational: for those of humanistic bent, France, and for those directly geared to social and economic change, the United States is the model, quite unqualifiedly worshiped, and the standard against which Turkish "backwardness" is judged.

[3] We may perhaps invoke such considerations to help explain the fact that, during World War II, several Japanese-American battalions, such as the famous 101st, performed extraordinary feats with the conscious intent of proving to an audience not physically present the 100 per cent plus loyalty of the Nisei, whereas segregated Negro battalions, less well educated on the average, had low morale and performed badly. In Korea, however, where Negroes as individuals were filtered into white battalions, they did very well: with the relevant reference group physically present, they were conscious of not wanting to "let the race down." In general, immi-

Another way of putting this is to observe that we often tend today to overestimate the tenacity of culture and of childhood socialization, and to underestimate—despite all the experience with migrations and large-scale acculturation—the ability of adults to absorb elements of a new culture and to undergo partial resocialization. The Turkish materials, not being longitudinal, give us very little direct evidence on this point, but there is one revealing exception in Lerner's follow-up interview with the village chief of Balgat, a tiny hamlet near Ankara. This chief, or *Muhtar*, had struck the urban interviewer in 1950 as "an unpleasant old man . . . mean and clever . . . the absolute dictator of this little village." With ceremonial politeness, he made it very difficult for the interviewer to meet other villagers alone; it would be demeaning, for instance, to have him interview a poor peasant; and, indeed, most of the villagers did make clear that "their" opinions were those of the chief who declared: "Yes, that is my main duty, to give advice. [Interviewer: What about?] About all that I or you could imagine, even about their wives and how to handle them, and how to cure their sick cow."

It would seem from this exchange that the chief could not project himself into the interviewer's place (conceivably, he aggressively did not care to), else he would quickly have realized that the latter *could* imagine advice on other matters than the cure and care of females.[4]

---

grants to the United States have become self-conscious of their ethnic identity only after arrival: the new setting forces a redefinition of the old one, especially after they have "filtered" in among nonethnics.

[4] In a discussion of self-conceptions as revealed through interviews done in Arkansas by the National Opinion Research Center in the wake of a disastrous tornado, Leonard Schatzman and Anselm Strauss observe that lower-class hillbilly respondents could not put themselves in the interviewer's place sufficiently to communicate to him a picture of what had occurred. They would plunge him *in medias res* without telling him so, shift place or pronoun without realizing that he could not follow, and so on. In contrast, better-educated respondents took care that the interviewer was led metaphorically through person, place, and time; could mark off digressions and hearsay as such; and otherwise could give an account that "made sense" across the experiential gap. Indeed, it is likely that they experienced the tornado differently—as "opposing" selves—or at least soon reinterpreted it as a news event such as happens to other people. See Schatzman and Strauss, "Social Class and Modes of Communication," *American Journal of Sociology*, vol. 60, 1954, pp. 329–38.

To be sure, we realize that one must be wary of comparisons between the lower class and the less enlightened in a modern "mass society" like our own and the tradition-oriented, the leaders and followers alike, in a pre-industrial culture. We realize, too, that the disaster-study material is

In the chief's interview, the grand themes of Turkish tradition resound. Asked what he wishes for his grown sons, he declares: "I hope they will fight as bravely as we fought and know how to die as my generation did." Asked about the British, he states: "I hear that they have turned friends with us. But always stick to the old wisdom: 'A good enemy is better than a bad friend.' You cannot *rely* on them. Who has heard of a son being friends with his father's murderers?"

However, such replies, traditional as they may sound, give the impression of a person who is not simply the unquestioning carrier of tradition: tradition itself seems to have become an "ism," a rather self-conscious one which quotes "old wisdom" rather than reflecting it. We learn that the chief has been away from his village in two wars—though he tells the interviewer, when asked where he would like to live: "I was born here, grew up here, and hope God will permit me to die here. . . . I wouldn't move a foot from here."

Even more unsettling, we learn that the chief, to please his sons, has bought a radio, and that every evening at six the leading villagers assemble at his home to hear the news broadcast from Ankara. Not being able to beat the devil (and many villagers, never having seen a radio, consider it literally the voice of the devil), he has sought to restrict him by partial incorporation: "We all listen very carefully," he said, "and I talk about it afterward." Are there any arguments about the news? "No, no arguments, as I tell you I only talk and our opinions are the same more or less."

Two things strike us here. In the first place, there *are* opinions. True, the terrain is traditional; for centuries Turkish peasants have had as a subject of village talk the absence of other Turks in a war abroad. Most opinions on these matters were worked out long ago and have been passed along. But something new is added when the old topic is transmitted as "hot news" simultaneously to groups formed throughout the Anatolian steppe, when certain types of information are incorporated by the urbane Ankara announcer that never figured in the traditional court chronicles of military campaigns, when the available stock of

---

susceptible of varying interpretations; for example, the possibility that the lower-class respondents were resentfully and at least semiconsciously making fools of the interviewers while pretending co-operation (or, possibly, that linguistic difficulties in the narrow sense, rather than broadly semantic issues, were involved). Nevertheless, there would appear to be some similarity in the lacunae of self-other awareness in these historically quite separate settings—a similarity reflected in analogous metaphoric patterns.

opinions is quickly used up and new ones must be prepared to meet the voluminous flow of varied items that comes anew over the radio each day. Thus, with media exposure, even the traditional Turks begin to acquire (and produce) views, not wholly proverbial, on a novel assortment of remote matters ranging from the American aid program to the decline of Western imperialism in Asia. While these same Turks could not conceive of themselves as responsible either for opinions or for affairs of state, they had taken the first step into modern times—into becoming as it were part of an audience-participation show, that is, indeed becoming a public with a public opinion.[5] In the second place, by acquiring a radio the chief had attempted to circumvent the fate that, in the Middle East as elsewhere, has overtaken ruling classes with the advent of the revolutions in technology and communications. Thus, in one Lebanese village, the chief had lost his monopoly of advice when villagers began turning to the young, lower-class bus driver for "the word," much as the American young have typically put their less hip, often foreign-born or rural-born, parents on the shelf. Balgat's *Muhtar*, thought devout and antisecular, had been flexible enough to extend the span of his leadership, over his sons and over his villagers, to the new medium, doling out the messages so that he might, in effect, circumvent them.

As the interviewer soon discovered, the chief's monopoly had already been breached by the village grocer. The latter, fearful about not making a good impression on the interviewer, made an even more unpleasant impression on him than the chief did: he seemed pretentious and out of place; as the interviewer wrote:

> The respondent is comparatively the most city-like dressed man in the village. He even wore some sort of necktie. . . . Although he is on the same level with the other villagers, when there are a few of the villagers around, he seems to want to distinguish himself by keeping quiet, and as soon as they depart he starts to talk too much. . . . He most evidently wished to feel that he is closer to me than he is to them and was curiously careful with his accent all during the interview. In spite of his unique position, for he is the only unfarming person and the only merchant in the village, . . . he is considered by the villagers even less than the least farmer.

[5] Cf. Hans Speier, "The Historical Development of Public Opinion" and Leo Lowenthal, "Historical Perspectives of Popular Culture," both in the *American Journal of Sociology*, vol. 55, 1950.

Understandably enough, it is precisely this middleman, this marginal man who could see himself as the interviewer saw him, who alone among the villagers could imagine himself living somewhere else, with a different style of life. He wanted to go to America, and to further probes, he declared: "I have told you I want better things. I would have liked to have a bigger grocery shop in the city, have a nice house there, dress in nice civilian clothes. . . . I am not like the others here. They don't know any better. And when I tell them, they are angry and they say that I am ungrateful for what Allah has given me."

Asked what he would do if President of Turkey, he did not hesitate: "I would make roads for the villagers to come to towns to see the world and would not let them stay in their holes all their lives."

The grocer had no formal education; he was poor—far poorer than the landowning chief. Yet he had "seen Paree"; he had been to Ankara to shop; and some villagers, though they might scorn him, came to him, of all people, for advice. What about? "What to do when they go to Ankara, where to go and what to buy, how much to sell their things which they take to Ankara."

All the old feudal issues, of bravery versus the cash nexus, are implicit in this revelation. The grocer is not yet a member of the elite, but the old elite is threatened by his presence, "fat shadow" though the interviewer called him. Torn between two worlds, he is self-conscious in the literal sense, as in his pathetic desire to impress the city-bred interviewer; he is the membrane through whom the new currents enter Balgat. The poor shepherd with whom the interviewer managed to talk despite the chief's ban was not allowed to hear the radio—"How can I go to the guest room? It is not for *us*"—and could only imagine killing himself if forced to leave Turkey—but even such a man could obtain through the grocer some indirect access to the imagery of the modern world.

The Middle East Research defined the grocer and his like as "transitional" Turks, a group differentiated by its at least moderate degree of exposure to mass communications despite lowly social and economic status. No ready occupational and demographic criteria distinguished the transitionals: in a village, one might find a farmer who listened to the BBC, though no wealthier or more literate than his neighbor who thought such listening impious; in a town, one might find a laborer whose communications behavior linked him with the cosmopolitan world of the coffee houses among a group of country-bred fellows who had as yet moved only physically from the farm. Very often, too, as with the grocer, these transitional Turks were unhappy—unhappy in a new, fatalistic way, that is. Their aspirations, for themselves and often for wider orbits, outran their possibilities. The grocer had seen in a movie what a *real* store might be like—"with walls made of iron sheets, top to floor and side to side, and on them standing myriads of round boxes, clean and all the same dressed, like soldiers in a great parade."[6] Whereas the traditional Turks spend their leisure, such as it is, in "doing nothing" or in visiting, these transitional "middlebrows" in more than half the cases spent it in attending to one of the mass media, and almost three quarters of them also took part in some organized leisure-time activity, such as sports, card games, or civic work.

The grocer, it turned out, was even something of a movie critic: "The Turkish ones are gloomy. I can guess at the start of the film how it will end. They are ordinary. But the American ones are not like that. They are exciting. You know, it makes people ask 'what will happen next?'"

Hollywood will be glad to hear that! Indeed, in making such a judgment, in which he stands at a distance from himself ("it makes people ask") and from his country, the grocer shows the subtle interplay that exists between self-consciousness and exposure to the mass media. The transitional Turks differ from their neighbors of similar status in the variables of self-attitudes—the ability for empathic self-projection—and behavior vis-à-vis the media, but in no other discernible way. While in some respects they resemble the "opinion leaders" who have been identified in some American studies,[7] they would appear to be less aware of their strategic position as middlemen in the flow of communication; they are rather potential middlemen, awaiting the further unsettling of the *Muhtars*—and possibly a lessened unsettling of themselves.

Envisaging the Grocer and the Chief as the symbolic protagonists of the drama of modernization, played out in a country which has cut the literate old off from the young by revolutionizing the alphabet, Lerner visited Balgat in the spring of 1954. The interviewer who had gone there in 1950 had meanwhile left to join the Turkish foreign service.

[6] The chief had seen several movies; he commented: "There are fights, shooting. The people are brave. My sons are always impressed. Each time they see such a film they wish more and more their time for military service would come so that they could become soldiers too." It is hard to imagine the chief regarding A & P tin cans as "a great parade."

[7] See Elihu Katz and Paul Lazarsfeld, *Personal Influence* (The Free Press, 1955).

Even greater changes, it was soon discovered, had come over the lives of the Balgatians. As a result of the fabulous election of 1950, which had turned out Ataturk's heirs and installed the Democratic party in the new nation's first free election, a road had been built connecting Balgat with Ankara, and a trip which had once been a good half-day's journey over rough terrain took merely half an hour by regular bus. The grocer's dream had come true, but meanwhile this unsung Prometheus had died.

However, the most astonishing news was still to come: the sons of the chief, trained to be stern soldiers as befitted the land-owning gentry, had changed their profession. They were shopkeepers: the younger a clothier, the elder—a grocer. Not only that, but their father was not without pride in them. Retroactively, we realize that all his talk, four years earlier, about his hopes for his sons' bravery and military glory must even then have been domestic psychological warfare, premised on his insecurity as to what his sons would actually do rather than on age-old warrior tradition. One of the sons even sold neckties.

Naturally, such a change did not stand alone; others no less momentous had occurred. In a month, after the coming election, Balgat was to be incorporated into Greater Ankara and be administered as part of that city; the chief declared: "I am the last *Muhtar* of Balgat, and I am happy that I have seen Balgat end its history in this way that we are going." The new ways, we asked, are then not bringing evil with them? The chief was far from bitter; he responded:

> No, people will have to get used to different ways and then some of the excesses, particularly among the young, will disappear. The young people are in some ways a serious disappointment; they think more of clothes and good times than they do of duty and family and country. But it is to be hoped that as the *Demokrat* men complete the work they have begun, the good Turkish ways will again come forward to steady the people. Meanwhile, it is well that people can have to eat and to buy shoes they always needed but could not have.

Even to the new ways of his sons, the chief seemed reluctantly acclimated:

> They are as the others. They think first to serve themselves and not the nation. They have no wish to go to the battle in Korea, where Turkey fights before the eyes of all the world. They are my sons and I speak no ill of them, but I say only that they are as all the others.

And we realize suddenly the pathos of the chief; he no longer strikes us, as he did the first interviewer, as mean and clever, but rather as a man whose bravery, far from instinctive, had now to be turned inward on his own reactions rather than outward in battle and command—he has come a long way toward the "opposing self," toward the modern sin of intrapunitiveness. Even if we assume that the chief's "real" attitudes changed less than did his behavior toward an interviewer who was a fellow Turk as against one who was an American, this very capacity to present markedly different opinions—to pull out on demand, so to speak, different file trays—would seem to indicate how shaky was his earlier adherence to tradition. In any event, the end of his chieftainship, and the shift in his sons' "calling," must have affected him profoundly, quite apart from conventional politeness to two city-bred interviewers.

Lerner counted sixty-nine radio antennae on the roofs—product of the new-found suburbanites' ability to earn wages in Ankara and to spend them on consumer goods. Hardly anyone farmed any more, and nearly everyone with whom the visitors from Ankara spoke had opinions about many matters.

In the United States today, with major immigration cut off and with the whole population more or less literate, urbanized, and mobilized, we are no longer daily reminded of the rapidity with which whole populations can become habituated to change and attuned to its various rhythms.[8] Nor save perhaps for Negroes from the Deep South who have moved to northern cities, are we reminded of the intense excitement which the first stirrings of literacy and of mass communication can generate among the previously inarticulate, unpoliticized peoples. With an organized social order, an accomplished industrial revolution, and an increasingly sophisticated consumership taken for granted, even the continued social mobility of American life, up the ladders of the educational system, no longer appears as revolutionary. Instead, American energies would appear to be increasingly channeled into the development of what we shall term the "mobile sensibility"—the personality so adaptive to changes through time, space, and empathy that displacement is its permanent mode.

The mobile sensibility is distinguished by its capacity for easy identi-

[8] Extreme instances, which nevertheless indicated the general tendency, were the cases before World War I of children from Central and Eastern Europe, brought here by their parents, moving in one fast jump from a traditional culture to the peaks of the contemporary mind or the intricacies of the contemporary market.

fication with new aspects of its environment. Linguistic forms no longer bind the self in quasi-Kantian constructions; perceptual forms are rearranged with relative ease, even while the objects "seem" are of course also transformed by the active personality. The psychoanalysts speak of projection (or introjection) but our interest here is not in the subtle details of theories of perception but in the large historical movements which bring enlarged capacity for projection or identification in their wake. In *The Lonely Crowd* this shift was described, as a first very rough approximation, in terms of a typology which saw inner-direction as developing out of tradition-directed cultures, and other-direction, with its increase in the mobile sensibility, as the product of a late stage in the development of the "modern" personal style—a state associated with routinized industrialization, economic abundance, and a plethora of mass communications.

Tradition-direction was defined, in *Faces in the Crowd,* in terms of "the impossibility of conceiving alternatives to the specific ways in which people in the given culture act, think, and believe"; more specifically:

> To conceive of the existing as "good" already belongs to more advanced mechanisms: for the tradition-directed person, what exists, for his group at any rate, is all that can exist. While the culture may institutionalize means of expressing certain dissatisfactions, as by joking, or through folk tales, there is no conception that the total shape of the society will change, or that man's way, for a given social station, will not be virtually the same for one's children and grandchildren as it has been for one's ancestors. . . . In America . . . too many alternatives (for tradition-direction to exist) are evident—evident even to the most isolated, the dullest, the most oppressed, or the most satisfied. There are no real traditions to which to conform; only false traditions, that is, ideologies.

It follows that an American can almost invariably project himself into the position of a newspaper editor or politician, and can connect the problems he faces with those "his" country faces. But when we ask the Turk here defined as traditional to make this connection, he fumbles. While if we ask him to name *his* biggest problem, he can say he is too poor and will in fact name an economic problem two thirds of the time (much as will both the modern and the transitional Turks), he is stumped when we ask him what is *Turkey's* biggest problem: he cannot "project" personal problems or link them with abstractions, "isms," and ideologies (only 8 per cent named economic problems of Turkey).

As against this, those we have defined as transitional Turks have moved a long way toward the awareness of alternatives for such abstractions as "Turkey" that accompanies the development of the mobile sensibility. In this group, more than a third of those who said their own biggest problem was economic, 21 per cent in all, named economic matters as the nation's problem. Similarly, if we ask the traditional Turk what he would like to know about America, he is likely in nearly half the cases to ask about concrete, personally related things: is it cold, will they be friendly to me, can I get a job; whereas only 15 per cent ask about more abstract matters, such as freedom of religion, and only 3 per cent about cultural matters, such as music. In contrast, 38 per cent of the transitional Turks ask about social order or ideology, and 9 per cent about cultural matters. Whereas nearly half of those classified as traditional Turks are unwilling or unable to express opinions on such matters as the likelihood of another war, or American or British policy toward Turkey, from 83 per cent to 90 per cent of the transitional Turks have opinions on these questions, approximating in this respect the opinion-proneness of the modern Turk. For the worldly modern, there is, of course, no difficulty in collating his personal problems and public problems; he can compare, equate, or differentiate them. He appears to possess aspects of the high self-consciousness and other-consciousness (if not always of what Trilling refers to as the "powers of indignant perception") which seem typical of the most advanced sectors of Western society. The most cosmopolitan Turks live in Istanbul, read *Time*, travel abroad, have British and American friends, and in most if not all respects are at home with the "international" (shall we say, late Bauhaus) style in personality as in architecture.[9] The modern Turk has projected himself on the world; he has taken the world inside himself.

We are far from understanding all that this may mean, but let us attempt to examine some of the implications. Our interviewers, it should

[9] An example is the high-school-educated well-to-do lady of leisure who, seeing Turkish movies as lying "heavy on one's soul," spoke of American films as follows: "I like films made in the U.S.A. because they have a grand style about them. It was apparent that no money was begrudged for anything, and even the underclothes of the stars which will not be seen are of the best quality. The technicolors are excellent . . . There are a great many actors and actresses so that one cannot get tired of seeing the same people all the time."

be recalled, do not tell us the proportion of these three categories in the Turkish population at large (we do know, from the 1945 census, that over 70 per cent of the population is illiterate); all our interviews permit us to do is to erect suggestive typologies, leaving the question of quantitative distribution and relative social and political power for further investigation. Nevertheless, even a few cases enable us to see that the modern Turk, largely urban and a member of the professional classes, exhibits the same principle of "the more, the more" which we find among Americans: if he belongs to any voluntary associations, he is likely to belong to several; if he reads any papers and journals, he will read several; if he has an organized leisure activity, he will have more than one—and each of these spheres is interrelated to the point or saturation or "communications overload." The transitional Turk is on his way to this point, but still has connections with, and shares features of, the traditional way of life. Perhaps the most significant finding is that the correlate of becoming "transitional" would appear to lie in projectivity itself: those Turks who are able to conceive of themselves as being somewhere else and doing something else have begun to be exposed and to expose themselves to the media, even though they may still be villagers, illiterate, and poor. To be sure, we do not know (despite the follow-up visit to Balgat) whether fact follows fiction, or life imitates art: other factors besides individual psychological bent help determine which Turks actually do begin the steps toward occupational and structural modernity. But what we do see is that the mobile sensibility can precede actual mobility (Robert K. Merton terms this "anticipatory socialization"), and that the media are harbingers, or perhaps more accurately indices, of the widening orbits of empathy, ideology, and self-awareness. They provide for the isolated transitional Turk a "secondary" public even before, so far as our data show, he has the support of a primary group. (The traditional Turk, of course, is still embedded in an oral tradition; even if movies are available to him, he thinks them either, as already indicated, the work of the devil or a waste of time; or, as one older farmer said: "I do not care at all and even if I had enough money, I would not buy a radio. [Why?] I don't like too much news." This same farmer also stated: "Novels are just nonsense stuff and they are not real." No image of the "opposing self" for him.

All this is obviously speculative. The very nature of the interview requires a certain ability to identify with others (as the Schatzman-Strauss materials amplify), and these interviews were done where they could be done, and not in a properly randomized way. Then, too, we lack participant-observation which would connect interview statements with "real-life" behavior, and conceivably would reveal unsuspected face-to-face support for some of those we have termed transitional Turks. Our typological scaffold rests, as such typologies generally do, on all too few cases.[10] Yet at the same time the increase in the mobile sensibility which these interviews hint at would seem to be connected, at the level of political life, with the often desperate and frenzied search in the Middle East for labels and categories of identity. The very term "Middle East" is a Western invention which native politicians have taken up, in an effort to impute uniformity and homogeneity to an area undergoing fantastically rapid flux and change. It competes with such other terms as "Arab World," "Muslim Bloc," "Fertile Crescent," all of which are more or less empty slogans when an effort is made to fix concrete boundaries or to take account of the sects and schisms among the followers of the Koran. The Turks are a bit better off, since Kemal Ataturk gave them an identity which has lasted for thirty years, but this may only mean that the models for imitation are allowed to swing in a wider arc. Whereas some Turks are angry with Americans because, as one put it, they "think we are living in the days of our ancestors," and thus show the sensibility of *arrivistes*, others express a belief that brings Condorcet to mind:

> Ever since I was a child I used to dream and think about people. I used to imagine all people equal, having nice homes. In my imagination I used to send their children to school and educate them. Now, as an adult, I know that America is the country I used to dream about.

Both the modern and the transitional Turks have the stuff that dreams are made of, but whether they have, or can acquire, the stuff for turning dreams into social and organizational reality is the problem that confronts them, as it confronts the other peoples whom, in our ambivalence, we no longer speak of as "backward" but euphemistically

[10] Nevertheless, it is encouraging that an analysis of over 2000 interviews done in the Middle East, in terms of latent structure analysis, indicated the high probability of the typology's usefulness as a predictive statement of "what goes with what" as modernization proceeds. A preliminary discussion of the typology appears in Lerner, "A Scale Pattern of Opinion Correlates: Communication Networks, Media Exposure, and Concomitant Responses," *Sociometry*, 16:266–71, 1953.

as "underdeveloped." While it is probable that the distribution of the techniques of industrialization and urbanization does not require the same inner-directed hardihood as their initial invention and promulgation, it is an open question whether a people can move without inviting chaos directly from a pre-industrial culture to the consumer mentality that accompanies the mobile sensibility.[11] It would seem that a strong support for communism in such countries comes from those who feel that the Puritan phase of "primitive accumulation" cannot be bypassed, yet do not trust their own and their fellows' ability to work and wait industriously for dreams to come true: in the East people look to dictatorship to get around vested dreams, as in the West to get around vested interests. The mobile sensibility has lost the constrictions that defend the tradition-directed person against novel ideological abstractions and has opened the way to the battle of slogans and parties. Yet these concerns, shared as they are with Point IV experts, applied anthropologists, and State Department officials, fail to capture the more deeply existential drama of self and society in Turkey and the other Middle Eastern countries. America has caught up with, perhaps even surpassed, Western Europe in its ambivalence toward the "opposing self," its growing doubt about linear progress and liberation. We look at the modern and transitional Turks, when they express roseate vi-

[11] All conservative economists, and many merely reasonable ones, tend to emphasize the need for some development of the austere virtues which lead people to save part of their income; and then to use their savings, when they do, for investment designed to increase the amount of wealth available for enjoyment in some postponed future rather than for consumption that enhances immediate gratifications. People can more easily organize their social values around so demanding a behavioral discipline when they have developed enough imagination to differentiate present from future in some such minimax calculus. What imagination provides is the capacity to invent and "savor" future delights. This sort of process, in which the expanding projectivity of the self makes it possible to overcome the demands for immediate gratification, is what we have been talking about under the head of "mobile sensibility." So Ragnar Nurske, after a lucid analysis of the economics of development, concludes that the matrix of basic decisions that make development possible lies in the domain of individual and social psychology. See Nurske, *Problems of Capital Formulation in Underdeveloped Countries*, 1953; see also Jacob Viner in: B. F. Hoselitz, *The Progress of Underdeveloped Areas*, 1952; Alfred Bonne, *The Economic Development of the Middle East*, 1945; Riesman, "Some Relationships between Technical Progress and Social Progress," *Explorations in Entrepreneurial History*, 6:3, 1954.

sions of our own country, as adults look at those vanishing children who are still able to believe in Santa Claus. Just as only an arrogant and heartless rich man can say to the poor man, "Why do you want my job, with my troubles and taxes?", so very few Americans are likely to say to the Turks, "Don't be like us."[12] In any case, our deeds would speak louder than words, and for us the most interesting question is, whether by the time the Turks and their like have caught up with their image of where we are now, we will have used our much more complex mobile sensibility to take us toward a more complex and valuable, rather than a merely cumulative, destiny.

[12] Recall in this connection the comments of the Muhtar of Balgat, whose traditional values and authority had both been radically undermined: "The young people are in some ways a serious disappointment . . . But it is to be hoped that . . . the good Turkish ways will again come forward. Meanwhile, it is well that people can have to eat and to buy shoes they always needed but could not have."

The Oral Tradition, the Written Word, and the Screen Image

(1955)

I want to deal in this essay with three large and general questions: first, what are the differences between cultures that depend entirely on the spoken word and those that depend on print; second, what will be the significance of the written word now that newer mass media, less demanding psychologically and yet perhaps more potent politically, have developed; third, what is likely to happen in those countries where the tradition of books is not fully established and where the newer media are already having a decisive impact. I shall deal with these questions, each of which deserves many books, suggestively rather than exhaustively; I shall browse, so to speak, among these topics, not worrying too much about digressions if they seem to shed light. Let me add that I am greatly indebted for guidance in this general area, and for this paper, to Mark Benney.

We need not be arrant materialists to realize that the form of transmission and storage of knowledge has immense relevance for its power and breadth and potential growth. The late Harold A. Innis of the University of Toronto took a rather crabbed, Spenglerian pleasure (in such books as *The Bias of Communications* and *Changing Concepts of Time*) in showing that, historically speaking, the materials on which words were written down have often counted for more than the words themselves. For instance, he argues that papyrus, being light and readily stored in a desert land, put the priests of Egypt in command of the calendar and, in Big Brother fashion, of social memory, and was essential to the spread of Egyptian dynasties in space and the hegemony of the priests in time. The clay tablets of Sumeria were put out of business by the greater convenience of the newer forms (much as many downtown movie houses have been put out of business by TV and the drive-ins). Perhaps it was understandable that a Canadian should be one of the first to study such problems systematically, after watching his country's forests being cut down on behalf of the *Reader's Digest* and other forms of American imperialism.

In the beginning—a beginning now so remote from our own experience that we have a hard time grasping it—the only word was the spoken word (though we may suppose that in virtually all cultures objects, including human bodies, were made to stand for other objects, that is, were regarded as symbols). Anthropologists no longer speak of the peoples they study—and they do still study peoples as well as powers—as primitives, let alone as savages (as Malinowski did); many prefer the less argumentative term "preliterate"—and I do not think they are wrong in making literacy a decisive dividing point.[1] While there are important differences, recently emphasized by the anthropologist Robert Redfield between the preliterate tribe, which depends entirely on an oral tradition, and the peasant culture where illiterate folk dwell within the moral and intellectual ambit of a great tradition of written literature, as in China or India or many other parts of the world past and present, we will not here be concerned with the differences, though we shall note the tendency, where the oral tradition is exclusive, for the old to have an exalted place as the storage banks of experience and entertainment, whereas writing, as in the example of Egypt, tends to foster hierarchies of skill along with those of age.

In Ruth Underhill's transcript of the autobiography of a Papago Indian woman are some passages which convey a sense of the impact of the spoken word in a culture where no other modes of communication compete with it. One passage goes as follows:

The men from all the villages met at Basket Cap Mountain, and there my father made them speeches, sitting with his arms folded and talking low as all great men do. Then they sang the war songs:

> Oh, bitter wind, keep blowing
> That therewith my enemy
> Staggering forward
> Shall fall. . . .

[1] However, some anthropologists insist on "nonliterate," which makes no assumption about stages of development or any imputation in favor of literacy.

> Many, many songs they sang but I, a woman, cannot tell you all. I know that they made the enemy blind and dizzy with their singing and that they told the gopher to gnaw their arrows. And I know that they called on our dead warriors who have turned into owls and live in the Apache country to come and tell them where the enemy were.

In the many passages of this sort that one can find in ethnographic accounts, we become aware of the immense emotional force that can be harnessed by the spoken word in such a group—so powerful here that at least in fancy it can shatter the morale of a distant enemy. On such an occasion, the quiet voice of the father is resonant with the memories of the tribe. And so, too, on less formal occasions, as when on long winter nights the Papago woman's brothers would say, "My father, tell us something," and the father, lying quietly on his mat, would start to recount how the world began. She continues:

> Our story about the world is full of songs, and when the neighbors heard my father singing they would open our door and step in over the high threshold. Family by family they came, and we made a big fire and kept the door shut against the cold night. When my father finished a sentence we would all say the last word after him.

Implicit here is the fact that a society dependent on oral traditions and oral communications is, by our standards, a slow-paced one: there is time enough, for grownups as well as children, to roll back the carpet of memories; nobody has to miss the ceremonies in order to catch the 8:05 the next morning from Scarsdale—or to run the train itself. To be sure, the teen-age girls today who get by heart the lyrics of popular songs do seem to have time enough on their hands to memorize verses, but even they must learn a new repertory every year and will surely not, as parents, sing these songs of their dating years to their own children. (In fact, as some studies done at Chicago by John Johnstone and Elihu Katz indicate, teen-age girls change their song preferences not only with age but with situation: in some groups they choose sad lyrics if they date often and are popular—possibly because they have plumbed the depths and learned that even if you get what you want you do not want it—whereas the wallflowers who date seldom or never are apt to like happy songs of successful love.)

What I have said needs to be qualified in several respects familiar to those of you who have done group singing informally. I do have the impression, strengthened by assiduous reading of jukebox labels, that there is a kind of sediment of tunes and ballads—"Stormy Weather" for example—which bind at least the jazz generations into an occasional songfest, more or less barbershop quartet style. Then there are the folk songs which many Antioch students and alumni probably have in common, as the highbrow variant of "Boola Boola" and "10,000 Men of Harvard." But for none of these songs is it terribly important to know the right words—the lyrics are not altogether meaningless even I suppose in the so-called "nonsense" songs, but neither do they encapsulate the history of the tribe or the patterns of heroic behavior.

What I am getting at is that the spoken or sung word is particularly impressive when it monopolizes the symbolic environment; but once books have entered that environment the social organization can never be the same again. Books bring with them detachment and a critical attitude that is not possible in a society dependent on the spoken word. We can occasionally have second thoughts about a speech, but we cannot hear it, as we can read a book, backward as well as forward—that is, the writer can be checked up on in a way that the speaker or, as we shall see, the movie-maker, cannot be. When a whole society depends on what individuals can remember, it can hardly help depending on every device of the demagogue and the poet: rhyme, rhythm, melody, structure, repetition. Van Der Kroef in a recent article on "Some Head-Hunting Traditions of Southern New Guinea," [*American Anthropologist* (1952) vol. 54, pp. 221–35] states:

> ". . . the names of neighboring friendly peoples and of specific locations are still given to dogs and pigs, supposedly in order that they may be better remembered. In some instances, as, for example, among tribes north of the Digoel River, names of woods, creeks, marshes are added to the head-name of the child, to indicate where the [head-hunting] victim was caught. It is important that these names be kept fixed in the memory of the people, for every head-hunting village has a definite area in which it may operate."

Beyond such devices, people tend to remember best the things they have felt most deeply: the memorable words in a culture wholly dependent on the spoken word will often be those most charged with group feeling; and we would expect communication to keep alive in an individual the childhood sense of dependence, childhood's terrors and elations, and something of its awe for the old. Indeed, one might argue that one can hardly speak of *individuals* in the modern sense in such cultures, since individuation depends to some degree on social differentiation and distance. Of course, this statement, like my other generalizations, has to be qualified. One thinks, for example, of the specialists on recollection who develop in some tribes, perhaps from among the more compulsive types; thus, among the Zuni Indians there are those who can recall the prayers for rain and other ceremonials with word-perfect accuracy—here the individual words have lost affective tone, and rote learning has taken the place of fireside forensics. The Zuni prayermonger, in his somewhat more individualized emotional make-up, seems to prefigure the monk of the Middle Ages, or the docile student who sometimes passes as the good student.

In significant ways, however, virtually everyone in a preliterate tribe is a specialist in the oral tradition. The anthropologist Fred Eggan, who has done field work in the remote islands of the Philippines, reports that messages are conveyed orally there with an accuracy that is fabulous to us, aware as we are through experience and experiment that a message or rumor need only pass through two or three of a daisy chain before becoming quite unrecognizable. For these tribesmen, words are like the buckets in a fire brigade, to be handled with full attention, while for us we feel we can afford to be careless with the spoken word, backstopped as we are by the written one.

But of course there is another sense, since we all began life as preliterates, in which our written tradition is backstopped by an oral one. The psychologist Ernest Schachtel, in his paper "On Memory and Childhood Amnesia," pointed out how the categories of the adult culture—which is largely the culture of the written word—blot out for most of us our childhood imagery—this gets lost not, as Freud thought, because it is sexual and forbidden, but because it is irrelevant to the communications we attend to as socialized, useful, adaptable, literate people. We still dream in the earlier, what Erich Fromm calls, the forgotten language, and our great artists often renew themselves and us by translations from that language into the agreed-upon written vernacular of the adult.

It would be interesting to know if mothers still read to children, now that TV is such an admirable baby-sitter for the baby-sitter. One might even suggest the possibility that reading to children (and having them in turn read to us) is one way to help establish an emotional relation to words which will later be taken out in books—for the analytic mode in which books can be read is itself of course the product of an emotional orientation foreign to many cultures and to many strata within our own culture.

Here again, of course, since even the most drastic and dramatic social changes are less than total, one can find preliterate precursors of contemporary modes. The proverb, as an invented repository of tribal lore and wisdom, appears in certain respects to be a kind of bridge between the oral and the written stages of history. Edwin Loeb, writing several years ago in the *Scientific Monthly*, proposed the hypothesis that the proverb, as a kind of abstract, generalizing, easily remembered statement about experience—the most literate, so to speak, of the preliterate styles of speech—is associated with cattle-raising people. It is in such relatively advanced, seminomadic people that the need for a distinct body of property laws first tends to be felt—to whom does the new calf belong?—and the proverb is a convenient mnemonic of tribal judgments. By the same token, proverbs may bespeak the replacement of matriarchal by patriarchal authority: the crescent power of abstractions over the concrete, of the *ex cathedra* over the spontaneous and parochial.

If, however, the parochial is to be transcended more completely, merely oral communications, even if codified into proverbs, must give way to more complex forms. We touch here on problems of the relation between linguistic forms and societal forms explored by such scholars as Susanne Langer, Dorothy Lee, and Benjamin Whorf—problems of tantalizing intricacy, where teleological solutions are at once attractive and suspect. At any rate, cases have been found where highly symmetrical, often geometric motifs of decoration have appeared in societies dependent on oral tradition at that point where, as we can retroactively see, a scribe turns out to be an essential figure—as if verbal and visual modes had been in some way complementary. But it would carry me very far beyond my own sphere of limited competence to discuss the dialectic between informative and affirmative modes of communication—between frozen metaphors (where a symbol no longer carries the affective freight it once did) and thawing traditions.

The shift to a literate culture, historically decisive as it is, does not of course occur all at once: only a tiny minority could read prior to the age of print, and the reading of manuscripts altered styles of communication rather less than one might today think. For one thing, manuscripts, having to be slowly deciphered, promoted memorization, which in turn promoted argument by quotation and commentary.

Manuscripts were often read aloud and, with their beautiful illuminations, were regarded not simply as rationalistic vehicles of knowledge but also as shared artifacts. By exteriorizing, by making palpable, the processes of thinking and discussion, they promoted individuation only partially, while also promoting adherence to tradition.

Indeed, even after Gutenberg (as Marshall McLuhan reminds us), it took time for men to learn to read books in the modern manner: they read aloud even when to themselves, just as they spelled freely and phonetically (until Samuel Johnson came on the scene). It is the Puritan who characteristically learns a silent, "unilluminated" reading, his head moving rapidly back and forth across the lines like a shuttle. Only at this relatively late point does the printed book open doors within as well as close doors without, and make good its invitation to isolation from the noise of others' presence.

The book is one of the first, and very possibly the most important, mass-produced products of the modern age, and its impact is an interesting demonstration of the simplistic falsity of the common notion that mass production per se brings about the massification of men—for the book, as I have already implied, tends to assist their individuation. A study by Eliot Freidson indicates that this may be true even of comic books for children; in interviews, children report that they associate the comics with being alone, just as they associate TV with the family, and the movies with the friends of their own age. However, the comic book, along with four-color advertising and picture magazines, may have brought back, as McLuhan argues, some of the qualities and emotional states associated with the manuscript era. As against this, the printed, unillustrated book imposes a direct consecutiveness and orderliness on the reader, implicit in its numbered pages, its table of contents, while it also allows the reader, as I remarked a moment ago, to turn back and forth to compare one statement with another. In this context, the librarians' Dewey decimal system, like microfilm or electronic scanning, reduces the import of the book as a physical object, while making more efficient its role as an impalpable carrier of information. (To be sure, a few authors, like E. E. Cummings, try to recreate spatial, palpable order or disorder on the page, perhaps as a kind of belated anti-Puritan rejoinder to the centuries of black columns and justified straight margins.)

I have been saying that the book, like an invisible monitor, helps liberate the reader from his group and its emotions, and allows the contemplation of alternative responses and the trying on of new emotions. Max Weber has stressed the importance of the merchant's account book in rationalizing the merchant and his commerce; and other historians have made familiar the role of the printed Bible in challenging the authority of the Roman Church. Luther, and especially Calvin, increasing by their doctrines the growing isolation of men, invited each pilgrim to progress by himself, Book in hand, while at the same time (as Fromm argues in *Escape from Freedom*) trying to institute a new authority in place of the old. But, as the dissident sects of Protestantism (and, indeed, of modern Catholicism) illustrate, the book tends to be a solvent of authority: just as there are still blank pages in the merchant's account book waiting to be filled, so there is always the question, when one has challenged traditional authority, "What next?" That is, the book with its numbered pages links yesterday to today in an orderly progression but encourages extrapolation into the future. (This is especially characteristic of the individual's own book, the diary which is the time-and-emotion study by which many men and women of the type my collaborators and I have termed inner-directed recorded the progress of their individuation.) I know no better description of this process than the opening lines of *The Pilgrim's Progress*:

> As I walked through the wilderness of this world, I lighted on a certain place where there was a Den, and I laid me down in that place to sleep: and, as I slept, I dreamed a dream. I dreamed, and behold, I saw a man clothed with rags, standing in a certain place, with his face from his own house, a book in his hand, and a great burden upon his back. I looked, and saw him open the book, and read therein; and, as he read, he wept and trembled; and, not being able longer to contain, he broke out with a lamentable cry, saying, "What shall I do?"

At the same time, while the printed book helped people, as in Bunyan's image, to break away from their family circle and parish, it helped link them into noncontiguous associations of true believers. Arthur E. Morgan, speaking in *Search for Purpose* of his childhood among small-town folk of limited horizons, remarks "This library [in the town] was like foster parents to me." Thomas and Znaniecki describe an analogous process (in their book on *The Polish Peasant in Europe and America*); the Polish peasant who learned to read and write became identified with the urban world of progress and enlightenment, of ideology and utopia, even while physically still in the peasant world. This identification had many of the elements of a conversion, print itself and the world it opened up being a kind of gospel. Today, in this country of near universal literacy we have forgotten the enthusiasm for print which can burst on people newly literate—the "each one, teach one" movements of Mexico, the Philippines, and elsewhere; the voracity for books (for what most librarians would define as good books) in the Soviet Union and other recently industrialized lands. (Indeed, it is probably not accidental that it is the great, largely self-taught industrialists, such as Carnegie, who have been among the most influential patrons and promoters of the library movement in this country—just as the self-taught printer, Ben Franklin, was one of the early pioneers.) Among the highly educated, and in the countries of long-established literacy, there is little comparable enthusiasm. We have become less excited about books as such, or even about "good books," and instead are more discriminating in terms of fields, of tastes, of literary fashions. Our world, as we know all too well, is full of many other things which compete with books, so that some of that minority who were avid readers as children, shutting out parents and peers with faces (as the latter would charge) buried in a book, are now buried as adults in activities that exclude books or make them simply one more almost limitless demand of what the well-thought-of person must attend to.

In any case, our experience in recent years with mass literacy and mass communications has generally been disillusioning—much as with universal suffrage. Thus, we no longer believe, as numerous thoughtful people did in the 1920s, that radio offers a second chance at animated adult education and civic literacy. Likewise, despite a few shining hours, few observers today regard educational TV as anything like an adequate counterweight to the endlessly smiling, relaxed informalities and (for many in the audience) lack of challenge of low-pressure uneducational TV. (Paradoxically, however, the coming of TV has given new possibilities back to the radio in the bedroom, for the TV audience is now the mass audience, and the radio can appeal to the wish for privacy, and to specialized tastes and minority audiences.) With rare exceptions, it is now the massness of the mass media, rather than their mediating and individuating power, which frightens and depresses many educated people —so much so that we frequently lose faith in enlightenment itself as a goal, let alone in the three easy lessons with which our predecessors sought to reach it. Sometimes, in fact, despair goes to such lengths that the writers of bombast on behalf of books, as if in answer to the spreaders of bombast on behalf of TV, are apt to urge that if only people read books once more, long and serious books that require close attention, the evils of the modern world would be undone and we would be saved.

The fact is, however, that books, whatever their liberating power in society as a whole, can be used, of course, in nonliberating ways. For instance, a child can be forced into slavery to print through parental fanaticism or pedagogue's pressures. Yet this happens less frequently today than heretofore. Indeed, we tend to think the education of John Stuart Mill by his high-pressure father, in which he learned to read at three and studied the classics before he was ten, as monstrous as it is amazing. We think the French and the orthodox Jews are cruel to make small children mind their lessons with no time out for sports, let alone for cultivating the "whole child." Psychoanalysts talk of the kind of characterological orality which has nothing to do with the oral tradition and everything to do with overambitious, overprotective parents who feed their *Wunderkind* on print when they cannot raise him as a Menuhin or a Heifetz. So far has this reaction gone that at a conference at Vassar several years ago, sponsored by the Bank Street Schools, the assembled anthropologists, psychiatrists, and educators were nearly unanimous in feeling that we could profit from the methods of child-training used in preliterate cultures and in rural India—that these methods (despite a good deal of rote learning) are more "natural" than ours and less crippling for mental health. The position that several of us took, that children like the rest of us had to shoulder some of the burdens of transmitting the cultural heritage, even if this meant a certain pressure on them to learn to read both words and music—this notion was regarded as an intellectual's defense against his own emotions and a cruel hangover from a patriarchal and puritanical past.

This conference helped prepare me for reading the debates that swirl at Antioch. Antioch, since Arthur Morgan's day, has been notable for its awareness of the human casualties unalleviated devotion to print can cause. And currently, in the *Antioch Magazine,* in the *Record,* in co-op reports and senior papers, in catalogues which bear the slogan "More than Books," and in speeches by President Gould and ex-President McGregor, one may vicariously be reintroduced to the problem of the role of books and bookishness at the college. An especially valuable article "Less than Books," by Judson Jerome in the *Antioch Magazine,* discusses anti-intellectuality and the general lack of privacy an activist, work-oriented campus imposes on the progressive, the prominent, and the devoted; another, which treats with sensitivity the drive for early love relations on a campus where intellect is not a defense against the affective life, develops a similar theme by indirection. On the whole, I was pleased to see these misgivings, this awareness that the wholesome, well-rounded communal life of the co-op may lack certain important imbalances—this awareness that a college can go too far in preparing young people for life, meeting life as adults experience it more than halfway, with the endless committee meetings, the civic responsibilities, and the bouts of going steady. (To be sure, as Kate Hevner Mueller observes in a recent issue of *Mademoiselle*, going steady is more constricting for college girls than for college boys, since the girls are useful to the boys insofar as they aid their careers rather than compete with them—indeed, out of a desperate fear of not getting married, they often end up captives of the husbands they think they have captured, sending their husbands through graduate school by subordinating their own intellectual interests to a job, to housework and child care, and the typing of doctoral dissertations. In this respect as in others, I would suppose that Antioch is more equalitarian and that Antioch graduates seldom divide their reading along sex lines, with the girls reading novels to justify the price they have paid for their own romance and the boys reading nonfiction as part of the price they still have to pay for their career ambitions.) Even so, looked at from one perspective, this college represents in extreme form the view that life prepares one for life. It is a challenge to an older view, more influential in theory than in practice, that withdrawal from life into the ivory tower and the library stack—withdrawal for a period of intense intellectuality and fierce discipline—allows one to emerge again into life without succumbing to it. As devout Catholics (and a few Protestant groups) sometimes take off from their daily concerns for what they term a retreat, a period of religious exercise and meditation, so the college years might be thought of as a retreat—a time of intellectual exercises and book-stimulated meditation.

But the general coed state-college pattern from which Antioch deviates in one direction (just as it deviates from the Ivy League colleges in another) imitates life without preparing for it, so much so that the BMOCs and rating-dating leaders are seldom likely to get over their premature success, let alone to live up to it. Antioch graduates are among the outstanding ones in the compilation of the careers of younger American scholars recently made by Professors Knapp and Greenbaum —evidence that whatever the loss of intellectuality involved in the Antioch pattern it cannot be very great.

Beyond all that, the enthusiastic response to Mr. Kettering's gift of a library is evidence if any were needed that the students, whatever their partisanships in other respects, are more unequivocally devoted to the life of the mind and to the books which nourish that life than students at campuses where far less is demanded in the way of unbookish pursuits. In my judgment, the Antioch experience is one further demonstration that far more can be demanded of young people—and, I would argue, of young people of all ages—than is suspected in most parental and educational quarters: the more they do, the more it turns out that they can do. This discovery, incidentally, is consonant with the recent findings of mass communications research that those who read the newspapers also listen to the radio and read magazines—one medium does not always drive out another, as is often feared, any more than one civic activity drives out another, but often one leads to tie-ins with the others. It is the people with jobs who get more jobs: the high-energy people of whom more is asked.

These considerations bring me back to the more generic problem touched upon at the Vassar conference, of whether young people can be asked to bear in their own persons the burdens of the cultural heritage of print. It seems to me that up to a point the society can ask this, can ask that individuals be compelled to acquire some one or more of the competences which are necessary if the past is to speak to us. The issue arises because the skills of reading, of singing, of playing instruments, must on the whole be acquired before the age of consent. But today there is a tendency not to ask children to do anything which they regard as stuffy, tiresome, or unpleasant. This comes out very clearly in responses to the first card of the Thematic Apperception Test, which shows a young boy staring at a violin on a table in front of him—people often interpret the situation as one of terrible constraint, and see the boy as wishing to go out and play baseball, kept in by a horrid witch of a mother. Less frequently, people will see the picture as symbolizing hopes for fame, in which the violin is a mere instrument for success; but I can't at the moment recall reading any protocols in which relation to music as such is referred to, let alone any in which the continuity of the musical tradition, or the eventual pleasures to be derived from participation in it, is mentioned or implied.[2] The violin, in sum, is seen as a rod to beat children with or a bridge to fame.

[2] Professor William E. Henry, an experienced TAT interpreter, tells me that he has come across hardly any themes in which either music or the sheer skill of performance is enjoyed, though one distinguished executive saw the boy as contemplating the music that is "in his fingers" with a mixture of ambition and delight.

In many societies the past has been a mortgage which really has crushed children, and the achievements of Greece did in some recent epochs result in a combined belittling of anything else and submission to classical rote learning. However, even with the small revival that the classics are having in our day at a few colleges, this fate is not a likely one, and the greater danger is that Americans, with increasing world power, will insist that everyone learn to speak American while not compelling our children to learn any other language—and in many schools not even our own in any full measure. Yet languages, like systems of musical notation, must be carried in the bodies of the living if the accomplishments and experiences of the dead are not to be lost to us. It may be that some residual feeling of this sort—some fear that children may be growing up as barbarians and away from us of the older generations—may be one element behind the ominous success of Rudolf Flesch's demagogic best-seller, *Why Johnny Can't Read*—a book that would lose the exaggerated edge of its power if *its* readers could read, or were not frightened. Flesch and his followers never ask the crucial question I am asking here, namely what distribution of not only reading skills but reading enthusiasms, for what systems of notation (including music, languages, and mathematics), is desirable if we are not only to pass on the heritage—the world's library of art and imagination—but also to contribute to it. They take it for granted that Johnny should read just because John Alden or John Adams did read: in the case of most of the reactionary critics of our public schools who are riding so high today, such terms as "heritage" are merely snob tags, status labels, which they can use to pull rank on schoolteachers, educationists, psychological counselors, and other relatively defenseless people. I suspect that many such critics would like to restore drill and to make reading more of a chore than it needs to be as a sublimated form of hazing the young, though some chore and bore elements will certainly be part of any educational program which aims to reach all who can possibly be reached by books or by any other media which connect people with a noncontiguous world, the world of yesterday and tomorrow as well as of the here and now.

There is, plainly enough, great irony in the fact that debate over whether or not children are given too comfy a time at school arises when the problems of production appear for this country virtually solved, and less and less is being asked of children in the way of contributions to the economy. Since black and blue print and heavy industry have historically accompanied each other, this relaxation should not surprise us, but it does present our culture with unanticipated problems—largely the problems of that postindustrial underemployment which is so very different in its moral and cultural effects from the underemployment of pastoral peoples in the pre-industrial world. Reuel Denney has pointed out ("The Cultural Context of Print in the Communications Revolution," *Library Quarterly*, October 1955) that leisure and abundance give to all branches of education more and more clients all the time, thus enlarging the number of Ph.D.s and hence the number of people who may pursue a vested interest in books in a beleaguered and dutiful rather than accessible and pleasurable spirit. He praises the paperbound book because it need not be treated with piety, because it invites casualness.

Certainly in an era of abundance we can afford to read books for pleasure, and it may on the whole be a good thing that a boy in school or a soldier in camp can pull out a paperbound book without feeling that there is anything esoteric or status-labeled in the act. Even so, casual pleasures in our society, hard as they often are to come by, will not suffice to absorb young people's energies and aspirations. On the contrary, young people need at some time in their lives to extend themselves, to work at the height of their as yet untapped powers (indeed, lacking better ways, some seek to do this in forms the society defines as delinquency). Since the world's work no longer offers this opportunity for exertion for most nonfarm Americans, we may think it fortunate—though in some respects arbitrary—that the world's storehouse of culture unfailingly does. While we can perhaps imagine a postliterate culture in which people are challenged primarily by other media than print and musical scores—and no doubt we have already a culture in which even in the most bookish strata many media co-operate, yet at the moment I think it is not just prejudice and snobbery which lead us to rely heavily on books as our traditional badge of enlightenment, and on libraries as the great storehouses of our culture.

Much as many sports and games we enjoy were once activities carried on for subsistence, like hunting and fishing, riding and do-it-yourself, so the music that was once part of religion; and the reading that was once part of religion, too, or of commercial development and social-class advancement, can now become, as it were, "sports" whose function for the individual is personal development and for the society the connection of individuals with one another through the shared enjoyment of symbolic forms which transcend individual capacities for day-to-day observation, forms which carry us, in Ortega's phrase, to "the height of the times."

For this to happen, however, our educational philosophy can profit by returning to a theme of Matthew Arnold in *Culture and Anarchy* and can view the school as training in those arts necessary for cultural transmission. To be sure, when one says this one conjures up visions of platoons of humanists denouncing pragmatism, vocationalism, and science, and insisting on a monolithic liberal arts curriculum for everyone. I want to make it clear here that I am not talking about everyone, but only urging that there be some schools which treat the curriculum as they treat the extracurriculum—as a challenge which is largely meaningless economically but something, like athletic skill, to be sought for its own sake and as part of a preparation for stimulating intercourse with others. John Stuart Mill was one of the first to argue that women ought to be educated to make men's environs and life more interesting, and in the same way we can argue that people should be educated not just to make a market for books, an audience for music, but to provide the members of a more attractive and open-ended social life.

Furthermore, there is no need to run away from the vocational benefits of a primarily antivocational curriculum. Those benefits are sometimes merely of a status sort: the engineer who can discuss Plato or Picasso may become a manager, while his classmate who has stuck to "fundamentals" may remain a section head. But this puts it too narrowly, especially for the future, when those who will manage industry in the era of automation will require the ability to handle much greater loads and overloads of symbolic material than at present. At the *Fortune* Conference on Automation, Dr. Cuthbert Hurd, the electronics director of IBM, wondered whether today's high schools could turn out the youngsters capable of the abstract and mathematical thinking that would increasingly be requisite—when every pressure would be on the boys to become "normal" in the sense of not caring to be prodigies, not caring to be immersed in some impersonal intellectual hobby. Norbert Wiener in his reflective account, *Ex-Prodigy: My Childhood and Youth,* indicates his wish for a less emotionally stunted upbringing, yet I wonder if he would have been happier in the end had his endowment of gifts, for which the culture would later find great use, been less strenuously cultivated? People find personal meaning in being of some use, and to give young people a chance to find that meaning and not be cut off from it by childhood slackness and indolence is one of the functions of what we might term the higher vocationalism—a bock-oriented but of course not antiscientific curriculum.

At an extreme, one might even consider it wise educational policy to lock children up (at some time before their majority) in a good library with good food and drink, alone and with paper and pencil but no other entertainment. We might first ask for volunteers and later conscript children who could endure it without cracking up—we would not, of course, want to push matters to the point of nurturing a rebellious anti-intellectualism or even Good Soldier Schweiks of the library. We do know that some children who have been made to practice the violin are later grateful to their parents, despite the evidence of the TATs, and I suspect that some who have been made to read do not regret it later on—even if they read as children out of loneliness, neurosis, or parental pressures. To be sure, we cannot take this later pleasure in reading at face value: there might be regressive elements in it, or resigned submission to cultural conventions as vindicated by the parents. But more positive elements are likely to be present also, especially in a life which, in an earlier phrase, is stressful with "going places and doing things."

It seems to me in any case that it represents a cultural advance when the young are no longer required to scarify their bodies as the price of admission to their culture's treasures and recognitions. But anyone who has seen in the Robert Flahertys' Samoan documentary film *Moana* how proud the young man is to receive the painful tattooings that mark his adulthood, or who has read ethnological accounts of initiations, can realize that young people do want to prove themselves—do welcome the endurance tests their elders inflict. I have been suggesting that we do not ask enough of the young, save in military service, to allow them to prove themselves, and I am also suggesting that initiation today as always is fundamentally symbolic and need not only and no longer be carried in bodily scars but can be "carried" internally—for instance, as experience induced by books. In place of the vision quest which led the Plains Indian youngster to face the desert alone, to discover his totem and his identity, I am suggesting that we substitute the solitary vision quest in the library.

These problems I have been discussing—and I cannot emphasize too strongly the tentativeness of what I have said—would be less important and less apparently insoluble if the book, and other printed matter, stood at the end of the road of social development, as was true from the fifteenth century to the end of the nineteenth. The sway of black print on white paper may be said to mark the epoch of the rise and increasing influence of the middle class—the class of clerks and bookkeepers, merchants and engineers, instruction-givers and instruction-readers, the class of the time-attentive, the future-oriented, the mobile. Reading and education were the highroads this class made use of to rise in the world and to move about in it during the great periods of colonization. Even the novel, denounced as frivolous and sensuous by the Puritans, had an important function in the changing society. I think not so much of its use as a device for reform and civic adult education, as in *Oliver Twist* or *Uncle Tom's Cabin*, as of its less obvious use as a device by which people might prepare themselves for novel contacts and novel life situations, a form of anticipatory socialization—that is, a preparation in imagination for playing roles that might emerge in one's later career. In fact, the very conception of life implicit in the notion of a career is facilitated by the dramatic structure of the novel, especially the *Bildungsroman*, with its protagonist, its interest in motive, its demand on the reader that he project himself into the experiences portrayed. In a society depending on oral tradition, individuals have life cycles—they live through childhood; they are initiated; they become adult; they grow old; they die—but they do not have careers in our abstract sense of the term. The novel of the nineteenth century, as its critics contended, doubtless disoriented many chambermaids and a few duchesses, but on many more occasions it helped prepare individuals for their careers in a disorienting world of rapid industrialization and urbanization, where, indeed, fictional moves and actual ones were not so unlike, and life and art could almost imitate each other.

The rise of the newer media of communication has coincided with a certain loss of power by the older, print-oriented middle classes. Yellow journalism, coming on top of universal suffrage, did begin to shake that hegemony. Indeed, the very term yellow journalism is significant as marking a change from the monotone of black on white (just as the fact that only 10 per cent of the cars turned out this year are black and all the rest are technicolor says a good deal about our loss of Puritan inhibitions!). The comic book, also, is part of this same revolution. If one travels on trains and sees, as one can do any day, Pullmans full of enlisted men reading nothing but comic books and an occasional picture magazine, one realizes how much the meaning of "reading" has changed from Cromwell's New Model Army with its Bibles and tracts. And of course the movies and broadcasting, while not displacing the book, do shake its monopoly and with it the monopoly of the middle class.

But the consequences of these shifts in the focus of attention and in the emotional impact of the media differ very much depending on whether one speaks of a country where print has long been institutionalized or of a country which had previously been largely illiterate. In the former, the shifts of power tend to be subtle and unclimactic. Thus, it is not a major revolution in America that TV has made preadolescent children even more hip than they were before, more apt to be one-up on their parents even about politics, more ready psychologically to empathize with other conditions of man than their own. But in the less industrially advanced countries the shift can be explosive. A study of foreign radio listeners in seven Middle East countries is illuminating on this score, for it enables us to watch, as it were in close-up, some of the processes Innis has traced historically. In many villages such people as the grocer who has a radio, or the young bus driver who has seen movies in the capital and can bring news of the great world, are displacing the village elders in positions of leadership. To rise in such a way, these upstarts do not need to acquire the stern discipline of the print-oriented person; rather, they need the same equipment American children have who go about in Davy Crockett suits—a willingness, often quite passive and unstrenuous, to let fancy roam at the dictates of the mass media. The political parties of the Middle East are now beginning to make use of this willingness, and as we all know programs can be fanatically pursued which promise to supply cars and cinemas to peasants who are told they can have these things without working, just as Americans do, if only they will vote and believe. Thus, in the illiterate and preliterate masses there tends to be created a new kind of literacy, an often terrifying emotional and political fluency, with all the emancipations of print and hardly any of its restrictions and disciplines.

An analogous point about the spread of ideas is made by Bertrand Russell in his *History of Western Philosophy*:

> . . . a philosophy, developed in a politically and economically advanced country, which is, in its birthplace, little more than a clarification and systematization of prevalent opinion, may become elsewhere a source of revolutionary ardour and, ultimately, of actual revolution. It is mainly through theorists that the maxims regulating the policy of advanced countries become known to less advanced countries. In the advanced countries, practice inspires theory; in the others theory inspires practice.

In Russell's sense, a movie image of life in Hollywood or New York, for all its documentary detail, is a "theory," and a radical one, when it appears on the screens of Nigeria or Indonesia or Lebanon.

The movies, of course, are a boundary-annihilating form, easily transmissible past linguistic and cultural barriers (as well as barriers of literacy). They may also be, as Arnold Hauser suggests in *The Social History of Art*, a democratizing form because of their mobility, the absence of traditional stage conventions and proprieties. Art historians have recently noted that when Renaissance painters shifted the Virgin Mary from front face to profile it marked a decline of Catholic religiosity and a less devout approach to the Trinity. The camera can be even more impudent, and can put aesthetic laws to use in all kinds of ways, leading the audience, as Hauser says, to the events, rather than leading and presenting the events to them, with the voyeuristic intimacy which we can see in such a film as Hitchcock's *Rear Window*. A movie can tell its story as though we are telling it to ourselves, or as though we are actually dreaming it; it can force us to identify with its chosen moods and people. The camera, by moving around, subtly invites us to embrace one character and exclude another—to look up and feel awe of a noble man or fear of a villain; to look down and feel contempt or pity. A sidelong glance of the camera alerts us for trouble— a right-to-left pan, reversing the right-handedness Hermann Weill discusses in his book on symmetry, invests people and places with a spooky feeling. I need not labor the catalogue of the director's powers, aided as they are by the near hypnotic effect of the concentrated brightness of the screen, while other sights and sounds (save in college-town theaters!) are at a low ebb. The movie is the novel in motion; it is potentially the least rationalistic, the most subjectivized medium. And like the broadcast, the rally, or the fireside council of the tribal chief, it demands attention now, this minute, in this time and at that place; unlike a book, it cannot wait for your mood, or your activity.

Where the movies and the book are both in circulation, the written word and the screen image compete in making our sensibility mobile and empathic, though for many of us even now the movies have pretty well replaced the novel as the powerful medium for anticipatory socialization. Conceivably, when every man has his own movie camera and home projector and his own movie library as we now have our record collections, he will become more critical and less vulnerable—this being the usual effect of do-it-yourself. Moreover, membership in film societies

literate society which might have moved away from print, or be skipping it, like these peasant communities of the Middle East just mentioned. In both, the encapsulating and isolating possibilities of print are absent; in both, symbols are given weight by their setting, by the local affective color so to speak, rather than by their logicality. But the social structure, of course, is very different indeed. The society based on oral tradition, with its dependence on the memory of the elders, links people together in small tribal groups and in their families. These people may be nomadic, but they are not socially and psychologically mobile in the modern sense; they are led by folk tales and songs to identify with the tribe as it has been and will be, or possibly with a legendary golden age, but they are not incited to imagine themselves outside its comforts and coherence. Sizable kingdoms, as in Africa, have been built on the spoken word, particularly where there are specialists in it, but empires large in space and durable in time require transportable information and some form of permanent record (of which proverbs may be one kind of early approximation). Moreover, the oral communication of a preliterate society tends to freeze the given social structure, though occasionally prophets can overleap the cellular walls of the tribe and bring about new structures. In contrast, a postliterate society would seem almost inevitably fluid, its people on the move, its structure unstable.

In other words, oral communication keeps people together, binds people to each other, while print in our day loosens these bonds, creates space around people, even isolates them in some ways. People who would simply have been deviants in a preliterate tribe, misunderstanding and misunderstood, can through books establish a wider identity —can understand and even undermine the enemies of home and hearth and herd. While the geographic migrations of preliterate peoples have something in common with the uncomprehending movement of flocks of deer, the readers of the age of discovery were prepared mentally for some of the experiences of their geographic mobility—they had at any rate left home in imagination even if they had not roamed as far or among as strange people as they were actually to meet. The bookish education of these inner-directed men helped harden them for voyages: they wanted to convert the heathen, civilize them, trade with them—if anyone changed in the encounter, it would be the heathen, while they, as they moved about the globe or up the social ladder, remained very much the same men. The epitome of this was the Englishman in the topics who, all alone, dressed for dinner with home-guard ceremonial, toasted the Queen, and, six months late, read with a proper sense of outrage the leader in the London *Times*. His ties with the world of print helped steady him in his course far from home and alone.

Today, the successors of these men are often other-directed; they are men molded as much by the mass media outside their formal education as by their schooling; men who are more public-relations minded than ambitious; men softened for encounters rather than hardened for voyages; if they move about the globe it is often to win the love of the natives or to try to understand their mores, rather than to exploit them for gain or the glory of God. Meanwhile, as we have seen, the natives (as they used to be called) are themselves in many cases on the move, and the sharp differences between societies dependent on the oral tradition and those dependent on print are tending to be less important with the coming of radio and film. Often the decisive difference is among the peasants themselves within a country now moving out of the stage of oral tradition—differences between those who listen to the radio and go to movies and those who shut these things out as the voice of the devil or as simply irrelevant for them. In the *Far Eastern Quarterly* [November 1955], Milton Singer describes the complexity of such differences in a South Indian province, where all levels of mediation exist between the peasant and the parochial and the Indian and the global. In the Middle East studies it was found that those peasants who listened to Radio Moscow or the BBC or the VOA already had, or perhaps acquired, a different sensibility from those who did not. The former were prepared in the imagination for more voyages than they were likely ever to make.

In "Self and Society: Some Observations on Turks in Transition,"[8] Daniel Lerner and I have traced the phenomenon we term "psychic mobility," the fluidity of identification which precedes actual physical movement, but which creates a potential for such movement. In some Lebanese villages, the young bus driver who visits the city or the young storekeeper who has a radio have become the opinion leaders, helping the villages make contact with an orbit in which their elders and chiefs, once looked up to as unquestioned founts of wisdom, now appear small and parochial. Peasants in the same village with the same occupation and the same income—that is, people not distinguishable by the usual demographic indices—are found to differ in their psychic mobility as marked by the degrees and forms of their attention to the

[8] See p. 402.

mass media. Of course, it may turn out that these newly and unevenly stirred masses are all dressed up in imagination with no place to go.

Despite a certain amount of indirect evidence concerning the new village elite of people who are there first with the most news of the great world outside, these investigations lack data as to whether peasants who are psychically mobile are isolated listeners or part of a group which mediates the media for them. Paul F. Lazarsfeld, Elihu Katz, and others have made it evident that in America people do not attend to the media as isolated atoms but as members of groups which select among the media and interpret their messages. Indeed, Father Coughlin discovered that he could not organize followers directly by his broadcasts but needed to set up, as he did in Boston and elsewhere, groups who would listen together—recreating, as it were, the tribal setting. (For one thing, in such a group no one would dare flick the dial.) Similarly, people go to movies in groups—especially the teen-agers who make up such a large proportion of the audience—and formal and informal fan clubs are of course a way of organizing these groups. Again, we see the idiosyncratic elements of print: people do not read in groups (though I suppose one would have to make something of an exception for textbooks and trots, both of which are often books only by courtesy), and the cubicle is as characteristic of the library as isolation is uncharacteristic of a modern movie palace (though the drive-in may in rare cases have brought it back).

Since the Middle East studies are based on interviews with individuals, and not on the observation of groups, we lack any reliable information on this point and tend to interpret the data as if individuals singly began those subtle psychological changes which are reflected in a decision to attend the movies in the nearest town or to listen to the radio in the nearest coffeehouse. Probably, it is not like that; probably, the moderns who listen and the ancients who don't are each in touch with one another and sustain each other. Lerner links psychic mobility with other-direction; that is, he connects it with the consumer mentality, the concern with others and how they evaluate themselves, the preoccupation with personal relations. It is strange to find something which looks like this urban American communications-conscious outlook in a Lebanese village which has not yet experienced the industrial revolution, and we are again struck with the possibility that the age of individualism —the age of the self-starter—may be an interlude between the age of the spoken and the age of the electronic word.

It is too soon, however, to say whether the epoch of print will be utterly elided in the underdeveloped countries, just as, with the coming of electrical and atomic energy, they may skip the stage of coal and water power. Conceivably, the movies and broadcasting will eventually help to awaken a hunger for print, when their own novelty has worn off and when they come to be used as tie-ins with print—as in "Invitation to Learning." Just as the barbarians of Europe in the Middle Ages pulled themselves up by Greek bootstraps, so the nonindustrial countries can for a long time draw on the storehouse of Western science and technology, including the science of social organization; and there are still enough inner-directed men in our society who are willing to go out and help build the armies of Iran and the factories of Istanbul. In this connection, it is striking that the Soviet Union, paying at least nominal heed to the scriptures of Marx and Lenin, has created what is in some ways a replica of the Victorian industrial world rather than the modern consumer world—so that treatises on Marxism and Hollywood movies may be seen as alternative lures to the pre-industrial nations, with national pride voting for steel plants and Karl Marx and personal taste for cars, Coca-Cola, and the stereotype of America. To be sure, communism may seem the quickest way to the consumers' utopia. (I should parenthetically add that the appeal to the consumer mentality in the East, the appeal of American luxuries, is almost never an intended propaganda move but rather a by-product of media forms coupled with American enterprise.)

In sum, it is apparent that the mass media, like other forms of technological innovation, bring about new polarizations in society and between societies. The readers and the nonreaders, the listeners and the nonlisteners, may belong to the same economic and social groupings, yet they have different values, different tastes, different turns of mind.

It is obvious in these last remarks that we touch on enormous problems—and "touch" is the right word, for that is all we can do here. But other remarks in this paper, too, though less apparently global, involve issues hardly less complex, issues of historical and comparative study. And even if my scholarship could cope with this task, as it plainly cannot, my value judgments would still be open to question, for books are fighting words, the gunpowder of the mind, and objectivity concerning them is for another planet, another day. In fact, on a number of the topics we have discussed, my own opinions have not been stable, and this essay has been, *inter alia*, an effort at personal clarification.

However, I can speak with some assurance on one point which often comes up when, as on this occasion, people discuss historical trends. Such discussion sometimes engenders a feeling of inevitability, and a cause is declared lost because not everyone votes for it and because research brings us the latest returns from the election. In this country, for instance, there are many educated people who fear that books are on the way out, that they are a lost cause against the newer media; they fear we do not have far to go before we have pocket-size TV along with wrist-watch radios, so that no one will ever have to reach for a book to escape from himself—nor will he want to in order to find himself. Plainly enough, one should note but not be too impressed by trends, that is, by the forlorn democracy of numbers (e.g., the depressing Gallup figures on the small percentage of book readers) as against the conception of democracy as a system that gives everyone a chance to make a play for his cause.

Yet one's own pleasure in books does not rest, beyond a certain break-even point, on the numbers who share such pleasures, but rather on the whole quality of life in a culture. What books can do for that quality, in broadening horizons, in encouraging fantasy, in promoting individuation, can in some measure be done by other media—witness the Third Programme in England, the great postwar Italian films, and some television drama and documentaries in this country. The newer media can be used to promote empathy and vicariousness in terms of emotional depth, and not simply in terms of political nationalism and consumer-goods sophistication. Even so, what the newer media can seldom do is promote privacy. The people on the TV screen are "company" for the viewer, even if they don't seek to make him a pseudoparticipant along with the rubberneck studio audience. The people in a book are "company" for the reader in a different sense: to "see" them the reader must make an effort, and he must do so—whatever guidance he gets from critics, teachers, and friends—in relative isolation. (In a recent cartoon, one person at a cocktail party asks another if he's read a certain book, and the latter answers, "Not personally.") In a world that threatens us with a surfeit of people, this role of the book becomes again as important as in the preliterate tribes where, also, there was no escape from others; and, as America becomes one vast continental pueblo, the book —whatever its residual trajectory as a revolutionary social force—comes into its own as a guarantor of that occasional apartness which makes our life together viable.

SECTION IV

Social Science Research: Problems, Methods, Opportunities

Preface

The operationalist in the social sciences who thinks of himself as hard-boiled is often possessed by a profound and even overwhelming epistemological skepticism as to how one can ever surely know anything. In his private and personal life he takes chances and makes guesses and generalizations like the rest of us, but as a scientist his ascetic canon seeks (usually, I believe, in vain) to eliminate all traces of the self and to generate fungible products that in principle could be duplicated in any laboratory. Such procedures are not to be sneered at by the more worldly and less pure, except when anyone insists that *only* through such procedures can we advance our understanding.

In an earlier essay, I discussed in some detail the reasons why I believed that social science in its present state of development needs to combine its separate pursuits with a more Gestaltist and inevitably loose-jointed approach to the questions raised by our reactions to the world in which we live.[1] In the case of my own work, I am chronically aware that little of what we think is so may actually be so—aware that, despite the great expansion, ingenuity, scope, and relative affluence of the social sciences in America, we remain in the dark as to many of the largest questions concerning what is happening in our own and other large-scale societies.[2]

[1] See "Some Observations on Social Science Research, *Antioch Review*, Vol. XII, pp. 259–78, 1951; reprinted in *Individualism Reconsidered and Other Essays*, pp. 467–83.

[2] It is sometimes said that if the social sciences had as much money available as the Manhattan Project or the Moon Shot or similar projects, it would be possible, if not to "solve" problems like those of war and peace and domestic strife, at least to overcome the immense lacunae of our understanding. This may be possible but I doubt it. I am inclined to think that the social sciences over-all have had nearly as much money as their more energetic personnel could wisely spend. It remains true that people, myself included, have had difficulty in getting grants and that good books sometimes have trouble getting published, while the young people who might

While there have been studies like Anne Roe's of the psychological orientations of more or less typical members of various academic callings, the subtle ways in which individual researchers get attached to particular lines of work have been little explored (this is one of the themes of my study of Veblen). In common parlance, research done at the call of a client is termed "applied," whereas research done at the call of a guild or a profession is regarded as "pure." But the guild itself can be a client in ways suggested in the essay on "Law and Sociology." The questions Robert S. Lynd raised in his book, *Knowledge for What?* seem no closer to being answered than when he wrote. In the last few years I have had an opportunity to talk to a number of non-American social scientists who have come to this country to see what they could learn from the much more highly developed and well-supported academic enterprises here. And I have got the impression that, in comparison to the seriousness of sociology in some foreign countries, the very refinement of American social science and its academic freedom have led to a growing divorce between what individuals as citizens are most concerned with and what individuals as researchers feel can be investigated with reliable methods.

Sometimes the visitors have come from countries where social science is a new enterprise or a poor one, or both, but vital and hopefully comprehensive. In Poland, for example, sociologists have worked courageously to substitute emprical data about how workers or peasants actually regard the regime for the usual dogmas and propaganda as to how

---

write such books are not given the opportunity. But on the whole such failures involve special problems of stickiness, marginality, or controversy, rather than problems of support for the area as a whole. I will grant that if there were a great deal more support, there would be more freedom of "waste" and the controversial good as well as the routine and fashionable mediocre would be more readily supported. But the results of bringing more people, both the able and the opportunistic, into the social sciences at the expense of fewer such people in other fields, remain questionable. And the distribution of funds within the social sciences as well as among them and other competing areas represents more general "decisions" in our society that also turn up in the way our imaginations work, in what we perceive and fail to perceive, in what appears problematic and in what we take for granted—all of which influence the sort of work that is done at least as much as the support that is granted. In *The Sociological Imagination* (New York: Oxford University Press, 1959), the late C. Wright Mills has some very perceptive and some very narrow-minded and egocentric things to say about these questions.

they should regard it; a public-opinion poll in such a country can be a tool, not only of manipulation, but for overturning established and hierarchical rigidities. In fact, many of the Polish intellectuals who sparked the rebellion of 1956 that brought Gomulka to power were sociologists or were influenced by the findings and ideas of sociology.[3] Similarly, in Yugoslavia and even in some small measure in the Soviet Union, social science research, as one harbinger of a freer, more open, and less fanatical society, has an unsettling and exciting quality.

I recall a conversation with a researcher from Yugoslavia who, at an informal gathering, asked a number of American economists, sociologists, and political scientists how we selected the topics on which we worked. The answers given him in the first instance were flip and cynical. One man said we watched our bright graduate students to see what would become fashionable and then worked on that; another mentioned the possibility of lucrative textbooks; still another said we worked on what the Ford Foundation wanted to spend money on. All this was characteristically deprecatory of our own commitments and priorities in that new-style American hypocrisy by which we understate, and perhaps come to disbelieve, our own ideals. Still it was plain that in this area, as in others, our abundance gave us a multiplicity of choices as compared to the Yugoslav, whose problems tended to be given him by state or social authorities rather than by the guild authority of his discipline.

To take another instance, a French sociologist came to see me because of his interest in studies of leisure and the consequences of automation. He was surprised to discover that I did not have a large staff engaged in answering the questions raised in some of the essays reprinted in this volume. He was even more surprised to find how little cooperation there was between economists and sociologists in making plans for the future of leisure. Indeed, like many Frenchmen who take planning for granted, he was astonished to be told, both by officials in Washington and by academicians, that "planning" was, if not a bad word in this country, at least a controversial one, that it was safer to speak of "forecasting," and that there was no over-all agency that planned research on long-run questions on the social psychology of work and leisure. It was a surprise to this man, as it has been to other visitors,

[3] I recognize that much of this initial enthusiasm and free-wheeling spirit has been lost in later restriction. Also the shiny and prestigeful American model of certain kinds of empirical research has sometimes had the effect of leading non-Americans to pale imitations of it rather than to more syncretistic adaptations.

can help put moviegoers in the director's place, can help them be more critical rather than so easily manipulated by him.

But all this betokens a society like ours in which radio and film are cumulative media for the better educated strata—a society in which a certain uneasy balance of powers exists among the media, a society in which the librarians have been vigilant of freedom while the movie magnates have generally failed to fight down their fears of the Legion of Decency and the other censoring groups who ultimately force sadism on the films in exchange for forbidden sex. In the Middle East, where the movies and radio arrive ahead of the book, there is no such balance —though I suppose Turkey comes paradoxically closest where Kemal Ataturk detached the young from even the literate old by imposing the Roman script: here the print-oriented are not simply the students of the Koran but are up-to-date and Westernized.

It is a truism that the revolutions which go on within countries, as the result of the uneven spread of new techniques and ideologies to the different strata, also go on among countries; and we are as accustomed to the term have-not nations as to the have-not classes. In microcosm we can watch the dispossession of the elders of Middle Eastern villages who lack access to news and images of alternative ways of life, and of consumer abundance; likewise, some of the very countries whose industrial and cultural development concided with the age of print are now under pressure from those countries whose development begins in the age of the screen image. Print, to be sure, still has prestige all over the world. The Western and Westernized statesmen now old enough to have power have mostly been nurtured on it, or at worst rebelled defensively against it. The model followed by the underdeveloped countries is, of course, profoundly influenced by the past triumphs of print, a process which makes it unlikely that they will skip the stage of print entirely. Thus, when it comes to describing what a country would look like where the oral tradition has been fragmented not under the impact of print but of broadcasting and the movies, we are still largely (despite striking developments in India) in the realm of science fiction rather than history.

Let me now go back to the beginning and recapitulate, from a slightly different perspective, the sequence I have here presented in impressionistic outline. First of all, we can see that a preliterate society dependent on the fluid, fugitive nature of the spoken word, may have certain resemblances, in the way its emotions are organized, to a post-to learn that books like *The Affluent Society* or *The Lonely Crowd* were speculative forays, not the result of elaborate institutional studies.

It may be that my own willingness to undertake such a foray reveals, in some slight measure at least, the feeling of the lawyer that he can master anything in a pretrial two weeks, that there is no expertise his own cannot readily subsume. When I was law clerk to Mr. Justice Brandeis, I became an "expert" in the making and shipping of berry boxes in one short spell, and in freight rate-making in another; for Lyne, Woodworth, and Evarts, I learned how to cross-examine heart specialists in insurance cases, and bits and pieces of paper-making for the reorganization of International Paper and Power. At the same time I came to distrust what the essay on "Law and Sociology" refers to as the "play it by ear" attitude of the bar. A good many lawyers and law teachers are inclined to feel that such fields as psychology or anthropology can be readily encompassed. In contrast, social scientists and many other laymen seem to me to stand too much in awe of the law, overestimating the difficulty of mastering its casuistries and forms at least for purposes of research.

The essay, "Law and Sociology," is in part an effort to overcome these misperceptions between lawyers and social scientists. It draws freely on my own limited opportunities to observe lawyers, and it adumbrates a program for field studies of the legal profession. In 1948 and 1949, while I was at Yale, I sought to introduce a few law students to the possibility of studying their own profession, encouraging them to use their summer vacations to interview members of the bar in their home towns. Many of these students lacked confidence that they, untrained in social science techniques, could actually do interviews—perhaps they had not yet gained the lawyer's confidence of which I have just spoken.[4]

---

[4] I would like to see much more widespread participation in the data-gathering processes of social-science research and for this reason have been interested in the "Mass Observation" movement in Great Britain. There are many nonrecurring situations that can be handled only by something akin to mass observation. For example, when General Douglas MacArthur came to Chicago after his recall from Korea by President Truman and paraded through the city, television presented him as the focus of enormous popular enthusiasm. However, Kurt and Gladys Lang led a group of graduate students who monitored the parade along its length, and their field reports indicated the holiday spirit of many of those who turned out to see MacArthur and the lack of intensity of their applause as he passed. So, too, when the sirens were let loose all over Chicago to signal the winning of the

Alexis de Tocqueville, a lawyer, had, of course, no such training; indeed, this is a theme of Robert Redfield's "The Art of Social Science" (*American Journal of Sociology*, Vol. LIV, November 1948, pp. 181–90). My essay, "Tocqueville as Ethnographer," seeks to understand something of the nature of Tocqueville's achievement, in comparison with that of other foreign visitors. It also touches on the perennial factors in American life that Tocqueville grasped.

Tocqueville and Beaumont, insouciant young aristocrats, had few qualms about how the Americans reacted to them; they felt no therapeutic mandate vis-à-vis America but were primarily concerned with developments in their own country. The team of social scientists who worked in the Canadian suburb they called Crestwood Heights, on the other hand, was intensely involved with the community, understandably fearful of doing it harm, and hopeful of being of some help in the sphere of education and mental health. The introduction I wrote to their book discusses these involvements and the new-found ethical responsibilities of researchers. These responsibilities operate at every step of the way: in selecting a community, in gaining entrée to it, in participant-observation of its affairs, in interviews and other contacts with individuals, and finally in reporting the results. I have encountered some of these problems in my own work since that introduction was written; and I can say only that in this area we proceed with many ambiguities, few guidelines, and intermittent anxiety.[5] I can well understand why researchers often prefer "subjects" who are not subjective, who cannot talk back, and who create no ethical dilemmas.

In "The Sociology of the Interview," Mark Benney and I discuss briefly the short history of social research based on any sort of formal interviewing or observation; and we suggest that such research arose, in the first instance, along lines of tension and cleavage in society. Or, to put it more accurately, such research tends to arise when social chasms and fissures, always present in some sense, come, with the rise of

---

pennant by the White Sox, a good many people thought atomic bombs were about to fall, and Professor Elihu Katz got a group of students to go out and interview people about their reactions. Students encouraged in this way to do interviews have gained an enhanced appreciation of the complexities and even treacheries of the data out of which generalizations concerning human behavior are developed.

[5] Cf. David Riesman and Jeanne Watson, "The Sociability Project: a Chronicle of Anxieties and Accomplishments," in Phillip Hammond, ed., *Chronicles of Social Research*, forthcoming.

democracy, to be regarded as problematic. A powerful and proud aristocrat would not think of making a systematic inquiry as to how his inferiors thought and felt; if he cared about the matter at all, he would believe he already knew—and his inferiors would take good care to preserve such illusions on his part as the price of comfort. The work of Tocqueville and Marx seems to me inconceivable without the French Revolution; and the rise of social research as a major industry reflects class conflict and change.

The flourishing of the public-opinion survey, especially in America, also reveals, as our essay contends, the democratic ethos, the view that everyone's opinion matters. The first systematic work I did on public opinion was an examination of the treatment by survey agencies and by interviewers of those minorities (usually 10 per cent or so of the sample) who have no opinion or venture none—and this in a situation where, unlike that of the Turkish peasants dealt with in "Self and Society," opinions are supposed to be free and everyone is supposed to have one.[6]

A few years later, with the assistance of Mark Benney, I began a more long-range study of interviews to try to understand the process itself better; I felt that the interview, as a sort of formalized conversation, could tell us a good deal about the attitudes of different groups toward their own convictions and toward expressing these to other people of the same or different sex or social class. We operated primarily not by adding our own few interviews to the enormous number done every year, but by what researchers call "secondary analysis"—examining earlier surveys to see what, for our purposes, could be gleaned from them about the process of interviewing.[7]

[6] See "The Meaning of Opinion," (with Nathan Glazer), *Public Opinion Quarterly*, Vol. XII (1948–49), pp. 633–48; "Social Structure, Character Structure, and Opinion" (with Nathan Glazer), *International Journal of Opinion and Attitude Research*, Vol. II (1949), pp. 512–27; reprinted in *Individualism Reconsidered* (The Free Press, 1953), pp. 492–507.

[7] In addition to the papers reprinted herein, the following also report on these investigations: "Some Observations on the Interviewing in the Teacher Apprehension Study," in Paul F. Lazarsfeld and Wagner Thielens, Jr., *The Academic Mind: Social Scientists in a Time of Crisis* (The Free Press, 1958); "Age and Sex in the Interview" (with Mark Benney and Shirley Star), *The American Journal of Sociology*, Vol. LXII, No. 2, September 1956, pp. 143–52; "Age and Authority in the Interview" (with June Sachar Erlich), *The Public Opinion Quarterly*, Vol. XXV, Spring 1961, pp. 39–56; "Some Observations on Interviewing in a State Mental Hospital," *Bulletin of the Menninger Clinic*, Vol. 23, No. 1, January 1959, pp. 7–19.

In this work I could never confine my attention to the interaction itself; the content mattered as well. This is so much the case that "Orbits of Tolerance, Interviewers and Elites," could quite as well have gone into the first section on "The Impact of the Cold War," although it is, in fact, a secondary analysis of the interviewing in Samuel A. Stouffer's *Communism, Conformity, and Civil Liberties,* and was first presented as a paper in a discussion of that book at the American Association for Public Opinion Research (AAPOR), the group of pollsters, market researchers, and academicians from a variety of disciplines who share a concern with survey techniques. (Nonprofessional readers are warned that some of this essay will be hard to follow, not merely because it takes for granted familiarity with the Stouffer volume, but because it assumes a certain knowledgeability about the survey process.) Similarly, "Interviewers, Elites, and Academic Freedom," returns to the same procedural or methodological concerns in an analogous context: a secondary analysis of the Lazarsfeld Teacher Apprehension Survey done for the Fund for the Republic.

The concluding essay, "The Study of National Character: Some Observations on the American Case," discusses the use of psychoanalytic typologies in social research, and, like the introduction to *Crestwood Heights,* considers the impact on educated readers of the sort of introspection engendered by such books as *The Lonely Crowd.* To illustrate: young people in college today frequently feel that the problem of their unique individuality and nonconformity is the all-important one; one psychotherapist has told me that this is the major presenting problem with which his college patients come. A confusion between a solipsistic egocentrism and autonomy is often made, and a contempt for the "masses" is cultivated by much of modern writing or read into it, whether the critics come from the social sciences or from literature. Some critics even talk as if they would like millions of people to disappear so that the country would be less crowded and frontiers open again; individuality is equated with individualism, and autonomy with elbow room. Such developments have been a factor in changing my own attitudes over the period represented by the essays in this volume. The tyranny of the majority takes different forms in many strata today from those it took when *The Lonely Crowd* was written, let alone the period in which Tocqueville wrote. Today private life and, in general, activities that do not enter the arena of the cold war are increasingly free from niggling or fundamentalist censorship and supervision. As Lipset and others have pointed out, there are times in American history when consensus and liberty seem to be the main problem and other times when equality and fraternity present themselves as major issues; there is an inherent tension between the fear of stability and the search for it.[8]

Despite the still powerful remnants of the booster spirit and the continuing optimism of perhaps a majority of Americans, there is a growing tendency to assume that America, if not the world as a whole, was better off in an earlier day and that at no earlier time were evils such as conformity (in the sense of excessive and unprincipled deference to others) so prevalent. I believe, as many essays in this book emphasize, that we are in terrible danger today, either of destroying ourselves and others by allowing mankind to blunder into war or of building up a garrison state, supposedly to defeat the totalitarian Communists. But in discussing these dangers I do not consider it helpful to let nostalgia blur our image of the American past, for this will lead us astray as to what we should do now. I do not regard the post-Civil War period and the post-World War I period in America as especially glorious. Ancestral political greatness does exist, in the Founding Fathers and their immediate successors and in rare figures since then. But men in public life today, if our own version of the cult of personality does not enter in, are sometimes unduly deprecated.[9]

American life in the 1960s seems to me less conformist, less cruel and barbarous, less oppressive of women and minorities, than at any time since the Civil War. It is these very emancipations, as they grate against values that are traditional but not really strongly held, that give rise to new waves of fundamentalism in politics, religion, and culture. Where we seem to have fallen short is in the gap between our opportunities and what our best intelligence tells us, and what we are actually able to accomplish. We are responsible for more people inside and outside America than ever before. Yet only a small portion of our greatly expanded educated population feels free enough, detached enough, well-informed enough to respond with independence to our danger and our opportunity. Our European "ancestors" having suddenly, if metaphori-

[8] I have found Seymour Martin Lipset's work particularly important in this area. See e.g., his essay, "A Changing American Character?" in Lipset and Leo Lowenthal, eds., *Culture and Social Character: The Work of David Riesman Reviewed* (The Free Press, 1961), pp. 136–71.

[9] Cf. my introduction to Stimson Bullitt, *To Be a Politician* (Doubleday Anchor, 1961).

cally, vanished, America finds itself an immensely and terrifyingly strong orphan asked to take charge of the inheritance while still hoping for one last fling. Regrettably—and this is quite a new thing in history at least since the Flood—that fling may be the world's last.

Law and Sociology
(1957)

RECRUITMENT, TRAINING, AND COLLEAGUESHIP

The different patterns of recruitment into law and into sociology and the different experiences of students and practitioners in both milieus are critical factors bearing on the relation between the two fields.

I cannot here delineate the immense variety of academic climates but will confine my comparisons to the leading law schools and graduate schools, respectively, and even within this group to a small minority of "national" schools. Nonlawyer readers should realize that the differences among law schools are enormously wider than those among medical schools, or even, in all probability, those among graduate schools of arts and sciences. That is, the gap is huge that separates the few, mainly Ivy League, law schools, that funnel their best graduates into leading firms and government offices, and the poorer (often proprietary) night schools that upgrade immigrants' children into white-collar work (though it should be added that this may often involve legwork such as bill collecting or ambulance chasing). In between there are private law schools that aim to be national, though they draw on a largely local clientele (for example, University of Pennsylvania, University of Buffalo); and state university law schools, some of which (for example, Michigan) are more national in purpose and market than others that dominate their locale (for example, the University of Washington).

As legal education at the state-university level improves and becomes more professional (with law professors increasingly taking graduate work in law at Harvard or Columbia), there is a pull toward "nationalization," which is also reflected in the upgrading of the law reviews. But the parochial pull in the other direction remains powerful, tied up as it is with the social mobility of disadvantaged groups, with the power of the local bar over bar examinations and admissions, and with the parochialism built into state decisions and courthouse folkways. A study by Carlin, *Lawyers on Their Own*, indicates that the overwhelming majority of practicing lawyers in Chicago are small entrepreneurs, practicing virtually on their own, and helping other small entrepreneurs (or small people who have trouble or a claim) through the interstices of the lower courts and lower bureaucracies, private and public; large affairs are concentrated in the hands of a relatively small group of lawyers, primarily the 7 or 8 per cent in the thirty-five largest firms that include fifteen or more lawyers, as well as a handful of lawyers practicing alone or in small firms or as house counsel in large corporations.[1] To repeat: I am not talking about the vast majority of lawyers nor the schools they attended (no doubt, a few of the nonprofessional lone practitioners went to leading law schools, but did not go on from there in the approved pathways). And even among the schools attended by the minority, there are still great differences: thus, Harvard, Yale, Chicago, and Columbia Law Schools all have somewhat different clienteles, markets, and forms of being national. Of necessity, in generalizing about these schools and their products, I shall overgeneralize.

My concern here, however, is less with legal education as a whole than with the law schools as a possible place for sociological work, and with the law professors in such schools as possible colleagues in interdisciplinary teaching and research. Furthermore, I shall have very little to contribute in this paper to the sociological study of the legal corpus or of major legal institutions. Sociology in its present phase can grapple with a profession or occupation; and, with its anthropological and social-psychological allies, it can seek to embrace a whole culture (if not too big); it can study stratification—and the way this shows up in jury deliberations or in the social mobility of lawyers. But, so far as I can see, sociology is not now prepared to embrace the legal order within its own categories in terms sufficiently detailed and concrete to shed new illumination. There is not only a certain intellectual impenetrability about the law, reflecting and resulting from the achievements of generations of jurists; there is an even more important factual impenetrability resulting from the sheer overwhelming and opaque bulk of data that must be mastered to link the empirical with the interpretive or the ideal-typical. And in the law, and even in its manifold branches, there is nothing so lucid, so condensed, so truly theoretical, as classical

[1] See Jerome E. Carlin, *Lawyers on Their Own* (New Brunswick, N.J.: Rutgers University Press, 1962). Carlin's data also indicate the relatively modest origins of the great majority of these lawyers—frequently from immigrant families of limited education.

price theory in economics. Law (or what Karl Llewellyn called "lawstuff") is everywhere in its impact; it is almost everywhere in such forms as judicialization and the use of precedent; and men trained in law (or at least graduates of law schools) can be found in many obviously significant social roles. No "pure theory of law" has won anything like universal assent, or even awareness, from students of law and jurisprudence; nor do we have an adequate theory to tell us, beyond semantics, when we are dealing with law, when with government, when with paralegal sanctions, and so on.

Correspondingly, to infiltrate the legal order-and-disorder with intellect and understanding remains, in the American scene, a task scarcely begun. The early advocates of sociological jurisprudence were unduly sanguine. Many of them hoped to storm the fortress of the law without extensive empirical work but with what now appear as semantic and epistemological slogans. The effect of these slogans was at first stimulating, especially when they were felt to be part of a general movement toward realism and debunking vis-à-vis American institutions. Now that the tasks loom in their true magnitude, I hope that scholars will nevertheless persevere. But I turn in these remarks to an oblique and indirect strategy of approach, via the sociology of the professions and of knowledge.[2]

THE COERCION OF IMAGES

Why is it, when lawyers and sociologists confront one another—though they would scarcely do so save peripherally if they were not in some measure marginal in their own guilds—that they do so as "representative men" of each? By assuming that their opposite number is central in his discipline, do they seek a firmer identity in their own? There is a tendency to talk about *the* law, *the* lawyer, *the* sociologist,

[2] For earlier efforts on my part to apply social-psychological concepts and methods to legal phenomena, cf. "Democracy and Defamation," 42 *Columbia Law Review* 727, 1085, 1282 (1942); "Legislative Restrictions on Foreign Enlistment and Travel," 40 *Columbia Law Review* 793 (1940); "Possession and the Law of Finders," 52 *Harvard Law Review* 1105 (1939) (making use of an amateur survey); "Law and Social Science," 50 *Yale Law Journal* 636 (1941).

Philip Selznick's "The Sociology of Law" [in Robert K. Merton, Leonard Broom, and Leonard S. Cottrell, Jr., eds., *Sociology Today* (New York: Basic Books, 1959)] seems to me a stimulating preliminary statement of possible stages in the development of such a sociology, as well as an indication of what some of the problems are that stand in the way.

very much as Americans abroad can hardly help being viewed as *the* American. It seems to me that mutual acculturation might begin with a more pluralistic set of images.

Sociologists tend to put lawyers in the role of the model lawyer, with a model constituency of people and problems. As seen from within, however, the legal profession is striking for the amorphousness of its boundaries, in comparison with the image of the "real doctor" operative among medically trained people. The ideal of the "real doctor" is so coercive an image that a man who, let us say, is an M.D. and a pathologist, or an M.D. and a hospital administrator, or an M.D. and a public-health man, or even an M.D. and a research clinician who does not have direct dealings with patients, is not considered fully a doctor.[3] He is apt to feel bad about it and to make the same sort of apologies that a dean may make to professors about being a dean. To be sure, lawyers do not completely lack comparably coercive images. One finds them operative in house counsel (that is, full-time salaried employees of an insurance company or other corporation) who feel themselves not quite lawyers, not quite independent professionals; one finds them occasionally in the government lawyer who has never tried a case and never had any of the appurtenances of starting at the bottom, but who went straight from law school to the FCC at $6000 a year; one finds them in the law professor who is at once pleased and a bit embarrassed if somebody brings him a trespass case or divorce case (I am talking of course about the full-time law professor), giving him the feeling that he has been initiated as a real lawman.[4]

[3] See Everett C. Hughes, "The Making of a Physician—A General Statement of Ideas and Problems," *Human Organization*, vol. 14, no. 4 (1956), p. 21. I owe a great deal to Professor Hughes for a way of looking at the intramural and extramural relations of the professions, and his work and that of his students tincture this article.

[4] In these images one can trace a variety of elements. One is nostalgia for an older tradition of the independent, down-to-earth professional man: for the cozy small-town general practitioner who knew everybody and could do anything. This is part of the antibureaucratic, "folk-society" ethos still so strong in American popular culture and intellectual culture, too. (One may compare the treatment of the professions in C. Wright Mills' *White Collar*.) There is the no less traditional romanticism that the work done at the bottom of the ladder—whether palpating a patient or trying a case—is somehow more real than the work entered, without apprenticeship, at the top of the ladder where the grass never grows. Involved, too, is American "thingmanship" and subtle anti-intellectualism. And this means that youngsters in a rapidly changing society enter callings such as the law under

Sociologists have often operated with an image of lawyers as men concerned with sanctions, with the enforcement of rules. This all too uncomplicated definition must make the lawman restive. For, as already indicated, the law-trained person is likely to be found almost anywhere in the American social structure. Precisely because the commitment of going to law school and the socialization that ensues for those who do go is less thoroughgoing than medical education imposes, and because, moreover, no Flexner Report has limited the numbers who can get a legal education,[5] the law remains par excellence the career open to talent. Librarian of Congress, president of Chrysler, Secretary of State, and at less exalted levels insurance executive, realtor, publisher —almost any managerial, commercial, or nonspecialized intellectual job you can think of—are within the reach of the law-trained man.[6] It is arguable that this escalator that the law provides is at least as important as a function of legal training as the functions more frequently discussed; arguable that the criminal law, or the sanctioning, legitimation, and interpreting functions, which Talcott Parsons among others has discussed, have no greater impact on the social order than this function of keeping open the channels of mobility for the boy who can talk, who is not too narrowly self-defined—who is a kind of roving fullback of American society and can and does go anywhere.[7]

---

the spell of an obsolescing image of the work done in them. And, as the callings themselves pass the point of no return, the captives in them may tend to feel displaced.

[5] There *was* such a report—the Redlich Report of 1914. But legal education has been an inexpensive moneymaker. Without laboratories, large classes can be managed, often brilliantly. And, as suggested at the outset, the law school world at large, with its support in the practicing and legislating bar, still clings to its night and proprietary schools and its often parochial standards of performance.

[6] In principle, one could imagine more relevant training for each of these careers—just as Freud, in my opinion rightly, envisaged more relevant training than medicine for the practice of psychoanalysis. For historical reasons, law school has visibly, in this country as abroad, remained the royal road. (However, it is my impression and that of other observers that many young men are perhaps somewhat less eager than heretofore to travel on a royal road—and, as indicated in the following footnote, other roads are now providing competition.)

[7] There are other competitive roads that, arguably, have a better chance in the future than law. There are the more technical roads, for example, economics or psychology, engineering or city planning, perhaps more adaptable intellectually in an age of automation; there are the still less technical roads, such as public relations.

THE SELF-CONFIRMING MYTH OF LEGAL EDUCATION

Is there anything the law schools do to facilitate this, or is it a purely accidental connection? I have elsewhere described the so-called legal mind, as selected and turned out by the best national law schools, as the nonlegalistic mind: the mind that has learned skepticism of abstractions and yet at-homeness with them.[8] The atmosphere of such schools, moreover, may help narrow the range of curiosity for some of the more humanistically oriented, but, unlike what sometimes happens in graduate school to social scientists, law students do not become more stupid and more cowed than they were as undergraduates. Or perhaps I should qualify this, bearing in mind the loss of curiosity and breadth of perspective that one often finds as students "progress" from their first to their final years in law school, especially if they are gifted but neither make the law review nor get involved in legal aid work. I should say instead that law students may get more stupid in the sense of a constricted *Weltanschauung*, more ready prey to a fundamental complacency; but at the same time they are apt to gain in confidence and craftsmanship.

This is a somewhat different process from that at work in comparable graduate schools, at least in the social science departments. Students in the latter emerge often less confident than they entered, less "promising." Just as they seldom get their doctoral degree within a regulation three or four years, but remain instead in an amorphous zone of delayed maturity; so they sometimes (unlike most law students) reach for an identity by incorporating a professor's definition of what they "are," while being subjected to his personal view of the "field" in grading, in thesis supervision, and orals.[9] In contrast, law students do not to the

---

[8] See David Riesman, "Toward an Anthropological Science of Law and the Legal Profession," *American Journal of Sociology*, vol. 57, pp. 121-35 (1951), reprinted in *Individualism Reconsidered* (New York: The Free Press, 1954), pp. 440-66.

[9] Of course, this puts in a bleak way an apprenticeship that can be, and sometimes is, a relationship in which there is learning and discipline on both sides. And it ignores the many schools where laxity and *laissez-faire* are more serious problems than subjection and fanaticism. The position stated above is based both on personal observation and on the report of the committee of graduate deans (working under the auspices of the Fund for the Advancement of Education) chaired by M. E. Hobbs and including Jacques Barzun, Peter Elder, and A. R. Gordon. Cf., for example, Jacques Barzun, *Graduate Student Study at Columbia* (extracts from the Dean's Report) (New York: Columbia University Press, 1957).

same extent find their identity as lawyers by "incorporating" their professors, who may or may not qualify as practitioners as well as teachers; and the system under which the law students operate is far more impersonal. People *do* get through law school in three years; there is very little of the protracted uncertainty of much graduate study, or of the umbilical clinging to one's teachers that failure to finish a thesis permits. This happens, in part, because law professors, whether full-time or part-time, are more worldly and better paid than most social scientists; they are intelligent but rarely intellectual; student devotion is nice, but they have alternative ways of "spending" their affects, and relatively little need constantly to prove the validity of their profession or their specialty through the shining eyes of indoctrinated students. The validity of their profession is only marginally in question: its success is historically solid and daily attested in the market place of American careers. Although, to be sure, sensitive lawyers and law professors suffer because of some popular disesteem for lawyers (though Supreme Court justices stood at the very top, even above physicians and physicists, in the National Opinion Research Center poll of the relative standing of occupations), and because they realize that some of this disesteem is deserved, it seldom shakes their belief in the legal career as such, but rather reinforces their belief in a variant model of it, such as the Brandeis-at-the-bar model, or the small-town independent lawyer model, or that of the crusading government lawyer.

Intellectual craftsmanship in the law, moreover, is a fairly visible and surprisingly unidimensional thing, so that law professors (with whatever unconscious injustices) can evaluate each other's competence rather readily, as mathematicians are said to be able to do, or organic chemists. Only an occasional heretic who tries something new creates problems for this system of ranking—and, just as Picasso might for once draw like Ingres to show he could do it, so such a legal scholar can often take a turn at the conventional games to maintain his professional standing. One has to be "real gone" to be read out of the fold, as Hohfeld was for some during his lifetime, and as perhaps Myres McDougal of Yale is now for anti-Lasswellians.

These comforts, as compared with the much more polemical situation in some branches of the social sciences and humanities, seem to me among the reasons that law professors, although they, like all teachers, can be wounded by their students, often, when they seek disciples, do so with twinkling eye and chastened zeal. There is a readier dialectical give-and-take in most good law schools than I have observed in graduate schools of arts and sciences at the same or comparable universities: the law student is encouraged, in part of course by forensic tradition, to talk back to his professors, even in huge classes, with a verve and lack of fear of what might happen to him that one finds less often in graduate school.[10]

If law is esoteric to the layman—without having to fight for its mystique, as psychology and sociology sometimes feel they must—it is not kept esoteric vis-à-vis the student who, after a year, can become a law-review editor, which involves sometimes editing his professors or taking issue with them in student notes and comments on recent decisions. There are some 150 law reviews, often subsidized by the school as part of its public relations work or as due its image of itself, and of course often also guided by the faculty. But there is, so far as I know, nothing comparable to this development in the graduate schools, despite the frequently lesser professionalization of the latter (or perhaps because of this). Although several interesting ventures have appeared lately (for example, among sociology students at Berkeley and anthropology students at Chicago), graduate students do not run the social science (or humanities) periodicals and lack the confident impetus this involves. Law-review and other law students more than compensate for the lacunae of their teachers by educating each other. And although this happens also in graduate school, it is less firmly institutionalized.[11]

The appearance of objectivity in law-school grading—and recall again that I am speaking here of the leading national schools—is part of one of the most remarkable self-confirming prophecies in vocational choice and selection. A young man who does well at law school in terms of its frequently numerical grading system is (barring an aggressively unfortunate personality) ticketed for life as a first-class passenger on the

[10] The Harvard Graduate School of Business Administration encourages a similar freedom, in large classes and small. Here, too, the case method reigns.

[11] Understandably, I find this contrast a source of sorrow. Whereas as a law teacher I was aware that my students "knew" ever so much better than I what the law was like, and hence rejected their faculty's innovations with Philistine abandon, as a sociology teacher I find students coming with little extra-academic sense of the field, and almost too ready to accept professorial models of life within it. However, I have the impression that contemporary law students are somewhat less Philistine and considerably less hostile to the social sciences than they were when I was a law teacher—part of a secular development in our educational system as a whole.

escalator for talent. Nicholas Kelley, not a naïve man, writes some revealing things on this score.

> A man . . . who wishes to prepare himself for corporation law will get himself into the best law school that will take him and will exercise all his powers to graduate as high as he can. Studying law in a good law school is stimulating, interesting and competitive. The marks that a good law school in this country gives are almost an unfailingly accurate grading of analytical power of mind and power to express it. Coming well through this testing and selecting process marks a man as valuable and promising for a wide variety of work even though he does not stay in the law.[12]

This is so thoroughly believed by victims as well as victors in the system that I have seen men of outstanding undergraduate attainment, Rhodes scholars and junior Phi Betes, let mediocre grades in law school convince them that they were mediocre men. In contrast, the law-review men went into the office of Kelley, Drye, Newhall and Maginnes and the other big corporate firms and had their chance to meet Chrysler Corporation executives, as Nicholas Kelley did, and thus to gain experience and connections that could later be used to prove that law school marks are infallible. Naturally, the confidence that comes of believing this—believing that one got one's start through ability and not looks or luck (confidence that in other versions has been part of the dynamism of the self-made man)—is purchased at the cost of others' being robbed of confidence.[13]

[12] The *Harvard Crimson, A Guide to Career Opportunities* (1956), p. 78.

[13] There is the more subtle cost for some of those who do well that they might have enjoyed doing something else even better; among their congeries of gifts, they prize what others prize and can seemingly measure. At the same time, since the law opens such a variety of doors, subsidiary or second-choice careers are available to many law-trained men who discover their hidden or suppressed talents after graduation.

A law-review editor, Robert A. Anthony of Stanford, wrote me the following comments on these matters in a letter:

"As to law review experience, there is in my mind no doubting its worth as a training beyond classroom learning. On the other hand, there is no doubting the arbitrariness of judging men for after life largely by the historical fact of their having done law review work (itself a reflection of first-year grades). Granting that law reviews are worth their cost, can the arbitrary status given by nonassociation with them be avoided? I don't see how. Even if there is money for a second-string intramural law review, as at NYU, the distinction will remain. The prestige of the first string is self-perpetuating. Is there any test to select law review men less arbitrarily than

SOCIOLOGISTS THROUGH THE LEGAL LOOKING GLASS

This confidence, as I shall try to show shortly, presents certain threats to interdisciplinary work involving lawyers. But before turning to this, I want to round out my comments on mutually coercive images by indicating that the lawmen have similarly hampering images of the social scientist. For instance, not many law professors realize the variety of intellectual pursuits that go under the label "anthropologist": human biology, archaeology, "primitive" cultures, modern nations, industrial enterprises and other reaches of applied anthropology, linguistics, and so on. There may be a sense in which some of these men are not "real" anthropologists: maybe they have to be kings of an Indian tribe, their tribe, to so consider themselves. But "the" anthropologist concerned with contemporary legal institutions (rather than with African legal forms) is likely to have his tribeship well behind him, and not to fit neatly into the law professor's simplified definition.

So, too, with sociologists, a group which today comprises a rapidly changing configuration of concerns. Sociologists used to come into contact with lawyers primarily in a mutual pursuit of relatively powerless and underprivileged groups: immigrants, criminals, juvenile delinquents, the insane, the generally disorganized. This was when sociology had as its clients the fringes of society to which the more vested academic interests had not laid claim, the way economists lay claim to the

---

by first-year grades? Again, it's hard to see how. Any other method would probably involve a gamut of more open competition and politicking which would heighten the abrasiveness of law-school life and put a premium on hateful sorts of aggressive self-assertion. . . . Perhaps as a phenomenon over time the status created by law review participation is shaking down a bit. Perhaps the profession has lived with non-law-review men long enough to appreciate the fact that some are as good as law review men. Surely there are plenty of solid non-law-review members of my class whose dignity and work quality has been maintained without a disruption of confidence. They are a good example for their less confident but equally endowed colleagues. Through the influence of such persons, both in law school and after, a dignity commensurate with ability should be attainable for the whole group of competent non-review men. The balance might quietly be redressed over time, without necessarily taking the form of an anti-intellectual revolt against the plutocracy of the law review elite. I suppose it all boils down to a matter of whether the non-review men can (as I think they can) pierce the transparency of the grading system enough to keep the quiet confidence that will best aid their success. . . ."

economy, political scientists to the state, and historians to all these things when dead. Today, as my preceding remarks have illustrated, sociologists are apt to take lawyers themselves for "clients" in the sense of an interest in studying the profession, its training, and its day-to-day life. Just as the anthropologists no longer stay put with their preliterates, the sociologists no longer concentrate on illiterates but lay claim to the highly literate and influential sectors of society. They are no more willing to stay in place in a mobile America than the lawyers are—though, unlike the lawyers, they make only an intellectual's, but seldom a consultant's, livelihood from other people's jurisdictional disputes.

SOCIOLOGISTS IN A LEGAL SETTING

In a law school or other legal environment sociologists and their intellectual allies are, of course, newcomers, and they often seek to behave in a way that will impress the lawyers. One can observe analogous tendencies when social scientists work in a medical environment and come up against psychiatrists and others who have acquired prestige and authority from having been tested in medical school (whatever may be the derogation they feel at not being "real doctors," as indicated above).

An aspect of the famous jury-recording case at the University of Chicago Law School furnishes an illustration. It is my impression that, in part, that situation arose because of some lawyers' desire to show their "hardheaded" colleagues of the legal profession that a study of experimental small groups, not legally called juries, was actually a study of juries. Lawyers and law professors, in my observation, are very apt to be scornful of the findings of social science. This is an offshoot of a professional self-image of omnicompetence based in some degree on the self-confirming tendencies mentioned above. It is also a reflection of the lawyer's wish to maintain a pattern of practice and teaching in which he can play by ear.[14] Science threatens this—just as the coming

[14] I have wondered whether this pattern has any connection with the English source of our law, for England is the country where the amateur is still an influential model, and it is bad form to be too clever, too farsighted, too technical. While our graduate schools are built on the German academic model, our law schools may reflect British values in somewhat greater measure, at least in this respect.

I think many students of the common-law tradition would agree that judicial amateurism is enshrined by the case-to-case workings of the common law; thus, it is well known that many judges resent (quite apart from

of automation and the enormous demands for planning threaten the similar "play it by ear" tendencies of old-fashioned business executives. Thus the lawyers were ready as professional skeptics to discount findings on juries—and the easiest way to do this was to say "they are not 'real' juries" (we are back again by another route at the intransigent "realism" of the lawyers' self-image). With some reluctance, the Chicago group was led into this trap of playing the other fellow's game.[15] But, on the whole, sociologists are not going to win by meeting the lawyer's presumed standards and momentarily impressing him. For the latter can always fall back on the clinching phrase—how often have I heard it used in interdisciplinary talk, "I don't know anything about it, but . . ." —a phrase that is always a preface to an ex cathedra opinion, as arrogant and impervious to "scientific method" as you please.

However inconvenient and irritating this arrogance may be—an arrogance akin to that of the man who has "met a payroll"—we should not forget its positive side, its value for the lawyer in opening many careers to him, as we have seen, and even for us in providing an occasionally useful corrective for inflated claims. But, speaking for myself, I must say that the atmosphere of a law school is too abrasive, too cocky, to make for an easy colleagueship on matters where the social scientist is apt to feel grave self-doubt—notably, at the frontiers of intellectual

---

content) the strait jacket that codes and legislation seek to impose on their wish to maintain an easy (or, invidiously, a "muddling through") fluidity in selecting which precedents in the armory of case-law to follow. The resistance most courts have displayed, until quite recently, to accepting sample surveys as evidence of public opinion (whether in libel cases, trademark cases, motions for change of venue, or other situations where an estimate of public opinion is relevant) would seem to me part of the same constellation of attitudes. (Some social scientists lay such matters to lag—a term that always seems to me the beginning of inquiry, not the end of wisdom; in any case, judges and lawyers in America have been fabulously inventive, for example, in the field of corporation finance, dragging the rest of society along.)

[15] There may sometimes be unintended advantages to social science in doing this. Thus, Julius Cohen, Reginald Robson, and Alan Bates at the University of Nebraska Law School conducted interviews throughout the state on popular conceptions of justice in adoptions and like cases; they engaged their respondents in strikingly argumentative and dialectical interviews, rather than the usual nondirective sort—not because they were being at the moment experimental in interviewing technique but in order to meet anticipated objections from lawyers that all they had gotten were off-the-cuff and ill-considered opinions.

work. If one is jogging along an already laid-out track—as one can so readily do in many fields of psychology—it is one thing, but if one is exploring rather new areas, with all the misgivings to which pioneering intellectual work is prone, then to meet constantly the really quite amiable needling of the skeptical lawman may be tiresome. A certain amount of cultism, even occultism, I am suggesting, is an almost necessary part of new intellectual enterprise, and although, like any other morale-building efforts, this can go too far and become an end in itself, it is part of the protection that uncertain activity demands.

Correspondingly, it is up to the lawyer-critic to make some effort to understand the terms and categories of the newer social sciences, with due sympathy for these problems of protection of novelty; of course, once the novelty wears off, what was once faddist language is either abandoned or becomes part of staple intellectual discourse and hence no longer recognizably exotic (this is what has happened to many terms and concepts in law and economics). By the same token law professors can sometimes serve social science in the role of amateur yet serious and reasonably acculturated critics.[16]

Many law professors have little understanding of this because they can live their whole lives as apparently active but intellectually passive feeders on the pulp of advance sheets daily turned out by the West Publishing Company, coupled with the superb index system that the legal profession has developed for itself.[17] The law professor can, like

[16] Willard Hurst of the University of Wisconsin Law School has made this point in correspondence. A good example is the careful examination by Walter Blum and Harry Kalven, Jr., of the University of Chicago Law School, of Samuel Stouffer's *Communism, Conformity, and Civil Liberties* (New York: Doubleday, 1955). They treat the Stouffer study as an exemplar of general methodological problems in public opinion research. Walter J. Blum and Harry Kalven, Jr., "The Art of Opinion Research: A Lawyer's Appraisal of an Emerging Science," 24 *University of Chicago Law Review* 1 (1956).

[17] Professor Albert Ehrenzweig reminds me that the indexing system presents the legal profession with many unsolved problems that would profit from sociological inquiry; for the decision by an indexer as to what a case is "about" may bury or mislocate its implications, as in any unimaginative system of semantics or filing. As the flood of published case law continues, only sloppily mopped up by restatements, texts, and annotations, those who would make sense of the law may be overwhelmed by the keys, the labels, intended to keep track of the material. Of course, United States Supreme Court decisions don't get "lost" this way: the justices themselves, their law clerks, and the bar and professoriate who follow these decisions find them manageable in scope and amount. And in the past a few voracious or im-

a book reviewer, depend on a steady supply, without the need many social scientists have to create their own data; he can say wherein this case is like that case, and not like some other case, and he, like his students, can take an endless delight in showing how the court forgot to take these and these things into account. Since judges (as the Blaustein and Porter book, *The American Lawyer*, shows) are less well educated than the average of the practicing and teaching bar, there is never any deficit of judicial limitations to be pointed out. This work of the law professor is so pleasant and so lacking in risk, and on the whole so well regarded if done in a craftsmanlike way, that it is a real sacrifice, a labor of love, for a law professor to get deeply involved in interdisciplinary exploration, since this means relinquishment of that sanctuary.[18]

The law students, as a whole, feel even less free to take social science too seriously, for they are still seeking sanctuary. A teacher who reminds them too much of an undergraduate social science instructor may

---

perialistic masters sought to keep track of cases in a single area of private law, as Wigmore did for evidence and Williston for contracts. But as "the literature" expands to include many intermediate courts of appeal and even of first instance, such heroic efforts at subsumemanship no longer suffice. It would be interesting to know how law students, trained toward coherence through mastery of selected cases, cope on graduation with the semiliterate products of the benches in their home jurisdictions—perhaps "play it by ear" may be an outcome of this encounter also.

There are other perspectives, however, in which the torrent of advance sheets would appear to be advantageous for legal education, if not for legal practice. For example, the fact that new decisions constantly impend is a kind of reminder of mortality to theoreticians: their concepts are apt to be "good for this trip only," and elaborate effort at the restatement of the law, even by the willful and ingenious, has definite limits. Other intellectual enterprises have methods for postponing the reckoning with discomfitting data (this sometimes gives them time to mature without being too much swayed by present trends and the hegemony of the hour), but a decision by a leading court can always surprise the law professor and hence teach him something. And the student can find in a new decision support for his earlier skepticism of his teachers' generalizations. Indeed, some of the often bracing intellectual climate of the best law schools is reflected in the fact that the law is not presented as something given, merely to be learned; too much discovery in other fields is presented to students as frozen metaphors and dead "results."

[18] Teaching law is only one of many avenues for the law graduate: not only does it select to begin with a small, more or less scholarly minority, but it continues to do so as the other alternatives (for example, practice, government service, the judiciary) remain alive.

threaten the still unformed crust of vocationalism. Even those students who will, on graduation or thereafter, not practice law in anything like the forms taken for granted in law school may want to try on the mask, the identity, of the "real lawyer" before modifying or exchanging it. A social scientist who comes bearing techniques—for example, for selecting juries by a rough SES (socioeconomic status) index or for interviewing witnesses with greater psychological acumen—may be well received by a minority of students, but only if he doesn't try to interest them in fundamental theoretical or methodological matters. Thus, the sociologist teaching in a law school, like one teaching in an engineering school, will tend to be forced into the role of salesman for his stuff (though he may have at the same time a certain freedom from some of the professional pressures he would face in a graduate school). And his success will in some measure depend on the attitudes toward him of his law professor colleagues—attitudes that the students, for reasons just indicated, will quickly pick up and magnify.

In this situation, the readiest accommodation of the sociologist in a law school setting is probably in terms of an unequivocal policy orientation, a direct concern with the potential relevance of social science for solving problems as lawyers see and present them, as against a more academic concern with theoretical understanding of legal processes. At its lowest level, social science provides new gimmicks to be used in advocacy. I believe this to be the function of the "Brandeis brief," an allegedly impartial but actually polemical use of documentation (largely economic) to overwhelm or provide new rationalizations for judges.[19] At a less forensic level, there is no doubt that a concern for policy often provides a common motivation for lawmen and social scientists. Yet the use of this concern as the principal lever for interdisciplinary projects frequently leads to the choice of a relatively unexamined standard policy topic from the law to be treated by a no less standard method from the social sciences. As Dean Edward H. Levi of the University of Chicago Law School has observed, this puts the social scientist in the role of an intellectual subcontractor, and it limits the extent to which he can influence law professors' thinking about what topics they might study

[19] Professor Paul A. Freund of Harvard Law School has pointed out to me that the Brandeis brief was originally designed to show that an impressive body of opinion could be mustered to support the judgment of a legislature against constitutional attack; its aim was to resist the "play it by ear" tendency of cavalier judges, but not to set itself up as a scientific arbiter beyond that.

and what categories they might discover, and hence minimizes his impact on legal education and the atmosphere in which law students develop. Although much useful work gets done this way, it is my belief that the most demanding and most potentially fruitful work requires a joint decision both on topic and method: a redefinition of the problem as presented by the lawyer and of the method as owned by the social scientist.

This is perhaps not so hard as it seems because, underlying the genuine concern for policy, there is a mutual but usually unavowed curiosity—an interest in knowledge for its own sake. The sociologists who came before the Rutgers Seminar on Law and Sociology generally assumed that the law professors are *that* interested in the traditional problems of the law: in the problems of social control, or of better legal aid, or of more humane or sensible treatment of insanity, and so on. The law professors tended to accept such ascriptions of motive, partly out of politeness, partly because the stated motives are part of the configuration, partly because, for reasons already indicated, well-understood and hence supposedly realistic motives seem truer than less palpable ones. Actually, I doubt whether most of the law professors at a seminar like this one would stay around if they were not intrigued intellectually—if they were not eager to see what kinds of birds sociologists are!

Let me return to the medical field for an illustration. When medical authorities turn to sociologists and anthropologists, it is surely in part because they want to run a more effective hospital or group health plan, or to bring better medical care to urban immigrants from the southern hills or Puerto Rican villages. But, having talked to a few of the doctors who have been leaders in extending invitations to social scientists, I am inclined to think that the joint concern for welfare is not the whole story on either side. The doctors come as one alternative to getting psychoanalyzed, or taking a trip to Europe or Japan: they are interested, and they want to see what we have to say. And I know that some of the sociologists go because they are curious about doctors: curious, and even sometimes quite hostile to the forms medical arrogance takes (we are all arrogant in our different ways, much as nations are), and envious of the glamour and prestige of the medical profession with its unbeatable combination of service, individualism, guild feeling, and science. These transactions tend to be covered over, just as in the case of the law, by talk exclusively of "problem-solving," "policy-orientation," or "basic research." I think we could be more creative in our meetings, and could more readily begin to invent topics and methods in the grooves of neither field, if we felt freer to recognize our fuller panoply of motives.

Sociologists, of course, have motives too; for some of us an aggressive lack of interest in policy problems occurred during our socialization in graduate school, since our teachers grew up in the generation when sociology was striving to become scientific, to free itself from association with socialism, social work, and other good causes. Many have observed how the sons of ministers substituted Science for God, the search for truth for the search for salvation or reform.[20] Thus, when a law professor comes to a sociologist because he is worried about the unequal distribution of justice, and regards legal-aid work as a drop in the bucket, the latter's preoccupation with methodology and lack of reformist concern may surprise him and send him back to his own devices.

DIFFERENCES IN LEGAL AND SOCIOLOGICAL STYLES

We may put this in terms of the different forms worldliness takes among sociologists and among law professors. The more sophisticated the former are, the more likely they are to be scornful of do-good activities (as professionals, if not as citizens). Yet, precisely in part because they eschew such activities, they often remain sheltered academicians in comparison with even the full-time law professors who bring the swish of practice, of affairs, into the atmosphere of a law school.[21] In a medical school, the arts of practice are carried in with the bodies of patients, emphasizing the split between the research-minded and sci-

[20] For fuller discussion, cf. my paper, "Some Observations on Social Science Research," *Antioch Review*, vol. 11 (1951), pp. 259–78; reprinted in *Individualism Reconsidered*, pp. 467–83.

An unpublished study, "Occupational Commitment of Graduate Sociology Students," done by Charles R. Wright of the Bureau of Applied Social Research, indicates that many students retained their personal definitions of the field, in terms of broad and philosophical concerns, in the face of a contrary emphasis on methodology insisted upon by the graduate faculty (and encouraged, I might add, by available job opportunities). Wright speculates as to why professionalization does not always take, and notes that many who resist it drift off into other fields without taking their degrees.

[21] To be sure, to some of the even more sheltered humanists on the faculty of arts and sciences, sociologists may appear to be extremely worldly men, a cliché's throw from Madison Avenue or the CIA or immersion in factory life or popular culture.

ence-minded temper of the professors in the preclinical years, and the practical and often business-getting arts emphasized by the Cadillacs if not the comments of the part-time men in the later clinical years. In the leading law schools, where only the Legal Aid Society, less prestigeful than the law review, has clients, and where the best students prefer to serve as clerks to judges when they graduate and thus continue for another year or so a law-review kind of existence, this split exists more *within* individual faculty members than between the men who teach in different years or even different courses. Recall that I am speaking of the major national schools, whose students envisage themselves, in the model case, as entering a large firm and hence a setting where their first "clients" are fellow lawyers rather than customers picked up off the street—a setting, that is, where they can remain somewhat impersonal and objective and not have to bend all efforts toward getting and retaining individual lay clients.[22]

The aroma of practical affairs is imported into such schools partly by men who have had bursts of practice, especially in the government, and partly by a sort of inside-dopesterism characteristic of the major law schools in which the factions of the Supreme Court (or sometimes, in addition, the United States Courts of Appeals) are refracted among the faculty who have been law clerks to judges or who know them personally or at least share a common culture. (It is this, *inter alia*, that makes the teaching of constitutional law in a law school so different from its characteristic teaching by political scientists, who are apt to take doctrine more seriously.) Moreover, a law school faculty is constantly engaged in consulting, so that, for example, Karl Llewellyn,

[22] The briefs written in these firms are, like the often anonymous law review note, usually colleaguial enterprises; their audience (and that of many documents, such as SEC registration statements) is primarily a legally trained official; moreover, the ties of large corporations to their law firms do not suffer from instability comparable to that of advertising agency accounts, allowing the law firm to maintain a certain professional dignity in its relation to corporate clients (and, on occasion, to exploit them).

In contrast, the small-time lawyer practicing on his own often must aim to impress his client rather than his adversary; and, like the doctor in general practice, he may worry about his deskside manner and his ability to deliver the goods quickly and visibly. The student who expects to become such a lawyer may find his professors often much too "impractical" and "highfalutin," and he may worry more about how to pass the bar examination (a routine left to cram schools by the leading university law schools) than about not knowing enough law when out in practice.

one of the law teachers who was an eminent intellectual and not only a very intelligent man, led another existence as a Commissioner on Uniform State Laws, meeting with bankers and manufacturers in efforts to unify commercial codes. Likewise, Herbert Wechsler, another intellectual, has been active on many consultative fronts, as in aiding the Department of Justice in drafting rules of criminal procedure and as Reporter of the Model Penal Code. Thus, even the more theoretically oriented among a law faculty are seldom theorists pure and simple.

The aroma of practice, moreover, is strengthened by the programmatic success of the movement of "legal realism" over the last generation. Realism in the law, like naturalism in the novel or behaviorism in psychology, is a convention, an artifice like any other theoretical approach; it highlights certain features of the legal process and underplays others. It leads in the classroom to an insistent emphasis on "what did the court really do?"—to an emphasis on the factual substratum rather than on the metaphysical "superstructure." (It is thus adaptable to American home-grown pragmatic Marxism or to Freudianism or to any other reductionist theory.) In the main, this movement has purged law schools of much that was dogmatic, legalistic in the pejorative sense, and ritualistic. But the victory—now taken for granted among the younger men and hence scarcely to be called a movement any more—has done nothing to repair the divorce between the law school and the other graduate schools. Since the better law schools (and this is to their credit) do not enforce a prelegal undergraduate curriculum (though a good many prelaw students do major in political science or economics), and since most law school courses emphasize casework and an ideology of empiricism, one can graduate from law school without having ever read any major abstract or theoretical works in the social sciences—neither Plato nor Max Weber nor Durkheim nor Marx.[23]

In comparison with a law school, a medical school is a far more complex enterprise: it treats patients; it aims at serious research; some of its teachers are scientists with Ph.D.s, for instance, in physiology. Although occasional law professors draft bills or codes, law school is primarily oriented to teaching and to conserving and ordering the corpus

[23] Conversely, the enthusiasm with which some first-year law students take to their studies is frequently the result of a reaction against "impracticality" and seeming lack of relevance or concreteness in their undergraduate courses: the case method attracts them by its plunge into a filtered documentary detail, and by its characteristic insistence (muted through growing epistemological sophistication) that it is factual and untheoretical.

of the law; ordinarily, what is called legal research is similar to the critical work done in some of the humanities: a tracing of influences, an appreciation of (judicial) styles, a critique of (judicial or legislative) work, or an anthologizing of cases (casebooks, however, are becoming more complex, garlanded as the cases are with references to materials that are increasingly drawn from outside the case law). In fact, some of the relatively casual quality of law schools, on the faculty side, in contrast to the greater intellectual tension in comparable graduate schools, may be due to the fact that research and "productivity" do not have the same primacy. Men can become professors in major law schools without any publications (other than their student work on the law review); and they can lead a life as capable teachers and consultants (for example, as arbitrators) with very little writing, none of it research, or at any rate none of it regarded as a contribution to cumulative scientific endeavor. There is seldom anyone around a law school (unless it be a social scientist on a temporary project) who brings another model of the scholarly career than this—anyone with a degree other than an LL.B.[24] Legal history, where it is taught as a separate subject and not as part of every subject, is almost invariably taught by law-trained men—who, with the lawyer's gift of omnicompetence I have discussed earlier, may have in fact become excellent historiographers but rarely have much contact with the members of the history faculty in the graduate school.[25] The principal beachhead of science that may be considered an established exception is the presence of economists at the Chicago Law School and formerly at Yale. Economics, in its law school versions, is a "hard" science, no less proud of its achievements than the

[24] There are some law librarians who have been trained in librarianship but lack a law degree; however, given the culture of law schools as I have described it, plus the complex filing and indexing tasks of the law, it is not surprising that most librarians in large schools do have an LL.B. Good M.D.s are scarce and need to be conserved for major medical tasks; good LL.B.s are more plentiful, hence available for paralegal work.

[25] Mark Howe teaching law to Harvard undergraduates is a hopeful exception. Harold Berman also teaches law to Harvard undergraduates—and to social scientists as well. And Willard Hurst at the University of Wisconsin Law School has long made common cause with social scientists.

Since presenting this paper at Rutgers I have had the opportunity to examine Harold J. Berman's *On the Teaching of Law in the Liberal Arts Curriculum* (Brooklyn: Foundation Press, 1956), a report of a conference at Harvard Law School; this volume develops many of the problems of law as a humanistic subject that are implicit in the foregoing.

law itself, and many of its disciples are far more rationalistic than most well-trained lawyers. Moreover, as implied earlier, economics possesses a resounding theoretical structure as inhospitable to most interdisciplinary work with "softer" and "newer" social sciences as the law has hitherto been. Some varieties of economics have proved practically useful in tax and especially in antitrust work.

It seems to me that it is, in part, just because full-time law professors have one foot in academia and because a few law schools have, with economics and occasionally government or planning, one foot in the social sciences, that further steps are so difficult. Many industrialists today, not to speak of merchandisers and advertising men, are far more committed to applied social research than most law schools are, whereas the law schools, in Lasswell's phrase, have restricted social science by partial incorporation. "I don't know anything about it, but. . . ." This really means, "I do know a little."

I have indicated how hard it is to interest law students in knowledge for its own sake, and that this intellectual allergy exists even among those many law students at the better schools who were humanistically inclined as undergraduates, for these often feel "we're in the army now," and hence are threatened by reminders of not wholly rejected concerns and curiosities. Moreover, since many law professors teaching first-year courses make it their business to root out ethical and other un-Holmesian approaches to law, the not-yet-solidified vocationalism of these students is given powerful faculty support.[26] Hence, the "show-me" attitude of much of the law faculty toward the newer social sciences is as nothing in comparison with the drive in the students to initiate themselves as completely as possible, burying self-doubts and alternative hankerings, in an unequivocally legal atmosphere. Conceivably, this drive is enhanced, as compared with earlier student generations, by the relative evaporation of political commitment[27] and by the momentum of the

[26] In fact, as with most narrow vocationalism, the sacrifices made on behalf of future practice are largely unnecessary, since the changing society with its changing career patterns makes much that is learned (including the seeming toughness of first-year attitudes) obsolete in the latter lives of many graduates.

[27] I do not refer here, of course, to the law students who are going to enter politics as part of their career plan, for example, by running for district attorney or joining the Young Republicans, for this is not the kind of more idealistic political commitment relevant to an interest in the social sciences.

desire of the young to anticipate the future by early marriage, early career choice, early settling down.

In the past ten years I have had a number of sociology students come to consult me about their decision to go to law school. Since I made the opposite switch, they are worried lest it turn out that I discovered something unwholesome about the law that they ought take into account. (I have told many of them, I might note, that if they will but keep their sociological eye, they can help cultivate the borderland between law and social science, since men with double training will increasingly find opportunities opening before them in interdisciplinary enterprise.) Almost invariably, in discussing their reasons for changing, these students have said that sociology is somehow not real, whereas law unquestionably is. Sociology is a goal or an attitude in the minds of men; law exists *out there*. In my opinion, they exaggerate the difference. Men worried lest what they are doing not be real are not inevitably going to find a less ambiguous identity in the law. But it remains true, I think, that the atmosphere of a law school, especially among the students, is far more monolithic in its belief in the reality of its activities than is the atmosphere of a sociology department, where competing definitions of what sociology "is," combined with the fact that parents and laymen generally have not the vaguest idea what it is, often gives chronic disquietude to the better students, for whom total immersion in such subfields as criminology or demography is not a complete answer.

The "play it by ear" approach of the lawman is part of the lawyer's relentless and in some ways admirable individualism, which is all the more striking because, in practicing law, he must so often counter the willful individualism of his clients. In spite of what I have said earlier about colleaguial work on briefs and memoranda, even a huge law factory has a more individualistic air than most corporate bureaucracies do—or, indeed, than most large hospitals do. The very universalism of the emphasis on grades, on performance, that one finds in law school tends to carry over into the big offices, at least in the junior ranks that are not responsible for getting or retaining business. Likewise, though a pair of law professors may coauthor an article or put together a casebook, a law school resists intellectual teamwork much as do men in the humanities, and sociologists are sometimes looked down upon for their presumed addiction to it. Moreover, the law professor, seeking to maintain the interest of large classes in an active dialectic, tends to cultivate his gifts as a showman—hence, as an individualist—rather more than do most teachers in the other graduate schools.

This Tocquevillian sort of individualism has been self-renewing in America, where its wastes and hazards, its egocentricities and eccentricities, appear to be justified by immense natural resources and where the mercantilist past has long been buried under the ideology of free enterprise. Moreover, the lawyer's individualism bears a paradoxical relation to the common-law tradition: that tradition seems in many ways irrational, out of tune with modern times and the scientific temper, yet it protects the lawyer's effort to maintain objectivity and distance from contending factions in public and private affairs; it gives him a foundation from which to move toward empiricism and objectivity. Working in a case-by-case, *ad hoc* fashion, the lawyer gains the ability (often warped, to be sure, in cases involving labor unions, real or alleged Communists, and so on) to resist the claims of fashion and fanaticism. The lawyer, much like the engineer or the businessman, prides himself on his directness and rationality; he tends to resist what he regards as the message of determinism—whether in his own buried psyche or in the society—in much work of the social scientist, and he also regards this work as oblique and indirect, not getting to the point. The lawyer does not regard society as the product of vast, impersonal, though conceivably comprehensible, forces; the universalism referred to above is more an insistence on equality and performance than an explicit ideology.

And, as already indicated, the lawyer is simply not impressed by the claims of the social scientist, any more than he is impressed by the plausible client's tale that may turn out not to be true; this skepticism is indeed an aspect of his individualism. (In this connection, who will deny that behavioral science, as a new, booming field, "made in America," has attracted many vulgar boosters, defensively boastful in the face of attack from the threatened, the snobbish, and the skeptical?)

Moreover, the lawyer's "play it by ear" tendency supports the wish most of us have, as adults, that we will not have to learn anything really new. I recall talking to a thoughtful practitioner who wanted to know what I thought of the new journal, *Behavioral Science,* and of the work of such model-builders as Herbert Simon, Jacob Marschak, and Anatol Rapoport. He really wanted to be told that I thought it was all the bunk, that it was not the wave of the future, and that he did not "have" to pay attention to it.[28] The eagerness of quite a few law professors to convince themselves that sociologists have nothing to say, that their vaunted methods are the imposing cover over the unimpressive hunches, occasionally has similar sources.[29] Naturally, the intramural arguments among sociologists can then be used, if caught wind of, to dismiss the whole affair.

One source of these arguments could, I think, be somewhat assuaged by training sociology students in the art of easy movement from one metaphorical or semantic scheme to another. I have, for instance, seen sociologists operating in a medical school who would insist on using a Parsonian frame of reference, or just as vehemently a non-Parsonian frame, clinging, with a defiance that would be admirable in a better cause, to the inessentials as well as the real contributions of the scheme. I think that, for the foreseeable future, sociologists need to learn to be friendly mediators among metaphors, never doubting that metaphors matter, but doubting whether they matter as much as the master's disciples aver. Yet, once we recognize that metaphorical schemes serve many social scientists as a magical penumbra, guarding against uncertainty (as in Malinowski's theory of magic), we cannot be too hopeful of fostering among students a more detached attitude toward such schemes and a greater willingness to move with linguistic ease and flexible freedom among them. Furthermore, we must also recognize that a certain amount of terminological solipsism has accompanied some of the most truly innovative work, as in psychoanalysis, as well as some of the unfruitful work. Such solipsism may serve to protect tentative gropings from too ready incorporation into the main body of accepted views, and psychoanalysis is an example of a movement that needed in its early stages to be protected from the overwhelming leveling power of common sense. Indeed, common sense, as we have already seen, frequently characterizes the law professor's impermeable defense against sociological or psychological experimentalism.

Some readers may wonder why I have talked about the opacity or rigidity of some sociological systems and not about the Anglo-American folderol of legalism that so many great writers have satirized. One per-

---

[28] Cf., for comments on judicial resistance to medical experts, Hans Zeisel, "The New York Expert Testimony Project: Some Reflections on Legal Experiments," 8 *Stanford Law Review* 730 (1956).

[29] I do not mean to suggest here that the sources of an idea are relevant one way or the other for determining the soundness of an idea. It may well be that the law professors are right.

sonal reason may be that I have never found legal jargon as forbidding as it sounds. With a legal dictionary and some guidance on procedural points, any literate person can read Supreme Court opinions, and many do so; and legal documents, with their attempt to foresee a variety of contingencies (for example, all possible orders of deaths in a family or partnership), seem to me easier to follow than many mathematical or philosophical arguments. But a more important reason for not emphasizing the impenetrability of legal discourse is that generations of law reformers since Bentham have done a great deal to put the law and its forms into basic English; moreover, the better law schools on which I have been concentrating in these remarks have been fighting ritualism and semantic silliness with marked success. The briefs produced in the major Wall Street and government law offices are models of clarity, marching with military precision to the points made, and using citations of previous authority with the finesse of a mutually understood shorthand, rather than as uninterpreted obfuscation. No wonder many judges crib from these briefs in writing their opinions. Indeed, the sense for style and elegance of form common among the best practitioners and professors is understandable in a generation nurtured on the opinions of Holmes, Cardozo, and Learned Hand, and taught to admire the simplicity and lack of pretense of some of the great state-court judges of the last century. The best law reviews are schools for condensed yet comprehensible writing far more than are the learned periodicals in other fields.

Correspondingly, once the law professor makes up his mind to it, he will have little more difficulty in understanding work in the less mathematical parts of social science than in other feats of translation that may come his professional way—as when he must master accountancy to grapple with tax problems, or technical matters in connection with patent law, or theories of oligopoly in antitrust law. A lawyer is, after all, supposed to be able to understand the problems of any client and to "talk his language." If he is prepared to give the time, his confidence will go a long way to level obstacles. Furthermore, he has little in terms of status at stake to block his learning in these areas, for his legal colleagues (as I found in my own case), not being in the main intellectuals, have less pride of system than intellectuals often possess, and the individualism of law schools means that a law professor who meets his classroom obligations can undertake almost any scholarly enterprise and count on a kindly if not always comprehending audience. True, a law professor who uses sociological jargon will meet with kidding, just as the sociologist himself will, and, if he forces his views, he will encounter resistances of the sort I have sought to portray. But the kidding will be unmalicious and he will have nothing to lose but his diet of advance sheets. Thus, I believe that generally the barriers of terminological nationalism are greater within the social sciences than between them and the fraternity of law professors.

INTERPERSONAL OR INTERDISCIPLINARY?

I was asked at Rutgers, as again during the Harvard Social Science Research Council Seminar on Law and Social Relations, for suggestions as to topics that lawyers and sociologists might jointly pursue. I felt able to say more about how not to choose a topic than about such choice in the abstract, for I insisted that people worked best at what interested them, and that one had to be flexible in interdisciplinary work in using the talents and interests the local setting provided. I added that I was unsympathetic to command performances based on some map of the gaps in social science integration or some judgment of a constituency as to what was important, for I had faith that if scholars are not entirely alienated from their culture, and not wholly constrained away from a vivid curiosity by their disciplines, they will be interested in what is important, and what is important will be interesting to them.

I think I can recognize some of the limitations of this position, as of theories of progressive education generally. Interest often follows rather than precedes effort, and sociologists, too, have their forms of playing by ear: as Professor Fred L. Strodtbeck has pointed out to me, our guild may prefer to pursue familiar problems of motivation and socialization rather than less familiar problems of structure and substance. And when I examine the work done by scholars in universities in comparison with applied work done in answer to some client's need, I cannot argue that the track of the discipline produces in general more seminal research than the quest of an answer to an extra-academic problem. Only a very rare person will be an intellectual self-starter.[30] And even

[30] Some problems probably cannot be studied at all without a client's invitation. But in the law, issues of entrée would seem to be surmountable by careful planning, in part because for a variety of reasons lawyers are far less self-protective as a guild than, for instance, doctors are. Professor Erwin O. Smigel of the Department of Sociology of New York University has found that even busy Wall Street lawyers will respond to long and searching interviews (indeed they would respond *only* to searching interviews that gave them an opportunity to confide in an understanding and disinter-

he needs to start somewhere (just as Freud started with patients who raised questions no one had been able to answer); a client's question can often be that "somewhere." Nevertheless, I think that really significant work must build its own track, one marginal both to the genres of the sociology of the professions and to the stock of problems the legal profession will bring to a seminar.

In my own talk at the Rutgers seminar I drew on studies that some participants undoubtedly thought frivolous. One study, by a graduate student at the University of Chicago, dealt with law students' luncheon conversation and one of its objects was to ascertain how the group socializes its members in the legal culture in their leisure time. (What he actually found, with one such group, is that they scarcely ever talked law, but rather what I might term office gossip, that is, the personalities and idiosyncrasies of the faculty, the students, and judges and other legal luminaries; also about TV personalities and other handy human fodder.)[31] I also mentioned Dan Lortie's study of practicing lawyers five years out of law school, in terms of their career alternatives, their judgment on their education, and the relation of their experiences to their earlier ideals of the life of the law. And I drew on published material, such as the Blaustein and Porter volume,[32] to shed light on

---

ested outsider). Likewise, Dan C. Lortie and Jerome Carlin have been able to go over records and life histories with lawyers in Chicago. [See Dan C. Lortie, *The Striving Young Lawyer: A Study of Early Career Differentiation in the Chicago Bar* (Unpublished Doctoral Dissertation, Department of Sociology, University of Chicago, 1958).] Courtrooms and cases, of course, are open to all. Members of the Jury Project at the University of Chicago Law School have found it possible to talk to judges as to how they would decide cases, and to trial lawyers about their tactics. Sociologists have not been around lawyers enough to wear out their welcome.

[31] Cf. Kenneth Feigenbaum, *The Limited Hour: A Situational Study of Sociable Interaction* (Unpublished Master's Thesis, Committee on Human Development, University of Chicago, 1958).

[32] Albert P. Blaustein and Charles O. Porter, *The American Lawyer* (Chicago: University of Chicago Press, 1954), pp. 187–88. They indicate that 12 per cent of law students decide on law before age fifteen, and 13 per cent after twenty-five. Thirty per cent of them have lawyer relatives, and 45 per cent have some interest in future political activity when they are in law school. Compare with this the relatively late decision that at least until quite recently was characteristic of students doing graduate work in the social sciences. See Elbridge Sibley, *The Recruitment, Selection, and Training of Social Scientists* (New York: Social Science Research Council, 1948), pp. 17–21.

the factors leading students to select law as a career. The image of the lawyer that the students appear to have when they turn up at law school seems to be framed—I go on very little evidence—by college campus politics, debating teams, and friends and relatives who tell a youngster that he will make a good lawyer (and who have perhaps business to throw his way when he does). In upper-class families, as Charles McArthur noted in longitudinal studies of prep-school boys at Harvard[33] the law sometimes comes close to being one ascribed career among very narrow alternatives. In ethnic families, in contrast, it is a form of mobility both for the individual and, through its ethnic "mouthpieces," for the group.[34] And not only the "mouthpiece," of course, but a symbolic figure, as the Italian judge rivals the Italian mayor as a sign to the Irish to make way for a new urban hegemony.

In the field of medicine we know (particularly from the studies by Hall)[35] that an able doctor of ethnic background sometimes can choose between the security of a practice within the ethnic community and its hospitals and the risks of the wider, ordinarily Protestant, medical world; he may try for the latter and, failing, be unable to fall back upon his alienated ethnic connections. The wider medical world usually has the attraction of higher standards, as well as higher prestige, and medical school may reshape a young man's aims toward an ideal of practice resembling that of his teachers in the big university hospitals. Likewise, the national law schools, while turning out many who will

---

Since writing the foregoing, I have profited from Wagner Thielens, Jr., "Some Comparisons of Entrants to Medical and Law School," in Robert K. Merton, George Reader, and Patricia L. Kendall, eds., *The Student Physician: Introductory Studies in the Sociology of Medical Education* (Cambridge, Mass.: Harvard University Press, 1957), pp. 131–52.

[33] Charles McArthur and Lucia Beth Stevens, "The Validation of Expressed Interests as Compared with Inventoried Interests: A Fourteen-Year Follow-up," *Journal of Applied Psychology*, vol. 39 (1955), p. 184.

[34] When recently an Indian came from one of the reservations to study anthropology at the University of Chicago, it was perhaps evidence that this native minority had "arrived" and no longer needed to send all its articulate men into law to fight for the rights of the tribe. Perhaps it also showed that anthropology had "arrived," and competes with the law as a way of fighting the battles of the underprivileged!

[35] Oswald Hall, *Informal Organization of Medical Practice: Case Study of a Profession* (Unpublished Doctoral Dissertation, University of Chicago Department of Sociology, 1944).

end up in a parochial orbit, set a model of performance before the alert students and, in addition, bestow prestige on certain fields of public and corporate law as fields in which these high standards may be obeyed. Surely one reason for the distaste with which the graduate of a major law school regards the criminal law and trial practice generally (not, of course, antitrust and like trials) is because these areas cannot be recreated in the law school image.[36] Corporate law, on the other hand, and many fields of appellate litigation, can be so created and recreated; for the finespun artifices of the legal imagination on which our corporate (and tax) structures rest rise far above the intellectual slums where, in the big cities, a largely ethnic bar carries on the Anglo-Saxon rites of trial by jury and "contaminates" the legal ideal with the demagogic practice.

So far as I am aware, not much is known about the way in which law students see these alternatives and choose among them, let alone what the contingencies are of their later careers. Recently, Dr. Osler Peterson of the Rockefeller Foundation made a study of general practice in North Carolina, visiting doctors and observing them in their day-to-day work. He and his colleagues were shocked by the low order of performance they discovered, and also by finding that standings in medical school made no difference in the low level to which the doctors sank. (In my own surmise, the high-ranking students who ended up

[36] In my brief exposure to trial practice, as a briefcase-carrying aide at Lyne, Woodworth, and Evarts, I quickly found how little of my book-learning was relevant. In studying the law of evidence in law school we had spent most of our time on the fabulous elaborations of the hearsay rule, which forbids, so it says, the introduction of hearsay testimony save in exceptional circumstances. In many trials I attended, it appeared that practically everything that went to the jury *was* hearsay which appeared to be admissible under none of the exceptions to the rule. In preparing trial briefs, I had begun by assuming that much of this testimony would be excluded. But I soon found that judges did not like to be deprived of hearing evidence that might be relevant, and that counsel, as previously stated, liked, along with judges, to play by ear, and resented any attempt to alter the live-and-let-live rules of the game as played in the courts in and around Boston. Even where a statute explicitly ruled out certain kinds of evidence, I found judges allowing it in "provisionally" and making clear their resentment of statutory curbs on looseness of presentation. To be sure, we could have appealed, but in most of these cases, where amounts involved were small and lower-court discretion large, my seniors sagely fought to win the jury and feared offending them by seeming to act like a brain-trust, limiting what they would be allowed to hear.

in small-town general practice may have felt a kind of destructive despair at their unanticipated fate, while the low-ranking students rose somewhat on discovering that, after all, they could be of some use.) These doctors lacked either clients or colleagues to keep them on their toes (it must be added that they apparently practiced an even poorer grade of medicine than had been taught the old-timers; they declined with the years, rather than remaining on a plateau). Would a study of the general practice of law find so depressing a story? Or does the occasional competition through the possibility of litigation act as a brake against the most abysmal sloppiness—at least where there is a chance that a gentlemen's agreement to cover for each other might be broken, as always seems more likely in the less guild-controlled legal profession than in medicine? Indeed, is the cynicism of the practicing lawyer less than that of the isolated doctor because his ideals were never so high, nor his training so exigent?[37] And because in most cases it is "only money" and not life that is involved? How many intelligently critical clients and demanding problems does a practicing lawyer need to keep mentally and morally awake?

Likewise, as a student of the dialectic between work and leisure, I expressed in the seminar at Rutgers an interest in the relations between a lawyer's life in and outside the law. Does the latter reflect, refresh, or reinforce the former? In the Auchincloss novels, the able and domineering lawyer is pictured as the unempathic spouse. Certainly the older tradition of the big offices was fiercely work-minded, and men enjoyed (while complaining about) the all-male atmosphere of night work as if they were in the Foreign Legion. Utter absorption was regarded as both essential for one's career and a test of one's manhood. Today, even the lawyer has been influenced by the revolution in attitudes toward leisure and the ideals of suburban *Gemeinschaft* and family life. Just as the armed services have difficulty in enforcing the arduousness of training routines, so with full employment the big offices can no longer afford to drive the young recruits with savage intensity; the man

[37] In two novels, James Gould Cozzens has concerned himself with the ideals of the two professions, as practiced in small communities. See *The Last Adam* (medicine) and *The Just and the Unjust* (law). The novels of Louis Auchincloss brilliantly portray the ethical temper of large downtown office lawyers; see, for instance, his discussion of the problem of partnership loyalty (akin to that found in advertising agencies) in *A Law for the Lion*, and his sensitivity to ethnic and social-class differences in *The Great World and Timothy Colt*.

in the gray flannel suit, fonder of his wife than of his work, now brings the pressure of his marginal utility to bear on the old Cravath firm. The study of law students' luncheon sociability I mentioned earlier first struck me as evidence that the students were relaxing at lunch from the rigors of their work, but I later doubted this and felt that law school itself was no longer quite the arduous quest that Nicholas Kelley speaks of; conceivably, the rate-buster or eager beaver may be under slight pressure even there. But we would need many diaries of law students as they go through their careers, and many studies of law schools such as Robert K. Merton and his associates and Everett C. Hughes and his are now making of medical schools, before we could begin to understand these changes.

This "interpersonal" approach to lawyers, as against an "institutional" approach to the law, led to what I regard as very clarifying criticisms from both law professors and sociologists at Rutgers—and again at Harvard.[38] Robert Rodes, now at Notre Dame Law School, expressed his point of view at the Rutgers seminar in the following manner:

> As a lawman, I am predominantly concerned with the law as a particular type of social control. That means that, professionally, I am very much interested in the behavior of other people, just as sociologists are; and this, it has seemed to me, is the fact that makes it promising for sociologists and lawmen to cooperate and pool their knowledge and resources. It also means, however, that *professionally*, the one person in whose behavior I am not interested is myself. The suggestion that sociologists cooperate with lawmen by studying them strikes me as a step away from interdisciplinary cooperation.
>
> If it is useful to sociologists to make the kind of studies you suggest, I would be very happy to cooperate—I'll be glad to help you fellows do your job by submitting myself as a specimen; but I don't see how the things you tell me about myself will help me

[38] Herbert Spiro, a political scientist at Harvard, suggested that my interest in motivation and interpersonal relations was very American, as compared with a Continental concern for institutional forms. And he felt that my frankness about the psychological sources of co-operation and competition among the disciplines put a tactless demand on the nonsociologists to be equally frank or to seem stuffy. He and others regarded the personality and culture approach with a distaste akin to that felt by British structural anthropologists. This and allied approaches, especially perhaps when brought home from the preliterate field, or from the clinic, do in my opinion raise serious problems for all participants, and not merely on the level of good taste. See my introduction to *Crestwood Heights*, p. 506.

do my job. I would be interested in the results intellectually; but they are outside my concern so far as my professional role is concerned.

There are, after all, several ways in which the lawman might tell the sociologist about himself, from the frame of reference of the professional lawman. We might consider such questions as whether sociologists, when they interview their subjects, are negligent if they trespass on the subject's privacy. If so, are they sued? What damages are awarded? Do they commit any crime? Are they in contempt of court when they "bug" juries? Does it constitute a legal defense that they are gathering data?

Sociologists might be interested in such analyses, but I don't think they would be professionally interested in them; and if I were to say that that is the only way in which lawyers are interested in sociologists, I think the sociologists would pack up and go home.

It may be that sociology is not yet ready to contribute major insights into law as a particular type of social control. If so, that would be interesting to know and it would be understandable; but the point I want to emphasize is that our major effort should be on the attempt to discover whether or not it is so. It should not—except insofar as sociologists would themselves profit—be on questions that are peripheral to the professional concerns of the lawyer, such as the nature of lunch-table conversations or whether it helps a lawyer in a big corporation to know how to play tennis.

These observations are well taken, and it is no answer to them to comment that Professor Rodes implicitly speaks for an older tradition—"a government of laws and not of men"—which many legal realists have sought to debunk. The belief of lawyers, that something called "the law" exists, has protected many clients from loss of rights and many counsel from too ready compromise and self-doubt; it has also been the source of willful stupidity, even fanaticism. But Professor Rodes's appeal is not merely for the rejection of gossip and other lowbrow concerns as fundamentally irrelevant: he is not simply setting up the "big power" world of social controls as more significant than the small power world of informal controls on the profession. Rather, he is asking, as his colleague Professor Thomas Cowan did in other terms, for help from sociologists in grasping the channeling of behavior by the legal structure. He would, I assume, be more interested in studies of decision-making among corporate executives to see to what extent the corporate income tax guided their investment and inventory policy than in studies of decision-making among law students as to whether to enter corporate work or not. Certainly, Professor Cowan, judging from his comments and his writings, felt that changes in legal and administrative constraints offered the social scientist ample opportunities for studies of change—opportunities that could even be enhanced by judicious legal experiment.

At this point in the Rutgers discussion several sociologists made common cause with Professor Rodes. Thus, Paul Massing raised the question as to what were the really important problems for American society that the legal order presented and implied that a sociology of the profession was at best a roundabout way to these problems. Likewise, Jackson Toby further clarified for the group the nature of disciplines as sets of abstractions. He declared:

> The significance of the kinds of observations you have been emphasizing, it seems to me, lies in their bearing on the *difficulties* of interdisciplinary research. That is to say, the role of the sociologist and the role of the lawyer are germane to the interdisciplinary task insofar as they create barriers to communication or motivated bases for noncooperation. As such, they are important for us to recognize. But their importance is not as foci of research; it is rather as *barriers* to interdisciplinary cooperation.
>
> In order to find common ground for some kind of interdisciplinary work, we have to look, not at the roles of lawyers or sociologists, but at the disciplines themselves, law and sociology. What we are trying to blend are not people but concepts and theories.
>
> It is true that the *discipline* of sociology does not exhaust the interests of sociologists, nor does the *discipline* of law exhaust the interests of lawyers. There undoubtedly are many kinds of questions in which the lawyer-as-intellectual and the sociologist-as-intellectual could be jointly interested; and they might very well profit immensely from cooperative research on such questions. But they would profit as individuals. The profit would not be to *sociology* or to *law*, unless the focus of activity is a central concern of law and of sociology.
>
> Sociology is one abstraction and law is another. When we keep this clearly in mind, we have the possibility of the blending of the abstractions by incorporation at strategic points of elements from the other field. But the more we focus on concrete persons, lawyers or sociologists, the less chance we have of learning from one another something about the respective abstractions which

make each field a *discipline* rather than a congeries of persons engaging in various kinds of activities and defense mechanisms.

In response to these criticisms, another sociologist, Alisa Lourié, sought to interpret my outlook, as well as her own. She observed:

> Lawyers and sociologists use different kinds of abstractions. "The law" is a tremendous abstraction; in a sense, "the law" doesn't exist; it is a fiction. The sociologist tends to operate on a lower level of abstraction. He is concerned with what people actually do, with patterns of behavior, of interaction. Law, of course, affects these patterns of behavior; but when the sociologist starts to talk about law, he almost automatically glides over into talking about lawyers and how they act.

"Lawyers and how they act" interests me, as Miss Lourié saw. But I am only one kind of sociologist—and not that kind all the time. I do not share the inverse snobbery that sometimes elevates "facts" and "what people actually do" into a behavioristic distaste for more inclusive concepts. True, at a time when I was less unfamiliar than I am now with European and American jurisprudence, I was depressed by the sterility of much discourse concerning law that seemed to me to take it out of the context of institutions, of lawyers, officials, clients, and other relevant publics and audiences. But, having seen in economics how much the system-builders have contributed in comparison with the institutionalists, I am even more convinced that there are no royal roads to understanding society, and that paths that strike any of us as unpromising may turn out to carry much intellectual traffic. Certainly, I would not agree with Mr. Rodes or with Mr. Toby that there should be a distinction between what sociologists do *professionally* and what they do as *intellectuals* or as individuals curious about their place and that of others in the scheme of things. On the contrary, one of the chief problems of being one of my versions of sociologist (the same holds for some versions of psychiatry) is that one never stops working. For example, when recently on a plane I chanced to sit next to a lawyer in a large firm who spends nearly all his time as counsel to a major airline, I interviewed him both about his role in helping to rationalize a once hazardous industry and about his feeling of possible imprisonment with a single—and extremely touchy—client. Did he have more in common with lawyers in general, with airline executives, or with the few people (some of them in the Civil Aeronautics Board) who shared his combination of vantage-points? How free was he, if he should get embroiled in some conflict with his client, to switch, after a dozen years of specialization, to some other field of law? And how long would the airlines, increasingly routinized, hold his interest? I began by chatting with him, but then felt impelled to reveal my own profession, while aware of the quasi-eavesdropping of what I had done, and the arguable violation of club-car norms. Novelists seem little troubled by the ethics of privacy, whereas thoughtful sociologists are greatly troubled. The latter are concerned lest their questions, even when invited, raise problems that had best be left untouched, and for which they lack any therapeutic magic. Unlike Mr. Rodes, they cannot close the office door and leave their profession behind.

Accordingly, I would not be entirely happy if Mr. Rodes should surrender his defenses and widen his definition of his own job and what might illuminate it. For, as I have already implied in commenting on the lawyer's traditional individualism and as I have emphasized in my article, "Toward an Anthropological Science of Law and the Legal Profession,"[39] the very distaste of many lawyers for knowing "too much" about personality may have certain advantages for the legal order. Tocqueville saw the legal profession in the United States as a link between the common people and the fragmentary elites of wealth and birth, and as a potential aristocracy. And the law in this country, despite elements of populism (as in the jury) and long-run obedience to public opinion, has been for better or worse a means of providing minority constituencies with an effective voice—a pattern sometimes supported today by the very fact that leading members of the bar are inner-directed men, able to defend the rights of clients in the face of public disapproval.

Thus, I know men in the older generation of large law firms whose perennial complaint is that their clients, individual or corporate, have no guts and will not, in litigation or other public forums, take an unpopular stand. Among these lawyers are some whose ferocity toward labor unions was forcibly muted by their clients' insistence that they had to "live with the bastards" even after winning a Labor Board or court case. But there are also some who have been prepared to defend men accused of communism or other outrageous views—and who have kept looking for harassed professors or suspended civil servants who

[39] *American Journal of Sociology*, vol. 57 (1951), p. 121.

would have the nerve to incur the publicity of a fight.[40] We know all too well that the law does not defend the voiceless, but, given the moderate immunity of some of the courts to immediate legislative rebuke, the voices of those who have but a small local constituency can be defended.[41] Even while violence flares about them, lawyers for the NAACP can be heard in southern courts, and the same relative freedom, partly aristocratic and partly professional, sustains judges and lawyers and the many law professors who have actively defended civil

[40] When, as has happened recently in Cleveland, in New Jersey, and elsewhere, lawyers become victims of "guilt by association" with their clients, this vital source of freedom is terrifyingly jeopardized. In fact the freedom has already been jeopardized, judging by the difficulties some men accused of subversion or disloyalty have had in finding counsel—particularly, respectable non-Communist counsel. I have the impression that some former Communists who have been encouraged by their lawyers to plead the Fifth Amendment before congressional committees have had the bad luck to fall in with Communist-controlled counsel because no other members of the bar seemed readily available to them (others, of course, still tied to the Party, would choose such counsel anyway). I need not spell out the sorry consequence, if not for the individual, certainly for the clarification of issues in the field of civil liberties—the committees, of course, wanted just such counsel to defend the people they harassed. Cf. my article, "The Supreme Court and Its New Critics," *New Republic,* July 29, 1957, pp. 9-13.

[41] A small example from private law may make the amplitude of my point clearer. When a testator died childless in a midwestern town, he left a moderate fortune for the study of cancer at an eastern university, and appointed a physician there as his executor. Local relatives questioned his sanity, whipping up xenophobia against the gift's going out of the state. The probate judge, with an election coming up, appointed a local attorney as coexecutor, contrary to the will. A good deal of pressure was brought against the university's counsel to permit this appointment to go through as a sop to local feeling—especially since it is so nearly impossible to impugn the "discretion" of the lower court; state law was cited to this effect. But the out-of-state counsel did not cave in, even when the probate judge's discretion was sustained in an intermediate appeal; they kept insisting that what was clearly an invasion of the testator's prerogative could not be "the law," no matter what more timid people argued. Their anger at finagling and injustice—at "particularism" in Talcott Parsons' terms—sustained them against the risk of further antagonizing the appointed coexecutor and the probate judge by continuing to litigate the latter's decision. Virtue won: the state's supreme court reversed the lower courts by a one-vote margin—and the probate judge was defeated for re-election. I am inclined to think that men more sensitive to public relations would not have carried the fight so far, nor have imagined that they could win it.

liberties against more subtle pressures to go along. The return to respect for *stare decisis* in a number of law schools reflects on the one hand the wider currents of the new conservatism and on the other hand a realization (perhaps most clearly elucidated by Mr. Justice Stone)[42] that judicial obstinacy may serve in the area of civil liberties to hold open the door of the future in a way that it has not always done in protecting property rights against regulation. Since I see the courts and the bar that serves and uses them as a countervailing power vis-à-vis parochial coercion, and see them in fact as making insufficiently self-conscious use of this power, I am not entirely happy with developments in our society that would rob the judge and lawyer of their protective insulation against preoccupation with public relations: we still need men who care more for what the books should say than for what people will say.[43]

[42] *United States v. Carolene Products Co.*, 304 U.S. 144, at 152–53, n. 4 (1938). Mr. Justice Stone's point, as I understand it, was that the courts should apply to governmental interferences with civil liberties severer standards—that is, lesser degrees of deference to the so-called legislative judgment—than in due process cases not involving freedoms of similar importance for the health and tone of free discussion; he felt that there is something irreversible about an interference with civil liberties. I think that, were he alive today, he would find much evidence (and too few justices) to support his judgment.

[43] To some extent, of course, these problems beset all professions that desire to establish professional distance from lay pressures and controls. Academic freedom, including power to set standards for admission to college, is cut from similar cloth. Correspondingly, there is always the danger that *public* relations will count too little, and *professional* relations too much—as when doctors gang up to curb public health programs (as, in Chicago, against free Salk shots), or when lawyers sell out their clients for fear of offending their brethren or offending a judge before whom they want to live to plead another day. Tension is inevitable here, and the public must remain a countervailing power against the profession, as well as vice versa. C. Wright Mills in *The Power Elite* (p. 289) links the corporation lawyer and the investment banker as go-betweens among the various elites of industry, the military, and the government. Correspondingly, he seems to give the lawyer little independent role but to regard him as a sort of high-class messenger who shares the values of his clients. Many lawyers themselves feel and fear this, and look back to an earlier day where they believe there was greater independence. Plainly, any study of the role of the corporation lawyer cannot be separated from the question whether he has any impact on his clients, as well as vice versa, and how if at all these interpenetrations are changing.

THE DANGER OF NEEDING QUICK RESULTS FROM RESEARCH

Yet such considerations, relevant as they may be for the recruitment and training of law students and for the understanding of the political and cultural leverage of the bar, do not help us very much in planning joint engagements of sociologists and law professors. In such planning it is important to know what one is up against. In areas such as crime and insanity, where legal processes are at once highly visible and almost surely inadequate, there is a fairly unequivocal invitation to the outsider to pitch in. The outsider also has access to appellate cases, especially in the public law fields, and he can be the beneficiary of the generations of law professors who have sought to reduce the chaos of decisions to some sort of order, at best "restating" it or at worst, as already indicated, indexing it under literal-minded headings. Even with respect to these cases, however, new modes of looking at the material, which could invite the attention of sociologists generally, are not easy to come by. Thus, it is possible to read upper-court cases with an eye for style, looking, for instance, for rococo or Edwardian modes of exposition, but this would only be the beginning in an effort to subsume the material under rubrics relevant for the understanding of American institutional life.

Beyond the decisions and, as everyone knows, more meaningful for the daily conduct of business and government is the more impalpable law-stuff of office practice. It is understandably easier for an anthropologist to make sense of a primitive legal system because, in the tradition of the one-man expedition, he can relate it to kinship and other structural elements, than for him to make headway with the problems created for the student of American law by its sheer bulk as it occurs in organizations large and small—for only a narrow definition of his task would limit him to the formally declared legal agencies while excluding from view the law-stuff that exists wherever judicialization and channeling of dispute go on. This material is frequently buried in files and memories and in commerical and governmental routines.

In this situation, the pioneering work of Underhill Moore, with its enormous input of labor always in danger of bringing forth a mouse, has had few successors; but it is this order of work that I believe to be necessary before the programs implicit in the comments of Messrs. Toby, Rodes, and Massing can even be glimpsed. I have indicated why the track of case criticism is so commodious and rewarding for legal scholars that lack of an audience among them for other types of work, such as Underhill Moore's, is not surprising.

On the sociological side, too, despite the current boom in the social sciences, most of us are unwilling to do what the physical scientists take for granted, namely, to undertake work that has very little chance of producing positive results, and then to report any negative findings. We are still sufficiently intellectual underdogs to need more "results" per year or per project than are likely to flow from the sort of immersion in day-to-day normative data Underhill Moore attempted. And this is not merely a matter of professional inferiority and misgiving. One should not underestimate the courage it takes to embark on a sea of data whose outlines cannot yet be mapped and through which no currents of established relevance already run. Just as economists prefer to study aggregates or models and not to take the chance of becoming participant-observers in a firm that might turn out at the end of years of work not to be "typical," or to be affected by influences from outside that could not be measured or even ascertained, so similar risks would attend a scholar who took the plunge in an effort to grasp the bearing of legal thinking (or thinking by law-trained men) on the conduct of life. Indeed, such a man would take even greater risks than an economist, for legal practice outside the case law is probably even more diversified in our society than is business. For the legal subcultures are nurtured by the "tariffs" of state and local boundaries, creating parochial idiosyncrasies perhaps even greater than those to be found in the subcultures of particular industries. For such work one would need the omnivorousness of an old-fashioned historian who is willing to plow through mountains of documents for an occasional clue, plus that eye for what goes together with what that constitutes the sociologist's imagination.

Tocqueville as Ethnographer
(1958)

America in the first half of the nineteenth century was visited by a large number of articulate and often distinguished travelers from all the countries of Western Europe. British Tories came to confirm their prejudices against democracy and a few radicals came to confirm their sympathies. Many, like Dickens, were interested in the novel achievements of American philanthropy: the care of the poor, the unlettered, the mill hand, the prisoner. (It would be a rare inquirer who came to America today to look at our prisons!) But while we read Dickens or Mrs. Trollope now because of their eye for local color and the picture of American manners they present, we do not read them to understand our contemporary America. Those who criticized our bad manners or described our quaint customs amuse us more than they interest or annoy us. It is to Alexis de Tocqueville that we continue to turn for understanding, because the issues that preoccupied him were those he saw as portentous for France and for all of Europe, namely, the consequences for liberty of the growing equality of condition. Although he gathered and had sent to him a great stack of documents on juridical matters, and although his notebooks describe places and scenes to some extent, Tocqueville lived during his journeys in his moral imagination. No other visitor has to my knowledge been so little distracted by the accidental and so sensitive to implication. This was especially the case with his reflective second volume of *Democracy in America*, which he published five years after the first. As he wrote, "On leaving the ideas which American and French society presented me, *I wish to set out the general tendencies of democratic societies of which no complete example yet exists.*"[1]

Tocqueville had come to this country in 1831 at the age of twenty-

[1] Quoted by J. P. Mayer, "Tocqueville's Influence," *History*, No. 3 (1960), Meridian, pages 87–103, on page 90.

six, along with his friend Beaumont, with whom he had secured a commission to look at American prisons and methods of penal reform. Although the young men did their duty by the prisons and wrote a report, this assignment proved a useful cover for their more important cultural mission—a mission complicated by the defensiveness of the Americans. As Beaumont noted, ". . . to be on good terms with them, you have to praise them a great deal. I do it with all my heart, without its affecting my manner of seeing. This national pride induces them to do everything they can to fascinate our eyes and to show us only the fine side of things; but I hope we will manage to find out the truth."[2]

Tocqueville, an aristocrat and a Catholic, had not come to America in the hope of finding a brave new world. Rather, facing the legacies of the French Revolution which had been for him part of both his family biography and the nation's fate, he came in order to understand better what might be in store for his own country and what might be done by wise policy to make the coming age of democracy and equality less despotic and more free. He put this serious mission into the introduction of *Democracy in America*:

> I confess that in America I saw more than America; I saw there the image of democracy itself, with its inclinations, its character, its prejudices, and its passions, in order to learn what we have to fear or to hope from its progress.

Democracy in America is singularly free of detailed descriptions of people and places. (Beaumont, in contrast, kept a sketchbook and Pierson's book reprints many of his drawings.) As I have indicated, Tocqueville's book is a work not of observation but of interpretation, particularly so in the second volume where he discusses potential supports and hazards for liberty, arising less in the juridical and institutional spheres than in the psychological and cultural ones. In envisaging what an "ideal" (that is, complete) democracy would be like were it to go further in the American direction—further, that is, away from where Europe presently was, he imagined himself into the mind of a citizen of such a nonexistent land and pictured for himself how all aspects of life, from the image of the Deity to articles of commerce and fictions of the mind, would look to such a hypothetical person. He deployed his actual experiences in America to illustrate rather than to bound or limit his conception. He did not ask himself whether the sailor who

[2] George Wilson Pierson, *Tocqueville and Beaumont in America* (Oxford University Press, 1938), pages 73–74.

told him that vessels were jerry-built because they would soon be made obsolete by the progress of invention was a typical American or not, for what he said fitted in with Tocqueville's vision. This inchoate method, if we may use so formal a term, was fundamentally aristocratic in the sense that not everyone would be equally good at it. Tocqueville founded no school and the centenary of his death in 1959 was little celebrated.

The America to which Tocqueville and Beaumont came (they made a side journey, useful for comparative purposes, to Quebec) consisted of thirteen million people. And young, smart French visitors were sufficiently rare to give them access to anyone whom they wanted to see. Furthermore, the absence of a French colony in the United States protected them from filtering their own impressions through an ideology already congealed among locally resident fellow-countrymen. At the same time, as Pierson's book makes plain in providing us with the detailed trajectory of the nine months the young men spent in this country, it is surprising how much Tocqueville transcended the prejudices of his informants, among whom were Hudson River patricians, embittered Federalist politicians, Catholic priests fearing the spread of Unitarianism, and men like Charles Carroll who regretted the passing of aristocratic forms. As scholars have pointed out, Tocqueville did go astray in some particulars (for instance, concerning the laws of inheritance), and he left America with apparently little sense of the importance of President Jackson and of what Marvin Meyers has called "the Jacksonian persuasion."[3] Yet Tocqueville liked America more than many of his conservative informants did and more perhaps than he had himself expected to: he liked the lack of servility, the freestanding quality of people who in his own country would be peasants, the self-reliant spirit and energy that he saw on all sides. For in the course of his travels he met innkeepers, traders, boatmen, and such.

There is, inevitably, a bias in such encounters, unless one supplements them with a sample survey or knows already where to look for those whom one will not ordinarily meet. The Americans who were visible to Tocqueville and Beaumont were naturally the more active

[3] See Marvin Meyers, *The Jacksonian Persuasion* (Stanford University Press, 1957), especially Chapter II. In Tocqueville's pages, one is not made aware of the extent and inanity of snobbery, such as emerges from Francis J. Grund, *Aristocracy in America: From the Sketchbook of a German Nobleman* (Harper Torchbook edition, 1959).

ones: the gregarious, the enterprising, the articulate, rather than the isolated and submerged. If they were farmers, they were more likely to be those up-and-coming ones who regarded their land as a property held for speculation than those withdrawn and secluded ones who regarded it as an inheritance to be conserved with a peasantlike tenacity. One finds in Tocqueville's pages neither the many indolent, self-indulgent, and shiftless frontiersmen, nor such groups as the pietistic Pennsylvania Dutch who even in today's America manage to seal themselves off in rural enclaves from currents of change. At the same time, the people Tocqueville did meet were precisely those who had more than a proportionate share in deciding what America was to be like. In that sense, the visitor's problem in discovering the typical was made easier by the dialectic his presence evoked.

There is evidence, however, that the image of America as a land of eager, enterprising, activist joiners and strivers has been overdone since the beginning. In frontier days, there were many who were isolated and unchurched, reached at most by an occasional revival. Today various researches show that the economic underdog and especially the older person is often entirely isolated: he may possibly be an inactive member of a trade union and an occasional churchgoer, but he is likely to have no other ties than this, beyond the pseudo-*Gemeinschaft* that television and the other mass media provide. (Church membership in terms of formal affiliation is much higher than in Tocqueville's day.) Granted these submerged exceptions, Tocqueville was nevertheless right to emphasize the difference between the mobile and fluid organizational life of the average American and the usual French encapsulation in the ties of family and parish. Tocqueville, like other visitors, stressed what we might call the associational literacy of the Americans, who on their own in a new country had learned how to form a committee, how to advertise it in the newspapers, and how to go on then to the next job that needed doing.

One large group of nearly silent Americans Tocqueville left largely to the researches of his fellow ethnographer, Beaumont; I refer to the slaves. Tocqueville was characteristically perceptive in seeing that the South was different and that the issue of slavery might lead to an explosion, and he was aware (as his later correspondence with Gobineau showed) of the dangers of racism; in *Democracy in America* he rejects racial and geographic explanations of national character. Beaumont's work, however, made it possible for Tocqueville to concentrate on the North and in this respect, too, on the American future. However, he was here before the coming of the railways and before industrialism had made any appreciable dent on the American landscape. Thus, he confronted a largely commercial-agrarian but pre-industrial culture and was not distracted from his main task either by the slavery issue, or by the colorful arguments over mechanization and industry: the factory system did not divert Tocqueville from the social system. Here, too, he foresaw more than he could actually see: he described some of the psychological reasons why mass production would appeal to the American market; and he expressed his fear that the Americans might succumb to a despotism of manufacturers facing laborers too handicapped by their dulling and constricting work to be free and mobile. Considering the small scale of industrial development in 1831, this glimpse of what America might look like in the age of the tycoon is even more startling than Tocqueville's famous prediction that America would have a population of one hundred and fifty million to face an equally powerful Russia for the destiny of the world. Even though Tocqueville continuously encountered American boasting (and its underlying defensiveness and vulnerability to criticism), it is doubtful whether these images of the future were simple transpositions of what his informants thought.

Tocqueville was protected against certain orders of mistake by being an aristocrat with a country seat. We can get a sense of this by comparing *Democracy in America* with Dickens' *American Notes*. Dickens, coming eleven years later, with a keen consciousness of the industrial blight and urban slums of Britain, was an eager visitor to the Lowell mills, precursors of modern welfare state capitalism. He seems not to have escaped a visit to a single charitable institution in Boston, whether for orphans or for the insane or for what we would today call juvenile delinquents—much as sentimental but uncritical visitors to the Soviet Union in the 1930s were taken on tours of similar institutions. But on the other hand Dickens was terribly upset by American crudity. He could not stand seeing unkempt men spitting on the carpets of the White House and lounging about without respect for the authorities; spitting got in the way of his vision, as it did for Mrs. Trollope—just as other coarse parvenu traits obscured the vision of many travelers and residents in the early years of the Soviet Union. The author of *Great Expectations* could not generalize from his extraordinary psychological understanding of individuals to a whole society of Pips, not all of whom were ennobled by the vision of Estelle. The picture he gives of America is colorful and, in details, accurate, as in his comments on American gregariousness or love of comfort, but it remains superficial. In contrast Tocqueville, less threatened by grossness, observed that Americans lacked both great coarseness and great refinement. And his personal sense of the qualities of an aristocratic milieu was used constantly as an intellectual foil in developing his abstract conception of "democratic nations."

Democracy in America is addressed primarily to Tocqueville's aristocratic and conservative French friends. It is the plea of a man who feels that a romantic conservatism which rejects democracy and all the institutions of the modern world is doomed to end either in despotism or inanity, and that liberty—the principal value in life for which a man should care—would be best preserved by working with, rather than against, the grain of modernity, the long, slow, centuries-old march toward social equality. Tocqueville pleads that democracy, although it will never be elegant and although it may not give adequate place to excellence whether in workmanship or in art, could nevertheless be tamed and tempered. The remedy for the evils of democracy is not a hopeless quest for reaction. (John Lukacs argues in his introduction to Tocqueville's *The European Revolution and Correspondence with Gobineau* that Tocqueville today would be out of sympathy with the conservatives' fear of socialism.) Democracy could be kept from becoming despotic and the tyranny of the majority moderated by providing, on the one hand, political bulkheads such as the Founding Fathers had fashioned and, on the other, a cultural style invigorated by the individual experience of citizenship and chastened by the restraints of religion (which Tocqueville saw not in terms of individual salvation but in terms of social cement). On so sober a platform, a Tory radical might unite with Matthew Arnold or with Tocqueville's friend, John Stuart Mill. It is a platform that attracts many Americans who want to surrender neither political democracy nor social equality, but who are afraid of revolutionary zeal, are not particularly aroused by injustice, and largely share the consensus Louis Hartz describes in *The Liberal Tradition in America*.

Tocqueville was impressed with the American separation of powers, as a therapy both for atomization and for excessive centralization—an attitude later strengthened by his work on *L'Ancien Régime*. He was also persuaded that the separation of Church and State strengthened religion, especially Catholicism, and was therefore a good thing for democracy. Indeed, the competing churches were for Tocqueville one example of what he regarded as the most efficacious and most characteristic American invention for the defense of political liberty, that is, the encouragement that liberty itself provided for forming decentralized associations. He saw political liberty as primarily an educational device that would teach men, reduced in individual stature by equality, to remain or become self-reliant and realistic. He regarded the town meeting as a principal school of this sort (not realizing from the accounts of his Whig friends the extent to which it had decayed). And, to his timorous and conservative compatriots, he emphasized the importance of America's bubbling associational life as increasing the distribution of political competence. Speaking of the democrat's "facility in prosecuting great undertakings in common," he declared:

> Political associations may therefore be considered as large free schools, where all members of the community go to learn the general theory of association. . . . Thus it is by the enjoyment of a dangerous freedom that the Americans learn the art of rendering the dangers of freedom less formidable.

Furthermore, Tocqueville insisted that the free press was essential as the organizational tool of associational life. By means of the press people learned that there were others of like mind with whom they could join when they could not know this automatically through membership in the same family or lifelong residence in a village. Accordingly, Tocqueville pictured Americans as busy with an infinite variety of associations, some private, some political, cannily making use of the newspapers as the basis for recruitment and excitement. (Curiously, he seems not to have reported the tremendous outcry against the Masonic order which was underway when he was here; his notebooks reveal his awareness of the kidnaping and murder of an ex-Mason that touched off this outcry, but Tocqueville gained little sense of what Edward Shils has called "the torment of secrecy," the fear of being on the outside, the fear of conspiracy, that was in 1831 already a dark undercurrent in American life.) Tocqueville's attention, however, was focused less on the Masons and other lodges (whose role in American life today seems much attenuated, perhaps in part because formality no longer seems interesting or worthwhile) than on the associations Americans formed to organize a church (parishes not being given in the landscape), to found a hospital, to crusade for temperance, to build a college.

Above all, he was tremendously struck with the perfervid political activity of Americans, which he seems to have taken as a regular feature of our national life and not as a periodic response to a leader and framer of issues such as Andrew Jackson. From his pages, one gets a picture of Americans marching forth from their domestic castles and from what he referred to as the dangerous solitude of the individual's own heart to learn the latest news of the courthouse, or to manifest their loyalties at a political rally—and to gain in this way a sense of confidence about what individuals when grouped together could accomplish, and a realistic awareness of the problems of the local and national life. Furthermore, he observed a kind of counterpoint between the easy gregariousness of politics and the exclusiveness of private life. Thus he wrote:

> The Americans, who mingle so readily in their political assemblies and courts of justice, are wont on the contrary to carefully separate into small distinct circles, in order to indulge by themselves in the enjoyments of private life.

Tocqueville's view of civic activity as perhaps the chief affair of the civilized and educated man has an Athenian style (compare the eloquent discussion in Hannah Arendt's *The Human Condition*). For Tocqueville, political liberty was itself of value, something that made men manly as well as averted the evils of social equality. But, by the same token, Tocqueville feared American individualism (a term he himself brought into use, but that he regarded not as we do, but as similar to egocentricity or solipsism), a withdrawal into "virtuous materialism" from the great and ennobling affairs of the common life. So, too, he saw in the "small distinct circles" an effort to establish a status denied by the formal institutions of democracy.

Tocqueville was aware from the European despotic example that governments could forbid associations and he warned against this. He pointed out that aristocratic nations, such as France had been, were chambered by castelike groupings; in such a society groups would be born, not made, just as men were born, not self-made. And since, as I have said, he believed such a form of social organization was doomed, he tried to persuade its residual cadres to welcome freedom of association as a guarantee of liberty.

Were Tocqueville to visit America now, he might well be alarmed at the ways in which individuals, called before governmental investigators, are asked to report on their ties with others and their informal as well as formal networks of association, so that the personal threatens to become political, and the political, personal. Tocqueville spoke of the bar as the most influential quasi-aristocracy in America (he had in mind the practicing bar rather than the Supreme Court, being largely unaware of the significance of John Marshall's decisions). But the role of the bar in recent years in defending freedom of association has not been impressive. Many lawyers have feared to take the cases of men accused of subversive activities or associations, lest they themselves be thought sympathetic to their clients. Thus, I have the impression that lawyers today are, if more professionalized than in Tocqueville's day, much less influential because of their reluctance to face popular distrust. The bar associations have done little to protect their individual members who take unpopular cases, and some have even gone so far as to attack the Supreme Court for those of its decisions which have sought to reinvigorate the freedoms both of speech and of association.

In fact, it is hard to see rising above the democratic plain any of the groups that Tocqueville thought might become potential aristocracies. Not, as I have just said, the lawyers, in spite of their numerical preponderance in Congress and state legislatures. And not the manufacturers, that is, the owning class whom Tocqueville thought of as potentially capable of oppressing their workers and becoming an oligarchy. Something like this did happen after the Civil War, in the period of the robber barons and the formation of great combines and trusts, and one could argue that in terms of discrepancies of wealth and power America between 1870 and 1900 differed both from the America Tocqueville saw and from the less ruthless managerial capitalism of today. In one important respect, however, as Louis Hartz has observed, post-Civil War Americans continued the movement toward equality, for by temporarily crushing the anti-industrial South they reduced all values to dollar values, and every man in principle became every other man's equal in the sense of having an equal opportunity to gain and to succeed. Certainly, men like Henry Adams felt that American life in the era of Grant had no place for an Adams: lacking were even the remnants of gentility that had survived down to the Civil War—remnants that had failed to impress Tocqueville perhaps because those who continued this tradition already felt themselves defeated (much as American businessmen today will tell all and sundry that it is impossible to make a fortune in one's lifetime because of taxes, although this is not the case). Thus, by overshadowing the competing echelons of land and family and of cultivated merchants, the post-Civil War oligarchy made in the end for a still greater equalitarianism.

Tocqueville had, however, one other candidate for hegemony, namely, certain groups of junior officers in the military establishment, and what he had to say about them makes all too uncomfortable reading today. I cannot think of another American visitor in time of peace and tiny armies who paid attention to this possibility. (Tocqueville was probably alerted to it by the wars unleashed by the French Revolution.) The military, of course, was one of the few groups, and the only influential one, having a code which played down the desire for material possessions. As Tocqueville wrote, the officer's "true country is the Army, since he owes all he has to the rank he has attained in it; he therefore follows the fortunes of the Army, rises or sinks with it, and henceforth directs all his hopes to that quarter only." There have been generals recently, notably General MacArthur, whose true country has been the Army, but it is on the whole surprising how much respect military men have for their civilian superiors in politics, and for their monetary superiors in big business: far from regarding the latter as vulgar men without honor and patriotism, the military in the absence of feudal traditions have lacked a counter-ethos. Correspondingly, the ambitions of individual officers for glory may be less important than the corporate ambitions of their arm of the service, tied in as each arm is with its defense contractors, its scientists, its friends on congressional committees or on the Atomic Energy Commission. In the era of the cold war, Tocqueville's prophecies about the military direct our attention in the right direction, but do not illuminate beyond that.

But in other respects and particularly in picturing the over-all psychology of what we have come to call mass society, Tocqueville's extrapolation of an America he saw into one he foresaw was prescient. Equality has gone much further, facilitated in part by public education (something to which Tocqueville adverted in his journals but did not think important enough for his published book). The fear of the rich that the poor would envy or unseat them has become in our day not merely an influence on public relations, but the source of a kind of social osmosis upward as well as downward in which numerous sons of the well-to-do search out the values of the less privileged for fear of missing something important and emancipating in life. In Tocqueville's day, what Americans wanted were the rights and privileges and possessions of other Americans, but today's Americans seem to me less greedy, certainly less greedy for possessions per se. And while Tocqueville saw Americans as endlessly energetic, moving eagerly onward and upward in economic activity and political caucus, it is my impression that many Americans today are less compulsively gregarious and somewhat more passive politically: what they want out of life is less easily defined—and less easily attained.

By the same token, Tocqueville's isolated individuals seem to me a good deal more freestanding than many Americans of today. While Tocqueville spoke of every man striving "to keep himself aloof, lest he be carried away by the crowd against his will," today there would seem to be less aloofness, more going with the crowd unconsciously, and at the same time a more desperate search for nonconformity. It follows that the self-confidence of Americans which so struck Tocqueville has also become attenuated, even though in the West and South one can still find old-fashioned representatives of it. The "small distinct circles" of private life into which Americans retire are increasingly those of the suburban P.T.A. or other neighborhood groups that avoid the more intractable issues either of the great metropolis or of the country as a whole. A great resurgence of the family, with people marrying at ever younger ages, has absorbed much of the leisure that Tocqueville thought would go into political and associational life. Contrary to what many think, the centralization of state power that Tocqueville feared has not come to pass in America: in many respects neither the several states, nor certainly the cities, nor even the federal government is strong enough for the burdens of making an affluent society also a civilized and humane one, even though our military and political leaders, in co-operative provocation with our enemies, may destroy the country and the world and en route oppress many individuals in the name of national loyalty.

Despite these dangers, American democracy remains a going, if threatened, concern, even though it violates many of the rules that Tocqueville's French conservative friends thought essential for civic order. But these rules were not of great importance for Tocqueville, who wanted to preserve from earlier times neither great refinement of taste nor feudal codes of honor (with their undercurrents of barbarity), but rather independence of mind and magnanimity of action. For the sake of a diminished servility and a wider ambiance of citizenship, he was willing to surrender many privileges from an earlier day. Moreover, he thought that the softening of manners that accompanied the growing equality of condition made men more human, for he did not wholly share the attachment of romantic conservatives then and now for the chivalric styles of the older nobility. In an extraordinary passage, he spoke of the way in which casual cruelty had become *démodé* even before the French and American Revolutions, remarking on the way in which Mme. de Sévigné could express a callous pleasure in public executions that a generation later would be inconceivable. He seemed to feel that there was something in the human career, linked to Christianity, which was responsible for a long, slow, and inevitable rise of equalitarianism, accompanied by a rise in sensitivity beyond the immediate enclaves of family and class. He did not delude himself that there were not losses in the democratic tide, for he was not entirely free of admiration for chivalry and punctilio, but he was quite willing to sacrifice these traditional virtues if the result would be an elevation of the mass of men and the disappearance of the abasement of the oppressed. What he feared was a new servility in which each man, respecting his neighbor no more than he respected himself, would respect only the serried and unranked mass of men. As he declared:

> Moralists are constantly complaining that the ruling vice of the present time is pride. This is true in one sense, for everybody thinks that he is better than his neighbor or refuses to obey his superior; but it is extremely false in another, for the same man who cannot endure subordination or equality has so contemptible an opinion of himself that he thinks he is born only to indulge in vulgar pleasures. He willingly takes up with low desires without daring to embark on lofty enterprises, of which he scarcely dreams. Thus, far from thinking that humility ought to be preached to our contemporaries, I would have endeavors made to give them a more enlarged idea of themselves and their kind.

Given the bombast and the big talk of many of the Americans he saw, Tocqueville drew here on his sense of the difference between the patrician ambition of those who are already in high place and the lesser vision of those who, motivated by envy, want merely to attain goals that are already there—in contemporary terms, the difference between Kennedy's personal pride and ambition for "his" country and Nixon's humble but even more egocentric drive to get to the top.

But such passages, in which Tocqueville extols what we today praise as individualism, must be set against his equally strong concern lest what *he* called individualism divide the nation into gangs of rapacious men pursuing an unenlightened self-interest. In the dialectic between individualism and solidarity, many intellectuals have tended (as has this writer) to stress the former—to the point where any eccentricity or idiosyncrasy, any rejection of the mass of men and their values, becomes praiseworthy, creating what Harold Rosenberg has dubbed "the herd of independent minds." An appropriately differentiated ethic for our own time barely exists and needs to be invented through experience; *Democracy in America* helps us to understand but not to solve our problem.

Introduction to *Crestwood Heights*
(1956)

When I was in the middle of the manuscript of *Crestwood Heights*, I had the good luck to attend a meeting in Park Forest, a new-model suburb which is comparable to Crestwood Heights in the intensity with which it has been studied. The meeting was addressed by William H. Whyte, Jr. of *Fortune*, its imaginative, incisive, and not unsympathetic main surveyor. En route to the meeting Whyte observed that, when he had been interviewing in Park Forest, he had had the strange feeling of being virtually the only male in the place during the daytime; the men were all at work downtown or in various plants around Chicago, and there were some joking references to his being loose in a harem. Moreover, the problems to which he had addressed himself in his justly famous series of articles on Park Forest had frequently been those felt most keenly by the homebound wives: problems of sociability and privacy in the rental courts; of the limits of idiosyncrasy in décor; of how to put down roots while remaining, on behalf of their husbands' careers, potential transients. At the meeting where he was asked to speak, however, Whyte was surrounded—and kept at a distance from the mixed audience—by a panel composed entirely of men; these, and their friends in the first several rows of the audience, asked him questions largely of a technical "male" sort, e.g., concerning social science methodology or zoning regulations; only one woman managed to get in a word during the entire evening. Many of the questions were hostile, and appeared to spring from resentment of the possibility or claim that an outsider could learn anything that was not obvious to the local experts and founding fathers of 1947–48, the date of first settlement.

This volume by Seeley, Sim, and Loosley makes several important contributions to understanding such encounters. A brilliant chapter is devoted to the triangle formed by male experts and researchers, their female clients, and the latter's husbands. The husbands work all day in the city; they pride themselves on being practical, no-nonsense men—

a pride partly maintained by polarizing themselves from their allegedly emotional, starry-eyed wives; they are willing to buy (and bury) social science in personnel and marketing departments (as one appurtenance, thanks in part to the corporation tax, of their being up-to-date), but not in affairs pertaining to their suburb and its schools. The wives have the leisure and education and energy to make a career out of suburbia— and to be anxious about themselves and their children. The social science experts, often marginal members of new professions, require lay co-operation in order to have subjects, financing, and the prestige sometimes denied them in the scholarly world. These experts, much like artists, appear male vis-à-vis their female clients, counselees, and devotees, but not quite manly to the latters' spouses. The experts also have the advantage of being in the community in the daytime, and of having prestige in the eyes of subsidiary experts such as schoolteachers, social workers, and other semiprofessionals of limited theoretical pretensions. It is understandable that the husbands, uneasy in any case because they are wedded to their work and only peripherally to their families, resent the experts with their psychological know-how, their intimate knowledge of the community, and their permissive notions of child-rearing (Whyte's notions were quite different, but this did not save him from triangulation).

The concern that Seeley, Sim, and Loosley have with this triangle and its dangers for all parties concerned—not least the expert, whose success with a lay public will divorce him still further from his academic colleagues—is part of a wider concern that runs through the book for the consequences of social research upon the communities (and other "objects") studied. Anthropologists have developed an ethical program to protect the tribes they visit from being unduly influenced by their presence, or that of other Westernized people; cultural relativism is part of this program, with its now much qualified mandate of equal detachment from all cultures, a mandate as it were of attachment to the principle of culture as such. In their efforts to combat the parochialism and ethnocentrism of missionaries and administrators, they have until recently been able to aim their research reports entirely at their audience at home; by definition, "their" tribe would not read what was written about them, and would presumably be disturbed as little as possible by having an anthropologist living unassumingly among them, seeking to learn their language and sympathetically to understand their values. But today it gets harder and harder to find "uncontaminated" tribes and to assume one can leave them that way (Mrs. Bowen's

Return to Laughter beautifully indicates the complexities and moral ambiguities involved), and as the world has shrunk anthropologists have become much more sensitive to their subjects. When the Lynds published their first *Middletown* book and when W. Lloyd Warner came back from an Australian tribe and started work on the "Yankee City Series," social science was directly plunged into the problem of reporting on its subjects to its subjects. Witness *Point of No Return*.

Seeley and his collaborators, like their predecessors in American community studies, have—unlike the *Fortune* articles—granted a kind of courtesy anonymity to their suburb, more as a sign of good will than in any hope that one can hide so distinctive a feature of the landscape as Crestwood Heights. But the authors collide, like Whyte, with a problem their predecessors only brushed against, for they are writing about *us*, about the professional upper middle class and its businessman allies, not about a New England museum for the upper class, such as Yankee City, or a small and rather parochial town in the South or Midwest, such as Jonesville or Elmtown. They are writing, as they are almost too aware, about themselves, their friends, their "type" (I "type" the authors, of course, no doubt unjustly, by treating the trio as if they were one person). Moreover, the enterprise on which they report involved much more than simply a one-shot data-gathering expedition; this was "action research," with teams of clinicians for the school children, discussion leaders for the schoolteachers and parents (as implied above, only the mothers, by and large, took part), and leaders of human-relations classes in the schools—classes in which the young people were encouraged, quite bravely, to bring up any problems of concern to them. In the high school, many of the suburban teen problems of parents, cars, sex, cliques arose, along with Crestwood Heights' exceptional sensitivity to interethnic (mainly, Jewish-Gentile) amity; there also arose some very probing questions concerning the search for personal identity and integrity. So intertwined, in fact, is the research with the community that this book gives the impression that its authors are still stuck in the tarbaby; their moral intensity about their task and their responsibilities both as researchers and as reporters is, in all its humorlessness and intensity, rare and admirable.

I have occasionally asked novelists how they feel about using their friends and families, barely disguised, in an autobiographical book. Usually, if they have thought about the question at all, the immensely powerful ideology of *l'art pour l'art*, developed for use against the Philistines, suffices to dismiss any scruples. Moreover, partly because of this ideology, writers have a vanity that researchers repress or seldom gain; as one, whose whole family garnishes a lurid novel, told me, "My book will be alive when all my family is dead"; his implication was they should be grateful for this immortality. To be sure, Randall Jarrell's *Pictures from an Institution* bursts with its tirade against a lady novelist who "heartlessly" cases a college community (the book in turn cruelly cases the lady). But Jarrell, as befits the author of *The Age of Criticism,* is unusually self-conscious about reflexivity for a literary man; most novelists so far as I can make out (Thomas Wolfe is a notable exception) take exploitation of their "material" for granted.

As I have implied, the consciences of the authors of *Crestwood Heights* are so involved with their research experience that I wish at times they had had the novelist's insouciance as well as the novelist's sensitivity to anxiety and other forms of mental suffering among the well-to-do. I myself often prefer, for reasons which I'm sure won't stand full examination, to suppose that social scientists exaggerate their power for weal or woe—hence in such cases as this their feelings of responsibility. Most social scientists, however, duck such moral issues by believing only in their subjects' subjectivity and not in their own, or by seeking to couch their findings in an opaque language which their subjects can presumably not decipher or which in any case is believed to be free from bias. Whatever discomfort is associated with the path chosen by Seeley, Sim, and Loosley, I will take it any day over the self-deceptions and ethical insensitivities of the majority. The authors of *Crestwood Heights* are not arrogant about their professional training (and they lack the innocence of supposing that technical terms can long conceal one's values); one result is that there is not a line in this book with which I would suppose an educated nonprofessional reader will have any serious difficulty. In some measure, I rather regret this, for it means that the writing, for my taste, is not sufficiently dense and allusive; everything is painstakingly spelled out. And in one respect this prolixity is perplexing, for if one assumes that readers and subjects are, apart from accidents of residence, the same people, then one would not need all the ethnographic detail that overburdens this book. Though the authors have a keener eye for moral impasse and arabesque than for the material culture or for the merely sociable, they insist on telling us what the houses are like, or the orbits of time and season, and there is a long chapter on summer camps that seems to assume that the reader will neither have seen such a camp nor sent his children there.

This chapter, incidentally, has a waspishness of tone—though not a penetration of idea—reminiscent of Mary McCarthy. And camps of course, with their pseudo-Indian lore, their parents who seek surrogates to toughen and discipline their children, their counselors who "goof off," are easy targets for satire. Elsewhere in the book, one feels that the authors are trying not to be too severe on their own kind, not to join the current intellectual critique of liberal, middle-class professional people, such as make up a considerable part of the population, as well as the leadership, of Crestwood Heights. But it is hard for description not to become parody when we are reading, not about strata or tribes remote from us, but about our own suburban (or in the case of the camps, in Spectorsky's phrase, exurban) life. Compare the following, from the description of a presumably typical family:

> Despite these separate rounds of activity, which intersect only occasionally (the husband states: "I am home so little, I only see the kids for an hour in the evening, that is if I'm not going off to a meeting"), the affection on the part of the children towards each other and their parents is demonstrative and this behavior is given high approval. . . . The giving of presents in this family is a highly regarded token of love and esteem. An equally strong norm, on the other hand, insists upon separate activities for each member of the family, with less frequent events in the nature of holiday or anniversary celebrations involving the whole group (the summer holiday together must be planned for a year or more in advance). Only a high degree of efficiency (faintly reminiscent of that of a well-run club or office) in operating the household makes this individualistic pattern of outside activities workable at all. The actual help given by the children can be symbolic only; more helpful, and unusual, is the presence of the same maid with this family over a six-year period.

Veblen knew that the apparently deadpan could be devastating, and part of Mary McCarthy's genius is to be able to say, for instance, that "the professor came into the room carrying his briefcase" so that the descriptive remark appears to undress him, to show him as he really ridiculously is, without pretense or illusion. But when I read such a passage as the one quoted above, and many like it, I wonder whether it is I who bring to the material a sardonic reaction or whether I find it there, in the use of the term "efficiency," in the comparison with the club or office, and in the awkwardness—neither quite jargon nor quite literature—of such phrases as "highly regarded token of love and esteem."

Readers will have to answer such questions for themselves, but it is part of the context that it is the very niceness of the Crestwood Heights people that lays them open to scrutiny either by the researchers or by the readers. The suburbanites (or at least the women and experts) invited the research team in; they welcomed long and probing interviews and tests, in a way that less agreeable and perhaps less vulnerable people would not have done. (It is perhaps an aspect of this ethos which leads Crestwood Heights, if not always to welcome the influx of Jews, at least not to tolerate any restrictions or quotas.) The same defenselessness of Crestwood Heights appears in its devoutness, the women's, that is, toward each passing fad in child-rearing, and in the social and psychological professions generally. The authors could not help but be struck by the way in which mothers rejected their own experience in favor of some formula—and if the researchers criticized the formula they were themselves in danger of becoming the new priests, only to be overthrown in turn. The anthropologist who goes into a culture that has successfully hardened against white contact does not face this danger, nor does the industrial sociologist, whom the workers in a factory regard as a tool or fool of management or of themselves. But every perceptive teacher does have the experience of fearing a discipleship which robs the student of independence, and might even prefer students' disdain to their passivity. As I have already indicated, it is the researchers' own niceness and defenselessness that makes them aware of the ethical ambiguities of their invasion of Crestwood Heights; under the circumstances, they could hardly be expected to possess the serene confidence in science, in evidence, that a Martin Arrowsmith struggled for. Moreover, Arrowsmith wanted to cure something obvious and concrete, something "outside," while the problems of Crestwood Heights are on another level. Possibly the very existence of the suburb itself (and the researchers studying themselves studying it) marks something of a retreat from the intractable problems of society, though it would seem fairer to say only that there is some loss of traditional forms of venturesomeness as the echoing internal frontier replaces the vanishing external one.

I have implied that the reader will not meet in this book people whom he doesn't know, though he may know himself and his setting better—I did—when he has gone through it. Reading, for instance, the extensive discussion of dating, it occurred to me that referring, as girls often do, to one of their number as "boy-crazy" is, among other things, part of an effort by the group to establish a norm to protect the skillfully slow "producers" against the awkwardly fast rate-busters: boys are the bosses, and a boy-crazy girl breaks down the oppressed group's effort to train themselves to restrain their zeal and to train the bosses to expect only limited and calculated returns from a series of graded incentives (cf. *Lysistrata*). Throughout the book, in fact, the high school students often seem to be more sophisticated and mature than their parents (they can also be contrasted with California and Massachusetts high school graduates who, as described in a report by Professor A. J. Brodbeck, exhibit a fear of anything serious or "controversial" coming up in class, and value above all cautious good manners and the cool approach). Regrettably, the Crestwood Heights study didn't last long enough to see whether the teen-agers became more stupid in later life and whether they became as sex-polarized concerning values as their parents are, with the father in charge of the department of realism (with sentiment his understudy), and the mother in charge of the department of utopianism (with practicality in reserve).

Or, to take another instance, never have I read a more searching account of why some reformers fear success and hence, as it were, plant the seeds of failure in their very attitude, finding in the hostility they arouse in others the alibi which will save them from recognizing their own volition in defeat. Another gem is the discussion of the semantics of "house" and "home"—though the suburb is Canadian, Americans will recognize the shadings.

In fact, there is almost nothing in the book which strikes me as peculiarly Canadian, although when I visited Crestwood Heights during the course of this research I felt I was in the presence of three provincialisms: toward London, toward Hollywood–New York, and toward Tel Aviv (there were not enough French Canadians or other Catholics to add Rome to the list). Thus, I surmise that the reader from Scarsdale or Flossmoor or Belmont will feel that Crestwood Heights is not so very different from suburbs he has known; and one of the problems of the book as a research document is its lack of comparative material. For there are things about Crestwood Heights which may be somewhat differentiating. As a suburb of one of Canada's largest cities, it is within the orbit of one of the few remaining financial bonfires in North America outside of our own Southwest: the province in which it lies is booming, and its menfolk in business are more likely to be the last tycoons than are businessmen in the tamer parts of Wall Street or State Street, just as pukka sahib attitudes lingered in the British colonies long after dying in the Colonial Office. If I am right about this, then the authors' discovery that there were two cultures in Crestwood Heights, that of the men and that of the women-cum-experts—cultures far more distinct than the nominal differences of Jew and non-Jew, upper middle and lower middle, professional man and businessman—would need qualification before being extended to the United States. Indeed, this sharp division of the sexes is reminiscent of an older America of tired businessmen and *The Male Animal,* in which women hauled their menfolk, not to the school psychologist or the PTA, but to the opera— an America that still persists in the midwestern towns and cities, and elsewhere, but which is fast disappearing . . . with what I have sometimes referred to as the growing homogenization of the sexes. This is the America in which I grew up, in which, save among a few seaboard aristocrats and Jews, the intellectual avant-garde was almost entirely composed of women—leisured housewives who read Joyce and Sherwood Anderson and Freud and even Einstein; an America in which men flaunted their Babbittry and women were Carol Kennicotts. Even in my own lifetime, this has drastically changed: the avant-garde exurbanites are men (and not only experts), and in many suburbs men as well as women read *The New Yorker* and learn to laugh ironically at suburban life and values.

In Crestwood Heights, however, one is confronted by men who apparently don't read anything and wives who will read this book and have read others like it. Yet in its tolerance for Jews the community is liberal and progressive for both sexes, and its large proportion of Jews also makes for idiosyncratic elements, which the book, not being comparative, cannot fully explore. For example, we do not know to what extent the Jewish couples contribute to the general profile of very distinct male and female cultures, since no quantitative data controlled for ethnicity are presented. It may be that the highly mobile Jewish businessmen, marrying somewhat more educated wives whom ethnicity robs of a wider choice, help give Crestwood Heights men their aroma of downtown "success" values as against the suburban "maturity" values of their emancipated and pampered, if patronized, wives. Or it may be, as I have already indicated, that this is the general Protestant Canadian pattern as well, where the women are exposed through the media to general North American currents against which the men are defended by their Big City work and their British-style clubs. We might get some clarification here if we knew how these Jewish and non-Jewish families voted; I am not sure whether Canadian Jews, though on the whole less organizationally differentiated than the immensely larger American

Jewish group, are as attached to the Liberal party by historical factors as American Jews are to the party of Roosevelt and Truman. . . .

As already stated, Seeley and his colleagues have written out of their intense moral, pedagogic, and democratic preoccupations for the lay as well as the professional reader; in doing so, they have followed the model of the ethnographic report on a primitive tribe, with its chapters on time, space, and architecture, on the family and on the life cycle, on ceremonial and associational life, and on belief systems. The difficulty of this model is pointed out in Robert Redfield's *The Little Community*, namely that once one leaves the isolated, preferably island, tribe, it is hard to know how to bound one's unit of study—in this case, how to know where Crestwood Heights ends and where Big City, or Canada, or North America, or the Jewish subculture, or the Western world begins. Indeed, as we have seen, the evidence goes to show that only the women live in Crestwood Heights, along with the young people and the professionals servicing both, while the men are, so to speak, visiting husbands from the bush—from the "real world" of Canada's booming economy; and by the same token it is the women who are cosmopolitan and who bring new foods, new practices, and new beliefs into the suburb. Seeley, Sim, and Loosley are at their best in delineating the subtleties of this division of labor and ideology between the spouses, showing how each provides a requisite countervailing power for the other, with the wives' covert practicality saving the men from the consequences, in dealing with their children, of the fathers' sentimental toughness and realism, while the men's overt practicality saves their wives from the consequences of too wide swings of idealistic faddism in the schools and in the too emancipated homes.

The authors also show, how both the parents look to the school and to such auxiliary institutions as the summer camp to mediate in their own struggles and to compensate for their own ambivalences. The school must teach co-operativeness and equality—yet prepare the children for competitive success. The school must treat each child as a unique individual—yet counter parental tendencies in this wealthy suburb to spoil the children. The school officials in this situation become accomplished diplomats, and their use of Home and School (PTA) meetings, where the parental pressures are nakedly revealed, is amazingly skillful. Yet here, too, there may be slight differences from comparable American settings, for educators seem to have a somewhat higher status and a surer intellectuality. And it would appear that there is a slightly greater tendency to send children away to boarding school than would be the case in a midwestern American city—an understandable tendency, since in boarding school the dirty work of discipline that mothers cannot and fathers and local public-school teachers dare not undertake can be accomplished behind the safe screen of distance and of social status. Furthermore, the authors observe that the teen-age children themselves cope with conflicting demands by organizing secret fraternities and sororities along ethnic lines—and then cleverly traduce parental efforts at suppression by "Moscow Subway" tactics: reminding the parents of their own country clubs, their own unmixed marriages, their own duplicities generally. One suspects that the maturity of the youngsters is in part the result of the conflict of cultures they must continuously reconcile at home and school. As already implied, I hope Seeley & Co. can go back in another twenty years and see what the youngsters of the 1950s have become.

Husbands and wives will enjoy reading [the book] together, for it marshals the arguments for a culturally produced sex difference in a way that undercuts much of the rhetoric of masculinists and feminists—and that raises profound questions concerning the identical education of boys and girls for differential life experiences. In Crestwood Heights at present the semantics of tolerance and the liberal taboo on biological ("racist") explanations make it difficult to discuss seriously either male-female or Jewish-Gentile differences—both are matters only for muttering in the clubs (or of vigilante tactics by the Canadian Jewish Congress); by full yet gentle exploration, this book makes the topic legitimate both in Crestwood Heights and in its analogues elsewhere.

Yet it is just this sort of reaction that Seeley and his collaborators, preternaturally aware of lay oversimplifications of science, view with foreboding; they want to better "their" community—yet leave it unharmed, its battle of the sexes unaffected. I understand this feeling all too well. I have wished many times, no doubt naïvely, that books of this sort could be read as the history of another time and place, or indeed another planet, curious and interesting but not a matter of the life and death of one's day-to-day existence. The authors shrink from the roles of prophet or practitioner—yet they know how an author's unconscious needs may push him toward a lay audience whose all too evident needs for rules of conduct press heavily upon him. No one of us alone, of course, can solve so general a problem. For that, social scientists will have to come to terms more frequently than they now do with their own temptations to grandiosity, to evasion of casuistical issues, and of their own involvement in what they study. But the audience cannot wait for that, or trust to it: to defend itself without resort to the easy road (polemically favored by some humanists) of antiscience, it can become more skillful in the consumption of social science (in part by contributing to it through Mass Observation and other ways of recruiting amateur sociologists), more habituated to its inroads on privacy and opacity, and more lively in its curiosity about the methods and mores of the social scientist.

The Sociology of the Interview
(WITH MARK BENNEY, 1955)

Sociologists certainly don't need to be told how crucial the interview has become as a mainstay of our research. We recently went through an issue of *Sociological Abstracts* and found very few studies reported (we leave out speculative papers) where the interview was not at some point employed; this was even the case where observational or psychometric techniques predominated. The same is even more forcefully true of research abstracted in the journal *Human Organization*. Other fashions in data-gathering may come and go, but the interview is definitely here to stay.[1] And it is here not only as a way of collecting

[1] What may not perhaps be sufficiently appreciated is the extent to which interviewing has become a staple industry in the business world. Last fall, *Business Week*, along with *Fortune* the most acute of the business periodicals, devoted a large section to "motivation" as the hottest thing in marketing. Last week (April 1955) at the meetings of the American Association for Public Opinion Research in Madison, two panels were given over to the same topic, a large fraction of the total program. Companies that would only two or three years ago have relied on design, engineers' judgment, salesmen's comments, and extrapolated sales curves for design and marketing strategy are now paying social researchers to conduct depth interviews to discover —to take one recent example—whether mothers will be made envious of their daughters when urged to buy Toni Home Permanent wave kits for their grammar school daughters, or—to take another example—whether Griesedeck's beer has lost sales punch in St. Louis because the brewery is somehow seen as declining in virility and glamour.

Likewise, a recent survey by the American Management Association showed that four fifths of the 180 companies which responded used personal interviews to determine the suitability of sales personnel—interviews, for the most part, rather than psychological tests. Indeed, Kephart, in his book, *The Employment Interview in Industry*, writes that over half the current labor force either changes jobs or takes new employment annually— and that all but a few of this 30,000,000 find "an interview the major factor in their new placement." (Newell G. Kephart, *The Employment Interview in Industry* (New York: McGraw-Hill, 1952), p. xx.

data about institutions and individuals, but also as one of our best laboratories for the study of interaction, of the Simmelian dyad and of other larger groupings. In social research, market research, industry, social work, and therapy, interviewing has become in fifty years a major white-collar industry—one of those communications professions which represents the shift of whole cadres into tertiary areas.

I

The history of the interview has yet to be written. The word itself harks back to the diplomatic encounters between heads of states during the post-Renaissance period of nascent nationalism; and the interpersonal conventions of the interview—its formality, equality, and transience—as then established, have been carried almost intact through all its subsequent cultural adventures. For most of modern history, of course, the convention of equality was possible only between states and their rulers; within the state formal communication was possible only by "prayer" and catechism; and a good deal of individuation between persons, and differentiation within a society, are necessary before the interview can be adopted widely as a communications device. In an absolutistic or tradition-directed society, such a form would be unlikely to emerge: there are no publics, and no public opinion—a theme stressed by Hans Speier in his article on the historical development of public opinion.[2]

The first newspaper interviews were with foreigners and with political opponents; when Horace Greeley sought out Brigham Young, leader of the sect against which he had been waging a bitter political campaign, asked him a list of prepared questions and printed the answers without comment, he not only invented the newspaper "interview," but also made it possible for people with deep-seated differences to get closer than ten paces. The interview proved to be a way of objectifying the controversy—a new form of conversation across the battle lines, as it were.

Indeed, while the interview came into being in the individualistic context of nineteenth-century journalism, it reached its modern development primarily as an effort to master the newly revealed conflicts and misunderstandings of a rapidly industrializing society. Thus, May-

[2] See Hans Speier, "Historical Development of Public Opinion," *American Journal of Sociology*, 55, 1950, 376–88.

hew (a newspaperman himself), Booth, Le Play, and Quetelet, in their pioneering efforts to understand the novel sorts of urban poor and working classes—classes no longer to be thought of simply as "the lower orders" whom the upper orders were supposed to understand as a matter of course, or could afford not to understand—resorted to systematic interviews and, in Quetelet's case, statistical treatment of them. These men, influenced by Comte and St. Simon, were no longer satisfied with illustrative "tales from the underworld"; they wanted, as it were, to create their own evidence, virtually to take their own census.[3] In this country, it is well known that the poor in the cities were ethnic; the existence of a problem of communication could not be hidden by feudal preconceptions. It would seem that sociology itself and one of its major techniques, the interview, are the product of a similar set of encounters between people in motion. Both were preceded by the novel, viewed as a form of report on the coming together of people of different social origins; for instance, the "proletarian" novel—Farrell, too, does this in a way—takes for its audience a kind of imagined interviewer from the upper classes.

II

Whether motivated by impulses of fear or reform, the early formal interviews by sociologists and social workers often assumed that the new people should become like the old people. For example, when some new housing was being planned in a Negro slum area in Chicago, teams of white and Negro interviewers talked to the slum residents to find out what kind of new housing they would like. One of the questions was: "How do you like it here?" and many of the slum dwellers replied, "I like it fine." The Negro interviewers were infuriated by this response and told the people they were standing in the way of progress of their race by having such an attitude.[4] It's clear in this case that the interview was used not so much to get information, as to give it, to bring pressure on people. This dialectic also besets social work interviews. However, many of the early sociologists were genuinely curious, whether or not they also wanted to change things; the "internal

[3] A. L. Bowley's application of sampling theory made the interview much more of an all-purpose tool than it had been for Booth and the other early surveyors.

[4] We owe this illustration to Professor and Mrs. Martin Meyerson.

anthropology" illustrated by Park, W. I. Thomas, and others at Chicago, was animated by a spirit of cross-class adventure.

At approximately the same time that Booth was asking questions among the poor of London, Freud was asking his patients—no less than the new urban poor the products of Victorian industrialization and development—to tell him all the hidden, all the unsystematic, all the previously disregarded aspects and incidents of their lives; and, beyond that, to enlighten him, through dreams and free associations, concerning the buried conflicts and misunderstandings, the internal "class war," of their lives. Like the great solo social surveyors of the last quarter of the nineteenth century, who also wanted to discover how the buried "other half" lived, Freud felt access to the buried "lower orders" within individuals had to be gained by a new technique; and this technique has provided another model for formal interviewing (the so-called depth interview), for analysis (the case study), and for asking questions based on a theory of the psyche ("projective" questions). The interviews currently conducted in this country move between the poles set up by Booth and Freud (there are, of course, many devices for linking the poles, such as those proposed by Lazarsfeld, Merton, and others), though perhaps we should regard the "nondirective" interview, as used in research and counseling, less as a variant of the Freudian, than as an independent tradition going back through Mayo to Charcot via Janet rather than via Freud.

Some social workers in this country[5] were familiarizing themselves with psychoanalytic concepts as early as the period just after World War I and were developing what we would today consider nondirective techniques in intake interviews. However, it would seem that the major impetus to spreading the gospel of the "rapport" interview—the opposite of the lawyer's courtroom cross-examination—was the famous study at the Hawthorne plant of the Western Electric Company in the late twenties. There Roethlisberger and Dickson and their coworkers developed by trial and error the values, therapeutic for the individual and morale-building for the group, of the informal or gripe interview. In these encounters, held on company time but under circumstances as neutral and uninhibiting as possible, the workers were encouraged to unburden themselves of whatever was on their minds—encouraged to

[5] And elsewhere. See, for example, Beatrice Webb: "Regarded as a method of investigation, the process of interviewing is a particular form of psychoanalysis," *My Apprenticeship* (New York: Longmans, Green and Co., 1926), Appendix B, p. 410.

talk about their troubles: troubles with their supervisors, with their fellow workers, with their families, and so on. The interviewers did not approve or disapprove of what they heard. They were not speaking for the company; they had no control over the workers. These interviews resulted in a lift to morale in the factory because, it would seem, the people got a chance to air their grievances. People accustomed to living in an authoritarian atmosphere experienced a nonauthoritarian interlude. They could make the white-collar interviewer listen. They could tell somebody off with no risk at all, although many who talked about factory grievances did not really expect the gripes wouldn't go any farther as the interviewers had promised: they hoped they *would* go farther, anonymously, and that as a result some changes would be made and somebody they didn't like would get fired. Actually nothing happened as a direct result of these interviews, but the workers interpreted subsequent changes as resulting from them.

In 1948 one of us accompanied Georges Friedmann on a visit to the Hawthorne plant to talk to the counselors. The program appeared to be getting stale. People were aware that nothing happened, nothing changed as a result of all the counseling interviews. We asked who counseled the counselors. They seemed cut off from the company as industrial-relations departments often are. The situation was no longer the same as it was when the program was inaugurated. There can of course be many and complex explanations for this change. The *élan* of innovation cannot be expected to last for decades. Yet it seems to us that one factor which might be important is the shift in the impact of permissiveness. When the program began, many employees at Hawthorne were poor, isolated, immigrant women who were intimidated by their bosses in the plant, at home, and in the precinct. Nondirectiveness in an aggressively directive milieu was therapeutically strange and novel; it still is for many GIs and for working-class and lower-middle-class folk who profit from Rogerian counseling. For such employees, talking to the interviewer meant a chance to form a "union of sinners"; they learned that they were not alone—that they would not be rejected for feeling the way they did. As the milieu is now less aggressively directive, so there's a different breed of girls working there now. Their job is more secure, they're better off economically, they're cockier and have more acquaintances that they can gripe to. It would seem likely that the interviewing program doesn't mean the same thing to them.

The Hawthorne experience would seem to raise a more general question about nondirective interviewing as well as counseling. Among those respondents and those many circles where the cult of permissiveness already prevails, and where a bland and unchallenging interview technique becomes a routine encounter to be handled by an equivalent blandness, we may wonder whether this form has not outlived its usefulness. In such cases it might be more productive to encourage more variegated conduct by the interviewer—conduct which could not so readily be handled by a falling back on the forms of informality. To put this another way: where respondents themselves have experienced a variety of interviewlike settings—among them nondirectiveness—they may take their cue as to how to respond in a particular case from the interviewer; and it becomes important to know whether there is anything in the relationship beyond its minimal novelty to evoke re-examination of self or situation. Indeed, we might mention in this connection the question we have put to a number of analysts as to why psychotherapy takes longer today, according to common report, than it did for equivalent cases in the first generation after Freud. When we suggested that this may be because patients are, as it were, "presocialized" as such, so that to discuss, let us say, sexual fantasies with an eminent physician is not particularly shocking; and, moreover, when free association along certain lines comes cheap and talk is no longer *ipso facto* dramatic and even traumatic—these analysts have tended to agree that such a diagnosis might make sense. They have all had the experience of interminable analysis with young people brought up in the quasi-therapeutic milieu and in an atmosphere of quasi-psychiatric lingo.[6]

III

Let us, however, before returning to the problem of rapport and nondirectiveness, contrast these contemporary settings of emancipation with the problem of interviewing in areas of greater self-constriction, among interviewees who do not have training in meeting strangers informally—the sort of training American urban and urbanized life so famously provides. When the National Opinion Research Center (NORC) interviewers from Chicago went to Arkansas after a tornado, they found it difficult with isolated and poor rural respondents to establish the sponsor's frame of reference: in ways described in an article by

[6] Lewis Dexter has commented on this by comparing the strains of young people immune to the older therapies with the strains of newer bug immune to the older antibiotics!

Leonard Schatzman and Anselm Strauss,[7] they would rebuff efforts to get a sequential account; rather, they would talk about their world ethnocentrically, as it were, and not invite the interviewer into it.

We ourselves have listened to a number of these same tapes, and in a few instances were driven to interpretations rather different from those of Schatzman and Strauss. For many respondents what mattered most was the theodicy problem: why had the disaster hit, killing those it killed and sparing others? Directly or indirectly, they wanted the interviewer's opinion, whereas the latter was trained only to want theirs —a technique which, coupled with hailing from Chicago and carrying tape recorders, gave an inevitable impression of godlessness. Once the respondent discovered that the interviewer was not going to debate theodicy, he either resignedly vouchsafed the minimum factual data called for by the embarrassed interviewer[8] or refused to make any effort to put himself in the interviewer's place. To be sure, many respondents did appear to lack the psychic mobility, the "projectivity" necessary for putting themselves in the place of the other; but so, too, did some interviewers.

What is involved here may become somewhat less unclear when we move from rural and remote America to try to conduct interviews in peasant cultures. Five years ago the Bureau of Applied Social Research at Columbia initiated interviews in seven Middle East countries, and we have read a number of interviews done in rural Anatolia and in Lebanon. When tradition-minded Turks were asked such questions as what were the main problems facing Turkey, they were stumped. They knew what faced *them*, but they could not identify with an

[7] "Social Class and Modes of Communication," *American Journal of Sociology*, Vol. 60, 1955, pp. 329–38. See also Raymond L. Gorden, *An Interaction Analysis of the Depth-Interview* (unpublished Ph.D. dissertation, University of Chicago, 1954).

[8] In "The Meaning of Opinion," (*Public Opinion Quarterly*, 12:633–48, 1949), Riesman and Glazer distinguish between "embarrassed" and "noncommittal" respondents (on the basis of other NORC surveys): the former wish to turn the interview into a sociable, friendly occasion, while the latter want to "give" no more than the minimum. In the Arkansas disaster survey, it was often the interviewers who, questioned by the respondents in an effort to make the encounter meaningful, reacted either as embarrassed or noncommittal. The deadpan tone of the latter, fending off unanticipated questions or disquieting revelations of respondent misery, often contrasted sharply in the tapes with the Biblical lilt of the respondents' initial comments (a contrast largely lost in transcription).

abstraction such as "Turkey"; they could not put themselves out of themselves enough for that.[9] Similarly, when they were asked where they would like to live other than in their village, they reacted in many cases by saying they could not conceive of this—they would rather die; whereas the modern Turk, oriented to mass communications, could readily pick his favorite world capital, such as Constantinople, Paris, or New York. The traditional Turk could not understand the play-acting or role-taking elements in the interview—a phenomenon not unconnected with his rejection of Turkish movies or radio as "unreal," and hence irrelevant for him. . . .

Undoubtedly an anthropologist would find these people accessible as informants, telling their tribe's stories or their own histories, but an interviewer has a hard time prying opinions from them, for they are only in the stage of "primitive accumulation" of them. As one thirty-year-old Turkish worker told an interviewer concerning an argument he had overheard about the wisdom of sending Turkish troops to Korea: "A silly argument. Nobody is asking our opinion. These are learned people. They know what is right and what is wrong better than we do."

To be sure, there are in this last answer elements one might readily find among the uneducated in this country. In Samuel Stouffer's book on public attitudes toward communism and civil liberties he reports asking people what are their main worries, and occasionally they say they aren't worrying about the planet—they pay taxes so that somebody else can do that for them.[10] However, when probed, such people *do* have opinions, and on such matters as war, peace, and wire tapping, opinions in the vein of those strata possessing greater education and articulateness. In contrast, the orbit of opinions maintained by the tradition-bound Turkish peasant, while it includes an age-old image of Russia as hostile and cruel, does not appear to transcend the orbit of unmediated experience. At the same time, there is some interesting evidence in these Middle East studies that those peasants who have allowed themselves to be exposed to mass communications are also those more capable of responding to the conventional opinion-frame of

---

[9] Somewhat analogously, lower-class Arkansas respondents were sometimes at a loss when asked, e.g., "How did your community (or Searcy or Judsonia) react to the tornado?" Such terms, beyond the kinfolk web, seemed to be too abstract.

[10] In *Communism, Conformity and Civil Liberties* (New York: Doubleday and Co., 1955).

the interview—it is as if mass communications train people in the personalized impersonality of the interview form, as well as providing a stock of opinions.[11]

IV

If we tie together what we said at the outset about the interview proceeding along lines of social and psychic cleavage and these all too fragmentary bits of cross-class and cross-cultural evidence, we may regard the spread of the interview into new areas as indicative of the spread of the modern temper, the modern forms of psychic mobility and communicativeness. Furthermore, whereas the first use of the interview is to get factual or objective information—for instance, who listens to the BBC—the interview increasingly tends to take as its overt topic the very subjective tensions which have, in general, brought the device into being, so that affective themes that once were secondary hindrances or byproducts become sought out for their own sake. One consequence is to shift the nature of the emphasis on rapport. This was once simply an instrumental device to get in the door and stay there while extracting information, and it of course must remain that with noncaptive interviewees; but the expanded use of the interview has made the encounter itself meaningful, the process as well as the product, as a quasi-transference, a symptom of the respondent's motivational patterns. Even demographers today are often interested in the census of feelings as well as of the traditional demographic facts.

And not only the researcher, but his subjects as well, are affected by the shift. Whereas, in the early days of social research, the tendency was for the lower-class respondent to be "captured" by the adventurous middle-class interviewer, today one reads more and more often of the captive interviewer, buttonholed by some Ancient Mariner of the country-club set, who uses the interviewer's innocent question about shaving-cream preferences to unburden himself of years of accumulated anxieties. In such circumstances the interviewer must maintain rapport not only with her respondent, but with her questionnaire and the time-schedule too; her problem is less one of being sociable, winning and sympathetic, than of persuading her respondent to be less so—to share with her the real and earnest tasks of information-gathering.

Much of this effort boils down to the truism that who you are may

[11] Cf. Lerner and Riesman: "Self and Society: Observations on Some Turks in Transition," p. 402.

speak louder than what you say. Interviewers often try to use the group memberships they share with the respondent in order to open up the channels of communication. We know, for instance, from work by Cantril and Stouffer that Negro respondents answer the same questions differently according to whether the interviewer is white or Negro; and Robinson and Rohde have shown that an interviewer with a Jewish appearance, or a Jewish-sounding name, affects what the respondent will express on anti-Semitic topics. Daniel Katz, Arthur Kornhauser, and Robert Merton have all shown that social-class differences can affect the interview product; and there is evidence, from the Office of War Information, that in certain circumstances local interviewers get significantly different results from nonlocal ones.[12]

Let us make clear that we are not suggesting that people are always more veracious when talking to interviewers from their own social class or ethnic group. Kornhauser's study showed that working-class interviewers in a Pittsburgh district got more prolabor responses from workers than middle-class interviewers did, and *The American Soldier* reports wartime experience that Negro interviewers "find" more antiwhite feeling among Negro troops than white interviewers do. Yet we face not always readily answerable questions as to which is the more valid response, and we can well imagine cases in which one's fellow group-member will evoke the stereotyped group feeling from which one can dare to free oneself when talking to a stranger.

Moreover, there is evidence, from Kornhauser's study and elsewhere, that interviewer training can go some way to minimize those disparities in group membership that are to some extent voluntary, such as social class, and a good interviewer can even go some distance to minimize involuntary memberships such as sex and ethnicity. Obviously, it matters what the topic is; the sex of the interviewer may be a reminder or barrier on certain topics and almost immaterial on others. (There exist, so far as we know, no research findings on the "shape" the interviewer is in—is he, for example, a Sheldonian mesomorph or an ectomorph?—though a paper by Jan Stapel in the *Public Opinion Quarterly* a few

[12] An excellent review of all these studies and additions to them are to be found in Herbert Hyman et al., *Interviewing in Social Research* (Chicago: University of Chicago Press (1954), c. IV. See also Robert K. Merton, "Selected Problems of Field Work in the Planned Community," *American Sociological Review*, June, 1947, pp. 304–12, which has some particularly valuable indices for rapport.

years ago discovered a difference in the political opinions of the fat and jolly as against the lean and hungry!)

Along with Shirley Star, we have recently completed a little study on sex and age as influencing communication in a mental health survey that Shirley Star directed in 1950. We chose sex and age as our group-membership characteristics for detailed investigation because, as Paul Sheatsley's NORC study and other data show, most survey and research interviewers are women; they are frequently housewives of that indeterminate age from thirty to fifty—indeed, research in this country depends (a) on the willingness of these women to put up with arduous if often interesting work for little pay—an indication of how much worse the privatized alternatives for educated but unskilled housewives are; and (b) on the ability of such women to go almost everywhere unescorted (though we recall the account one gave us as to how she would pick up a cop, tell him some story as to how she was afraid of her husband, and get him to wait outside when she went into an apartment in a tough neighborhood).

Moreover, we saw sex as interpenetrating with age to give individuals perhaps their most exigent role definitions in America, so much so that social class even at its most imperative may be seen as a form of defining differential sex behaviors at different ages.[18] We looked for questions where there might be variations depending on the age and sex of the communicators; unfortunately, we could not run comparisons by social class since most interviewers are almost necessarily from the middle class, the class which is trained in the white-collar tasks of communication and record-keeping. One question on the survey asked the respondents to consider the behavior of a young woman named "Betty White," to suggest "causes" for her schizophrenic conduct, and to say whether they think she is mentally ill. Of the national sample of 3500, 333 or 9.4 per cent gave answers indicating a sexual etiology, and we ran the cards to see which interviewers dealing with which respondents got proportionately more and less of such answers. It turned out that male interviewers got 60 per cent of responses that could be characterized as sexual from other males—and male interviewers under forty got a somewhat larger percentage than males over forty. Female interviewers likewise did "better" with females, but not as markedly so,

[18] We followed here the lead of Talcott Parsons' paper (on "Age and Sex in the Social Structure of the United States," *American Sociological Review*, October 1942, pp. 604-20) as well as his more recent discussions of the socialization process.

since only 54 per cent of their sex responses were from women—an indication, it may be, that women present a somewhat more neutral stimulus in the interview situation than men do, though it is probably also the case that the women interviewers were on the whole the more experienced and tenacious. Furthermore, female interviewers under forty got sexual responses from 16 per cent of their respondents, while those over forty got only 10 per cent—a difference that may in part represent the greater ease of communication between young women and in part the reminder-value of the interviewer herself that the imaginary Betty White is both young and a woman. (We got a rough measure of ease of communication by constructing a scale of satisfaction with the interview from data given by the interviewer concerning the respondent's co-operation and frankness, and we found there that older interviewers get more evasive responses than younger ones but are more readily satisfied with what they do get.) Young men interviewed by young men are least likely to mention sex in answer to a general question as to causes of insanity but are also least evasive when the interviewer probes about sex.

V

Interpretation of such findings is as yet extremely tentative and preliminary. We expect to find at work in material of this order secular trends regarding knowledge of sex as a factor in mental illness and regarding freedom of expression on the topic—trends that may perhaps operate most powerfully upon women.[14] In general, we may say that women interviewers do not appear to the respondent as "doctor, lawyer, merchant chief," and they may be somewhat more neutral as to occupation than men on the whole are.[15] By the same token, they may be less useful as interviewers once we begin to use interviews "anthropologically" rather than "social-psychologically"—that is, once we go after elite[16] groups, and highly specialized occupational groups rather than

[14] See a similar study reported in Hyman et al., *Interviewing in Social Research*, pp. 154 et seq.

[15] A male interviewer, unless clearly a student, will often seem "unsuccessful," while the role of housewife-interviewer is more indeterminate, with its quasi-amateur standing.

[16] I am not happy with the term "elite," with its connotations of superiority. Yet I have found no other term that is shorthand for the point I want to make, namely that people in important or exposed positions may require VIP interviewing treatment on the topics which relate to their importance or exposure. (D.R., 1955.)

the man in the street, or in the *n*th house. In dealing with such groups, the interviewer often needs to show—casually, not by a speech—that he shares a common class or occupational culture with the respondent if he is to be told the secrets of the occupation or power group; he needs the right mixture of the insider's semantics and the outsider's detachment; if he appears too innocent, as many women automatically would, it would seem hopeless to the respondent to communicate with him; if he appears too knowing, there may be no pleasure in instructing him, or indeed there may be fear and competitiveness. But at this point, the interview is no longer being used to communicate information from less privileged respondents to more privileged sponsors but rather as one of many techniques of communication within the highly differentiated occupational cultures of the upper strata. And by the same token, it is not nondirective, but probing and intrusive. We are reminded of the answer William H. Whyte, Jr., of *Fortune* gave one of us when we asked how he had managed in several months to find out so much about Park Forest, a new Chicago suburb. Whyte said: "You sociologists waste a lot of time worrying about securing rapport. I just wade in, ask what I want to know, and get the story." To be sure, it is not only women and sociologists who today are preoccupied with rapport; Whyte and a few other journalists, along with Groucho Marx, are among the few who are relatively impervious.

Fortune, however, like the Census Bureau, can get past certain gatekeepers we can elude only by generous doses of rapport. Rapport in the interview often means calling on group memberships shared with the respondent to obscure the lines of social cleavage which lead to the respondent in the first place. "Just between us girls" may obscure class differences; a generalized human friendliness shown by talk about the common coin of the weather or sports is advised by most books on industrial interviewing as a way of overcoming the cleavage between management and the worker. Rapport, that is, follows the lines of presumptively shared group memberships rather than of interest and ideology as such.

In the important book which Herbert Hyman and his collaborators have written on the interview, a case is presented in which rapport was superlatively good—both parties reported afterward how much they had enjoyed the encounter; it had been, Hyman says, "in the nature of two women friends having a 'hen party.'" Yet there is some evidence that the respondent, just because she liked the interviewer so much, wanted to learn the latter's opinions and felt pleased that, as she said, "we seemed to agree in our ways of feeling." Hyman speculates that the the respondent tailored her views to her image of this nice interviewer's views. And he contrasts this encounter with the case of a very hostile and aggressive respondent (who appeared to the interviewer to be pleasant enough, a case of parataxis or distortion) where nevertheless the interview "worked" in the sense of producing apparently reliable information. Indeed, it is our observation that interviewers and respondents are both likely to misjudge rapport (just as one finds in the analytic interview), and to give rather different accounts of feeling-tone when interviewed later about the interview.

Moreover, we think it is a prejudice, one often based on psychoanalytic stereotypes, to assume that the more rapport-filled and intimate the relation, the more "truth" the respondent will vouchsafe. In *Dynamics of Prejudice,* Bettelheim and Janowitz report on an interview study of ethnic attitudes among returning GIs. The interviews were done by young women who began by asking the veteran to tell them about their war experiences. Rapport ("tea and sympathy") was often intense[17]— and prejudice likewise. Reading the materials, we have the impression that the interviewees were on occasion using big talk to make an impact on the girls—as if the violent anti-Negro emotions were in some instances a kind of boasting, conceivably less "real" than the more conventional attitudes a more superficial encounter would have engendered. Obviously, as Bettelheim and Janowitz fully realize, it is a question of levels and alternatives and a question of what we are interested in—or, indeed, of social structure as well as of psychic structure—what we consider to be "deep" and hence sociologically meaningful. Certainly many interviewers, judging from interviews we have had with them, regard an interview as a good one in which intimacies are revealed, in which the respondent reveals marital or sexual problems for example, and in the NORC data and elsewhere we have found evidence that a respondent who truthfully answers "no opinion" or "don't know" is often considered unsatisfactory. In fact, in the literature and manuals on interviewing there is much more said on how to get the respondent to talk, to reveal himself, than on what seems to us the equally pressing problem of getting him to stop talking, to interrupt the flow of legend and cliché with which rapport-filled interviews often overflow.

In this connection, some comments by Cannell and Kahn of the

[17] See *Dynamics of Prejudice* (New York: Harper and Bros., 1950), pp. 10–11.

Survey Research Center are interesting. The Center asked respondents who had been interviewed in the annual Survey of Consumer Finances concerning their incomes, savings, and buying plans to comment by mail about their reactions to being interviewed. The authors declare:[18]

> Their replies were more often couched in terms of the personal relationship and personal qualities of the interviewer than in terms of the content of the study or the apparent purpose of the inquiry. Typical comments mentioned the fact that the interviewer was a very understanding person or that the interviewer had a keen insight into the respondent's situation.

Since interviewees are free to refuse and break off, it is understandable that interviewers will want to structure the encounter in an engaging conversational way, assisted by the semantics of many focused interviews which lead from one topic to another by easy stages and such phrases as "do you happen to know" or other ways of making light of any lacunae of information or derelictions of conventional civic duty. And financial data are, according to one set of NORC interviewer reports, and according to what many interviewers have told us, the most disagreeable to get, more so than sexual attitudes.

Yet, as this last example may imply, interviewers and interviewing agencies can easily develop conventions, based on their own traditions and needs, which blind them to other possible modes of maintaining the interview as a going concern. Often the interviewer will find it hard to get information he himself would not readily vouchsafe. Thus, on the Mental Health study previously referred to, the interviewers themselves first took the interviews and, upon reading these, one can find many who were uncomfortable about sex and mental hygiene generally; we have some impressionistic evidence that they sometimes communicated this and "found" an equally disquieted respondent. Conventions of what one tells and withholds vary, of course, among the classes, regions, and ethnic groups of this country, and the interviewer may easily project her own misgivings into the situation.[19] Often the best interviewers appear to be those who first persuade themselves as

---

[18] See C. F. Cannell and R. L. Kahn, "The Collection of Data by Interviewing," in Leon Festinger and Daniel Katz, *Research Methods in the Behavioral Sciences* (New York: Dryden Press, 1953), p. 356.

[19] Interviewing agencies are themselves subject to similar sensitivities, and very widely in the extent to which they feel justified in collecting religious, ethnic, and political data about the interviewers they employ.

to the vital importance of the survey and everything in it, and they seldom encounter refusals or withholdings.

VI

It would be a mistake, however, to assume that the respondent is merely passive in all this, and can never take over the interview and talk to the sponsor, if necessary over the head of the interviewer. Likewise, many respondents will gladly share the trained interviewer's task-oriented conception of the encounter: the opportunity to help the interviewer in her task is frequently exploited to minimize status differences. Viditch and Bensman provide an illustration in their article on "The Validity of Field Data"; there they report.[20]

> In a difficult joint interview between a husband and wife, which required them to discuss certain problems, respondents would remind their spouses of failures to fulfil the instruction to "discuss" with the remark that "this is not what they wanted." When couples failed to fulfil the instructions and saw that they had failed, they frequently apologized for their "ignorance" or ineptitude, and usually expressed a hope that they might be of further help on another occasion.

We suspect that what we would find, if we were able to hold interviewer-effect constant, would be much the same gamut of attitudes among respondents that Gregory Stone and his colleagues have found to exist among women shoppers, where some are "economic men" and others personalize the relation to the sales clerk or the store and still others grind an ideological ax by shopping in their neighborhood stores out of parish loyalty.[21] But of course the interviewer herself by her very presence, by the identifications she cannot help creating, does a lot, especially in unstructured situations, to cue the respondent—the "Sheriff-effect" operates here too. Many studies have shown that this is not a question of bias in the direction of the interviewer's own opinion; indeed, studies now under way at Cornell indicate that those students make the best fieldworkers who are the most judgmental, the most pas-

[20] *Human Organization*, vol. 13, 1954, pp. 20–27.
[21] See, e.g., Stone, "City Shoppers and Urban Identification: Observations on the Social Psychology of City Life," *American Journal of Sociology*, vol. 60, 1954, pp. 36–45; also Stone, William H. Form, and Hazel B. Strahan, "The Social Climate of Decision in Shopping for Clothes," *Journal of Home Economics*, vol. 46, 1954, pp. 86–88.

sionate about their values—once they can learn to go after those values in a roundabout way through reliable and objective interviewing.[22] Rather, as many studies have shown, and as these remarks have already implied, interviewing itself is a middle-class profession, in pursuit of middle-class concerns: in matter and manner these tend to set the stage. The results secured are not necessarily misleading, once we can allow for the "ether drift" produced by this factor, as it operates through the personalities and schedules with which respondents are confronted in survey research.

Sometimes, however, as we well know, the results can be misleading. Not long ago, a study in a Hawaiian shipping company, done by means of interviews conducted by an outside agency, showed that middle management was discontented, but that the workers were quite satisfied. A short time later the workers surprised everyone by going on a bitter strike. Another look at the interviews showed that the workers didn't think of their problems as gripes. The form of the interview drew out the complaints of middle management, but not those of the workers. Not till the latter struck did they succeed in their communication.

One of us has previously reported on a somewhat analogous experience in the Elmira election study of 1948.[23] There some workers in pre-election interviews would say that they were against the Taft-Hartley law, that they were union members and thought well of the union, that they would like Truman for a lodge brother, and so on, but when asked their vote intention said they planned to vote for Dewey. The interviewers in such cases did not for the most part challenge the respondent; they did not say: "Look here. You tell me you are for the working class, and that you think Truman is, yet you intend to vote for Dewey. How come?" Such conduct might have decimated the panel; it also ran against the grain of the accepting nondirective role—a role which, one might argue, is conventionally suited to women in our

[22] See Stephen A. Richardson, *A Study of Selected Personality Characteristics of Social Science Field Workers* (mimeo., 1954).

[23] See "The Meaning of Opinion," note *supra*, at p. 13. See further: Bernard R. Berelson, Paul Lazarsfeld, William M. McPhee, *Voting*, Chicago: University of Chicago Press, 1954; Chapters 7 and 12 of this report on the Elmira Study deal with the rallying to Truman of previously ambivalent voters and give substantive reasons for their shift of attitude apart from the interviewing context—on the basis of the total survey it is hard to say to what degree the interviewing could itself have helped better to predict the late rise of the Democrats.

society unless they wish to be labeled back-seat drivers in the lower-middle class and "castrating females" among the college-bred. However, later investigation showed that those workers who had expressed themselves in the way described frequently ended up voting for Truman, and it may be that a more challenging interview might occasionally have brought this "truer" intention to light. Tentatively, we interpret this Elmira experience less in terms of conscious duplicity by a working-class respondent concealing a pro-Truman outlook (although no doubt this occurred) than in terms of the interview confirming the respondent's unthought-out assumption in Dewey's favor in so heavily Republican an environment as Elmira; he would as little think of Truman as of cussing the nice interviewer out.[24]

VII

Since the emphasis on rapport is so beautifully compatible with many current tendencies in American life, it is not surprising that we sometimes find interviews used to discover things which demographic data can more easily and more accurately reveal. An example is a survey which was reported on at an AAPOR meeting in 1950. The millers had engaged a market-research firm to do interviews with a national sample on people's attitudes toward bread, in an effort to discover why bread consumption was declining. The researcher reported woefully

[24] Since writing the foregoing, we have come across the ingenious experiment done by Lieutenant Arthur Greenberg in an election study in 1952 (under the direction of Professor Lester A. Guest at Pennsylvania State University). One control group of respondents was simply asked conventionally whether they were going to vote for Eisenhower or Stevenson and what reasons they would give to support their choice; an experimental matched group was told: "Now we are going to play a game. Pretend that I am someone you want to convince of your vote intention, and tell me why I should vote for . . . (whoever was the respondent's choice)." When the respondent gave reasons, the interviewer was coached to say, "You're getting warm," or "You're not getting very far," but not to go beyond those probes. Respondents played the game eagerly, and it turned out that the range of reasons they gave for voting for their candidate was fuller, and more vivid, than was the case with those who were polled in the conventional way; moreover, this initial difference carried on throughout the interview, although the dialectical technique was used only at the start.

See also the interesting comments on S. F. Nadel's "bullying" technique (as described in Phillip H. Lewis' "The Field Methods of S. F. Nadel") in *Anthropology Tomorrow*, Vol. 3, May 1955, pp. 14–23 (a publication of the anthropology students at the University of Chicago).

that it was dreadfully hard to interest people in talking about bread— even "motivational research" couldn't get very far, nor did it become clear from what respondents said why they had stopped eating bread, save for those women who were dieting. Yet, as Hans Zeisel pointed out in discussion, if we studied census data on urbanization and on the shift away from manual labor, we could clearly demarcate the areas of declining bread consumption all over the Western world: people moved from country to city, from factory to office, but didn't know that this would leave them eating fewer loaves.

The point is that we are oriented to people; we want response and respondents. A form of communication which typically allows or even encourages the subordinate to reveal rather than suppress affects in the course of conveying information appears to us as democratic; the liberation of affect in the interview confines both parties to the "human" level, even while it may misleadingly elevate the respondent to the level at which "everybody" votes for Dewey, or at least votes, contributes to the community chest, and possesses a driver's license (all items overstated on surveys).

As democratization spreads, moreover, through the interview and symbolized by the interview, interviewers themselves may be expected to become increasingly sensitive to the encounter with the working class. Even now, every effort is made to reduce questionnaires to words of one syllable—so much so that educated respondents are hard put to it to fit their complex reactions into the dichotomized simplicity imposed by the questionnaire.[25] Interviewers are trained to use slang and colloquialisms; and doubtless many of the social gestures they make before beginning the formal interview are designed to put lower-class respondents at their ease—well-trained employment interviewers have indeed institutionalized this to such degree that they customarily call their informants by their first name. In our Kansas City Study of Adult Life, the interviewers trained in the University of Chicago ethos have been very sensitive to the problems of rapport with lower-class respondents, and have actually sometimes found them easier of access than upper-class members. The middle class has always been the mediating class, the communicating class, and it is arguable that it now talks down almost as readily as up.

[25] Cf. K. W. Back, R. Hill and J. M. Stycos, "Interviewer Effect on Scale Reproducibility," *American Sociological Review*, vol. 20, 1955, pp. 443–46.

A useful example appears in the book by members of the Yale Department of Psychiatry: *The Initial Interview in Psychiatric Practice*.[26] The book contains three verbatim reports of "intake" interviews, along with comments by the authors; it is one of a number of recent publications which creditably reproduce complete interviews taken from wire recordings (in this case one can get the recording itself as well) and which enormously facilitate the kind of "secondary analysis" toward which these remarks of ours are intended to throw out introductory leads and highly tentative generalizations. The second interview in the Yale book is done by a third-year medical student with a working-class man, a truck driver, who suffers from headaches. The student is frightened; he makes many errors; yet he establishes contact; neither the patient's slang nor his sex life throws the student off—both are men and can share aspects of a male culture which is above, or below, class.

It is often, however, much more difficult to get in touch with a patient who lives in a Tennessee Williams kind of world of artificial gentility and movie imagery. The third interview in the Yale book is one with a young schizophrenic woman who is, we assume, of lower-middle-class origin but who has stocked her imagination with upper-class symbols of sensibility. The doctor in this case is able and sensitive, but his qualities of empathy and reassurance do not seem to suffice for a woman whose urgent problem is to communicate the special quality her world has for her. Every so often he makes contact, but she is far too elusive and allusive, and, concluding that she cannot communicate with this inquisitive stranger, she withdraws still further, appears still more obscure.

It is of course hard if not impossible to say whether a therapist of wild fantasy like Harry Stack Sullivan or John Rosen might have given her at least the illusion of being understood; there are times when the Yale therapist appeared to get her point without her noticing the fact. In some nondirective interviews which we have read, however, it would seem that empathy is not enough for a patient faced, through experience or class origins, with themes alien to the therapist's own outlook. Likewise, therapists (whose own class origins have probably shifted) may be relatively more sensitive today, as compared with the situation a generation ago, to differences "downward" than "upward" in the social structure. Many of our students appear to be more willing to learn some-

[26] Merton Gill, Richard Newman, and F. C. Redlich, *The Initial Interview in Psychiatric Practice* (New York: International Universities Press, 1954).

thing of the language and semantic forms of the lower strata than of the less numerous but no less differentiated upper strata. Just as Freud revolutionized psychiatry by making the feelings of women as well as the pains of men medically relevant, so one aspect of the democratic revolution has been to make relevant not only the feelings of the boss or monarch but also the feelings of the depressed classes—the groups we might delimit as those for whom nondirectiveness has been emancipating; and it is sometimes a corollary that only those feelings are "allowed" that can be widely communicated and shared.

VIII

For the therapist and counselor, however, there remains one monarch, one authority, to protect him from the ultimate consequences of encouraging the flow of affect upward in the social system: this authority is the clock, to which both parties in the relationship are trained to be subordinate. The clock is at once a reminder that the day's work brings many tasks, and an enabling agent for the interviewer's task-orientation as contrasted with his mood-orientation. But as we know the mandate of the clock does not run in all jurisdictions. Alice Bauer, who has done some interesting work on problems of interviewing Soviet refugees for the Russian Research Center at Harvard, says that when the work-minded Americans tried to get the respondents in the camps to stick to the point, the latter took this as a slight on their own idiosyncratic humanity and the tale it alone had to tell and sabotaged the interview by refusing to open up. Only when the interviewers encouraged the respondents to express their private biography, to vouchsafe events and attitudes which were their very own, would they later be willing to volunteer the more standardized types of information concerning, for instance, the extent of Party membership in their office or plant. Not only did this mean very protracted interviews but also the creation of entangling dependency relations in which the interviewers were haunted by the personal plight of their respondents and could not easily at night shut out the day's encounters. There are evident resemblances between these interviews and those done in Arkansas by the NORC disaster team—there, too, the mandate of the clock did not run and interviewers, once invited into the respondent's world, found it hard to take their leave. We suggest that while in both cases the disaster was the proximate cause of this refusal to be bound by temporal norms, the cultural factors were the more important ones. Indeed, in our Kansas

City study, it would sometimes seem that old age is for many a kind of chronic emergency, chronic disaster, and that the old, once they are treated with an interviewer's patient civility, have a hard time letting go —we may judge by the many interviews, scheduled for an hour and a half, which run to four hours or more. (The interviewers we refer to were mostly trained people on salary, not being paid by the hour.)

To be sure, what the schedule of appointments is for the therapist and interviewer on their own home grounds, the schedule of questions or of foci is for the interviewer doing a house-to-house or street survey. Likewise, the notes on a clipboard or a tape recorder are a reminder that the sponsor's ghost hovers over the conversation, objectifying it. (One of the topics our Interview Project is examining is the different symbolic meanings of notes and recordings for different sorts of respondents—for old and young, for the science-minded and the haters of gadgets, and so on. Very likely, as Shirley Star has pointed out to us, these meanings are not highly structured for a great many respondents and the definition of their meaning lies in the interviewer's hands, and how he or she feels —the Yale psychiatrists who published their initial interviews have some observant things to say of the anxiety-provoking effects on them of knowing they were being "overheard," anxieties they sometimes tended to project onto the patient.)

In these remarks, we have confined ourselves to the areas we know best (or least inadequately), and not presented as we would like someday to be able to do, a more formal and systematic ecology of the interview: a statement as to who interviews whom, for what purposes, in what contexts, and with what effects in the country at large. We do know that the interview is taking on something of the nature of a *rite de passage* as one moves from one institution to another, from school to army to job to other jobs and finally to the gerontological social worker; we know that our semantics are changing, so that we are likely to say "I'm going for an interview about a job" rather than "I'm going to see a man about a job"; and we know that play-forms of interviewing on radio and television programs, where an audience member is interviewed by a master of ceremonies, are becoming an increasingly popular entertainment. These images and experiences, it would seem, help to pretrain, one might almost say precode, people to become respondents, and the media certainly play a vital role in defining what is public opinion and what is private opinion, what is important and what is peripheral. As the formal research interview grows, it itself feeds into this process, while in turn drawing for its forms on current conversational styles.

Our image of a not too distant America is of a series of groups in the opinionated strata preforming themselves into Lazarsfeldian panels and only waiting for the interviewer to turn up to quiz them! A procedure that began as a way of relieving and releasing social tensions and individual ones is developing, like other industries and institutions, a certain functional autonomy, transcending the imperatives of personal and cultural dissension that called it into being. While motivation research may for a time reduce the number while stepping up the intensity of market research interviews, it would seem that the interviewer—already a standard figure in cartoons—will become as omnipresent a figure in the society of the future as the investigator. But whereas the investigator is a figure of fear, even when we have nothing to hide, the research interviewer, with his conventions of transience, personalized impersonality, and protection for anonymity, more often than not leaves a pleasant afterglow. At its best, the interview is an exchange of intangibles in which both parties gain in esteem and understanding, and nobody loses.

Orbits of Tolerance, Interviewers, and Elites
(1955)

Recent poll data, and particularly Professor Samuel A. Stouffer's *Communism, Conformity, and Civil Liberties*,[1] raise an almost infinite series of questions concerning what might be termed the ecology of tolerance for political and cultural dissent; they show, on a great variety of civil-liberties issues, that the educated are relatively more tolerant than the uneducated—this is the most salient difference, even when one sorts it out from age, income, and region; that the young are more tolerant than the old; men than women; people in the Far West and East than in the South and Midwest. "Tolerance," of course, is a word of many meanings; I shall not seek to unravel them here, but rather to develop Stouffer's own conclusion that tolerance as he defines it goes together with wide orbits of education, work, and travel; I shall hope to clarify his and similar data and to suggest some of their implications for the future of political leadership. And since I believe that the data may be somewhat clarified by a better understanding of the methods used in obtaining them, I want to dwell on some of the interviewing problems involved, and especially on Stouffer's innovation in interviewing simultaneously a national cross-section and a sample of "community leaders" —mayors, bar association presidents, PTA heads, DAR regents, and so on. This research design is a contribution to our understanding of the institutionalization and rationalization of political attitudes, but one requiring development of a more systematic distinction between anthropological interviewing of informants and poll interviewing of respondents on such bifurcated political surveys.

[1] New York: Doubleday, 1955. For discussion of the poll data, see Nathan Glazer and S. M. Lipset, "The Polls on Communism and Conformity," and Lipset, "The Sources of the 'Radical Right,'" both in Daniel Bell, ed., *The New American Right* (New York: Criterion Books, 1955); see especially pp. 197–99 and sources there cited. The latter of these is also reprinted in Daniel Bell, *The Radical Right* (*The New American Right*, revised and updated) (New York: Doubleday, 1963).

I

As if Maxwell's demons occasionally slept and occasionally guarded the gates of privilege, two processes appear to be going on simultaneously in this country: homogenization and differentiation. Equalization is proceeding between city and country, between the social and occupational strata, and between the sexes—this we know or think we know from many sources; by the same token, differentiation proceeds among the age-grades, and remains large (as we shall see) between North and South and between the college-educated and those of lesser academic exposure. And as soon as we move away from the gross demographic variables which, as it were, populate the boxes in polling studies, we find enormous polarizations of opinion: between, for instance, the tiny minority (in Stouffer's data, less than 1 per cent) who are worried about the state of civil liberties and the overwhelming majority who have other things (and often literally, things: cars, diseases, houses, etc.) on their minds. Pollers, however, are not happy if they have 99 per cent in one cell and 1 per cent in another—even if the latter, on a national sample survey of adults, number a million people concentrated in certain crucial callings; thus, Stouffer does not linger over the fact that while among the college educated as a whole 5 per cent are much troubled over erosions of freedom, the figure rises to 12 per cent among the presidents of County Bar Associations in his subsample of community leaders—a possibly significant index (speaking here socially, not statistically, for the numbers are small: cf. note 33, infra) of the role or potential role of the bar and judiciary as professional protectors of civil liberties.

Nevertheless, what he does do is to compare this special population of leaders, found in towns and cities of 10,000 to 150,000 population, with the whole nation, with the "more interested" part of it, and with people at large in the same cities as the leaders. In every such comparison, the leaders, exposed as they are to wider orbits of communication, give more tolerant, more differentiated responses; this is true even of the heads of the DAR and of the American Legion. Unfortunately, no direct comparisons are made between educated leaders and those equally well educated and otherwise demographically similar who are not leaders.[2]

[2] In a helpful discussion of an earlier draft of this paper, Professor Stouffer called my attention to the table on page 104 which indicates that 79 per cent of the college-educated community leaders are among the "more tolerant" on his scale of tolerance, as compared with 66 per cent for the general college-educated population (p. 90).

However, when we see that the leaders of labor unions are not as tolerant as Chamber of Commerce presidents, we can suppose that the latter are the better educated—while the former would perhaps be even less tolerant (and thus resemble the noncollege educated more closely) were they not exposed to communications from the Democratic party and the national headquarters.

In an analysis along these lines, it might turn out that education plays its decisive role in making for what is here defined as tolerance because for many it constitutes acculturation to the ideology of the assured and successful, and that this leads (in Merton's distinction[3]) to "cosmopolitan" leadership, while "local" leadership involves becoming a middleman of tolerance, exposed on the one side to the tolerant views of the social elite and on the other to the more xenophobic and intolerant views of the constituency from which one sprang and on whose votes one still depends. Indeed, the cosmopolitan leaders who, before they were put into leadership roles, might have expressed an unequivocal ideology of tolerance, might be exposed through leadership to less tolerant opinions which they partly undermine or sabotage in protecting their "classmates" but also partly succumb to; along such lines, I suggest, we must explain the Stouffer finding that mayors and school board presidents are the most reluctant among his fifteen leader categories to allow a Communist the right to speak (save for the DAR regents and women's-club presidents who are, of course, less intolerant than women in general), for these are presumably the holders of the most vulnerable positions who have to face the music from both the tolerant elite and the intolerant majority.[4]

[3] See Robert K. Merton, "Patterns of Influence: A Study of Interpersonal Influence and of Communications Behavior in a Local Community," in Paul F. Lazarsfeld and Frank Stanton, eds., *Communications Research 1948–1949* (New York: Harper & Bros., 1949), pp. 180–219.

The decisive role of education in making for tolerance is further suggested by Herbert Hyman and Paul Sheatsley's evidence that differences in ethnocentrism can be as readily correlated with differences in formal education as with differences in character structure. See their article, "'The Authoritarian Personality'—A Methodological Critique," in Richard Cristie and Marie Jahoda eds., *Studies in the Scope and Method of "The Authoritarian Personality"* (Glencoe, Ill.: The Free Press, 1954), pp. 50–122.

[4] Lewis Dexter has suggested to me that it would be worthwhile to reinterview many of these men after they had retired from office and were presumably no longer exposed either to the tests of action or to communica-

It would be an error for those who have not read the Stouffer book or other poll data to infer from this that the community leaders are particularly enlightened: one can qualify as "more tolerant" on Stouffer's scale even if one's views would mark one as reactionary in academia, and I think it would be more correct to say that even the least liberal of the leaders does not share the general bigotry of the population when it comes to such matters as irreligious or socialist books or speakers or teachers. And such a division is of course the general poll experience: on every issue where orbits of experience matter, education (whatever may be bound up with it as an index: social class, energy, exposure to diverse or proper views, etc.) is crucial.

However, Stouffer reports an exception to this general rule: when he asked his respondents what the best way was to stop the Communists in Europe and Asia, whether by fight, flight, talk, withdraw (or don't know), the community leaders gave virtually the same answers as the general sample, differing by at most 2 per cent. Thus, 20 per cent of both groups opt for allowing the Communists to take over Asia; 59 per cent or 57 per cent would fight to prevent this; and 21 per cent or 23 per cent don't know. Perhaps a further breakdown would show that this really startling identity is spurious—is the result of differences canceling each other out; for instance, the leaders' greater ability to differentiate may lead some to reject the given alternatives and answer "don't know" out of wisdom, whereas among the general sample "don't know" is more likely to mean "don't care": the paucity of alternatives may be the reason why leaders and led are herded into the same boxes. However, we must remember that these are *community* leaders being asked about international matters—matters outside their usual orbits of experience if not of discourse, matters on which it may be that both they and the population at large must accept the dimensions structured for them by national leaders and national media.

To carry this further, we should look at the functions of the institutions in which these leaders are officeholders. They form an unsystematic and unrepresentative sampling of interest groups and social groups, and perhaps only four of the fourteen could normally be expected to have an institutional policy in the field of international af-

---

tions from both camps—a problem somewhat analogous to that raised by *Voting* concerning the softening of polarizations between political campaigns. Cf. Bernard Berelson, Paul F. Lazarsfeld, and William McPhee, *Voting*, (Chicago: University of Chicago Press, 1954), Chapter 13.

fairs. It is as policy makers or policy interpreters that the local leaders tend to rise through their organizations, and thus to differentiate themselves from the rank-and-file; they expect and are expected, in the area of their organization's interests, to be "advanced." But to the degree that their organizations don't have to have policies on such matters as foreign relations, they cease to be leaders in any important sense; that is, their opinions on these matters are not likely to be argued on a platform, let alone put to a vote.

Even so, I remain perplexed: it is hard to find in poll-data cases where elite or educated and popular opinion converge so closely. Historical trends are relevant: the National Opinion Research Center and other surveys show that since World War II the lower classes' perennial distrust of Russia (as of other foreigners) has grown somewhat, while the educated classes, less immune to the news and its interpretation, have moved much more—from relative friendliness to a position much closer to that of the uneducated.[5] However, as Glazer and Lipset point out in their article in *The New American Right*, the upper strata, once convinced of the dangers of Soviet imperialism, are much readier to make sacrifices at the behest of the military and civil leadership than the lower strata whose xenophobia includes distrust of army brass and of appeals for sacrifice.[6] But this again leaves me bewildered in the face of the identical elite and general willingness in the Stouffer survey to fight in Asia—and I fall back on the possibility that the weight of an opinion to this effect differs in the several strata, or the hardly more

[5] Paul Sheatsley at the AAPOR meetings in 1955 presented the following example: in 1947, 44 per cent of grammar school graduates would deny a Communist the right to speak on the radio as compared with 78 per cent in 1954, while in 1947, 31 per cent of the educated would deny the right as against 71 per cent in 1954. Stouffer's Appendix E cites many similar studies and throughout he makes use of polls to give historical depth to his own survey results.

[6] See "The Polls on Communism and Conformity," in Note 1, *supra*. Paul Sheatsley has called my attention to an October 1955 NORC poll in which people were asked, "If Communist armies attack any other countries in the world, do you think the U.S. should stay out of it, or should we help defend these countries like we did in Korea?" Of the college group, 66 per cent answered "help defend"; of the high school group, 51 per cent; and of the grammar school group, 46 per cent. This is the typical pattern. In the light of this and other polls it would seem that the phrase, "fight in Asia," brings to those with more education an image of very concrete consequences, whereas those with less education need a more specific reference to Korea before they back away from the consequences.

statisfactory explanation that a national consensus among all classes can be reached where decisive events, remote from both community leaders and followers, can be decisively interpreted from the top.

A similar tendency to convergence, but only among businessmen, is to be found in an MIT study of attitudes toward the tariff.[7] In a poll in 1938, 7 per cent of big businessmen favored high tariffs as against 42 per cent of men in smaller business; by the time of the 1954 MIT survey, 41 per cent of men in firms of over 1000 employees wanted lower tariffs as against 37 per cent in firms of from 100 to 999 employees. Bauer believes that between the two dates, the more world-minded views of top business leaders had trickled down to the rest of the business community, though size of firm—a rough index of breadth of orbit —still made a measurable difference. However, on a national cross-section, education serves as usual as a decisive dividing point: Bauer cites a Roper poll showing that extreme free traders are more apt to be Republicans—61 per cent to 39 per cent—whereas extreme protectionists are more often Democrats—56 per cent to 44 per cent, but this in turn is an artifact of education, since the more highly educated are more likely to be well-off Republicans, so that a college-educated Democrat will as frequently be an ultrafree trader as his Republican counterpart.

II

Education itself is not unrelated to region; Warner and Abegglen show that Ivy League colleges, and eastern schools generally, contribute disproportionately to top business careers.[8] Stouffer's data on regional variations in tolerance for dissent are among the most fascinating in his book; our problem is to seek to relate them to a theory of orbits and communication. The South, not surprisingly, is by far the least tolerant section; yet, as we have already seen, southern men who go to college end up about as tolerant as those of like education in the Far West, the most tolerant section; of course, Southern narrowness of orbit is part of a socio-economic pattern in which relatively few do go to college. Eastern college men are somewhat more tolerant than Far Western ones (perhaps in some part because of the greater number of Jews), but among those of lower education the Far West is more tolerant than the

[7] A preliminary report by Raymond A. Bauer appears in *Fortune*, Vol. 51, April 1955, p. 238.
[8] See W. Lloyd Warner and James Abegglen, *Big Business Leaders in America* (New York: Harper & Bros., 1955).

East; perhaps the "wide people" go to the open spaces in fact as well as fancy. What lowers the level of tolerance in the Midwest is the lack of differentiation between metropolis, small town, and farm there; rural attitudes, that is, retain a greater hegemony—in that sense, the Chicago *Tribune*, with its slick city merchandising of rural suspiciousness, is not unrepresentative. Conrad Arensberg marshals evidence to show that patterns of city settlement in the Midwest trace back to European patterns very different from those of New England or the South;[9] do we meet these ancient legacies in Stouffer's findings? Are the cities of the Plains, whether they began as trading centers or mill towns, less cosmopolitan than the ports of either coast? Are the orbits shorter that bring people from Kentucky to Detroit or from the Ozarks to Kansas City than those that bring Richmond Negroes to Harlem or Iowa readers of Cowles newspapers to San Diego? As an aspect of this, are the kin ties of farm-born city people closer in the Midwest than on either coast?[10]

National merchandisers such as Sears, Roebuck, having found that regional differences in consumer styles are disappearing, are dispensing with regional catalogues;[11] moreover, ads for consumer goods in farm journals, wherever issued, tend to approximate urban norms.[12] Professor Reuel Denney, inquiring about bobby sox styles at Stephens College, reports that the girls recognize three: an Eastern casual type; a Midwest neat, low type; and a Far West high style (the South, a "colony," does not appear to have a style of its own). At any rate, the regional differences in psychic and political tolerance that Stouffer dis-

[9] "American Communities," *American Anthropologist*, vol. 57, 1955, pp. 1143–62.

[10] E. Z. Vogt has some suggestive comments on orbits of travel among rural Texans, bounded by cultural compatibilities, kin ties, and traditions of movement, in "American Subcultural Continua as Exemplified by the Mormons and Texans," *American Anthropologist*, vol. 57, 1955, pp. 1163–72, cf. pp. 1166–67.

[11] Louis Harris, to whom I am indebted for many valuable suggestions, believes that Sears may draw from different strata in different regions—a difference hidden by uniformity of sales; his own observations as an interviewer in many parts of the country indicate that differences in styles remain substantial.

[12] Henry Carsh, a graduate student in sociology at the University of Chicago, made a content analysis of *Ebony* which indicated how the ads increasingly featured Negroes—a sign of differentiation—although in activities which stressed their similarity to white middle-class norms.

closes are sizable. For example, Table 2 in Chapter 5 shows that at the grade school level only 4 per cent of Southerners living in medium-size cities classify as "more tolerant" as compared to 35 per cent in the Far West; among high school graduates living in large cities 57 per cent classify as "more tolerant" on both coasts, as compared with 42 per cent in the Midwest and 26 per cent in the South.

Among community leaders, however, as we would expect, these differences are much reduced, with those in the South and Midwest far more tolerant in comparison with the nonelite in their own region than those of the generally more tolerant East and West. That is, the elite and the overlapping group of the male college-educated are nationally fairly homogeneous—one thinks again of Merton's "cosmopolitans" in his Rovere study who read *Time* and are members of the school and library boards. Short of graduation from college, however, Southerners are far less tolerant than similarly-educated Northerners; this means that the college graduate in the South is, in these respects, quite sharply cut off from the rest of the community, including even those with some college attendance, for although education is everywhere associated with tolerance, the gradations are much less steep in the North. Moreover, much the same is true in the South for metropolitan communities against smaller cities, though in this dimension there are substantial differences in the East as well.

Ethnic data would add to our understanding of this material. Farm and metropolis in some Midwestern areas are linked by ethnic homogeneity, whereas ethnic and religious factors divide New York City from upstate. How complex these factors can be is illustrated by James M. Shipton's study of intergroup images and attitudes in "Bay City."[13] This is a Massachusetts manufacturing city of some 50,000, with a Catholic majority. Lower-class Protestants in the city are the most anti-Semitic group, while Protestants of higher status are least anti-Semitic; the Catholic strata are in between, with lower-class Catholics less intolerant than equally disadvantaged Protestants, and higher-status Catholics more intolerant than their Protestant class peers. To venture an interpretation, it would seem as if Yankees of higher education share an Enlightenment (and perhaps in some cases also an Old Testament) culture with the Jews and a prejudice against the Irish Catholics, while

[13] *Reference Groups in the Formation of Public Opinion*, unpublished preliminary report, Center for Field Studies, Harvard Graduate School of Education, 1955, Part I.

the lower-class Protestants feel an envy and resentment akin to that which many urban Negroes feel for the Jews. These Protestants feel tension between their social status and their economic status of the sort Richard Hofstadter and Talcott Parsons both describe in their articles in *The New American Right*. Meanwhile, the Catholic group may be moving away from the Jews, with whom they were often politically linked in an earlier day, in part as the result of their own Americanization and in part as a result of diverging attitudes toward foreign policy— attitudes that are driving some Catholics out of the Democratic party.

For indeed political parties operate, as S. M. Lipset states in a recent article, [14] much as churches and colleges do—they may lead people into an orbit outside their rural or ethnic or class base as unwilling or unwitting captives of an idea (tolerance, for instance) which is historically linked to the party's platform, premises, and promise. The lower classes tend to vote Democratic, as data from the Centers' and other polls indicate, because of underdog attitudes toward government spending, control of business, and like matters; this links them by organizational and rhetorical ties to a party which has historically stood for free trade and which has been pulled and pushed by events and leadership into favoring civil liberties and restricting xenophobia. The polls, in other words, pull asunder what the parties join together; they show the popular and Populist roots of xenophobia. Thus, the Democratic party county chairmen in the Stouffer elite sample are less tolerant than their presumably better-educated Republican opposite numbers—but no doubt, as official Democrats, they are more tolerant than their kin among the uneducated and, as partisans, possibly more tolerant in practice than the Republican chairmen.[15] But to explore this further we would need to study elites within the elites (as the MIT reciprocal

[14] Delivered at the Milan Conference of the Congress for Cultural Freedom, September 1955.

[15] In view of the small numbers, and the differences between the NORC and AIPO halves of the sample, such interpretations rest of course on shaky foundations in the data. Cf. note 33, infra. An interesting Gallup poll of a special population was made by mail ballot in November 1955, among Democratic county chairmen across the country, asking them their candidate preferences and expectations. Their *preferences*, e.g., for Stevenson, 42 per cent, and for Kefauver, 14 per cent, did not depart too widely from those of rank-and-file Democrats; but their *expectations*—the party ties that bind—were for Stevenson 78 per cent and Kefauver 3 per cent. See AIPO release of December 6, 1955.

trade study has been doing), right up to the very top of the several relevant hierarchies.

III

As every study director knows, no public opinion poll, no matter how large or how imaginatively stratified the sample, turns up enough cases (or data) to answer the questions its results raise. Even Stouffer's 5000 rapidly melt when, for instance, he wants to see whether age is correlated with intolerance once one holds education, region, and urban-exposure constant. What I have been doing here is to read his book and related polls as detective stories in which the reader must supply essential clues. One such clue turned up in a study of a well-to-do Canadian suburb which examined in close detail the different value structures of men and women.[16] The men are, in their ideology, fairly rugged individualists, while their wives believe in co-operation and groupism; yet, when it comes to dealing at home or school with their own children, it is the wives who defend them against patriarchal legalism and who insist on their right to be idiosyncratic. It is possible that somewhat comparable ambiguities are involved in Stouffer's finding that women, though they are less tolerant politically, as already implied, answer a question as to whether children should be made to conform to group norms with somewhat greater tolerance for differentiation than the men do.[17] It would seem that fathers want children prepared "realistically" to cope with the tough world: the fathers, that is, move in orbits that lead to political aeration and domestic severity. Indeed, the greater political intolerance of women can in part (as Glazer and Lipset also suggest) be linked with their cultural role of protecting the young: it is, the Stouffer study makes clear, "insidious" teachers they fear, and ideas and books—not sabotage or direct political threat. Their limited orbits make them vulnerable to the charge that their children are being corrupted; and of course the "heritage" groups of the DAR or Colonial

[16] See John R. Seeley, R. Alexander Sim, and E. W. Loosely, *Crestwood Heights: A Study of the Culture of Suburban Life* (New York: Basic Books, 1956), Chapter 14.

[17] This question is one of several Stouffer uses to develop a scale for psychic as distinguished from political tolerance. His research strategy here pays tribute once more to the fruitfulness of *The Authoritarian Personality* —a tribute I am particularly glad to echo because I have elsewhere criticized some of the political and conceptual premises of the Berkeley Study.

Dames accept the pedestal position of women and the protective morality that goes with it.[18]

I have heard tell of a women's group in a Chicago suburb, first organized around a PTA, that campaigned for the Republicans in 1952, very largely on an anticorruption, anticrime plank, and now is finding new protective activities in an anticomics crusade.[19] And I recall the grimness of my own reception when I spoke several years ago to a politically active women's organization and criticized Kefauver and his TV hearings as a lure for the unpolitical, a mobilization of the indignants, and a distraction from more important issues (as well as a danger to the usefulness I see in the urban boss and his brokerage among fanatical ethnic groups and ideologies); a men's group of like education, perhaps worldly-wise and cynical, would have gotten the point more easily—possibly, too easily.

Though American women do not bind their feet, as Chinese women once did, it remains true that at every class level save the very top (and perhaps among the Bohemians) they get around less than men do.[20]

---

[18] There is some evidence in the Stouffer book and his *Look* articles that people would accept the verdict of their school board that there are no Communists in the schools more readily than the verdict of top federal officials concerning the government, let alone local industrialists and union leaders concerning a defense plant. The school boards are relatively trusted because they are locally run and hence "democratically" sensitive to parochial vigilance; indeed, in the Bay City studies (see note 13 above, as well as publications by Peter and Alice Rossi), it is apparent that the school board is less susceptible to the values of the Protestant elite, though of more concern to them, than the city government as a whole. The Minute Women and like groups feel that schools, libraries, and other cultural institutions, along with pets (foils for antivivisectionists) and faucets (sources of God's unfluorinated water), are within their proper orbit.

[19] Cf. John E. Twomey, "The Citizens' Committee and Comic-Book Control: A Study of Extragovernmental Restraint," *Obscenity and the Arts*, an issue of *Law and Contemporary Problems*, Vol. XX, 1955, pp. 621–29—a study of the organization and procedure of the Chicago Citizens' Committee for Better Juvenile Literature, a women's group.

[20] One illustration is Mirra Komarovsky's study, discussed in "Some Continuities and Discontinuities in the Education of Women," p. 324, showing that, despite the breakdown of the double standard, women don't as often go away to college and that when they do they don't go away as far as comparable men do. Fred Strodtbeck, studying with his characteristic ingenuity husband-wife interaction, has shown great differences among ethnic groups in the degree to which the wife takes initiative in settling dis-

Louis Harris presents evidence—which many trade union officials would confirm from their own experience—as to the greater political conservatism of women, or more precisely their relatively apolitical outlook on politics, which led them in recent years to voice a greater fear of corruption and suspicion of malfeasance among the Democrats in Washington than their menfolk did.[21] He suggests that the homebound political feet of many women made Eisenhower, the candidate "above politics," appealing enough to lure them to the polls. And the kinds of effort, high-minded as well as low-minded, which have been made in recent years to get out the vote often bring the uninformed and indifferent to the ballot box when, in my judgment, they should have been allowed to remain audience rather than actors and counted as "don't knows" until they widen their grasp of political communications.

One form of such communications is the public-opinion survey which seeks to ferret out the "vote" even of those women who would not actually venture to the polling booth. Women interviewers find fairly ready access to privatized housewives: because they are women, they are not seen by respondents of limited contacts and education as threats to self-esteem; and to get the interview many of them not only make it a practice to dress down,[22] but also to chat with the housewife about her

---

agreements: in most groups she is the mood-engineer and not the decision-maker in the family, though in the Jewish group she comes closest to command position. See Fred Strodtbeck, "Family Interaction, Ethnicity and Achievement," in a Social Science Research Council monograph edited by David C. McClelland.

March found that the wife's prominence in political discussion decreases as the discussion moves from local to foreign to labor affairs. Since his women are members of the League of Women Voters and women with quite wide orbits of experience, this restriction by area is particularly interesting. See James G. March, "Husband-Wife Interaction over Political Issues," *Public Opinion Quarterly*, Vol. XVII, (Winter 1953–54) No. 4, pp. 461–70.

[21] *Is There a Republican Majority?* (New York: Harper & Bros. 1954), Chapter 7. Cf. interviews with housewives quoted by Samuel Lubell, *The Future of American Politics* (New York: Harper & Bros., 1951), pp. 217–18. Angus Campbell, Gerald Gurin, and Warren E. Miller, *The Voter Decides* (Evanston, Illinois: Row, Peterson & Co., 1954), pp. 154–55, present evidence that sex differences were small in the actual 1952 vote, although women were somewhat less issue-oriented and more candidate-oriented than men.

[22] While very high heels may in some circles be an American equivalent of bound feet, some interviewers carry a change of shoes with them—wearing high heels when they interview in upper-income areas, and loafers in

geraniums, her children, or whatever other conversation pieces can disguise a political poll as a sociable affair. Thus circuits of domesticity can get linked up with circuits of political communication, and in a fashion as idealistic as it is often misleading, everyone who can walk and talk is counted as a political animal.

I had these matters very much in mind when, in the spring of 1954, a male student in a seminar of mine at Johns Hopkins conducted some telephone interviews. He phoned people in the Baltimore phone book, picking an initial letter and then going at random, asked them if they had been listening to the [McCarthy] hearings, and if so then a few questions about their reactions (which were frequently highly cynical, of a plague-on-both-houses sort). When housewives answered, some refused to talk with him: they said they would call their husbands—politics was their husband's sphere. Of course, the student would try to get an answer out of them, but many would, though timidly, insist on bringing their spouses to the phone. Though the project was dropped before anything like a sample was garnered, it did turn out that in virtually all such cases the husband declared himself an ardent McCarthy supporter: it was our impression that the authoritarianism which led to so clear-cut a division of labor within the family would also be reflected in admiration for the toughness and apparent clarity of Senator McCarthy.[23] There is plenty of impressionistic evidence that many women admired his posture of virility, while protecting themselves from recognizing their deeper motivations by accepting the Senator's story that he was cleaning out Corruption and Communism.

Obliquely, moreover, we may relate the housewife's suspiciousness—an element in her rejection of the phone contact—with her presumptive intolerance. We know from *The Authoritarian Personality* and analogous studies that cynicism and suspiciousness are often psychodynamically linked with authoritarianism (*vide* many items on the F-scale.)[24]

---

lower-income areas; gloves, hat, earrings, and makeup also compose part of the alternative kit; occasionally, too, an interviewer will wear a fur coat in one area, a cloth coat in another.

[23] "The idea that 'woman's place is in the home' is apparently accepted by most women. . . ." T. W. Adorno, et al., *The Authoritarian Personality* (New York: Harper & Bros., 1950), p. 116; for slight evidence that women are more ethnocentric than men, see Table 14 on p. 125, while political agreement (irrespective of party) with one's father correlates highly with ethnocentrism, p. 192.

[24] See, e.g., *Ibid.*, pp. 411–12: many high-scoring interviewees questioned the purpose of the interviewers and resented "prying into their business."

And we also know from poll data that xenophobic unwillingness to trust others is found in the same low-education stratum where fear of imminent war and political xenophobia are strongest—the conditions of lower-class life do not encourage trust. While of course it is difficult here to distinguish character structure from class-bound cliché, the fear of many housewives that an interviewer, especially if male, is trying to sell them something, would seem to reflect both early conditioning and later interpretations of a very narrow experience. The husband is more likely to have faith in his sales resistance, in part because he has had to endure the give-and-take of his associates at work. If they support his convictions (in the fashion demonstrated by the Sandusky and Elmira data on voting behavior as correlated with views of friends and clique-mates[25]), he will have "the strength of ten" at home, while his wife needs merely to be bored by incoming mass media concerning politics in order to continue to defer to him (whatever her repressed suspiciousness of him too). His encounters, in other words, bring to his politics a certain patina of realism, and, in an interview, a certain dialectical facility, while his wife remains a *femme couverte,* at best able to repeat his views, without qualification or critique.

There were, however, several exceptions to our experience in the telephone interviews that housewives who called their husbands to the phone would have ardent McCarthyite spouses, for there were families of old-world outlook where the husband was a staunch union man and Democrat and the wife had trouble with the English language—here it seemed to me that we came upon a peasant patriarchalism different in quality from the authoritarianism of at least more superficially Americanized folk. And by the same token such housewives might be expected to be less accessible to the public opinion interviewer, certainly less likely to hear and be influenced by get-out-the-vote propaganda, and in any case less likely to be citizens.

IV

In sum, then, the reaction of housewives and of other women to the interview situation gives us clues to the understanding of Professor Stouffer's finding that women are less willing than men to tolerate

[25] Cf. Bernard Berelson, Paul F. Lazarsfeld, and William N. McPhee, *Voting* (Chicago: University of Chicago Press, 1954), chapter 6.

political and religious nonconformists.[26] Lower-class men in an interview will often express themselves with bravado and assurance, whereas women of similar origins will often doubt themselves—a mistrust which may then color the content of what they say. Even so, it is not entirely clear why women, who as various studies show are more empathic than men, should register on Stouffer's scales as almost invariably more intolerant. No doubt, Stouffer is right that housewives are less exposed to competing value systems; moving in narrower and more self-selected orbits, they lack confidence in their own powers to rebut "subversion"; their suspiciousness is therefore the other side of their gullibility.

More puzzling, however, is Stouffer's evidence that workingwomen are scarcely if at all more tolerant than housewives of comparable class position (using education as an index of class)—and markedly less tolerant than men in the same occupational group. I would suggest that this finding be interpreted in terms of the only partial widening of orbits that work brings to the average woman in factory and office. She is ordinarily at work not because of an occupational commitment but because of a domestic one, or waiting for one: the job is a way of filling and refilling the hope chest, and the woman's eye is on a home freezer or the costs of a baby rather than on rising in a career or through a union-powered escalator for the group. Workingwomen tend to bring domestic concerns to their talk at the factory as they sit around a table wiring relays (*vide* the Hawthorne Plant studies); nor do they talk politics in the public utility office where George Homans recently investigated the cash posters,[27] nor in the employment agency where James Carper interviewed the office staff.[28] For another thing, as these

[26] This holds whether the breakdown is by age, education, or region, but not among farmers: there men cluster about the midpoint of the scale of tolerance, while the women tend to be more polarized both on the tolerant and the intolerant sides, conceivably because some attend to farm-and-home programs while their husbands are isolated from contacts by the nature of their arduous work.

[27] "The Cash Posters: A Study of a Group of Working Girls," *American Sociological Review*, Vol. XIX, pp. 724–33, 1954. In correspondence, Professor Homans tells me that these women not only consider politics dirty but also divisive, as talk of religion would also be. The fear that political talk would destroy friendship groups would appear to reflect not only tact but the seriousness with which politics might be taken, were it brought up; whereas among men, more hardened to talk about "dirty" games, camaraderie could more readily survive political bluster and banter.

[28] An unpublished study, reported on in part at the Midwest Sociological Society meetings, Des Moines, April 22, 1955.

illustrations indicate, women at work tend to be given sedentary assignments; they are not likely to be in the maintenance crews from which, as Sayles and Strauss and others have noted, a disproportionate number of union activists and officials are drawn.[29] Whereas to many European observers American women appear as quite emancipated, Stouffer links the intolerance and conservatism of women to the fact that they go to church more regularly than men do, and churchgoers in general rank as less tolerant on his scales. Conversely, women who do not attend church tend to approach the level of tolerance of men of like education. In the South, women who go to church are not liberated even by college attendance—37 per cent of them are "more tolerant" on Stouffer's scale as compared with 38 per cent of Northern women *high school* graduates who are churchgoers, and with 67 per cent "more tolerant" among male churchgoers, both North and South, who have been to college. It would be interesting if one could break this down further by type of college the Southern women attended: whether the "female seminaries" which seldom uproot them from home-and-church or the larger coed schools or relatively liberal colleges like Randolph-Macon or the Women's College of North Carolina. And we miss, too, ethnic and denominational breakdowns (other than into Catholic and Protestant) which would separate, for example, Episcopalians from Fundamentalists in the South, and Polish from Italian Catholics in the North.[30] For churches obviously differ very much in the degree to which they freeze or widen the orbits of their parishioners. Ideally, moreover, we would like to be able to compare people who have remained in the church they were born into and those who have moved among denominations—primarily, of course, among Protestants; but the matter is complicated by the mobility of the churches themselves, and it is this "mobility" of institutions which makes any simple index of geographic or denominational mobility quite unsuitable when we are trying to understand what

[29] Cf. L. R. Sayles and George Strauss, "Occupation and the Selection of Local Union Officers," *American Journal of Sociology*, Vol. 50, 1953, pp. 585–91.

[30] Jewish women, of whom 68 per cent are "more tolerant," average a tolerance akin to that of the (mostly male) community leaders discussed below, while among Jewish men, 79 per cent are more tolerant—a finding to be explained in terms of many historical and current political factors, but also not unconnected with Strodtbeck's data on relative equality in family roles.

are the channels which put people into the wider and more cosmopolitan circuits.[31]

On Stouffer's tolerance scale, the DAR regents and the Women's Club presidents ranked lower than any men in the leadership group save commanders of the local Legion post. I wish he had interviewed League of Women Voters chapter heads, for I believe he would have found these women more tolerant politically and psychologically than virtually any men's group outside of journalism[32] and the universities: League women (and top-flight interviewers) often use their freedom from routine jobs to make a career out of widening their orbits and continuing their education.

V

Stouffer did have his own interviewers (NORC and Gallup) answer his questionnaire.[33] And recently Mark Benney and I had the oppor-

[31] And of course any large church is itself a congeries of channels. For probably not untypical contrasts between the men's Bible class and the liberal minister's sermon at a midwest middle-class church, see my article, "Some Informal Notes on American Churches and Sects," *Confluence*, Vol. IV, pp. 127–59, especially at pp. 143–46, 1955.

[32] Of the community leaders the newspaper publishers rank as the most tolerant, with 73 per cent in the extremely tolerant group and only 1 per cent among the least tolerant. Even publishers, let alone rank-and-file newspapermen, can hardly avoid breadth of orbit and have a vested interest in civil liberties.

[33] Thanks to Professor Stouffer, Mark Benney and I, in collaboration with Shirley Star, are now engaged in analyzing these returns. On the basis of earlier data, we would expect to find the NORC interviewers a good deal more liberal. Tables 1–4 in Chapter 2 of Stouffer's book indicate considerable disparities in the responses of community leaders by interviewing agency; for example, 85 per cent of Community Chest chairmen interviewed by NORC would allow atheists the right to speak, as compared with 65 per cent interviewed by AIPO [Gallup]; conversely, 62 per cent of Democratic party local chairmen interviewed by AIPO would allow Communists to speak, as compared with 50 per cent interviewed by NORC. These differences do not appear to form any consistent pattern related to presumptive ideological differences in the agencies; in any case, given the small numbers involved, they are not "significant" and more or less cancel each other out in the over-all tolerance scales. However, Herbert Stember has shown that NORC interviewers got a good deal more side-comment than the AIPO group, and more politically tinted responses to open-ended questions about the interviewee's worries—perhaps they just kept respondents

tunity to interview some of the NORC interviewers who had also worked on the Stouffer study; interested as they very generally were in civil liberties, they found this study, like their other politically oriented surveys, greatly rewarding as an opportunity to contribute to the processes of political enlightenment, including their own (though at the same time often distressing to them because of the low level of tolerance and concern which they found).[34] A few of these interviewers appeared to have husbands considerably less liberal and open-minded than they were—husbands uneasy about the political implications of such surveys as Stouffer's (notably so in the South), and sometimes "putting their foot down" against interviewing at night, or in certain neighborhoods, or on certain topics. In such cases it was plain that an element in the intolerance of women was the desire of their husbands to restrict them; undoubtedly, for women to take their work and the big political world more seriously, and thus expand their orbits, men will have to fear and patronize them less.

The willingness of many women to face their spouses' ire and their respondents', and to go anywhere and see anybody about often touchy political issues, for $1.25 or so an hour (and they frequently, out of diffidence, understate their hours), makes political communication through the polls economically feasible and technically reliable. And, as I remarked earlier, their role as women enables them to pose as political amateurs when they interview in the strata of limited horizon and of intolerance for the new and strange. By virtue of that role, they can encourage shy and hesitant respondents that their answers or failures to answer are just what the doctor in charge of the survey ordered, and not seem insincere. But this advantage with those of restricted orbit be-

---

talking (being used to longer, more open-ended interviews anyway) until they got onto politics. See Charles H. Stember, *The Effect of Field Procedures on Public Opinion,* unpublished doctoral dissertation, Columbia University, 1955.

[34] We met these interviewers as the result of having been asked by Paul F. Lazarsfeld and Louis Harris to make a report to the Fund for the Republic concerning the adequacy of communication in the Teacher Apprehension Study sponsored by the Fund and directed by them; on this Study 2500 college social science teachers were interviewed by Roper and NORC, and Benney and I interviewed in turn some 50 of the more than 150 interviewers. We are indebted to Lazarsfeld and Harris, and to the two interviewing agencies, for their openness and co-operativeness.

comes in my judgment a disadvantage when these same interviewers are sent to interview officials and other elite members.[35] . . .

VI

The early fact-finding survey was developed out of an interest in specific groups—eminent scientists, in the case of Galton; slum-dwellers, in the case of Booth; adolescents, in the case of Hall. And when Beatrice Webb interviewed trade union leaders or government officials, her bluestocking manner, her name, and her confident knowledgeability might intimidate interviewees but would hardly let them dismiss her with easy answers. The journalist finds out as much as he does because he pretends to know it already—and at times because he doesn't care too much for rapport of the easy social sort. Such interviews with informants require different preparation beforehand and different perceptiveness on the spot than the characteristic survey of our day with relatively uninterested and uninformed respondents—respondents who (as Stouffer has pointed out to me in connection with his own survey) may look to the better-informed interviewer for cues as to how to deal with an area in which they are not deeply involved and hence have not structured.

Implicit in what I have said is the notion that there is no perfect interview and that every encounter conceals as well as reveals. In the field of civil liberties, we may want to know how people sound off, what their official rhetoric is, as well as how they might act if an issue were to confront them realistically. More experimental interviewing at retail rather than wholesale might disclose wider ranges of potential behavior than the more monolithic type of survey, but no matching of interviewer to respondent can ever guarantee full and free communication at all levels. However, there seems to me to be a danger that, when we return to the older tradition of studying elites and other special groups, we will use the new tools of the nation-wide survey—tools attractive in their efficiency and near omnicompetence—without sufficient retooling.

Recently, for example, when the editor of this issue [Ithiel de Sola Pool] and his MIT colleagues wanted to study the attitudes of leading businessmen toward reciprocal trade, they employed NORC to interview 900 heads of companies. For this sort of politically searching and serious work, NORC interviewers, as I have already implied, possess

[35] CX "The Sociology of the Interview," p. 517.

exceptional interest and capability, yet it is doubtful whether they would in general manage to impress businessmen as *au courant* with business problems and reciprocal trade technicalities—though to the extent that these can be made matters of mood and affect rather than technique, a good interviewer working with an educative schedule might manage well enough (apart from the point that some heads of companies are in this field amateurs, glad not to have their special competence put to the test).[36] With awareness of these difficulties, the Center for International Studies at MIT used its own elite to conduct a number of unstructured interviews with businessmen, union leaders, and politicans; having had the opportunity to read a number of these (with identifying data removed), I am confirmed in my belief that even very busy men enjoy talking to outsiders who already grasp the relevant technicalities and are genuinely curious and alert as to the issues—something that has also been my own experience both as interviewer and as respondent.[37]

It will obviously be a long time before the national survey agencies seek to develop various special cadres of interviewers for work with special populations. To maintain such a staff would be terribly expensive, since the special gifts making for accessibility to one group might foreclose one from entry to another,[38] and since there would be great

---

[36] Conversely, the interviewers' own education was enhanced by the encounter: 56 per cent of the seventy interviewers, being polled later, said they had become more favorable to businessmen, many commenting on their breadth and lack of greed, while others were impressed by their courtesy and friendliness. See an unpublished memorandum by Ithiel de Sola Pool and Raymond A. Bauer, "How Pollers See Businessmen," January 28, 1955, summarized in *The Journal of Commerce*, February 15, 1955.

[37] Reviewing his own work in the MIT and comparable studies, Lewis A. Dexter has pointed out that in some cases he had to make vividly clear in a moderately subtle manner that he did not conform to the style of the stereotyped academician, the free trader, if he was to be taken into the confidence of the leadership of some high tariff circles; at this point, survey interviewing becomes a problem in establishing, as an anthropologist might, that one is neither quite in nor quite outside of a secret society or religious cult. Cf. Dexter, "Role Relationships and Conceptions of Neutrality in Interviewing," *American Journal of Sociology*, Vol. 62, 1956.

[38] Merton faced an analogous problem when he wanted simultaneously to approach the authorities in a housing project and the tenants; in such a study, careful selection can replace the providential matching on which a national survey largely must rely (apart from FEPC, agencies are understandably reluctant to get social class and ethnic data from their interviewers,

administrative problems of maintaining a staff of selective usefulness at widely separated sample points. Moreover, the diligence and conscientiousness in following instructions so typical of the docile woman student and the agencies' old-hand interviewers make difficult the alternative course of retaining the staff on a particular survey so that they might be able flexibly to meet the requirements of a highly literate group of highly placed respondents.[39]

Stouffer, at any rate, attempted nothing of the sort, but, as already indicated, administered the same questionnaire via the same agencies to his national cross-section and to his community leaders. Arguably, these leaders don't regard themselves as so distinguished as to feel, for example, that a male interviewer from a "name" agency like Gallup is not worth communicating with on a "man-to-man" basis; arguably, the interviewers were as alert and intelligent about the issues of civil liberties as these only moderately select respondents (some of the NORC interviewers told us they were disappointed in the lack of sophistication of some of the leaders), who were not told they were selected by virtue of their roles. Yet we must ask: are the questions on Stouffer's schedule really, as they verbally appear to be, the same questions when presented to leaders as when presented to an area sample? Does not the interviewer need to show that he grasps the special situation of the leader and is not presenting him, as the average poller may appear to do, with a stock situation calling for a stock response? Unless, as may often happen, we specifically want the stock response.

Many interviewers, as I have said, are "unaverage" (more so, possibly, than some study directors realize); doubtless, they are frequently able, no matter what the wording of the survey or the strictness of their

---

though many insist on a kind of minimum presentability). See Robert K. Merton, "Selected Problems of Fieldwork in the Planned Community," *American Sociological Review*, vol. 12, 1947, pp. 304–12.

[39] Stember's study of the handling of free-answer questions on the Stouffer study by the two agencies illustrates how powerful is the force of an agency's "house style" in guiding its interviewers through unfamiliar terrain. As already indicated, the AIPO staff got considerably less side comment, and somewhat less differentiated answers, than the NORC staff, while the latter, possibly anticipating political replies to open-ended questions, may in some subtle way have gotten more of them than more neutral interviewers would have. It should be emphasized, however, that these differences are relatively small, and that Stouffer's coding procedure made them irrelevant, save as the richer free-answer material supplied him with illustrative quotes.

training and supervision, subtly to adapt a schedule for a particular respondent—their eagerness to do so is whetted by a desperate desire to avoid refusals and break-offs. These interviewers apparently look upon the refusals and break-offs as personal rebuffs and defeats rather than as just the luck of the trade.

While public opinion pollers have often sifted their universe to eliminate, for instance, nonvoters or children or, occasionally, the uninterested or uninformed (Stouffer, working in this tradition, has breakdowns between the more and the less interested), in general they have adhered to an admirably insistent democratic ethos in tapping the voiceless as well as the vocal, the timid as well as the salient. And, as already indicated, something of this ethos has influenced, at least at top levels, the selection of interviewers by major agencies, so that they would hesitate to sort out, in any systematic way, those poorly equipped for elite interviewing (FEPC laws might in any case impose something of an obstacle).[40] In contrast, anthropology is democratic vis-à-vis cultures as such—each counts one—but vis-à-vis individuals it is fully conscious of their location on charts of prestige and influence. Whether in an African kingdom or an American factory, it always cases the joint, looking for lines of connection: its tradition is sociometric even when it becomes perhaps a bit uncomfortably conscious also of problems of sampling and quantification. It is hard to imagine an anthropologist who is the full inheritor of a tradition of amateur adventure and upper-class cosmopolitanism writing *The American Soldier,* although in that enterprise Professor Stouffer and his colleagues also studied special populations and elites within them.

Such considerations bring us back to the question of the role of the legal and constitutional systems, and of institutional controls generally —these being less affected by individual attitudes than public opinion data or even voting data are: it is a truism that social structure regulates the psychic structure which might otherwise, free of constitutional and institutional forms, run or ruin the country. In surveying community leaders as well as every *n*th house, Stouffer helps us understand why dissent still exists in this country in spite of the twenty-one house-

[40] Mark Benney and I, for instance, have talked to quite a few excellent all-purpose interviewers who fear or are nervous with their "A" respondents (ordinarily, their quotas include only a handful of them, so that experience accumulates slowly). Many save their A's for last, after they have become letter-perfect and familiar with objections on respondents of lower status and less unnerving impatience.

wives whom he quotes who talk very much like the agitators' clichés in *Prophets of Deceit*.[41] Conceivably the community leaders lack the courage of their convictions or ambivalently enjoy the dirty work done by vigilante groups, but these leaders are in turn subject to communications from other leaders and, as already stated, to control from other institutions. Indeed, if we add the Decatur and Elmira designs to Stouffer's, we can go on to ask who are the opinion leaders—either with respect to child-training or more directly political attitudes—for the "community leaders"; who are the people with whom they discuss these matters, and the media to which they attend; and what are the cross-pressures in families and friendship groups which may be conducive to tolerance or to closure. One would still sample, but on the basis of far more complex judgments, and along more sociometric lines.

But it would go much too far to say that, since social structure (including the courts and the legal profession) channels psychic structure, we can safely ignore the latter and its pathologies. Margaret Mead, in a thoughtful comment, has criticized the approach that Richard Hofstadter, Glazer, and I, *inter alia*, have taken to these matters, calling it "isolationist" in its concentration on domestic developments as against viewing American discontents as an understandable reaction to Soviet imperialism and America's new and difficult role in the world.[42] Stouffer, likewise, appears to suggest that Soviet moves are primarily responsible for the lessened ambit of tolerance that the polls reveal. Data quoted earlier in this article certainly show the radical shift toward intolerance not only toward Communists but toward socialists, atheists, and so on, both among the elite and the entire population in the years

[41] See, e.g., the Indiana housewife who says: "They're creeping in [the Communists] in places and poisoning the minds of young people in education with things that are contrary to the Bible." (Stouffer, p. 161); or the New Jersey housewife: "It's like a germ. It can spread. Communists are a danger when they talk to ignorant people. . . . I think ignorant people are most likely to become Communists, but, still, I always had a feeling that Mr. and Mrs. Roosevelt may have been Communists" (Stouffer, p. 162). Cf. Leo Lowenthal and Norbert Guterman, *Prophets of Deceit* (New York: Harper & Bros., 1949).

[42] "The New Isolationism," *American Scholar*, Vol. XXIV, 1955, pp. 378–82. Mead refers to Hofstadter's "The Pseudo-Conservative Revolt," *Ibid.*, pp. 9–27, and to Riesman and Glazer, "The Intellectuals and the Discontented Classes," *Partisan Review*, Vol. XXII, pp. 47–72, 1955; both reprinted in *The New American Right* and *The Radical Right*, note 1 above.

since 1947, the years of the cold war. Yet the quotations Stouffer presents from interview material provide some evidence that those whose orbits are narrowest, who know and care least about world affairs, are those most likely to want to curb librarians and teachers; if they see a threat in domestic communism, this would seem to be a rationalization of their generalized fear and suspicion—a permission granted to their fear by their leaders' domestically focused interpretations of world events, plus such windfalls as the Hiss case.[43] Indeed, many of the people who, in Stouffer's poll and others, can't recall the name of an investigating Senator or don't know who Hiss is, nevertheless "vote" their presently encouraged fear of subversive books, people, and ideas. Mass communications help provide these people with the rationalizations to defend their way of seeing, or not seeing, and if the Soviet Union were conveniently to vanish tomorrow, these people might not allow themselves to notice its absence, should the domestic situation continue to put pressure on them.

To argue this way obviously does not mean to deny the role of war and foreign relations in influencing the leaders who either can channel, exacerbate, or partially dissipate discontent rooted in domestic psychic and social strains. Moreover, even if only a relatively small percentage of educated people swings with the tide of external events, this of course may suffice to alter decisively the balances of opinion and power in the country at large. Nevertheless, any student of poll data, congressional hearings, and the media must be struck with the fact that some positions can easily be defended rhetorically, and others not. The cold war makes it hard to resist the almost physical force of the argument: "Would you want your child taught by a Communist?"—just as the desegregation struggle makes it harder for the southern liberal to face once more: "Do you want your daughter to marry a Negro?" Low tolerance for ambiguity plays into the compelling nature of such punch lines, whereas the liberal position, being more differentiated, takes longer to spell out and, outside of simple economic contexts, is therefore harder to sloganize.[44] If this is so, it says something about our culture

[43] Likewise, Stouffer's data imply that some liberals who underplay the threat posed by domestic Communists are often rationalizing their judgment that the congressional committees chase only witches.

[44] The University of Chicago Law School's Jury Project has been asking jurymen of different occupational strata who they would like to have on a jury in a case involving them. Prior to the deliberations, jurors tended to

generally, about the things that strike us (because we select them) as salient, as real.

It also says something about the nature of our political campaigns which serve to summarize and sloganize underlying attitudes for which the public rhetoric may as yet be unavailable, especially for those of lesser education. By emphasizing the personal qualities of candidates, one can avoid taking a stand, even with oneself, on such basic issues as war or peace, segregation or integration, civil liberty or civil restriction. The campaign (as the voting studies have shown) helps supply "reasons" to defend one's choices. To be sure, it may in some circles be "impossible" to vote for "that man," but one can still do so in the privacy of the booth or of the public opinion poll. It would be much more impossible to tell even oneself that one would do something so rhetorically indefensible as to allow a Communist to "poison the minds of children" or to profit from the sale of his books to a government agency.

VII

And this brings us back to the social rhetoric of the interview. As just pointed out, the more differentiated positions take longer to state—unless the interviewer and respondent can share a subculturally provided shorthand—and even the open-ended approach may not gather in the small but structurally significant groups who feel cramped by the frame of the questionnaire or the fairly self-evident time limits of a door-to-door survey. This may be one reason why Stouffer's scales give so little place to those who see both a domestic Communist threat and

---

prefer to be tried by persons of like status. This stereotypic response shifted when, after the face-to-face experience of the deliberations, they were asked to indicate before whom of their fellow jurors they would prefer to be tried. It then turned out that the lower occupational groups would prefer to be judged, not by their social-class peers, but by the top occupational group of proprietors and professionals (their peers are a second choice); it is as if they recognized the greater tolerance, fair-mindedness, and resistance to rhetoric of the men of higher education (they tend to reject women of whatever class). Conceivably, they have enough awareness of their own suspiciousness to prefer not to be judged by those who are like themselves. (I owe this information and other suggestions to Professor Fred Strodtbeck.) Indeed, reference to the Jury Project reminds us of another example of the difficulty of stating a complex position, namely that in the recent uproar there was no way of quickly and easily defending the "bugging" of the jury.

a domestic anti-Communist one—and are tolerant of dissent; not only do the variations within this group disappear if one is looking for large quantitative breaks, but even before this happens the variations may be washed out by the precoding of the questionnaire itself.

Somewhat analogous considerations apply to Stouffer's second and third questions, which asked people whether they worried more or less now than they used to, and what about. They did not bring up, save in some 8 per cent of the cases, the sorts of political concerns and dilemmas we have been considering here, but rather such concerns of limited orbit as health, personal relations, the job. Most respondents are "normal" in the sense that, asked "how are you?" they answer, "I'm fine," rather than submitting a bill of political complaint; and when asked what worries them, they see the interviewer, trained as she is to gain rapport, as inviting them to a sociable "domestic" conversation, in which they feel free to share with her their private worries over secrets and subversives as well as over health and wealth. Many do not see her, that is, as a *public* but as a private opinion poller; she comes into their orbit and is made at home, while at the same time in the dialectic of the encounter (as panel studies might more fully show) the interviewee is somewhat pried loose from previous apathy and narrowness—as the interviewer through her work certainly is. It is in a way surprising how few people, when asked in an interview what worries them, say they don't know: "worries," it would seem, are on hand, like the weather, as conversational coin. I am not contending, as some have, that Stouffer would have found more anxieties about political and civil liberty had he probed in depth; rather that when private opinion, made for casual interchange, is fed back through the polls as public opinion, it may tend to harden unduly, to become grotesque or exaggerated, with a private if emphatic rhetoric gaining fierce momentum in this echo.

VIII

The younger generation, as has become notorious, is not fierce about anything, and they show up in Stouffer's study, as well as in other polls, as far more tolerant than the old, even with education held constant. While it is not always easy to distinguish this tolerance from indifference to the ideological concerns of an earlier day,[45] there

[45] I am indebted to Nelson Foote for this idea and other suggestions. *Voting* (note 4 above) presents evidence that the young, by virtue of their indifference, prolong for a time the party identifications of their parents—

would seem reason to suppose that the life-conditions of the young make for a wider cosmopolitanism than their parents possessed; to be young today means to have a larger orbit than the previous generation; TV (whatever its hazards), the car, the armed services, the near universal high school and widespread college provide "nationalizing" experiences and encourage the decline of regional and rural parochialisms. Moreover, though women are not drafted, they are getting around more outside the home, while men take more part in the domestic circle and the care of children, thus developing a greater equality on psychic and political issues between the spouses and in turn between them and their children.

Yet it goes without saying that all such homogenizations work both ways. Nicolas Rashevsky or Stuart Dodd could no doubt figure out how the not entirely random collisions of young people, as more and more of them become educated through high school and beyond, will increase the contacts of the intolerant with the tolerant, in situations, like the Army, of mutual give-and-take. The chances are that the educated will have more contacts (as they have more of most everything else) and, in politics and perhaps in child-rearing, will be more influential.[46] However, it is conceivable that the Stouffer data showing that college education in the Far West leads to comparatively less tolerance vis-à-vis other strata than in the East and South is partly due to the pattern of collisions there and the generally lower class consciousness of the Far West: if, as a study in Ventura, California, indicates, physicists and skilled workers become not only neighbors but friends,[47] the lines of influence will not run only one way. And

---

and today's young voters are the children of the New Deal; this would make them receptive to the Democratic line on civil liberties. It doesn't follow, of course, that they will become reactionary and intolerant as they get older: what happens to them will depend on their history as well as their prehistory.

A recent Gallup poll provides further evidence of the sharpness of age-graded differences: 47% of those 50 or over declare themselves Republicans, as against 31% in the 21 to 29 age group and 33% in the 30–49 year old group. See AIPO release, December 1, 1955. It is the old Republicans who have been left behind on the farms and in the small towns—and who want Taft or his successor to make them young again.

[46] Cf. Elihu Katz and Paul F. Lazarsfeld, *Personal Influence* (Glencoe, Ill.: The Free Press, 1955), chapter 12.

[47] Cf. S. Stansfeld Sargent, "Class and Class Consciousness in a California Town," *Social Problems*, Vol. 1, 1953, pp. 22–27.

similarly we must take the trend poll data which Stouffer cumulates to mean that the leaders, though ever so much more tolerant than the population as a whole, have given ground considerably on fundamental civil liberties points—have perhaps done so particularly where a short-form rhetoric was not available which would serve at once to defend one's own values and to conciliate the unenlightened. The very tolerance which shows up in Stouffer's scales may have made them vulnerable to the majority's intolerant views, once the polarizing processes of politics, discovering fertile ground in the area of civil liberties, forced these views on their attention.

Homogenization, which attracts the tolerant and equalitarian, frightens those who depend for security on the differentiations of privilege. The very fact that tolerance has become the ideology of many of the educated, of top executives and the social elite, makes it possible for anti-elite groups to gather around the partisans of intolerance (without always sharing whatever psychic reasons for intolerance the latter have). Both political parties appeal to both camps, avoiding the Armageddon that extremists in each group might independently seek. And, while the tolerant young are not apt to turn up as community leaders in Stouffer's elite sample, their representatives have some national influence through their slots in the newer quasi-political professions such as TV and public relations. Yet neither they nor the community leaders may decide the future. Precisely because expanding orbits of tolerance and acculturation hold the center of the stage in our prosperous and mobile America, nativist reactions—back to the home, the parish, the region, the ethnic group, and the nation—lurk always in the wings.

Interviewers, Elites, and Academic Freedom
(1957)

This paper explores the reactions of academic social scientists toward being interviewed about issues clustering around their academic freedom and their fears for its invasion, issues which concern many of them directly, and the rest vicariously. The interviews—2500 of them—took place in 1955 in the course of a survey of "teacher apprehensions" commissioned by the Fund for the Republic and undertaken by Professor Paul F. Lazarsfeld.[1]

Many sensitive issues were probed in the course of the questioning: not only about whether one was apprehensive or not, vis-à-vis McCarthyism or analogous local pressures, but also about one's relations with students, fellow teachers, and the Administration; one's pedagogical values; one's estimate of the professor's status in the eyes of the community. Professor Lazarsfeld had done informal "pretesting" by canvassing the literature on academic freedom and by asking colleagues to tell him of their anxieties and worries, past and present; and he was well aware of the heavily affect-laden nature of many questions he would want to ask. But when the questionnaires at last went out into the field (subsequent to a more formal pretest of the near final questionnaire), convoyed by interviewers from Roper and the National Opinion Research Center, even the careful specifications given the interviewers could not guard against often violent reactions by respondents—reactions to what they regarded, alternatively, as an inept questionnaire, an incompetent interviewer, or a methodologically or politically misguided project. At a number of colleges and universities, the interviewers could hardly have been received with more uneasiness and hostility had they

---

[1] For a preliminary report, Paul F. Lazarsfeld and Wagner Thielens, Jr., "Social Scientists and Recent Threats to Academic Freedom," *Social Problems*, 5 (Winter 1957–58), pp. 244–66.

been immigration agents asking in an immigrant slum area about citizenship. While such abrasive encounters were, overall, in the minority, their occurrence nevertheless sheds light on the interplay of a sensitive issue, academic respondents, and nonacademic interviewers. It was not so much that the respondents were afraid of disclosure as that the collision of a hot subject and a cool methodology (and an occasional carefully "cool" respondent) engendered resentment. Not all social scientists, and assuredly not all academicians, are willing respondents in the best of cases—as anyone can discover who seeks to do research on a college campus; and not even the practitioners are immune to ambivalence toward the scientific method, when it comes close to home.

Sociologists have, in fact, increasingly come close to home as, gaining status and self-confidence, they have no longer confined their researches to marginal or captive groups about whom some elite wanted information—such groups as workers, soldiers, prisoners, immigrants, patients, and students. They have begun to interview big businessmen, legislators, high military officers, doctors and lawyers, and, at long last, even each other.[2] But if the topic is one of any importance and touchiness, problems of access and rapport arise when sociologists seek to use with elites the same well-watered techniques for establishing at once the right amount of distance and the right amount of intimacy they have traditionally used with what Veblen called the underlying population. The more distinguished a person is in fact or feeling, the less likely he may be to want to play the role of respondent as distinguished from that of informant. To be sure, if he is sampled as a member of the general population he may be sufficiently responsible to play his assigned role, especially if he is asked about matters concerning which he has no special competence by virtue of his position. And Samuel Stouffer in his survey of attitudes toward civil liberties provided a marginal case, for while he administered the same questionnaire both to a national cross-section and to a sample of "community leaders" (such as bar association presidents, mayors, leading publishers, and so on), he was still dealing with leaders in relatively small communities and many of them

[2] Cf., e.g., Erwin O. Smigel, "Interviewing a Legal Elite: The Wall Street Lawyer," *American Journal of Sociology*, 64 (September 1958), 159–64, and Harry V. Kincaid and Margaret Bright, "Interviewing the Business Elite," *American Journal of Sociology*, 63 (November 1957), 304–11, and, in general, the issue on the interview, *American Journal of Sociology*, 62 (September 1956).

were, in fact, hardly different from the man on the street in terms of special competence or responsibility in the area.[3]

In general, when such efforts to approach elites misfire we do not hear about it, for if negative findings are seldom reported in the social sciences, absence of findings because the study couldn't get started are reported even less. We do not hear about the pretests that warn people off from studying a certain community, and even in the Teacher Apprehension Study I wish more were known and reported about those cases where college presidents did not give permission for the investigation to proceed and where, in consequence, it was dropped—testimony in my opinion to the fact that such colleges should be black-listed by the AAUP while being highlighted for study by those social scientists who have as much courage as they have curiosity. Moreover, in most surveys of elites there is no feedback from respondents after the fact (panel investigations would be another story). Indeed, social scientists who do large-scale surveys are seldom made aware of the consequences of the interview for their respondents, since, as we all know, the work becomes increasingly bureaucratized, with the study director further and further away from the hazards and potentialities of the field work. Sociology has only the glimmering shadow of the powerful tradition of field work in anthropology, an initiation that everyone, to be a full member of the group, must at some time share. Thus, sociologists may be protected all their lives by the hierarchy of supervisors and other "field hands" from having to face many ethical and practical dilemmas of their calling. They are seldom either tempted to "go native" nor, unless by chance they are interviewed as dwellers in an nth house in some survey, do they long remember what it is like to be treated as a native, as a respondent.

When, however, in the spring of 1955, Professor Lazarsfeld undertook this survey of college social science teachers concerning their experiences with and attitudes toward academic freedom, he was of course aware of the possibility of passion, distortion, and resentment; he considered that the interviewers even from two leading agencies might not invariably find a ready entrée to the academic mind. He invited me, as someone interested both in interviewing and in academic freedom, to check his findings retroactively by a qualitative study of interviewers

[3] See Samuel Stouffer, *Communism, Conformity and Civil Liberties* (New York: Doubleday, 1955), and my discussion in "Orbits of Tolerance, Interviewers, and Elites," p. 540.

and respondents—by what might be called a live but partial secondary analysis. (I had myself, prior to the invitation, been sampled as a respondent in the study, as had my colleague who worked with me, Mark Benney.) With Professor Lazarsfeld's encouragement, I interpreted my investigation as covering not only the adequacy of the interviewing in its own terms, but also as an effort to see what the respondents, neither constrained nor prodded by a formal interview, might feel to be the salient problems of academic freedom at their college—issues which they had felt, for whatever reason, unable to communicate to their interviewer in the original survey. Moreover, I soon discovered that reactions to the survey could frequently be important clues to the nature of freedom at the particular college and thus could provide material ancillary to that gathered in the original survey.

Only social scientists were interviewed, in part on the ground that they had been under the heaviest pressure. Among them were many men accustomed to doing surveys, and many others, particularly in political science and history, accustomed to deriding them. But even in the former group there was much antagonism, sometimes on methodological grounds, and sometimes on grounds of the alleged political bias of the questionnaire. Social scientists were by no means regularly good "patients" for other social scientists: at a number of leading universities (including my own) angry respondents had felt almost insulted to have to discuss the intangibles of academic freedom with interviewers not always or wholly acculturated to academia. At most colleges where such reactions occurred, angry reactions were dissipated in talk, and in only a handful of cases did they lead, in the face of the conciliatory tactics of the interviewers, to a refusal to be interviewed or to a break-off in the midst of the encounter. But at one leading college the faculty felt strongly enough to hold meetings of protest and to draft a round-robin letter to Robert Hutchins, the president of the sponsoring Fund for the Republic, attacking the ineptness of the questionnaire, casting doubt on any possible good results, and suggesting that the "enumerators" were incompetent.

Whereas Professor Lazarsfeld's survey took soundings at 165 colleges, representing the range of all accredited institutions, denominational and secular, private and state, liberal arts and four-year teacher's colleges, our own follow-up could not sample this range adequately. We talked to about a quarter of the 212 interviewers who had worked on the study; we visited colleges mainly in the North and East, and among these mainly the more distinguished ones where the reactions had been most intense; and we tried in each case to triangulate encounters by interviewing the interviewers at those colleges, by reading the interviews they had done, by talking to some of their respondents, and by using such other evidence as we could gather in a brief visit to get a feel for the climate of academic freedom at the institution. In addition, we sent a mail questionnaire (to which we got a 55 per cent return) to some 750 of the respondents, asking them to describe their interviewer and to tell us the extent to which the original survey tapped areas they considered salient for academic freedom, and the extent to which they felt constricted by the questionnaire or by the interviewer.

At leading institutions where respondents had been irritated, they often assumed in an almost ethnocentric way that other professors elsewhere would be equally irritated. But it did not take long to discover that not all professors teaching in the social sciences at American colleges consider themselves members of an elite or anything like it. I speak here not of their conscious views, but of their unconscious reactions to being interviewed on the one hand by professors from the University of Chicago, and on the other hand by, as one of them said, "a little girl who could probably check soap without any trouble." There were many professors, as it turned out, so humble as to be glad to be respondents. Far from assuming, as many leading men did, that only a peer, a colleague, should have been sent to interview them, they felt deferential to the "lady from the Fund," asked her where they could get work like hers, or in slightly better situations exploited the opportunity to learn something from her about survey methodology. Naturally, the problems of academic freedom faced by such respondents had often little enough to do with McCarthyism or, indeed, with any recent national political events: freedom for them might consist of the privilege of rejecting an occasional ill-prepared student or even flunking him, or the privilege of teaching fewer than five courses (ranging from European history, when anybody turned up who wanted it, to criminology to educational psychology), or even the freedom to talk with a visitor who had not been cleared with the president's office.

But let us start our discussion at the top of the academic ladder where in some of the Ivy League colleges professors teaching in such fields as history, political science, and economics look down on the methods, the people, and the projects of sociology, and felt free and individualistic enough to resent being made *respondents* when—could they have chosen the occasion and the hour and the audience—they might not have been unwilling to be *informants*.[4] And at similar colleges, and throughout the gamut of social science disciplines, there were professors who felt that interviewers without social science training could hardly be expected to grasp or record the subtle differentiations necessary for describing the climate of freedom in so complex an institution as a college, or the apprehensions of so complex a constituency as themselves.[5]

At once, we realize that whatever the impact of McCarthyism on protest beyond the groves of academe, it remains a characteristic of leading liberal colleges and universities that a critical temper is taken for granted within the institution. Respondents, in talking with Mark Benney and me as well as with each other, were highly articulate about defects in the survey, or indeed, in our own investigation. They felt correspondingly free to be critical of the way the country was run, or their own institution or department. Ordinarily, their criticisms indicated their involvement both in the topic of academic freedom and in the technicalities of research. But there were times when I felt their criticisms of the Teacher Apprehension Study were disproportionate, indicating a displacement of affect, and thus a symptom of a certain malaise, a certain lack (whatever the formal protections) of free-wheeling intellectual freedom. Just as left-wing sectarians attack each other more than they tackle the omnipotent Right, so survey specialists attacked Paul Lazarsfeld who, whatever his "crimes," had not seriously jeopardized their academic freedom!

In contrast, at more somnolent or intimidated colleges, it did not occur to any respondents to criticize the survey or its emissary: at such colleges, many of the interviewers had a much livelier interest in academic

[4] In reflecting on Professor Daniel Lerner's article, "The 'Hard-headed' Frenchman: On Se Defend, Toujours," *Encounter*, 8 (March 1957), pp. 27–33, I was struck to see how greatly some of the more recalcitrant professors in the Teacher Apprehension Study resembled the French political and cultural leaders who bitterly or wittily refused to be treated as plain respondents, but who graciously consented to help the American study director frame questions which would not antagonize other Frenchmen— and of course in the process revealed their own opinions.

[5] The attitudes of these men resembled the problems faced by University of Chicago graduate students trying to make contact with rural Arkansans to discuss a tornado that had devastated the latter's homes. Compare Leonard Schatzman and Anselm Strauss, "Social Class and Modes of Communication," *American Journal of Sociology*, 60 (January 1955), pp. 329–38.

freedom than did their respondents, as well as a keener concern with methodology. At such colleges, it was the social grace of the interviewer, her ladylike charm, that got her by a suspicious president (who might regard the Fund for the Republic as subversive) and sustained an interview of an hour or more with a professor only minimally involved in the topics inquired about and perhaps restive as a result.

Yet there are never simply two parties—interviewer and respondent—involved in a survey; over them both hovers the ghost of the sponsor, and occasionally of the agency as well. The highly involved professor, confronted with an interviewer whom he felt to be poorly educated, could nevertheless seek—as in fact it was intended he do—to talk with Paul Lazarsfeld or the Fund for the Republic (and Robert Hutchins) over the interviewer's head, much as someone might irritably conduct an important conversation over a sputtery party telephone line. Comparably, the politically conservative or reactionary professor, hostile to the Fund and angry at any assumption that academic freedom was in jeopardy, or that teachers were apprehensive, could use the occasion of the interview to express these resentments and vehement convictions, even where, as often happened, the interviewer was herself politically liberal, a member of Americans for Democratic Action, or otherwise concerned with civil liberties. What was striking in both cases was the degree of trust placed in the interviewer, partly because she was misperceived as sharing the respondent's own orientation more than in fact she did, and partly because survey research has built up confidence in the neutrality and confidentiality of its field forces. There were cases, for instance, where an interviewer went to a college with a feeling, "What's wrong with these professors anyway that they object to taking an oath: they have our kids on their hands, don't they?"—yet listened attentively to the respondents' contentions and emerged with far more sympathetic appreciation of the academic perspective, having tipped her hand to none but the most hypersensitive and anxious respondent at the outset. And here the fact that most of the interviewers were women, accustomed to listening to men, not easy to type occupationally, made it perhaps easier for the respondent to believe his interlocutor was within political range—or comfortably indifferent to politics.

Before the survey got under way, there were some misgivings that professors with a "past"—Wallace voters, for instance, or ex-fellow travelers—would be reluctant to disclose their attitudes or reveal their apprehensions, especially perhaps to interviewers whose manner did not convey a ready sympathy with attitudes which in the general population might be regarded as subversive. It is hard, of course, to speak with certainty on such matters, but our impression is that academicians of this sort were often fearful but rarely silenced; they were glad for the opportunity to unburden themselves to the representative of the Fund, and they were not so intimidated as to need much reassurance as to the latter's confidentiality. Matters were different, of course, in some of the more impoverished colleges where a dictatorial president would eavesdrop on the Fund interviews; or would (as in a case mentioned to me by Everett C. Hughes) open all mail addressed to "his" professors; at several small teachers' colleges, the presidents interposed themselves between us and their faculty members; and the latter, not surprisingly, tended to claim, "We have all the academic freedom we want here"—a pretty sure sign they hadn't the vaguest idea what it was (or thought it the better part of wisdom to play dumb).

At such colleges, the survey often seemed to speak the language of another world. At some small denominational colleges, for instance, not McCarthyism but evolution was the salient issue of freedom; not freedom of research, but, as already indicated, freedom to teach fewer than a dozen courses in as many widely scattered fields of "social science." The interviewer's problem at such a college was often to see if the depressing homogeneity of response was in any degree factitious: that is, were there exiled in these academic wastelands any men who would be only too happy if they could claim to have an academic freedom problem as a sign that some constituency thought their teaching mattered? Or, to take another example, were there among the sometimes rather unworldly nuns teaching at a small Catholic college for girls any who did not wholly share the complacent view that they possessed to the full all the academic freedom consistent with Catholic doctrine—a complacency facilitated by the fact that the college, run by one of the teaching orders, was freer from the pressure of trustees or local businessmen than comparable Protestant or publicly controlled institutions? It could not be easy for the interviewer, confronting gracious nuns perhaps for the first time in her experience, to probe for the slight nuances of difference that might betoken dissent, rather than to accept the apparent uniformity of response. (Indeed, as is usual where free-answer material is desired, probing behavior proved the most difficult to standardize; some interviewers irritated their respondents by continually asking "Anything else?" after the respondents had already made clear their minimal involvement and "know-nothingism," while others, awed by their respondents or fearful of getting a bad name at a college before finishing the job there, let their respondents early in the game define the amount they would "give.")

At leading colleges, on the other hand, respondents often felt frustrated because not all questions called for free answers but instead for answers in terms of precoded categories; and the interviewers, faced with insistence that "the question can't be answered 'yes-or-no,'" sought with varying success to pin respondents down. Historians and political scientists were perhaps especially apt to resent what they considered a denial of their own or their college's individualism by the questionnaire's insistence on comparability of response. It was hard for some interviewers not to give such men the impression, even on free-answer questions, that what was wanted was a minimum of response—here it was the "training" of respondents that was partly at issue, and their inability or unwillingness to differentiate changing styles within a single questionnaire. But on the whole, we are inclined to think it was the training of the interviewers that led to great variations in what they regarded as proper length of response; those impatient of qualifications soon succeeded in cueing most of their respondents to their attitude, while those eager for expansiveness and side comment could likewise usually succeed in conveying their definition of the encounter to the respondents. (To be sure, there were cases where the interviewers, in the grip of some garrulous or egocentric professor, were unable to terminate an interview which ordinarily took one-and-a-half to two hours in less than three, four, or five hours.) However, even where parataxic misperceptions occurred between the participants, it was often clear from the record that the study director had gotten relevant information even while the respondent felt he had not been asked the right questions by the right person.

I have been concentrating on the difficulties and leaving aside the many encounters that went swimmingly. While, in the lower reaches of academia, aspirations for freedom were low to match the opportunities for it, so that here the survey often seemed either irritating or irrelevant, in the large middle range of institutions were the colleges that were under the most severe pressure, those publicly controlled universities that harbor high aspirations for freedom but often have pliable presidents and regents more attuned to the state legislature than to the standards of self-restraint not uncommon among trustees in the Ivy League. Many professors at such places were so grateful to the Fund for doing the survey, so eager to talk, and so democratic in judging the interviewer, that they overcame their technical misgivings about surveys or their feelings of constraint in the wording of particular questions; the survey seemed to be addressed specifically to them. And when respondents reacted in this way, they could manage to overcome considerable obstacles in felt deficiencies in the interviewer; they could recruit her, as had been intended, as a temporary amanuensis—while she, in the diligence characteristic of her kind, could respond despite her own inadequate preparation. Overall, more than three quarters of the respondents to our mail questionnaire felt they had managed to get their story across to the interviewer.

Part of our concern in the follow-up study was to discover who, in fact, were the interviewers. We found that they could be divided into two main categories: the "market researchers," and the "bluestockings."[6] In general, the former were apt to be older and more experienced, to be married to small businessmen, to belong to garden clubs and similar voluntary organizations, and to find support in the arduous and often anxiety-provoking tasks of their trade in personal loyalty to other members of the agency. Correspondingly, in relating to their academic respondents, these market-research interviewers tended to emphasize the social along with the intellectual elements of the encounter; they enjoyed meeting distinguished, and frequently polite, men as a change from house-to-house canvassing concerning beer preferences or simple pre-election questionnaires. They tended to interpret their task as saving money for their agency by getting as many interviews done in a day as was compatible with not cutting respondents off (but, as I have remarked earlier, some respondents did get the feeling they were being cut off): their definition of interviewing emphasized comparability as against idiosyncratic detail, and their norms of time rested on interviews averaging twenty minutes or less, so that they hesitated to press respondents—obviously busy men—beyond the hour between classes that was all many had available.

The bluestockings were ordinarily younger, less experienced, married to professional men (including teachers), a number of them Jewish. Their source of morale lay in devotion, not to the personnel of their agency, but to the impersonal topics and themes of social science or social policy; those in this group who worked for NORC appreciated

[6] While in general the market researchers worked for Roper and the bluestockings for NORC, the market researchers did not all work for Roper, nor the bluestockings all for NORC. The best interviewers in each agency resembled each other more than they resembled the average in their own organization.

the university connection and the cosmopolitanism of "National Opinion Research Center." While often horrified by the political apathy or bigotry of respondents, they had learned to sublimate their personal reactions in the service of science; they appreciated less seeing how other people lived as people than how they talked and felt as citizens and political men. Thus, they related to their academic respondents in terms of the concepts and problems of academic freedom. Accustomed often to interviews lasting several hours or more and, as young and highly educated women, brought up in the Age of Psychology, they expected respondents to spend two hours discussing their apprehensions and attitudes—while it did not occur to the market researchers that men might enjoy discussing for several hours subjects such as their fears.[7] Some of the bluestockings impressed respondents as too eager to collect atrocity stories of violations of academic freedom; others seemed too aseptic even to professors devoted both to research and to freedom; thus, one of the more characteristic bluestockings, herself a member of the American Civil Liberties Union, left a number of her respondents in discomfort because of her neutrality, for they wanted some recognition of their college's admirable devotion to freedom, and not a merely clinical technique.

This last instance is illuminating, for here highly involved respondents, precisely because of their involvement, were not satisfied with mere competence on the interviewer's part, and some of them, being social scientists, felt a certain anomaly in their own reactions. In wanting more, in seeking "therapy" as well as "diagnosis," they somewhat resemble the patients in a medical clinic whose reactions to initial interviews were studied by Norman Polansky, Jacob Kounin, and their coworkers;[8] these patients, who often felt that their problems had been

[7] There may have been a few bluestockings so very acculturated to academia that they felt diffident, even on so important a topic as academic freedom, about taking the time of leading professors with whose work they were familiar. But, on the whole, their great political concern overrode more private or personal concerns.

[8] See Jacob Kounin, Norman Polansky, Bruce Biddle, Herbert Coburn, and Augustus Fenn, "Experimental Studies of Clients' Reactions to Initial Interviews," *Human Relations*, 9 (December 1956), 265–93, especially pp. 268–69. This paper notes the reluctance of interviewees, when interviewed concerning their feelings toward their social worker, doctor, or other interviewer, to express negative reactions; this "accent on the positive" was of course also a problem for us in getting professors to express freely their

understood, still felt dissatisfied at frustration of what the authors speak of as "relationship needs," i.e., warmth and "personalization" of themselves as individuals by the doctor. In contrast to this situation, there were a few cases where the academic respondents, dealing with a subject that was an emotion-laden one for them, preferred a professional interviewer whose uninvolvement was somehow reassuring, at least where such neutrality was not felt as symptomatic of the anti-intellectualism of the wider nonacademic community. And this interpretation depended a good deal on the general climate of fear or freedom at the college, and the extent to which local or national xenophobias were salient at the time of the interview.

Indeed, on the whole, reaction within an institution to the interviewer and the survey was seldom an idiosyncratic matter; at the more liberal or avant-garde campuses, the survey was much discussed because of its topics; whereas in the sleepier, low-level institutions it was discussed because of its rarity as an event—as at the colleges where the "lady from the Fund" was photographed with the president or asked to address the assembled social science faculty on survey methods. Such discussion frequently occurred despite the usual instructions given by the interviewers to their respondents not to discuss the questionnaires until the interviewing was concluded at the college—instructions more often obeyed in the less critical-minded institutions (save in those where reactionary hostility to the Fund, to the name Lazarsfeld, or to Columbia University, entered as an incitement to group discussion and definition of the event).[9] Understandably, not all campuses were equally en-

---

criticisms of their interviewers, even though we made clear that we were not checking up on the latter or reporting to their agencies. We developed rough indices of criticism which satisfied us that those academicians who were most involved with the problems of academic freedom were, on the whole, also those least hesitant to notice deficiencies and comment on them; after all, this is in some measure the professor's "business."

[9] Such objections on the part of reactionaries often fastened on particular questions in order to prove the alleged leftist or liberal bias of the survey. Thus, respondents asked why there were not more questions permitting them to expose the pressures they felt from their liberal colleagues, from foundations, and so on. To some very conservative men teaching in impoverished colleges on meager salaries, the very ability of the "enemy" to set afoot so elaborate and carefully worked-out a study must have seemed an affront. This whole question of the conservative reaction to the questionnaire is fully dealt with in Paul F. Lazarsfeld and Wagner Thielens, Jr., *The Academic Mind: Social Scientists in a Time of Crisis* (Glencoe, Ill.: The Free Press, 1958), chapter 5.

gaged in reaching a group consensus concerning the survey's aims and emissaries; conditions were very different in a small, cohesive college in a hostile or indifferent community, or in a Catholic college with a resident faculty of priests or nuns, than in a "street-car university" whose faculty, often largely part-time teachers, scattered after their evening classes to a dozen different suburbs and had little feeling of identity even with colleagues in the same department, let alone with the institution as a whole. Still, where there was such a consensus, it occasionally mattered a good deal who were the first respondents, since it was they who set the tone by which later ones interpreted "their own" experience. And it is of course relevant in this connection that interviewers who found the assignment novel and perplexing sometimes put the survey's worst foot forward in these initial encounters, since by the nature of the case they could not follow their usual practice of trying out a difficult interview with a presumptively easy-going respondent—as, for example, when they "practice" on Negroes or other lower-class folk before filling their quota of upper-class and middle-class respondents.[10]

Let me repeat that I am concentrating in these remarks on what could be learned from a study of the interviewing concerning the climates of freedom and constraint in American academic life, and concerning the problems faced by social scientists when they become objects as well as subjects of their own procedures. That is, I am not engaged here in evaluating the effectiveness of the interviewing in its own terms (I concluded that it was, in fact, quite effective), but rather in seeing what variations in ease or difficulty of communication can reveal in their own right apart from the content of what is communicated. In any case, the survey could not possibly be judged—nor would Professor Lazarsfeld want or expect it to be judged—on the basis of majority or even overwhelming majority vote, for in a survey of elites (and I would think in most opinion surveys) not every individual counts one: in the Teacher Apprehension Study, for instance, those who have something to say and are apprehensive and silent might count much more than those who bear the title "professor" by grace of semantic generosity.

There were many respondents who were both apprehensive and

[10] A number of interviewers did, in fact, run through the interview with a college-educated person: spouse, child, fellow-interviewer, or friend. But those who needed such practice most were least apt to have opportunity for it.

articulate. Having been neither silent nor stupid in the face of McCarthyite pressures, they not only had had something to say to the interviewer but had already spoken out to their students and to other constituents, for which they either had been under attack or had realized they might become targets: the very awareness that had made them apprehensive also had made them sensitive to defects in the culture and not merely complacent fellow travelers of "the American way of life." And, as the Lazarsfeld and Thielens volume encouragingly shows, many of these professors, despite their apprehension or even because of it, "fled forward" into the very traps set by reactionaries and became defiant, more vigilant and energetic protectors of academic freedom than if they had not been threatened. But many others, of course, neither free enough for defiance nor cowed enough for total submission, were (as it seemed to me from my work on the study) gravely damaged by repression: some withdrew into safe specialisms and minutiae; others balanced every criticism of America with a self-demeaning, even though factually correct, criticism of communism; others were only vaguely and uneasily aware at the time of the interview that their feeling of moral potency and responsibility had become eroded with compromise and caution.[11] And at the bottom of the academic pile, as I have already stated, were men who could only be flattered if they should ever hear of Robert Hutchins' declaration that "teachers are scared," because, quite apart from those numerically not negligible teachers who were reactionaries to begin with and hence could feel relieved when the climate of the country at large more closely approximated their own values, many other professors started life so scared that shifting winds of national doctrine could not shake them any further.

When I began my work on the Teacher Apprehension Study, I was inclined to believe that the harm done to the academic profession by McCarthyism had been grave but still somewhat exaggerated.[12] Perhaps such exaggeration was rife before McCarthy's censure and down-

[11] In several striking cases, respondents realized after the fact that their animus toward the questionnaire was touched off by their unwillingness to face their "escape from freedom" during the cold-war years.

[12] Cf. my essay "Some Observations on Intellectual Freedom," *The American Scholar*, 23 (No. 1, 1953), pp. 9–26, reprinted in *Individualism Reconsidered and Other Essays* (New York: Doubleday Anchor Books, 1955).

fall, and, as I contended in the article just cited, led to panic in the face of attack. Today, however, it seems to me that the sophisticated academic community faces the opposite danger, of assuming that the wave of reaction ended with McCarthy.[13] Indeed, by the spring of 1955 when the survey was made, many professors in the better protected and, by the same token, more distinguished institutions, told the interviewers that "the worst was over," and that the survey had come too late. Such a judgment now strikes me as a bit complacent and as representing the provincialism of the cosmopolite. The survey did not come too late in the majority of state universities, where freedom is always precarious. It had not come too late in the denominational colleges of middle rank, nor in the occasional urbane and even Bohemian college located in a small rural community—nor did it come too late to the rare vocal antisegregationist teaching in a southern college so encapsulated in its community as to lack the protection that, for instance, the University of Virginia and the University of North Carolina give their faculties by their tradition of gentlemanly freedom.[14]

To be sure, "too late" in these last remarks refers to the interviews themselves and the sense they gave beleaguered professors that influential colleagues were concerned enough about their plight to inquire into their experiences; for many such men, the survey itself, even if nothing had ever been published, was therapeutic, as it was in another way for those men who were given an opportunity to review experience and listen to themselves in areas of tension and discomfort which they had tended to shut out of conscious awareness. A number of respondents were in fact quite grateful for this opportunity, and said as much to the interviewers or to us.

[13] Taking the academic profession as a whole, however, McCarthyism probably did less damage there than to the civil and especially the foreign service, to the general conduct of debate on foreign policy, and hence to the chances of peaceful survival in a turbulent, fast-changing world. Moreover, the fight for domestic civil liberties necessarily distracted many academic people from critical attention to foreign policy, though the waning of criticism has many other roots as well.

[14] On the whole, the "ecology" of colleges matched the ecology of the interviewing staff: despite the fact that there was no deliberate matching of interviewers and respondents (though where choice was possible, the agencies used their better interviewers), regional and rural-urban differences tended to put the more experienced interviewers at the doors of the more academically demanding colleges, which were also the ones, in the main, presenting the greatest challenges.

This group, however, was a small minority in comparison with those professors who, to hear them talk, considered academic freedom as at best a very peripheral subject—men who read nothing more "subversive" than *The Saturday Evening Post* or *U. S. News and World Report*. As we have seen, many reactionaries reacted to the study with indignation, but a larger number of apolitical men regarded it as either a chore or a pleasant diversion from even more routine matters—at one teachers' college in the Middle West, respondents made bets with each other about who could get through it fastest (the record: 41 minutes, as against an over-all norm of perhaps an hour and a half). In talking with the interviewers and reading their job reports, I was struck by the fact that, taking the academic profession as a whole, most respondents (whatever their later complaints to their colleagues or to us) were civil and genial when being interviewed. Only rare "characters" were acerb or refused to be interviewed. The great majority, in their ready candor and their lack of intellectual arrogance, were like millions of other Americans: they did not dream that they should be considered an elite. Others reasoned with themselves that if some people are going to get information others will have to give it: they felt a little as I do when I religiously fill out even the silliest of market-research questionnaires as a kind of professional comity. They responded to the demands of the interview as interpreted by the interviewer patiently, pleasantly, unassumingly.

Indeed, one could wish for the sake of academic freedom that they had had a good deal more arrogance, for their willingness to put up with a questionnaire many considered Philistine or oblique to their problems and an interviewer who sometimes frustrated rather than facilitated communication—this willingness is the other side of an equalitarian permissiveness which has often led to inner vulnerability (as well as political defenselessness) in the face of Populist attacks on intellectuals and on the universities.

The Study of National Character:
Some Observations on the American Case
(1958)

I shall try in these remarks to put into perspective certain problems in the study of national character. My procedure will not be technical and systematic, but speculative and fragmentary. I shall take my mandate broadly to touch on a variety of styles of thought and thus address myself not only to the sociology of society but also to the sociology of knowledge. My emphasis will be on national character, not as historians have traditionally used the concept, but rather in terms of the inquiries that have resulted from the confluence of psychoanalytic or Gestalt psychology and cultural anthropology. This confluence, going back to Sapir and others in the 1920s, is hardly more than a generation old. It received an enormous impetus in the Second World War when anthropologists, who had examined the relations of culture and personality in small preliterate societies, turned their attention to assessing the morale, the vulnerability, and the approachability of enemy and allied states. Ruth Benedict's book on Japan, *The Chrysanthemum and the Sword* (1946), is one of the best known examples; work was also done on Burma, on Rumania, and by the psychoanalyst Dicks and others on Germany and the Soviet Union. Margaret Mead's book on the United States, *And Keep Your Powder Dry*, which appeared in 1942, was a wartime effort to understand the sources of American morale as well as part of the perennial effort of a highly self-conscious nation to understand itself. In the war, it was important to know how the Japanese would respond to an occupying army; or in what ways American GIs and British Tommies might misunderstand each other; or how American housewives would alter their food habits under rationing when this involved a break with an ethnic heritage. Such imperative curiosities helped overcome the reluctance of anthropologists and psychoanalysts to enter the areas already pre-empted by historians, political scientists, and occasionally a sociologist, particularly when they could not make use of their technique of the long-term field expedition and had instead to rely on secondary sources and to infer much more than they could observe firsthand.

Work in this genre, originating with the war, set a pattern or style of study that was continued by the Research on Contemporary Cultures, first directed by Ruth Benedict and then by Margaret Mead.[1] Members of the separate disciplines, including many anthropologists, strongly objected to this approach, partly on justified grounds that it ignored history, was more unsystematic than necessary, and lumped subgroups together on the basis of inadequate sampling. But partly the work seemed just too vague and impressionistic to appeal to young men and women interested in quickly gaining an unequivocal professional identity and in exploring some of the problems, at once technically exacting and intellectually challenging, that have come into prominence recently. Only a few departments of anthropology carry on research in national character or culture and personality at present, and the only sizable project I am familiar with is that being conducted at Harvard by John W. M. Whiting. For the most part, the psychoanalysts have gone back to their patients, the anthropologists to their tribes.[2]

A few historians, however, more venturesome than their fellows, have begun to take an interest in this area. David Potter, in his book *People of Plenty* (1954), has sought to assimilate the studies that have been done on American character by nonhistorians and to link them to more traditional historical perspectives. Elkins and McKitrick

[1] See, for general review, Margaret Mead and Rhoda Métraux, *The Study of Culture at a Distance* (Chicago, 1953). This project, of course, was not the only work on national character, but is used illustratively here. Mention should be made of the comparative study by Francis Hsu, *Americans and Chinese: Two Ways of Life* (New York, 1953). A full bibliography can be found in Alex Inkeles and Daniel J. Levinson, "National Character: The Study of Modal Personality and Socio-Cultural Systems," *Handbook of Social Psychology*, ed. Gardner E. Lindzey (Cambridge, Mass., 1954), II, 977–1020.

[2] It should be noted, however, that at the meetings of the American Anthropological Association in Washington in November 1958, John J. Honigman declared that a survey had shown that as much work in culture and personality had been done in the last few years as in the immediate postwar period. It would be necessary for a fuller appraisal of the true situation to compare these publications, both in scope and number, with work in other expanding fields of anthropological research.

have employed psychoanalytic and anthropological research in their work on slavery in the Americas.[3] A year ago, William L. Langer in his presidential address to the American Historical Association stressed the importance of psychoanalytic studies for the understanding of historical development.[4] Since in larger perspective it does not matter which guild, which discipline, does the work that needs to be done, and since I myself feel that tribal or national character cannot be understood without history, I would be very happy if historians went ahead to make their own a borderland now only laxly tended by other social scientists.

History is often said to be an ideographic or descriptive study, as distinct from the nomothetic or generalizing social sciences. In preference to these rather formidable terms, I want to fall back on the old dichotomy between the romantic and the classic, though I shall use these labels in a somewhat special way, one which, however, is applicable not only to the study of national character but to almost any sort of study of man. What I shall call the "classic" approach aims primarily at generalizations that could in principle be true at any time and place, whereas the "romantic" is concerned with a particular people, in a particular time and place. The problems that bother the classicist tend to be given him by his discipline and hence often appear to be objective, while the romanticist is apt to allow the problems that bothered the people he is studying to bother him also. The historians and other humanists who have for a long time been interested in national character have been attracted to the particular, even the parochial; they may have a yearning for wider generalizations in a more classical mode but they manage to resist it. The yearning may be an element in their frequent resentment of interlopers from alien fields who talk about "the" Russian or "the" German or "the" American character, as well as the often much greater resentment against Spengler or Toynbee, who seek to impose a grand design on history and to cultivate categories that are transnational and go beyond the common sense that serves the average historian for a psychology.

In contrast, the "classic" approach focuses on social forms rather than content (a fragile distinction at best). The classic mode tends to be detached from time and place and generally in the past (though not

[3] Stanley Elkins and Eric McKitrick, "Institutions and the Law of Slavery," *American Quarterly*, IX (1957), 3–20, 159–79.

[4] William L. Langer, "The Next Assignment," *American Historical Review*, LXIII (1958), 283–304.

inevitably) has surrendered the attempt to cope with social change. We see this approach in one of its purest forms in the work of economists who build models under which all deployment of resources and all choices among them in any society can be subsumed. As Carl Kaysen put it at a meeting, the input-output scheme of Leontief could in this way handle the choices Eskimos make, or even that seals make, assuming we could infer the preferences and energies of seals from observing their behavior.

Talcott Parsons has been much influenced by such models used by economists and has, in turn, influenced them; and while much of his work deals with very concrete problems of contemporary America, his book *The Social System* (1951) and other writings comprise an effort to find categories within which any society in any historical period could be described—such categories, for instance, as those of universalism versus particularism, or of achievement versus ascription. Other scholars have written in a similar vein. Thus Florence Kluckhohn's distinctions between "being," "becoming," and "doing" represent an effort to embrace all possible societies in terms of their orientation toward time and toward movement and achievement[5]—although, to be sure, being and doing are concepts particularly suitable to the American experience and the present American ambivalence. Likewise, one finds in a paper by Clyde Kluckhohn and Henry Murray on the determinants of personality formation the typically classic statement that every man is in some respects like all other men, in other respects like some other men, and in still other respects like no other man.[6] Such a statement clarifies what one might discover in any conceivable society; and pushed to its extreme the classic approach becomes a set of abstract logical statements.

No doubt this dichotomy between the classic and the romantic approaches is itself classic. Correspondingly, none of the writers I have mentioned is, of course, a pure case of either type, for all are very much concerned with what is happening now in these United States. I think we need both the classic and the romantic approaches to the study of national character, or rather we need the dialectical tension between them; and in that sense the not wholly integrated or assimilated pressure for concreteness from historians on the one side, and for

---

[5] See Florence L. Kluckhohn, "Dominant and Variant Value Orientations," in *Personality in Nature, Society, and Culture*, ed. Clyde Kluckhohn and Henry A. Murray, 2nd ed. (New York, 1953), pp. 342–57.

[6] *Personality in Nature, Society, and Culture*, p. 53.

generalizations from more neophyte social scientists on the other, can be as productive as it is often contentious and dismaying.

This dialectical tension can be felt in the way others have used Freud's own originating concepts in the study of national character. And Freud *is* the originator here, not because his is the soundest and safest guide among the available systems of psychology, but because his is the most provocative and alive. His assumption that all men pass through a series of psychosexual stages—principally, the oral, anal, and genital—led in the hands of his disciple, Karl Abraham, to the further development of the concept of the anal character, the concept, that is, of a person who is frozen at or who has regressed to the anal state, and who continues to live as an adult in a metaphorical image of that state. The biological universalism of Freud is "classic" in its style, and, although it is dynamic when applied to an individual life cycle, the same universalism is often static when the organic metaphor of the individual life is extrapolated to the culture at large and one speaks of a whole culture as "anal" or "oral" as the case may be.

Freud himself, however, in *Moses and Monotheism,* one of his last works, sought to deal with what was for him a concrete historical problem in national character, namely, why the Jews had maintained for centuries a particularly ascetic religion, with only one God and severe inhibitory rituals. And he sought to answer his own question in terms of a reconstructed historical event, the killing of the Egyptian leader, Moses, by rebellious Jews, and the remorse that followed from this, recreated anew in each generation of Jews by quasi-Lamarckian and quasi-cultural processes. *Moses and Monotheism* is thus a study in the origins and present import of Jewish national character. In its cavalier way of handling data, both about Biblical history and comparative religion, this book illustrates a highly characteristic procedure whose vices are evident enough but whose virtues need also to be understood. For the psychoanalysts have had the temerity to tackle whole cultures in an effort to link the creation of a particular type of character structure in childhood to the adult society's mode of production, love, war, folklore. Indeed, in the sensitive hands of Erik Erikson, this highhanded method becomes a way of explaining how two American Indian tribes have organized the psychosexual stages on life's way, perpetuating themselves through time by inculcating in the children the orientations that will "make sense" in the natural and human environment the adults must cope with.[7] For example, he shows how the Yurok

[7] See Erik H. Erikson, *Childhood and Society* (New York, 1950), Chapter 4.

Indians, living by and preoccupied with a salmon river on the Northwest coast, construct their houses, their view of the world, and their day-to-day imagery on the "oral" analogy of the river's mouth.[8] In all such work, there is an effort to see what goes with what, what hangs together, how a society channels its drives of sex and aggression, and it is this that has been a factor in the encouragement given historians (as Richard Hofstadter points out)[9] to think in terms of configuration and style, and thus to delineate patterns as well as to describe events. (To be sure, historians have worked this way in the past when they have allowed themselves to refer to a period as "baroque" or to speak of the "romantic era," but the psychoanalytic impetus involves a more explicit linking of individual motives to large societal forms.)

Moreover, the psychoanalytic contribution not only introduced new and often grandiose styles of generalization; it also insisted on the importance of previously neglected aspects of day-to-day life—underprivileged data, we might say, with which only a few of the more social social historians had concerned themselves. Fleeting memories, dreams, the games of children, the modes of weaning—all became the stuff of history. And I think we see here one reason why so many anthropologists found in Freud, despite his obvious ethnocentric biases, a compatible figure, for they, too, had an interest in underprivileged orders of data—data from tribes without writing, without a navy, without what used to be called "culture." Furthermore, anthropologists had necessarily been forced by the nature of their one-man expeditions into a kind of amateurism in which the art, the economics, the mythology, the child-rearing practices, the legal system, and the kinship system were all within their purview, needing to be organized in some holistic way. When anthropology was poor, it could not afford to send more than one person to one place, and the tribes, too, were poor in the sense that they could not protect themselves against white contact and could not be assumed to remain intact for the next field trip. Moreover, when anthropology was poor, anthropologists were autocratic and aristocratic; by this I mean that, like the early psychoanalysts, they were prepared to generalize on the basis of scanty evidence even when they could have no assurance that another research

[8] See Erikson, *Observations on the Yurok: Childhood and World Image* (University of California Publications in American Archaeology and Ethnology, Vol. XXXV, No. 10; Berkeley, Calif., 1943).
[9] In *The Varieties of History*, ed. Fritz Stern (New York, 1956), p. 362.

worker might automatically duplicate their account. They practiced an art requiring confidence in themselves and imagination as well as ability to observe and record. Today, I suspect that this is changing. Neither anthropologists nor psychoanalysts are an esoteric elite seeking to rub the noses of their fellow men in what is common or vulgar. What was esoteric has become part of our daily life, and anthropologists, now belonging to a stronger and more well-endowed profession, are also burdened with observational and analytic games at which any number can play, if they have bought their chips at the proper graduate school.

At the same time, of course, it has become possible to rectify some of the excesses of the early enthusiasts. Scholars are, for the most part, not so sure as Freud was that they know what is "basic" in a particular culture. To be sure, the psychoanalyst Abram Kardiner and his anthropological coworkers have developed a concept of "basic personality" in which what is basic depends on psychoanalytic preconceptions as to what is most important to man in his culture. If one deals with a small tribe or enclave, the shortcomings of this approach are apt to be covered up by the ability to relate everything to everything else, so that religion, for instance, may appear, not as the heritage of a specific tribal history, but as the reflection of childhood training and parental aggression. But as soon as one moves into a more complex and differentiated society, what is basic for one group may not be basic for another, and groups may struggle to define what is to be regarded as "basic" for the society as a whole. To understand such a struggle, one needs not only life histories, but history, as a number of anthropologists are aware. Irving Hallowell, for example, in studying Canadian Indian tribes, has gone back to the early Jesuit accounts, the so-called Jesuit relations, concerning the same tribes he has worked with in the field, in order to discover what is truly basic in the sense of more or less permanent and what, though it may strike the fieldworker as significant, may perhaps be ephemeral.[10] Likewise, when Erich Fromm was working (with the late Ralph Linton) on materials from Truk, he went back to the accounts of early Spanish and later German visitors to Truk in order to show that the "hoarding" or anal-sadistic orientation he found in the contemporary Trukese reflected, not presently prevailing conditions of peace and plenty, but earlier conditions of

[10] See A. Irving Hallowell, "Aggression in Saulteaux Society," *Psychiatry*, III (1940), pp. 395–407; and the essays collected in his *Culture and Experience* (Philadelphia, 1955). Work by A. F. C. Wallace could also be cited.

famine and warfare that, through parental transmissions, had left their mark in the tribal character and social institutions.[11] So, too, Geoffrey Gorer, for his recent book, *Exploring English Character*, not only employed an elaborate questionnaire among Englishmen now alive, but also sought to discover through historical evidence how and why the British became a law-abiding people.[12] Works such as these are more sober than the earlier works, but they have not surrendered either the concern for underprivileged data or the effort to relate the rivulets of individual motives to the turbulent streams of history.

At the same time, the introduction of new materials, such as poll data, when combined with an interest in history, presents us anew with the problem faced by the social historians: that records are largely the product of the more articulate strata and that it is never an easy task to infer and reconstruct how ordinary people in an earlier time were brought up to think and feel. We cannot interview the dead. We can see what this means when we examine two studies, *The Authoritarian Personality* and *The Lonely Crowd*, as I should like to do now.[13] Neither of these (despite the subtitle of *The Lonely Crowd*) can quite be termed studies of *national* character, because their focus is on salient strata within a population rather than on a total population but they do attempt to make the linkage between a more or less psychoanalytic approach to individuals and certain historical questions.

The Authoritarian Personality took off from the near contemporary scene of fascism in Germany and the possibility of incipient fascism in America; but its method is primarily clinical, focused on the psychodynamics of individuals as revealed in interviews and projective tests. From these individuals a picture is in turn built up of the structure of authority in the family, with overbearing but conventional authority in childhood seen as the basis for sadomasochistic and intolerant disposi-

[11] The work was done in a seminar at Yale in 1948–49 at which George P. Murdock and Ward H. Goodenough reported on their observations in Truk. I speak here of my own recollections of the seminar, which I attended, as Fromm has not published his work on Trukese character.

[12] Geoffrey Gorer, *Exploring English Character* (London, 1955). See especially Appendix I.

[13] Theodor W. Adorno, Else Frenkel-Brunswik, Daniel J. Levinson, and Nevitt Sanford, *The Authoritarian Personality* (New York, 1950); and David Riesman, with the collaboration of Reuel Denney and Nathan Glazer, *The Lonely Crowd: A Study of the Changing American Character* (New Haven, 1950).

tions in later life, and in the larger world of politics. Thus, the family is seen as the microcosm of society, as well as the transmission belt for its imperatives. Yet we wonder in reading this book whether the authors, had they had access in their sample to seventeenth-century Puritans in New England, would have regarded them as authoritarian and, if so, how they would explain the rise of political democracy in just such a setting. And we might conversely ask to what extent tolerant and permissive families, highly democratic, arising in twentieth-century America, might seem quite pliable in the face of an authoritarian political and cultural regime. For the historian realizes as a matter of course that institutions mediate between the family and society. And, if that is so, individual character structure may not necessarily be the most salient element for historical development at a particular time. Anonymous individuals possessing certain character orientations in common may provide both an active and a passive audience for a dictator, and thus play a part in his rise to power. However, any large-scale industrial society, whatever its numerically preponderant national character, is bound to have enough sadists and bureaucratic authoritarians available to do the dirty work of totalitarianism, provided other historical conditions are present. Correspondingly, within wide limits a totalitarian movement can create its own audience, and destroy or intimidate the rest. It is unduly complacent of Americans to assume that "it can't happen here," and that Hitler's rise to power can be attributed to "the" German character and hence "the" German family; this assumption is also an historicist fallacy, for there were many accidents in Hitler's rise to power and his stay there, as he himself well realized, and the authoritarianism that surely existed in sections of the German lower-middle class (as it exists in sections of the American working and white-collar classes) was but one predisposing factor among many.

Many published criticisms of *The Authoritarian Personality* have been made,[14] my own among them, and I do not want to add to them here, for the book deserves the great impact it has had; it did try to link the most intimate and the most impersonal realms of contemporary life. Had the book been written to the mandates of all-inclusiveness that might have saved it from criticism, it would have been so "classic"

[14] See particularly *Studies in the Scope and Method of "The Authoritarian Personality,"* ed. Richard Christie and Marie Jahoda (Glencoe, Ill., 1954).

as to lose interest for us. The point is rather to see what next steps can be taken, on the one hand to bring institutions into the picture, and on the other to look for comparative cases, both historically and cross-culturally, where a similar pattern of child-rearing coexists with a different set of institutions and a different social climate in the culture at large.

The Lonely Crowd resembles *The Authoritarian Personality*, which appeared at the same time, in its effort (far less systematic, to be sure) to deal with a historical problem that is broader than genitality and narrower than fate. It is a "romantic" book in the sense that its focus is less on man in general than on specific social strata in a specific historical setting. Just as *The Authoritarian Personality*, as a study in the social and psychological sources of prejudice, transcends the American case, though its interviews and tests happen to be with Americans, so *The Lonely Crowd* aims at understanding the social and psychological consequences of the shift from an industrial to a postindustrial culture—a shift most pronounced among the highly educated and urbanized members of the American middle classes, but one that could in principle be traced in other affluent or near-affluent societies elsewhere than in America. Nevertheless, in its tentative suggestions linking demographic, technological, and cultural patterns, *The Lonely Crowd* touches on a theme more characteristic of classic than romantic works; so, too, in its discussion of three modes of adaptation: autonomy, adjustment, and anomie. Even so, this latter typology, influenced as it was by the writings of Erich Fromm, moves quite far from the biological base of many typologies, whether we think of Freud's oral, anal, and genital, or, at a different (nonpsychoanalytical) level, of Sheldon's mesomorph, endomorph, and ectomorph. For, by beginning with the problem of conformity and autonomy, the typology is already a socially patterned one, and of course it reflects the very specific preoccupation with socialization, conformity, and individualism found in the educated and sensitive strata in the United States today.

To my way of thinking, typologies are scaffoldings, good for a single building only, and needing to be scrapped when the movements of history and of thought present us with different problems and different ways of perceiving problems. I am reminded of a letter I received recently from a sociologist in Ethiopia who was trying to apply the scheme of *The Lonely Crowd* to developments in that country. I know almost nothing about Ethiopia, but I have felt, perhaps unfairly, that there was at work here the attraction that schemes of any sort hold, if they are at all plausible and if they have either two or three or some other magic number of boxes. I felt that if one were beginning work in Ethiopia undistracted by America, one would almost certainly develop a different typology to deal with what was most important there. For one thing, different traditions are differentially fragile to the inroads of the modern industrial world, and I would like to see studies of national character in the so-called underdeveloped countries that took account of this. At any rate, the typological concepts of *The Lonely Crowd*—"ideal-type" concepts, in Max Weber's sense—were framed in terms of what seems to be presently happening in those countries where industry is already well established, where the physical plant and the social organization for mass production and mass consumption have been installed, and where, consequently, the character structure necessary for developing such organization may no longer be so essential. I think of the United States today as the chief exemplar of postindustrial culture (Sweden may be another), and my concern is with what this means for the development of character and of institutions, especially those institutions that, through the family, the mass media of communication, and the schools, influence the training of the oncoming generation.

In contrast to most of the studies I have mentioned, my collaborators and I in *The Lonely Crowd* did not move outward from individuals toward society, but rather the other way round; we started with society and with particular historical developments within society. We did not concern ourselves, moreover, with all classes of society, but primarily, as already indicated, with the upper social strata, particularly with what has been called the "new middle class" of salaried professionals and managers. We assumed that there would be consequences for individual character in the loss or attenuation of the older social functions on the frontiers of production and exploration and the discovery of other frontiers in the realm of consumption and personal relations. We did not assume that an individual would be the replica of his social role, but rather that there might be great tension between an individual's search for fulfillment and the demands of the institutions in which he had a part, or from which he felt alienated.

It is implicit in what I have just said that the inwardness of individuals is only awkwardly if at all captured by a typology designed for the understanding of large-scale social change. It is easier to classify individuals by means of typologies developed by psychologists for just this purpose, and thus we can say of someone that he is an "oral" or "receptive" type, or a "sadomasochistic" one, and take account of much that is relevant about him as an individual in doing so. But it is much harder, if not impossible, to classify a particular individual as other-directed or inner-directed, and when we have done so, we may have made a statement that helps explain his social or occupational role but not much else about him, not what we would most care to know about him if we were his friend.

I would like to illustrate some of these problems of relating work on national or group character to concrete situations and concrete individuals by drawing on several recent studies in which social scientists have attempted to develop tests or measures for inner-direction and other-direction in individuals. Thus, a few years ago Jacob W. Getzels developed what he termed the I-O, or inner-other, scale, and administered it to a group of air force officers who were teaching at an air force academy.[15] What he did was ask them to respond to a group of statements or slogans that expressed inner-directed or other-directed ideologies, as the case might be. At the same time he collected psychological and behavioral data on these same individuals. But when he compared the way they answered the I-O scale to what he knew of them personally, he was perplexed—until he discovered that those who, on the basis of other evidence, he would classify as principally other-directed, had answered *all* his slogans in the affirmative, including those designed to betoken inner-direction. Conceivably this says something about certain types of career officers or "organization men," as well as about the ways in which other-direction might manifest itself in a certain social stratum. I am fairly sure that Harvard students or University of Chicago students would not manifest other-direction on the same scale.

In this connection, an investigation reported by Michael S. Olmsted is interesting.[16] He asked a group of Smith College students to say whether they considered themselves more inner-directed or other-directed than their parents, "most of the boys you know," the "average" girl at Smith, and their particular friends at the college. They tended to regard themselves as considerably more other-directed than their fathers (and slightly more so than men in general), and as more

[15] Personal communication. Getzels' collaborator in this work was Egon Guba.
[16] Michael S. Olmsted, "Character and Social Role," *American Sociological Review*, LXIII (1957), pp. 49–57. I am indebted to Professor Olmsted for helpful suggestions.

inner-directed than Smith girls in general. Olmsted has suggested that there may be differences based on sexual role at work here. While Smith girls would like to think of themselves (in my judgment, not inaccurately) as more independent than the majority of women, they are fully alive to the pressures toward compliance that young women —and their mothers as well—are under. However, when they interact casually with other girls, they are apt to be aware only of the compliance, and not of the underlying resistance to it that they themselves and their close friends often harbor—one reason, Olmsted proposes, why the girls who label themselves as "inner-directed" (40 per cent of the respondents) believe themselves to be more atypical than in fact they are; they may, of course, also enjoy regarding themselves as more independent than the "average" even of Smith girls. However, the image the Smith girls have of their fathers is blinkered by the fact that they do not see them at work, in the world in which they interact with other men, but only at home, and probably infrequently at that. Likewise, the fact that they see boys as slightly less "other-directed" than girls may reflect the fact that they see boys mainly on dates, when the culture places the initiative in the latter's hands. Consequently, they may somewhat overestimate the independence of the menfolk, at least vis-à-vis other men—and then we must ask whether this overestimation, when the men are aware of it, may help foster the very independence it attributes to them, or in some cases, when they cannot live up to feminine expectations, weaken them further.

I think we can see, both in this and in the previous study, that it is extremely difficult empirically to separate character structure from behavior, and to sort both out from the haze, the fog, of ideology that clouds our perception of ourselves and others. There is also the problem, when the Smith girls compare themselves with their parents, of distinguishing between those generational differences that are due to chronology and those that bespeak a genuine historical shift. Thus, it would appear that the adolescent may go through a stage in which he is becoming independent of his parents by what seems like overdependence on his peers—a stage of other-direction and role-diffusion; when he in turn becomes an adult, he will appear to be more independent of peers, with values closer to those of inner-direction.[17]

Some interesting empirical confirmation of this hypothesis has re-

[17] Cf. Erik H. Erikson, "Ego Development and Historical Change," *Psychoanalytic Study of the Child*, II (1946), 359–96.

cently been provided by a questionnaire study of 2500 ninth- and tenth-grade students in middle-class New Jersey high schools.[18] In this research the students were asked to respond to a series of vignettes of which the following is an illustration:

> Helen and Dick are what you would call all-round. They're pretty smart, but not too smart, good-looking, but not exactly the movie type. They play on the teams but aren't top athletes. In short, they seem to be pretty good at almost everything although not outstanding in any one way.

Or, another example:

> George and Lucy each live pretty much in a world of his (or her) own. Each feels that his (her) own thoughts and own reading are in a way more important than the day-to-day struggle to do well in school.

The students were asked to judge many such vignettes in terms of their own values, what they thought the popular members of the class would want their friends to be like, what their parents would expect of them, and what qualities they thought would be helpful to them as adults. I cannot go into all the complexities of this work, or into the problem of separating professed values from character structure. One conclusion, however, emerges that is quite striking: perhaps a majority of the teen-agers are not geared wholeheartedly to the values they attribute to the peers with whom they are attending school, but have also incorporated adult values, both those they attribute to their parents and those they expect to hold themselves when they in turn are adults. They possess, as it were, a double consciousness of themselves now and themselves later, living at once in the present and in the future, and sharing both the good-time and popularity goals of their peers and the more achievement-oriented and studious goals of their adult mentors. It seems to me that they can do this in part because they have eliminated from what a sociologist would call their reference groups any models that unequivocally challenge the prevailing compromise on values in which the parents give their sanction to teen-age frivolities up to a

[18] Matilda White Riley, John W. Riley, Jr., and Mary E. Moore, "Adolescent Values and the Riesman Typology: An Empirical Analysis," in *Culture and Social Character: The Work of David Riesman Reviewed*, ed. by Seymour M. Lipset and Leo Lowenthal (Glencoe, Ill., 1961).

point, while the teen-agers in turn accept adult goals up to a point. Thus, George and Lucy who live in their own private worlds are rejected (though not by any means overwhelmingly), but the person with mediocre aims is also, while not rejected, not highly approved of. In this system, people can be both popular and studious up to a point, both compliant and independent up to a point—as I interpret the results, the rough edges of all character types and all ways of life have been smoothed down, and a wide tolerance is extended to values that, in an earlier day, might have been more sharply polarized.

Possibly, we see at work in these questionnaires some of the reasons why we refer to adolescents today as teen-agers rather than simply as "youth": the latter term has a futuristic ring, implying that youth will do things and change things, while the term "teen-ager," used by teen-agers themselves, has a highly self-conscious but also patronizing quality, referring as it does to a kind of protected or encapsulated and not quite real life, and used as it also is to justify what an earlier generation would have considered inane, while making clear that it is but a stage, like being a sophomore, that will pass with time.[19] In this case, the researchers concluded that the high-school students are, for the most part, neither inner-directed nor other-directed but both at once—carefully uncommitted occupants of the middle way.

Let me mention just one other study, also done with young people, because it brings us back by another route to Freud's heroic efforts somehow to link the biological with the psychological and both with culture. In this research, two psychologists (Elaine Graham and Harriet Linton) worked with forty-two freshmen at Brooklyn College, administering both an attitude test, by which one might differentiate inner-directed from other-directed attitudes, and also a test of spatial orientation, the Witkin tilting-room-tilting-chair test, which measures a person's ability to respond to inner cues as against environmental ones. In this test, a person is put into a tilting chair in a tilted room, and asked to move the chair until he feels upright. Some subjects are deflected or distracted by the tilted room, and these are termed field-dependent, whereas others show little influence and are termed self-orienting. The investigators found that those who were other-directed in terms of their psychological tests were also likely to be field-dependent, while those who were psychologically more inner-directed were also among

[19] I owe to a conversation with Eric McKitrick my awareness of the importance of the substitution of the term "teen-ager" for that of "youth."

those who were able to use bodily cues in adjusting the tilting chair.[20] I would expect that this seemingly physiological reaction is itself part of a complex syndrome, not unrelated to childhood training and cultural norms.

Moreover, all such work that deals in an intensive way with living respondents gives rise to problems similar to those we discussed in connection with *The Authoritarian Personality*. We would like to know, for example, how in the nineteenth century young people might have responded to the Witkin test and whether in fact more people today than in an earlier day are field-directed, either somatically or psychologically. What my coworkers and I did when we were working on *The Lonely Crowd* was to look for individuals who might in some way speak for the nineteenth century—those who, by reason of location or occupation, were less directly in the path of modernization, people who were not in the new middle class, people who were not yet members of the affluent society. But obviously we could not assume that such people are always preserved specimens from an earlier era. If they still cling to traditions, they are apt to do so self-consciously rather than to take them for granted. Their relative isolation compared with that of others changes their situation, hence, in all likelihood, their attitude and eventually their character structure.

Consequently, the best that we could do in our study was to examine secondary sources, historical writings and travelers' accounts, and to infer from these some hypotheses as to whether American national character has changed in substantial segments of the population in the last generation or so. Talcott Parsons and Winston White have recently written a paper arguing that fundamental orientations have not changed, that the American is still, as he was in Colonial times, oriented to performance and achievement, not to hedonism or consummatory pleasures.[21] What appears as change, they suggest, is the altered situation in which these drives manifest themselves. The home no longer

[20] See Elaine Graham Sofer, "Inner-Direction, Other-Direction, and Autonomy: A Study of College Students," in *Culture and Social Character*, 316–48; also Harriet B. Linton, "Dependence on External Influence: Correlates in Perception, Attitudes, and Judgment," *Journal of Abnormal and Social Psychology*, LI (1955), 502–7, and Harriet B. Linton and Elaine Graham, "Personality Correlates of Persuasibility," *Personality and Persuasibility*, ed. by Carl I. Hovland and Irving L. Janis (New Haven, 1953).

[21] Talcott Parsons and Winston White, "The Link between Character and Society," in *Culture and Social Character*, pp. 89–135.

is the seat of a family firm engaged in producing agricultural commodities or in running a small business. It is, rather, engaged in the "production" of children who must be trained and encouraged to take their places in the demanding professional and managerial system; and the parents must seek to succeed in this more intangible realm as they might once have sought to show a profit, to increase the acreage, or to build up an inheritance for their children. The American, Parsons and White believe, still judges himself by his output; it is only that a different kind of output is in demand—and is permitted—today.

Similarly, when one reads Tocqueville or the accounts of other nineteenth-century observers, one often has the impression of meeting the contemporary American, for these observers commented on our gregariousness, our lack of arrogance or hauteur in the European sense, the hegemony of children, the love of comfort, and many other things that seem to us characteristically contemporary. No doubt, these observers were struck by the differences from the Europe they knew, and this may have alerted them to incipient trends that have become much more pronounced with time.[22]

In considering such questions, we must ask ourselves what it is we are most interested in, that is, what do we regard as most important for us at the moment—and these, as I have indicated, are questions of a romantic rather than a classic order. We know that, when we deal with Americans, we deal with people who, at least outside the South, lack feudal traditions, a strong established church, and extended family ties. We know that we deal with people who believe themselves to be pragmatic and sometimes are, who, on the whole (again outside the South), are optimistic, for themselves, their children, their community, and their country; and with people who are extremely mobile both in terms of rank and of region. The American of today and his ancestor of a hundred years ago are much alike if we range them for example against the South American, the Asian, or the African.

[22] In an earlier discussion of some of these themes, "Psychological Types and National Character: An Informal Commentary," *American Quarterly*, V (1953), 325–43, I raise the question whether social-class differences or national ones are more important today in comparing groups within the Western industrial world. Recent comparative studies indicate that, contrary to imagery and ideology, social mobility is no less great in Europe than in the United States; and of course there is much evidence that similar cultural tendencies, often labeled "Americanization," are occurring among young people in Europe.

But if we concentrate on the differences, I think we find important ones both in outlook and in situation. The American of the nineteenth century was, I suggest, oriented toward people because his attitude was (in the terms of Erich Fromm in *Man for Himself*, 1947) exploitative, or if a woman, receptive: whereas the upper-middle-class educated American of today tends increasingly to be oriented toward people, not because he wants something specific of them, but because he wants direction, resonance, response. If this be exploitation, it is of a very intangible sort, like that of roommates who take turns in discussing their problems and love affairs with each other. There has been a general tendency, facilitated by education, by mobility, by the mass media, toward an enlargement of the circles of empathy beyond one's clan, beyond even one's class, sometimes beyond one's country as well. That is, there is not only a greater psychological awareness of one's peers but a willingness to admit to the status of peer a wider gamut of people, whether in one's own immediate circle or vicariously through the mass media. The problem for people in America today is other people. The social and psychological landscape has been broadened in a sense because those other people are more in number and possibly in heterogeneity than ever before. But other figures in the landscape—nature itself, the cosmos, the Deity—have retreated to the background or disappeared, with the result that aspects of character that were always in some sense "there" or available become more salient, and other aspects recede.

Many people have read *The Lonely Crowd* and other similar writings to mean that things were better before the day of relative material abundance, permissive child-rearing, progressive education, and the omnipresent mass media. Such books, too, have become involved in the usual and age-old transatlantic arguments about the supposed superiority of European culture. It is an unavoidable dilemma of romantic research that it confronts us with ourselves in this direct way, whereas research in the classic tradition, which treats what is happening now as merely an instance of a general case, seems less likely to make for self-consciousness, although at its deadpan worst it may make for unconsciousness.

The wartime studies of national character ran these risks only in an incidental way, for they were undertaken in the hope of being able to cope better with our enemies, our allies, and ourselves. After the war, the State Department realized that men who were to represent this country abroad should understand not only the language and culture of the country to which they would be assigned but also should become more self-conscious about American culture, and be aware of what sorts of biases they would typically carry with them, and what sorts of culturally patterned dangers, such as despising the natives or wanting to go native. Thus, the Foreign Service Institute began some searching studies of American culture. Work of this sort, while beginning with very concrete and even chauvinistic aims, has also tended to transcend its military or cold-war origins and to add to the traditional ways in which we as a people have sought to understand who we are and how we compare with and differ from other countries.

I can imagine a future, however, in which we shall begin to worry less about the specifically American identity and the American character—a worry that among other things exhibits on the international scene feelings of rivalry and even inferiority engendered by domestic conditions. And in that case we shall begin asking whether nations are the most appropriate boundaries for investigating what it is that social groups have in common. It is in some ways convenient and it is certainly topical to do research on "the" Americans or "the" Russians, but a wider perspective might lead us to highlight, for example, the possible similarities in character structure of Russian *and* American managers and technicians, or in the character of factory workers in Australia, Sweden, and the United States. Men like Barrington Moore, Jr., and Alex Inkeles, in making comparative studies of the institutions of the whole industrial world, are moving in this direction.

Let me make clear that I am not recommending here the planetary perspectives of the classicist. It would be premature to say that nations are no longer important, when they have the power of life and death over us all; and when, since social character is the legacy of history, there will remain for a long time differences in national character just as great as differences in character arising from occupation and class. It is only the fantasy of a brave new world that there is no national character but only a group character, conditioned in the laboratory to order and to be ordered, and where a relic of individualism and parochialism is merely the result of an oversight.

Still, as we all know, fantasies when believed in sometimes have a way of making themselves come true. Social science today is increasingly feared as a hidden persuader or manipulator of men, while a generation ago it was primarily admired as a liberator. The study of national character, as of other motivational patterns, can be put to manipulative use, to be sure; the best defense against this that I can see is inoculation by greater knowledge. Moreover, it is no longer possible for people, especially in this country, to remain unself-conscious about personal and group identity; and it is not desirable, for I believe that such knowledge, as well as knowledge of social science in general, can still be liberating.

But it is in this last regard that social science, as presently practiced, seems to me weakest. We find it easier to describe the limits on human conduct than the areas of freedom and amorphousness. Studies of national character tend to strike a deterministic note, even when, if they are grounded in history, they show how great and dramatic have been the changes in a nation's ethos within the period of a century or less. It is frequently said that the world is getting more homogeneous, and that enclaves, whether national or regional, are bound to disappear, provided we do not all disappear. There is truth in this, of course. But it is also true that the differences among men that will increasingly matter will not arise from geographical location and will hence be more within the realm of the individual. Indeed, the importance of the individual in setting a model for the character of a group has been insufficiently studied by social scientists, though we all know in a general way how identification with great historical figures is one way by which we avoid the parochialism of our particular birth in a particular family. We are only beginning to understand the power of individuals to shape their own character by their selection among models and experiences. I can envisage a world in which we shall become more different from each other than ever before, and in which, as a result, national character will be an even more elusive concept than it is at present.

Acknowledgments and Notes on Previous Publication

1. "National Purpose" was first published in the *Council for Correspondence Newsletter*, June 1963, pp. 5–12.

2. "The American Crisis" was first presented at an informal discussion among congressmen and others in Washington, D.C., June 1960, and first published as "The American Crisis: Political Idealism and the Cold War," in *Commentary*, Vol. 29, No. 6, June 1960, pp. 461–72, and in *The New Left Review*, No. 5, Sept.–Oct. 1960, pp. 24–35. It was reprinted in *The Liberal Papers*, edited by James Roosevelt (Quadrangle Books and Doubleday Anchor Books, 1962).

3. "Reflections on Containment and Initiatives" was delivered at the annual meetings of the American Sociological Association, Washington, D.C., September 1, 1962, and was first published in the *Council for Correspondence Newsletter*, February 1963, pp. 21–30. It appeared in shortened form as "Containing Ourselves," in *The New Republic*, Vol. 148, April 6, 1963, pp. 14–17.

4. "The Nylon War" was first published in *Common Cause*, Vol. 4, No. 6, 1951, pp. 379–85, and reprinted in *Christian Century*, Vol. 48, No. 18, p. 554, in *Etc.*, Vol. 8, No. 3, pp. 163–70, and in *New Problems in Reading and Writing*, edited by H. W. Sams and W. F. McNeir (New York: Prentice-Hall, 1953), and in my book *Individualism Reconsidered* (Glencoe, Illinois: The Free Press, 1954). It was reprinted with a new epilogue in *Preventing World War III: Some Proposals*, edited by Quincy Wright, William M. Evan, and Morton Deutsch (New York: Simon and Schuster, 1962).

5. "Some Observations on the Limits of Totalitarian Power" was prepared for a symposium in 1951 on totalitarianism, arranged by the American Committee for Cultural Freedom in New York City, and was first published in *The Antioch Review*, Vol. 12, No. 2, 1952, pp.

155–68. It was reprinted in my book *Individualism Reconsidered* (Glencoe, Illinois: The Free Press, 1954).

6. "The Cold War and the West: Answers Given in a *Partisan Review* Symposium" was first published in a symposium "The Cold War and the West," in *Partisan Review*, Vol. 29, No. 1, Winter 1962, pp. 63–74.

7. "Careers and Consumer Behavior" was first published in *Consumer Behavior*, Vol. II, edited by Lincoln Clark (New York: New York University Press, 1955). It was reprinted in *A Modern Introduction to the Family*, edited by Norman W. Bell and Ezra F. Vogel (Glencoe, Illinois: The Free Press, 1960).

8. "A Career Drama in a Middle-aged Farmer" is based on a memorandum of 1953 submitted to the Kansas City Study of Middle Age and Aging, thanks to a Carnegie Corporation grant to the Committee on Human Development, University of Chicago. It was first published in *Bulletin of the Menninger Clinic*, Vol. 19, No. 1, January 1955, pp. 1–8.

9. "Work and Leisure: Fusion or Polarity?" was a publication of the Center for the Study of Leisure at the University of Chicago, supported by a grant from the Behavioral Sciences Division of the Ford Foundation, and was first published in *Research in Industrial Human Relations: A Critical Appraisal*, edited by Conrad M. Arensberg, et al. (New York: Harper and Brothers, 1957). It was reprinted in part in *Way Forum*.

10. "Leisure and Work in Postindustrial Society" is developed from a lecture, given on January 27, 1958, in my series on "The American Future" sponsored at the University of Chicago by the Division of the Social Sciences and the College. It is a publication of the Center for the Study of Leisure. In footnotes I have sought to take account of some of the points raised in the question-and-answer period which followed the lecture. I have drawn on an earlier article, "Abundance for What?" reprinted here on p. 103. It was first published in *Mass Leisure*, edited by Eric Larrabee and Rolf Meyersohn (Glencoe, Illinois: The Free Press, 1958).

11. "Some Issues in the Future of Leisure" is a publication of the Center for the Study of Leisure and was supported by research M-891 grant from the National Institute of Mental Health. It was first published in *Social Problems*, Vol. 9, No. 1, Summer 1961, pp. 78–86 and reprinted in *Work and Leisure: a Contemporary Social Problem*,

edited by Erwin Smigel (New Haven: College and University Press of New Haven, 1962), pp. 168–81.

12. "Sociability, Permissiveness, and Equality: A Preliminary Formulation" was supported by research grant M-891 from the National Institute of Mental Health, Public Health Service, and was first published in *Psychiatry: Journal for the Study of Interpersonal Processes*, Vol. 23, No. 4, November 1960, pp. 323–40.

13. "The Suburban Dislocation" is a publication of the Center for the Study of Leisure. I have drawn for this article on research conducted by Rolf Meyersohn, Research Director of the Center, and Robin Jackson, Research Associate; and I am indebted to Nathan Glazer for helpful suggestions. The paper was first published in *The Annals of the American Academy of Political and Social Science*, Vol. 314, November 1957, pp. 123–46.

14. "Flight and Search in the New Suburbs" was originally presented at a symposium on "Suburbia, the New America?" at Smith College, April 1959. It was first published in *Forum*, The University of Houston Quarterly, Vol. 3, No. 3, Fall 1959, and reprinted in *The Grécourt Review*, Smith College, and in *Community Development*.

15. "Autos in America" is a publication of the Center for the Study of Leisure. The paper was first presented in an address at Carleton College, April 1956, where it drew on Eric Larrabee's "Autos and Americans: The Great Love Affair," in *Industrial Design*, Vol. 2, No. 5, October 1955, pp. 95–98. We are indebted to Reuel Denney for helpful suggestions. The paper was first published by Carleton College, *The Voice*, Vol. 22, 1957, pp. 4–18; then in *Encounter*, Vol. 7, No. 5, May 1957, pp. 26–36; and in the present version in *Consumer Behavior: Research on Consumer Reactions*, edited by Lincoln Clark (New York: Harper and Brothers, 1958).

16. "Abundance for What?" was first published in *Problems of United States Economic Development*, Vol. I (New York: Committee for Economic Development, 1958). It also appeared in *Bulletin of the Atomic Scientists*, published by the Educational Foundation for Nuclear Science, Inc., 935 East 60th Street, Chicago 37, Illinois, Vol. 14, No. 4, April 1958, pp. 135–39.

17. "The Found Generation" is developed from an address presented to the Harvard College Class of 1931 Symposium in Cambridge, June 11, 1956, and was first published in *The American Scholar*, Vol. 25, No. 4, Autumn 1956, pp. 421–36.

ACKNOWLEDGMENTS AND NOTES ON PREVIOUS PUBLICATION 607

18. "Some Continuities and Discontinuities in the Education of Women" was first given as the Third John Dewey Memorial Lecture at Bennington College on June 7, 1956. The cross-reference in the title to Ruth Benedict's article, "Continuities and Discontinuities in Cultural Conditioning," *Psychiatry*, Vol. 1, 1938, pp. 161–67, is intended to acknowledge her stimulation in this area (to which she returned in another perspective in her book on Japanese character, *The Chrysanthemum and the Sword*).

The text printed here was first published by Bennington College and has been revised to include matters raised in the discussion following the lecture; it has profited also from discussion of the panel on Utilization of Human Resources of the Rockefeller Brothers' Fund, and from a Conference on Education held at Vassar in the fall of 1956. For opportunity to work on these questions, I am indebted to a grant from the Carnegie Corporation.

19. "The Search for Challenge" was first presented as a lecture at the University of Chicago as part of my series on "The American Future"; the present version was given as an Inaugural Lecture at Kenyon College in October 1958, and appeared in the *Kenyon Alumni Bulletin* in the January-March 1959 issue. It was republished in *New University Thought*, Vol. 1, No. 1, Spring 1960, pp. 3–15; and more fully in the *Merrill-Palmer Quarterly of Behavior and Development*, Vol. 6, 1960, pp. 218–34. Both the address and the discussion that followed were tape-recorded. The ideas presented here were also discussed in a lecture at Monteith College of Wayne State University in 1959. In each case, extensive discussion followed the talk and gave me the chance to qualify issues too flatly and simply presented here. Some of the objections are reflected in footnotes to the tape-recorded text, but the latter remains virtually unchanged and is republished here despite my dissatisfaction with it, because I believe that the issues of Utopian thinking are urgent, so that even my errors and oversimplifications may widen discussion beyond the audiences heretofore addressed.

I am indebted to the Carnegie Corporation for a grant that has facilitated work on matters discussed in this lecture; the lecture also reflects the concerns of the Center for the Study of Leisure.

20. "The Social and Psychological Setting of Veblen's Economic Theory" was first delivered as a lecture to the Economic History Association, Bryn Mawr, September 1953. It was later reprinted in *The Journal of Economic History*, Vol. 13, No. 4, 1953, and in my collec-

tion of essays, *Individualism Reconsidered* (Glencoe, Illinois: The Free Press, 1954). In the footnotes I have taken account of some of the points made in the discussion following the presentation of this paper to the Economic History Association. I gratefully acknowledge many helpful suggestions from Staughton Lynd.

21. "The Relevance of Thorstein Veblen" draws on an essay in *The New Statesman*, April 9, 1960, and the Introduction to the Scribner Library edition of my book *Thorstein Veblen: A Critical Interpretation* (New York: Charles Scribner's Sons, 1953); the version here presented was published in *The American Scholar*, Vol. 29, No. 4, Autumn 1960, pp. 543–51.

22. "Self and Society: Reflections on Some Turks in Transition" was first published in *Explorations*, University of Toronto, June 1955, pp. 67–80. See also Daniel Lerner with the collaboration of Lucille W. Pevsner, *The Passing of Traditional Society: Modernizing the Middle East*, with an introduction by me (Glencoe, Illinois: The Free Press, 1958).

23. "The Oral Tradition, the Written Word, and the Screen Image" was first presented as a lecture delivered in connection with the dedication of the Olive Kettering Library, Antioch College Founders' Day, October 1955, and based on a series of studies of the Center for the Study of Leisure. It was first published by the Antioch Press, 1956, and was reprinted in part as "Books, Gunpowder of the Mind," *Atlantic Monthly*, Vol. 200, December 1957, pp. 123–26, in *Explorations* No. 6, July 1956, pp. 22–28, in *Explorations in Communication*, edited by Edward Carpenter and Marshall McLuhan (Boston: The Beacon Press, 1960), and in *Essays of Our Time*, edited by Lisle Hamalian and Edmund L. Volpe (New York: McGraw Hill, 1960).

24. "Law and Sociology" was first presented at a seminar on law and sociology at Rutgers Law School and edited from the tape-recorded address and the ensuing discussion. Publication of my Rutgers lecture in the *Stanford Law Review*, Vol. 9, July 1957, pp. 643–83, has garnered helpful criticisms, which I have sought to take account of in this revised and expanded version. It was reprinted in *Law and Sociology*, edited by William M. Evan (Glencoe, Illinois: The Free Press, 1962). Work on the problems discussed in this article has been facilitated by a grant of the Carnegie Corporation for studies of higher education and has also benefited from discussion at a conference on Higher Education, sponsored by Carnegie, at Princeton in April 1957.

See Earl J. McGrath, ed., *The Carnegie Conference on Higher Education* (New York: Carnegie Corporation, 1958), pp. 98–112.

25. "Tocqueville as Ethnographer" was the opening lecture in my series on "The American Future," given at the University of Chicago in January 1958. It had been published in part as "Tocqueville and Associations: An Introduction," *Autonomous Groups' Bulletin*, Vol. 12, 1956, pp. 1–3, and was published in its present form in *The American Scholar*, Vol. 30, No. 2, Spring 1961, pp. 174–87. I am indebted to J. P. Mayer, George W. Pierson, and Melvin Richter for their studies of Tocqueville and for specific criticisms.

26. "Introduction to *Crestwood Heights*" is from *Crestwood Heights: A Study of the Culture of Suburban Life* (New York: Basic Books, 1956).

27. "The Sociology of the Interview" was an address delivered at the Midwest Sociological Society meetings, Des Moines, April 22, 1955, and was first published in *The Midwest Sociologist*, Winter 1956, pp. 3–15. Thanks are due to the Social Science Research Committee of the University of Chicago, and the Foundations' Fund for Research in Psychiatry for support of the "Interview Project," directed by me and Mark Benney; this article reports some of the project's initial preoccupations.

28. "Orbits of Tolerance, Interviewers, and Elites" was first presented as an address at a symposium on Samuel Stouffer's *Communism, Conformity, and Civil Liberties* (New York: Doubleday, 1955) at the meetings of the American Association for Public Opinion Research, Madison, Wisconsin, April 15, 1955; it was first published in *The Public Opinion Quarterly*, Vol. 20, No. 1, Spring 1956, pp. 49–73.

29. "Interviewers, Elites, and Academic Freedom" was supported by a grant from the Foundations' Fund for Research in Psychiatry. An earlier version of this paper was presented at the Twentieth Anniversary of the Bureau of Applied Social Research at Columbia University, April 1957. It draws on the Teacher Apprehension Study, directed by Professor Paul F. Lazarsfeld of Columbia University for the Fund for the Republic; for details see *The Academic Mind: Social Scientists in a Time of Crises*, by Paul F. Lazarsfeld and Wagner Thielens, Jr. (Glencoe, Illinois: The Free Press, 1958) and my chapter therein. I am indebted both to the Fund and to Professor Lazarsfeld for an opportunity to work on these materials. The paper was first published in *Social Problems*, Vol. 6, No. 2, Fall 1958, pp. 115–26. See

also my article "Academic Freedom and the Press," *Forum,* The University of Houston Quarterly, May 1958, pp. 31-34.

30. "The Study of National Character: Some Observations on the American Case" was first presented as my Inaugural Lecture as Henry Ford II Professor of Social Sciences, Harvard University, December 1958. It was first published in the *Harvard Library Bulletin,* Vol. 13, No. 1, Winter 1959, pp. 5-24. See also my article (with the collaboration of Nathan Glazer), "The Lonely Crowd: A Reconsideration in 1960" in *Culture and Social Character: The Work of David Riesman Reviewed,* edited by Seymour Martin Lipset and Leo Lowenthal (Glencoe, Illinois: The Free Press, 1961).

Index

Abegglen, James, 545
Abel, Theodore, 86fn., 219fn.
Abraham, Karl, 588
Abundance, xiii
Acheson, Dean, 34, 70
Accidents, automobile, 288–89
Adams, Brooks, 23, 385
Adams, Henry, 9fn., 388–9, 501
Adenauer, Konrad, 18, 42, 78, 98
Adorno, T. W., 552, 591
Africa, 438
Air Force, 14
Algeria, 94; war with France, 63, 95
Allen, Frederick Lewis, 227fn.
Alsop, Louis and Joseph, 73, 302
Amana Society, 117
American Anthropological Association, 359
American Association for Public Opinion Research, 451, 517fn., 534
American Association of University Professors, 570
American Automobile Association, 136
American Civil Liberties Union, 578
American Committee on Cultural Freedom, 6, 80
American Federation of Labor (AFL), 74
American Home, 120
American Journal of Sociology, 259
American Legion, 541, 556
American Management Association, 517fn.
Americans for Democratic Action, 81
American Sociological Association, 14, 65
American Soldier, The, 526
Americans for Democratic Action, 574
Amherst College, 330
Amish culture, 116–117
Anaheim, California, 303
Anderson, Jackson M., 150fn.
Anderson, Sherwood, 513
Ankara, 406–11
Ann Arbor, Michigan, 111
Anthony, Robert A., 462fn.
Anti-Communism, 38–39, 80–92

Antioch College, 330, 362, 365, 373, 421, 427–9
Architectural Review, 255
Arendt, Hannah, 6, 7, 81, 84, 86fn., 88fn., 90, 500
Arensberg, Conrad, 546
Argyris, Chris, 48
Aristophanes, *Lysistrata*, 512
Arms race, 182
Arnold, Matthew, *Culture and Anarchy*, 432
Arrowsmith, Martin, 511
Articles of Confederation, 27
Aspen, Colorado, 253
Aswan Dam, 306
Ataturk, Kemal, 403fn., 415, 437
Atomic bombs, 3
Atomic Energy Commission, 29, 62, 502
Auchincloss, Louis, 483
Auden, W. H., 291
Automobile manufacturing, 21–22
Automobile Manufacturers Association, 293
Avery, Sewell, 302fn.

Bach, Johann Sebastian, 178fn., 239, 345
Back, K. W., 535fn.
Baker Workshop, 324
Bales, Robert F., 118fn., 199–200, 204fn., 213
Baltimore, Maryland, 135, 256
Baltzell, E. D., 132fn.
Balzac, Honoré, 128
Bank Street Schools, 427
Bar Harbor, Maine, 134
Bartok, Bela, 345, 364
Barzun, Jacques, 459fn.
Bates, Alan, 465fn.
Bateson, Gregory, 146, 335
Bauer, Alice, 537
Bauer, Catherine, 234
Bauer, Raymond, 7, 545, 559fn.
Bauhaus, 234–5, 413
Beats, 371–2, 400
Beaumont, Gustave de: 449, 494–9

Beauvoir, Simone de, *The Second Sex*, 331
Becker, Howard S., 176
Behavioral Science, 476
Bell, Daniel, 12fn., 172, 173fn, 291fn, 540; *Work and Its Discontents, The Cult of Efficiency in America*, 171fn.
Bell Telephone Company, 232, 364
Bell, Wendell, 228fn.
Bellamy, Edward, 353, 363; *Looking Backward*, 307, 377
Beloit College, 325
Benarik, Karl, 230
Benedict, Ruth, 585; *The Chrysanthemum and the Sword*, 584
Benney, Mark, ix, 87, 123fn., 287, 418, 449, 450fn., 517-39, 556, 561fn., 571
Bennington College, 324, 329, 333, 334, 337, 345, 347, 362
Bensman, Joseph, 532
Bentham, Jeremy, 478
Bentley automobile, 277
Berelson, Bernard R., 533fn., 543fn., 553fn.
Berenson, Bernard, 378
Berger, Bennett, 258, 259
Berger, Clarence Q., 178
Berger, Morroe, 219fn.
Beria, Lavrenti, 59, 68
Berkeley, University of California at, 258, 461
Berlin Crisis, xiv, 24, 53, 56fn
Berman, Harold J., 473fn.
Bettelheim, Bruno, 7, 91, 223fn.; *Dynamics of Prejudice*, 530
Better Homes and Gardens, 120
Bible, 375
Biddle, Bruce, 578fn.
Bion, W. R., 200fn.
Birnbaum, Norman, 87fn.
Blackett, P. M. S., *Studies of War*, 61fn.
Blaustein, Albert P., *The American Lawyer*, 467, 480
Blegen, Theodore, 376fn.
Bliven, Bruce, Jr., 303fn.
Blood, Robert O., Jr., 326
Bloomberg, Warner, Jr., 107, 122-23, 147-161, 178fn, 291
Bloomfield Hills, Michigan, 20
Blue Cross, 303, 320
Blum, Fred H., *Toward a Demcratic Work Process*, 160

Blum, Walter, 466fn.
Boat, Marion D., 228fn.
Boder, David P., *I Did Not Interview the Dead*, 86fn.
Böhm-Bawerk, 379
Bolsheviks, 80, 385, 396
Bonne, Alfred, 416fn.
Booth, William, 519, 520, 558
Borah, William E., 393fn.
Borgatta, Edgar F., 205fn.
Borth, Christy, 293
Bossard, J. H. S., 128
Boston, 241; West End, 109
Bourne, Randolph, 388
Bowen, Elenore, *Return to Laughter*, 507-8
Bowles, Chester, 45fn.
Bowley, A. L., 519fn.
Boy Scouts, 190, 360
Bradley, General Omar, 52
Bradley, Phillips, 134fn.
Brady, Dorothy S., 122fn.
Brandeis, Justice Louis D., 270, 448, 460; "Brandeis brief," 468
Brandeis University, 330
Brando, Marlon, 343
Bright, Margaret, 569
British Broadcasting Company, 32, 525
Britten, Benjamin, 345
Brodbeck, A. J., 512
Bronfenbrenner, Urie, 61
Bronx High School of Science, 243fn.
Broom, Leonard, 456fn.
Brown, Harrison, 167fn.
Bryan, William Jennings, 377
Bryn Mawr College, 325, 347
Bryson, Lyman, 136; *The Next America*, 164fn.; *Facing the Future's Risks*, 337fn.
Buffalo, New York, 259
Buffalo, University of, 454
Buick automobile, 124, 126, 130, 156, 273
Bulletin of the Atomic Scientists, 34
Bullitt, Stimson, 10fn.; *To Be a Politician*, 105, 452fn.
Bunyan, John, 425
Burke, Edmund, 91
Business Week, 301, 517fn.
Butler, Samuel, 375

Cadillac automobile, 124, 126, 127, 273

INDEX

Caldwell, Erskine, 177
California, 236, 240, 313
Calvin, John, 425
Calvinism, 84fn.
Camp William James, 362, 365
Campbell, Angus, 551fn.
Canada, 181, 278, 506-16; U.S. border with, 56
Canadian Jewish Congress, 515
Cannell, C. F., 530-1
Cantril, Hadley, 76, 526
Cardozo, Justice Benjamin, 478
Cargo cults, 163
Carlin, Jerome E., 480; *Lawyers on Their Own*, 455
Carnegie, Andrew, 250fn., 426
Carnegie Corporation, 342fn.
Carnegie, Dale, 250fn.
Carper, James, 169, 554
Carroll, Charles, 495
Carsh, Henry, 546fn.
Cash, W. J., 135
Castro, Fidel, 66
Cather, Willa, 377
Census Bureau, 529
Central Intelligence Agency, 28, 67
Central Park (New York), 247fn.
Chaplin, Charlie, 206
Chapman, Dwight, 346-7
Charcot, Jean Martin, 520
Charm, 129
Chaucer, Geoffrey, 328
Chiang Kai-shek, 42, 98
Chicago, 125, 160, 240, 241, 242, 243, 268, 448, 455
Chicago Federal Reserve Bank, 287
Chicago Tribune, 273, 546
Chicago, University of, 5, 108, 111, 124, 131, 390, 420, 461, 480, 535; Center for the Study of Leisure, 246, 248, 311; The College of, 330, 347; Law School, 455, 464, 468, 473fn., 563fn.
China, 419
China, Communist [People's Republic of], 14, 60, 64, 73, 75, 94, 99, 100
Chinese Communists, 6fn., 15, 17, 82fn.
Chinoy, Eli, 170fn., 236fn.
Christie, Richard, 592fn.
Chrysler Corporation, 130, 274, 458
Chrysler, Walter, 272
Churchill, Winston, 13

Cincinnati, 269
Civil Aeronautics Board, 487
Civil rights, 40-41, 48-49
Civil War, 4, 34, 167, 189, 392, 452, 501
Civilian Conservation Corps, 111, 362
Clark, J. B., 374, 379
Clark, Lincoln, 113, 233fn.
Clarke, Alfred C., 178-79
Coates, Willson, 386fn.
Cobalt bomb, 31
Coburn, Herbert, 578fn.
Coca-Cola, 114, 441
Cohen, Julius, 465fn.
Cohen, Morris, 378
Cold War, xiii, 18, 29, 38, 50, 77, 93-101, 396
Coleman, James, 343fn.
Coleman, Richard, 135
Colm, Gerhard, 304
Colorado College, 325
Columbia University, Bureau of Applied Social Research, 372, 402, 523; Institute for the Study of Human Variation, 279fn.; Law School, 454, 455
Comic books, 114
Committee for Economic Development, 110, 301
Common Cause (magazine), 76
Communism, 64-65, 99-100
Communist Manifesto, 81
Communist Youth Festival, 38
Community Chest, 20
Comte, Auguste, 383, 519
Concord, Massachusetts, 314
Condorcet, Marquis de, 356, 415
Congo, 15
Congress, 9-11, 501
Congress of Industrial Organizations (CIO), 74
Constantinople, 524
Constitution, 42
Consumer Reports, 135, 137, 270
Consumers Union, 130
Continental automobile, 282
Cornell University, 329, 532
Cort, David, 287fn.
Corvette automobile, 273
Cottrell, Leonard S., 197fn., 456fn.
Coughlin, Father, 440
Council for Correspondence, 11-12
Cowles newspapers, 546

Cozzens, James Gould, 483fn.
Cowan, Thomas, 485-6
Crane, Stephen, 394
Crockett, Davy, 435
Cromwell, Oliver, 434
Cuba, 93, 94
Cuban missile crisis, 14-15, 17, 60
Culture, traditional versus popular, 164
Cristie, Richard, 542fn.
Cummings, E. E., 424

Daily News, 71
Daimler automobile, 277
Damascus, 253
Dartmouth College, 310fn., 362
Darwin, Charles, 374, 390
Darwinism, 382-3, 398
Daughters of the American Revolution, 540, 541, 542, 556
Day, Chon, 288fn.
Dean, James, 216, 285
Dearborn, Michigan, 271
Debs, Eugene V., 388, 396
Decatur, Illinois [?], 562
Defense, Department of, 14
DeGaulle, Charles, 54, 98
Democratic Party, 10-11, 130, 307, 542
Denmark, 189
Denney, Reuel, 124, 137-8, 220fn., 310fn., 431, 546
DePauw College, 325
DeSoto automobile, 130, 274
Détente, 59
Deterrence, 31-32
Detroit, 152, 156, 234, 236, 266, 270, 546
Deutscher, Irwin, 131fn.
Devers, General 52
Dewey, John, 46, 325, 338, 382, 383, 390, 399; *Human Nature and Conduct*, 390
Dewey, Thomas, 533-4, 535
Dexter, Lewis, 522fn., 542fn., 559fn.
Dickens, Charles, 493; *American Notes*, 497, 500; *Oliver Twist*, 434; *Great Expectations*, 499
Dicks, 584
Dickson, 520
Dillard University, 330
Dior, Christian, 296
Disarmament, 48-49, 50
Disneyland, 303

"Dissaving", 119-120
Doblin, Jay, 280fn.
Dobriner, William, 242fn.
Dodd, Stuart, 566
Dos Passos, John, 396
Doubleday Company, 348
Dreiser, Theodore, 377
Drucker, Peter, 278fn; *Concept of the Corporation*, 171fn., 236fn.
Dubin, Robert, 185
Duesenberg automobile, 277
Duesenberry, James, 119fn.
Duffus, R. L., *The Innocents at Cedro*, 270
Dulles, Allen, 95
Dulles, Foster Rhea, 147fn.
Dulles, John Foster, 18, 21
Duncan Hines, 291
DuPont Corporation, 300
Durant, William C., 272
Durkheim, Emile, 194, 385, 398, 472

Earl, Harley, 273
Ebony, 135
Edsel automobile, 22fn., 274, 294, 297-9
Eggan, Fred, 422
Egypt, 418-19
Ehrenzweig, Albert, 466fn.
Einstein, Albert, 513
Eisenhower, Dwight D. ("Ike"), 18, 21, 52, 57, 59, 65, 100, 111, 251, 252, 261, 321, 551
Eisenstadt, S. N., 217, 342; *From Generation to Generation, Age-Grades and the Social Structure*, 338
Elder, Peter, 459fn.
Elmira, New York, 533-4, 553, 562
Emerson, Ralph Waldo, 162, 314, 388
Engels, Friedrich, 383
England, 464
Ennis, Philip, 240fn.
Erikson, Erik H., 348, 358, 588-9, 596fn.; *Childhood and Society*, 83fn., 218fn.
Erlich, June Sachar, 450fn.
Eskimo, 398
Ethiopia, 593-4
Exner, Virgil, 275

Fabian Society, 9fn.
Farley, James, 211
Fascism, 83

INDEX 615

Fava, Sylvia Fleis, 228fn., 242fn.
Fay, Sidney B., 396fn.
Federal Bureau of Investigation (FBI), 81
Federal Communications Commission (FCC), 457
Federal Housing Authority (FHA), 278
Federal Reserve Board, 302fn., 304
Feigenbaum, Kenneth D., 202fn., 480fn.
Fenn, Augustus, 578fn.
Festinger, Leon, 531fn.
First World War, 3, 4, 34, 351, 394, 452, 520
Fisher, Irving, *Capital and Income*, 379
Fisher, Janet, 119
Fisher, Robert M., 228
Fisher, Roger, 57
Fisk University, 330
Fitzgerald, F. Scott, *The Great Gatsby*, 195
Flaherty, Robert, *Moana*, 433
Flesch, Rudolf, *Why Johnny Can't Read*, 430
Fleisher, Alexander, 150fn.
Flexner Report, 458
Florida, 236
Foote, Nelson, 171fn., 197fn., 223, 565fn.
Ford automobile, 115, 130, 258
Ford, Edsel, 271
Ford Foundation, 447
Ford, Henry, 164, 271-3, 276, 293
Ford, Henry II, 21
Foreign Service Institute, 602
Forge, Andrew, 281
Form, William H., 532fn.
Forster, E. M., 207
Fort Worth, Texas, 234, 292fn., 305
Fortune, 20, 21, 121, 125-26, 259, 301, 432, 517fn., 529
Fourier, Charles, 146
France, 3, 15, 17, 73, 105, 331
Franco, Francisco, 74
Frankel, Ernest, 230fn.
Frankel, Lee K., 150fn.
Frankel, Max, 170fn.
Franklin automobile, 271
Franklin, Benjamin, 426
Freedgood, Seymour, 20
Freedman, Mervin B., 332
Freidson, Eliot, 117-118, 424

French Revolution, 6, 450, 494, 502
Frenkel-Brunswik, Else, 591
Freud, Sigmund, 46, 197, 216, 349-50, 385, 390, 401, 422, 458fn., 480, 513, 520, 522, 537, 588-90; *Moses and Monotheism*, 588
Freudianism, 472
Freund, Paul A., 468fn.
Friedman, Milton, 304
Friedman, Rose D., 122
Friedmann, Eugene A., 150fn., 236fn.
Friedmann, Georges, 521
Friedrich, Carl J., 3
Fromm, Erich, 107, 172fn., 260, 333, 339, 344, 422, 590; *Escape from Freedom*, 425; *Man for Himself*, 46, 601; *The Sane Society*, 151; *The Art of Loving*, 223fn.
Fuchs, Klaus, 34
Fueloep-Miller, René, 209fn.
Fund for the Republic, 571

Gabain, Marjorie, 117fn.
Galbraith, John Kenneth, *The Affluent Society*, 166fn., 180fn., 182fn., 184fn., 349, 448
Gallup poll, 33, 442, 560, 566fn.
Galton, Francis, 558
Gandhi, Mohandas K., 270
Gans, Herbert J., 108-109, 227fn., 372
Gardner, John, 342fn.
Garland, Hamlin, *Main-Travelled Roads*, 394
Gary, Indiana, 153, 178fn., 236
Gavin, General James, 30
Geddes, Patrick, 236
Geer, Blanche, 176
General Electric, 71, 232
General Motors, 20, 130, 173fn., 266, 272-3, 384
Germany, 3, 7fn., 81, 90, 105
Germany, East, 17
Germany, Nazi, 230fn.
Germany, West, 15, 16, 18, 181, 307
Gestapo, 84
Getzels, Jacob W., 595
Ghana, 222
GI Bill, 364
Gilded Age, 134, 307, 389
Gill, Merton, 536
Glazer, Nathan, 12 fn., 115fn., 216fn., 450fn., 523fn., 540fn., 544, 549, 562

Gobineau, Arthur, 496
Godfrey, Arthur, 216, 243
Goffman, Erving, 209fn.
Going steady, 339-40
Goldwater, Barry, 10
Gomulka, Wladyslaw, 447
Goodman, Paul, 111; *Growing up Absurd*, 46, 107, 186; and Percival Goodman, *Communitas*, 152, 229-231, 234, 253, 257, 358, 359fn.
Gorden, Raymond, 523fn.
Gordon, A. R., 459
Gorer, Geoffrey, 72-73, 591
Gould, Samuel, (former President of Antioch), 427
Gouldner, Alvin, 147
Graham, Elaine, 598, 599fn.
Graham, Martha, 324
Grant, Ulysses S., 4, 501
Great Books, 189
Great Britain, 105, 173, 203; attitudes toward nuclear disarmament, 32-33
Great Depression, 111, 254, 310, 311, 327
Greece, 430
Greeley, Horace, 177, 518
Greenbaum, J.J., 428
Greenberg, Lieutenant Arthur, 534fn.
Greenberg, Clement, 164fn.
Griffin, S. F., 55fn.
Grodzins, Morton, 5
Grosse Point, Michigan, 271
Gruen, Victor, 234, 292fn., 305
Guba, Egon, 595fn.
Guest, Lester A., 534fn.
Guest, Robert H., 170fn.
Gurin, Gerald, 551fn.
Gutenberg, Johann, 424
Guterman, Norbert, *Prophets of Deceit*, 562
Gutman, Robert, 265

Habenstein, Robert, 131-2
Hall, 558
Hall, Oswald, 481
Hallowell, Irving, 590
Halperin, Morton, 53
Hammond, Philip, 449fn.
Hand, Justice Learned, 478
Handlin, Oscar, 392, 393fn.
Hansen, Ralph, 285

Hare, A. P., 205fn.
Harlem, 185, 546
Harper's, 259
Harper's Bazaar, 136
Harrington, Alan, *Life in the Crystal Palace*, 193fn.
Harris, Louis, 546, 551, 557fn.
Hartz, Louis, 4fn., 501
Harvard Business School, 128, 230
Harvard College, 127
Harvard Graduate School of Business Administration, 461fn.
Harvard Law School, 57, 324, 454, 455
Harvard University, Russian Research Center, 537
Hauser, Arnold, *The Social History of Art*, 436
Havemann, Ernest, 325
Havighurst, Robert J., 150fn., 236fn.
Hawkins, Charles, 204fn.
Hegel, G.W.F., 383, 390
Heifetz, Jascha, 427
Heimann, Paula, 200fn.
Hemingway, Ernest, 362
Henderson, H., 227fn.
Henry, William E., 429fn.
Herald Tribune, 71
Herzog, Herta, 224
High School of Music and Art (New York), 243fn.
Higgins, Marguerite, 326
Hill, R., 535
Hillman Minx automobile, 281
Hindemith, Paul, 364
Hiroshima, 28, 100
Hiss, Alger, 563
Hitchcock, Alfred, *Rear Window*, 436
Hitler, Adolf, 3, 7fn., 83, 592-3
Hobbs, M. E., 459fn.
Hodge, General, 52
Hoffa, Jimmy, 57fn.
Hoffer, Eric, 177fn.; *The True Believer*, 84
Hofstadter, Richard, 391, 392, 548, 562, 589
Hohfeld, Wesley N., 460
Holiday magazine, 238
Hollywood, 284, 436
Holmes, Justice Oliver Wendell, 478
Homans, George C., 554; *The Human Group*, 199
Hoover, Herbert, 73

INDEX

Hopi Way, 19, 353
Horton, Donald, 203fn., 243fn., 248fn.
Hoselitz, B. F., 416fn.
House Armed Services Committee, 60fn.
House Beautiful, 120
House Committee on Un-American Activities, 74
Household magazine, 250
Hovland, Carl I., 599fn.
Howard University, 330
Howe, Mark DeWolfe, 473fn.
Howells, William Dean, 394
Hsu, Francis L. K., 117fn., 585fn.
Hudson River, 329
Hughes, Emmett, *The Ordeal of Power*, 21fn.
Hughes, Everett C., 91fn., 128, 142-3, 149, 175, 283, 457fn., 484, 575
Hughes, H. Stuart, 11
Huizinga, Johan, 147fn.
Human Organization, 517
Humphrey, George, 300, 302
Hungarian Revolution, 8
Hungary, 17
Hunt, Everett, 342
Huntington, Samuel, 61fn.
Hurd, Cuthbert, 432
Hurst, Willard, 466fn., 473fn.
Hutchins, Robert, 571, 581
Huxley, Aldous, 89; *Antic Hay*, 358; *Brave New World*, 174, 354
Hydrogen bomb, 165, 234
Hyman, Herbert, 526fn., 528fn., 529-30

ICBMs (intercontinental ballistic missiles), 15, 59
Icelandic sagas, 398
Illinois Central Railroad, 160
India, 94, 419, 437
Indo-China, 73, 94
Indonesia, 436
Industrial revolution, 148
Ingres, J. A. D., 460
Initiation, 433
Inkeles, Alex, 585fn., 602
Innis, Harold A., 435; *The Bias of Communications, Changing Concepts of Time*, 418
Installment buying, 119-120
The Intercollegian, 110fn.

International Business Machines (IBM), 432
International Paper and Power, 448
Interviewing, 517-583
Iowa, 546
Iran, 441
Istanbul, 413, 441
Izvestia, 354
Ivy League, 310, 330, 339, 343, 454, 572, 576

Jackson, Andrew, 56, 302, 393fn., 495, 500
Jackson Park (Chicago), 247fn.
Jackson, Robin, 248fn., 311
Jaguar automobile, 127, 273
Jahoda, Marie, 542fn., 592fn.
James, Henry, *The Bostonians*, p. 330
James, Rita M., 204fn.
James, William, 5, 353, 382, 390, 399
Janet, Pierre, 520
Janis, Irving L., 599
Janowitz, Morris, 19, 52, 63-64, 193fn., 228fn., 240; *Dynamics of Prejudice*, 530; *The Professional Soldier*, 30fn., 52 fn.
Jantzen bathing suits, 281
Japan, 3, 13, 53, 65, 73, 93, 100, 101, 105, 189
Jarrell, Randall, *The Age of Criticism*, 509; *Pictures from an Institution*, 207, 509
Jeep, 270
Jefferson, Thomas, 351, 352, 392, 393fn.
Jerome, Judson, 427
Jim Crow, 280, 285
John Birch Society, 11, 194fn.
Johns Hopkins University, 28, 552
Johnson, Alvin, 378, 384
Johnson, Samuel, 424
Johnstone, John, 420
Joyce, James, 364, 513

Kafka, Franz, 371
Kahn, Herman, 53
Kahn, R. L., 185fn., 531fn.
Kaiser, Henry J., 274
Kalven, Harry, Jr., 466fn.
Kansas City, Missouri, 127, 131, 135, 138-9, 241, 360, 546
Kansas City Study of Adult Life, 535

Kansas, University of, 176
Kant, Immanuel, 308, 377, 379, 382, 390, 412
Kardiner, Abram, 590
Katona, George, 119, 122, 131, 136, 233fn., 278, 302fn., 304
Katz, Daniel, 526, 531fn.
Katz, Elihu, 238fn., 409fn., 420, 440, 448fn., 566fn.
Kaysen, Carl, 587
Keats, John, *The Crack in the Picture Window*, 259
Kefauver, Estes, 548fn., 550
Kelley, Nicholas, 462, 484
Kelly, Grace, 319, 320
Kendall, Patricia L., 481fn.
Keniston, Kenneth, 110fn.
Kennan, George, 4, 101; BBC lectures, 32-33; *Russia, the Atom and the West*, 33fn.; *Russia Leaves the War*, 396fn.
Kennedy, John F., 10, 16, 26, 37fn., 62, 94, 111, 504
Kennedy, Robert Woods, *The House and the Art of Its Design*, 128, 233fn.
Kentucky, 546
Kephart, Newell G., 517fn.
Kettering, Charles Franklin, 428
Kerr, Clark, 155
Keynes, J. M., 380
Keynesian economics, 5, 34, 49, 106, 180, 182, 300, 307
Khrushchev, Nikita, 15, 17, 35, 57fn., 62, 66, 94, 98
Kiehl, Mary L., 290fn.
Kincaid, Harry V., 569fn.
Kipling, Rudyard, *Just So Stories*, 220
Kissinger, Henry, 55
Kitt, Alice S., 114fn.
Klee, Paul, 358
Klein, Melanie, 200fn.
Kluckhohn, Clyde, 587fn.
Kluckhohn, Florence R., 337fn., 587
Knox College, 325
Kogon, 86fn.
Komarovsky, Mirra, 325, 328, 334, 340, 550fn.
Koolaid, 118
Koran, 415, 437
Korean War, 4, 15, 34, 53, 56, 67, 74, 75, 371, 448fn., 524
Kornhauser, Arthur, 526
Kounen, Jacob, 578

Kouwenhoven, John, 232, 277fn.
Kozelka, Robert M., 290fn.
Kravchenko, Victor, 84
Kremlin, 70, 72
Kris, Ernst, 87
Kroeber, Alfred L., 282, 349
Kroger Food Foundation, 113, 116
Kronenberger, Louis, *Grand Right and Left*, 155
Kuhn, Manfred, 116-117
Kuznets, Simon, 121
Kawkiutl, 380

LaFollette, Robert, 388, 393
Lake Success, 70
Land, Edwin, 47-48
Lane, Robert, 4fn.
Lang, Kurt and Gladys, 448fn.
Langer, Susanne, 423
Langer, William L., 586
Laos, 93
Lardner, John, 293fn.
Larrabee, Eric, ix, 30fn., 52, 107fn., 121, 175fn., 187fn., 230fn., 270-299
LaSalle automobile, 273
Lassalle, Ferdinand, 377fn.
Lasswell, Harold, 283, 380, 460, 474
Latin America, 95
Lawrence, D. H., 155
Lawshe, C. H., 147fn.
Lazarsfeld, Paul F., 158fn., 219fn., 248fn., 409fn., 440, 450fn., 520, 533fn., 542fn., 543fn., 553fn., 557fn., 566fn., 568-83
Leaders, importance of personal qualities, 19-21
League of Women Voters, 268, 556
Lebanon, 436, 439
Lee, Dorothy D., 225fn.. 232, 423
Legal education, 454-92
Legion of Decency, 437
Leites, Nathan, 7, 87
LeMasters, E. E., 130
Lenin, V. I., 441
Lenski, Gerhard, 202fn.
Leontief, Wassily [?], 587
LePlay, Pierre Guillaume Frédéric, 519
Lerner, Daniel, 372, 402, 439, 573fn.; *The Passing of Traditional Society*, 163fn., 168fn., 351
Levi, Edward H., 468
Levinson, Daniel J., 585fn., 591fn.

INDEX 619

Levittown, New Jersey, 109
Levittown, New York, 259
Levittown, Pennsylvania, 132, 259
Lewin, Kurt, 204
Lewis, Phillip H., 534fn.
Liberal Papers, 9
Liberal Project, 9, 30
Library of Congress, 458
Life magazine, 11, 24, 259, 277, 287fn., 324, 338
Lifton, Robert J., 6
Lincoln, Abraham, 57
Lincoln automobile, 127, 271, 273
Lindzey, Gardner E., 585fn.
Linton, Harriet, 590, 599fn.
Linton, Ralph, 590
Lippitt, Ronald, 200fn., 208fn.
Lippmann, Walter, 30, 74fn.
Lipset, Seymour Martin, 4, 12fn., 451, 452fn., 540fn., 544, 548, 549, 597fn.
Little League, 177, 321
Little Rock, Arkansas, 194
Llewellyn, Karl, 456, 471-2
Locke, John, 391
Loeb, Edwin, 423
Loeb, Martin, 146
Loewy, Raymond, 150, 275
London, Jack, 378fn.
Loosley, Elizabeth W., 197fn., 227fn.; *Crestwood Heights*, 506-516, 549fn.
Lortie, Dan C., 480
Louisiana, 297
Lourié, Alisa, 487
Lowell, Massachusetts, 174
Lowenthal, Leo, 158, 177fn., 248fn., 407fn., 452fn., 597fn.; *Prophets of Deceit*, 562
Lubell, Samuel, 54-55, 260, 551fn.
Luddites, 172
Lundberg, G. A., 229fn.
Lunt, P. S., 120fn.
Luther, Martin, 425
Lynd, Robert S., *Knowledge for What?*, 446; *Middletown*, 508
Lynd, Staughton, 371, 376, 388-401
Lyne, Woodworth, and Evarts, 448, 482fn.
Lynes, Russell, 121, 129, 285

MacArthur, General Douglas, 52, 53fn., 448fn., 502
Maccoby, Michael, ix, 13, 36fn.

MacDonald, Dwight, 3
Machiavelli, Nicolo, 389
Mad magazine, 358
Mademoiselle magazine, 129, 327
Madison Avenue, 357fn.
Maginot Line, 78, 395
Malenkov, Georgi, 59
Malik, 70
Malinowski, B. K., 419, 477
Malthus, Thomas R, 356
Manhattan Project, 445fn.
Manifest Destiny, 23, 167
Mannheim, Karl, 309
Manus, 350-1
Mao Tse-tung, 42, 75, 95
March, James G., 551fn.
Market research, 295
Marmon automobile, 271
Marquand, John P., 227; *Point of No Return*, 508
Marshall, John, 501
Marshall Plan, 38, 44, 231
Marschak, Jacob, 476
Marx, Groucho, 529
Marx, Karl, 148, 168, 307, 356, 375, 379, 383, 397, 441, 450, 472
Marxism, 48, 49, 472
Masculinity, American need to prove, 35-38
Massachusetts Institute of Technology, 545, 548, 558; Center for International Studies, 403, 559
Massing, Paul, 486
Maxwell, Elsa, 203
Maxwell's demons, 541
Mayer, J. P., 493fn.
Mayhew, 518
Mayo, Elton, 147, 159, 520
McArthur, Charles C., 133, 312, 481
McBride, Mary Margaret, 243
McCall's, 155
McCann-Erickson market research firm, 274
McCarthy, Senator Joseph, 34, 393, 552
McCarthy, Mary, 363, 510
McCarthyism, 95, 357, 568-83
McClelland, David C., 551fn.
McCone, John, 95
McDougal, Myres, 460
McGraw-Hill, 302fn.
McGregor, Douglas, [former President of Antioch], 427

McKitrick, Eric, 585–6, 598fn.
McLuhan, Marshall, 424
McMahon, Mrs. Edna, 386fn.
McNamara, Robert, 14–15, 21, 27, 54, 60fn.
McPhee, William M., 533fn., 543fn., 553fn.
Mead, Margaret, 38, 191, 202, 326fn., 332, 333, 350–1, 355, 562, 585; *And Keep Your Powder Dry*, 584; *Soviet Attitudes toward Authority*, 84; *New Lives for Old*, 163fn.; *Male and Female*, 289
Mechanics Institutes, 189
Meier, Richard L. 167
Melman, Seymour, 44; *The Peace Race*, 105
Melville, Herman, 353
Mencken, H. L., 389
Mennonites, 283
Menuhin, Yehudi, 427
Mercedes-Benz automobile, 131
Mercury automobile, 115, 130, 273
Merton, Robert K., 114fn., 219, 414, 456fn., 481fn., 484, 520, 526fn., 542, 547, 559–60fn.
Métraux, Rhoda, 585fn.
Mexico, 261, 426; war with, 23
Meyers, Marvin, 495
Meyersohn, Rolf, 187fn., 188fn., 238fn., 248fn.
Meyerson, Margy Ellin, 287fn., 519fn.
Meyerson, Martin, 519fn.
Michigan Bell Telephone Company, 358
Michigan State College Social Research Service, 129
Michigan, University of, 314, 326, 358, 454; Survey Research Center, 108, 278
Midas, Margaret, 155fn.
Mikoyan, Anastas, 68
Military service, 314, 336fn.
Military services, 4
Mill, John Stuart, 427, 432
Miller, Arthur, 198fn.
Miller, D. N., 228fn.
Miller, Warren E., 551fn.
Miller, William, 10
Mills, C. Wright, 107, 166, 198; *The Power Elite*, 490fn.; *The Sociological Imagination*, 446fn.; *White Collar*, 457fn.

Mills, Theodore M., 204fn.
Milwaukee, 160
Minneapolis, 244
Minnesota, 129
Minute Women, 550fn.
Missouri, 106
Missouri Compromise, 61
Mitarachi, Jane Fiske, 273fn.
Mitchell, General Billy, 52
Modigliani, Franco, 302fn.
Money-Kyrle, R. E., 200fn.
Monopoly, 358
Monsanto Chemical Company, 285
Montgomery Ward, 302fn.
Moore, Barrington, Jr., 602; *Soviet Politics*, 84
Moore, Harriet, 120
Moore, Mary E., 597fn.
Moore, Underhill, 491–2
More, Sir Thomas, *Utopia*, 349
Morgan, Arthur E., *Search for Purpose*, 425, 427
Morgenthau, Hans J., 4
Morison, Elting E. ed., *The National Style, Essays in Value and Performance*, 13fn., 23fn.
Morse, Nancy, 169, 237fn.
Moses, Robert, 293
Mount Holyoke College, 329, 347
Movie, drive-in, 252fn.
Mowrer, O. H., 337fn.
Mozart, Wolfgang Amadeus, 178fn., 239
Mueller, Kate Hevner, 428
Mumford, Lewis, 247, 249, 364; *The Transformations of Man*, 162
Munich, 10, 98
Murray, Arthur, 210fn.
Murray, Henry, 587
Mussolini, 20
Mutual Security Act, 38
Myrdal, Gunnar, 85–86

Nadel, S. F., 534fn.
Nagasaki, 28
Nash automobile, 281
National Association for the Advancement of Colored People, 489
National Association of Manufacturers, 302
National Institute of Mental Health, 108

INDEX

National Opinion Research Center, 405fn., 460, 522, 527, 530, 531, 537, 544, 556–8
National purpose, 8, 20–27
National Purpose, The, 24
NATO, 14, 15, 16, 54, 55, 64
Navaho, 404
Nazism, 7fn., 19, 53, 64, 80, 100
Nebraska, University of, Law School, 465fn.
Negroes, 106, 185, 204, 261, 404fn., 411, 546
Neumeyer, Martin and Esther, 147fn.
Neutra, R. J., 128fn.
Neutron bomb, 101
Newcomb, Theodore, 333
New Deal, 9, 49, 566fn.
New Guinea, 359, 421
New Haven, Connecticut, 269
New London, Connecticut, 45
Newman, Richard, 536fn.
Newman, Thomas M., 290fn.
Newman, William, 227fn.
New Masses, The, 81
New Orleans, Louisiana, 194, 253, 305
Newport, Rhode Island, 134
New School for Social Research, 386fn.
New York City, 20, 241, 268, 283, 292–3, 436, 524
New Yorker, The, 314, 513
New York University, 462
Nicolson, Harold, 221
Niebuhr, Reinhold, 36
Nigeria, 253, 436
Nisbet, Robert A., 107fn., 219fn.
Nisei, 404fn.
Nixon, Richard, 504
Norris, Frank, 394
Norris, Senator George, 393
North Carolina, 482
North Carolina, University of, 582
North Carolina, Women's College of the University of, 329
Nuclear arsenals, 16–17, 18, 53, 65
Nurske, Ragnar, 416fn.

Oberlin College, 329
Oedipus, 85
Office of War Information, 526
Oldfield, Barney, 293
Oldsmobile automobile, 130, 271
Olmstead, Michael S., 595

Opel automobile, 298
Oppenheimer, J. Robert, 165
Ortega y Gasset, José, 432
Orwell, George, 89, 90; *1984*, 82, 98, 354; *Down and Out in Paris and London*, 311
Osgood, Professor Charles, 58–60, 63, 77
Oxford University, 111
Ozarks, 546

Pacifism, 3–4, 4 fn., 32
Paddleford, Clementine, 210fn.
Page, Charles H., 219fn.
Pakistan, 38
Paliau, 351
Panyushkin, Ambassador, 70
Papago Indians, 419–20
Parent Teacher Association, 503, 513, 540, 550
Pareto, Vilfredo, 380, 385
Park, Robert E., 520
Park Forest, Illinois, 109, 129, 227, 243, 259, 507
Parrington, Vernon, 394
Parsons, Talcott, 118–119, 136, 200fn., 340, 458, 477, 489fn., 527fn., 548, 599; *The Social System*, 587
Pasternak, Boris, 39
Patten, Simon, 376–7
Patton, General George, 52
Peace Corps, 26, 49, 100
Pearl Harbor, 3, 13, 98
Peirce, Charles, 382
Pennsylvania, University of, 364, 454
Pentagon, 53, 65, 299
Peterson, Osler, 482
Peterson, Warren, 150fn.
Petrov, 84
Philadelphia, 256, 261, 269
Philippines, 73, 422, 426
Piaget, Jean, 117fn., 222, 358
Picasso, Pablo, 432, 460
Piel, Gerald, 34, 106fn.
Pierce-Arrow automobile, 271
Pierson, George Wilson, 494
Pittsburgh, 269
Planned Parenthood League, 74fn.
Plato, 389, 432, 472; *The Republic*, 349
Platt, John R., 5, 167fn.
Plymouth automobile, 130, 274
Pohl, Frederick, "The Midas Plague," 175

Poland, 8, 94; social science in, 446–7
Polansky, Norman, 200fn., 208fn., 578
Polaroid camera, 267
Polaris submarine, 77
Politburo, 72–3
Politics (journal), 3
Pontiac automobile, 273
Pool, Ithiel de Sola, 43, 558, 559fn.
Populism, 61, 391–4
Porter, Charles O., *The American Lawyer*, 467, 480
Portugal, 71
Potsdam agreement, 56
Potter, David, 111; *People of Plenty*, 585
Potter, Robert J., ix, 108, 190fn.
Potter, Stephen, 315
Pravda, 354
Presley, Elvis, 163, 216
Prohibition, 290
Prometheus, 410
Proust, Marcel, 358
Public Health Service, 311
Public Opinion Quarterly, 526
Pueblo Indians, 398
Puerto Rico, 185, 261, 469
Pullman cars, 434
Pullman, Illinois, 267
Pullman plant, 174
Puritanism, 84, 148, 151, 169
Puritans, 6, 272

Quality Courts Unlimited, 291
Quebec, 495
Quetelet, 519

Radburne, 234
Radcliffe College, 319, 325, 330
Radio Moscow, 439
Railroad Brotherhoods, 74
Rambler automobile, 294
Rand Corporation, 28, 29, 29fn., 30, 37fn.
Randolph-Macon Woman's College, 329, 555
Rapoport, Anatol, 476
Rashevsky, Nicolas, 566
Raytheon, 44
Reader, George, 481fn.
Reader's Digest, 419
Rebel without a Cause, 284, 360
Red Cross, 22
Redfield, Robert, 419; *The Little Community*, 514

Redlich, F. C., 536
Reed College, 330
Redl, Fritz, 200fn., 208fn.
Redlich Report, 458fn.
Reimann, Guenter, *The Vampire Economy*, 88
Reischauer, Edwin, 95
Reiss, Albert J., Jr., 178, 228fn.
Renaissance, 345, 436
Renault automobile, 297fn.
Republican Party, 10, 295, 300, 307
Reuther, Walter, 294
Ribicoff, Abraham, 288
Richardson, Jane, 282
Richardson, Stephen A., 533fn.
Richmond, Virginia, 546
Rickover, Admiral Hyman, 46, 264
Ridgeway, General Matthew, 30
Riesman, David, *Faces in the Crowd*, 216fn., 412; *The Lonely Crowd*, xiv, 107, 111, 113, 168, 171, 197fn., 328fn., 412, 448, 451; *Thorstein Veblen, A Critical Interpretation*, 333fn., 375
Riley, John W., Jr., 201fn., 202fn., 597fn.
Riley, Matilda White, 597fn.
Roberts, John, 290
Robinson, 526
Robson, Reginald, 465fn.
Rockefeller Foundation, 482
Rockne, Knute, 274
Rhode, 526
Rodes, Robert, 484–8
Roe, Anne, 446
Roethlisberger, 520
Roland, Albert, 250
Rolls Royce automobile, 277
Rolvaag, Ole Edvart, 376
Romney, George, 21, 22, 294
Roman Catholic Church, 425
Roosevelt, Eleanor, 562fn.
Roosevelt, Franklin D., 56fn., 396, 514, 562fn.
Roosevelt, Theodore, 23, 37, 362, 393, 395
Roseborough, Howard, ix, 107, 113–137
Roseborough, Mary E., 204fn.
Rosen, John, 536
Rosenberg, Bernard, 107fn.
Rosenberg, Harold, 504

Rosenstock-Huessy, Eugen, 362
Rossi, Alice and Peter, 550fn.
Rostow, Walt W., 13fn., 23fn.
Rotary, 201fn.
Rousseau, Jean Jacques, 374, 391
Rousset, David, 86fn.
Rovere study, 547
Rowntree, B. Seebohm, 122
Roy, Donald, 185
Rudikoff, Sonya, 334
Ruesch, Jurgen, 146
Rusk, Dean, 54
Russell, Bertrand, *History of Western Philosophy*, 435-6
Russell Sage College, 329
Russia, 524
Rust brothers, 165
Rutgers Seminar on Law and Sociology, 469, 479, 480, 483

Sagan, Françoise, 343
St. John's College, 347
St. Louis, Missouri, 156, 242
St. Simon, Claude Henri, 383, 519
Salinger, J.D., 400
Sandburg, Carl, 285
San Diego, 546
Sandusky, Ohio, 553
Sanford, Nevitt, 224fn., 332, 591fn.
San Francisco, 258, 259, 268
Santa Claus, 417
Sapir, Edward, 584
Sarah Lawrence College, 329
Sargent, S. Stansfield, 121, 566fn.
Saturday Evening Post, 158, 583
Saudi Arabia, 297
Savonarola, 231
Sayles, L. R., 555
Scandinavia, 398
Scarsdale, New York, 243fn., 420
Schachtel, Ernest, 422
Schatzman, Leonard, 405fn., 414, 523, 573fn.
Schelling, Thomas, 55
Schlesinger, Arthur, Jr., *The Vital Center*, 23
Schmoller, 375, 390
Schumpeter, Joseph, 307, 376, 380
Schwartz, Richard, 310fn.
Scientific American, 107, 238
Scott, Sir Walter, 392

Sears Roebuck, 75, 121, 136, 302fn., 546
Second World War, 3, 4, 13, 19, 28, 31, 34, 45, 53, 57, 101, 106, 141, 146, 153, 238, 273, 296, 300, 313, 327, 361, 364, 396, 404, 544, 584
Securities Exchange Commission, 471
Seeley, John R., *Crestwood Heights*, 197fn., 227fn., 451, 506-516, 549fn.
Selznick, Philip, 456fn.
Seventeen, 129
Sévigné, Mme de, 504
Sex roles in sociability, 223-225
Shartle, Mrs. Doris B., 313fn.
Sheatsley, Paul, 527, 542fn., 544fn.
Sherif-effect, 532
Shils, Edward, 4, 5, 19, 118fn.; *The Torment of Secrecy*, 34
Shipton, James M., 547
Shriver, Sargent, 111
Shulberg, Bud, *What Makes Sammy Run?*, 26
Shulman, Max, 227fn.
Sibley, Elbridge, 480fn.
Sim, R. Alexander, 197fn., 227fn.; *Crestwood Heights*, 506-516, 549fn.
Simmel, Georg, 196, 198, 252, 286
Simmelian dyad, 518
Simon, Herbert, 476
Singer, Milton, 439
Slater, Philip E., 200fn.
Slichter, Sumner, 301
Sloan, Alfred, 297
Smigel, Erwin O., 479fn., 569fn.
Smith, Adam, 148
Smith College, 325, 595-6
Snow, C. P., *The Two Cultures and the Scientific Revolution*, 401
Social Darwinism, 23
Social Research, Inc., 120, 273
Sociological Abstracts, 517
Sofer, Elaine Graham, 599
Sombart, Werner, 375, 390
Sorel, Georges, 385
Sorokin, Piritim A., 178
South Pacific, 98
South Vietnam, 93
Soviet Union, 5fn., 13, 14, 15, 23, 29, 41-43, 54-66, 80-92, 93-101, 105, 170, 173, 232, 426, 441, 447, 497, 544, 562

624 INDEX

Spectorsky, A.C., 227fn., 510
Speier, Hans, 407fn., 518
Spencer, Herbert, 355
Spengler, Oswald, 418
Spier, Robert, 284
Spiro, Herbert, 484fn.
Sputnik, 8, 181, 295, 307
Stakhanovites, 354
Stalin, Josef, 6, 13, 68, 105
Stalingrad, 354
Stalinism, 81–82
Stanton, Frank, 158fn., 248fn., 542fn.
Stapel, Jan, 526-7
Star, Shirley, 450, 527, 538, 556fn.
Stassen, Harold, 62, 397
State Street, 512
Steffens, Lincoln, 252, 261
Stein, Clarence, 247
Stein, Gertrude, 326
Stember, Herbert, 556-7fn., 560fn.
Stephens College, 329, 546
Stevens, Lucia B., 133fn., 312fn., 481fn.
Stevenson, Adlai, 548fn.
Stock, Dorothy, 200fn.
Stone, Gregory, 157fn., 228fn., 532
Stone, Justice Harlan Fiske, 490
Stouffer, Samuel, 265, 268, 526; *Communism, Conformity and Civil Liberties*, 33, 451, 466fn., 524, 540-67, 569-70
Stowe, Harriet Beecher, *Uncle Tom's Cabin*, 434
Strahan, Hazel B., 532fn.
Strategic Air Command, 24, 29, 44, 181
Strauss, Anselm, 203fn., 251fn., 405fn., 414, 523, 573fn.
Strauss, George, 555
Stravinsky, Igor, 324
Strodtbeck, Fred L., 204fn., 479, 550fn., 564fn.
Strong Vocational Interest Inventory, 336
Studebaker automobile, 271, 274, 281
Stutz Bearcat automobile, 271
Stycos, J. M., 535fn.
Sullivan, Harry Stack, 536
Sumeria, 418
Sumner, William Graham, 90, 383
Supreme Court, 460, 466fn., 470, 478, 601
Survey Research Center, University of Michigan, 185fn., 302fn.

Sussman, Marvin, 120, 153fn.
Swados, Harvey, 187fn.
Swanson, G. E., 228fn.
Swarthmore College, 330, 342
Sweet Briar College, 329
Switzerland, 307
Szilard, Leo, 4, 43

Taber, John, 300
Taconic State Parkway, 242fn
Taft-Hartley law, 533
Taylor, Frederick Winslow, 153
Taylor, General Maxwell, 30
Teacher Apprehension Study, 568-83
Teller, Edward, 29, 62
Tennessee, 253
Tennessee Valley Authority, 163, 231
Test ban, 17, 78
Texas, University of, 130
Thelen, Herbert A., 200fn.
Thematic Apperception Test, 429, 433
Thielens, Wagner, Jr., 450fn., 481fn.. 568fn., 579fn.
Thomas, W. I., 382,520; *The Polish Peasant in Europe and America*, 425
Thompson, Dorothy, 362
Thoreau, Henry David, 250fn., 289, 400, 401
Thurber, James, *The Male Animal*, 513
Time magazine, 310, 314, 322, 413, 547
Times of London, 439
Toby, Jackson, 486-7
Tocqueville, Alexis de, 134, 232, 242, 329, 330, 345, 449, 450, 476, 493–505, 600; *Democracy in America*, 52fn., 162, 226, 398
Tolstoy, Leo, 355
Toronto, University of, 418
Totalitarianism, 6–8, 64–65, 80–92
Toynbee, Arnold, 349
Tregold, R. F., 147fn.
Trevor-Roper, Hugh, *The Last Days of Hitler*, 88fn.
Trilling, Diana, 330
Trilling, Lionel, 86, 413; *The Opposing Self*, 402
Trippe, Juan, 74
Trollope, Anthony, 246
Trollope, Frances Milton, 493, 497
Truman, Harry S, 34, 68, 75, 448fn., 514, 533-4
Tupholme, Renée, 230

INDEX 625

Turkey, 402–17, 437, 523–4
Tuskegee Institute, 334
Tuxedo Park, 134, 392
Twain, Mark, *A Connecticut Yankee in King Arthur's Court*, 392; *Huckleberry Finn*, 392
Twomey, John E., 550fn.

U-2 spy plane, 37, 98
Ulbricht, Walter, 17, 42
Ullman, E. L., 150fn.
Underhill, Ruth, 419
U.S. News & World Report, 583
U.S.S.R., 13, 18, 67–79, 300, 353
United Auto Workers, 173fn.
United Nations, 66, 100, 338
United States Information Service, 76
United States Court of Appeals, 471
Urban renewal, 261, 269
Utopian thought, 89, 96, 98, 229–230, 234, 348–67

Vandenberg, General Hoyt, 72
Van Der Kroef, 421
Van der Rohe, Mies, 234, 304
Varga, 68
Vassar College, 332, 337, 342, 346, 347, 427, 429
Veblen, Thorstein, xiii, 25, 111, 126, 153, 160, 175, 186, 194, 198fn., 209fn., 270, 272–3, 276, 285, 293, 371–2, 374–401, 446, 510, 569; *Imperial Germany and the Industrial Revolution*, 399; *The Nature of Peace*, 394, 395; *The Theory of Business Enterprise*, 398; *The Theory of the Leisure Class*, 372, 390, 397, 398
Ventura, California, 121
Vermont, 190
Veterans Administration, 141, 145, 146
Veto groups, 111–112
Vidich, Arthur J., 532
Vienna, Communist Youth Festival, 38
Vietnam, 53, 55
Viner, Jacob, 416fn.
Virgin Mary, 436
Virginia, University of, 582
Vogt, E. Z., 546fn.
Voice of America, 72, 75, 403, 439
Volkswagen, 270, 294, 297

Wagner, Richard, 239, 324

Walker, General, 53
Walker, Charles, *The Man on the Assembly Line*, 170fn.; *Steeltown*, 154
Wall Street, 72, 272, 312, 391, 478, 512
Wallace, Henry, 574
War, 4; moral equivalent for, 65–66
War of 1812, 56
Warner, Lloyd, 120, 545; Yankee City series, 508
Washington, University of, 454
Waskow, Arthur, 14fn., 16fn., 77fn.
Watson, Jeanne, ix, 108, 190fn., 213fn., 449fn.
Watson, Tom, 393fn.
Weaver, Henry G., 274fn.
Weaver, John D., 194fn.
Webb, Beatrice, 520fn., 558
Weber, Max, xiv, 385, 425, 472, 594
Webster, C. K., 346
Wechsler, Herbert, 472
Wehrmacht, 19
Weiland, J. Hyman, 284fn.
Weill, Hermann, 436
Weimar Republic, 235
Weiss, Robert S., ix, 107fn., 108, 169, 184–95, 237fn.
Weisskopf, Walter, 332fn.
Welfare state, 180
Weller, George, 314
Wellesley College, 345
Wells, H. G., 249fn.
Wescott, Glenway, 397
West, Patricia Salter, 325
West Publishing Company, 466
Westchester County, New York, 262
Western Electric Company, 520
Wheeler, Harvey, 244fn.
Wheelis, Allen, *The Quest for Identity*, 350fn., 361, 400fn.
White, Lynn, Jr., *Educating Our Daughters*, 330
White Sox, 449fn.
White, Winston, 599
Whiting, John W. M., 585
Whitman, Walt, 162, 353, 367
Whorf, Benjamin, 423
Whyte, William F., *Street Corner Society*, 147, 199
Whyte, William H., Jr., 124–25, 129fn., 215fn., 227, 241, 322, 506–7, 529; *The Organization Man*, 231

Wiener, Norbert, *Ex-Prodigy, My Childhood and Youth*, 432
Wigmore, John Henry, 467fn.
Williams College, 333
Williams, Tennessee, 536
Williston, Samuel, 467fn.
Willkie, Wendell, 397
Wilson, Charles, 21
Wilson, Woodrow, 4, 393fn., 394-6
Winnetka, Illinois, 243fn.
Wisconsin, University of, 9fn.
Wobbly (IWW) workers, 377, 381
Wohl, Richard R., 203fn., 243fn.
Wohlstetter, Albert, 29
Wolfe, Thomas, 509
Women's College of North Carolina, 555
Wood, Robert, *Suburbia, Its People and Its Problems*, 259, 267
Woodward, C. Vann, 393
Works Progress Administration, 108, 362

Wright, Charles R., 470fn.

Yale University, 310, 448; Department of Psychiatry, 536, 538; Law School, 455, 473
Yalta agreement, 56
Yellowstone Park, 305
YMCA, 190, 360
York, England, 122
Young Americans for Freedom, 97
Young, Brigham, 177, 518
Young Republicans, 474fn.
Yugoslavia, 76, 94, 105, 189, 447

Zaslavsky, David, 69
Zeisel, Hans, 477fn., 535
Zinsser, William K., 202fn.
Znaniecki, Florian, *The Polish Peasant in Europe and America*, 425
Zuni Indians, 404, 422